Tiflis

Derbend

Caspian

Sea

Baku

Saliany

BAIJAN

Tabriz

Astara

mia

Resht

Tekke Turcomans

Ashkhabad

Geok Tene

To Merv and Herat

ELBURZ

Astrabad

Kazvin

Tehran

Meshed

Farimun

Sulimaniya

RUSSIAN SPHERE

Khorasan

AFGHAN-
ISTAN

Kirkuk

Hamadan

Kasr-i-Shirin

Qum

Dasht-i-Kavir

Kermanshah

Kashan

Ferdaus

hdad

Tabas

Ctesiphon

Nain

Birjand

ylon

Isfahan

PERSIA

Dezful

Shuster

Yezd

DASHT-i-LUT

Ahwaz

ARABISTAN

Abadeh

Basra

Behbehan

NEUTRAL SPHERE

SHAMIYA

Muhammerah

Zubair

Shiraz

Kerman

Shatt-al-Arab

KUWAIT

FARS

BRITISH

SPHERE

in

Dahana

Bushire

TANGISTAN

BALUCH-
ISTAN

Al Hasa

Hormuz

Persian

Henjam

Bandar Abbas

Lingeh

BAHRAIN

Gulf

Straits of Hormuz

Jask

Makran

Sea of Oman

ch

Riyadh

Hofuf

ARIDH

OMAN

ey

- - - Boundaries of Syrian provinces
of Ottoman Empire, 1914

+—+ Railroads to 1914

— — Boundaries of Anglo-Russian
spheres of influence agreed in
St. Petersburg, 31 August 1907

+++ Proposed or unfinished lines

0   100 200 300 400 500 Miles

Kilometres 0   200   400   600   800

G000241585

The Illicit Adventure

H. V. F. Winstone

The Illicit Adventure

*The Story of Political and Military
Intelligence in the Middle East from
1898 to 1926*

JONATHAN CAPE
THIRTY BEDFORD SQUARE LONDON

First published 1982
© 1982 by H. V. F. Winstone
Jonathan Cape Ltd, 30 Bedford Square, London WC1

British Library Cataloguing in Publication Data

Winstone, H. V. F.
The illicit adventure: the story of political and
military intelligence in the Middle East from
1898 to 1926.
1. Intelligence service—History
2. Near East—History
I. Title
355.3'43   DS49
ISBN 0 224 01582 6

Typeset by Phoenix Photosetting, Chatham
Printed and bound in Great Britain
by Mackays of Chatham

For Sarah

Contents

Preface   xi
Acknowledgments   xiv

1 The Battlegrounds   3
   'See the Conquering Hero'   3
   Military Intelligence   6
   Of Freemasons and Jews   8
   Of Turks, Arabs and Christians   11
   'No entanglement with Wahabees'   14

2 Footprints in the Desert   17
3 The Seeds of Revolt   37
4 The Lion and the Eagle   75
5 Murder at Hail   97
6 War: Most Urgent   124
7 The Flickering Flame   143
8 Councils of War   161
9 The *Intrusives*   172
10 The Siege   201
11 Aaron and Jamal   224
12 The Sharif's Revolt   240
13 Von Stotzingen   269
14 War and Peace   279
15 Requiem for Victory   315

   Appendix A: The Arabs   365

Appendix B: Structure of the British Military
   Intelligence Organisation, General Staff
   Cairo   384
Notes   385
Bibliography   488
Index   511

Illustrations

Plates

between pages 80 and 81

1 Professor Koldewey, head of the Deutsche Orient Gesellschaft
2 Germans at Kalat Shergat
3 Gertrude Bell at dinner with the German team in Assyria

between pages 112 and 113

4 A page from Gertrude Bell's field notebook
5 Dr Andrae with gazelle at Assur
6 Ibn Saud at Basra

between pages 272 and 273

7 Shakespear going ashore at Bahrain in 1914
8 'Women' of the Howaitat tribe
9 Sir Percy Cox with Kurd and Arab shaikhs, 1918

between pages 304 and 305

10 No. 1 Squadron, Royal Air Force Mail Service
11 Sassanian arch and palace at Ctesiphon
12 Colonel A. C. Parker
13 T. E. Lawrence and Gertrude Bell in Egypt, 1921

Figures

		page
1	Shakespear's route log at Zarud	120
2	Intelligence Section, GHQ Basra's pocket map of Mesopotamia	202
3	Christmas card from Intelligence Section, Basra	207

4   Mesopotamian campaign victories listed in
       Intelligence Section's 1917 Christmas card   211
5   Greetings from 'Intelligence', 1918–19   219
6   Greetings from 'Intelligence' after the move
       from Basra to Baghdad   222
7   Colonel Parker's diary, October 1916   249
8   Letter from the Sharif Faisal to his brother, Ali   253
9   Letter from T. E. Lawrence to Colonel Parker   264

Maps

Endpaper   The Ottoman Empire in Asia, Persia
              and central Arabia before the First World War
1   Early twentieth-century journeys in Syria and
       Kurdistan   18
2   Journeys in Ottoman Syria, 1905–6   29
3   Routes of Aylmer and Butler, Carruthers,
       Aaronsohn and Musil, 1908–10   38
4   Routes of Leachman and Shakespear, 1910   55
5   Routes of Musil, Gertrude Bell and Lawrence,
       1911–12   79
6   Routes of Raunkiaer and Leachman, 1912   90
7   Routes of Gertrude Bell, Lawrence and
       Woolley, 1914   108
8   Routes of Gertrude Bell and Shakespear, 1914   121
9   Routes of Shakespear and Musil, 1915   156
10   Routes of German agents through Mesopotamia
       and Persia to Afghanistan, 1914–15   169
11   The administrative regions of Ottoman Syria   184
12   Division of the Arab lands in accordance with
       the Sykes–Picot agreement of 1916   242
13   Division of the Arab lands by the Mandates
       issued at San Remo in April 1920   344

Preface

I set out to tell the story of the Arab Bureau, to write about those men who dreamt their dreams dangerously in the openness of day, whose faith 'sold them into slavery', a splinter group who fought their own war within a larger conflict, fashioned their own ends and devised their own strategy.

But that was Lawrence's story, and as far as it went it could not have been better told. I soon saw that I was pursuing phantom figures, that the desert revolt which the men of the Bureau fostered with youthful enthusiasm and which focused on Arab leaders who were British pensioners in Cairo and Turkish servants in Mecca, Madina and Damascus, had unsuspected origins. I began to look afresh at the policy-makers and their henchmen, at the soldiers and agents, spies and camel dealers, at the travellers and explorers and their guides and contacts; and inevitably I was taken backwards and forwards in time in the search for cause and outcome. I looked especially at the intelligence and secret political files of all sides, of Turks, Austro-Hungarians, British, Germans, French, Zionists, Russians, the canvas stretching all the while from Berlin to the Yemen, from London to Simla, central Asia to the Red Sea coast. It took three years to trace the few surviving relatives of the chief actors in the drama, and even longer to sift through the massive official record now available to supplement the tales already told and published by the soldiers and 'politicals' who took part; and the one led me to a suspicion, at first nagging and then conclusive, that the other, the official record, was as revealing for what it did not contain as for its actual content.

Through the interest and generosity of relatives and friends of some of the chief personalities in my story, I was able to piece together a detailed account of British intelligence activities in the area conveniently covered by the term 'Middle East'; and I discovered from long-forgotten letters and diaries that in important respects I and other writers had been led woefully astray by official versions of events. In particular I was able to build up a much closer picture than I had previously gained of the long conflict between two of the principal departments of state in the British administration, the Foreign and India Offices. In the end I came to the conclusion, remarkable though it may be, that these two bodies devoted a larger part of their energies to spying on each other and countering each other's schemes, than to undermining the activities of the enemies of imperial Britain in the east. But I must not anticipate my own story or proffer conclusions before presenting the evidence. I acknowledge gratefully the many people who helped to set me on my right path, often opening up archives in their care which they had never looked into until I approached them. Without their help much of what follows could not have been written.

Even at a remove of seventy years I cannot divulge all my sources. A few custodians of private papers have asked for confidentiality and I have respected their wish. Some questions of life and death remain unanswered. Those who knew the truth are mostly no longer with us to tell; some of those who survive remain loyal to oaths of secrecy, an unfashionable attitude nowadays but one that I would not wish to abuse.

Though I have departed a long way from my original plan, the Arab Revolt still lies at the heart of the story, the flowering of ambition among a few Arab intellectuals and power seekers in the settled lands around the peninsula before and during the First World War, the controversial instrument of wartime policy-makers among the Entente powers, and the seed of perpetual unrest and danger in the modern world. The break-up of the Ottoman Empire and the schemes and disputes of the great powers which accompanied that agonised death and dismemberment present any writer with a pretty skein to unravel.

This is, as far as I can make it, a truthful account of events told through the diaries, recollections, letters and published accounts of those who took part, as well as through official records. I have tried to let them speak and to tread warily the well-worn paths of dispute in which Arab and Jew, Briton, Frenchman and Turk are most liable to hurl profitless abuse at each other. All the same I have used a pejorative title and that at least commits me to the proposition that I am dealing with matters of doubtful propriety, and though sides are not taken easily or lightly in the division of illicit spoils or the distribution of poisoned waters, it would be dubious caution to avoid all comment and to rely solely on bland statements of fact. Decisions taken in the heat of the moment, compromises forced by war, are too readily judged with Olympian certainty by those of us who can look back from lofty towers. But in the present age even the most secure towers are becoming infirm. History is catching up with us and verdicts are having to be made anew. Then imperial prestige and loyalty were the issues; territories won in war the prize. Now it is oil and claims to diminutive homelands that underlie bitter conflicts, senseless acts of violence, and the most sophisticated intelligence war in history. It is a story without a foreseeable end.

1982   H.V.F.W.

Acknowledgments

So many people have helped in the preparation of this book that I can claim space for no more than the barest mention of them. Some made substantial contributions, researching for me in distant archives; others merely conveyed messages. I thank them all and hope that none will be offended by equality of recognition. I must make just one exception, however. Immediately before his tragic death I was in correspondence with Earl Mountbatten of Burma about the battles inside and out of the Admiralty when his father was First Sea Lord. Lord Mountbatten responded to my questions with all the generosity which writers, historians and others who encroached on his time and patience took for granted, and I would like to express my own gratitude.

Otherwise, I thank: the directors, librarians and archivists of the Foreign and Commonwealth Office, India Office Library and Records, Ministry of Defence, Public Record Office, British Library, Royal Geographical Society, Royal Central Asian Society, House of Lords Records, in London; the Goethe Institute and the German Historical Association, London; Auswärtiges Amt, Bonn, and the Militärgeschichtliches Forschungsamt, Freiburg im Breisgau; Ministère des Affaires étrangères, Paris; the Aaronsohn Museum and Archive, Zichron Yakov; the Royal Sussex Regimental Association; the Middle East Library, St Antony's College, Oxford; the Royal Air Force Association; the municipality of Boulogne-sur-Mer, and the Chamber of Commerce of the same town; and the editor of *Air mail* magazine.

I also thank most sincerely: Mr C. H. Imray, Mme Magali Chappert, Mrs Jill Stevens, Air Chief Marshal Sir Brian Burnett, Mr Douglas Burnett, Mr John Locke, Mr George B. Blaker, Mr Rupert Lancaster, Mrs Valentine Vester, Lady Plowden, Mrs Mary Wilson, Major G. Horne, Mrs Rosemary Carruthers, Mr K. J. Philippides, Miss Jacqueline Williams, Mr

Nial Charlton, the Baroness Elles, Ms Rosemary Meynell, Mr
Derek Brown, Mrs Anne Edgerley, Mr Robert Lacey, Mr and
Mrs F. C. S. Lorimer, Major-General J. D. Lunt, Mr Heinz
Rosinger, Sir Victor Goddard, Wing Commander R. H. Mc-
Intosh, Mr C. Cook, Wing Commander E. J. G. Hill, Mme Col-
ette Douadarth and Mlle Douadarth, Mr J. Bodem, Mrs Sarah
Hilborne, Lieutenant-Colonel Gerald de Gaury, Dr Saad
Allam, Oberstleutnant Dr Rhode, the late Mr Lionel Jardine,
Mr Frank Stafford, Mrs Zahra Freeth, Mr William C. Tice, Mr
F. J. Elvy and Mr J. F. Elvy, Dr Maria Keipert, Dr Eva Strom-
menger-Nagel, Mr Christopher Gordon, Mr Frank Stafford,
Mr Z. Ahmed, and from my own family, Joan, Jill, Ruth, Diana
and Jo.

Credits

The author and publishers are grateful to the following for per-
mission to reproduce photographs and figures in the book: Ger-
trude Bell Photographic Archive, Department of Archaeology,
University of Newcastle upon Tyne, 1, 2, 5, 6, 9, 11, 13; Mr
George B. Blaker, Figs 2, 3, 4, 5, 6; Mr C. Cook, 10; Mrs Anne
Edgerley, 12, Figs 7, 8, 9; the Private Papers Collection, Middle
East Centre, St Antony's College, Oxford, 3; Royal Geographi-
cal Society, 4, 8, Fig. 1; Times Newspapers Ltd, 7.

'Thus said Jesus, upon whom be peace,
The world is a bridge, pass over it,
but build no house upon it.'

Akbar's inscription
at Fatehpur-Sikri (Agra)

1

The Battlegrounds

'Let the Turks now carry away their abuses in the only possible manner, namely by carrying off themselves. Their Zaptiehs and their Mudirs, their Bimbashis and their Yuzbashis, their Kaimakams and their Pashas, one and all, bag and baggage, shall, I hope, clear out from the provinces they have desolated and profaned.'

W. E. Gladstone, 1876

'See the Conquering Hero'

Suddenly, in the last days of the nineteenth century, the hotels of Syria, Mesopotamia and Persia filled with new breeds of men. Staff officers of the British, Indian and German armies, railway engineers, archaeologists, insect collectors, bird watchers: they came in uniform and civvies, bowler hats and *topis*, professorial floppy hats and even Arab *kaffiyas*, armed with field glasses, cameras, butterfly nets and revolvers. They came in the back-wash of the German Emperor's pronouncement, and soon their spies and agents proliferated in the towns and villages of the desert lands.

'Tell the three-hundred-million Moslems of the world that I am their friend,' the All-highest had proclaimed at the glittering dinner held in his honour at the *serai* of the Wali of Damascus on a wet and cold November evening in 1898. A week before he had journeyed through the valley of Ajlan, imbibing the scenes of Joshua's victory over the Amorites, to the Church of the Holy Redeemer, where a band greeted him with 'See the Conquering Hero', and the choir burst forth with 'Tochter Zions freue Dich'; on that same day Major-General Sir Herbert Horatio Kitchener arrived at Charing Cross station in London to the strains of 'See the Conquering Hero', to receive the gratitude of Queen and country for his defeat of the Khalifa's army in the Sudan; on the day after a young lieutenant of the Sirdar's army, Winston Spencer Churchill, enthralled a meeting packed to overflowing in London's dockland with a rousing speech on the 'Crowning Victory' at Omdurman.

The *Drang nach Osten* had begun in earnest. Arabs with their own brand of blarney named the German Emperor *Hajji*, the Pilgrim, after he had repeated his words of friendship at the tomb of Saladin and laid a wreath which bore the message 'Wilhelm II, Emperor of Germany and King of Prussia, in memory of the hero Saleh-ad-Din, son of Ayub'. But Wilhelm failed to see the irony implicit in his unbeliever's tag and wore it proudly. The twists and turns, the intrigue and political in-fighting which followed Germany's imperial declaration of leadership in the Islamic world are not easy to set out or to follow. A few disparate and seemingly unconnected asides are called for.

The new men and a solitary woman arrived along with the automobile and the telegraph. Politicians, administrators, academics, explorers, military and naval intelligence officers, practised spies: all were bent on doing (or undoing as the case might be) the Kaiser's bidding, equipped on the German side with singleness of purpose, divided on the British side by an obsessive fear of the Teutonic opposition and a growing conflict between Whitehall and the Viceroy's Government in India.

Hajji Wilhelm, for ever dipping the royal finger in the German Foreign Office gravy and unforgiving of anyone who failed to inform him of the most trivial development in the Islamic territories, and Kitchener – the dour, taciturn Sirdar of the Egyptian army and hero-figure of the British public – were to become the dominant personalities in the battle for ascendancy. But at the turn of the century the two great proconsuls, Curzon in India and Cromer in Egypt, stood sentinel over the imperial lifelines, hawkish guardians of Suez, the conduit of the British Empire and of the Persian Gulf, its strategic armature; and keeping a weather eye on the forbidden lands of central Arabia which lay between.

By 1903 Curzon had reached the end, effectively, of his viceroyalty. Following the Boer War he committed the most serious error of his political life by talking the Government into letting him have Kitchener as his Commander-in-Chief. These two resolute, imperious, immovable men – one of few words and even fewer friends, the other gregarious, brilliant and articulate, friend of Kipling and Oscar Wilde, blessed with 'the stature of Apollo and the complexion of a milkmaid' – came to blows over the Viceroy's established right to a say in the organisation and deployment of the Indian army through the Military Member of his Council. Kitchener would admit of no interference, and like Tweedledum and Tweedledee the contestants agreed to have a battle. Kitchener, with powerful friends in London and a reputation with the British public which politicians ignored at their peril, won the day. Curzon came home by way of the Gulf, with a great armada of the 'Indies' fleet to impress on Persian and Arab rulers great and small, on German and Russian and anyone else who cared to see, that Britannia was still the incontrovertible mistress of the seas, and that the Gulf remained a British lake. It was a bitter-sweet end for the apostle of Empire, but at least he returned to his long political ostracism in the glow of naval prowess and in the aftermath of the last great assertion of imperial pride before the long rule of the Liberals set in and Europe became the dominant factor in political debate and strategic planning.

A salutary warning had been wrung from Lansdowne by persistent parliamentary questioning, which was there for the world to see and hear: 'We should regard the establishment of a naval base or a fortified post in the Persian Gulf by any other power as a very grave menace to British interests, and we would certainly resist it with all the power at our disposal.' Curzon had captured in his younger days the spirit of the struggle now unfolding between Europe's most powerful nations:

> Turkestan, Afghanistan, Transcaspia, Persia – to many these words breathe only a sense of utter remoteness or a memory of strange vicissitudes and of moribund romance. To me, I confess, they are pieces on a chessboard upon which is being played out a game for the domination of the world.

A century after those words were written men would still say Amen. But in the first decade of the twentieth century there was a realignment of forces. Germany quickly ousted Russia and France from the table. Old enmities gave way to the Anglo-French-Russian Entente. Germany, already in bed with what its wittier politicians called the 'Habsburg corpse', began to look with increasing favour on Ottoman Turkey in the last days of Abdal Hamid, the tyrant-Sultan who was beset with the contradictory evidence of his reputed 30,000 spies, castigated by one of his own as the 'Whore of the World'.

In the shadow of a collapsing Ottoman Empire and a bankrupt, ungovernable Persia, and of massive commercial investment in those territories by German bankers and railroad builders, Britain decided to put its intelligence-gathering services in order.

Military Intelligence

The lessons of the Crimea had given rise to the old Topographical and Statistical Department of the War Office, the embryo of military intelligence. The Franco-Prussian War had given a salutary warning to generals and politicians that the mobilisation and rapid movement of armies demanded reliable information. The occupation of Egypt and the Sudan campaigns reinforced the warning. In 1887 the title 'Director of Military Intelligence' was coined, and in the same year a liaison officer from the Indian army was appointed to the DMI's staff.

Lord Northbrook, ex-Viceroy of India, General Brackenbury, Wolsley's intelligence officer in the Nile Campaign, Lieutenant Evelyn Baring of the Royal Artillery (Lord Cromer to be), Captain Hozier (father-in-law of Winston Churchill), Colonel Sir John Ardagh, the monocled sapper who saw the Prussian army march into Paris, and Sir William Nicholson, Adjutant of the Indian Army: these were the pioneers, greater and lesser, in the 1880s, of the military intelligence service which developed out of the reverses of the Egyptian and Sudan campaigns, and in response to the achievements of the Prussian army. Sometimes they were referred to in the popular press as the heads of the Secret Service, a misapprehension which survived late into the twentieth century.

Just before the defeat of Balfour's Conservatives in 1905, the War Secretary, Arnold Forster, introduced a new chain of command to the army based on the Prussian model, with a General Staff and a Directorate of Military Operations which embraced intelligence and took it away from the jealous rivalries of the Quartermaster General and the Adjutant-General which had dogged it since the Crimea. Major-General Grierson became the Director of Military Operations or DMO, and his intelligence sections were designated MO1 to MO4, the most active being MO2 under Colonel W. R. 'Wully' Robertson, the only officer of the army who actually rose through the ranks to carry a Field-Marshal's baton in his knapsack and who was to become Chief of the Imperial General Staff at the high point of the First World War. MO2 was responsible for all foreign intelligence, and from the sub-division of duties at that time derived the misnomer 'Middle East', which had been used to signify Persia and the Gulf territories since the Congress of Berlin but was now made to include everything from Egypt to India.

In 1906, military intelligence was moved from The Mall to the new War Office building in Whitehall, frowning from a majestic height on the older citadel of the Admiralty across the road. In 1907, MO1 became responsible for strategy and war games, MO2 as before dealt with Europe, the Ottoman Empire, Austria–Hungary and Abyssinia, MO3 combined Persia and India with Asia, America and Russia. MO4 retained its topographical and map-making role. And two important new sections were created: MO5 for counter-espionage, internal security and 'special' duties; MO6 for medical officers on foreign duty.

A significant division of duties was decided on in 1906 when General Spencer Ewart took over from Grierson. The Indian War Office, whose intelligence staff was organised on a system similar to London's, took over Arabia south of a line drawn from Aqaba to Basra, excluding Asir, Hijaz and Yemen. The rest of the Arabian peninsula, and the Ottoman territories of Syria and Mesopotamia, remained the provinces of MO2 in London. The first act of the new DMO was to order a *Military Report on Syria*, which replaced an earlier and most inadequate document called *Military Report on Arabia*. The new secret guide was compiled in collaboration with Admiralty staff and was largely the work of the stalwart old soldier who was Britain's military attaché at Constantinople, Colonel Francis Maunsell, and the enthusiastic young gentlemen who were known as honorary attachés at the Embassy such as Mark Sykes, Aubrey Herbert and George Lloyd. Between them they covered much of Kurdistan, Syria and Mesopotamia in their journeys and reported what they saw faithfully. But of course Maunsell had professional agents working for him, like the experienced Colonel P. H. H. Massy, who travelled widely in Anatolia and Kurdistan between 1893 and 1903, as well as two able young intelligence men – Harry Pirie-Gordon, an archaeologist working for the Admiralty, and Captain Smith of the Royal Engineers. Maunsell finished the work on which the report was based by the end of 1905; just in time, for by then the British Government under its new Liberal leadership had conceded to Germany a prior place in the affairs of the Ottoman Empire, and Maunsell had become an embarrassment. He was sent to Macedonia as a staff officer with the *gendarmerie* there, but retired after a year in mixed anger and frustration to the padded armchairs of the United Services Club in London, and to the War Office in Whitehall and the Royal Geographical Society in Savile Row, between which establishments he carried on a fruitful association with old friends as they passed through on their way to or from the deserts and metropolitan centres of the Middle East.

Germany's Secret Services had been weakened by the union of the German states, but the hard core of Prussian brilliance had survived the reign of Wilhelm II and the eclipse of the old master, Bismarck. In 1893 Baron Max von Oppenheim, Jewish archaeologist and *bon viveur* who was known in Egypt as 'The Spy', had toured from Damascus through Mesopotamia to the centre of British Gulf intelligence, Jask. By the turn of the century he was the chief of the Kaiser's intelligence services in the east, working through an establishment of studied respectability in Berlin, the Institute of Archaeology at 75 Wilhelmstrasse, reporting to Dr Zimmermann the principal Under-Secretary of Auswärtiges Amt, the Geman Foreign Office. Three years after his Gulf tour, in 1896, the German businessman Herr Wönckhaus, director of a Hamburg export–import company set up his stall at Lingeh on the Persian side of the Gulf, ostensibly to collect and sell sea shells, though he saw more profitable avenues to exploit in the service of the Fatherland.

Of Freemasons and Jews

France, Russia and Austria-Hungary followed suit and re-organised their intelligence services as they began to adapt to the new alliances among the powers and the new balance of muscle-power in the strategically vital territories between Egypt and India. The reshuffling came just in time. In August 1906 the merchants of Persia rebelled against the oppressive regime of the Shah and sought refuge from his police in the garden of the summer residence of the British Legation. There they drew up their country's first Constitution, which the Shah signed reluctantly two months later.

In the following year the Young Turks, who had long plotted the downfall of the old 'Fox', Abdal Hamid, from Paris and Salonika, Athens and Constantinople itself, marched on the capital and proclaimed the Constitution, which Midhat Pasha, the most respected of Ottoman politicians, had drawn up in the year of the Fox's accession, and which was disowned a year after he occupied the throne. Throughout the Ottoman Empire the peoples danced in the streets: Arabs, Turks and Kurds, Armenians and Greeks, Albanians and Jews. For a moment the word on every tongue was *Hurriye* – freedom. The word had a very English connotation. The excited crowds pushed and shoved their way over the Galata bridge and up to Pera, where the British Embassy stood beyond the green turf of its own cricket field, and carried the new Ambassador, Sir Gerard Lowther, aloft from his carriage to the Embassy steps. But it was short-lived joy. Lowther and his chief dragoman and closest adviser, the red-moustachioed Catholic Irishman, Gerald Fitzmaurice, had no time for the raw new men, preferring the 'aristocratic trades union' of the old diplomacy, of tried and trusted men. They saw a conspiracy of Zionism and Free-masonry in the revolution, the 'Flowery Revolution' as it came to be called.

Fitzmaurice spoke Turkish perfectly and had shown great courage in opposing his hosts during the Armenian massacres at the turn of the century. He bitterly disliked both Turks and Kurds. When Aubrey Herbert sang the praises of the latter race to him on one occasion he replied: 'Yes, a remarkable race. I don't know of any people I'd sooner have to help me – in a surprise attack on unarmed peasants.'

Germany, guided by its majestic Ambassador, von Bieberstein, and its ambitious sovereign, saw its opportunity. The Young Turks were admittedly a motley crew and traditionalists of the 'blue-blood and red-tape' school could hardly look with equanimity on their invasion: Talaat the post-office clerk, a hard man bursting with 'brutal *bonhomie*', a light in his eye 'rarely seen in men, but sometimes in animals at dusk'; Enver, slight and dapper, Italianate, given to admiring himself in mirrors and shop windows; Karasso the Jew, dreamer and financial wizard;

Javid, another Jew, accountant extraordinary and Anglophile; Ahmad Riza, President of the new Chamber of Deputies, bone-headed and immovable; Rahmy Bey, pro-British and gentlemanly; Izzat, nominally second secretary to the Sultan, who had feathered his nest by patronage and wire-pulling and was said to be the richest man in Turkey. Theirs was the new power, though not for a further five years were they to gain absolute dominion. Abdal Hamid survived the revolution by a year before he was sent into exile and succeeded by his benign brother, Mehemet V Rashid.

A new regime came to govern the four-hundred-year-old Empire of the Ottoman Turks, to fight for its own life in the face of internal strife and outside interference, and to perpetuate the terrible persecution of Armenians, Greeks and other Christian minorities which had begun in the last decade of Abdal Hamid's reign.

When the Persian *majlis* met for the first time on 7 October 1906, the Shah Muzaffer ad-Din was too sick to smoke the traditional pipe at the opening ceremony. He died a few days later and his successor Muhammad Ali Mirza pledged himself to stand by the Constitution. But tribal ambition and the conflicting aims of Russia and Britain reduced the new order to chaos. On 31 August 1907 the two great powers decided to divide and rule. On that date Sir Arthur Nicolson, the Ambassador at St Petersburg, and Alexander Isvolsky, the Russian Foreign Minister, signed a Convention which set out the spheres of influence of the two nations in Persia, Afghanistan and Tibet. Persia was divided into three, with Russia predominant in the north and Britain in the south-east. The oil-bearing central region was designated neutral. The Persian Gulf was specifically outside the scope of the Convention and Russia continued to recognise Britain's prior position along its coasts. In July 1909, with the country still in revolt, Shah Muhammad Ali took refuge in the Russian Embassy from the Bakhtiari tribesmen who hammered at the gates of Tehran. On 15 July his son Sultan Ahmad, who was thirteen years old, was proclaimed his successor.

In these events too, the influence of Freemasonry if not of Zionism was suspected by some who observed them closely. The Masonic lodges of Salonika and Turkey proper had close connections with the Grand Lodges of India, and Indian Freemasonry was fraternally allied to the lodges of Basra, which

had existed since 1839. The most influential of all the Masons of
the Middle East was probably Shaikh Khazal of Muhammerah,
the tiny principality on the Persian side of the Shatt-al-Arab.
Khazal was the almost inseparable companion of the Shaikh of
Kuwait, guardian of the oil installations of southern Persia, a
loyal ally of Britain from the turn of the century, and Grand
Master of all Freemasonry in Mesopotamia. He was also a close
associate of men in Turkey and Persia who were instrumental in
both revolutions. For good measure he was on intimate terms
with Abdal Aziz ibn Saud of Riyadh and with Arab officers in
the Ottoman army who within three years of the Young Turks'
revolution were plotting the overthrow of the new regime, with
Ibn Saud as their titular leader. Following the Persian revolution
Russia intervened on behalf of the deposed Shah Muhammad
Ali. The leader of the powerful Bakhtiari tribe, Hajji Ali Kuli
Khan, who was friendly towards Britain, went to Muhammerah
to confer with Shaikh Khazal before leading a successful march
on Tehran and forcing the Russians – who sought to reinstate
Muhammad Ali – to withdraw. Khazal promised neutrality on
the question of the Constitution.

Of Turks, Arabs and Christians

The last noteworthy journey into the Arabian interior in the
nineteenth century was that of an aristocrat of the Habsburg
Empire, Baron Nolde, in 1893.

At that time Muhammad ibn Rashid ruled all the heartland of
Arabia from his capital, Hail, which lay about 450 miles
south-west of Baghdad and a little farther south-east of
Damascus. The Turks occupied the coastal region of Al Hasa in
the Gulf, which they had captured from the Sauds in 1871 with
the aid of the Shaikh of Kuwait. The substance of Nolde's
conversations with Muhammad ibn Rashid was never revealed,
but Ibn Rashid had designs on Kuwait and on Al Hasa, and as
Nolde worked for the Czar's Secret Service it may be assumed
that his purpose was not entirely divorced from Russia's ancient
ambition to find a warm-water port in the Gulf, or from an
impending show of Russian diplomatic and naval strength in the
region.

The Austrian travelled farther south towards Riyadh after a
lengthy stay in Hail, but his devious mission and the rigours of
the desert seem to have turned his mind. He went back to

Damascus and from there made his way not to Vienna or St Petersburg, but to London. He booked into Long's Hotel in New Bond Street, where he remained for almost exactly a year, communicating with the Russian Embassy but otherwise in almost total isolation, locked in his room, until one day in March 1895 a maid opened his bedroom door to find him lying in a pool of blood, an elephant gun close by. He had left a note addressed to the Russian Embassy announcing his intention of taking his life and asking that a small sum of money in his London account should be used to give him 'a decent burial'.

Nolde's host, Muhammad ibn Rashid, among the greatest of all Arab leaders, died on 3 December 1897 from arsenical poisoning. Foreign gold, it was said, was sowing division in the ruling house of Hail. Six years earlier, in 1891, he had forced Abdurrahman ibn Faisal, the senior surviving member of the Saud family of Riyadh, who were the hereditary rulers of the central province of Najd, to flee with his sons to the protective custody of the Shaikh of Kuwait. In 1896 that Shaikh, Muhammad ibn Sabah, was murdered by his half-brother Mubarak, who became the chief mandarin of all Arabia in his heyday. Mubarak began to plot the restoration of the authority of the Sauds in Arabia at the moment of Muhammad ibn Rashid's departure.

Anarchy reigned on the Persian side in Makran and Arabistan, and a British official of the secret telegraph station at Jask was murdered. Germany appointed its first Vice-Consul at Bushire, and Russia sent a team of medical officers there to study a non-existent outbreak of the bubonic plague. The Turks used the same excuse to send a team of sanitary inspectors to Bahrain, but the Royal Navy prevented them from going ashore. France obtained a monopoly of archaeological exploration rights in Persia, and within a year Germany was granted a 'preferential right' to build a railway from Constantinople to Baghdad and beyond to the Gulf, and exclusive access to the archaeological sites of Mesopotamia. Russia appointed a Consul-General at Isfahan, where, as the British Foreign Office was quick to note, she had no commercial interests. The Turks demanded that Mubarak of Kuwait should acknowledge their authority over his territory and told him he was their *kaimakam* or Governor. Mubarak turned in vain to Britain. In April 1897 Greece threatened to annex Crete and Turkey declared war on her.

In 1898 Russia sent an officer of 'special ability' to its

Consulate at Baghdad, and both France and Russia sent warships to prance impudently before the Royal Navy's Gulf fleet. A Turkish invasion of Kuwait threatened. Austria and Germany withdrew from the European concert, and just before the Kaiser set out for his visit to Constantinople and Palestine, Britain's Ambassador in Berlin, Sir Frank Lascelles, had urgent words with him. But Omdurman seemed for the moment to renew John Bull's vigour. In 1899 the Resident in the Persian Gulf was given permission by Whitehall to make a secret pact with Mubarak. Modelled on an earlier treaty with the Sultan of Oman, it bound the Shaikh not to sell or lease any part of his territory to foreign powers without the consent of Britain. It was, in fact, designed simply to countermand German and Russian rail schemes, and gave the Shaikh precious little in return. He was to be offered a single payment of £5,000 (less if the Resident could get away with it) or an annual subsidy not to exceed £200. The Shaikh's brothers, Hamud and Jabir, were so incensed by the terms of the deal that they refused to witness the document. Eventually Mubarak was paid £1,000. He was offered better terms by both France and Russia, but the less-than-generous treaty was ratified in February 1899. A month later the Russian gunship *Gilyak* appeared and its Captain paid a polite call on Mubarak, while a Turkish naval force assembled offshore.

Though Britain's navy kept the rival forces at bay, it can hardly be said that Whitehall or the Indian Government (which was allowed little freedom of manoeuvre despite Curzon's protestations) were resolute in the matter. It was of course the time of the Boer War and both London and Simla had other problems to contend with. In September the Ambassador at Stamboul, Sir Nicholas O'Conor, delivered a 'stern warning' to the Porte. He reported back that the Sultan was 'greatly disturbed' by his language. In April 1900 O'Conor told the Sultan: 'HMG could not view with indifference any action which would change the status quo or give another power rights over territory belonging to the Shaikh of Kuwait, while not wishing to interfere with the Sultan's authority, etc.' Two years later the Foreign Office was telling the Viceroy: 'HMG acknowledges Kuwait to be part of the Ottoman dominions, subject, however, to the qualification on which we have always insisted, viz. that the Sultan's authority was of an insubstantial character.' That communication was intended for onward transmission to the Sultan, but Curzon refused to countenance it.

While these political events were taking place the warriors of the desert were fighting for their places in whatever territorial concert might emerge.

'No entanglement with Wahabees'

Muhammad ibn Rashid's successor, Abdal Aziz ibn Mitab, was a brave and accomplished leader, but he feared his own regicidal family so acutely that he never entered his capital at Hail during his reign, though some of his children remained there. The battles which followed his accession in 1897 were to be portrayed vividly by that most articulate traveller in the Arab lands, Gertrude Bell:

> Human nature being what it is – and at bottom the same in the Arab as in the European, pugnacious, ambitious, covetous, sometimes loyal but mainly treacherous, occasionally enlightened but always restless – the tribal fights in the Shamiyah desert may be expected to exhibit the same to and fro, change and interchange of alliances, as may be found in . . . Europe. The redeeming feature of the picture is its comparative bloodlessness.

When Sadun Pasha, chief of the mighty Muntafiq tribal alliance of the Euphrates, raised his standard, Abdal Aziz ibn Rashid, the head of the Shammar tribe, had declared: 'This cannot be. There cannot be two standards in the desert.' And in 1901 Ibn Rashid came to take down the standard of Sadun Pasha. But the chief of the Muntafiq and his ally, Ibn Suwait of the Dhafir tribe, stood firm and Ibn Rashid retreated, to return when the element of surprise was with him. At the subsequent Battle of the Reeds in the marshy territory of southern Iraq, Ibn Rashid won a decisive victory, though Gertrude Bell exaggerated somewhat when she compared it with Hastings or Waterloo. Sadun licked his wounds and made an alliance with Shaikh Mubarak and the exiled Sauds who now lived in Kuwait. They joined battle with Ibn Rashid at a famous Arabian war ground, Sarif on the plain of Tarafiyah, but again the Shammar were victorious. The Ottoman Government, seeing which way the wind blew, decided to back both Ibn Rashid and Ibn Sadun and to bring those chiefs together by offers of gold and territory.

Mubarak, just as sensitive to the nuances of desert war, went to the man who was known as the 'Butcher of Basra', his friend Sayid Talib, son of the Naqib, who was head of the orthodox or Sunni Moslem community of Basra, offering him 3,000 lira to persuade the Turks to seize Sadun Pasha. Sadun was invited to Sayid Talib's home, and in the night was taken aboard a Turkish gunboat, and thence transported to Aleppo, where he died in a prison cell. Sadun's son Ajaimi took over the leadership of the Muntafiq and showed himself to be a fine soldier; but perversely he went over to the Turks, who had so treacherously seized his father, and turned his back on Britain.

These conflicts between the tribes of eastern and central Arabia and the subsequent appearance of a Shammar army within Mubarak's territory, supported by a substantial Turkish force gathered at Basra, posed a serious threat to Kuwait and to Britain's position in the Gulf. But that threat was nullified early in 1902 by the dramatic seizure of Riyadh by the exiled Abdal Aziz ibn Saud, son of Abdurrahman al Saud; an event which brought to the Arabian political scene a man of great stature who was an implacable enemy of the Turk. From the first he held out his hand to Britain, but despite the efforts of the Indian Government and its servants in the Gulf, Whitehall was to reject his offers of friendship and alliance. Britain's Foreign Office continued to refer to Ibn Rashid of Hail as the 'Amir of Najd' and the Viceroy, Lord Curzon, continued to insist that Whitehall should reconsider its position now that the powerful Muhammad ibn Rashid had gone and Ibn Saud had returned to Riyadh. A complex web of intrigue was woven in the train of that event. In January 1902 the Turks occupied Mubarak's territory at Safwan, Umm Kasr and Bubiyan island. In March Ibn Rashid asked the Wali of Basra to help subdue the 'revolt' of Ibn Saud, telling Constantinople that Britain was trying to gain a foothold in central Arabia through Ibn Saud. And in September there was an attempt to take Kuwait by *coup de main*, led by Mubarak's half-brother Yusef and two disaffected nephews. The invaders were intercepted at sea by HMS *Lapwing*, but a British sailor was killed in the ensuing fracas, which led to an insistent demand for punishment. In the debate which followed these events the Foreign Office asked Sir Nicholas O'Conor to lay down the law and he did so in a memorable edict: 'No entanglement with Wahabees.'

In a note on the position which Britain found itself in at a time when German pressures and the changing allegiances of the desert became irresistible, the Foreign Office composed an essay, as much for its own consumption as for any other party, in which it said:

> But the whole history of the Persian Gulf, whether in the time of the Portugese, the Dutch, or the English, has shown that commercial prosperity inevitably leads to political hegemony, and in these circumstances it is a matter of grave concern whether, on political grounds, exceptional measures should not be taken to facilitate British enterprise in the Persian Gulf, and to neutralize the efforts being made to undermine our existing position.

2

Footprints in the Desert

The twentieth century began with some tentative first footings. Gertrude Bell, thirty-two years old and the favoured daughter of a wealthy English ironmaster, entered Jerusalem in December 1899 in time to see in the new century amid the teeming, multi-national throng of the Holy City. She had been introduced to the German Emperor in the year of his journey to Constantinople and Palestine, and now she stood where he had made his gesture to the Christian community in the Church of the Holy Redeemer.

She stayed at the Hotel Jerusalem, within two minutes' walk of the German Consulate, where she spent most of her time in the company of the Reich's envoy, Dr Friedrich Rosen, whose family she had known since a girlhood visit to Persia, where Rosen was then the German Minister, and her uncle, Frank Lascelles, the plenipotentiary of Britain.

While in Italy on her way out Gertrude had met the English archaeologist, Dr David Hogarth, who, like his German counterparts, was the scholarly link between his country's intelligence service and the men of academic reputation who were to work for it in the Ottoman lands. She set off early in January 1900 on a journey that encompassed both tourist attractions and strategically important railway and military installations, starting out with the Rosens but parting from them after a few days and going on with her own guide. She was on the move for almost six months, visiting Ain Musa, Madeba, Kerak, Wadi Musa, Deraa, Salt, Bosrah, Jabal Druse, Damascus, Palmyra; places where revolt had threatened or was soon to threaten; places on the Hijaz railway, which the Sultan's engineers with German assistance were currently building between Damascus and Madina. She photographed people and places and made copious notes and drawings, chiefly of Islamic and Crusader buildings and historical sites, but much that she recorded had a usefulness to the map makers and topographers of MO4 and the Royal Geographical Society in London.

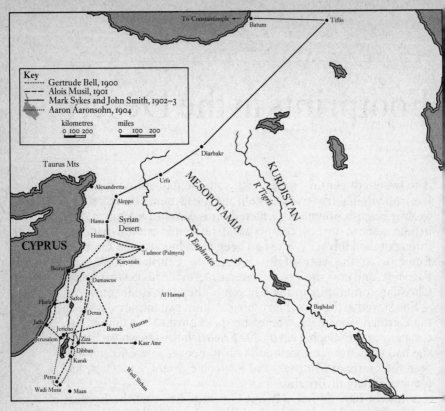

Map 1   Early twentieth-century journeys in Syria and Kurdistan

She was a familiar caller at the homes of the Bessam family in Damascus and Beirut. The Bessams were perhaps the richest and most powerful merchants in northern Arabia and Syria, protectors and helpers of Charles Doughty and many another Victorian traveller, suppliers to them of the official guides, the *ageyl*, whom Ottoman regulations stipulated must accompany any voyager in the Arab territories. Muhammad al Bessam, head of the family and son of Doughty's generous host Abdullah, was immersed in the conflicts of the desert and privy to the secrets of its princes.

As Gertrude and the rest of the *cognoscenti* jostled with pilgrims and sightseers, they paid increasing attention to the Turkish garrisons at Damascus, Deraa, Mashetta, Kerak and Maan. Here a new brand of Turkish soldier, and Arab soldier in Turkish uniform, goose-stepped on the parade grounds, trained by the old hero of the Franco-Prussian war, Field Marshal von der Goltz, and his military mission at Constantinople. As the visitors made notes and took photographs, a German railway engineer, Herr Meissner, was engaged in building the 900-mile track from Damascus to Mecca (though in the end he only reached Madina) along the old Hajj route trodden by countless men and camels in the past 1,300 years. The great political achievement of the Sultan, a train ride to the annual pilgrimage, had become one with military strategy, with the movement of supplies and armies, and the first European visitor to take a close look at the new route after the Englishwoman Gertrude Bell, was a Bohemian Jew of the Austro-Hungarian Empire, Alois Musil.

Musil stepped into Syria as Gertrude left, in July 1900. He too was cutting his teeth, photographing the inscriptions and wall paintings at the eighth-century Islamic castle of Amra in Moab, of which he had heard when a student at the Jesuit College in Beirut. His was the first eye-witness account of that early and singular repository of Islamic art. He was to return in the following year to complete the work of recording and preserving as much as he could of the paintings. And over the next few years he was to cross time and again the paths of Britons and Germans as they searched for ancient artefacts and surveyed the deserts; hearing much of each other, but taking care never to comment on each other's activities, except in secret reports.

Musil was to become the most accomplished and tireless member of that select band of scholar-travellers who were to follow a handful of Victorians into the depths of Arabia. A cosmopolitan citizen of the Habsburg Empire, he was usually identified as an Austrian. He took the name Shaikh Musa in Arabia.

He was born in 1868, fourteen days before Gertrude Bell, at the Czech town of Mahren, and was educated at the old Catholic university of Olmutz. He was ordained in 1891, gained a doctorate in theology in 1895, and went on to study Oriental languages at Paris, Beirut, Cambridge and Berlin. He was a brilliant student, and his ability to speak fluent Arabic at an early age and to engage in Koranic disputation with the best divines of the East soon came to the attention of the authorities in Vienna. As a student he was introduced to Herr Thomasberger, an officer of Austro-Hungarian military intelligence, at the Military

Geographical Institute of the Habsburg capital. He returned from Syria to his first university at Olmutz in 1902 to become professor of Old Testament studies, and did not revisit the Arab lands for six years. The years 1902 to 1904 marked the quiet before a storm of desert reconnaissance and espionage. Only the irrepressible Mark Sykes, back from the Boer War and determined to cement his position as the expert among politicians on matters Arabic, ventured into the Syrian and Mesopotamian outbacks, accompanied by an old friend from Cambridge, John Smith, with whom he argued incessantly. The two men split up at Aleppo, Sykes going on to the Taurus mountains, Smith diverting to Kurdistan and the Russian border at Tiflis. Between them they covered a good deal of ground and gained useful information on the tribes of the Euphrates valley and the hilly lands between Turkish and Russian territory. The journey took them well into 1903, when Sykes returned to England to marry Edith, the daughter of Sir John Gorst, Member of Parliament for Cambridge University. Sykes's father had increased his allowance from £2,000 to £4,000 a year, and the young man who was more inclined to prudence in his personal relationships than in his political actions, decided that he could afford the luxury of a family life. He and his wife spent their honeymoon in Constantinople, to which city Sykes was to return in 1905 as honorary attaché. Curzon in India and Cromer in Egypt were the men for whom he had the highest regard and to whose authoritative stature he aspired, but even they failed to measure up entirely to his proconsular standards.

As the German assault on Britain's position in the Persian Gulf gained impetus, the Balfour administration made decisive moves towards securing the position of Turkey as a buffer between competing European powers and the Indian Empire. Balfour and his Liberal successors sought to maintain the *status quo* by giving sanction to the Ottoman Empire in Asia and bolstering Turkey's European dominions. But to India the game looked different. The Indian Government saw an urgent need to establish friendly relations with the most reliable rulers and tribal leaders on either side of the Gulf, most of whom were at daggers drawn with the Sultan of Constantinople.

On 8 February 1904 Mr Brodrick, the Indian Secretary, sent a telegram to Curzon 'with the concurrence of Lord Lansdowne'. It read: 'The previous sanction of His Majesty's Government must be obtained before any steps are taken with a view to entering into closer relations with Najd, or to sending agents there.' Ibn Saud, who had re-established the authority of his family at their capital of Riyadh, was at the time engaged in desultory battles with Ibn Rashid, whose Turkish-armed badawin army was to be a thorn in the Saudi warrior's side for some years to come.

On 4 February the India Office had received a request from India for permission to send an agent to Riyadh to obtain reliable information on the progress of events. Lord Lansdowne and his Ambassador in Constantinople, O'Conor, 'concurred . . . as to the inadvisability of sending a special emissary to Riyadh or Najd'. And in December 1904 Lansdowne was even more emphatic. He told the Secretary of State for India, who of course relayed the statement to Simla: 'It should be clearly understood that the influence and interest of HM Government are to be strictly confined to the coast-line of Eastern Arabia, and that no measures are to be taken, or language used, which might appear to connect them even indirectly with the tribal warfare now in progress in the interior.' In the shadow of the Foreign Office ruling the invasion of the desert became the province of the expert, of the military intelligence officer and the civilian agent, representing not so much the interests of opposing powers as the conflicting interests of departments of state within the British administration.

In February 1904, as the Foreign Office slammed the door on the Indian Government's plans in central Arabia, a young Jew of exceptional gifts made his first journey of substance in the Syrian desert. His name – Aaron Aaronsohn – might have been chosen to predestine him to the tasks he set himself in the Bible lands. Stockily built, with fair wavy hair and blue eyes, and with an iron will, Aaronsohn carried on his broad youthful shoulders the aspirations of a people cowed by the long misery of their subjugation in the European pales of settlement, demoralised to the point where few of them had the will to fight for anything save day-by-day survival in a largely hostile world.

Aaron Aaronsohn was different. He was cosmopolitan, vigorous in body and mind, widely read in areas which would arouse no great rabbinical enthusiasm, and at the age of thirty he was one of the world's most respected experts in agriculture and agronomy. He feared no one, and rejected no one from his vision of a Palestine or Eretz Israel which, through his knowledge and the combined resources of Arab and Jew in developing the agriculture of the region, would become, if not paradise, at least a land of plenty. He was among the first to advocate the use of Arab labour on farms, a policy to which many of his neighbours were bitterly opposed.

He was taken to Palestine in 1882 at the age of six from his Rumanian birthplace, Falticeni. His father, Ephraim Fishel, was a hard-working and successful farmer; his mother, Malkah, a devoted wife. They set up their home at Zichron Yakov near Mount Carmel and became respected pioneers of the agricultural settlements which owed their origin to the philanthropic and autocratic father-figure of world Jewry, Baron Edmond de Rothschild. Aaron had studied at the Grignon agricultural college in France under the patronage of Baron Rothschild and later worked as an instructor at one of the Baron's estates at Mullah in the Druse country of Syria. He soon discovered that the Druse shaikhs who sold the land to the Rothschilds had deceived their purchaser. The terrain was infertile and useless. When he told his employer the facts, Rothschild replied that he had been sent there to concern himself with agricultural matters, not to question the sagacity of his employer.

Aaronsohn went on to Anatolia, where the Turks, who had heard of his reputation in Palestine, put him in charge of research at a large and prosperous estate known as 'The Devil'. His relations with the Turks were good and he made a number of useful contacts, but the job did not last long. He had become friendly with an engineer named Joseph Treidel and a Russian agronomist, Dr Selig Soskin. The three men, with little money between them, set up a Bureau for Technical and Agricultural Survey, the idea perhaps deriving from the Baron's unfortunate purchase from the Druses. The new association took him home to his family, from where he and his colleagues were able to make tentative probes into the Palestinian desert looking for plants, mineral deposits, water, and so on, analysing their finds when they returned to Zichron Yakov. Aaronsohn always rode his trusty mare Fahra, never a camel, and usually slept rough, wrapped in his *abba*, the woollen coat of the Arab. The Bureau attracted important customers from Germany, America, France and Britain, not all of whom confined their interest to agriculture. In 1904 Aaronsohn welcomed to Haifa a German scientific deputation.

It was the year of Herzl's death. The Jewish national home for which the Austrian had fought and conspired remained a distant dream. Two years earlier Herzl had talked to Joseph Chamberlain, the Colonial Secretary in London, of an alternative homeland. The wasteland of Sinai was mentioned, but Cromer in Egypt would not hear of it. Cyprus and even Mesopotamia, then part of the Ottoman Empire, came up for discussion. But the Zionists themselves were largely – and often angrily – opposed to alternative schemes. Palestine was the promised land. No other would do.

To the young man who now set off on the first of several exploratory journeys through the waterless wastes of Transjordan and Sinai the arguments were irrelevant. He had little time for alternative homelands, and even less for the nostalgia of his fellow Jews, for their constant wailing and ever-present sense of injustice. For him the opportunity was there in Palestine to be grasped by men of energy, good will and vision.

The vain effort of the Kaiser to intercede on behalf of the Zionists in 1898 during his visit to Constantinople was still fresh in the memory. So was Abdal Hamid's message of two years before. Following a visit to the Sultan by Herzl in June 1896, when he offered to 'regulate the entire finances of Turkey' in return for Palestine, Abdal Hamid told Herzl's friend Philipp Michael de Newlinski:

> If Mr Herzl is as much your friend as you are mine, then advise him not to take another step in this matter. I cannot sell even a foot of land, for it does not belong to me, but to my people. My people have won this Empire by fighting for it with their blood and have fertilized it with their blood. We will again cover it with our blood before we will allow it to be wrested from us ... The Turkish Empire belongs not to me but to the people ... Let the Jews save their billions. When my Empire is partitioned they may get Palestine for nothing. But only our corpse will be divided. I will not agree to vivisection.

Aaronsohn made his way by the Dead Sea to Transjordania, accompanied by the German scientists Blanckenhorn and Benzinger, the first part of the journey being by rail. He kept an immaculate diary in French. On 4 February 1904 they picked up their Arab guides Salim and Muhammad Rashid at Ras Mersid on the west coast of the Dead Sea and then rounded the lake as they progressed to the fortress town of Kerak, almost in direct line with Sodom and Gomorrah, Benzinger and Blanckenhorn making careful note of phosphate, bitumen and asphalt deposits, Aaronsohn concentrating on the flora of the region and water, vital to travellers and armies. Their twelve-day outward trip resulted in the discovery of three hitherto unknown water sources.

It was not a particularly long or difficult journey. But it had proved productive for the German contingent, who had photographed the troops at Kerak marching in German style with new uniforms, somewhere between khaki and green in colour, which made them almost indistinguishable from troops of the fatherland. They had found interesting phosphate deposits. They had touched on the Hijaz railway at Mashetta and Kalat Ziza. And they had made pictures and notes on plant life which would eventually find their way into the scientific press of the world.

They arrived at the Hotel Jordan in Jericho at 6.30 pm on 6 March. Aaronsohn's diary recorded: 'Petrides n'est pas là; sa soeur s'offre pour le remplacer auprès de moi. All right! Soirée passée à causer avec Anglais et Anglaises.' Who were the English whose appearance at the hotel in Jericho was sufficiently important for Aaronsohn to make a diary note?

Staying in that remote and mysterious city at exactly that time was a young naturalist fresh from Trinity College Cambridge with an almost predictable name – Carruthers. Douglas Carruthers was to become one of the last if not *the* last, of the gentlemen participants in the Great Game, anticipating Kipling as they made their way across desert and veld on that long trail where 'the wildest tales are true and the men bulk big on the old trail'. For the moment he too was learning the ropes, establishing contacts, following Herr Meissner along the Hijaz railroad. He was to become closely associated with the cartographical division of military intelligence, MO4. For the moment, however, he was a 'private citizen' in search of the oryx, that elusive and beautiful creature of the desert which ancient voyagers had thought was the unicorn and which, like the gentlemen explorers, was soon to fade from sight. He went down to Maan, where Arabia Petraea joins the Hijaz, where the railway would eventually turn off towards Madina, the Prophet's city, and then he went north to the Syrian desert. We know no more of his wanderings in 1904.

We know, however, that his journey went on into 1905, for he relates in a footnote to stories of later travels that he met Gertrude Bell for the first time in Damascus in April of that year: 'after over a year in Syria, I came into Damascus from the Palmyrene Desert, and on entering the Victoria Hotel found an English lady holding conversations in French and Arabic with the cosmopolitan crowd that was usually to be found there. She had just come in from Jebel Druse.'

Es-sitt, the Lady, arrived in Beirut on 18 January 1905, and two days later was at Dumeir, the Turk garrison town east of Damascus, 'deep in the gossip of the East'. She travelled back towards the Syrian coast – Ain al Kantarah, Haifa, Jerusalem – arriving just in time to have dinner with Mark Sykes and his wife on their honeymoon. Edith made a stout effort to keep the conversation within civilised bounds, while the two travellers engaged in an unseemly effort to outdo each other in their knowlege of people, places and affairs, their friendships with men of influence in London, Syria and Constantinople. Gertrude was kind about her hosts in letters home. She found them 'delightful'. Sykes had much harsher and ruder things to say. Gertrude set off towards the Jordan bridge on 3 February, and Sykes left on a leisurely journey by way of Damascus and Alexandretta to Constantinople. Gertrude, who always used silver cutlery and drank from crystal glasses in the desert, and whose trestle table was laid with the finest Irish linen, admitted that she travelled comfortably, 'but not like Lord Sykes!'

She was making her way to the stony desert of Hauran, to Jabal Druse, a place of increasing interest to Constantinople and London as the warlike inhabitants of that region carried on their bitter struggle with Moslem neighbours and the Turkish *gendarmes*. The area from the Damascus hinterland for hundreds of miles down to Wadi Sirhan (the nearly impenetrable gateway to central Arabia), and beyond to Jauf (then occupied by Ibn Rashid), was the traditional territory of the great Anaiza tribal confederation. But of all the enemies of the Druses, the Bani Sakhr took pride of place. Gertrude had begun to come close to the politics of the desert and the rivalries of its tribes:

Between the Bani Sakhrs and the Druses there is always blood. There is no mercy between them. If a Druse meets an Ibn Sakhr, one of them kills the other. Now one of my muleteers is a Druse. He has to pass for a Christian till we reach the Jebel Druse, 'for', said Namoud, 'if the Sakhr here' (my hosts of last night you understand) 'knew that he was a Druse, they would not only kill him, but they would burn him alive'. Accordingly, we have re-baptised him, for the moment, and given him a Christian name.

When at last she found the homeland of the Druses towards the end of February she found 2,000 horsemen ready to take off for an encampment of the Bani Sakhr. A month before the tribe had carried off 5,000 sheep from Druse grazing grounds. 'Tomorrow the Druses are going forth to recapture their flocks and to kill every man, woman and child they may come across.' Letters home bore the address *Umm al Rumanin*, 'the Mother of Pomegranates – but there aren't any', telling of the hostilities between her beloved Druses and their many enemies.

She stayed at Damascus in early March, making excursions to Baalbek and Aleppo, which by then were connected to Damascus by rail, and mingling with the international fraternity of the Victoria Hotel. She went on to Constantinople, where she enjoyed a restful cruise aboard O'Conor's yacht *Imogen*. A young Foreign Office apprentice, Percy Loraine, had just arrived and thus another life-long friendship was forged in a network of diplomats and high officials strung across the world. Among old acquaintances, Aubrey Herbert was about to embark on a journey down the Red Sea to the Yemen, where Italy was threatening war if the Turks did not prevent attacks on its ships; while Mark Sykes went off to Anatolia and Kurdistan on a final errand for the disgruntled military attaché, Frank Maunsell. The Foreign Office ban on travel in central Arabia prevailed, but activity on the edges showed a marked increase.

On 3 December 1905 Aaronsohn set off again, this time along the route of the Hijaz railway. He was accompanied by Blanckenhorn and they went by train to Deraa, the junction of the Hijaz line with the French-owned link from Haifa. They spent their first evening 'chez Miglievitz', 'chef du mouvement' of the railway, who was entertaining the much sought-after Meissner Pasha, accompanied by two young ladies. A game of tennis was in progress when the visitors arrived. Aaronsohn excused himself from dominoes after dinner so that he could write letters, and doubtless write up his diary. He engaged the services of a young Arab guide, Tuman al Hajji, and went off next day through the volcanic Hauran to Maan, where they met a familiar Frenchman, an agent of the Deuxième Bureau by the name of Delor. On to 'rose-red' Petra and back to Deraa and Meissner Pasha. Aaronsohn's notebooks were filling rapidly with the names of rare plants, the locations of water wells and Turkish garrisons, and the not-so-rare representatives of the European powers.

Aubrey Herbert, that gentle and improbable parliamentarian and intelligence officer – 'of crystal, unearthly goodness' as Sir Ronald Storrs put it – arrived at Hodeida in the Yemen in 1906, having set off from Constantinople in the previous August with his friend Leland Buxton.

Herbert's excursions into the Balkans and the Anatolian and Arabian wilds defied his own physique and the accepted constraints of desert travel. Each year his eyesight faded perceptibly and he learnt to type blindfold so that when his sight went completely as he knew it would he could still labour at his manuscripts. The experiment was not always successful. A report from the Embassy was addressed to the Foreign Secretary, Lansdowne, as 'My Dorl' and contained a number of other errors. It was later used by the Foreign Office as a guide to intending diplomats on how not to compose communications to the Foreign Secretary. He learnt, too, to love his fellow men despite their all too apparent wickedness. He became attached to the famous dogs of Stamboul, the wretched creatures that were used as scavengers to keep the streets clean, until the Young Turks despatched them to an uninhabited island in the Sea of Marmara, where they starved slowly and painfully, attempting to eat each other as they died.

He and Buxton spent some time with Storrs in Egypt before sailing down the Red Sea to Jiddah. They arrived at Hodeida almost a year after setting out, Herbert all the while singing the praises of the Turkish soldiery, many of them from the Balkan territories of the Ottoman Empire, and most with the lives of a good few Armenians or Kurds to their account. Herbert wrote:

Generally speaking, he [the Turkish soldier] had been exiled from his own country from three to ten years, and sometimes for even longer; he was paid the regal sum of four francs a month; he had campaigns behind him and campaigns before him, a very precarious reward in victory, almost certain death in defeat. Beside the elusive Arab, who took a hundred grinning shapes, he had to fight the poisonous desert heat of the lowlands and the fierce cold of the high mountains with the same equipment, and through it all lavished praise upon the goodness of Providence and upon the mercy of his own wise Government.

Even the sceptic Buxton was convinced. 'We agreed that the Turkish private soldier was an heroic figure.'

Herbert and Buxton went through sandy desert and flower-carpeted fields, skirting mountains and breathing the 'delicious air of the highlands', meeting a few Jews at Menakah who had survived the famine which had reduced their population by half in the past year or two, to Sanaa, where they were entertained by an Italian merchant, Signor Caprotti, who wore the fez and shared the almost universal belief of foreigners that British policies were devised with the greatest subtlety and cunning, and that the British political and military intelligence services were incomparably the best in the world. Italian disasters in Abyssinia in recent times were, he said, 'a calculated part of British political schemes'. The Englishmen were dumbfounded by his insistence on the 'extraordinary intelligence' of their fellow countrymen.

On Christmas Day 1907 they arrived at Muscat aboard the SS *Africa* from Aden, having travelled with a Britisher who had become a naturalised German and was known as 'Wolff', though that was not his real name. He sold aphrodisiacs to the Yemen Arabs, which were made up by his handsome travelling companion, a fictitious doctor who claimed to have made the pilgrimage to Mecca and was known as Hajji Ali. The Englishmen thought there was more to their travelling companions than met the eye.

Herbert's meagre physique was not up to so long and arduous a journey. He was taken ill aboard the *Africa* and was confined to bed at Muscat. It says much for his astonishing will-power that he went on by ship to Basra and then travelled overland through Babylon and Karbala, the city of the Shia martyr Husain, and on to Baghdad, Damascus and Jerusalem before returning by boat from Beirut to Smyrna and thence to his post at Constantinople.

On 8 May 1906 Aaronsohn set off again, this time from the Hotel Grossman in Tiberias on a short but remarkably profitable journey to the Golan Heights in Galilee. Apart from a call at the laboratory

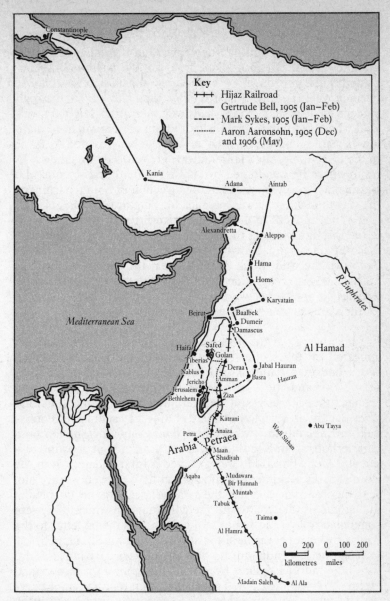

Map 2 Journeys in Ottoman Syria, 1905–6

of the scientist and Christian Zionist, Dr Torrance, to collect meteorological information for his colleague Treidel, this was essentially a botanical trip. Since 1902 when he was working for

Rothschild, Aaronsohn had been aware of the concern of agriculturalists at the deterioration of the world's wheat stocks. Cultivated since the dawn of civilisation, the precious seed had become weakened by intensive inbreeding and was increasingly subject to disease. Nobody had ever found the original stock, wild wheat or emmer, from which the basic ingredient of mankind's staple food derived. By 10 May he had reached Muzarib in the direction of the Haifa railway. He returned to Tiberias by train, where he was joined by another agricultural scientist, Dr Bermann. They went north in the direction of Safed, parting on the way to make separate searches for botanical specimens.

Aaronsohn went to the village of Rosh Pinah and as he wandered through fields at the foot of Mount Hermon he made the discovery of his life. Blowing gently in the breeze was a stem of *Tritticum,* the wild wheat. Within a year the young man who so far had sought recognition in an indifferent world, was famous. Articles and lectures were eagerly requested by the learned journals and societies of the western world.

In 1907 a young army officer who mocked and courted danger appeared on the scene. Lieutenant Gerard Evelyn Leachman was a one-man band; all the heroes of Rider Haggard, *Boys' Own Paper* and the North-West Frontier rolled into a single frame; lithe, fearless and belligerent. One of three sons and three daughters born to Dr and Mrs Albert Leachman of Petersfield in England (his two brothers died in infancy), he left both Charterhouse and Sandhurst without academic or sporting distinction of any kind. He was gazetted a First Lieutenant in the Royal Sussex Regiment in 1900 when he was twenty years old. Arriving in South Africa in the same year, he was so appalled at the fatigue of the troops and the conditions in which they were compelled to live and fight that he wrote a personal letter to the King. Authority never held the slightest fear for Leachman.

When he left India on the first day of February 1907, bound for his home in England by way of the Gulf and an overland journey to Syria, he carried with him a high reputation for bravery and insubordination. He had fought with distinction in the Boer War and later on earned the grudging respect of Curzon by defying an absolute ban on travel in Tibet, except with the approval of 'the highest authority' and going alone deep into the Dalai Lama's territory. He set himself a single, uncomplicated task in life, the defence of the Empire, and he often behaved as though he carried the entire burden of that struggle on his shoulders. So devout and proud a patriot might have been expected to see Curzon's point of view in India, but the army was entirely on Kitchener's side. In a letter home Leachman observed that his Commander-in-Chief was subdued. 'George Nathaniel sits on him as he sits on everyone. Very unpopular.' He visited Hormuz, Bandar Abbas, Bahrain and Bushire as he made his way along the Gulf to Basra, keeping a 'guarded' diary as he went.

The Persian navy – some six vessels of which the flagship was the gunboat *Persepolis* – was anchored off Bushire. Leachman noted that the Hamburg–Amerika line, which had begun its Gulf service the year before his arrival when the gleaming white *Candia* made a stately voyage from port to port, dispensing champagne and 'Deutschland über Alles' as it went, was now offering the Turks and Arabs free passage to Cairo and Jiddah for the Meccan pilgrimage. He spent a few days in Basra and then went by river boat to Baghdad, and thence along the Euphrates. On its bank he picked up two Armenians stripped of their clothing and all other possessions. 'The more I see of Turks the more I loathe them,' he observed.

He went overland to Aleppo, staying for one night at the Aziziyah Hotel, where he came to blows with a German officer in 'defence of the Empire', before taking the train to Damascus, Beirut, Mersina and Constantinople. He arrived at the Ottoman capital just ahead of Gertrude Bell and another countryman, Captain William Shakespear. He reached England on 18 April 1907 and a few days later was called to the War Office, where he was interviewed by the head of MO2, Colonel J. A. Haldane. The DMO had recently passed to Haldane a note from the Chief of Staff in India, General Beauchamp Duff, suggesting that there was an opportunity 'for non-official travellers to explore inner Arabia'. Beauchamp Duff wanted to use civilians travelling as businessmen under the aegis of the Indian Government. Haldane saw a brighter prospect in Leachman.

For several years the tribes of Syria and the northern deserts of Arabia had been relatively quiet. In 1908 they burst into life like dormant buds at the end of a long winter, as if stimulated by the changing climate of the world without. It was the year of the *Ittihad ve Terraki*, of Union and Progress and the high optimism of the millions who aspired to freedom in the Ottoman Empire; of the seizure by Austria–Hungary of Bosnia and Herzegovina, of renewed clamour for enosis in Crete, and of Bulgaria's declaration of independence from the Ottoman Empire. It was the year in which Britain sent a naval mission to Constantinople led by Admiral Sir Arthur Limpus, to counter the prestige of von der Goltz's military mission in the immediate aftermath of revolution, and to look closely at that strategic bottleneck, the Dardanelles. The year of war games in Whitehall and of H. H. Asquith's tenancy of 10 Downing Street. The year of the establishment of a Zionist office in Palestine, adroitly disguised as a bank. The year in which prominent Arabs set up secret societies – civil and military – in the chief provinces of the Empire. And the year in which Britain and France engaged in secret naval discussions, though committing nothing to paper.

Such events were trifles to the princes of the desert, for as yet they knew little of the world beyond Stamboul, and little enough of that despised place.

At the end of 1907 two seasoned British army officers, Captains Butler and Aylmer, who had been on staff duty in east Africa, returned home on leave by the somewhat circuitous route of Baghdad and Wadi Sirhan.

They arrived in Baghdad in January 1908 and set off hastily with their 'guide and friend' Muhammad al Mathi of the Bishr section of the Anaiza tribe. Their route took them to Kubeisah, a small Turkish garrison a few miles away from Hit on the Euphrates, and then across uninhabited gravel desert in a southwesterly line to the district of Awaj. They eventually joined the caravan trail from Najaf to Jauf, passing through the territory of the Dulaim tribes, whose tents they estimated to number 13,000, and noting on the way 'the supreme idleness of the badawin' and the rigmarole of camel discipline. They also noticed that their headdresses, red and blue spotted *kaffiyas,* were made in Manchester, England; and observed the tell-tale cough of consumption which had spread like wildfire in recent years.

They met groups of the Slubba on the last stage of their journey, the great hunters of the desert, childlike and bearing their poverty with fortitude, for they knew that if they ever accumulated a few sheep or camels the badawin would steal them. Tinkers, musicians, poets and hunters, they believed themselves descended from the original inhabitants of Arabia and they had been taught by endless persecution to accept joy and sorrow equably. They played a tune on their reed pipes for the visitors and pointed out their route.

The traveller to Jauf came first to Sakaka, an oasis covered with trees 'yielding delicious fruits', with three or four hundred houses and a population in those days of some 1,700. And there was sweet water in abundance. Merchants there traded with the Shia cities of Karbala and Najaf in Mesopotamia. Jauf itself, about thirty miles from Sakaka, lay in a basin about two miles across. At that moment the highly prized town belonged to Hail, though before the Rashid family usurped the authority of the Sauds in Najd it had belonged to the southern dynasty. Its governor in 1908 was Faisal ibn Rashid, cousin of Abdal Aziz ibn Mitab al Rashid, the warrior prince of Hail who had been killed in battle with Ibn Saud two years before.

Abdal Aziz ibn Rashid left four sons, of whom three were in Hail, Mitab, Mishal and Muhammad. The first of them, Mitab, succeeded to the throne at the age of twenty. The family connections of almost any Arab family are hard for the outsider to understand, for often sons take the names of fathers and grandfathers and it is not uncommon for there to be two important princes with exactly the same name at a given time. Thus Abdal Aziz ibn Rashid was the son of Mitab and was succeeded by his own son, Mitab. A few more family details are necessary, however. Abdal Aziz had five cousins, Majid, Salim, Saud, Sultan and Faisal, sons of Hamud, the son of Obaidallah, who favoured the Wahhabi house of Ibn Saud at Riyadh.

When Mitab, the son of Abdal Aziz, had been on the throne for six months his cousins Sultan, Faisal and Saud suggested a picnic party just ouside Hail and accompanying slaves were asked to give a display of riding skills. The Amir and his younger brothers, Mishal and Muhammad, together with their first cousin Talal, watched the horseplay with rapt attention, and while they did so the three sons of Hamud went behind them and shot each of them in the back. All were killed instantly except the youngest, Muhammad, who was five. He was badly wounded and was taken to his mother, the sister of the culprits, who nursed him back to health. But no sons of Abdal Aziz were to be left alive. As the young Muhammad lay in bed recovering from his wound, his uncle Saud went to his sister's home and cut the boy to pieces in front of the demented mother. Sultan, the eldest surviving member of this band of ruffians, became the Amir of Hail in 1906, and he was still on the throne when Aylmer and Butler arrived in the domain of Hail in early February

1908. His brother Faisal was Governor of Jauf. The British officers had no idea what to expect of their host. They only knew that his reputation was none too savoury.

'We found Faisal ibn Rashid sitting in a low room, the roof of which was supported by solid pillars. All round the sides of the room were spread carpets, on which sat his viziers and members of his court.' The English officers were received by the reprobate Prince, who asked many questions about England, its King and late Queen.

'I honestly think he considered he was treating us well in not taking all that we had, and turning us adrift to die in the desert,' said Butler. Even so, he fleeced them of their guns, watches, compasses and most of their kit.

They left Jauf after five days, making across Ruwalla territory by the eastern edge of the Wadi Sirhan to the Hauran country of the Druses. They stopped at Kasr Azraq, where the headman told them that he had two months before cut down the rotting remains of his predecessor, who had been left hanging by the Druses in his own doorway as a punishment for killing one of their number.

They arrived in Damascus with horns of Arabian oryx given them by Faisal ibn Rashid, who was about to take flight from Jauf in the face of another desert *coup*.

Aaronsohn made several return visits to the Safed region, where he found further samples of the wild wheat. In March and April 1908 he made his most extensive journeys in the wilderness. With Blanckenhorn at his side once more he set off from As-Safa at the southern end of the Dead Sea, through the dry wadis of Arabia Petraea to the territory of the Atiyah tribe at Finan. Then back to As-Safa, where units of the Turkish army were parading and both men took photographs of the Soldiers of the Prophet in their last days under the regime of Abdal Hamid. Within two months those troops would join others throughout the Empire in a wave of mutiny and British and Russian delegates would meet to plan the disposal of Europe's 'sick man'. 'Orient and Occident are no longer divided,' wrote Blanckenhorn over the entwined emblems of oak leaf and corn sheath, demonstrating perhaps an awareness of the success of his Emperor's policies.

In the same region he and Aaronsohn ran into a tribal group dressed in distinctive indigo *thobs* or long outer garments, the Howaitat, who occupied the desert region between Sinai and

Wadi Sirhan and whose principal shaikh was the roughneck
Auda of Abu Tayya. They returned along the Dead Sea coast to
Zerka and Hamam, where they obtained more photographs of
Turkish camps, and of local citizens protesting about military
service, which was compulsory for Arab and other Ottoman citizens. They went on to Jericho, where the German scientist
Professor Watzinger awaited them, then to Tel Nimrin, Jeriah,
and Tel deir Alla, where a badawin girl appeared smoking a long
pipe. Professor Blanckenhorn found more asphaltic deposits. It
was an arduous but successful journey, and the last that Aaron
Aaronsohn was to make for some time. In three years he had
obtained massive evidence of the plant life and mineral deposits
of the Syrian and Jordanian deserts. He had mapped much of
the natural water supply, correctly positioned a number of townships wrongly placed on British, German and French maps, and
made innumerable contacts among the consuls, *mudirs, kaimakams* and professional advisers from Ghaza to Beirut, from
Maan to Damascus on the now completed Hijaz railway.

He returned to Safed and the hills of Rosh Pinah and Lake
Tiberias in 1908 with a new companion, Avshalom Feinberg, a
young man who matched Aaronsohn himself in enterprise and
skill as a desert traveller. Feinberg was known among the Arabs
of the desert as Shaikh Salim. They were accompanied by
Aaron's sister Sarah, an 18-year-old girl whose beauty had
about it a fragile, vulnerable quality. They stayed with Dr Torrance in Tiberias and listened not for the first, or last, time to
the theological premise of that scientist and Christian Zionist,
that the return of the Israelites to Palestine would be the har-
binger of the second coming of Christ.

On his return to Zichron Yakov, Aaronsohn received a pressing invitation from the US Department of Agriculture to visit
America. He left for the United States at the beginning of 1909
and was offered the chair of agriculture at Berkeley, California.
But he did not intend to slumber in academic pastures or to stay
away for long from Palestine, Eretz Israel of the Jews. He met
the distinguished jurist, Judge Brandeis, Dr David Fairchild of
the Department of Agriculture and Henrietta Szold, the wealthy
49-year-old editor of the Jewish Publication Society. All were
greatly impressed by him and he returned home with funds and
enthusiastic support for the setting up of an experimental agricultural station.

Alois Musil had been given leave by the University of

Vienna, where he was now Professor of Biblical Studies, to make an extended journey during 1908–9 in western Palestine and along the Euphrates. As Aylmer and Butler reached Damascus, and Aaronsohn noted Turkish army dispositions by the Dead Sea, Musil was camped at Dumeir, a little way to the south-west of Damascus, arranging his cartographic material with Thomasberger, who was known in the desert as 'Tuman', and awaiting the arrival of Nuri ibn Shalan, paramount Shaikh of the Anaiza tribes and Amir of the Ruwalla. At the time, May 1908, Prince Nuri was the involuntary guest of the Turkish Governor of Damascus.

The cast was almost assembled, though one or two of the principal actors had yet to appear.

3

The Seeds of Revolt

'Why, O Musa, with the help of Allah, could I not found a dominion there, like that which Ibn Rashid has founded?'

The Prince Nuri ibn Shalan pointed south-east towards Jauf. Nawwaf, Nuri's eldest son, had left with the best men of the Ruwalla tribe and the fastest she-camels two days before them, while the Prince and his Austrian guest, who had persuaded the Wali of Damascus to give him his freedom, stayed in Dumeir for Ramadhan. It was 6 January 1909 when they approached the 'brow of Syria', the Wadi of Sirhan; Musil the learned Jewish theologian and Nuri Shalan, the proud old Arab, riding together with the Prince's slave-minister Amr at their side, and Nuri's falcon chained to his camel saddle, alert eyes blinking from behind its scarlet hood. Four slaves and a scribe rode close behind them.

'I could subjugate the whole of North Arabia, O Musa. Let Ibn Sa'ood rule in the South.'

'If Allah wills it,' replied Musa.

'Allah has willed it,' said Nuri ibn Shalan.

Musa sketched and made notes as he travelled and his host, who was a cosmopolitan among desert princes, indulged him in the habit, though other chiefs forbade so irreligious a practice. A fierce *shimal* blew as they marched over the volcanic territory between the great wadi and Jauf, and progress was slow. It was the route that Aylmer and Butler had taken in the opposite direction a year before, and much had happened in the interval at the Rashid strongholds of Hail and Jauf.

Before they left Dumeir, merchants from Jauf had brought news of Ibn Shalan's hereditary enemies. The Amir Sultan, who had succeeded to the title after the bloodbath in which he and his brothers had destroyed the family of the Amir Abdal Aziz ibn Rashid, was himself killed by his brother and fellow murderer Saud in May 1908, as Aylmer and Butler made their way from Jauf

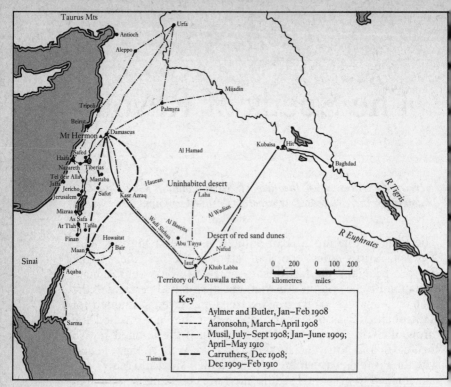

Map 3   Routes of Aylmer and Butler, Carruthers, Aaronsohn and Musil, 1908–10

to Damascus. But Abdal Aziz had another son, also named Saud, who was born of his second wife, who came from the family of Ibn Subhan. The boy was rescued by a slave and was taken by his mother's relatives to Al Madina in the Hijaz, where he was now in the care of the Sharif, Husain of Mecca, just restored to his position in the Holy City following the Young Turks' revolution.

At the time of his brothers' murder he was six. Now, two years later on the death of his uncle, Sultan, his supporters brought him back and with the support of powerful forces within the capital restored him to the throne, killing Saud, the brother of Sultan, who had claimed the amirate, along with all his followers. Faisal, the only survivor among the homicidal brothers who had committed the atrocity of 1906, deserted the Governorship of Jauf and sought sanctuary with Ibn Saud at Riyadh. Thus, Saud ibn Rashid, an eight-year-old child, ruled at Hail. And to make matters more difficult for those who wish to explain or understand the history of central Arabia, his chief minister was named Saud. He was Saud ibn Subhan.

These matters were the portents of other changes to come and of much discontent. He who ruled the whole of central Arabia, as did the Sauds a century earlier, and the Rashids at the end of the nineteenth century, could dominate the entire peninsula. He who wanted to control the periphery had better divide the centre.

Nuri ibn Shalan recognised the supreme authority of Ibn Saud and was well disposed to the young Amir of the south. And Ibn Shalan was now supported by Austria with the knowledge of the German Emperor. When he was at camp with Nuri at Dumeir, Musil had entertained Talal, chief of the Bani Sakhr tribe, to whom the Turks had given the title Pasha and a yearly subsidy, but whom they had since left in the cold: the completed Hijaz railway enabled them to transport their own troops to the territory he had once policed for them. Musil had given Talal a letter to an agent in Jerusalem, who had instructions to hand to the Arab chief six thousand rounds of ammunition for Mann-licher carbines already supplied by Musil's Government. It was the first of many shipments of guns and ammunition that Austria was to give to Arab forces in the Syrian desert.

On Thursday 4 February the Prince's party was at Subih among the sand dunes of the Great Nafud desert. A messenger arrived, yelling at the top of his voice as he approached: 'Nawwaf has taken Jauf!' He dismounted his camel and told them that two days before Nawwaf had led his force unopposed into Jauf and had proclaimed his father Amir of the oasis and all its environs. Nuri remained at camp at the watering place of Al Haujah to the north-west. Musa galloped with the yelling badawin to Jauf to meet Nawwaf, who was already installed in Faisal's mud-brick palace. According to Nawwaf, his father had received messages in Damascus from Ibn Saud and Faisal ibn Rashid telling him of events at Hail, of Faisal's dash to Riyadh to escape the new regime of the infant Saud ibn Rashid, and inviting Nuri to take possession of Jauf. Perhaps Nuri feared reprisals by the Shammar army of Hail, for he stayed in the desert and did not go to his capital for several months. But within three days all the surrounding tribes had sworn allegiance to him through his son. Shaikh Musa rejoined Nuri three days after entering Jauf.

As he arrived at Nuri's camp news of yet another homicidal assumption of power came from Hail. Hamud ibn Subhan, the uncle who had rescued the young prince Saud and who had recently brought home the infant, himself assuming the role of regent, had died from poison two months before, though the event had been kept secret until then. It was a strange if timely series of events which led by a succession of murders to the position which now prevailed, for Hamud it seemed had been done to death at the instigation of his brother, Zamil ibn Subhan. And Zamil, who became regent for the young prince, was well disposed towards Ibn Saud at Riyadh.

The Subhans were closely related by maternal links to the collateral branch of the ruling house of Hail, the family of Obaid, or Obaidallah; and that family was traditionally loyal to the Wahhabi doctrine of the southern dynasty, unlike the descendants of Abdullah ibn Rashid, who despised the puritanism of the Sauds.

As he waited to move on from the stony expanse of the Hamad desert Musil met Shaikh Auda Abu Tayya of the Howaitat, who called at the camp of Nuri ibn Shalan at Al Haujah. Here was the lovable reprobate who in time to come was to manifest to the world an oversize vision of the badawin leader, roguish, bellicose, and perverse, surrounded by tribesmen dressed magnificently in *thobs* of indigo, or riding to the desert raid with bandoliers across their chests and spotted *kaffiyas* worn high and proud on their heads; accompanied by womenfolk of extravagant beauty, eyes glittering like diamonds through the slits of their *burqas*.

The old Shaikh had returned from an act of robbery on the Bani Hutaim, but had met his match in a Shammar raiding party who intercepted him on his way to Nuri ibn Shalan in the hills of Misma. A bullet had shattered his elbow, not by any means his first war scar, nor his last. The irascible Auda had seared his damaged limb with a hot iron by way of traditional badawin surgery, and had it bandaged in his own tent. It had swelled and was giving him great pain. Musil applied antiseptic treatment and re-bandaged it, and Auda decided that the gifted doctor Shaikh Musa must accompany him until his arm was better. And so the Austrian marched south across the hot waterless waste towards Taima behind the banner of the Abu Tayya.

Returning to Nuri's camp through Wadi Sirhan, Musil saw the last lion ever to run free in Arabia shot by a tribesman. As he went, he was photographing, drawing, collecting specimens of plant life and rock and earth, recording even the lyrics of songs sung by lovesick boys and girls of the Howaitat and Hutaim, Shammar and Ruwalla, as they lamented and serenaded in the still cool nights. He arrived back in Damascus in May 1909. By June he was on his way again to the camping ground of Prince Nuri at the south of the Hamad, inspecting the now crumbling remains of Kasr Amr, whose wall drawings he had copied on his first visit as a student. His journey came to an end on Saturday 19 June, when he returned to Damascus and straight away filed a report to the Austro-Hungarian Embassy at Constantinople. Nuri had told him that he (Musa) was 'dearer to him than his first-born son, Nawwaf'.

The universities have been traditional hunting grounds of the Secret Services of most European nations, and the nurseries of subtle and sometimes devious minds. They also provide the choicest forms of academic cover. The 'honest seeker', archaeologist, botanist, geologist, ornithologist even: all give scholarly justification to the tasks of looking in strange places and recording the evidence of eyes and ears. The anonymous men who seek out the desired talents can seldom have alighted on a better prospect than David George Hogarth, Winchester and Magdalen, Oxford, with firsts in mods and humanities, tutor at his old college by the year 1886, patriot and man of Empire, with a poor opinion of 'men in the lump', and a disdain for democracy. His qualifications were impeccable, and as luck would have it he was attracted to a career in archaeology.

Of course family and social connections are not without importance in such matters, and here too Hogarth was blest. By one of those strange chances which so often determine human affairs, it was the Church that set him on the path of espionage. His father, the Reverend George Hogarth, himself a scholar of merit, was acquainted with Professor Palmer before the latter's untimely death in the Sinai desert, where he had been sent with the intelligence officers Gill and Charrington and £30,000 in gold in the wake of the occupation of Egypt. Hogarth was also well known to a dynasty of Oxford Arabists and students of the Semitic races, the Margoliouths. David Margoliouth occupied the chair of Arabic at Oxford, and in turn was well acquainted with the head of the London School of Oriental Studies, Denison Ross. Ross was to become a 'special adviser' to the Director of Military Intelligence, and from about 1896 was active in helping and assessing likely candidates for service in the Middle East. His first and most inspired find was Gertrude Bell, for a woman with an ability to speak Arabic, the resourcefulness to survive long spells in the desert, and a keen understanding of archaeology and ancient architecture to justify her travels, was at that time almost too good an intelligence prospect to be true. Gertrude was at Lady Margaret Hall, Oxford, with Hogarth's sister Janet. Hogarth's father had another clerical friend, the Reverend Henry Thomas Armfield of Leeds; and Armfield's daughter married the naval officer William Hall, who became the first Director of Naval Intelligence when a staff was formed at the Admiralty in 1882 in the aftermath of the occupation of Egypt and the mishaps of the Sinai expedition.

Between 1887 and 1907 the dapper, autocratic Hogarth with his goatee beard and peremptory air of academic certainty had served with a number of archaeological expeditions. He was in Asia Minor under Sir William Ramsey, the famous epigraphist and historian of early Roman and Byzantian churches, who sent him off to Greece to learn his craft. He then served in Paphos, Ephesus, Knossos and Crete with Sir Arthur Evans, the Keeper of the Ashmolean Museum at Oxford; and in Egypt with the British Museum team at Assint. In 1897, while digging in Crete at the time of the joint effort of the European powers to expel the Turks, he acted as correspondent for *The Times*.

In 1897 he was appointed director of the British School at Athens, and in 1909 succeeded Sir Arthur Evans at the Ashmolean. Meanwhile he had published several books which had firmly established his reputation as a scholar with precise views on the Ottoman Empire, especially the Levant and the Arabian peninsula. During his travels in Asia Minor he met another Englishman who, like most of his contacts, flits in and out of the story of British involvement in the Arab countries – Valentine Ignatius Chirol, who was forty-eight years old at the turn of the century and who started work as a clerk in the Foreign Office in 1872. Chirol had been Consul-General in Berlin and had travelled extensively in Asiatic Turkey, Egypt, Persia and India, was on terms of close friendship with Charles Hardinge, the Foreign Office Under-Secretary who was to succeed Lord Minto as Viceroy of India, and with Gertrude Bell. In 1899 Chirol succeeded Sir Donald Mackenzie as director of the Foreign Department of *The Times*. He too had written a number of books on the East. He bore the fetching nickname Domnul, given to him when he was working in Rumania, apparently a colloquial term for the true-blue Englishman. The cogs of military and naval intelligence, foreign news-gathering and genuine archaeological inquiry therefore meshed nicely in the recondite world of David Hogarth.

One actor who had been waiting impatiently in the wings made a fleeting appearance on-stage in the summer of 1909, raw and a little uncertain of his way but determined to master the habits of the people he moved among. Thomas Edward Lawrence was a small, physically delicate man, just over five feet five inches in his socks, and twenty-one years old when he arrived in the Levant aboard the SS *Mongolia*, armed with Baedeker, an *irade* signed by Curzon, some maps in need of updating given to him by the young archaeologist working for naval intelligence, Harry Pirie-Gordon, and a camera – uncommonly for the time equipped with a telephoto lens – supplied by David Hogarth.

In his first year at Oxford in 1905 Lawrence had become friendly with another bright spark, Leonard Woolley, junior Assistant Keeper of the Ashmolean under Evans and Hogarth. Lawrence, whose subject was medieval history, showed a keen interest in pottery and ancient buildings and he made a number of useful finds among the rubble of building and road works going on in Oxford at the time. Woolley left in 1907 to join the University of Pennsylvania dig in Nubia, and Lawrence was awarded an exhibition at Jesus College.

The first decade of the century brought radical changes to Britain's military intelligence organisation, as the threat of war between the powers waxed and waned, as unrest in the Ottoman Empire produced revolution and the Balkan wars, and as the Greeks of Crete rebelled against the Turks for the second time. In 1906 the Turks had seized Aqaba in British-administered Sinai, but they withdrew before the expiry of an ultimatum. In 1906, too, a War Office *Report on Arabia* pathetically thin in topographical content, was superseded by the *Report on Syria*, containing much more information mostly supplied by Colonel Maunsell before his peremptory dismissal from Constantinople.

Hogarth's men were to provide Britain's counterpoint to the highly skilled operations of the Deutsche Orient Gesellschaft, which by 1908 was well established along the Euphrates and Tigris. By the time Hogarth's team arrived in Syria the threat of conflict had reached the point where the War Office had decided no longer to publish details of 'special duties' conducted by the Directorate of Military Operations. The affairs of MO2, embracing Germany, the Near East (Egypt, Syria and Asiatic Turkey), France and other territories, were put in the hands of Colonel Count von Gleichen, ex-chief of intelligence in Cairo and military attaché in Washington and Berlin. India and the Arabian peninsula became the parish of Colonel J. A. Haldane in a newly constituted MO3.

In 1908, just before the Committee of Union and Progress (CUP) came to power and soon after Abdal Hamid had ordered an extension to the Euphrates branch of the Baghdad Railway, crossing the river at a point close to Carchemish, Sir Gerard Lowther was asked to apply to the Sultan for permission for a British team to dig there. By a happy chance the British Museum owned the lease of a site there, just outside the village of Jerablus. Hogarth went out to start the dig in the late summer of 1908.

In the following year, after consulting with Hogarth, Lawrence decided to submit a thesis on the military architecture of the Crusader fortresses for his degree. Thus, in June 1909 he left on his first journey to the Middle East. He arrived in Beirut on 6 July with the vague plan of completing a 1,000-mile walk through Syria. In fact he took a fairly leisurely stroll along the coast road to Nabatiya and the southern end of the Lebanon mountains, swimming in the river Litani, acquiring a guide and asserting early on that 'Baedeker drivels as usual architecturally'. Then he worked his way inland to Safed, near the scene of Aaronsohn's momentous discovery and site of the hospital of the London-based Mission to the Jews, whose director Dr Anderson and his assistant Nora Harrison had shown the young Jewish agronomist generous hospitality when he visited the region in 1906. Then down to Lake Galilee and Tiberias to visit another friend of Aaronsohn and other Syrian travellers, Dr Torrance, whose optimistic view of Palestine's future was shared by few of the Jews or Christians who called on him, though most of them were keenly interested in his detailed knowledge of the Syrian terrain.

Lawrence doubled back to the coast at Haifa by way of Nazareth and the slopes of Mount Carmel, and then returned to Beirut. At Jubail he called at the American Presbyterian school presided over by Miss Holmes, and met a Quaker-educated teacher there, Miss Faridah al Akleh, who took him for a German tramp. In a relatively brief acquaintanceship with Arabs, Jews and Gentiles in the Holy Land Lawrence had already formed some definite views. Observing the squalor of badawin life and the luxurious vegetation of the Jewish colonies and smallholdings, his thoughts turned to biblical Palestine: 'Palestine was a decent country then, and could so easily be made so again.

The sooner the Jews farm it all the better: their colonies are bright spots in a desert.'

His route is not easy to follow from here on. Only his letters home to his mother and brothers offer support for the supposition that he visited the places he intended to go to. And from the beginning Lawrence combined a power of invention with sharpness of mind which made him a formidable adversary and a subject of unique fascination to the biographer. From Beirut he went on to Syrian Tripoli and by 22 September he was at Aleppo. From there he seems to have gone across the Euphrates to Urfa and the hideouts of the twelfth-century Assassins south of the Taurus mountains, sleeping on the roofs of Arab houses or wherever else he could find a cool berth for the night. Then back to Aleppo and down the Hijaz line to Homs, Hama and Kalat Husn, 'the finest castle in the world', now a Turkish penitentiary to which Gertrude Bell had helped to transport two handcuffed prisoners five years before. At this time Lawrence spoke to his hosts mainly in French. He had mastered no more than the customary greetings in Arabic and few of them spoke English. He went on to that other famous fortress town, Kerak, by the Dead Sea.

He had been provided with an armed escort at Aleppo. But on 22 September when he reached Kerak he wrote home to say that his money had run out, his boots were 'porous' and his feet blistered, and that he was returning to England. His camera had been stolen at Urfa. Pirie-Gordon's map had become bloodstained. Pirie-Gordon himself had been attacked by Kurdish tribesmen somewhere between Aleppo and Urfa. It was probably in order to meet Pirie-Gordon that Lawrence crossed the Euphrates to Urfa.

In a letter which was held back from publication by his brother until 1954, Lawrence had said that he could not take any interesting film of the site he visited because of the theft of his camera. 'I really meant to,' he added. In his first journey to the East he had shown himself to be a tough and courageous young man, who was willing to endure a great deal of privation for King and Empire. It is equally certain, however, that his accounts of journeys in Syria and the northern domains of the Ottoman Empire are scant in detail, seldom more than half true, and hardly ever easy to follow. His power of invention, often demonstrated as much by the curious process of contrived omission as by what he actually says, is manifested in the earliest of his letters from the East. But the same omission of vital facts is characteristic of the letters, books and articles of other travellers of the time: and perhaps the most curious fact of all is that the principal wanderers in these desert lands, though they knew of each other and of each other's missions, hardly ever referred to their fellow travellers, even in private correspondence, though they stayed in the same hotels and crossed paths in the same barren stretches of country.

Leachman reappeared at the dawn of the century's second decade, to be quickly followed by a procession of civil and military agents whose activities took on an air of increasing urgency. He arrived at Baghdad on 2 December 1909 after a journey which took him from Karachi to Muscat, Bushire, Muhammerah and Basra. In each place he stayed with the Political Officer or Resident. The capture of Jauf by Nawwaf ibn Nuri Shalan and the consequent extension of Ibn Shalan's dominion over the desert regions of Syria were certainly topics of discussion, as was the strengthened position of Ibn Saud at Riyadh.

The Foreign Office had reaffirmed its ban on travel in central Arabia in November 1906 and again in April 1907. It found a willing ally in the Secretary of State for India. Morley told the Viceroy firmly, 'No incursions into the central region'. Constantinople underlined O'Conor's dictum, 'No entanglement'. Ibn Saud had asked for British protection and the Resident at Bushire had asked for guidance. 'Tell him no reply can be expected,' Morley told the Viceroy curtly.

But Ibn Saud did not acknowledge Ottoman suzerainty. And Ibn Saud now had a well-disposed and powerful friend in the north. Zamil ibn Subhan was secretly sympathetic to the Wahhabi Amir of Riyadh and was in close touch with him through the refugee, Faisal ibn Rashid. Zamil saw his nephew Saud ibn Abdal Aziz grow into a handsome boorish lout, while the desert expanse of Jabal Shammar was rife with feuds and discontent. Settlers and Shammar badawin fled south to the territories of Ibn Saud, lands which a decade before had been part of the ordered empire of Muhammad ibn Rashid. Around Jauf townsmen and nomads sought the protection of Nawwaf ibn Shalan. The oasis of Taima, one of Ibn Rashid's richest possessions, deserted the ruler of Hail and asked the Turks to provide a garrison. At the end of 1909 Zamil ibn Subhan recognised Ibn Saud as his overlord in secret discussions conducted through Faisal ibn Rashid.

Faced with a rapidly changing balance of power in central Arabia which could have the most damaging consequences for Britain's own position in the Gulf and among the coastal shaikhdoms over which the Viceroy held sway, the simmering conflict between the Government of India and the Foreign Office came to the boil again. Even under the sick and compliant Viceroy, Lord Minto, the Government of India had been unwilling to sit back complacently while an uncontrolled chain of events threatened its naval bases, its lines of communications and its authority.

Kuwait was the watchtower from which events in central Arabia could best be observed, and in 1904 a tentative move towards involvement in the affairs of Ibn Saud and Ibn Rashid had been made by appointing a mild and competent army lawyer, Lieutenant-Colonel S. G. Knox as Political Agent to Shaikh Mubarak. But Foreign Office injunctions to observe but not to interfere had been strictly observed. Just after Knox's appointment, when the Turks were using Abdal Aziz ibn Rashid as a battering ram against Ibn Saud and the father figure of Arabian politics, Shaikh Mubarak, the appointment was thought likely to embarrass the Ambassador at Constantinople and Knox was withdrawn on the pretext of illness. He returned after an absence of nearly a year, but he had little influence on proceedings in the interior. 'I very much fear that the present Cabinet will have nothing whatever to do with Central Arabia,' the Resident, Percy Cox, told him in 1906.

By 1907 the attempts of Britain's representative to control the artful Shaikh of Kuwait had become hilarious. On 27 July the Political Agent at Muhammerah, McDouall, wrote privately to Knox in Kuwait to tell him of rumours that Mubarak wanted to be rid of him and proposed to smuggle a lady into his bedroom to compromise him. On 5 August Knox replied: 'Thanks for warning . . . but it is an impossible scheme.' Knox also referred to 'the mischief' of Mubarak and his friend, Khazal of Muhammerah, and of their contacts with German agents of Wönckhaus. In June 1908, Knox wrote to Cox: 'Mubarak must, I think, be brought to his bearings and taught his place . . . we can't take all his bluff lying down.' In July: 'Shaikh is, I am afraid, intriguing in all directions . . . impossible to place the smallest reliance on his statements.' August: 'We have got Shaikh Mubarak alarmed and in a yielding mood.' By September Cox was alarmed. 'There is no doubt that Shaikh Mubarak is suffering from

mud in the head . . . you on the other hand are inclined to be
much infected by the atmosphere of your surroudings . . . He is a
difficult character. Would a better class of dragoman help?'
wrote the Resident. The need for a new and stronger Agent was
apparent.

In April 1909 Captain William Henry Irvine Shakespear was
appointed in his place. Some eight years spent in the Indian
Political Service had demonstrated that this Englishman with
the most English of names was made of stern stuff. He had been
Cox's deputy since the new Resident took over at Bushire in
1904, combining the role of Consul to Bandar Abbas with that of
First Assistant at the Residency and he had come into immediate conflict with the Russians and the Persians. During his
Persian term the Indian Government decided to build a new telegraph station at Bandar Abbas to supplement the exposed Jask
station, and it was decided to make it part of the consular complex on the sea front, some way from the centre of town. The
Persian builders, egged on by the Russians, started to erect it in
the town without consulting the Resident or the Minister in
Tehran. Shakespear allowed them to proceed until it was half
constructed and then called in a party of Bluejackets, who stood
over the contractors while they pulled it down brick by brick.
The Russian, Ovseenko, was appointed 'on special duty' to Bandar Abbas soon after the episode, and he and Shakespear quickly
came to blows.

The newly appointed Political Agent adhered firmly to the
edict of Britain's finest Consul in the East, Claudius Rich, who
exerted a dominating influence over the Baghdad Residency in
the early days of the nineteenth century and who left for his successors a rule for dealing with Oriental despots: 'Nothing but
the most decisive conduct will do; any other will increase the
insolence of his disposition.' But Shakespear was not xenopho-
bic. Though he disliked Persia, that 'pestilential place', he
admired the tribesmen of the Indian frontier, of Afghanistan
and Arabia, and he entertained a burning ambition to explore
inner Arabia and to meet its ascendant star, Ibn Saud. As soon
as he arrived in Kuwait he began a series of journeys into the
interior of eastern and central Arabia that were to make him one
of the most proficient and productive of all desert explorers, and
to build him an everlasting reputation among the tribes as the
single outsider who moved among them as a friend and equal.
He acquired a fine she-camel, which he called Dhabia, a pack of

hunting salukis, and a falcon which he trained to fiendish performance and which he named Shalwa. With his animals and his
faithful retainers he made a princely passage through the
Dahana, the largely unexplored region of dunes and red sands
which sweep from the Nafud of the north, around the Tuwaiq
hills, Palgrave's 'Caucasus of Arabia', and disappear in the
sands of the Rub al Khali, the Empty Quarter in the south. He
began to investigate the flanking belts of scrubland and stony,
sandy wastes called Dibdibba and Summan and Hadjarah, and
the coastal strip of Al Hasa; and he sailed the Gulf with spectacular skill in the Agency yacht, *Lewis Pelly*. But not for some
twelve months was he to meet Ibn Saud.

Leachman and Shakespear had a great deal in common, with
some essential differences. Both had immense physical strength
and proven ability to survive in the most unwelcoming terrain
and among the most treacherous of peoples. As army officers
they had both achieved reputations for courage and endurance
under adverse conditions. Shakespear, with a long family tradition of service under the Raj to look to, was born into the practice as well as the concept of Empire. 'Waterloo' Arthur
Shakespear, who was listed at the Duke's Ball, and Sir
Richmond Shakespear of Afghan and Khivan fame were two
distinguished ancestors among many who had served in India
for more than a hundred years. Shakespear's accomplishments
were those of the more popular army officer and administrator.
Modestly equipped academically, his schooldays at Portsmouth
Grammar School and King William's College in the Isle of Man
had been marked chiefly by sporting success. He was good at
rugby football, and cricket, and an outstanding yachtsman.

The lanky Leachman was gifted neither academically nor at
sport. Only rifle shooting appealed to him at Charterhouse. His
sinewy strength seemed to explode from his tall, languid frame,
like the pounce of the wildcat. Many an Arab chief was to go in
fear of him; others nursed grievances over the years and swore
revenge. Shakespear, on the other hand, though he was
hot-tempered and capable of using fists and gun without too
much premeditation, was generally content to win the friendship
of Arab chiefs and tribes by example, by his prowess as a horseman and rifle shot, as a desert traveller and Gulf sailor, and
more especially as a hunter among huntsmen.

When he reached Baghdad, Leachman stayed with John Gordon Lorimer, the Scot whose stewardship of the Residency

there compared favourably with the legendary regimes of predecessors such as Rich and Rawlinson. He would normally have
had to apply to Lorimer or to Percy Cox for authority to travel in
central Arabia. But he had no need to do so. He already had
permission from MO3 in London to travel into the interior.
Whitehall had decided to find out for itself – in the teeth of its
own edicts – what was happening in Ibn Saud's domain.

At the end of December 1909 Leachman had left the Baghdad Residency in disguise for a two-week journey to the Shia
cities of Karbala and Najaf, putting to the test for the first time
his ability to survive incognito among the most fanatical Arabs.
He seems to have succeeded, for he returned to the hospitable
and keenly interested Lorimer on 25 Janury none the worse for
wear. Already there were signs that Leachman was being
watched by the Turks. His biographer Bray, who himself travelled the same paths at this time, was to write: 'Even at this early
stage in his wanderings Leachman's diaries are very guarded
regarding important matters.'

On the way to Baghdad he wrote to his mother: 'Just a line to
say that I am off today on my travels. I have been so rushed
lately.' There was no further word from him for five months,
when he wrote home again:

> I warned you I could not tell you where I was going . . . I
> have been making a great and to a certain extent an unsuc-
> cessful attempt to reach the unknown parts of Central Ara-
> bia. The Turk for some reason objects to ambitions of this
> kind so I have had great difficulty in getting away.

In the months between those letters he had been involved in
one of the most adventurous and dangerous excursions into the
interior ever undertaken by a European. He had walked deliberately into a bloody battle between the two biggest and most warlike tribes in Arabia, the Anaiza and the Shammar. And as he did
so, Shakespear was invading the deserts to the south of his path,
Douglas Carruthers was advancing through Wadi Sirhan and the
northern Nafud, on a 'hunting expedition', and Musil was packing his bags once more for a journey along the Hijaz railway.

After some days of preparation at Baghdad, where he stayed
with Daud Bey Daghistani, the son of the Wali of Mosul, and
after some hard nights of boisterous party-going and debauch-
ery, Leachman finally set off in the direction of the Rashid

capital of Hail on 3 February. Again he wore Arab dress, and by now he spoke a fairly fluent form of Najdi Arabic which was to stay with him for the rest of his life.

His party was led by Shaikh Majid ibn Ajil, who was connected by marriage to the young Amir of Hail. They made for the Darb Zobaida, the ancient pilgrim route from Najaf to Hail and Madina, joining up with the caravan of Shaikh Abdullah, who belonged to the Abda Section of the Shammar. On 13 February Leachman was seated in a tent of the Amarat listening to tales of Musa an-Namsawi, Musil the Austrian. To quote Leachman's biographer again, Musil was 'doing for the Turks and Germans what Leachman was doing for his own country. Musil was no soldier, but he was an expert intelligence agent and his splendid work was spread over more than twenty years of indefatigable labour.'

As he listened to Majid's friends talking of 'Musa' in the tent of the Amarat, Leachman became aware of a disturbance. As his own party had marched along the Darb Zobaida with its huge force of Shammar badawin to the fore, another army had marched in parallel, the eastern Anaiza of Fahad Bey ibn Abdal Mehsin ibn Hadhal. Although nominally under the authority of Nuri ibn Shalan, the paramount chief of that great tribal federation, Fahad Bey was a law unto himself. Old and nearly blind, ponderous in speech yet still in his advanced years an expert horseman, he was one of the most respected princes of the desert. After dark his men raided the camp of the Amarat, who were of the Anaiza federation but always at daggers drawn with their consanguine tribes and thus often camped with the Shammar. Many prisoners were taken and the harem tent was looted, but as is the badawin custom the women were unharmed. Majid alternately demanded and pleaded as the attackers swept through the tents, taking everything of value and rounding up men and animals. Leachman was taken with other prisoners to the Anaiza camp, where he met Fahad Bey, his features 'sunk into the lifelessness of clay'.

This was but a taste of events to follow, a normal tribal raid, and Fahad was generous to his guests. Leachman sat silently through most of the haranguing between old enemies who knew each other well. The prisoners were allowed to return, stripped of their belongings, to their own force. Next day Leachman met a party of Slubba who told him that almost all the Anaiza were on the warpath and moving towards Ibn Rashid's capital.

A camp of the Madan Shammar was attacked on 14 February,

but two of the Anaiza raiders were killed and some booty stolen on the previous day was restored to its owners. By the 17th they were in the valley of Jumaina, where some 3,500 Anaiza tents were pitched, a small part of the force gathered for the assault on Jabal Shammar. But the Anaiza were surprised by the sudden appearance of the Shammar, and Leachman could only stand and watch as an orgy of looting and killing took place before his eyes; men and young boys, horses and camels, were indiscriminately slaughtered while women rushed past the Englishman pleading with him to take their jewellery and keep it safe until after the battle. Of the vast Anaiza camp not a vestige remained, except for the great white tent of the Prince Fahad. Zamil ibn Subhan, the Regent of Hail, had said that enemy chiefs must not be attacked, and the old man was able to rejoin his tattered army on the way to the village of Ghuribiya. While the looting was at its height Leachman sat in the tent of another Fahad – Fahad ibn Dughayim, 'a true badawin' – writing letters. Intruders rushed in and out of the tent and the tall, bronzed Englishman who was easily taken for one of their kin cursed them and told them to get out of his light. With a candle burning at each side of him he went on writing. A youth who saw his favourite uncle killed in the skirmish shot himself in front of Leachman. It was a violent baptism.

Leachman and the Shammar were on the march again during the same night and soon they could see a fairyland of lights in the valley which lay before them, thousands of camp fires glowing, bursting into flame then dying away, for they approached the assembled Shammar army of Zamil ibn Subhan, the Regent of Hail, who was called Ibn Rashid for courtesy's sake.

Leachman was to remain at the camp of the Regent and the young Amir, who was his ward, for five weeks. He gained a valuable insight into the politics and relative strengths of the forces in desert Arabia which must have kept the DMO and the Foreign Office occupied for many a day. He was received at the camp by Abdullah ibn Mubarak al Faraiq, standard bearer of the royal household, 'gorgeous' in his gold-threaded *abba*, and was soon engrossed in the bloody history and insane rivalries of his hosts.

During his first week among the Shammar there was heavy rain. On the first day, 18 February, he was taken to the great white marquee of Ibn Rashid, where the impressive Zamil greeted him with an unexpected smile and the direct unblinking

gaze of an honest man. With him was the young Amir, Saud ibn
Abdal Aziz, 'a beautiful, bad-tempered little boy'. The infant
Saud was already a good horseman, and riding appeared to be
his only accomplishment and amusement. He told the Englishman as they talked, rain beating down on the tent, that he was
weary of attending the *majlis*, the daily parliament and law court
of his elders, and Leachman could see his point.

The Englishman spent a few days travelling among the tribes
with the war-scarred Abdullah ibn Mubarak, before that warrior
departed for Hail leaving Leachman the poorer by a golden
sovereign and the richer for a luscious kiss on the mouth delivered at the last moment.

Zamil refused Leachman permission to go on to Hail, and so
he was confined to the Shammar camp until given authority to
go back to Baghdad. On 20 February he started to write a long
letter to Shakespear in Kuwait.

Dear Shakespear

I know you by name from Gibbon in the Intelligence at
Simla. I am here at camp with Ibn Rashid near Hail. Three
days ago I was with a very large mass of the Anaizah on
their way to attack Ibn Rashid. In the evening the Rashid
appeared and utterly defeated the Anaizah who got away
with their camels only. Rashid's men looted thousands of
tents. I took refuge with some Shammar who were prisoners with the Anaizah and with whom I had been for a
few days before they were captured.

He went on to detail the latest happenings within the
Rashid family, adding: 'The Regent wants news of his victory to
resound as much as possible.' He asked Shakespear to take
delivery of his mail in Kuwait and concluded:

They say civil war has broken out in Ibn Saud's kingdom, between his two brothers. I believe this is true. You
know who the rival factions are so I won't bother you with
details.

Sincerely,
G. LEACHMAN

The letter bore the address 'Camp of Ibn Rashid, three
days' march from Hail' and was dated 23 February.

He finally left the royal encampment on 25 March, bidding a fond adieu to Zamil and 'the little Amir' and joining a caravan bound for Khamasiya, where he met up with Ibn Sadun, chief of the Muntafiq tribes. He wanted to go to Kuwait to meet Shakespear, but he was compelled by an order sent on from Zamil, the Rashid Regent, to turn back before he could join the road to Kuwait and find out at first hand what was going on between Ibn Saud, Shaikh Mubarak and the British Agent. Shakespear had been at camp a stone's throw from where Leachman and Ibn Sadun now wandered, making his own observation of preparations for a desert battle the results of which, in the form of human debris, surrounded Leachman and the chief of the Muntafiq.

The two most remarkable Arabian travellers of the early twentieth century were destined never to meet. Leachman's return journey, though it was wide of its intended path, was almost as eventful as his outward mission. But Shakespear takes up the story. He turned up in Kuwait on the last day of February with a diary full of valuable exploratory notes and some colourful vignettes of princely intrigue. While camped at Halaiba on 15 February, a discreet distance from his compatriot's path, he picked up news of the feud in Ibn Saud's family which Leachman had mentioned in his letter. As he talked to men of the Mutair tribe round the coffee hearth he heard of an attempt to murder the Saudi Amir by the administration of poison. The culprits were two cousins of Abdal Aziz, claimants to the throne which the young Ibn Saud had occupied in January 1902.

The *Gonsul* as the Arabs usually called him, or *Skaishpeer* when they were on familiar terms, was the first outsider to hear the story of this latest attempt at a homicidal assumption of power in Najd, and as is the way in the desert he was treated to the abstruse history which went with every badawin tale, much of which he knew already though some was novel to him. Since the return of Ibn Saud to his capital, Riyadh, following his celebrated attack on the fortress of the Rashid Governor, Ajlan, he had welcomed back from exile almost all the displaced members of his family, including the sons and grandsons of his uncle Saud, who claimed a prior right to the title 'Amir of Najd'. And it was in pursuance of that claim, presumably, that two of the grandsons, Ibn Saud's second cousins, set out in 1910 to poison him. The young men responsible were hurrying across the desert to Al Hasa, where they hoped to find protection with the

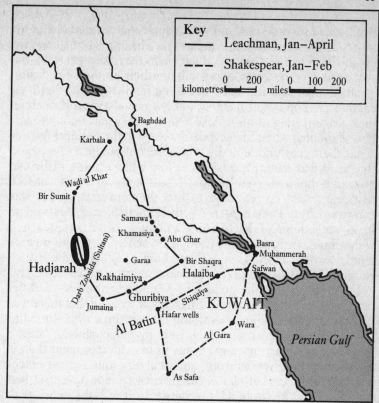

Key
— Leachman, Jan–April
--- Shakespear, Jan–Feb

kilometres 0   200   miles 0   100   200

Baghdad
Karbala
Wadi al Khar
Bir Sumit
Samawa
Khamasiya   Abu Ghar
Basra
Muhammerah
Hadjarah   Garaa   Bir Shaqra   Safwan
Rakhaimiya   Halaiba
Darb Zobaida (Sultani)
Ghuribiya   Shiqaiya   KUWAIT
Jumaina   Al Batin   Hafar wells
Wara
Al Gara   Persian Gulf
As Safa

Map 4   Routes of Leachman and Shakespear, 1910

Ajman tribe, when Shakespear heard of the discovery of their murder attempt.

By the time the Englishman arrived back in Kuwait, a very much alive Ibn Saud and his brothers were waiting for him. Shakespear was anxious to learn in detail the fortunes of the family of Al Saud in the complex realignment of tribes and princes which had been taking place over the past decade; since, in fact, the equilibrium of Arabia had been upset by the death of the all-powerful Muhammad ibn Rashid in 1897.

He joined Shaikh Mubarak and the Saudi princes on the night of his arrival, 28 February 1910, taking dinner with them in the vast and ugly palace of mud brick which was the home of the mercurial Mubarak. It was a formal occasion. The old Shaikh

and the Englishman knew each other well by now; well enough
to have had several stand-up rows which commended one to the
other. But several of the Sauds eyed Shakespear suspiciously,
especially Saad and Muhammad, a moody pair who did not
share the easy, outgoing personality of their brother, Ibn Saud.

Shakespear and Ibn Saud got along famously from their first
encounter. The Political Agent did not reveal a great deal about
their first meeting in his official report – they met again the following evening when Shakespear was host at the Political Agency
– but there was undoubtedly talk of recent political events and
Ibn Saud was naturally anxious to know the attitude of Britain
now that he had established his authority in Najd. Shaikh
Mubarak could be relied on to fuel the conversation. He was
compared by a contemporary with Richelieu, and was said to
have 'something of Richelieu's ambition as yet unquenched
within him'. In 1903, when Curzon presented him with a cere-
monial sword, he exclaimed: 'Now I am a soldier of the British
Empire!' To Britain he remained something of an enigma.

It is unlikely that the politics of Arabia were neglected at the
dinner table, but in his report Shakespear insisted that there was
no political discussion. Describing his meetings with Ibn Saud
and Mubarak, he confined himself to personalities. 'Shaikh
Mubarak was even more generous in his entertainment than is
his usual very generous wont, and at a very rough guess entertainment and presents for these princes cannot have cost less
than £20,000,' he wrote. Of the young Amir of Najd, he wrote to
his chiefs: 'Abdal Aziz, now in his 31st year, is fair, handsome
and considerably above average Arab height . . . He has a frank,
open face, and after initial reserve, is of courteous and genial
manner.' The brothers, he reported, were of 'dour and taciturn
manner'. He concluded:

> Abdal Aziz in particular, is a broad-minded and straight
> man . . . His reputation is that of a noble and generous
> man who does not descend to mean actions . . . Abdal Aziz
> did not discuss politics with me beyond remarking that he
> thanked God there were no Turks nearer his capital than
> al Hasa, and that the English, as friends and brothers of
> Mubarak, were themselves his brothers and friends.

Shakespear was to become the lone protagonist of the Saudi
Amir's cause, though backed judiciously by Percy Cox at Bushire

and by the Viceroy. Leachman became the lookout of the War Office: a dashing, irrepressible invader of forbidden regions at the heart of Arabia, without political commitment, simply doing the job asked of him with little care for the consequences to himself or to those he observed.

Mubarak and Shakespear said farewell to the Sauds on 4 March. Six days later the Amir and his brothers were back in Kuwait with a ragtag army, and the oasis of Jahra was thick with unkempt soldiers of the desert and their animals. Leachman was still at the royal encampment of the Shammar. Shakespear discovered that Mubarak and his 'son', as he called Ibn Saud, were preparing a raid on the army of Ibn Sadun. Shaikh Mubarak's son Jabir took charge of the Kuwait troops. Ibn Saud commanded the cavalry. They set off on 11 March for the plain between Rakhaimiya and Ghuribiya west of the Batin depression which marked the undefined boundary between Kuwait and Najd. Two days later they suffered a humiliating defeat. Ibn Sadun's disciplined tribal army decimated the Saudi-Kuwait force.

When Leachman reached the battlefield on 30 March, five days after leaving Ibn Rashid, he found the area littered with the corpses of the combined army. Vultures and jackals had devoured most of the victims' flesh, though a few bones were still clad with noxious remnants of human tissue. The appearances of Mubarak's army on the battlefields of Arabia were seldom distinguished.

On 31 March Leachman received a message from Zamil ibn Subhan telling him to find Ibn Sadun, who eighteen days before had won a great victory over Ibn Saud and Jabir ibn Sabah. By 1 April he had joined up with the Muntafiq, and was able to give a first-hand account of that powerful tribe. Of Ibn Sadun: 'A most delightful man. I was more at ease with him than anyone.' By repute Mubarak of Kuwait was not, he said, as good a man. News came that Ibn Saud was preparing another attack on the Muntafiq, and Shakespear confirmed that new preparations were afoot at Jahra. As Mubarak and the Saud family sorted men and camels under the eye of one Englishman, another marched with the army of Ibn Sadun, an army 'martial and inspiring, with Sadun at its head'. But the Saudis and the Kuwaiti Shaikh thought discretion the better part of valour on that occasion. Shakespear had given them a stern warning not to resume the fight. The badawin were released from Jahra, and Ibn Saud and his family returned to Riyadh.

Leachman left Ibn Sadun with regret, 'this fine old man, so up to date and so courteous, a very rich and splendid soldier, and a cordial enemy of the Turks, whom he had beaten in fight on many occasions'. But the Muntafiq leader was about to be betrayed to the Turks, and his son Ajaimi take over the leadership. Ajaimi became the bitter enemy of the betrayer, Sayid Talib, and perversely the ally of the Young Turks in Mesopotamia. Leachman arrived back in Baghdad on 21 April, draped in his customary disguise, with 'inviolate pride in himself as an Englishman', to make his report to London through the military attaché in Constantinople.

In February – while Leachman and Shakespear were attending to the tangled affairs of Ibn Rashid, Ibn Saud, Mubarak and Ibn Sadun – Douglas Carruthers was at Maan as the guest of Meissner Pasha. He was officially hunting the white oryx, and he found that Meissner had two of these magnificent creatures as pets in his garden at the garrison station on the Hijaz railway where he had his temporary home. Carruthers enjoyed a hospitable stay and then went off with Bani Sakhr tribesmen through Wadi Sirhan into the Nafud desert, close to Leachman's route, ostensibly in search of the wild variety of a creature that had all but disappeared from Arabia.

And on 21 February Musil had left Vienna in response to an urgent telegram from the Austro-Hungarian Embassy in Constantinople asking him to report for a journey along the Hijaz railroad. He was to compile detailed maps of the region between Maan and Al Ala in the Hijaz. He arrived in Damascus on 21 May in the customary guise of Sayid Musa, accompanied by Thomasberger and Leopold Kober, a Viennese geologist. They went by train to Maan to meet Meissner.

While the Austrian mapped and measured along a remote stretch of the Hijaz railroad, his English counterparts were engaged in conflicting activities in the hinterlands of the Persian Gulf. Shakespear and Leachman shared two close contacts in India – Captain C. M. Gibbon of the Royal Irish Fusiliers, who was working for the DMO'S Intelligence Department, and Captain F. Fraser Hunter of the Survey of India, who in 1906 joined with Lorimer to supplement his *Gazetteer* of the Persian Gulf with maps and topographical detail, an undertaking which was to remain on the 'Secret' list until 1930 when it was declassified, but marked 'for official use only'. Shakespear was also in frequent touch with Lorimer, and at about this time they devised a system of keeping each other in touch with events without treading on the toes of the Foreign Office, through a newsletter which circulated only to the most trusted of their colleagues. Lorimer's loyalty was divided by a strange arrangement through which the Baghdad Residency was primarily responsible to the Ambassador at Constantinople though it was maintained by the Government of India. Just as oddly the Basra Consulate was manned by a servant of the Levant Political Service, F. E. Crow, who though responsible to the Foreign Office through Constantinople was in 'demi-official' touch with Lorimer and Shakespear. Shakespear was also in regular contact with HMS *Sphinx*, the 'communication' ship of the Royal Indian Navy in the Gulf, and with Maunsell, who was working for MO3 and spending much time in the map room of the Royal Geographical Society.

In 1910 the intelligence activity of the Political Agent was put on to a regular footing. Arms trafficking had intensified through the intervention of Germany, and Bahrain and Oman, once the hunting grounds of the French, were now threatened by the dealings of German agents. Simla was working with the DMO London to trace a long line of intricate business dealings between the Gulf states, Constantinople and Paris which resulted in continental and even British arms being purchased by the Germans and distributed through Turkey to Persian dissidents, Afghans, Omanis and the North-West Frontier tribes. The Indian Navy was on constant alert in the Gulf.

On 16 September 1909 Gibbon had written to Shakespear: 'Am sending you a couple of reproductions of our new secret maps of the country in your neighbourhood. Corrections please.' In the same month the Government of India told the Resident at Bushire: 'Political Officers may correspond with Intelligence Branch on matters relating to a) details of routes, b) enquiries of a specially secret character respecting persons employed by the Chief of Staff for reconnaissance purposes. Copies may be sent to you except on case of (b).'

And on 4 November Gibbon wrote again: 'Considering the importance of your *raj* and its surroundings if you have an opportunity of doing anything when you happen to be on tour we shall be very much indebted for your efforts.'

Shakespear had already become a familiar figure at the helm of the *Lewis Pelly*, navigating the troubled waters between Basra and Oman with complete assurance. In April 1910 he took aboard for the first time the new Staff Officer appointed to Jask as head of Gulf Intelligence, Major Standish Craufurd, heir to the barony of Kilbirney and a Gordon Highlander. The squat, peppery Scot, whose task it was to put an end to the activities of the pirates and gun-runners and to counteract the work of the German agents, became Shakespear's closest colleague in the Gulf and his almost constant companion aboard the *Lewis Pelly*.

The problems posed for 'field' officers in the Gulf territories by foreign infiltrators and national trouble-makers came close to home for the Viceroy's Government in the first few years of the century.

The rising tide of nationalism in the first decade of the twentieth century caused near panic in India in the following year. Late in August 1911 there were frantic comings and goings at the government offices in Simla. Documents were piled high in a room marked 'No Admission', and along the corridor in the palatial setting reserved for the highest councils of state a large green-baize covered table and the chandelier above it could just be discerned through a thick cloud of cigar and pipe smoke. Closer inspection revealed at one end of the table the tall, neat figure of Field-Marshal Lord Nicholson, Chief of Staff of the British army, and at the other Sir Charles Cleveland, a massive, tight-lipped man with bulldog jaw and the shoulders of a rugby prop forward, the Inspector-General of Police and chief of the Indian Secret Service. Ranged alongside them were Sir Henry McMahon, the new Foreign Secretary in the Viceroy's Government, and the civil and military elite.

Officially the meeting had been called under Nicholson's chairmanship to review expenditure on the armed forces of India, which, at that time, consisted of 70,000 white troops and 140,000 natives who were charged with the task of protecting the eastern Empire from outside attack and from internal disruption. In fact the meeting was concerned with the growing international threat of terrorism and insurrection.

When it came to Sir Charles Cleveland's turn to speak there was a hushed silence while the solitary, taciturn figure sought for words. When he found them, he uttered them sparingly, almost inaudibly:

> It is not only that we have to deal with political agitation, which in general is working more or less openly, but with sedition which is being fostered in baffling secrecy. Unrest . . . is on the increase . . . like some hidden fire. If it is suppressed in one

direction it breaks out in another. These outbreaks . . . are inter-connected and highly organised and my impression . . . is that they are controlled by one great intellect; but whose? So far . . . unfortunately . . . with all the machinery at our disposal . . . we have been unable to discover.

Officers of civil intelligence and the army staff were taken aback. They were less inclined than the Secret Service chief to see a brilliant conspirator, a universal Kropotkin or political Svengali, as the cause of the ferment which raged from central Europe to North Africa and central Asia; rather they saw a shift of equilibrium, the shared aspirations of Asiatics who had formerly been content to accept an inferior place in the world but who now saw their opportunities in the astonishing growth of Japanese power at one extreme and the sudden break up of the Ottoman Empire at the other.

These officers had seen an awareness of the vincibility of Europe enter the minds of Asiatics from the frozen wastes of Manchuria to the deserts of Arabia. And they had seen the rising power and influence of Germany give credence to the Kaiser's words of 1898. The sun had yet to set on the British Empire but it was no longer an unimaginable contingency. And in the climate of uncertainty produced by Britain's timidity and Germany's single-minded endeavour, the trouble-makers, the anarchists and professional revolutionaries saw their chance.

In 1908 there had been a series of outrages in India and several pro-British Indian officials had been murdered. In an attempt to stem the tide of rebellion Lord Minto had appointed an Indian to his Council, but that measure had little effect. The punitive measures taken by Kitchener, then in his sixtieth year and his last few months as Commander-in-Chief, were no more successful in halting the wave of crime and political outrage. Troops of the Indian army were being suborned, and the immense Moslem population of the country was unsettled by events in Constantinople, for they, more than any other community of Moslems, were loyal to the Sultan Caliph. In December 1908 the Criminal Law Amendment Act was signed by the Viceroy in Council, enabling secret societies to be suppressed and trials of anarchists to be expedited. In 1909 the Minto–Morley reforms, which aimed to give educated natives more say in the country's affairs, were greeted non-committally by Indians and denounced as unconstitutional and a step towards Home

Rule by a majority of the British press, which saw in Morley's approach to India an extension of policies already being adopted towards Ireland by the Liberal Government. In 1912, less than a year after Cleveland's pessimistic words, Bengal revolutionaries came into the open and threw a bomb at the new Viceroy, Lord Hardinge, wounding him and killing an attendant. Aubrey Herbert saw it all as the 'beginning of the end of Empire'.

Bray had arrived in Simla from Damascus bearing tidings of revolt in the Arab lands. He had applied for permission to travel north into Asiatic Turkey before returning to India, but was told by the War Office that the Foreign Office forbade further excursions into the Ottoman vilayets. Anatolia and Asiatic Turkey generally were recognised as 'a German sphere of influence'. If Whitehall insisted that the corridor to India must be protected by the maintenance of the *status quo* in the Ottoman dominions, field intelligence men must carry out their tasks as best they could; but carry them out they must, or be overwhelmed by the opposition.

The gathering in Damascus from which Bray went hot foot to Simla was far from being clandestine. It had the appearance of a well-publicised Secret Service convention, with invited guests from several sides. The ancient city of Syria had become a metropolis of spies and agents. Damascus in those days was not just an Oriental city. It was *the* Oriental city, a symbolic place of splendour and bustling activity, its gleaming domes set in a crust of grey and white, speckled with green trees and flamboyant fruits. It was a favourite resort for the tourist and the 'official' visitor, a keystone of the Arab world, a hotbed of intrigue among Arabs and the European powers.

In August 1910 a silent war began to take shape in the Syrian desert, between a Turkish force and the Druse inhabitants of the Hauran region, a war which was never reported in the world press, apart from a few officially inspired statements issued in Constantinople. Before the fighting began two English intelligence officers arrived on the scene: Leachman, who had hardly taken breath after his journey into the Shamiya, and Captain F. E. Packe of the Welsh Regiment on the staff of the DMI in Cairo, Colonel Lee Stack. They were followed by Simla's men, C. C. R. Murphy and N. N. E. Bray.

The Turkish army under the command of General Sami Pasha was assembled at the rail junction of Deraa in the first three weeks of August. Overall control of the expedition was in the hands of Field-Marshal Fetki Pasha, commander of the Fifth Army Corps at Damascus. The British staff officers estimated the size of the force gathered some 1,300 kilometres down the Hijaz railroad to be about 21,000 men, chiefly reserves from the Fifth and First Armies, and part of a regiment of cavalry from the Fifth Army Corps trained by Major von Hochwaechter, one of von der Goltz's instructors. Field- and mountain-guns and a few machine-guns constituted the main armoury.

This was to be an object lesson in the strength of the Ottoman army under its new leadership; a lesson to one of the most courageous and recalcitrant populations of the Empire which would spread to Arabs throughout the peninsula and convince them of the folly of resistance and insurrection. It would demonstrate that never again would the Druses re-enact their famous victory of 1896, when the army of General Abdullah Pasha was defeated at Ezra.

On 19 September the Turks were disposed for battle. The 1st Division under Colonel Abdal Hamid Bey was at Deraa, the 2nd Division under Colonel Ali Bey at the key point of Kharabat al Ghazala; and an independent brigade under Colonel Naji Bey held a line of villages west of Suareidah and Shuhba. At the end of the month Sami Pasha's army emerged from the yellow-ochre plain of Deraa and marched across the dull stony Hauran. As they did so another British officer appeared in Damascus, Captain Stewart F. Newcombe of the Royal Engineers, one of Cairo's staff officers on 'Special Duty'. Newcombe, an outstanding mathematician, educated at Felstead and the RMA Woolwich, was thirty-two years old in 1910. He was already familiar with the northern deserts, having taken over the mantle of Kitchener, Condor and their successors, wandering through that ill-defined region which the world called Palestine on behalf of the DMI Cairo under cover of the old Queen's Exploration Fund. He preferred to ride a horse on his frequent and lonely excursions – he often surveyed the desert entirely on his own – but he was an accomplished camel rider when put to it. His features were sharply chiselled, and he usually wore Arab headdress. His sensitive skin went raw as soon as it was exposed to the sun, and so he was known to his colleagues as 'Skinface'.

The two Turkish divisions headed for the Druse heartland villages, while the independent brigade straddled the pathways leading from the desert to the Hijaz railway and Damascus, where the Druses could count on many supporters. On 21 Sep-

tember, to the surprise of the Turks and the assembled representatives of British intelligence, the chief of the Druses, Yahya
Atrash, came out of the desert with five companions carrying a
white flag. All were immediately arrested and imprisoned by the
Turks. The news soon spread among the Arabs of Syria, who
saw the event as just one more example of Ottoman perfidy. As
one of them remarked to Murphy: 'One hole more or less in a
strainer makes no difference.'

None of the officers who descended on the hotel which British and German agents generally favoured, the Victoria in
Damascus, had described the region in which the fighting was
now taking place. But Gertrude Bell, ever anxious to keep her
family informed, had done so ten years earlier on her first visit to
the Druse country. From Konawa, reputed burial place of the
prophet Job, she wrote:

> 'My faith' it was cold. I thought the bare plateau on the top
> of the ridge would never end ... I saw its [Konawa's]
> ruined temples standing up on a spur of the hills. It was
> splendidly placed; one looks down all across the great
> Hauran plain ... the streets are paved with red paving ...
> On the north side of the town is a deep rocky valley with a
> stream at the bottom and willows growing in it. There is a
> tiny theatre among the willows ... The Jebel Druse end in
> tiny volcanoes, the beginning of the purely volcanic Lejah.
> It all looks black and uncanny – 'unheimlich'. – There's a
> cuckoo here; let me quickly write and tell the *Spectator*.

She had also described briefly the chief of the Druses,
Yahya Atrash Bey, at his fine house in Areh. 'He is the most
perfect type of Grand Seigneur, a great big man (40 to 50 I suppose) very handsome and with the most exquisite manners.'

On 23 September 1910 an official Turkish communiqué
announced: 'Yahya Atrash, the chief of the rebellious Druses,
has surrendered unconditionally with two companions to Sami
Pasha. Several other chiefs came in yesterday.'

It was not an accurate account. There was more fighting.
Indeed, on the night of 30 September the sky was illuminated by
fires along the Jabal Druse, the mountainous range in which that
equivocal race – part-Muslim part-Christian, and loved by
neither – isolated itself from the marauding world without. It
was the war signal of the Druses. But it was intended only to

deceive the Turk. When Sami Pasha returned to his base at Soueda he took 350 conscripts with him as fodder for the Ottoman army. Altogether the Turks lost 93 killed and wounded and the Druses between 400 and 500 according to their own figures. British intelligence estimates were of 60 Turkish casualties and fewer than 400 Druses. Either way, the Druse chief had been advised of Sami Pasha's intention to use his people as an example, and had pulled the rug from under him by surrendering before the battle had begun in earnest.

Sami paraded his troops and the spoils of war through the bazaars and narrow streets of Damascus, claiming a famous victory; and the British officers sent their versions of events to the military attaché at Constantinople and the DMO at Simla. They had learnt a good deal about the Ottoman army's performance and morale.

'Thick-set, sturdy men, well clothed and well-armed, but poorly shod,' was the general verdict. Most of the men of the *Redif* or reserve units seemed to be in every way superior to the *Nizam* troops, Christian regulars mostly from Anatolia and the Greek-speaking dependencies who were being tried out in the Hauran. Drill, after nearly twenty years of von der Goltz's Prussian-style instruction, characterised by a military correspondent of the time as, 'Right turn, left turn, take the beggar's name down', was described in the report of the military attaché at Constantinople as 'slovenly'. The field force had adopted Arab headdress of *kaffiya* and *agal* and wore bandoliers across their chests. Most of their rifles were new and of German and Austrian manufacture, but the soldiers of the Prophet never cleaned their guns. The expeditionary force used heliographs but the resultant signalling was deplorable. They were also issued with field telephones, which were quite useless since they had received no instruction in their operation. Progress was noted in their approach to sanitation, which had led to massive outbreaks of dysentery in past campaigns. Altogether, British army intelligence appeared to be the only substantial beneficiary from the campaign.

The real test of the new Turkish army was about to begin as the Druse expedition came to its close. It was to be witnessed by yet more observers from the British army. In November Major C. H. Leveson and Captain G. P. Knott from the Egyptian General Staff booked in to the crowded Victoria Hotel.

It was late in November when Sami Pasha was instructed by

Marshal Shevket Pasha, the War Minister, to send a small force to Kerak to strengthen the garrison there while instructions regarding the enrolment of conscripts were being issued throughout the Empire. After the ease with which the Hauran expedition had been accomplished the Porte had no doubt that the same result could be achieved at the southern fortress town. Sami Pasha, the most senior Arab in the Ottoman army – with a keen understanding of the working of the Arab mind – was opposed to the idea, but the Wali of Damascus advised the government to go ahead.

The intention to strengthen the garrison and raise recruits among the local population was communicated to the shaikhs of the Kerak district and the news soon spread to the tribes, who decided that the scheme was not for them. Before Sami had despatched his reinforcements the local commander ordered fortified posts to be set up on the outskirts of the town to form a warning girdle against tribal infiltration. By 4 December sixteen posts, each with two field-guns and forty rifles, were established. In order to man the posts the commander had denuded the citadel of its trained men. The shaikhs, seeing their opportunity, waited until sundown and then ordered the tribesmen to fire on their Turkish masters. In a few hours the town which had attracted so much attention from foreign agents in the recent past was overrun by Arabs, who occupied the roofs of houses and swarmed along hillside roads to the high fortress itself, shooting every Turk they encountered. The men at the outposts were picked off one by one, with the exception of two men at each post who were impressed into joining the Arabs and storming the citadel. The fortress defences were stormed before midnight, the treasury and the bazaars looted, and the *Régie* tobacco money, the property of the International Debt Commission in Constantinople, taken.

When almost the entire Turkish complement of 800 men had been wiped out and every portable object looted, the Arabs made their way to the near-by Hijaz railroad, where they wrecked five stations including Kerak itself and damaged others. They pulled down the telegraph wires and cut down the poles, tore up some eighty miles of railway, killed a number of officials, and held up a train, which was looted and then set fire to. After four days, before Sami's troops were anywhere near the scene of chaos and mutilation, they disappeared as suddenly as they had come, leaving the Turkish General Staff to contemplate the ill-fortunes of war. The world had no more knowledge of this event than of the Druse campaign which preceded it.

While these unrecorded disturbances were taking place in the Syrian deserts there were outbreaks of war and localised violence all over the Middle East. There were riots in Baghdad and Basra, the Italians prepared to invade Tripoli, the last Ottoman stronghold in North Africa, rebellions broke out in the Yemen and Asir, the Balkans were in ferment, and the Sharif of Mecca, taking advantage of the rift in the Saudi ruling family caused by the Amir's cousins, the *Araif*, sent an army into Najd under the command of his second son Abdullah. Ibn Saud's supporters in the Trucial states rebelled and Bluejackets went ashore. *Status quo*, a concept dear to Sir Edward Grey, had become an empty phrase.

The events of the Middle East were of minor importance compared to the daily calamities of the Balkans and Ireland, but they helped to stoke the fires of international conflict. It was no coincidence that 1911 was the year in which the Official Secrets Act found its way on to the statute book.

In January 1911 Gertrude Bell joined the assortment of British observers and agents in Damascus. Everyone except Murphy, who had travelled down to Kerak to see events for himself, viewed the proceedings from the Victoria Hotel, and some of them from an even better vantage point, the International Club formed by a group of German offices at the instigation of Major von Hochwaechter, the officer in command of cavalry. The Germans were naturally suspicious of the English in their midst, but they preferred their company to that of the despised Turk. Rule 4 of the International Club's conditions of entry stated: 'No fez-wearing citizen is permitted to become a member' – a poor response to the Young Turks' elevation of the German Empire to a position of unchallenged supremacy in their dominions. But alliances of convenience are usually fragile.

Knowing the methods of their hosts the British officers took care to protect themselves from the wiles of glamorous women, but even so Bray was nearly poisoned by one – an Egyptian lady who was in league with the hotel manager. She found her way into his bedroom and after an interesting interval of conversation suggested coffee. The Englishman was suspicious, and when the coffee arrived he declined to drink it despite the lady's encouragement. When she had left he tested it and found that it contained arsenic.

The most important piece of intelligence picked up by British agents during the Damascus episode of 1910–11, however, was the murmur of desert revolt. Leachman had left early in the Hauran campaign, returning to Baghdad to report to the Resident, Lorimer, and to Constantinople. But before doing so he had met with Arab officials of Al Ahad, the military wing of a secret society with branches throughout Syria and Mesopotamia. Newcombe, Murphy and Bray had met with officials of the organisation too. They heard of a coming together of Arab chiefs to stage an armed rebellion. Plans would have to be laid carefully and the date and names of the leaders kept secret for the time being. But the conspirators were quite clear that they looked to Britain for support in throwing off the Ottoman yoke, and that as soon as they had evidence of that support they would provide all the details in confidence. That was the gist of the report which, with minor variations, reached the DMI Cairo, and the army intelligence departments in London and Simla at the conclusion of the Damascus affair in 1911. But there were two significant details. The Arab officers had decided unanimously that Ibn Saud should be asked to lead the revolt, and that Basra should be its flashpoint.

The Foreign Office diary for 29 May 1911 recorded:

Najd affairs. Despatch from Bushire forwarding report from Political Agent, Kuwait, recording conversation with the Wahhabi Amir of Najd as to relations with HMG and Turkey. Captain Shakespear's view of situation is that the hatred of the Turks is becoming so strong throughout the Peninsula that it may unite the tribes in a common revolt.

Shakespear had left the Political Agency late in February, accompanied by his now familiar retinue of servants, *rafiqs* (tribal guides), camel *jemaders* and animals. His salukis yelped and pranced among the camels as they sampled the freedom of the desert after weeks of confinement in Kuwait. Shalwa the hawk was perched on the back of the she-camel Dhabia, chained to its owner's wrist. A now familiar desert caravan was on its way to join the shaikhs of the Bani Khalifa, who had policed Ibn Saud's territory of Al Hasa for its Turkish occupiers in recent years. And Ibn Saud was on his way from Riyadh to camp with his army at the wasteland of Thaj, where once a rich city known to Greece and Rome had stood. He had arranged to meet the Political Agent there, and the Al Khalifa, who recognised his claim to the Gulf coastline of Najd even though they ruled it for his enemies.

It was a pleasant journey through lush hunting country. As was his custom, Shakespear travelled with the combined resources of the trained soldier, the professional explorer and the English gentleman. Several cases of his favourite drink, sparkling Moselle wine, were strapped to his pack animals, as were such delicacies as *marrons glacés* and tinned asparagus for the evening snack after a day's work. These were what he called 'Europe' days. Days spent in abandonment to the joys of the wide open spaces, interrupted only by his obsessive occupation with map projection and note-making as he made his way at leisure, pipe in mouth, *topi* on his head to protect face and neck from a benign spring sun.

He was a star among the Arabs and they watched and served him with admiration and devotion, but he kept his distance from them and only when invited by the desert princes to their homes and tents did he share their food. He knew that an upset stomach, or worse, was the inevitable fate of those Europeans who tried to ape their hosts' habits of life; he admired the badawin in his turn, but he was no sycophant. Years later Lawrence was to hear tales of his exploits and to write:

> Many of the *ageyl* . . . had travelled with him, as escort or followers, and had tales of his magnificence and of the strange seclusion in which he kept himself day and night. The Arabs, who usually lived in heaps, suspected some ulterior reason for any too careful privacy.

He rode and hunted with his hosts, but he worked and ate and slept privately. His mission was confidential. Prying eyes were common enough in the desert and news spread like wildfire from hearth to hearth in a land where word of mouth counted for telegraph and newspaper.

The dividing line between Al Hasa and Kuwait was ill defined. As a despairing Foreign Office Under-Secretary wrote when trying to assess the limits of British involvement: 'The limits of Kuwait have never been accurately, or indeed, even approximately, defined.' At any rate the army of Ibn Saud, led by its banner proudly displaying the *Kalimah*, the word, 'No God but God and Muhammad his messenger', met up with

Shakespear and the Khalifa shaikhs on 7 March at Ellaimiya in the tribal territory between Kuwait and 'Turkish Najd'.

They camped near Thaj, where Shakespear found the first stones to be discovered in eastern Arabia bearing inscriptions in the ancient language of the south, Sabaean, the tongue of the Queen of Sheba. On the way Shakespear had heard of more troubles in the kingdom of Ibn Saud; of the Amir's recent problems in dealing wth his cousins the *araif*, 'the lost ones', who still made loud claims to the throne of central Arabia; and of the activities of the Turkish vassal, Sharif Husain of Mecca, who was leading a Turkish-backed badawin army into Asir, the land between the Hijaz and the Yemen, to attack the usurper Sayid Muhammad al Idrisi, who had seized the territory a year before. But the most important disturbance of all had been a battle waged between Ibn Saud and the Sharif's army in October of the previous year. As the Saudi Amir had pursued his rebellious cousins, who were living in the Hariq district, he sent his favourite brother Saad into the tribal district of the Bani Ataiba to recruit reinforcements for his army. Husain's son Abdullah, knowing of the rivalry in the Saudi ruling camp, had led a force into the region and Saad walked into his arms. Ibn Saud was forced to leave his army at Hariq in the charge of his kinsman Fahd ibn Muammar, the Governor of Kharj, while he went off to rescue his brother. Fahd was successful in preventing the *araif* pretenders from setting up a rival seat of government, and they eventually took refuge with the Sharif. Ibn Saud was also successful in rescuing his brother, but he had to make concessions to Abdullah ibn Husain, and the world press had reported a resounding victory for the Sharif, the man the Turks and the European powers called the 'Amir of Arabia', the man in whom the Young Turks were now inclined to place their faith rather than their old ally Ibn Rashid.

Shakespear was about to hear the story of these and other events from the mouth of Ibn Saud himself. Ibn Saud was little known to the outside world at this time, and Shakespear's descriptions of him were the first to reach the west. But Shakespear was not a keen observer of his fellow men; he was the surveyor *par excellence*, an utterly reliable recorder of fact and material detail. He was no poet. It was left to others who came after him to describe the personality and human qualities of the princes and tribesmen of the interior.

Over six feet tall, Ibn Saud had broad, powerful shoulders, an athletic figure clean-cut and symmetrically developed, with all the grace of the polished Arab nobleman and an open countenance which invited confidence; his frequent gestures 'accentuated the beauty of shapely hands'. Such was the impression made on an English missionary attached to the American Mission of the Dutch Reformed Church, Dr Mylrea. Gertrude Bell described him as 'a great kingly-looking man, like an Assyrian picture', but she had not met him when she wrote those words; she was relying on the impressions of her chief, Sir Percy Cox.

A man of devout faith, it seemed, but not of bigotry. 'I will follow my Prophet absolutely. Not even a fly will I offer any other religion,' he told Mylrea. He did not like turncoats. 'I do not understand men who adopt foreign faiths,' he told Shakespear. He was, in the tradition of his family, a follower of the unitarian teachings of the Wahhabi sect, whose sword – according to Charles Doughty – 'repressed even the disorders of the desert'. But he did not always approve of the iconoclasm of his co-religionists.

By 1911 a new discipline had emerged among the Wahhabis of the settled agricultural region of the Artawiyah in the north of the Sudair. Musil had been the first outsider to notice this fiercely intolerant restatement of a puritanical faith which was called by its founders Al Ikhwan, the Brotherhood. For the moment, however, Ibn Saud was content to observe its hold on a small settled region. He had other more pressing matters on his mind, and he made sure that his English guest was left in no doubt as to their substance.

Shakespear's report to Resident Cox at Bushire was dated 8 April 1911. It told of a most cordial reception. 'Abdal Aziz gave me the impression of being endowed with a particularly straightforward, frank and generous nature . . . I frequently discussed matters of doctrine, custom and religion . . . I was habitually addressed as *Brother*.' Shakespear was careful to say in his report that he had not encouraged the Prince of Najd to discuss politics; and that he himself had merely listened. Ibn Saud had insisted on 'showing his heart' however, and he wanted more than anything to enter into treaty relations with Britain. There was the customary preamble abut the history of the House of Saud, which was always on the tip of his host's tongue: the conquest of the Wahhabi dominions – virtually the whole of the Arabian peninsula – by Ibrahim Pasha of Egypt; their reconquest by the Amir's great-grandfather, Turki; the ruin of the kingdom brought about by the rivalry of his own father's brothers, Saud and Abdullah; the visit of Britain's Resident, Lewis Pelly, to Riyadh in 1865 (an occasion on which Pelly remarked that the Wahhabis had been 'newspapered into an exaggerated notion of their own importance'); Ibn Rashid's occupation of southern Najd; and his own *coup*, in which he and some forty trusty companions had retaken Riyadh from its Rashid governor. Ibn Saud talked too of his skirmish with the Sharif in the previous year. He had made no promises and given no written assurances, he told Shakespear.

Ibn Saud expressed bitter resentment of the continued Turkish occupation of Al Hasa. He added that he was not alone in his hatred of the Turks. Then came the admission of plans which Britain's intelligence men had heard about in Damascus, plans which involved many of the leading citizens of Syria and several Arab officers in the Ottoman army. Shakespear's report revealed that almost all the chiefs of Arabia were in correspondence with each other about combining 'to attack the Turks simultaneously and drive them out of the country', with Ibn Saud at their head. Yahya of the Yemen, Sayid Muhammad al Idrisi of Asir, the chiefs of the northern tribes (including the most powerful Nuri ibn Shalan of the Ruwalla), and other 'responsible Arabs' were named. Ibn Saud had also received overtures from Ibn Rashid. But the Saudi leader was unwilling to commit himself at the moment, said Shakespear, as he had 'unhappy recollections of how the Turks came to be in Hasa'.

Ibn Saud's fear, which he expressed in this reference to the Turks' conquest of Al Hasa, showed that he believed there might be a traitor in the Arab midst. Mubarak, his protector and mentor, had led the invasion of Al Hasa in company with Sadun Pasha, Talib and Khazal of Muhammerah in 1871, and he still kept bad company, but in 1907 the Shaikh had signed a binding treaty known as the Bandar-Shuwaikh lease with Britain and it was surely inconceivable that he would betray his 'son' and the Arab cause to the Turks now that he was officially allied to Britain. It was more probably Sayid Talib whom Ibn Saud had in mind. Talib was the most ruthless and unprincipled swindler in the entire story of modern Arab politics. In 1902 he had been made Governor of Al Hasa, but his regime was so cruel that even the Turks were forced to remove him. He had been the catalyst in bringing Mubarak and his friend, Shaikh Khazal of Muhammerah, into the Ottoman fold to attack Al Hasa, and he remained the richest and most feared link in a chain of trouble-makers and gun-runners which stretched from Paris to the North-West Frontier. Sayid Talib was a man to watch, and even Ibn Saud feared his influence. All the same, rebellion was clearly in the air and Ibn Saud was the inevitable focus of Arab ambition.

Whitehall was fearful and divided in its response. The Foreign Office had at that moment decided to embark on negotiations with the Young Turks through Ambassador Lowther to recognise Ottoman authority throughout the Arabian peninsula except for British strongholds in the Gulf. Ibn Saud would be recognised as Turkey's *mutasarif* in southern Najd.

The Political Agent's remarks were, as Sir Arthur Nicolson of the Foreign Office observed, 'well worth reading'. Shakespear had concluded: 'If a combination were to take place between the principal leaders in Arabia – and the fact of a serious discussion of a simultaneous revolt between men of such widely divergent religious tenets as the Imam Yahya and the Wahhabi Imam makes such a union at least possible – I am inclined to the opinion that a revolt is not only probable but would be welcomed by nearly every tribe throughout the Peninsula.'

The Foreign Office received Shakespear's report at the beginning of June. It was quickly into its stride. 'We could hardly at present make use of the overtures of the Wahhabi Amir as a weapon to fight the Turks with,' read a Foreign Office minute of 7 June. 'This is something to bear in mind if our negotiations with Turkey do not go right,' said another. The India Office, on the same day, mollified the Foreign Secretary by repeating earlier objections to 'a policy of adventure in Central Arabia', but stressing that,

in view of the intractable attitude of the Turkish Government in the Persian Gulf, it is important that His Majesty's Government should leave none of the weapons at their disposal unexamined . . . and it is evident that one of these is such a response to the overtures now made by Abdal Aziz bin Saud as would render the position of the Turks on the Arabian coast of the Gulf untenable.

That somewhat Machiavellian approach came from Sir Richmond Ritchie, W. M. Thackeray's son-in-law, who occupied the senior Under-Secretaryship at the India Office.

Shakespear left his host in late March to the accompaniment of a pressing invitation to visit the Saudi capital. Now on terms of the most intimate friendship with the Amir, he promised that he would call. But he was beaten to Riyadh by a most amiable and gifted young Dane with pronounced German connections, and by his own countryman, Leachman.

4

The Lion and the Eagle

'The gods were jealous of any man, or any nation, who was pre-eminently powerful, fortunate, or prosperous.'

Herodotus

By the second decade of the twentieth century the tenuous Entente between Britain, Russia and France was a political reality, as was the equally tenuous Triple Alliance of Germany, Italy and Austria-Hungary. The great Empires of the European powers were ranged against each other, with a single exception, and Germany began to look with increasing favour in the direction of Constantinople, pursued by the jibe of the day, 'Deutschland über Allah'. Britain responded by negotiating an Anglo-Turkish Convention which would regularise the Ottoman possessions in the Middle East and the British protectorates of Aden and the Gulf.

1911 was a year of disaster for the Ottoman Empire. Albania, emulating Samson, built a temple of service to the sultans, and in its presumption tried to lift the roof. The structure collapsed around its ears and the European Empire of the Turks disintegrated in the Balkan Wars of 1911–13.

Kitchener, deprived of the prize of the Viceroyalty by Morley, who told the King that the C-in-C India had become 'hopelessly idle', arrived in Cairo on 28 September 1911 to take the place of Eldon Gorst, Cromer's successor. Kitchener's stay in Cairo, three eventful years in which several attempts were made on his life by nationalists, found added enlivenment in the companionship of his Oriental Secretary, Ronald Storrs, who, unlike his austere chief, was devoted to beautiful women, good food, music, literature and chess. He was fastidious to a degree in his habits and choice of friends, catholic in his tastes; and a witty and outrageous snob.

The new chief wore the proconsul Cromer's mantle easily, never failing to let Abbas Hilmi know who was the true ruler of Egypt. Gorst, on the other hand, had always treated the Khedive with studied deference, addressing him as 'Your Majesty'. 'It costs no more than Lucky Jim, and gives so much more pleasure,' said Storrs. Gorst advised the old man, Kitchener cajoled him. Yet Kitchener won the approval of most Egyptians, 'a manly man', they called him, though his own countrymen were inclined to think his administration effete, even effeminate. Events in the Moslem world were about to present him with an opportunity to exhibit his strength not only to potential enemies within Egypt but also to fellow countrymen who had denied him his fondest ambition.

Germany had been granted far-reaching privileges under the Ottoman Capitulations, to sweeten the Anglo-French Entente of 1904, including the right to appoint officials to key posts in Egypt. Two eminent diplomats were sent to Cairo to supervise the interests of the Reich, Count Bernstorff and Prince Hatzfeld. They quickly turned their charm and confident grasp of affairs to the task of undermining the Khedive's confidence in Britain, ably abetted by 'The Spy', Baron von Oppenheim. While they went about their tasks in Cairo, Enver Bey, the military attaché in Berlin, and the peripatetic von Oppenheim entertained lavishly in Germany and Constantinople. The Countess Keller, lady-in-waiting to their Imperial Majesties, who had accompanied the Kaiser to the Turkish capital in 1898, and the Countess Schlieffen, wife of the Prussian Chief of Staff, often shared the role of hostess. Sayid Talib, the *agent provocateur* of Basra, was entertained on several occasions, as were the Pan-Islamic agents who came in increasing numbers from India, Afghanistan and even the United States to assist in the 'struggle' against British imperialism. The new Ottomans dreamt ever more hopefully of an alliance with Europe's mightiest military power, and perhaps of hegemony over Islam into the bargain.

Political conflict and civil war in the Balkans, north Africa, Yemen, the Gulf and Ireland stretched the resources of all the major European powers involved from 1911 onwards. One immediate response was the wholesale reorganisation of their intelligence services. Remarkably in the second decade of the twentieth century Germany's was the Cinderella of the European Secret Services, relying chiefly on a small but active naval department controlled by Captain von Tappken, the civilian von Riechter, and on the Eastern Bureau of the Foreign Office. In 1912 Colonel Nicolai was appointed head of the army *Nachrichtdienst*, the equivalent of Britain's Military Operations intelligence division. Nicolai spoke fluent Russian and may have been of Russian origin. His eastern 'arm' was Colonel Frobenius, who journeyed incognito in the Arab world under the name of Abdal Karim.

Britain's Middle East intelligence was given a fillip in the early years of the century by the enterprising work of the Commander-in-Chief in the Mediterranean, Admiral Fisher. 'Through the patriotism of magnificent Englishmen', mostly merchants, he was able to fix up important 'forwarding stations', the most significant of which was at Piraeus just outside Athens. It reported, like its German, French and Russian counterparts, to Berne, where Britain's European network was controlled by 'M', or 'Maurice'.

In Whitehall, the Francophile Irishman Henry Wilson took over as DMO from Spencer Ewart. He kept in close touch with the French Chief-of-Staff, General Foch, and his military attaché in London in the conviction that war with Germany was imminent and inevitable. India, the Gulf, Aden and Persia were taken over by MO1 from MO3; and MO2 became responsible for the Ottoman Empire, including central Arabia.

Following the Russo-Japanese war the Czar's Okhrana fell into the clutches of the French Deuxième Bureau, and between them the two organisations effectively penetrated the German army. The chief of Austro-Hungarian counter-intelligence, Colonel Redl, was working for the Okhrana and passing on to Russia the secrets of the Alliance.

While intelligence became more competitive and unscrupulous, politicians and civil servants in Whitehall, in the Wilhelmstrasse, the Peterhof and the Quai d'Orsay addressed themselves to the complex problems of the world with growing uncertainty and suspicion, still wearing frock coats and sometimes writing with quill pens.

Amid all the other world problems of 1911, the Entente's resolve had been put to its first real test when the German gunboat *Panther* appeared at the Moroccan harbour of Agadir. Lloyd George, speaking in July, called it 'a deliberate provocation', and said that 'peace at that price would be a humiliation intolerable for a great country like ours to endure'. The German

Ambassador at Marrakesh at the time was the urbane Dr Rosen, who thought with some justification that Britain and France had 'over-reacted absurdly'.

War was averted. But no sooner had the Agadir crisis been resolved than Italian troops invaded Tripoli and the Dodecanese islands. Trouble came to the Balkans too as Bulgars and Serbs began to negotiate an alliance which gave rise to the creation of the Balkan League with Greece and Montenegro, as a counter to the massacres of Christians in Macedonia which had continued unabated since the Young Turks took over from Abdal Hamid.

To rub salt into European wounds, the Imam Yahya declared *jihad* against the Italians in the Yemen and allied himself firmly to his old enemy the Turk. Sir Edward Grey stepped up the pace of negotiations with Turkey's plenipotentiary in London, Tewfiq Pasha, and showed him all the treaties with Arab leaders, except the one which effectively wrecked the Turco-German plan of an outlet for the Baghdad railway in Kuwait, the Bandar-Shuwaikh lease of 1907.

Sir Edward Grey's uneasy vision of a world fast crumbling around him was reinforced. One of the Foreign Secretary's Liberal colleagues had described him as 'that weak-kneed invertebrate politician'. But the squire of the Foreign Office stood firm amid chaos. When the Albanian Conference broke up in London early in 1913, its British member, Lord Newton, Lansdowne's biographer, declared in his exasperation: 'Sir Edward Grey is a phenomenon in our national life. He is above criticism. He is something between the laws of first-class cricket and the Ten Commandments.'

David Hogarth assembled a team of diggers at the mound of Jerablus on the Syrian side of the Euphrates in February and March 1911. The last of the British assistants to arrive was T. E. Lawrence, who had travelled via Constantinople (which he had reached in mid-December 1910), Beirut and the American Mission school at Jebail, where one of the lady missionaries helped him brush up his Arabic. He followed a strange tadpole-shaped path: Mount Carmel, Nazareth, a visit to Dr Torrance at Tiberias, across country by the Haifa railway to Deraa and then northward by the Hijaz line to Damascus and on to Aleppo and Jerablus, the site of ancient Carchemish in Kalti of the Hittites, which he reached at the end of March.

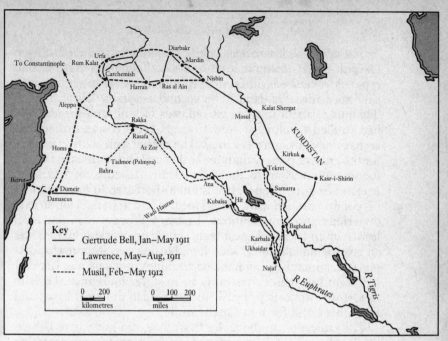

Map 5   Routes of Musil, Gertrude Bell and Lawrence, 1911–12

The chief and his two senior assistants were already hard at
work with their Arab task force, digging away at the mound
which Sir Henry Layard had persuaded the Sultan to lease to
Britain some fifty years before, and where Hittite inscriptions
had been identified in the 1870s.

But digging was by no means the only activity. The attention
of the Britishers was focused keenly on the activities of a team of
German engineers near by, who by coincidence had begun to
build a rail bridge over the Euphrates at almost the same
moment. The Baghdad railway was by now a *fait accompli*, the
physical evidence of Germany's predominance in Asia Minor,
and if the Foreign Office in London had conceded that position
to the Reich with a sigh of relief after years of financial pressure
on Turkey by the German bankers and in the face of the equally
undesirable prospect of Russia building a line from Erivan
through to a warm-water port in the Gulf, the army and navy
intelligence departments had no intention of letting the project
go unobserved. They wanted to know its exact route, its gauges,
its weaknesses, its military usefulness. Hogarth was working for
both the British Museum and for the Director of Naval Intelligence, and if either had a prior claim on his services at this time it
was the DNI.

The senior assistant was a bluff, opinionated epigraphist from Oxford, Dr R. Campbell Thompson, Fellow of Merton, and reputed to be the meanest man with money ever to set foot outside his native Scotland. The second assistant, like Campbell Thompson about thirty years old, was of a different stamp. He had studied theology at New College, Oxford, and drifted into archaeology through a fascination he shared with contemporaries for the ancient pottery finds and other artefacts of the past which found their way in to the Ashmolean Museum, of which he became Deputy Keeper. It was but a short step to the service of his country in such work as Dr Hogarth had in train. Tall, strong, imperious and conscientious, Leonard Woolley was the ideal leader of an archaeological team. His hard-working nature was an inspiration to those around him. He was easy if somewhat distant in manner, but emphatic on all things; not a man to state his case with less than earnestness, or to suffer fools at all. Early in 1911 he was working primarily in the Nubian desert of Egypt and flitted back and forth to Carchemish.

The latecomer to the team, Lawrence, did nothing to lighten the burden of intellect which descended on the unsuspecting township of Jerablus. Assyrian, Greek, and Roman history, the military pros and cons of the structure of the medieval fortress, the provenance of a pottery shard: such were the topics of conversation as the Britishers viewed the scene though their field glasses and took photographs of the Germans through their telephoto lenses, while von Oppenheim's men working by the Euphrates viewed them through identical Zeiss binoculars and photographed them through identical Zeiss lenses. Hogarth was to write of Lawrence in retrospect:

> Besides being anti-official, he dislikes fighting and Arab clothes, Arab ways, and social functions, civilized and uncivilized. He takes a good deal of trouble about all things but quite a great deal about repelling people whom he attracts . . . It is better to be his partner than his opponent, for when he is not bluffing, he has a way of holding all the aces: and he can be ruthless, caring little what eggs he breaks to make his omelettes . . . He should go far; but it may be driving lonely furrows where at present few expect him to plough.

Viewed from an even greater distance, the report is in parts as quirkish as its subject, but it serves for the moment to give visual

1   Professor R. Koldewey, head of the Deutsche Orient
Gesellschaft team at Babylon, photographed by Gertrude Bell in
1911

2 Germans at Kalat Shergat (Assur), photographed by Gertrude Bell in 1909. From left Backmann, Andrae, Jordan and Hendricks

3 Gertrude Bell at dinner with the German team in Assyria. On her left is Dr Andrae, expedition leader; next to him is Dr Preusser, chief German agent on the Euphrates during the First World War

anchorage to one of our four men in the Syrian desert; men who were to play a lively part in the affairs of the Middle East in years to follow, reared on the precepts of Empire and service, yet questioning creatures, inclined to the high-Toryism of the Milner and John Buchan brand, devotees of the Round Table, somewhat Francophobe, and decidedly clever.

Hogarth returned to London in April and Campbell Thompson took over as expedition leader, and his pay was therefore increased from a pound to thirty shillings a day, no mean remuneration for a relatively inexperienced archaeologist in those days. Lawrence was getting by on an Oxford demyship of £100 a year obtained for him by Hogarth.

In May the party received a visitor from across the river. 'We are expecting Miss G. Bell,' Lawrence had written to his brother a month earlier. She arrived on 18 May, a female whirlwind that had blown across Syria and Mesopotamia in the first four months of the year, enchanting and exasperating in turn, invading the camps of the German archaeologists of the Deutsche Orient Gesellschaft, and advising and listening to the great man, Professor Koldewey of Berlin. She got to know his assistants at the excavations, where the streets and palaces of ancient Sumer and Akkad and Babylon were being uncovered with Teutonic thoroughness and skill – Dr Andrae, Wechsel, Conrad Preusser, Willi Bachmann, Moresch, Julius Jodrell; she filled her notebooks with plans of buildings, inscriptions in Arabic, Syriac and the cuneiform, messages from her hosts, details of roadways and mountain paths. She had stayed with the Resident, J. G. Lorimer, in Baghdad, 'an exceptionally able man'. She had enjoyed long fireside chats at Kalat Shergat with Preusser, Oppenheim's man among the German archaeologists, whose news-agents were already spread along the Euphrates and were thick in the holy cities of Najaf and Karbala. Her notebook contained the name of a German art expert, Dr Goyer, whom she met at Hatra, capital of Parthia in the days of the Roman Empire. Goyer was later to be connected by British intelligence with the distribution of arms to the Euphrates tribes. Gertrude had made a riverboat journey with the surveyor Sir William Willcocks, one of Britain's keenest intelligence brains in the East, mapping likely routes of the Berlin–Baghdad railroad from Baghdad to Basra. 'A twentieth-century Don Quixote', she called him. She had visited the widows of Abdal Hamid's ally among the Kurds, Ibrahim Pasha, the most beautiful of them by repute having made a deep impression on her. Her ever-present servant Fattuh, a Syrian Christian, was not so impressed. 'Hiya rajul!' he shouted as Gertrude praised the old lady's looks on the way from Diyabakr to the camp at Carchemish. 'She is a man!'

She was by now famous for her exploits in the Arab lands. Her book *The Desert and the Sown* had proved a best-seller in Britain and America, telling of her early travels with the 'careless rapture' of youth. Now in the year of her most important journey in the Ottoman Empire *Amurath to Amurath* had been published. It had been well reviewed by her friend, Valentine Chirol, in *The Times,* attracting attention more for her dedicatory epistle addressed to Lord Cromer, than for its actual content. Liberty in the Ottoman lands was her theme, and she told *The Lord:* 'The banks of the Euphrates echo with ghostly alarms; the Mesopotamian deserts are full of the rumour of phantom armies; you will not blame me if I passed among them *trattando l'ombre come cose salde.'*

She entered the tents of Campbell Thompson and Lawrence with no lightness of tread. She took a quick look at the excavations going on around her and told C.T., as he was always called, that his methods were 'prehistoric'. Compared to the careful work of the Deutsche Orient Gesellschaft, the pioneers of the new digging methods which substituted trowel for pickaxe, they were. But C.T. was not amused. She caught her first sight of Lawrence. 'He is going to make a traveller,' she wrote to her stepmother. She stayed with the archaeologists of Carchemish for some five days, and doubtless spoke of many things besides the world of antiquity. After both sides had demonstrated their ability to put on an impressive display of erudition they calmed down, and parted with 'mutual expressions of esteem'. It was the beginning of a long collaboration between Hogarth's men and his single woman agent.

Campbell Thompson left for home to marry in July and Lawrence and Woolley began to talk of closing down the Carchemish site some six months after they had started digging. But they went on in a desultory way. Lawrence left on 12 July on a lone journey across the river to Tel Ahmar, the Red Hill, where the Germans were digging and where Gertrude had been a month or so before. His letters reveal nothing of his purpose. Six days later he was at Urfa, on the road to Jerablus and Aleppo, where he met a 'massive' group of German rail engineers. He photographed everything in sight, usually working from a distance with his telephoto lens, at a couple of miles it was 'rather better than the naked eye!' he told his mother. At Beirut he met Miss Holmes of the American mission school.

He started to find refuge from about this time with James Elroy Flecker and his wife, who had gone to live at Areya in the Lebanon. Flecker began to look forward to his visits, to talk of literature and Oxford, and to hear tales of 'the astonishing boy's adventures'. In 1912 Flecker wrote, 'except Hogarth and his two fellow archaeologists intermittently resplendent on the way to or from Carchemish we never see a civilized soul'.

Carchemish was now simply a base for increasingly important espionage work, although after a year the excavators had dug through the layers of Ottoman, Abbasid, Roman and Hellenic occupation and had reached the Hittite zone.

In May 1911 as Woolley, C.T. and Lawrence chatted of antiquity and other things with their new found companion 'Gertie', Shakespear arrived home in London, remaining for the Coronation of George V in June before going on to India. He motored across the sub-continent in his single-cylinder Rover to Delhi for the Coronation durbar in December. He arrived back in Kuwait in January 1912 to find that a good deal had happened in his absence. Shaikh Mubarak told him laconically that he had been visited by a strange Englishman called 'Lachman' with 'some Arabs' and that he had sent them packing.

In the previous November Leachman had arrived in Basra from India, where he lodged with an Arab friend. The Arab is not named in Leachman's diary, but there is every indication that he was an associate of Sayid Talib, who at the time was trying to induce Constantinople to recall the Wali of Basra and to appoint him in his stead. A British resident in Basra recalled Leachman: 'In the same way that his appearances were sensational, so were his departures. He would dine with you and say "Good night" and that was the last that would be heard of him for perhaps months, when he would suddenly appear again ... Leachman was indeed playing a lone hand.'

In a letter to his father dated 13 November Leachman had said:

I am leaving here tonight and going down by desert to Kuwait, near which place I pick up a crowd of Arabs and go away down to a place not far from Riyadh in the centre

of Arabia. I think I have a very good companion and I am
going with a type of Arab well known for their straightness
and broadmindedness, so things should be all right. In case
anything should happen . . . I have left your address here
with a man who will inform you.

He left the house of his Arab friend at 3 a.m., disguised in Arab
dress. With a few rowdy companions he made his way to Zubair
and then took the road to Raudhatain in the north of Kuwait.
There a further party of noisy, ill-dressed Arab townsfolk joined
them, and they went on along the sandy road towards the oasis of
Jahra, from where they intended to branch off to Rigai in the
direction of Riyadh. But Shaikh Mubarak had received
warning of the venture and sent a party of horsemen to intercept
the Englishman and his band of thieves. They were taken before
the Shaikh, given a severe dressing down and sent back to Basra.
'A miserable failure' was Leachman's own description of the
venture. 'The Shaikh was rather offensive,' he thought.
    Not even the intemperate Leachman could have imagined that
he would succeed in making a journey with a party of Iraqi and
Kuwaiti rowdies through tribal areas deep into the territory of Ibn
Saud unless he had reason to suppose that his path had been
smoothed by somebody. The hand of Sayid Talib must be suspected, since he was engaged in ambitious political schemes at
the time which had a good deal to do with the Anglo-Turkish
discussions, and with the death of his arch-enemy, Sadun Pasha,
in a Turkish gaol. Nor would Leachman have invaded Shakespear's patch without the permission of higher authority on the
British side. When he heard about it Shakespear described the
adventure as a 'masquerade', adding: 'I don't exactly burn with
affection or admiration for Leachman.' The rival claims of London and Simla had driven a deep wedge between two of the most
able Britons in the Middle East. As it happened the Shaikh was
forewarned and the journey cut short before anyone came to
grief.
    Leachman had applied originally to the India Office for per-
mission to travel to Riyadh. In August 1911 he wrote to his parents:
'I don't know what has happened about my leave, but I imagine
that Lord Crewe is at present contemplating it and intending to
refuse me permission to travel, in which case I will have to revert
to subterfuge.' In fact, Morley's recent successor at the India
Office did refuse him permission.

But the plans for an Arab rebellion which had been rumoured at Damascus in 1910 were coming to fruition. At a time when Britain and Turkey were deep in the throes of drawing up their Convention, when German penetration of the area was increasing day by day, the War Office was anxious to know what was going on, though it had to work within the framework of the Foreign Office ban on travel in central Arabia and in the knowledge of the Indian Government's close ties with Mubarak and Ibn Saud through Shakespear. The need to obtain information became urgent in the latter part of 1911, as a German agent set out for Riyadh and Wönckhaus agents began to put pressure on Mubarak.

Two years before, MO3 in London had received news from Copenhagen of discussions among a party of Danes under the patronage of Admiral P. de Richlieu, the President of the Danish Royal Geographical Society, regarding a proposed expedition to the Gulf and central Arabia. As soon as the Foreign Office was told of the scheme, Grey instructed his Ambassador, Sir Alan Johnstone, to inform the Danish Foreign Office that Britain would not be well disposed to any such expedition. Johnstone reported back that his representations had been conveyed to the Geographical Society in Copenhagen, but that the Society had not been 'very helpful'. On 22 December 1909 he sent Grey a copy of a letter from Professor Olufsen of the Society setting out the purposes of the expedition, which were said to be 'geological, ethnographic, archaeological, linguistic and botanical'. The argument raged for two years, during which time Sir Edward Grey did everything in his power to forbid British as well as European incursions. Even Captain Hunter, the official cartographer to the Survey of India and the man responsible for bringing War Office maps of the area up to date, was forbidden to enter the Arabian interior.

And during the same period Shakespear in Kuwait reported increasing pressure on Shaikh Mubarak by Germany to permit the Wönckhaus company to set up an office in his territory. On 9 April 1911 Shakespear informed the Resident that ten days before Shaikh Mubarak had received a letter from the German Consul at Basra, Emil Ackloni, with another from the Wönckhaus company manager at Basra (an Englishman of German nationality named Thomas Brown), dated 23 March. They simply informed the Shaikh that it was proposed to open an office in Kuwait. Brown's letter did not mince matters: 'We have appointed, as an agent in business, Abdullah bin Ustad Ahmad, who is also empowered to appoint an agent to assist him ... We hope you will co-operate with our Agent ... and that you will pay him your attention with a view to assisting him in the requirements of business.' Addressed to Mubarak Pasha ibn Sabah and not as was the Turkish habit to the 'Kaimakam' or Governor of Kuwait, it was delivered in Arabic with a German translation.

In July, Simla had told Cox at Bushire that he and Shakespear should continue to resist the pressure from Wönckhaus but that Britain could not legally impose a ban.

While on leave in England, Shakespear had told the India Office's Political and Secret Department: 'I take every opportunity of reminding Shaikh Mubarak that the efforts of Wönckhaus & Co. to obtain a footing in Kuwait appear to have other than purely legitimate commercial ends in view.' He had warned Mubarak that the most active supporter of Wönckhaus was the Shaikh's own Customs Master.

German moves to extend their hold in the Gulf through a Wönckhaus agency in Kuwait were being renewed in Shakespear's absence when, at the end of 1911, the Dane, Barclay Raunkiaer, arrived in Basra as the guest of the Wali. Just before he reached Kuwait, the Shaikh was approached by Abdullah 'Germani', who arrived in Kuwait on 19 January complete with his office furniture. He told Mubarak, 'he did not know if he was aware of the friendly interest and solicitude with which His Imperial Majesty the Sultan watched him [Shaikh Mubarak] and his doings and how HM was continually sending messages to the local authorities to safeguard the Shaikh's interests in every way'. He then set about criticising British intervention in the state. Mubarak replied: 'At a critical juncture in my affairs the British Government interfered to protect me and landed soldiers who threw up entrenchments and, owing to their kindness and firmness the danger passed away.' Abdullah 'Germani' was sent packing.

Britain had successfully opposed the expedition planned by the Royal Danish Geographical Society. 'We have told Alan Johnstone that it is as well the Danish Government should know that we have an eye on these proceedings,' the Foreign Office told the India Office, after the discovery that Admiral de Richlieu had extensive holdings in Far Eastern railways and was actively interested in the Baghdad rail scheme. But military intelligence in London and Simla and the Foreign Office had reckoned without the ability of the youngest member of the proposed party and of his German contacts to break through official barriers. They had reckoned too without the ability of Simla intelligence to be just as devious as its London counterpart.

Barclay Raunkiaer left Denmark alone on 12 November 1911 bound for Constantinople, the day before Leachman set off on his abortive excursion to the Arabian interior. Although the Royal Danish Geographical Society had cancelled the expedition, it had not withdrawn its patronage from Raunkiaer after the new British Ambassador, Sir Conyngham Greene, told the Danish Government that Britain was unable to afford the expedition protection or help. In fact, two members of the original party were given permission to travel to 'Turkish Arabia' – Raunkiaer and the intended leader, Lieutenant Davidsen. But Davidsen went to Cairo, intending to join his colleague later in Arabia. He was kept under close surveillance by Kitchener's secret police chief Philippides, and in the end gave up the struggle to reach Arabia.

Raunkiaer, travelling through Turkish-held territory, made a speedy journey to Baghdad, where he arrived at the beginning of December. The British Consul in Basra, F. E. Crow, expected him to make straight for the southern city and then to go on to Kuwait and Najd along the route which Leachman and his Arab followers had intended to travel, presumably to monitor the Dane's progress and contacts or even to waylay him. But Raunkiaer would have spoiled the plan even if Mubarak had not. He stayed over a month in Baghdad, where he was received enthusiastically by the Wali and by the German Consul. It was not until early January 1912 that Lorimer was able to report from Baghdad that the Dane was on his way by paddle steamer along the Tigris to Basra, accompanied by a Christian guide he had picked up in the city.

In Basra too, the likeable , frail young Dane was warmly welcomed by the Wali Hassan Riza Bey, by the German Consul and the managing director of Wönckhaus, Herr Harling, even by Mr Van Ess of the American mission of the Dutch Reformed Church, and by Russia's Consul. He stayed at the International Hotel and several conversations with the Wali were noted. They always spoke in German without an interpreter.

In February 1912 Shakespear was able to report: 'A traveller arrived in Kuwait on 29 January overland from Basra, describing himself merely as a traveller of Danish nationality wishing to go to Hofuf. His name is Barclay Raunkiaer.'

Shakespear added a note to the effect that the Dane was poorly equipped for his task, spoke good English but no Arabic, and was at present lodged with the Shaikh. The Resident informed 'Foreign' at Simla and asked Shakespear to keep him in the picture. Within a few days the Political Agent was told by India: 'Please give Shaikh of Kuwait a hint that Government of India do not desire that the Danish explorer should be given any facilities.' A copy of that request was of course sent to London and conveyed to the Foreign Office.

Shakespear had one of his frequent outings with Standish Craufurd aboard the *Lewis Pelly* while the young Dane waited in the Shaikh's palace, observing its routine and the daily activities of the old man's slaves as they ran riot around the mud-brick ramparts. Shakespear and Craufurd had a great deal to talk about after the former's return from the Coronation durbar. Apart from Wönckhaus's persistence in trying to seduce the Shaikh and Raunkiaer's sudden appearance, there were other ripples on the surface of Shakespear's pool. The Shaikh had uncovered a 'plot' against himself – a frequent enough occurrence – supposedly led by one of the town's richest merchants, Saqar al Ghanim, and several of his own nephews. Al Ghanim had been clapped in gaol and the nephews sent to join the Shaikh's son, Salim, in exile at Basra. The Shaikh's exiled relatives were becoming a positive embarrassment to Britain since they represented a fertile source of discontent for the Germans and Turks to exploit, and because they were constantly engaged in dubious schemes of both financial and political complexion with Sayid Talib. It was decided that Shakespear should take a firm line with Mubarak over his treatment of family and friends, and that despite Whitehall's instructions he should discreetly help the Dane on his way and keep his ear to the ground to discover his contacts and proposals. It was clearly important for the Government of India to know exactly what were the plans of Raunkiaer's masters, and there was no better way to find out than to let him make his journey and leave Shakespear to find out as much as he could from the desert grapevine.

'He will travel with the next large caravan to Buraida,' reported Shakespear at the end of February, on his return from a pleasant sea voyage round the Bahrain pearl banks with the intelligence chief from Jask. 'He carries a letter to Ibn Saud [from Mubarak].' Raunkiaer left Mubarak's town on the first day of March. By mid-month he and his companions were at the great walled town of Buraida in Kasim, the Dane sick with something akin to dysentery, hardly able to stand and dreading the journey across a thousand miles of forbidding desert territory. As Shakespear had predicted he was ill-prepared for such a venture. But he was a resolute young man.

'Henceforth we shall have no caravan to rely upon,' he wrote in his diary. 'Alone I must ride to Riyadh in these wretched conditions, with a following of only four men, protected by four carbines.' On 20 March he noted: 'I employ my time in rearranging my effects ... Diaries, sketch maps, drawings, photographic aparatus, and other essential equipment are stowed away in a pair of saddle bags, which I shall keep on my own camel, so as to be fairly sure of not losing my records, unless at the same time I lose my own life.'

His guide was trying to induce the Amir of Zilfi to provide an escort to the next point on their route, Ghat. But the chiefs of the towns and villages on the way were reluctant to help him. His Arab companions paid coffee calls on friends as they went through the wilderness towards Jabal Tuwaiq, the high range that leads down to Al Aridh and Riyadh; but nobody invited Raunkiaer to the coffee fire. He thought of turning back to Kuwait, but he knew that he must not lose his nerve. 'I saw myself riding, as the sum and total of my whole adventure, into Kuwait, presenting myself before Shaikh Mubarak and being received at another place with an ironical Anglo-Saxon smile.' He had observed the wry smile of the Political Agent as he left, and he did not want to see it again in the emptiness of defeat.

He went on towards Ghat, sick and weak, 'and in danger of betrayal' in the heart of Arabia. 'I felt almost as if I had met my own ghost, and little if at all able to resist giving away to sheer fatalism.' As he approached Ghat camel riders came out to hand him a letter telling him that he would not be welcome in the village. When he reached his destination the Amir was frigid, though mutton was brought to the Dane's party from the town. And at Ghat he had his first contact with homosexuality in central Arabia.

> Later on in the evening I was honoured by a visit from a rather feminine-looking young Arab and his more normal

friends. The feminine person from Ghat wears a black coat but with that exception only white, and he is beardless – an indecent fact which he seeks to hide by drawing his *kaffiyah* over his face right up to his nose. He is one of the youths kept in all central Arabian towns by those surfeited with such joys as earthly houris are qualified to impart!

When Raunkiaer's party arrived at Riyadh towards the end of March they were little more fortunate than they had been all along. Ibn Saud was away, but Raunkiaer was received with kindness and good humour by the Imam Abdurrahman, his father. On 28 March the Dane noted: 'In the course of this afternoon I am to have an audience of the Imam ... All necessary measures for the protection of an unbelieving dog in this city of the fanatically orthodox are to be observed.' The meeeting took place in the date gardens said to have been planted by Mahbub,

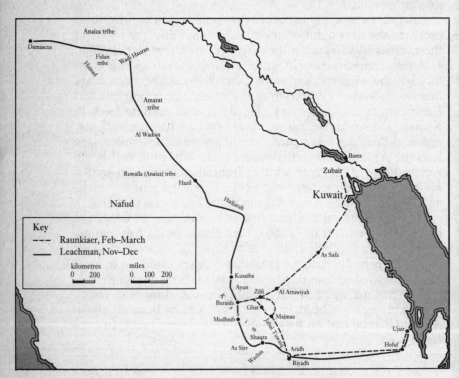

Map 6   Routes of Raunkiaer and Leachman, 1912

the emancipated slave who became chief minister of Faisal the Great, Abdurrahman's father. Now there was less to fear, fewer Saudi spies to watch the stranger's every move; but still the strict rules of abstinence, still the unfamiliar rigour of Wahhabi doctrine. 'Abdurrahman is a marvellously handsome man, whose whole appearance bears the mark of adventure and splendour. He suggests a living episode of the *Thousand and One Nights*, – this amiable but austere old man with eagle eye and white beard'. They engaged in frank discussion about Kuwait, 'the bone of contention between England and Germany', about the respective interests of Britain and Turkey in the peninsula and its surrounding territories, about the Turco-Italian war now raging in Tripoli and the Yemen, about the relative strengths of the European powers. And when he had finished trying to persuade the friendly old Imam, who in any case left all such matters in the hands of his son, Abdal Aziz, the young Dane concluded: 'In the matter of Afro-Asiatic politics, I could do no more than confirm the chieftain's deep-rooted belief in the hegemony of the British Empire.'

Raunkiaer went home in June 1912. When he reached Copenhagen he expressed his eternal gratitude to Shakespear for removing the 'insuperable objection' of his Turkish and German contacts from the old man's mind. Admiral de Richlieu promptly sent the thanks of the Royal Danish Geographical Society to the Foreign Office for the help rendered their protegé by Captain Shakespear, and by Captain D. L. R. Lorimer in Bahrain, who assisted the sick traveller on his way home. Sir Edward Grey promptly demanded that Shakespear and Lorimer be hauled over the coals by the Resident.

As Raunkiaer arrived at Riyadh to find that Abdal Aziz, warned of his coming, had taken himself off on a 'raid', Shakespear made a dash along the Shaq depression towards Ibn Saud's camel grazing grounds in the Dahana. If they met, there is no record even in the most secret files of the Indian Government. But it would not be the only time that the Arab chief and the Englishman had met covertly, without the knowledge of government, though the DMO's department at Simla was usually kept informed. The need for information and contact was so much at variance with official policy at this time that both the Whitehall and Simla ends of military intelligence were compelled to act in defiance of the rules.

Two years after his return to Denmark, in 1915, Raunkiaer

succumbed to the disease that had wracked his frail body with a dry cough and aching weariness while he traversed the desert. He was only twenty-seven when he died.

Musil returned as the Dane departed, this time accompanied by no less a fellow traveller than Prince Sixtus of Bourbon, son of Robert, Duke of Parma, a young man close to the thrones and power centres of Europe. Musil's companion of past journeys, Thomasberger, was with them, as were the Czech's faithful servants, Bader and Muhammad, keepers of the vast store of provisions and surveying equipment which Shaikh Musa always had with him on his journeys.

They spent most of February 1912 in Damascus, where they took soundings of the talks still going on between the Arab chiefs, conspiring to enter into the secret councils of desert princes and influence their alliances. They were officially intent this time on recording a string of heights between the Palmyra desert and the southern Euphrates, and then travelling across southern Mesopotamia to Baghdad and Samarra. It was a journey of impressive extent and, as it proved, accomplishment.

They left Damascus on 15 March 1912 and went by way of Homs and Al Bahra to Tadmor, ancient Palmyra, and on to the Euphrates at Rasafa. Then they rode for some 600 miles along the great river to Ana and Ramadi until they turned sharp right into the desert where the vast ruin of the Abbasid palace at Ukhaidar stands as a lone reminder of human habitation, the palace that Gertrude Bell had measured and dissected a year before and was presently making into the subject of her latest book. On 27 April they arrived at Najaf or Meshed Ali, back on the Euphrates, to behold the 'golden gleaming dome of Ali', the holiest of holies of the Shia Moslem. Then on to Karbala, the city of the martyr Husain, where the ethereal dome and beautiful tile work of another magnificent mosque pays earthly tribute to the second martyr of the faithful of Persia and Iraq – like its sister mosque down-river, an ever-present reminder of deprivation to the world's most devout fanatics. And with its crowds of fanatical pilgrims, in 1912, it was a glittering reminder of the harvest of disaffection which could be sown by Turkey and Germany should British India ever need to occupy the swamps and deserts of southern Mesopotamia.

Musil, the Prince of Bourbon and Thomasberger went on to Babylon, Baghdad and Samarra, meeting the Germans who were digging and observing patiently as they had done for more than a decade now, laying bare the bones of the first civilised communities, planting their agents, givers and receivers of news, in the most strategic places, on the land routes to Persia, Afghanistan and ultimately India; on the route to Britain's oil supply line at Ahwaz and Abadan across the Shatt-al-Arab. The vicious circle of espionage was becoming confusing through its sheer symmetry. Prince Sixtus, a French citizen by birth, brother-in-law of the heir to the Austro-Hungarian throne, was shortly to become a go-between of the Triple Alliance and the Entente powers. For the moment, however, he served the Emperor Franz Joseph and the world's most ruthless Secret Service.

Musil and his companions were about to discover that others were capable of underhand tactics. As they returned to the Syrian side of the Euphrates on 26 May, they were set upon by Shammar tribesmen who had been instructed to lay in wait for them by Saud ibn Subhan, the hooligan chief minister of the young Amir Saud ibn Rashid at Hail. The Austrian party was lucky to escape without loss of life, but hundreds of photographic plates, map projections, route surveys and notes were taken, and almost certainly handed over to Constantinople. They had to rely on memory in making their reports to their own Embassy in Stamboul and to the Military Geographical Institute in Vienna. The attack took place at Abu Harara, a village between Rakka and Zabid on the way to Aleppo, where they arrived exhausted and stripped of all but their clothes in the evening of 30 May. It was the end of Musil's penultimate journey in the Arab lands. Not until the world was at war did he make a last and most adventurous bid to influence events at the heart of Islam.

Across the river Tigris that ever-turbulent nation, Persia, was in disarray. Another Shia shrine was the centre of attention in the spring of 1912, the mosque of the Imam Reza at the holy city of Meshed, one of the most beautiful buildings in the world. A Russian protégé, Sardar Yusef, was murdered by a Persian mob in its precincts, while Britain's emissary Percy Sykes looked on helplessly. Russian troops bombarded the sacred building in retaliation. In 1909 the regions of Fars and Kerman had been in a state of great agitation, and in July of that year forty sepoys with a Maxim gun were sent from the Bushire Consular Guard to Shiraz to contain the disorders there.

While the British and Russian Ministers wrestled in Tehran, Percy Cox, the Resident at Bushire – 'Cokus' to the Arabs – had to deal with a situation which became more dangerous as each day passed, and Germany appointed a new Consul to that unattractive seat of the Governor of the Gulf Ports.

The German who arrived in Bushire in the summer of 1909 was a man of egregious good looks and a somewhat aggressive manner with the unforgettable name of Wilhelm Wassmuss. His mission was said to be directed to establishing equality of shipping rights for Germany, but his close contact with Wönckhaus and the general unrest in Persia suggested that his brief was more extensive. Wassmuss gave 'Cokus' the once over and decided that he had met an adversary of a most aggravating kind: cool, complacent, privileged and essentially English. The bluff German was no match for the diplomatic skills of the British Resident, but he had a distinct appeal for the Persians, and was soon a popular figure among them. 'What is the authority for this *Drang nach Westen?*' he would demand of Cox. Cox would reply calmly: 'We have policed these waters for sixty years, our privilege here is part of our imperial necessity, and as for respecting Persian integrity, if it wasn't for us there wouldn't be such a thing.'

Wassmuss, just twenty-nine and bristling with energy and patriotism, did not stay long, though he was to return in due course. After exactly a year he was sent back by the Auswärtiges Amt to his previous post in Madagascar, his blue eyes, marble-white skin and long golden hair being lost to the gaze of the Persians and Gulf expatriates for the time being. Dr Helmuth Listemann returned to his old post. A dapper man with a Kaiser moustache and the practised manner of the German diplomat, Listemann fitted much more easily into Cox's scheme of things.

In December 1909, Sir Richmond Richie of the India Office noted that India, as often in the past, would have to find the money for Persian extravagance. He told the Foreign Office: 'It will be very easy and not unreasonable for Indian politicians to ask why they should pay for the security in Persia of a constitutional system strictly denied to themselves.'

The attempt to straighten out Persia's financial problems concerned Russia as well as Britain; and the Shah's Parliament made its first real attempt to come to grips with the matter by appointing the American, W. Morgan Shuster, as its financial adviser in 1911. Recommended by the US Treasury Secretary, Shuster was the ideal man for the job; honest to a degree which was said to have caused 'embarrassment' to the administration in his previous job, and of great force of character, he fought a one-man war against the conflicting imperial interests of Britain and Russia. He arrived at a time when Germany was intent on intensifying that rivalry and so preventing a combination hostile to its own interests.

Before Shuster's arrival there had been an attempt by Russia to reinstate the deposed Shah Muhammad Ali, who had lived in exile in the Caucasus for four years. In August 1911, a few months after the American had taken up his post, an army led by the renegade Arshad ad-Dowla marched on Tehran. Bringing up the rear was Muhammad Ali, with a false passport and an escort of Okhrana agents. Shuster was largely responsible for organising resistance to the invaders. Arshad was captured and executed, and the remarkable Shuster was execrated by both sides. Even Soviet historians were later to describe him as the 'agent of American imperialism', while the Czar's men regarded him as the 'agent of British imperialism'. In the end Britain agreed with Russia that an end would have to be put to his activities, which they believed threatened the Anglo-Russian agreement. On 24 December 1911, after less than a year in office, with the Persian *Majlis* surrounded by protesting Bakhtiari tribesmen, Shuster was dismissed, and the *Majlis* disbanded. In London Grey observed: 'He attempted what was good, but what could only be done by force; and there was no force available for the purpose.' Barclay, the British Minister in Tehran, said: 'It's enough to make the angels weep . . . I *really* liked that man.'

A Treasury *gendarmerie* was proposed before Shuster's dismissal, and the American wanted to make Britain's military attaché, Major C. B. Stokes, its commander. Russia, and more remarkably, the British Foreign Office, opposed his appointment, and in the end a force of Swedish-officered policemen was recruited. From the beginning the Swedes showed distinct pro-German sympathies. Stokes was accused by the British Minister of being 'fanatically anti-Russian, also anti-British'. He was also accused of being a rabid supporter of Persian nationalists. His 'nationalist' activity was almost certainly designed to win the confidence of tribal leaders whom the Germans were wooing most successfully in 1911. But in Persia, as in Arabia, the Foreign Office and British intelligence appeared to be at odds. The man who might have prevented Germany from gain-ing a stranglehold on the tribal leaders was to find himself a few years hence in Mesopotamia, as a member of the military intelligence service, fighting a rearguard action against the machinations of the Germans in the south of Persia, led by Wilhelm Wassmuss. For the moment he was in disgrace.

5

Murder at Hail

In October 1912 the Resident at Bushire received an application from Leachman for permission to travel in central Arabia. Two months earlier Leachman had made a similar application to the India Office in London, which had been turned down by Lord Crewe. Cox was in England on leave at the time and his second assistant, A. T. Wilson, wrote to Shakespear asking his advice, saying that Cox was anxious to do everything possible, 'privately' to help. Shakespear was hotly opposed to Leachman, being allowed to travel 'after his masquerade here last year'.

Leachman was in England when the Gulf officers were discussing his application, having arrived from India in April. He noted in his diary 'strong support from military authorities' with regard to his projected journey. He also noted the generous support offered by the Royal Geographical Society.

He left the London docks bound for Beirut on 17 October, nine days before Bushire received his request. Leachman, the uncompromising patriot, never wasted time. Eight days after leaving England he was in Damascus with the authority of the DMO, Henry Wilson, upholding the honour of the Empire in the face of an almost orchestrated assault on his presence by German and Austrian soldiers and officers who now swarmed through the streets and hotels. As a young subaltern in South Africa he had prayed that peace would not be granted 'till no man either of present or future generations could doubt our victory'. Now that war with the Central Powers was generally regarded as inescapable he spoke of those who would leave Arabia to the misrule of the Turks or the ambition of Germany as 'traitors'.

German and Austrian agents were trying desperately to bring the Arab chiefs into the Turkish fold, he noted. On 2 November he wrote to his father telling him he would be off next day, not indicating where he was going but saying that he should be in

Basra or Kuwait in about three weeks. He left for Dumeir and the central Arabian route in pouring rain, his camel squelching and sliding in sandy mud, taking the old Damascus–Baghdad camel-post road.

He travelled with Muhammad al Bessam's *ageyl* and a mysterious Arab companion who was identified as Saleh, who joined him at the National Hotel in Damascus. In a letter home he said simply that he knew the man well and that he 'had just arrived from Baghdad and was agreeable to go anywhere with me'. Leachman does not record any dates, but there are clues in a subsequent report.

'On the twenty-eighth day from Damascus at nightfall we reached the outskirts of Kusaiba, the border town between the territory of Ibn Rashid, the Shammar Amir, and Al Kasim,' he says. Thus he had arrived in the territory of Ibn Saud some 800 miles from his starting point by the beginning of December. He crossed a route taken only the year before by Musil as well as the Jauf route of Aylmer and Butler, and met several of Musil's guides on the way and some desert characters, one of whom composed a poem in his honour, though neither the recital nor the reward came up to expectation.

Leachman was a fine horseman and a good if reluctant camel-rider: 'The Badawin is very kind to his camel, and in return the Arabian camel is a very different animal to the ill-mannered, treacherous variety encountered in India,' he noted. As he wandered through Kasim towards the neighbouring townships of Buraida and Anaiza, he recalled that the Turks still laid claim to the district. At Ayun on the Buraida road he was introduced to the local chief, the brother of his companion, who 'whispered in his brother's ear that I was an Englishman and received in return strict injunctions from him to say that I was to pass myself off as a Musalawi, or inhabitant of Mosul in Mesopotamia'. The travellers were given a dinner in their honour at Ayun, and Leachman's meat went down the wrong way.

He eventually passed the way of famous predecessors through Buraida and Anaiza, the great towns of Kasim; through gates that had admitted Palgrave, Wallin, Huber, Doughty and few others from the outside world, testifying like them to the 'remarkable business proclivities' of the natives, and to their 'bigoted and fanatical' nature.

Leachman did not record the date of his arrival, but we know from another source. On Christmas Day Shaikh Mubarak told

Shakespear that a European had arrived at Buraida accompanied by a servant and interpreter and that they had been there for some 'twenty days'. If that was so, Leachman had now traversed some 900 miles of the most difficult and hazardous desert in the world in the incredibly short time of one month – an average of thirty miles a day over rock and sand dunes, and precipitous outcrops.

On 23 December Mubarak had been told that Ibn Saud had sent horsemen to take the traveller to him. Leachman took the road on towards Jabal Tuwaiq which Raunkiaer had used a few months before and then on to the Shaqra road which only Captain Sadleir had taken before him, in 1819 when he went in pursuit of the Egyptian Ibrahim Pasha. Leachman arrived under escort at Riyadh at the turn of the year.

> Very soon we were escorted to an upper hall overlooking
> the bazaar and the town, and here we were greeted by
> Abdal Aziz, the Wahhabi Amir himself . . . He is a man of
> about forty, 6 feet in height and broad in proportion, with a
> strong though kindly face and the simplest of manners. He
> shook me by the hand and put me at my ease at once by the
> friendliness of his greeting, and a long conversation
> ensued on the news of the outside world, especially the
> Turco-Balkan war.

That was all that Leachman ever recorded of his conversation with Ibn Saud. He listened as all visitors must to the story of past fortunes in the family of the Sauds, and he was treated with great courtesy and kindness, both by Ibn Saud and his father the Imam Abdurrahman. But the Amir was suspicious of his purpose.

He met Ahmad ibn Thaniyan in the town one day, the son of a noble family of Najd, whose mother was Circassian, and who had been educated at Constantinople. They discussed the geography of Arabia at length, but no matters of political moment it seems. Ibn Saud would not fall in with the Englishman's wish to travel south by way of Jabrin, and so Leachman made for the Al Hasa coast, through the gravelly outskirts of Riyadh and the Dahana sandbelt. Eight days out from Riyadh he entered Hofuf, a town of 30,000 inhabitants many of them Wahhabis, where he was 'most hospitably' received by Turkish officers. Then to Ujair and across the Gulf to Bahrain, where his friend Macpherson was staying. 'Hullo, got anything to eat?', said Leachman as he barged into his friend's house. He looked like a 'long cadaverous and altogether filthy Badawin', according to his host.

The journey was supposed to be one 'of the first geographical importance'. He did admittedly map one small part of the Kasim route accurately and he correctly placed the town of Hazil in north Arabia which Wallin, the nineteenth-century Swede, had misplaced. But the significance of his remarkably swift descent on Riyadh in the face of Sir Edward Grey's strict ban on travel in central Arabia, was assuredly other than geographical.

In March 1913, within a few weeks of Leachman's departure from Riyadh, Shakespear made a sudden journey to Khafs, one of Ibn Saud's favourite camping grounds, without discussing the trip with the Resident or consulting him as to the advisability of a visit to the Amir at a time when Britain was about to sign a treaty with Turkey which had important long-term implications for central Arabia.

The Political Agent, like Leachman, was a man of gritty determination; but unlike the more impulsive Leachman, he was circumspect in his dealings with Arab chiefs. Leachman, over the years, enjoyed a love-hate relationship with the princes of the desert, being inclined to lash out when they rubbed him up the wrong way. Shakespear, even in his close relationship with Ibn Saud, was usually formal and politically on guard. Thus his journey in the spring of 1913 was, on the surface, surprising.

There were many reasons why the Political Agent should have wished to talk to Ibn Saud at that time; and an overwhelming reason why he should not have done so. At the end of November 1912, he had warned the Resident that new trouble was brewing in central Arabia, in the shape of a squabble between Zamil ibn Subhan, the Regent of Hail, and Saud ibn Saleh, the Chief Minister. In early December Mubarak made an unannounced departure from Kuwait and stayed at his citadel at the Jahra oasis; and on the 22nd of the month he departed aboard his yacht for Muhammerah to consult with the conspiratorial Shaikh Khazal. At the beginning of 1913 the nationalist committees in Beirut and Damascus had nominated Ibn Saud as 'the natural champion of the Arab peoples', and had begun to plan the long-awaited uprising which would be preceded by a secret gathering in Kuwait early in 1914. On 4 January 1913 *The Times* of London reported: 'Disturbances feared in Constantinople. Movement for Arab Empire.' The plans of the Covenant, as Al Ahad came to be called, and of the other nationalist committees, had come into the open at the time of counter-revolution in Turkey. 'Conspiracy in Turkey', read *The Times*'s main headline on 28 February. Sayid Talib, anticipating the plans of the Covenant, threatened revolution at the head of the Gulf, there were riots and murder in Basra, and Consul Crow called in a warship to anticipate the plans of the Naqib's volatile son.

All these matters concerned both Shakespear and Ibn Saud, and the latter had plans of his own in the light of events in Constantinople. But overriding everything was the fact that on 10 February Hakki Pasha, ex-Grand Vizier at the Porte, was sent by the hard men of the CUP to Berlin and London, to finalise the Anglo-Turkish Convention; a document which would recognise that Ibn Saud was an Ottoman subject and that he would become the *mutasarif* of the Government in Najd. Only the most urgent business could have encouraged Shakespear to make an unscheduled call on his friend the Amir at that moment.

Nevertheless he left the Agency on 13 March, a few days after returning from a voyage to Kubbar island aboard the *Lewis Pelly*, where he met C. C. R. Murphy, who had taken over from Craufurd as Gulf intelligence chief. He took a familiar route and by mid-month was at Majmaa in the Sudair, having passed through Ibn Saud's camel-grazing territory in the Dahana. He was royally entertained at the village of Harma by an acquaintance who often visited Kuwait, Abdullah ibn Askar, and the two men enjoyed a smoke while Ibn Askar brought Shakespear up to date with the affairs of Najd. The 'old soldier' told him that Ibn Saud was presently camped at Khafs, some sixty miles to the south through some of the most difficult terrain in the region.

Shakespear's party left Camp XV in the Sudair on 27 March and battled through craggy hills and passes to Tamair and across the Khazza ridge in three days, arriving at the Amir's camp on 30 March. They left five days later on 4 April. During Shakespear's stay he and the Amir were locked in conversation for hours on end, often with Ibn Saud's brothers and with Ibn Jiluwi the Amir's cousin and the strong man among his political counsellors. Not a word of the conversations was ever recorded in the political files of Whitehall or the Indian administration, however, or in personal letters or notes.

His journey back to Kuwait was relatively slow, taking sixteen days, and in the course of it he kept travel notes which were out

of character with all his other log books. He was a most immaculate explorer, noting every detail in a careful hand in his notebooks before he went to sleep each night. But on the Khafs
journey he scribbled illegibly, as though irritated and totally out
of sorts. It is impossible to tell his exact route from the pages of
the travel diary. He arrived back in Kuwait on 20 April.

A few days after his return to Kuwait Ibn Saud's army moved
south-east from Riyadh towards the Gulf. By the second week
of May they had taken the key town of Katif. Turkish reinforcements were sent from Basra on the British ship *John O'Scott*, but
by the end of May the Saudis had recaptured the whole of the
vital seaboard of Al Hasa, which had been under Ottoman occupation for forty-two years. Abdullah ibn Jiluwi, Ibn Saud's lieutenant at the taking of Riyadh ten years before, was made the
first Governor of the province under the new regime, and he
ruled with an iron hand. Whitehall was not amused. It had
accepted Turkish authority over Al Hasa as a provision of the
Convention. Cox at Bushire passed on to the Government
Shakespear's assurance that he had discussed 'nothing but personal matters', and that not a word of official business passed
between them. The reprimand was fierce. The Political Agent
must not meet with Arab chiefs in the future, 'at any time, in any
circumstance', without the prior approval of HMG, the Foreign
Office told the India Office, who told McMahon, the Indian
Foreign Secretary, who told Cox. While Shakespear was away
on his clandestine mission a high-powered oil delegation had
visited Kuwait from India, and had found 'the chances favourable', after viewing the oily deposits of the Burqan region. But
Shakespear had more pressing matters on his mind.

On 20 September 1913 Bray arrived at his old stamping
ground of Damascus. Norman Bray flitted between Simla, London, Cairo and Damascus during the years between 1905 and
1914, yet he was on the unattached list for the entire period. Not
until 1916 was he put on the 'Special' list, but in the interval he
had unhampered access to the General Staff offices in London.

'My immediate task was to make friends with all and sundry,'
he noted in 1913. He took his brief literally. He had a number of
meetings with his own Consul at Damascus, George P. Devey,
and with Henry Cumberbatch from Beirut, one of the most
experienced of Britain's consular men in the East, and the skilled antagonist of the French representative at Beirut, M.
Georges Picot, who more than lived up to the assessment of

Nicolai of the *Deuxième Bureau*, 'Beware! It is brutal and efficient.' But Bray concentrated on the Turkish and German officers, especially the aggressive cavalry instructor, von Hochwaechter. The Germans were not exactly friendly, but the polo pitch provided a useful meeting point. Most of all he spent his time in conversation with Arabs of Al Ahad, their revolutionary fervour stimulated by the failure of the *Ittihad* to fulfill its early promises of equality under the Cresent flag.

'Understanding has been reached with some of the most powerful Arab chiefs and tribes,' he said, and even Christian leaders and Druse chiefs were involved. 'With the exception of Ibn Rashid, ruler of Hail, who was definitely pro-Turkish, and the Imam Yahya of Yemen, replies had been favourable.' Definite plans had been laid for revolt. He did not know that Sayid Talib had already undermined those plans. He attended several meetings of Al Ahad and had secret talks with one of its most sensible and moderate leaders, the Syrian Christian Haddad, who spoke to him of *liberté spirituelle*. Bray seemed confident that the Turks and Germans were as yet ignorant of the conspiracy, but he was wrong, for Musil was kept informed by Nuri ibn Shalan and through him Vienna, Berlin and even the Quai d'Orsay were following closely the plans of the desert princes. The significance of the journeys of Leachman and Shakespear, and of Raunkiaer, to Ibn Saud began to emerge as the plans for an Arab rebellion against the Turks gained momentum. Britain's warring administrations in Whitehall and Simla kept their separate vigils. Shakespear and Leachman were the only agents with the experience and resourcefulness as desert travellers to take on the most dangerous and exhausting journeys into the interior, but others were soon on the move around the edges of the peninsula, and deep enough into the lands of Ibn Rashid and Ibn Saud to observe their movements and plans. Bray kept his ear to the ground in Damascus, acting as liaison between the War Office in London and Simla intelligence.

While Britons and Germans, and other nationalities besides, rubbed shoulders in the clubs and bars of Damascus, the Young Turks were busy with political problems at home. Strictly speaking they had never attained the power which the revolution promised them. In January 1913, however, they staged a second and decisive *coup* a fortnight after new outrages against the Armenians were reported from the town of Hadjin. Jamal Bey, the picturesque ruffian of the party, walked into the Sublime

Porte one day to be greeted by the new Grand Vizier, Mahmud Shevket Pasha.

'Jamal Bey,' shouted Shevket above the hullabaloo, 'I want you to take over as military commander of Constantinople, at once.' Inside the building lay the corpse of Nazim Pasha, the grand old liberal of Turkish politics. With him perished the hopes of all who still believed that there was hope for the Ottoman Empire. Azmi Bey, the most sinister figure in the capital, became Chief of Police. With Jamal and Talaat in the saddle, soon to be joined by Enver, the friend of Germany, the Young Turks were at last in charge.

Henry Morgenthau described the scene when he arrived as Ambassador from the United States at the time of these events:

> Like American cities it [Constantinople] fell into the hands of irresponsible elements because the real hard-working citizens are busily engaged in daily tasks and have no leisure for public matters. Abdal Hamid, the great assassin, had been replaced by his gentle brother Mehemet V . . . but that was not the reality.

Indeed. The gaols were full to overflowing, and one of their inmates was an Arab officer of the Ottoman army who had won renown in the Turco-Italian war, and who had been instrumental in clearing Constantinople of counter-revolutionaries in an abortive attempt by old-guard supporters to regain power in 1911. His name was Aziz Ali al Masri, a founder of Al Ahad. But his greatest crime was to have questioned the military leadership of Enver in the Tripoli campaign. The charge on which he was arraigned was one of 'embezzling public funds', to the tune it was claimed of £30,000. He was found guilty and condemned to death, but Britain stepped in to save him. Kitchener sent the Vice-Chancellor of the University of Cairo to plead for him, and there were some tough words from Britain's Embassy. It was probably the French journalist, Georges Rémond, who obtained his release, however. He met Jamal at a party and told him, 'Aziz may possibly be an Arab revolutionary . . . but he is certainly no thief.' Jamal wrote to Enver, and Aziz was sent to Cairo, banished from the Empire he had served well, and leaving behind his sword as a token that he would not take up arms against it.

There were other important political arrests after the *coup*.

The resurgent Young Turks were determined to dispose of the opposition this time, and to break the spirit of revolt in the Empire. But the old 'radicals' fought back. By mid-summer Shevket himself had been murdered. It was he who had sent Hakki Pasha to London to sign the treaty that had been under discussion while Britain and Germany contended for the hand of Islam in central Arabia, in Damascus, Tehran and Baghdad.

At the beginning of the year Gertrude Bell had written a famous letter to *The Times*: 'It is not the loss of a friend for whose strength and fearless honesty I had a high esteem and regard that sharpens my words. It is the apprehension that . . . the murderers of Nazim Pasha may be a . . . knell sounding the doom of Turkey.' Sir Gerard Lowther reinforced his warnings of the influence of Freemasonry and Zionism, and shortly after decided to retire to his farm in England. Sir Louis Mallet, Grey's right-hand man at the Foreign Office, was sent to replace him as Ambassador.

Aubrey Herbert arrived in Constantinople soon after the Young Turks' final *putsch*, to a bleak, cold and apathetic Bosporus. The capital was virtually under siege as Bulgarian forces occupied Adrianople. Councils were divided between Anglophiles and Germanophiles and wounded soldiers learnt to count in English to take their minds off mutilations for which there were neither doctors nor medicines to offer the prospect of repair. Herbert's notebook paid tribute to the land he loved with all its faults and wicked extravagances. In April 1913 a new peace was signed with the Balkan countries. But in July the Turks reoccupied Adrianople in defiance of the great powers and war broke out again. Herbert sensed the tragedy of the protracted conflict and burst into satirical verse:

> So now the twilight falls upon the twice betrayed,
> The *Daily Mail* tells England
>   and the *Daily News* tells God,
> That God and British statesmen
>   should make the Turks afraid –
> Who fight unfed, unshod.

Bray remained in Damascus in December, making his daily round of bars and clubs, listening to the Germans as they chattered endlessly about the Berlin–Baghdad railroad, 'blind to the feelings of the people of the region and thinking only of strategy'.

Out of the blue appeared the *de facto* ruler of Turkey, Enver

Pasha, resplendent in the uniform of a general, with the strutting gait of the cartoon military dictator. He was there to inspect the Damascus garrison.

> During the visit several Turkish officers with whom I was on friendly terms, informed me that a programme of intensive training was shortly to be commenced, and which was to be completed by July 1914. I asked the reason for this haste and the choice of the month of July. They replied rather vaguely that Russia was unostentatiously increasing her effectives on the Armenian frontier and that Turkey had to prepare for any eventualities in that quarter.

Late in 1913, while Bray was still in Damascus, Gertrude Bell arrived back there. Their respective hotels, the Palace and the Victoria, were a stone's throw from each other alongside the Wali's *serai*, but neither mentioned the presence of the other in letters or subsequent accounts of their visits. Gertrude had been given Foreign Office permission to travel from there to Hail, and Sir Louis Mallet had obtained the Porte's approval for her journey.

At Jerablus on the Euphrates, Lawrence and Woolley maintained the appearance of digging at the site of ancient Carchemish, though the expedition was officially at an end, and Lawrence heard stirring tales from the Arabs of 'Mister Bell'. The German engineers and their Arab railroad squads still worked near by on the construction of a bridge. In Palestine and Sinai Captain Newcombe wandered, still 'on special duty' under the auspices of the Exploration Fund, appointing and instructing his agents with renewed urgency, doing the daily work of ten men.

In Kuwait Captain Shakespear was making final preparations for a long-proposed trans-Arabian expedition which would embrace a call on Ibn Saud at Riyadh, though Foreign Office approval, very necessary after the meeting between the Political Agent and the Saudi Amir at Khafs, had not been granted. Nevertheless, the Indian Government was determined that Shakespear should make the journey and the Viceroy, pressed by the General Staff, was taking up his case. Sir Percy Cox, knighted in the Coronation honours list of 1912, had moved to New Delhi (the centre of government decided on at the Coronation durbar of 1911) as Foreign Secretary, and J. G. Lorimer, a firm supporter of Shakespear's pro-Saudi stance, had taken over as Resident in the Persian Gulf. The consequent interaction of personalities and events in the first three months of 1914 was to build up into one of the most arcane episodes in the modern history of the Arab lands.

Before setting out on her most ambitious journey to date into central Arabia Gertrude Bell had met Douglas Carruthers in London and tried to talk him into accompanying her. He was unable to join her however, and so she set off alone. Lawrence at Carchemish obviously knew that she was on her way eastward. On the day that she left Damascus for the Syrian desert, 10 December 1913, he wrote to his brother: 'Miss Bell passed straight through from Beirut to Damascus . . . and will not visit us till Spring.' The source of his information is not far to seek. Gertrude carried with her three pieces of scrap paper torn from a notebook containing about thirty place names, dotted in approximate geographical position. On the front sheet she had pencilled: 'Plans and notes on buildings and following needed by Mr Hogarth.'

By coincidence she had shared a cabin on the SS *Lotus* on her way from England to Beirut with Miss Winifred Baird, who was on her way to India to marry Shakespear's brother, Henry. Gertrude wrote to her stepmother from the ship: 'I know about his [Henry's] brother: he is a very able man in the Persian Gulf.' She little knew how close she was to come to him in days ahead. She progressed south-eastward from Dumeir, as if she was going to Baghdad, and then sharp west towards the Hijaz railway, making notes and drawings of Hogarth's nominated places as she went, and taking innumerable photographs: Adhra, Ghadir, Burqa, Jabal Sais, Kasr Amr, Kharaneh, Mashetta, Ziza on the railway, Bair. If Carruthers had not been able to go with her, he was at least able to arrange for her to have his very reliable guide of years past, Muhammad al Murawi, which was fixed up through Muhammad al Bessam. 'I want to cut all links with the world,' she declared. 'The road and the dawn, the sun, the wind and the rain, the camp fire under the stars, and sleep, and the road again.' But things were not to be quite as idyllic as that. Her loneliness and solitude rested heavily on her in the long days and nights, and she had vital matters to attend to before she could cut the thread of civilisation and turn south-east again for Hail.

On 28 December Lawrence and Woolley departed suddenly from Carchemish, leaving their German neighbours to collect

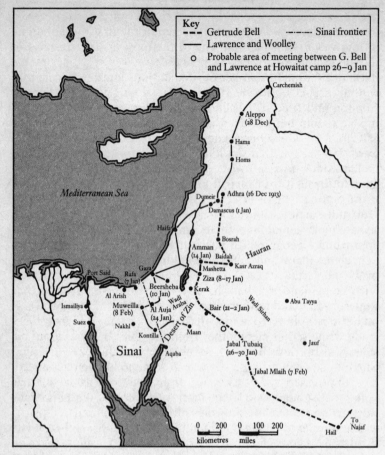

Key
- – – Gertrude Bell   – · – · – Sinai frontier
- —— Lawrence and Woolley
- o   Probable area of meeting between G. Bell and Lawrence at Howaitat camp 26–9 Jan

Map 7   Routes of Gertrude Bell, Lawrence and Woolley, 1914

granite from the excavation site for their building operations while they went down in the footsteps of the Israelites to the Wilderness of Zin. Neither could assert with Moses: 'O Lord, I am not eloquent.' They were most argumentative and articulate men. But on this occasion they were less than forthcoming.

Woolley averred that he and Lawrence 'went down into Sinai because the Egyptian Exploration Society wanted some archaeologists to follow in the footsteps of Moses.' Sir Frederick Kenyon, Director of the British Museum, friend of Hogarth and a man with high contacts in the Foreign Office related within two years of the journey that the British Museum asked if they could carry out an 'archaeological survey in southern Palestine for the Palestine Exploration Fund'.

The report which the two men wrote after the journey suggested nothing at all of archaeological investigation but much of biblico-geographical conjecture. It was dedicated to 'Captain S. F. Newcombe, R.E. Who showed them *the way wherein they must walk, and the work that they must do*'. Newcombe, an excellent engineer and surveyor and expert on the heating of buildings, would not be the choice of most authorities as a guide to the 'archaeological investigation' of Sinai. He insisted later that the dedication was a 'leg pull'. It is not without significance that at the time of their journey Kitchener in Cairo was giving a good deal of thought to the security of his front door, and to the choice of Arab allies should Britain need them in any war threatening the Suez Canal. Until 1883 the Egypto-Turkish frontier had been fixed as a line running from Suez to Al Rafa, a point between Al Arish and Gaza. The peninsula south of that line was officially Ottoman territory up to 1906, but from 1883 Britain dominated it from the fortress of Nakhl by the same uncertain proxy with which it ruled Egypt.

The Military Governor of the region from 1906 to 1912 had been Major Alfred Parker, nephew of Lord Kitchener. Educated at Harrow he had joined the Royal Sussex Regiment in 1895 and served in the Egyptian Army from 1899. He succeeded a short, stubborn, indefatigable officer, Colonel Alwyn Jennings Bramley in the hot and lonely seat of the Governor's residence. In 1912 Parker went off to take command of the Abbasia Police School at Cairo and was succeeded by Captain C. S. Jarvis, who like Jennings Bramley, wrote interminable articles about the tribes, the biblical past and the flora of Sinai for the journal of the Palestine Exploration Fund. All three were staff officers of exceptional ability, and all were to play important parts in the British adventure in the Arab lands which had begun to unfold in earnest at the beginning of 1914.

Woolley and Lawrence appeared to be restricted for time, 'six weeks' from starting out according to their own account. They arrived at Damascus on 1 January 1914 and came down the railway to Ziza, where 'Gertie' was held up by Turkish officialdom in her attempt to leave for Hail. After the arrival of Lawrence (her 'beloved boy') and Woolley, she changed her intended path via Jauf to one which took her south to the region of Taima and then in a straight line east to her destination. Thus she was able to pass through territory only mapped sketchily so far by the Italian, Guarmani, and by Carruthers and Musil between Jabal Shammar and the Hijaz railway.

In the meantime Woolley and Lawrence went to Beersheba, and set out with Newcombe on 10 January. At Gaza they had met the missionary, Dr Stirling, big in bulk and mind, whose only condition for treating the sick and injured was that they listen to a sermon first; and the Consular Agent Knesevich and his son Emil, men well known to Aubrey Herbert, and to Aaron Aaronsohn and Avshalom Feinberg. At Beersheba they were received by the Kaimakam, Erfah Bey, 'free from the widespread suspicion of map makers'.

The travellers from Carchemish told more of Newcombe's than of their own activities: 'Off each morning with his guides, returning to camp at dusk where he went on working in his tent until about midnight, knowing where every one of his workers and agents was and keeping the details in his head, relishing the Spartan simplicity of his life.'

Woolley and Lawrence parted from their mentor at Esbaita and went on into the wilderness of Al Tih in ancient Edom, which Aaronsohn had traversed in 1908, and then to the plateau of eastern Sinai in country 'too detestable to merit comment from earlier travellers'. 'And they removed from Ezion-Geber, and pitched in the wilderness of Zin which is Kadesh.'

Kadesh is preserved in the spring of Ain Kadeis in present-day Sinai, but it could not have provided water for the 6,000 Israelites who were about to see the Promised Land. But five miles to the north-west lies ample water at Ain al Kudairat, the source of the fertility of the valley of Kudairat, and it was here, at the point from which the spies of Moses set out after the 'miracle of water' into the Valley of Grapes, that our twentieth-century spies separated. Woolley went north through the Negev towards the land of the Philistines, arriving back at Gaza on 22 February.

Lawrence's movements are not so clear. He gives us little detail of his movements between Kudairat and Aqaba, and then through Wadi Araba to Maan. But he must have hurried, for a few days after reaching the old Pilgrim road, now the Hijaz railway, he had sped on along Wadi Araba. Gertrude had finally left Kalat Ziza with her manservant Fattuh and her guides on 17 January. On the 25th she was able to write: 'Tomorrow I hope we shall be guests of the Howaitat. The big tents cannot be far away.' Two days later she was among the Howaitat in the region of Wadi Sirhan, being entertained by Muhammad, brother of the chief, Auda: 'A magnificent person ... He carries the Howaitat reputation for dare-devilry written on his face – I should not like to meet him in anger.' Auda, whom Lawrence was to meet in years to come and to make into the most famous of Arab shaikhs, was away raiding when Gertrude was at his camp.

In late January Gertrude moved on with a party of Howaitat in the direction of Bair, the place on Hogarth's list where she would normally have turned off towards Jauf. Instead she moved south-east towards Jabal Tubaiq. It seems that Lawrence in the meantime had travelled due east from Maan through stony desert towards Tubaiq, where he met up with Gertrude again, and she photographed him in the colourful indigo-dyed dress of the Howaitat among a group of women, the wives of Muhammad abu Tayya. As the men of the tribe are said to be the most handsome of Arabs as well as the most belligerent, so the women are robust beauties, and Lawrence, with his clean-shaven face peering through a distinctive headdress, did not look out of place. Neither Lawrence nor Gertrude ever mentioned the meeting, but her photographic plates told the story of a clandestine parley. He returned to Carchemish, where he joined Woolley in March. She took the road down to Taima close to the border of the Hijaz and then went on a straight, arid and scarcely populated path to Hail.

She wrote as she left the shaikhs of the Howaitat: 'I made great friends with Muhammad. He is a good fellow and I liked and trusted him ... And I fancy that when you have drunk the milk of the naga over the camp fire of Abu Tayya you are baptised of the desert and there is no other salvation for you.'

The story of Gertrude Bell's journey to Hail, of her imprisonment in the guest house of the Rashids, her determined arguments with Ibrahim, the brother of Zamil the Regent and the uncle of the Amir, as she stood on her dignity when deprived of money and freedom, her bedroom conversations with Fatima, the Amir's powerful grandmother, and Turkiyyeh, the chatterbox of Hail, while she was holed up for two weeks, were once part of the legend of Arabia as seen by Britishers who only dimly imagined its vast deserts and unpredictable tribes. It was a favoured topic for school essays in England until the 1930s, when another legend swept everything before it. Hers was a brave and formidable undertaking for a lone woman; and a woman at the lowest ebb of a highly charged and emotionally frustrated life. But the vital event of her visit occurred not in the crenellated mud-brick castles and palaces of the Shammar fortress, but outside in a drama which must claim a high place even among the princely excesses of the Rashid family.

The Amir of Hail, the young Saud ibn Abdal Aziz al Rashid, was away on a 'raiding' expedition when Gertrude arrived on 24 February. He was accompanied by his villainous, squint-eyed cousin and namesake Saud ibn Saleh as Subhan, and by the Regent Zamil ibn Subhan, uncle of both men. They were still away two weeks later, somewhere in the Great Nafud desert, when she left Hail for Baghdad. There was an air of conspiracy at Hail, which was closely associated with events elsewhere in Arabia involving Britain, Turkey and Ibn Saud.

The British troopship *John O'Scott* had been used to transport Ottoman militia to Al Hasa and in its embarrassment – for Sir Edward Grey and Hakki Pasha were about to initial the Anglo-Turkish Convention in London – the British Government even offered Indian troops to help stem the Saudi tide. Eventually the Turkish garrisons escaped to Bahrain and Qatar, and Ibn Saud demanded their expulsion. Britain was forced to comply, especially since the Saudi leader promised the Resident that he would 'represent the Turks as Governor' and would 'undertake to ensure the tranquillity of the district'.

For a moment the battle between India and Whitehall centred on Cox, Shakespear and Ibn Saud. 'I gather privately that FO are much frightened by Sir Percy Cox and Shakespear,' Sir Thomas Holderness of the India Office wrote to Sir Louis Mallet in July. They suspect them of 'all sorts of designs', he added. And there followed an affirmation of one of the profoundest problems facing central government when far-flung imperial interests are at stake: 'It would be a pity if we said or did anything that would discourage the local people from saying what they think, and encouraged them to say what they think they are expected to say.' Lord Crewe agreed with his Under-Secretary.

Noting the events of May 1913 the Foreign Office observed: 'Shakespear spent four days with Ibn Saud in April.' In the margin Under-Secretary Alwyn Parker had written, 'Pity'. And alongside a summary of Shakespear's observations there appeared a pencilled, 'Nonsense'.

4 A page from Gertrude Bell's field notebook, signed by members
of the German expedition at Babylon

5 Dr Andrae with a gazelle at Assur in 1911

6   Ibn Saud, photographed by Gertrude Bell at Basra in 1916

Nevertheless the Indian Government decided to send Cox
and Shakespear to see both Mubarak and Ibn Saud in July as
the Convention neared the point of signature. Grey insisted that
a meeting with Ibn Saud should await the completion of the
treaty, which 'would not be long delayed'. Ibn Saud was still
demanding the expulsion of the Turkish garrison from Qatar as
the summer came to its end in one of the hottest years in the
memory of Gulf residents. In October the Foreign Secretary in
Whitehall was still stalling. He could see 'no such urgent or
paramount necessity' for troops to be withdrawn from territory
'which has been theirs since 1872'. The note containing Grey's
comments on Ibn Saud's demands had been preceded by a
reminder that: 'Shakespear is in future to confine his activities
strictly to the limits eventually assigned to Kuwait under the
Anglo-Turkish Convention.' But if the Foreign Office seemed
on the surface to be anxious to implement the letter and the
spirit of the conversations with Turkey, its actions were open to
question. In July a highly secret meeting took place between
Shaikhs Mubarak and Khazal and a British delegation aboard
the warship, HMS *Sphinx*. The Shaikh of Kuwait was told the
terms of the Convention and warned to keep all foreigners,
including the Turks, and especially Wönckhaus, at arm's
length. A few days after the meeting and the signing of the Convention, the Foreign Office suggested that the Shaikh should be
approached with a view to granting Britain an oil concession in
his territory.

By October 1913 Ibn Saud was in total control of Al Hasa. On
4 November Sir Louis Mallet wired from Constantinople to tell
the Foreign Secretary that the Turks were about to accept
defeat and 'to recognise Ibn Saud as the mutasarif in Najd', the
Ottoman Governor of the region. But Ibn Saud had other plans.

Shakespear was to hand over the Kuwait agency to his successor, Colonel Grey, in early January 1914. No love was lost
between the two men. In December 1913 Shakespear carried out
his last official function as Political Agent. Cox had decided not
to go himself to Ibn Saud and so Major Trevor, the Political
Agent in Bahrain, was called down to accompany Shakespear;
the Foreign Office clearly did not trust the latter on his own.
Their task was to convince the Amir that he must accept the
conditions of the Convention. According to Shakespear's report
Ibn Saud was told that he must come to terms with the Turks.
He replied that he 'would gladly accept British suzerainty over

his territory'. Britain's envoys replied that such an arrangement was 'out of the question'.

The Turks were not as fussy about the small print of agreements as Sir Edward Grey appeared to be. At the very moment when they led Whitehall to believe that the inheritance of Najd was settled, that they would recognise it as a Turkish dominion under the governorship of Ibn Saud – thus nullifying the loss of Al Hasa – they were taking part in negotiations with Ibn Rashid's agent in Constantinople, Rashid Pasha (who was unrelated to his namesakes), with the aim of supplying arms to Hail with which to attack Ibn Saud in the south. In December 1913, 6,000 Mauser rifles, some 60,000 cartridges, a Daimler motor car, and a large sum of money were sent by the Hijaz railroad to the station of Al Muazzam near Taima, whence they were taken along the road followed by Gertrude Bell on her way to Hail little more than a month later. The regent Zamil ibn Subhan had demonstrated the strength of his loyalty to Ibn Saud in the five years that he had ruled in the stead of his young nephew. In 1910 he had attacked the Wuld Ali tribe and the Wuld Suleiman for alleged compliance with Turkish orders in the region of the Hijaz railway, and later had attacked the Turkish garrison at Taima, beheaded Arab supporters of the regime and set up his own Governor. In 1913 the Young Turks had decided on a trial of strength within the ruling house of Hail and sent these massive gifts of arms to the eighteen-year-old Prince Saud and his hooligan kinsman Saud ibn Saleh as Subhan. Ibn Saud, hearing of Turkish plans, sought to reinforce his ally and to use the pretender in his midst, Faisal ibn Hamud al Rashid, to that end. Shakespear, his own loyalty stretched by the deep division between London and India over the very question of involvement in Arabian matters, was to become dangerously immersed in a conspiracy among the Arab princes. A good deal of his time at Khafs in the summer of 1913 had been taken up in discussions with Faisal ibn Hamud.

Shakespear handed over the Agency's secret papers to Grey on 19 January 1914, and set out on the familiar route of the Buraida caravan by way of the Batin on 2 February. Of the entourage that had gone with him on previous expeditions into the Arabian hinterland only Dhabia, his pampered she-camel, remained. The badawin of the eastern deserts would reminisce over camp fires for generations to come about his escapades, his hunting expeditions and strangely secluded passage among them during his four eventful years in the Gulf. They were sorry to see him go. Shalwa, the falcon, and the salukis had been distributed to Shaikh Mubarak and his crony Khazal of Muhammerah. *Lewis Pelly*, his beloved yacht, was handed over to his successor with as much misgiving as were the affairs of the Agency itself.

He had told Cox, who was now acting Foreign Secretary at Simla in place of McMahon, who had gone to London on lengthy furlough: 'Of course I shall be careful to avoid all politics.' The new Resident, J. G. Lorimer, had told him a few days before he left Kuwait: 'It is your duty to your country and yourself to start without delay.' Loch at intelligence wished him 'God speed' and looked forward to hearing from him.

The *shimal*, the biting, sand-infested north wind, had blown incessantly for the first six days, so that it was impossible to pitch their tents. The Englishman and his companions marched day and night and made slow going, bivouacking for a few hours when tiredness made it impossible to continue. The camels were exhausted and close to collapse by 8 February, and one of them produced an offspring which had to be put in a cradle on its mother's back. In the dreadful conditions of wind and rain in the first week of the journey they could not halt for man or beast. One of the guides, Ali the Ajmani, decided that he was being taken to the end of the world and refused to go on. Shakespear tried to soothe him, then threatened to beat him if he tried to desert. But Ali disappeared in the night and was never seen again.

By mid-month the weather had improved and they were on the route followed by Palgrave, Raunkiaer and Leachman to Riyadh, having taken a sharp left turn at the sands of Al Bittar towards the Tuwaiq escarpment and Zilfi. They left Zilfi on 28 February and that evening arrived at Ghat, set in a gorge of the Tuwaiq hills, where Shakespear was entertained by the Amir Saad ibn Abdal Mehsin as Sadairi, a kinsman of Ibn Saud on his mother's side.

Sadairi had fourteen coffee pots on the boil, and the two men recalled that they had met at Khafs. On to Majmaa and the string of eighteen villages of the Sudair that lead down to Aridh and Riyadh through undulating country which is watered here and there to provide crops of wheat and grazing land. At Majmaa he met his old friend, Abdullah ibn Askar, who had also been at Khafs. Abdullah's brother, Hamid, had been killed at the taking of Hasa nine months before. There were many other meetings with the warriors of Thaj, Khafs and Hasa on the way through the Sudair. He arrived at Riyadh on Monday 9 March.

> *10th March, Tuesday:* A more-or-less Europe morning and bath; then the horses arrived to take me to town. Rode in and was a bit late for Abdul Aziz's *majlis* but early enough to see Masaud as-Suwailim and a number of the children; also others I knew ... Then went to see Abdurrahman ... Returned to palace and bucked a bit with Saad ... [afternoon] found Abdal Aziz with a bad head so talked to Saad and Abdullah and had evening meal with them ... another talk with Abdal Aziz after which rode home by moonlight, read and went to bed early.

Shakespear never stayed in the palaces of the Arab princes. He had no great liking for Arab food and he refused to give up his evening glass of whisky, his Moselle with dinner and his pipe in the cool of the evening. He camped among the date plantations and went into the town each day, attending the Amir's morning parliaments and having innumerable meetings with him and his family; and a number of disputes.

Abdal Aziz was in a bad temper during much of the Englishman's visit. His eyesight was beginning to deteriorate from the constant glare of the desert light and he suffered from severe headaches. And events of recent months had caused him anxiety. He was still worried about British and Turkish plans and was convinced that the two nations were colluding to deprive him of his independence. His English friend and adviser was in a difficult position as he tried to reassure the Saudi chief, while remaining loyal to his own country and balancing as best he could the divergent attitudes of the Indian and home Governments towards central Arabia. Meetings were usually held at the home of the Amir's secretary, where only those who were directly concerned with the secret matters under discussion were present; even the Amir's brothers were excluded. Abdullah ibn Jiluwi, the cut-throat Faisal ibn Hamud, Ibn Saud and Shakespear were often locked in discussion and dispute for hours on end, with only the faithful secretary to overhear their plans and disagreements. The talks centred chiefly on the urgent need to settle the disputed leadership of the Shammar at Hail now that Ibn Saud had taken control of Al Hasa, in order to secure his position throughout Najd.

When the time for departure came, however, the two men rode out of Riyadh together, the green flag of the Sauds in front, its message emblazoned in white: *La illah il allah wa Muhammad rasul allah*. 'There is no God but God and Muhammad is his messenger.' The Amir, Shakespear noted, was the most striking figure he had met in Arabia on his fast and lean black mare, and was surely destined to rule over the lands which his forefathers had won so bravely and lost so foolishly.

They marched together for four days during the second week of March, Shakespear giving talks at the morning *majlis* of the shaikhs about the rudiments of wireless telegraphy and modern warfare, and attending to their ailments as they surrounded him with their sores and ills, mostly requiring more expert attention than he could offer. 'Another long buck with Abdal Aziz,' he noted on 15 March. He sent a letter off to Mubarak in Kuwait, paid farewell calls and set off towards Buraida on the 16th. Ibn Saud had left him with a new guide, Thami the Shammari, for he was going on to the lands of Ibn Rashid.

Before leaving Riyadh Shakespear learnt that Lorimer was dead. He received a message from Loch, his friend from intelligence at Simla who had moved into the Bushire Residency as Lorimer's first assistant, to the effect that the Resident had been killed by a self-inflicted gun wound. Lorimer had been Shakespear's closest confidant in the past few years. He had died on Sunday 8 February, less than a week after the Political Agent's departure.

Saddened and not a little surprised by the news, Shakespear made his way towards Anaiza and Buraida in Kasim. He spent several days in hard bargaining for camels and *rafiqs* at the latter town with the Amir Fahad ibn Muammar, the least hospitable of Ibn Saud's allies on the route. When he left Buraida he had an upset stomach and a sore throat, a heavy *shimal* was blowing, and he was harassed by a mob of camel dealers and venal badawin who were constantly cadging baksheesh. On 6 April they arrived at the watering place of Zarud. The water turned out to be 'the colour of urine' and according to Shakespear tasted like it. His stomach was not improved by having to drink it. At this point he made an unexplained decision. He had almost certainly intended to take the direct route to Egypt through Hail. He carried a letter from Mubarak addressed to the Amir Saud ibn Abdal Aziz al Rashid, which read:

An Englishman named Shakespear is visiting you in order to buy horses. He requires from six to eight animals for adornment and according to the ties of friendship between our two great nations, our Happy Arabian State and the the Great and Glorious English State, it is our duty and yours that we guard this man and help him.

Route logs and private diary become suddenly deceptive at this point. The names of companions began to emerge from his notes, and it seems that they were making the decisions about the route.

On Tuesday 7 April as they approached Zarud his private diary recorded not merely the quality of the water but one or two matters besides. 'On until we joined up with the other Ageyls camped on an open plain. Tremendous crowd of camels now.' There had been no mention of 'other Ageyls' until that moment. The traveller simply doesn't pick up 'Ageyls' in the desert.

8 April: Howling north wind. My cold has got down into my chest and given me a cough now. Camped early. [This was camp 49.] Afternoon went to coffee with Ali al Muta-wah. Conversation mostly of Saleh al Mutawah and what his fate might be, either lost his way or murdered, as nothing heard of him for the last 21 days, since in fact he left Buraidah and parted from some other Arabs two days later, taking only one man with him. His henchman Saleh al Humaidi looking very gloomy.

9 April. The log book records: 'Halted at Camp 49.' It shows bearings on thirteen place names in the vicinity of their camp from angles given him by Saleh al Humaidi. Hail was about seventy miles as the crow flies to the south-west through almost uninhabited desert. His private diary records: 'Everyone rather depressed as still no news of Saleh al Mutawah in spite of men having been sent to look for him.' He had coffee with Al Ribdi, a camel dealer. 'Beastly cold.'

10 April (Friday). 'Halted at Camp 49.' More sightings are recorded. Private diary notes: 'Another Europe morning . . . halted waiting for return of some of the searchers of Saleh.' Later: 'The excitement of the day was the arrival of a man from Ibn Rashid, Hamdani by name, who quite usurped my hon-oured place at the coffee hearth. Brought news of Saleh al

Mutawah being alive and having strayed, so we shall meet him after a day or two, as camels being sent for him.'

11 April. Travel log. They left camp at 6 a.m. and travelled for 1 hour and 40 minutes before pitching camp 50. Thus they had been stationary for four days in a deserted region in the easternmost corner of Jabal Shammar. Shakespear's private diary records: 'A silly march . . . merely to change grazing, apparently . . . Judging by the talk we are apparently going by the Khall route via Jubbah. I hope so as it will be new ground entirely.' In the course of their 'silly march' they crossed the Darb Zobaida, Gertrude Bell's route from Hail exactly a month before.

12 April. 'Halted at camp 50.' The diary tells us – 'A Europe morning . . . Tremendous thunderstorm afternoon and evening . . . managed to fill two skins from pool before it dried up . . . Saleh al Mutawah is reported to have arrived.'

13 April (Monday). 'Halted at camp 50.' Shakespear noted in his diary: 'After breakfast walked over to see Saleh al Mutawah, after having sent him Bin Maamar's letter of recommendation. Found him very pleasant and affable and rather like his look.'

14 April. 'Halted at camp 50.' Shakespear wrote in his diary: 'False alarm about marching. Got up extra early and everything ready, only my tent left to take down when Saleh ordered halt. Damned annoying . . . Opinion now seems to be that we shall probably go by the Haianiyah road.' Saleh was giving the orders now.

15 April (Wednesday). 'Left camp 50, at 6 a.m.' At last they were on their way, his Arab companions making for Damascus, he traversing the long way round the north of Jabal Shammar to Ibn Shalan's dominion of Jauf and then through the territory of Auda abu Tayya to Wadi Sirhan, Jabal Tubaiq and the border post of Kontilla in Sinai.

Nowhere does Shakespear say anything of his conversations with Saleh al Mutawah or his confederates. There is not the slightest indication in documents or diaries of what was happening during those days of patient waiting in the desert. In fact, it was not until 1917 that Douglas Carruthers, in correspondence with Murphy at Staff HQ, India, and Shakespear's brother, gave an indication that the trans-Arabian crossing was not entirely what it seemed.

However, the Political Agent did give a matter-of-fact account of proceedings which came to his notice four days after he left his Arab friends when he was at the wells of Hayaniya. On 19 April his private diary read:

REMARKS	WATCH TIME	SET. 100	BETWEEN POINTS			DAILY TOTAL		RUNNING TOTAL	
			Hrs.	Mi.	Miles	Hrs.	Miles	Hrs.	Miles
Brought forward								349⅔	
11ᵗʰ April Saturday								938½	
Left Camp XLIX	6·0	310							
passed pattes of									
main Haj route between	7.20	240	1	20	3½				
Hadra & Shaiba		55°							
of the Darb Zubaida									
passed Wadi Zigat	7.30		·	10	½				
mound square 'ofood'									
Camped in same									
Khub 1½ from the									
Wadi Zigat Camp L	7.40		·	10	½				
To Wadi Zigat		193	1	40	7½				
Camels going fairly									
2 ¾ mph.						13	22		
								351	
								943	
CARRIED OVER								351	943

Fig. 1   Shakespear's route log during his enforced halt at Zarud, while he was waiting for Saleh al Mutawah, who had been sent to warn Zamil, the Regent of Hail, of an attempt on his life

Heard startling news about Ibn Rashid today. It appears that a letter was received yesterday from the Ageyls on ahead [his earlier companions] to say we ought to hurry as Ibn Rashid had murdered Zamil ibn Subhan ... This took place nine days ago [that is 10 April], and the manner of it was thus: Apparently the Shammar have evinced a want of faith in Saud ibn Abdal Aziz's ability to be their Amir, and having showed plainly that they thought Zamil ibn Subhan

should be the Amir . . . young Saud ibn Rashid and Saud
the son of Saleh ibn Subhan put their heads together and
determined to clear Zamil and his intimate friends out of
the way. When they mounted and were on the march
somewhere near Abu Ghar, a slave came up from behind
and shot Zamil in the back, killing him outright. Seeing
this, Zamil's brother and some others jumped on to their
mares and made off. They were rounded up however and
then killed out of hand . . . Men were sent off to make sure
of Hail, and young Ibn Rashid now hopes to make the
Shammar want him as their Amir! A low-down crime, as
but for Zamil young Saud ibn Abdal Aziz would not be
alive now.

It was the only contemporary account of a murder which was to
end the prospect of a revolutionary alliance of the Arab tribes,
and of peace in central Arabia.

Abu Ghar was not on the route which Saleh al Mutawah took

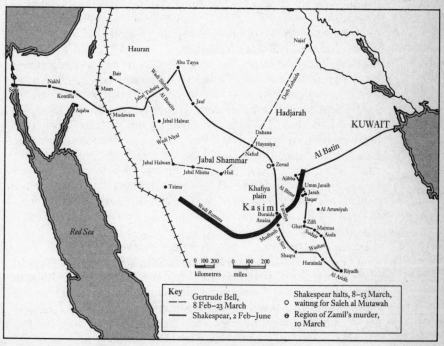

Map 8   Routes of Gertrude Bell and Shakespear, 1914

when he left Buraida for Jabal Shammar on 13 March, several
days ahead of Shakespear and his party. The murder occurred at the time that Saleh was reported lost in the desert and
camel riders were despatched to find him. Saleh's arrival at
Shakespear's camp was preceded by that of Ibn Rashid's messenger, Hamdani. And Saleh al Mutawah was none other than
Leachman's mystery companion on the 1912 journey to Ibn
Saud's capital.

For clues to the Englishman's part in the events of April 1914
we have to turn to the Austrian records and the testimony of
Musil, who was never far from the scene of major events in the
Arab lands and who had the confidence of the knowledgeable
Nuri ibn Shalan.

At the end of 1913, when Rashid Pasha went to Damascus for
talks with the French Consul at Beirut, the devious M. Georges
Picot, he was concerned with larger matters than the supply of
arms to his chief, Ibn Rashid. According to Musil, the plan was
to make Jabal Shammar a protectorate of France. The tricolour
would thus fly in the back yard of Syria, a territory in which
France had assumed a moral responsibility, and an acquisitive
interest, since the days of the Crusades. Musil also insisted, on
the evidence of tribal leaders, that Shakespear visited Hail during those blank days from 7 to 12 April when he was allegedly holed
up at Zarud, about seventy miles from the Rashid capital. These
were days of almost no activity according to Shakespear's travel
log, except for a few indifferent astronomical observations. His
private diary recorded only his conversations with Al Mutawah's
brother, when they suspected that Saleh had been murdered. In
fact it was Zamil the Regent who was murdered on 10 April,
while Saleh was somewhere in the vicinity, clearly trying to warn
him of impending danger. Musil also insisted that Shakespear,
confronted with the death of the pro-Saudi Regent and the need
to head off Picot, had made a secret compact with the pro-Turk
Minister, Saud ibn Subhan. It is an almost inconceivably conspiratorial theory, suggesting as it does that one of the most diligent of all desert explorers had falsified his travel notes. A more
likely explanation is that Saleh al Mutawah, having sped to the
scene of the murder to warn Zamil on behalf of Ibn Saud, sent a
representative of the Rashids to Shakespear after the deed was
done, and that any message that the Englishman had for the
Minister Saud was carried back by Hamdani.

'Ibn Saud, outraged by the breach of peace and the murder of

Zamil, declared that he would not treat with the murderer and peace-breaker and would instal Faisal ibn Hamud,' wrote Musil, who six months later was to visit Jabal Shammar as the last representative of Europe before war brought about a new divide in Arabia. Whatever the exact details of the assignations and power struggles of April 1914, no further facts can be elucidated, except the most indubitable fact of all, that the Arab Revolt, the promised rebellion of the Princes of the peninsula under the banner of Ibn Saud, at the instigation of Arab officers in the Ottoman army, had been crushed in embryo.

While this Byzantine drama was being acted out in Jabal Shammar, Abdullah, the second son of the Sharif of Mecca, who knew of the plans of Al Ahad though he resented Ibn Saud's leadership, arrived in Cairo to speak to Kitchener. He was followed by Shakespear, who arrived at the Residency on 26 May, weather-beaten after a journey of nearly 2,000 miles through largely unexplored desert, confident in his knowledge and appreciation of Arabian affairs. He was quickly deflated. The Resident and the Sirdar Wingate were, he said, 'inclined to exaggerate the influence of the Sharif'. He found that the 'local bigwigs had 'only sketchy information on central Arabia'. He wrote briefly to Ibn Saud before embarking for England.

Gertrude Bell had gone on to Palmyra soon after her return to Baghdad at the end of March, and while the murder of Zamil was being perpetrated she was on her way from the ancient ruins of the Syrian desert to Damascus. 'The man of Najd came to me,' she said.

'Have you news of that which passed in Hail since you left?'

'Of Ibrahim?'

'No, God save you, but what has befallen Ibrahim?'

He looked at me in silence and drew his fingers across his throat.

6

War: Most Urgent

'It is the practice of both sides to accuse their enemies of the guilt of first alliances; and those who fail in their negotiations, are loudest in their censure of the example which they envy, and would gladly imitate.'

Gibbon, *History of the Decline and Fall of the Roman Empire*

Matters which may seem diffuse in time of peace are marvellously concentrated by war. The threads of negotiation and investigation, of clandestine arrangements and secret treaties which occupied a handful of European and eastern schemers and potentates in the first thirteen years of the twentieth century knitted into a many-coloured coat in the sweltering summer of 1914.

To the brink and beyond, honourable intention necessarily vied with *realpolitik* and subterfuge among men whose political lives had been dedicated to the notion that peace should be purchased at almost any price. Souls were searched in vain on that fateful first day of August when Germany and Austria–Hungary declared war on Russia, and Anglo-French contingency plans were conveniently forgotten.

Even on 3 August, when Germany declared war on France, Grey thought it necessary to tell the British Parliament that 'its liberty of decision was not hampered by any engagements entered into previously without its knowledge'. It was a tormented Liberal Cabinet which was forced to declare a state of hostility on 4 August.

Kitchener, on leave from Egypt and about to return to his post in Cairo when the crisis reached its height, was persuaded to stay and take over the War Office. War without Kitchener in charge of the nation's fortunes was unthinkable to the British public. But it was to Prince Louis of Battenburg, the First Sea Lord, on whom the public turned its back and on whom the press (converted from an almost universal pacifism to hot-headed patriotic fervour overnight) vented its wrath, that Britain owed its first act of self-preservation. On Sunday 26 July, at the end of the annual fleet manoeuvres, Prince Louis decided not to stand down the ships but to put them on a war footing. No minister was available for consultation, but Churchill, the First Lord, agreed with the decision after it had been made. 'We had the drawn sword in our hand,' Prince Louis told the King with quiet pride. But his political chief was about to hand the sword to the enemy and the Royal Navy to feel its cutting edge.

Just as politicians refused to acknowledge their obligations to France until German aggression forced them into red-faced compliance with the Entente compact, so they refused to accept the existence of the war plan of 1906, which had been brought to prominence by the Agadir crisis of 1911. When the die was cast the Government acted as though Britain retained freedom of action within the Alliance. The half-hearted Allied cause was helped early on by a fortunate circumstance. Russia's Commander-in-Chief, the Grand Duke Nicholas, had the Central Alliance plan in his pocket, betrayed to him by Austro-Hungarian intelligence, and success at Galicia might have been compounded by decisive victory in Prussia had his generals not met more than their match in Hindenburg and Ludendorff at Tannenberg and the Masurian Lakes.

On 2 August two German battle cruisers were reported to be victualling at Messina in Sicily, although Italy had reneged on the Triple Alliance of 1882 and declared her neutrality, the term Triple Alliance giving way to Central Powers. On the very day that Britain went to war with Germany a drama of the seas was about to set the seal on an alliance between the Central Powers and the Ottoman Empire which had already been secretly negotiated by the German Foreign Office and a group of Young Turks led by Enver, though several of Turkey's chief ministers, including the Grand Vizier, were opposed to the bargain.

Admiral Lord Fisher, not a man to mince words, had suggested to Edward VII in 1908, when Germany's secret warship building programme had been uncovered, that a pre-emptive strike should be delivered against the Kaiser's navy, thus emulating Nelson at Copenhagen. The analogy was not strictly accurate historically, but the proposal itself was enough to bring forth the riposte: 'My God, Fisher, you must be mad!' The King added that he agreed with Fisher that war with Germany was inevitable.

Fisher had departed angrily from his post in 1910, and two elderly and ineffectual admirals had filled the void until the end of 1912 when Prince Louis appeared. Fisher had seldom seen eye to eye with Winston Churchill, who had opposed his six Dreadnoughts in 1909, but in November 1911 he wrote a most prophetic letter whilst on holiday in Lucerne: 'My only two visits to Winston were fruitful. I tell you (and YOU ONLY) the whole secret of the changes! To get Jellicoe C-in-C of the Home Fleet prior to 21 October 1914, *which is the date of the Battle of Armageddon.*' In terms of an impending Turco-German alliance, and of the humiliation of the Royal Navy, the Admiral's estimate was a mere fortnight out.

The two German cruisers, *Goeben* and *Breslau* meandered through the Mediterranean during the five weeks between the Sarajevo affair and the declaration of war. On 2 August, as Germany and Turkey signed a secret treaty of alliance, Wangenheim, the German Ambassador, and Liman von Sanders, military adviser to the Turk and Commander of the Ottoman First Army, jointly wired the German Admiralty asking it to order the two cruisers to sail for Constantinople. On 4 August the secret Berlin transmitter *Nauen* signalled the Admiral aboard *Goeben*: 'Proceed to Constantinople.' The first move in a game cleverly devised to make the alliance a military reality was afoot. The extent to which Britain abetted that plot and kept its ally France in the dark can be ascribed to only three possible causes: stupidity of an incomprehensible order, treachery, or a deep-laid plot which went badly awry.

Enver issued an order for the Dardanelles to be kept open for the German warships as soon as the request was made to the German Admiralty. The Grand Vizier, Said Halim, promptly rescinded Enver's order and sent a telegram to the German Commanding Officer aboard the *Goeben*, Admiral Souchon, telling him that he could not sail for Constantinople 'because of political circumstances'. Souchon, instructed by Berlin two days later, ignored the telegram and set sail.

There followed a pursuit which was to become famous in naval history, and to end in a remarkable victory for the brilliant German Admiral, who took on the might of the Royal Navy's Mediterranean Fleet, and his brave and resourceful crew.

At a meeting on 1 August between Paul Cambon and Grey, the French Ambassador had exclaimed: 'All our plans are arranged in common. Our General Staffs have consulted. You have seen all our schemes and preparations. Look at our fleet! Our whole fleet is in the Mediterranean in consequence of our arrangements with you and our coasts are wide open to the enemy. You have laid us wide open!' The French fleet might have helped to prevent the humiliation of the *Goeben* and *Breslau* incident had its Commander-in-Chief been warned of what was happening. But Churchill gave instructions to Admiral Milne, the Commander of the Mediterranean Station, forbidding him to contact his opposite number in Algiers.

It needs no accomplished naval geographer or strategist to explain that there are only two outlets from the Mediterranean to the high seas, the Straits of Gibraltar and the Suez Canal, and that both were impassable without British authority. It was only necessary to send a battleship to patrol the Dardanelles outside territorial waters to declare game, set and match. Sir Berkeley Milne, 'Arky, Barky' to his men, a 'flatterer of royal ladies', decided to embark on a chase from one end of the sea to the other, from Algeria, Malta and Sicily to Turkish waters. *Goeben* if not its sister ship could have outpaced his own older vessels (it had British turbines), but in the event it had to protect the *Breslau*, which was damaged by gunfire. 'Pretty little *Breslau*, I wonder what will become of her,' remarked Souchon during the chase. *Goeben* had been given a frantic boiler refit at the Austrian Adriatic port of Pola in the few days before war was declared. She had to be nursed by her engineer during the subsequent pursuit in which Souchon demanded full speed for hours on end.

When the dapper Milne was appointed to his command by Churchill, Fisher wrote to the First Lord: 'I fear this must be my last communication with you . . . you have betrayed the Navy . . . you are aware that Sir Berkeley Milne is unfitted to be the senior admiral afloat,' and he told Lord Esher, 'Winston, alas! (as I have had to tell him) feared for his wife's social ostracism at the Court,' which had made Churchill bow to the royal wish and appoint Milne. 'A wicked wrong . . . Milne is an utterly useless commander,' Fisher wrote. The man in charge of the other camp was of a very different cast. Souchon was short and stocky with a Prussian head containing a Huguenot mind, 'looking more like a parson than an admiral', according to America's Ambassador at the Sublime Porte, Morgenthau.

From the moment the Admiralty received information that the Germans had fuelled at Messina until the conclusion of the pursuit eight days later, the British fleet was at sixes and sevens, with Churchill at the operations desk in the Admiralty Building firing off signals to a perplexed and confused Flag Admiral, suffering as he was to write later 'the tortures of Tantalus', while the intelligence department tried desperately to crack the German code and decipher the signals between *Goeben* and Berlin. And while Rear-Admiral Troubridge aboard the flagship, HMS *Defence*, with the First Cruiser Squadron, eight destroyers and the battleships HMS *Indomitable* and *Indefatigable* went after them, the real drama was being played out in the *Goeben's* engine-room:

> In silence, but pluckily and undismayed, the stokers stuck to their work . . . the sweat ran in streams down their gleaming torsos. The searing heat from the furnaces burned the skin and singed the hair . . . it was here that the issue was being fought out . . . Four heroes, four plucky shipmates, paid with their lives in that hell of toil.

And while that hell of toil raged, and an almost inconceivable train of errors emanated from Whitehall, Constantinople awaited the arrival of two ships which in a matter of days had become the most famous vessels afloat; and politicians and diplomats worked feverishly to push the Sublime Porte into war on the one hand, and to encourage its neutrality on the other.

Ambassador Louis Mallet wanted the Porte to ratify the 1913 Convention, but by now the Young Turks were not anxious to be bound by its terms: they had more profitable plans in mind and were already demanding a large loan from Berlin, which Chancellor Bethmann Hollweg was most unwilling to grant, though the Kaiser eventually approved it. The aim of the CUP was to abolish the Capitulations, under which Germany was a major beneficiary. Baron Hans von Wangenheim was too strong for Mallet. An aristocrat of the old Prussian school, absolutely assured of his own judgment and of the rightness of his role, he often lectured Morgenthau, saying that mankind was 'divided into two classes, the Governing and the Governed', and insisting: 'We in Germany keep our governing class pure, unmixed of blood.'

Morgenthau looked on awe-struck during these critical days

when Wangenheim ran rings round his British adversary and round the Turks. The Sultan himself, the gentle and retiring Mehemet V, now aged seventy, told Mallet that he was determined to keep Turkey out of the war, that he retained 'an unalterable friendship' towards England. Morgenthau watched as German diplomacy, 'in its most ruthless and most shameless aspects . . . with wonderful skill manipulated the desperate and corrupt adventurers who controlled Turkey in 1914 into becoming an instrument of Germany'.

The secret Turco-German alliance of 2 August had been signed by Germany on the condition that Turkey contracted to take action against Russia 'worthy of the name'. None the less Enver looked the Russian military attaché in the eye and told him that the Ottoman army had no designs on his country.

While Wangenheim, looking like the Rock of Gibraltar, made his way each day between Pera and the Porte in old Constantinople, his massive frame 'pulsating with life', Mallet sat patiently in the diplomatic quarter hoping for a gentleman's agreement with the old guard, Said Halim, the Grand Vizier, and the Sultan himself, not to enter the war on the Entente side but to remain neutral. Wangenheim had no great love for the Turks, indeed he despised them, but he was now acting under the direct instructions of the Kaiser, to bring the Turkish Empire into the struggle. Britain made his task doubly easy. Its one strong man in Constantinople, the vastly experienced dragoman Fitzmaurice, refused to go along with Mallet's polite diplomacy towards Enver's gang and Wangenheim. He was said to 'twist the Ambassador round his little finger'. He was not popular either in Constantinople or Whitehall for his outspoken opposition to the CUP and the Germans, and as the crisis reached its height he was recalled to London on the extraordinary ground of being 'too anti-German'. But as T. E. Lawrence – one of his detractors – remarked, he was 'eagle-minded and iron-willed'. He alone among the British was a match for the opposition, but Britain had decided to play the game softly. 'He rebuffed every advance of the Young Turks,' said Lawrence. In any event, the game was lost before the combatants came into the arena.

At the end of July, just before the *Goeben* episode was about to explode, the Turks informed Britain that they wished to take delivery of two Dreadnought class ships which they had ordered from the Armstrong-Vickers yard in 1911. The ships now named the *Sultan Osman I* and the *Rashadieh*, had been fitted out and paid for, and the crew, trained by Britain's naval adviser in Constantinople, was waiting to take delivery.

On 1 August Enver had secretly promised to direct the ships to German ports, but the Grand Vizier found out and told Wangenheim that he was opposed to such a step, being anxious not to give Britain an excuse for impounding them. But the decision had already been made in London. A few months earlier Rear-Admiral Limpus, who had been naval adviser to the Ottoman Ministry of Marine since 1912, had written to Churchill giving him the terms of the new naval agreement with the Turks, which presupposed continued co-operation between his mission and the Ottoman Marine Department, now under the political control of Jamal, the ex-military Governor of the capital.

Also on 1 August a detachment of Sherwood Foresters had gone aboard the ships at Devonport, where their fitting out and trials were completed. The First Lord had decided that the Government could not permit the ships to be handed over to a foreign power. The Turks were ordered home. Mallet begged Grey to counsel patience, and even as the anger of the Enver faction reached boiling point and the *Goeben* and *Breslau* were nearing the end of their historic voyage, Said Halim was pleading with Britain to keep Admiral Limpus and his naval mission in Constantinople in the hope that the pro-German faction could be warded off.

By 7 August a full-scale row had broken out between the commanders of the British ships in the Mediterranean and Admiral Milne at Malta. The German vessels were steaming for the Aegean, with *Breslau* falling back from her faster companion. HMS *Gloucester* closed on the smaller ship and began firing with her 6-inch guns. *Breslau* returned the fire. On the 8th Souchon wrote in his log: 'We have shaken off pursuit . . . but Dardanelles still a long way off and not enough coal to get there!' The German admiral could not contact Constantinople directly and had to use a passenger ship near by to relay his messages. At dawn on the 9th he was desperate for coal and anchored in a bay off Denusa near the Greek island of Naxos. Three days earlier the Greek Prime Minister, Venizelos, who was already in communication with Britain regarding a proposed joint assault on the Dardanelles, sanctioned the fuelling of the ships. There was no sign of their pursuers. On 10 August, as they made their way from Naxos, Souchon received a message from *Nauen*: 'It is of the greatest importance that you go to Constantinople as quickly

as possible in order thereby to compel Turkey to side with us on
the basis of the treaty that has been concluded. The ambassador
has been informed direct.'

Later that day Souchon wrote:

> At 1600 hours we saw . . . the plain of Troy and the Hel-
> lespont. The entrance appeared free. With great anxiety
> and everyone at their battleposts, ready to open fire, we
> entered the Narrows. I signalled by semaphore to Cape
> Helles: 'Send a pilot at once.' A Turkish destroyer
> approached us. He had a signal flying: 'Follow me.' I gave
> the hand of the Turkish staff officer a friendly squeeze. He
> spoke German . . . Our breakthrough had succeeded.
> Each man had done his duty.

And while Souchon and his ships made their dramatic entrance,
Enver, still in conflict with the Cabinet, was in conference with a
German staff officer who had just arrived from Berlin, Colonel
Kress von Kressenstein. 'Kress' reported that the Turkish com-
mander at Chanuk in the Dardanelles required instructions
regarding the German ships.

> ENVER: I must consult the Grand Vizier.
> KRESS: I must have an immediate answer.
> *(Silence.)*
> ENVER: They are to be allowed to enter.
> KRESS: If the British warships follow they are to be fired
> on?
> ENVER: I must consult my colleagues.
> KRESS: I must have an answer.
> ENVER: Yes.

Next day, 11 August, the Turkish army mobilised and the
knives were out in the Admiralty. Churchill wanted Rear-
Admiral Limpus to take command of the Eastern Mediterranean Squadron, but Grey, advised by Mallet, vetoed the idea,
saying it would provoke the Turks. It was all too much for Limpus: a non-smoker all his life, he took to smoking large cigars,
even in his bath. On 14 September Grey sent a personal note to
Mallet telling him to use 'any discretion you desire to secure the
withdrawal of Britain's Naval Mission'. The next day Limpus
took his leave of Jamal, who was 'disappointed', Talaat who was

'embarrassed', and the Grand Vizier, who confided that he was
'tired and angry with the military brutes'.

Soon after Rear-Admiral Wilhelm Souchon hoisted his flag as
Commander of the Mitelmeer-Division of the German navy in
October 1913, he submitted a report on the British fleet to the
Marine Office in Berlin which inevitably arrived on the royal
desk. The all-highest wrote famously in the margin: 'John Bull
always wanted to spit in the soup.'

The crass errors of judgment at the Admiralty in the first
week of war gave support to more than the Emperor's disdain.
As the 'brilliant and pungent' Deputy Director of Naval Operations, Captain Herbert Richmond, was to observe after six
weeks of wartime bungling and frustration: 'We are the most
appalling amateurs who ever tried to conduct a war.' And of the
Chief of Naval Staff, Admiral Sturdee: 'Everything was impossible to this absurd historian.' Richmond was to pay dearly for
his opinions, but the man who bore the brunt of the misguided
indignation of the public and the outrageous calumnies of the
press was the First Sea Lord, who was 'trying to play a professional hand despite Churchill's assertive role'. Before the end of
the year Prince Louis of Battenburg would be forced to resign
and the 70-year-old Fisher be recalled to the post. In the meantime Prince Louis ordered the Commander-in-Chief
Portsmouth to hold a Court of Enquiry, at which Milne was called to give evidence and Troubridge was arraigned. The
Rear-Admiral in charge of the Cruiser Squadron was held to be
entirely responsible for the fact that the two German battle-
cruisers outwitted his own squadron, two ships of the line
and several destroyers. But in justice he was acquitted. Milne
was recalled and left on half-pay for the rest of the war.
Churchill remained First Lord of the Admiralty for the time
being and began to turn his mind to another adventure.

Germany was not slow to rub salt in the wound. Five days
after the *Goeben* and *Breslau* entered the Straits, the Royal Navy
had still neglected to plug the route. A German merchantman
proceeded along the same sea path laden with mines. It was
smuggled to Chanak. And on 15 August a double line of contact
mines was laid across the entrance to the Dardanelles. More
mines were laid on the 19th, and at the same time Hotchkiss
guns were mounted on both sides of the Straits to reinforce the
minefields. On 27 September Liman von Sanders ordered the
closing of the Dardanelles, and the manning of the artillery by

German naval gunners. All this despite the fact that Turkey was
still a neutral power. Sir Louis Mallet was still talking to the
Grand Vizier, still seeking the ratification of a treaty which
would guarantee in effect the neutrality of the Ottoman Empire,
with Britain's support for its crumbling Asiatic Empire.

The war on land in Europe was going badly for the Allies.
Kitchener was at odds with the Commander-in-Chief in France
and few of the Generals would speak to each other or to their
French counterparts. Whitehall and the Quai d'Orsay were in
disarray. The Kaiser had told a group of German politicians on
the day Britain declared war: 'I no longer recognise parties. I only
know Germany.' The matter was somewhat more complicated
for his cousin George V in London and his ministers. All the
same, the politicians and the high commands of the Central
Powers, and their ally presumptive in Constantinople, had their
problems too. While Constantinople celebrated and the hero of
the hour, Admiral Souchon, announced amid the popping of
champagne corks that Turkey had purchased *Goeben* and *Breslau*
from Germany for the Black Sea fleet, Baron Wangenheim was
in touch with the Foreign Office in Berlin announcing Enver's
wish to send a joint Turco–German mission to India and Afghanistan. According to Enver, revolutionary movements in North
Africa, India and Afghanistan were 'waiting to be exploited by
German officers, who should work with the Turks'. Holy war
had a sure appeal to the Moslem fanatic, and Enver proposed to
make the most of it, using the Sultan, his virtual prisoner in the
Yildiz Kiosk, to lend the Caliph's authority to the call to arms. It
was the first recorded reference to a mission that was to have a
profound effect on the conduct of the war in Mesopotamia and
the Gulf, and little though the actors in the drama knew it at the
time, was to prove instrumental in bringing the United States
into the conflict.

On 27 August Baron Max von Oppenheim, that 'chattering
egotistical Jew', as Hogarth called him, sent a telegram to
Wangenheim telling him that fifteen Germans including three
doctors and an animal handler had been appointed for the
Afghan mission and were ready to leave Berlin for Baghdad.
The leader of the expedition was Oskar von Niedermayer,
twenty-nine years old, who had studied geography and geology
at Regensburg Gymnasium, belonged to the Persian Bahai sect
and had travelled in the two years before the war in Persia and
India on the strength of an allowance from the Princess Theresa

von Bayern, using the Moslem identity of Abdal Wahhab. In 1913 he had been the guest of the British military representative in Meshed, Colonel Percy Sykes. At the time of Enver's report to Wangenheim, Oberstleutnant von Niedermayer was serving with the 10th Royal Bavarian Artillery in France and was hurriedly recalled to Berlin by von Oppenheim. Before the contingent left Berlin a row broke out between the Foreign Office and the General Staff over the composition and purposes of the mission, and it was decided to send two missions. The first of the parties was in Constantinople on 21 September ready to leave for Aleppo.

While these preparations were being made, Enver was busily playing off the Entente powers against each other. During those eventful first days of August he told the Russian military attaché that Turkish mobilisation was in no way directed against Russia. The Russian Ambassador, apparently relieved, told his Foreign Minister, Sazanov, that Turkish preparations were not directed at the Entente, and Sazanov expressed the hope that Turkey would maintain her neutrality. Russia, in turn, would respect Turkish territorial integrity if Turkey honoured foreign concessions in the Empire.

There were tense scenes at meetings of the ottoman Cabinet and a row over the use to be made of the *Goeben* in the Black Sea broke out between Enver and Jamal, the Marine Minister. Intelligence officers and politicians in London, St Petersburg (or Petrograd as it became in 1914) and Paris were following events with insight since the Russians were receiving details of cables between the Austrian Ambassador, Pallavici, in Constantinople and the Foreign Ministry in Vienna. Enver, always artful in negotiation, had suggested to Wangenheim that if Germany did not respond to his overtures he would, with heavy heart, have to side with the Entente. But in the end it was fear of Russian ambition which drove the majority of the CUP into the alliance.

On 9 October it became apparent that the 'War Party' had finally won the day. Four days earlier the Kaiser had bowed to Turkey's demand for money and agreed to send two consignments of £1 million (Turkish) each by train through Rumania, in bullion. Enver had asked for £T5 million. The first consignment arrived in Constantinople on 16 October; the second turned up five days later. On the 15th Prince Said Halim had told Mallet that Turkish troop movements 'on the Egyptian frontier and elsewhere did not predicate an aggressive movement'. By then King

Carol of Rumania, who was pro-German, had died and on the 23rd the Rumanian Government closed the frontier to supplies for Turkey. Enver's trump card had been played just in time, though the German Emperor's decision was entirely political in inspiration; he had no love for Enver, though he once found him 'likeable', as did Churchill (who met him at military manoeuvres in Germany in 1909). But after the cold-blooded murder of Nazim Pasha in 1913 the Kaiser had ordered that he was never to be allowed to return to Germany.

On the day that the first gold consignment arrived in Constantinople a British Expeditionary Force nominated 'D', left India in forty-seven ships with sealed orders, under the command of Brigadier-General Sir Walter Delamain. And on that day also, Lord Cromer came out of retirement to deliver a paper to the Cabinet in London on steps to be taken in the event of war with Turkey.

Events crowded in as October 1914 drew to a close. On the 21st Enver assumed the title of Vice-Generalissimo of the Turkish army, admitting pride of place in rank to the Sultan alone. On the 23rd the British Expeditionary Force 'D' anchored off Bahrain, and Murphy, the Staff Officer sent down from Jask to join it, was despatched ashore to arrest the managing director of Wönckhaus, Herr Harling. As Murphy and his escort burst into the German's office he was holding a letter to the German Consul at Bushire giving details of the British force. His facts were correct: 5,000 men were on their way and a further 10,000 ready for embarkation at Karachi. Murphy recalled as he went through Harling's papers that when Wönckhaus first arrived at Lingeh in 1896 and started to collect sea shells, his entire visible possessions were three wooden boxes which he placed in a row at night to sleep on. By 1914 his company was one of the richest and most powerful in the Gulf.

On 26 October, Mallet's military attaché, Colonel Cunliffe Owen reported that a special train had left Aleppo for the rail bridge at Jerablus with two German and four Turkish naval officers, 100 Turkish sailors and large quantities of ship's tackle. They were on their way to Basra with a consignment of mines for the Shatt-al-Arab.

On the 27th and 28th, the British Cabinet considered intelligence reports that German submarines were being transported by rail to Constantinople. On the 27th the Ottoman fleet under Souchon set out into the Black Sea on a mission of war, though ostensibly searching for a Russian mine-layer. On the 28th a joint Russo-British Commission sent to arbitrate in an eighty-year-old frontier dispute between Persia and Turkey hammered in the last demarcation pillar at the foot of Mount Ararat. On the 29th Turkish torpedo boats attacked Odessa, and strafed coastal villages, while Sir Louis Mallet tried still to persuade the Young Turks to remain neutral.

On the same day Lord Fisher was re-appointed to his old job as First Sea Lord in London, following the forced resignation of Prince Louis. 'Resurrected! Again!' exclaimed the old sea-dog. On the 30th an advance British force disembarked at Shaikh Khazal's port of Muhammerah. On 31 October Sazanov recalled his Ambassador from Constantinople and announced that the Turks, in concert with Germany, had been guilty of an act of war. On 1 November the Grand Vizier sent an apologetic note to Sazanov through the French Ambassador. Sazanov replied that war would be declared unless Turkey expelled all Germans from its territory. The British and French Ambassadors promptly left the capital. On the next day the Viceroy of India issued a proclamation stating that in the event of war Britain would respect the sanctity of all Islamic holy places, and the Egyptian administration declared a state of martial law.

On 2 November the Czar declared war on Turkey. The next day Britain had put the issue beyond doubt with an act which in the long run was to prove even more majestic in its stupidity than the débâcle of August. Vice-Admiral Sir Sackville Carden, who had succeeded Milne as Commander-in-Chief, was ordered to make a punitive strike against the Dardanelles forts. Some 150 Turks and Germans were killed and the new Turco-German alliance was cemented beyond anything the Kaiser or Enver could have achieved in concert. More importantly, ample warning was given to the enemy of the need to reinforce the Straits and the Gallipoli Peninsula. Admiral Jellicoe, after the war, described the first Dardanelles bombardment as 'an unforgivable error'. On 4 November Britain and France declared war on Turkey.

On 23 November, Field-Marshal Freiherr von der Goltz, who had been made Military Governor of Belgium soon after the declaration of war, was recalled to army headquarters in Berlin. On the next day he was appointed Supreme Commander of Turco-German forces in Mesopotamia, to the consternation of General Liman von Sanders, who had been made Commander-in-Chief by the Turks.

As telegrams flew around the world: 'War – Most Urgent', and European war became world war, Niedermayer's unhappy band was on its way across the Taurus mountains, arriving at Aleppo on 13 December. They had been joined by Wilhelm Wassmuss, still with his long locks of now greying hair, his white skin and blue eyes like lapis lazuli; but more restrained in manner, the professional agent to his elegant fingertips. He had not changed sufficiently, however, to weather the burden of discontent in the German party with which he had joined forces in Constantinople. Animosity between him and the other members of the party, which had already been separated from the original contingent, was inflamed to a point where several members of the Niedermayer group petitioned Berlin demanding the recall of Wassmuss. Wangenheim was instructed to suggest a compromise; Wassmuss should travel with Niedermayer in one party, while the others made their way separately to Persia, that 'showplace' of English and Russian rivalry.

On Turkey's entry into the war Ajaimi ibn Sadun, the chief of the Muntafiq, had declared his loyalty to the Sultan, and he had already become a serious obstacle to Britain's efforts to prevent the infiltration of enemy agents into Arabistan. Shaikh Ghadaban of the Bani Lam on the Persian side was also anti-British. The khans of the Bakhtiari tribes occupying the forbidding country of Fars between Shiraz and the Gulf ports had declared their neutrality.

Niedermayer and Wassmuss left Aleppo with the Turkish officer Rauf Bey on 26 December and arrived at Baghdad to pick up their Turkish collaborators two days later. The army command in Baghdad made it abundantly clear that whatever Enver and the German General Staff might arrange, no love was lost in the new alliance. There would be no Turkish participation in the scheme, but a separate party would be sent under Rauf. Suleiman Askari Bey, the Turkish Commander in Baghdad, decided that in view of the landing by British forces at Basra, the German contingents would have to make their own way into Persia without escort, taking either the mountainous route through Mosul and Kurdistan or going down river from Baghdad to a point below Kut-al-Amara and thence cutting across into the Bakhtiari tribal territory of Arabistan. One party made its way by the former route. Niedermayer and Wassmuss took the Tigris route, travelling in separate groups.

In January Berlin had sanctioned the second Afghanistan mission under the command of a consular officer, Werner von Hentig. He had been in the Washington Embassy and had met the Indian revolutionary and pro-German Barakat Allah at San Francisco. Barakat Allah, now Enver's man in Kabul, was busily laying the groundwork, trying to persuade the Amir of Afghanistan, Habibullah, to take up arms on the side of the Central Powers and attack India. On the way von Hentig was to meet another Indian dissident whose activities in America and Europe had excited the interest of British intelligence, Mahendra Pratap of the Berlin Indian Committee and an old friend of Baron Oppenheim. The second German party did not leave Berlin until 14 April. They were accompanied by a Turkish officer, Kasim Bey, described by Hentig as a 'useless dolt'.

The German expedition, overall, represented one of the most remarkable exercises in logistics of modern times. Hundreds of men, thousands of animals and vast stores of arms and equipment were transported over some of the world's most inhospitable wastes, over thousands of miles of swamps and deserts and rivers. Doctors, dentists, veterinary surgeons, mechanics, accompanied these astonishingly dedicated Teutons on their mission of disruption.

According to a British intelligence officer who had served at Bushire since December 1912, C. J. Edmonds of the Levant Consular Service, Wassmuss arrived back in Persia with Dr Theodor Linders and two unnamed Indian revolutionaries at Shuster in about the middle of February 1915. On the 22nd they set out for Shiraz, by way of Behbehan, leaving a trail of disruption and a growing thirst for *jihad* behind them. They were being shadowed closely by British agents working for Basra GHQ. Wassmuss was bound ultimately for Bushire, where the German Consulate-General and the British Residency had kept a watchful but friendly eye on each other until the outbreak of war. The German establishment was a large rented building about two miles from the town, and the Consul-General Dr Helmuth Listemann had led a somewhat solitary life since the parties and the polo matches had ceased in the previous August. Wassmuss had, of course, been to Bushire briefly in 1909 and had returned temporarily in 1913. He became a familiar and much-liked figure whose receptions were famous in the diplomatic community. He travelled extensively in Tangistan and came to know the area well.

When Wassmuss arrived back in Persia the British Residency was in the charge of Lieutenant-Colonel S. G. Knox, Shakespear's predecessor at Kuwait. Cox was now with Expeditionary Force 'D' as its Chief Political Officer, stationed at Basra. The first assistant at Bushire was Captain W. G. Neale; Captain E. W. Noel, heir to the earldom of Gainsborough, a dashing young officer with something of Leachman's madcap temperament, was number two. C. J. Edmonds was acting Vice-Consul. The Residency was guarded by the 102nd Bombay Grenadiers, who had relieved the 2nd Rajputs a few months before the German intervention.

Listemann was still in charge of the German Consulate at the declaration of war. A recent addition to the German community was Karl Eisenhut, the new agent for Wönckhaus, who had arrived with his young bride to take up residence at a house about half a mile from the Consulate.

The Persian Governor of the Gulf Ports, Ali Muhammad, had been to school in England, spoke the language perfectly and was a jealous guardian of Persian rights, but was on good terms with the Resident, as he had been with Cox. The most important chief of the region was Haidar Khan, whose tribal parish, called Hayat Daud, was thirty-five miles north of Bushire along the coast. His influence was widespread and he was a shrewd man, dedicated to law and order and the suppression of piracy, and his family had been the recipients of a royalty on ships crossing the bar of the Shatt-al-Arab since the early days of the East India Company. In contrast the Tangistanis along the coast south of Bushire were the custodians of a long tradition of piracy, smuggling and blackmail. One of their leaders, the Khan of Burazjan was constantly in trouble with the Persian Governor and the British Resident.

On 6 March 1915, Neale received a telegram from intelligence at Basra telling him that the German party had left Behbehan in Haidar Khan's territory on the 2nd and instructing him to send Noel to Haidar Khan to arrange for the chief to arrest the Germans when they passed through. The mission was successful: the German caravan was surrounded and captured some miles inland by tribesmen led by the Khan's brother. But jubilation turned to dismay when Neale and Edmonds decoded another message from Noel telling them that the most important member of the party, Herr Wassmuss, had disappeared in the night. He had made his way down a ravine behind his tent and set off in bare feet until he was able to hitch a donkey-ride, in the direction of Burazjan.

Noel, who had found a useful supply of gold sovereigns and thousands of inflammatory pamphlets in Persian and English in a satchel left behind by the German, went off in pursuit. But Wassmuss, doubtless concealed by the Khan of Burazjan, was not to be found. Indeed, he was to remain at large for the rest of the war.

Neale and Edmonds realised as soon as they had deciphered Noel's telegram that they must arrest Listemann and Eisenhut before they were able to join up with Wassmuss and concert whatever plan Berlin had prepared for them. But clearly the British were acting illegally. Persia was a neutral country and Britain's long-established commercial and political rights on the Gulf coast gave the Residency staff no rights to commit acts of war. Such considerations do not seem to have concerned Edmonds and Neale unduly. They drove in separate horse-drawn carriages to a pre-arranged point where they were met by army detachments. Neale was accompanied by a party of sepoys under Captain Oakes to Old Bank House, where the Eisenhuts were asleep in bed. Edmonds, accompanied by Lieutenant Withers of Army Intelligence and a detachment of sepoys under Captain Warton and the subaltern Hastings, went to the Consulate about half a mile away.

Hastings was a lively young man who just after the declaration of war had climbed the flagpole on top of the German consulate and replaced the imperial flag with the Union Jack. The dapper Consul Listemann was waiting at the bottom of the flagpole when Hastings returned to earth. Now Hastings was sent to disturb the doctor once more. He had to position an army detachment between the consular buildings and an adjacent fishing village. But as they took up their positions a chorus of barking started up, first from one dog and then from what seemed like hundreds of the creatures. Persian guards at the Consulate began to fire wildly. There was a crash of glass as Hastings dived through a window and made for the Consul's bedroom. When Warton and Edmonds arrived Listemann was looking dazed and Hastings wore a broad grin. On a bedside table were several empty bottles of German beer and a bottle of grenadine syrup.

'Oh, it's you again, Hastings, is it?', remarked the dazed Listemann. Then he clicked his heels and introduced himself to Warton. Turning to Edmonds he said: 'You are a member of the regular Consular Service and you must know that what you are doing this night is strictly contrary to international law.' Edmonds replied rather weakly that he was not there to discuss international law but to effect an arrest. A Persian guard had galloped off while the arrest was being made to inform the Governor, an eventuality the Englishmen had hoped to avoid. The mild-mannered Listemann was marched off hurriedly in his dressing-gown, with Edmonds asking him for his keys. 'Keys! Keys!' shouted the German, as he flung a handkerchief and box of matches on to the floor. 'These are all you allow me to take, and you ask me for keys!' They had to walk the half mile to the Old Bank House, where the Eisenhuts were being arrested by Neale, who greeted the Consul with the words: 'Sorry to disturb you, Dr Listemann, but war is war, you know.' The German's 'Kaiser' moustache bristled.

The two parties were ushered into separate carriages and with their escort galloped to Dastak, a cove near the old town of Reshire, six miles from Bushire, where they were to be put aboard the Indian Marine *Nearchus*.

The Englishmen returned to the German Consulate, where they were met by a jubilant Withers. In a chest-of-drawers in Listemann's bedroom, kept in handy proximity so that they could be destroyed in emergency, an act forestalled by Hastings's sudden entry, and wrapped in several pairs of long-johns, he had found two German cipher books. The Consul had been unable to destroy them, so sudden was Withers's entry.

The German archives were intact. They contained ample corroboration of reports that agents were to be infiltrated into Persia to sabotage the Indo-European submarine cable at Reshire and to bring Tangistani tribemen into a devastating rebellion. The find of the cipher codes was to prove one of the most precious discoveries of the war. But Wassmuss remained at large, and his escape was to prove costly.

The position in Persia at the outbreak of war has been stated with commendable simplicity:

> Persian neutrality could be maintained only by the un-neutral presence of British and Russian troops on Persian territory. So long as these troops remained passive the Persian Government would never declare war on the Allies. The aim of the Germans was to provoke the British and Russians to abandon their passivity.

Oil was not yet the touchstone of rivalry in the east, but the refinery at Abadan and the oil pipeline from the fields of Masjid-i-Sulaiman to the Shatt-al-Arab were of vital concern to Britain and its allies; and six days before the declaration of war in Europe the Anglo-Persian Oil Company was taken into national ownership at the instigation of Lord Fisher and Winston Churchill. In February 1915 a scheme conceived by Niedermayer was carried out by a party of German auxiliaries. Parts of the pipeline were cut and fires started along its length; and the junction of the Karun river and the Shatt-al-Arab was blocked by the sinking of a German vessel that had been trapped by the British arrival. They were the first and last acts of sabotage on the oil installations in the course of the war, and the damage was soon mended.

7

The Flickering Flame

'The Turks will go and the English will rule Turkish territory; the punishment of God for their bad treatment of Arabs. Therefore, my son, you and I must follow the wishes of the Glorious Government, for therein lie our interests.'

Shaikh Mubarak to Ibn Saud, October 1914

While Musil was in Constantinople in October 1914, receiving instructions from Enver, Captain Shakespear was commuting between the Foreign, India and War Offices in London at the beck and call of Sir Edward Grey, Lord Crewe and his friend, Lieutenant-Colonel Maunsell, who was now handling Turkish affairs for military intelligence under Major-General C. E. Callwell, who had succeeded Henry Wilson as DMO in August.

Whereas Shakespear's observations had hitherto been brushed aside by a succession of Under-Secretaries, his opinion was now courted by the highest officials in the land, and he was about to depart on a vital mission. He was to return to Arabia as Political Officer on 'Special Duty', charged with the task of ensuring that in the event of Turkey entering the war the tribes and their chiefs would join the side of the Entente, if requested to do so, and that they would otherwise observe a strict neutrality. Ibn Saud, the only Arab leader with a voice among the most powerful tribes, had been told only recently that he must accept Ottoman authority over his lands and his affairs, and that he could expect no help from Britain.

Shakespear sailed from Southampton on the SS *Arabia* on 10 October. His ship docked at Bombay, where he transferred to the British India steamship *Chakhdara*, which took him to the Shatt-al-Arab. He stepped ashore on 30 October at the anchorage of the British Expeditionary Force some fifteen miles from the date plantations and the Turk fortress at Fao, where he was met by Major Murphy. He handed Murphy his confidential diary and other secret papers before leaving.

It was announced at the beginning of November that the Viceroy would be arriving from India in December and Shakespear was asked to wait to see him and the new Commander-in-Chief. He insisted that he had definite instructions from London, however, and that his mission was of the utmost urgency. He remained with the force throughout November for consultations with Sir Percy Cox and Sir Arthur Barrett, who took command during the month, long enough to witness the death of yet another of his close friends in the Gulf, young Birdwood, Lorimer's first assistant and the man who completed his *Gazetteer*. Birdwood had jointed Force 'D' as soon as it arrived and was hit by shrapnel at the Battle of Saniyah on 16 November, the first time in history that British troops engaged in combat with regular Turkish-speaking soldiers of the Ottoman Empire. Shakespear was also there long enough to see heavy casualties among the Dorsets, the Mahrattas and Punjabis in the early battles in the swamps and slime of Mesopotamia in the first month of war, to see the indecision of the commanders, and the bravery of the injured as they were carried aboard the *Chakhdara* to be taken to hospitals in India. Long enough to observe: 'Thank God I'm not with the army. I'd be court martialled within a week.' He left on 18 November, three days after British troops marched into Basra and raised the Union Jack over the residence of the Governor, Colonel Subhi Bey, who escaped to fight another day, and Percy Cox made a speech to the assembled force. The German Consul and five agents were arrested.

Interest in the mission to Ibn Saud had declined noticably while Shakespear was with Expeditionary Force 'D'. The army was advancing. The Turks, despite new Mauser rifles and gleaming bayonets, were on the run. The need for allies in far-off deserts had diminished. As Shakespear left the Shatt-al-Arab, he noticed that among the little ships gathered on the river for war service, tied up beside paddle-steamers and pleasure craft that had been brought from Britain and India, was his beloved *Lewis Pelly*, pressed into service as a river tugboat.

All was not shipshape in the domain of Shaikh Mubarak either. While the Expeditionary Force battled through mud and tempest, Sayid Talib was on his way from Basra to Kuwait as the emissary of Enver, though he was open as ever to a higher bidder. In fact, he had been offered a pension by Britain, through

Shaikh Khazal of Muhammerah, the Persian citizen whose independency embraced Ahwaz and the oil pipeline. On 16 November Grey, the new Political Agent in Kuwait, had written to Resident Knox at Bushire to tell him that Shaikh Mubarak's agent in Basra, Abdal Aziz ibn Salim, was on his way to Kuwait with Sayid Talib.

The devious Talib eventually arrived to tell Grey that he had resisted an invitation to go to Constantinople, and was on his way to Ibn Saud to attempt to induce him to rise against the British Government and support the holy war, though he would nevertheless like to place himself at the disposal of Britain. If he was known by the Turks to be making that offer, however, he feared for the lives of his family who were still in Basra. He left with Grey new terms for his co-operation with Britain. Later he asked Grey if he and Mubarak had come to an agreement about using his services, or about the terms which he had presented at an earlier meeting with Shaikh Khazal, to wit a large sum of money (unspecified) on account, an annual retainer, the guarantee of his properties in and around Basra after the war and the promise of the governorship of the province of Basra.

Grey reported to the Resident on 17 November:

At about 2 p.m. (today) the above mentioned Abdal Aziz bin Salim came to inform me that Sayyid Talib and his accompanying party of twelve men had decamped unknown to the Shaikh, and were on their way to Jahra and thence to Buraida where the Amir Saud is at present. His object in coming to Kuwait was thus made clear. It was to sound me as to the possibility of obtaining better terms for his friendship than those he had refused, and, through me, to obtain a further offer from you.

Grey told Knox that after the escape of Talib the Shaikh of Kuwait had remarked that 'Sayid Talib now has every door closed against him.' Grey thought the old man was very pleased to see the back of his visitor. 'His own view is that the Turks invited him to Constantinople to put him to death, and that they have now turned him out of Basra.'

Shakespear had had a good deal to do with Sayid Talib over the years since his arrival in the Gulf as a young man in 1904. While on leave in London early in 1914 he told the India Office: 'The man [Talib] is a strong, wilful, utterly unscrupulous character usually heavily in debt and therefore importunate.'

Now he was caught up in Talib's web of intrigue and in the almost incredible folly of his own successor, Grey. In the previous April, while Shakespear was camped on the edge of Ibn Rashid's territory, the Saudi Amir had received an urgent message from Mubarak, instigated by Grey, to go to the Subahiya wells in Kuwait. On 20 April Crow, the Consul at Basra, had telegraphed Constantinople to tell the Embassy that a Turkish mission was on its way to Kuwait. Crow's message referred to the formation by the Turks of a commission to include the Chiefs of Staff at Basra and Baghdad and the *mutasarif* of Hasa, none other than Sayid Talib. It was to be sent to Al Hasa, where Talib was to arrange a takeover by the Turkish Government.

On the same date Knox said that Major Trevor, the Political Agent at Bahrain, believed that Ibn Saud would treat with the delegation, though Mubarak thought otherwise. Unwilling to deal with Grey in Kuwait, Ibn Saud had kept in touch with Trevor. Two days earlier Knox had sent a mysterious message to Trevor, asking him: 'Could you inform our friend that the individual he proposes to meet left Kuwait on March 25th? If so please do: Hope in this way to make Abdal Aziz pause.'

On 16 April, Ibn Saud had written to Mubarak:

> In agreeing to approach Kuwait I have obeyed your instructions as regards obedience and submission to *our* Government, but you know well with what contempt and disdain the officials of [that] Government have treated me, and you have seen the patience with which I have submitted to their conduct all these years notwithstanding that I never once experienced anything from them which could console me. Now, heaven be praised, I am in a position to do great things, even as far as Iraq, were it not for the fact that I do not wish to be the cause of further difficulty to the Government and revolution on the part of those Arabs.

Grey described it as 'an interesting piece of Oriental diplomacy'.

An interesting piece of occidental diplomacy was in the wind. The Turkish delegation, led by Sayid Talib, was on its way from Basra aboard the Anglo-Persian Oil Company's ship SS *Ferrara*, to be entertained by Shaikh Mubarak and Colonel Grey in Kuwait, while they waited for Ibn Saud to make his unenthusiastic way to Subahiya. The Political Agent's scenario ran thus: Shaikh Mubarak's investiture with the Ottoman order of

Osmanieh would take place on the next day (23 April). And the Shaikh would show them Ibn Saud's letters to him on the subject of their meeting, which was intended to restore Ottoman authority in Al Hasa through Sayid Talib, and, incredibly, in return for the Amir's submission to their scheme, of which Britain was fully aware, they would give verbal but *not* written permission to him 'retake Qatar and Trucial Oman when he wished'. Those lands had not been under Saudi control since the days of the first Wahhabi Empire in the early nineteenth century. Sayid Talib's delegation was finally led out to meet Ibn Saud at Subahiya. Perhaps the British officials involved in this attempt to promote the Ottoman cause had in mind a statement made by the Viceroy to Whitehall at the conclusion of the Anglo-Turkish negotiations in September 1913:

> There can be no doubt, so far as India's interests are concerned, that the existence in Asia of a strong Turkish power, friendly and reformed, will be a safeguard against interference with India from the West, and it might even be the indirect means of Persia's integrity being maintained. We have nothing to fear from Turkey.

The Foreign Office in London noted: 'It would be a serious prospect for India if the partition of Turkey ever eventuated.' Hardinge in India and Mallet in Constantinople were in cordial agreement. Mubarak did not turn up to meet Ibn Saud, but Colonel Grey eventually arrived on the scene. The Turks had presented a treaty for signature, appointing the Amir their mutasarif or Governor in Najd, and promising him an annual pension if he signed. Ibn Saud at first refused. Pressed by Grey, however, he finally put his signature to the document. When the great prince of the desert, the lifelong friend of Britain and enemy of the Ottoman power, asked Grey what he should do just before putting his name to the document, Grey replied tersely: 'You can expect no help or guidance from Britain.' Shakespear was to find out the rest from Ibn Saud himself.

In May 1914 when Shakespear was camping at Nakhl in Sinai on his way to Egypt, he had informed Constantinople that a consignment of arms was on its way along the old caravan road to Hail to encourage Ibn Rashid to wage war on Riyadh. The information was ignored. But on 23 June Ambassador Mallet sent a jubilant telegram to the Foreign Office: 'Bin Saud has

accepted position of Wali and Commandant of Najd. Acknow-
ledgement that he is Ottoman subject and will hoist Ottoman
flag. Sultan has telegraphed Talib congratulating him on success of his connection.' A copy of the treaty between Ibn Saud
and the Ottoman Wali of Basra dated 15 May 1914, was found by
British troops within a few days of their entry into Basra. It
marked the end of Ibn Saud's confidence in Shaikh Mubarak,
and of his trust in Britain. With the treaty was found an undated
letter from Ibn Saud to Sayid Talib, who it seems had reminded
the Amir of his duty and allegiance to Islam and the Porte, and
had betrayed the correspondence to the Turks. Ibn Saud told
him: 'It is these people [the British] whose good qualities cause
the countries of the world to remain in repose, whom we know
and on whom we depend, and do not wish to displease.'

The Viceroy told London after the event, 'negotiations nearly
ended in a free fight between Abdal Aziz and the Bimbashi
[Turkish officer] over the question of a Turkish garrison at
Katif'. And Mallet in Constantinople wrote to the Foreign
Secretary of the 'suspicion created in the Turks' mind' by the
visit of Shakespear to Ibn Saud in 1913, and of 'the dilatory and
obscure methods of Oriental diplomacy'.

On his arrival in Kuwait at the end of the year, Shakespear
wrote to the Resident:

> I reached Kuwait on 18 November and learnt from Lt.
> Colonel Grey that Sayyid Talib had left on the 16th inst. with a
> small following of some 50 men ostensibly for Najd to inter-
> view Bin Saud . . . The Sayyid was ordered by the Turks to go
> to Najd and secure Bin Saud's co-operation; feeling nervous
> as to his own position in the event of our occupying Basra
> Sayyid Talib endeavoured to secure terms from HMG; news
> of his negotiations would appear to have reached the Turkish
> officials in Basra for Sayyid Talib seems to have apprehended
> the direct consequences to himself and his family if he
> remained in Basra.

Shakespear was confident that Ibn Saud would be circumspect in
his dealings with the 'plausible' and 'unscrupulous' Talib. All the
same he wrote a letter in Arabic to Ibn Saud warning him of Talib's
possible treachery and sending a translation to the Resident:

> And verily I have heard in Kuwait that Sayyid Talib fled
> from the Turks at Basra to Kuwait and after some days here

fled to you. And our esteemed friend Shaikh Mubarak as-Sabah has informed me of his tricks and mischief and I also take the opportunity of explaining to you what curious things he has done.

In 1911 Talib had visited Kitchener in Cairo and the Viceroy in Simla armed with notes of introduction from Consul Crow at Basra. In October 1914 the new Consul at Basra, Bullard, sent on a note from Talib to Lord Kitchener, offering his services to Britain. Two weeks later the 'Butcher' of Basra was summoned to Constantinople.

During October there had been a flurry of correspondence between London, Bushire and Kuwait. Messages from Sir Edward Grey, Lord Crewe, the Viceroy, the Resident and Shaikh Mubarak had been transmitted to Ibn Saud, who was raiding the turncoat Mutair and Ajman tribes in the hope that a sharp lesson in loyalty might restrain their habit of siding with others against him when the spoils were tempting enough. By mid-November the Wahhabi Amir was at Buraida. A letter from the Shaikh of Kuwait had brought a promising response from Ibn Saud in early October, carried by his kinsman Abdullah ibn Jiluwi, the Governor of Al Hasa. Colonel Grey had telegraphed Bushire: 'Ibn Saud is with us.' That was before war was declared with Turkey. But it was a premature note of joy. Ibn Saud was biding his time. Ibn Rashid, encouraged by Enver, was raiding his territory in Kasim and the rival tribes at the centre of Arabia were spoiling for a fight.

By December Shakespear was tying up loose ends in Kuwait, waiting for the Amir's call. By now the journey had obviously taken a dangerous turn. The Englishman had been told to stay with Ibn Saud and if necessary to take up residence at his capital. News of an impending fight to end the Rashid dynasty of Hail came to Kuwait and Shakespear prepared to join what looked like being a full-scale fracas: a military solution to a political scheme in which Shakespear had so recently played a clandestine part. On 7 December the invitation arrived from Ibn Saud's camp near Buraida. Shakespear had a presentiment of trouble. On the 11th he wrote a letter to Grey, with whom he was still on the most distant terms, asking him to inform his mother 'in case I should get snuffed out in the desert'. And less than a week before, on 5 December, he had composed his last will and testament. For almost all his adult years he had flirted with danger, as a desert explorer of exceptional bravery and thoroughness; as a pioneer motorist among the unfriendly hills and precipices and even less friendly tribesmen of Persia and Anatolia; as one of the earliest aeroplane pilots; as a Political Officer and agent of military intelligence. It had never once occurred to him to make out his will. He did so now, with Grey and the Agency clerk, D'Mello, as his witnesses.

He left Kuwait for the inner desert along the familiar path of Al Batin on 12 December. He spent Christmas Day at his own camp near the Hafar wells before turning off towards As Safa and the Dahana sand belt. He arrived at Ibn Saud's camp near Majmaa on the plain of Arma on the last day of December. Abdal Aziz was in a good mood and welcomed his guest warmly, but it was not long before his anger with Britain and Shaikh Mubarak over his treatment at the Kuwait meeting was evident. They moved on towards Zilfi.

Shakespear's letters from Camp XXI central Arabia to the Resident at Bushire and to his brother in India expressed his own as well as the Amir's displeasure. He told Knox on 4 January:

> Bin Saud was completely detached from the British Government when I arrived ... Abdul Aziz, who is animated by an intense patriotism for his country, a profound veneration for his religion and a single-minded determination to do his best for his people ... trusted the British Government as no other ... now he is asked to commit himself to open war with his most powerful and bitter enemies by a power which six months before told him it could not intervene on his behalf and left him free to do a deal with the Turks.

In a report to Cox at Basra he remarked: 'It is unnecessary for me to recall what passed between Bin Saud and Grey.'

Sayid Talib was at camp with Ibn Saud when Shakespear arrived. The Amir was advised in no uncertain term to despatch him back to Basra. Cox made him Britain's house guest in India. Once the hooligan of Basra had been dealt with, Ibn Saud and his English visitor got down to the business of hammering out a treaty of alliance which would give military and financial protection to the Saudi leader and ensure his support for Britain's wartime cause. While their negotiations were in progress they had a visit from an emissary of Abdullah ibn Husain, son of the Sharif of Mecca, who wanted to know if Ibn Saud proposed to lend his support to the Sultan's call for *jihad* and to the plan of Enver's ambassadors that he, Ibn Saud, should harry the British in the Basra region while the Sharif and Ibn Rashid guarded the western and northern boundaries of Arabia. Shakespear advised the Amir to tell the Sharif to temporise with the Turks and to promise nothing. The emissary returned with a verbal message from Ibn Saud and a copy of the Viceroy's promise to protect the Holy Places.

Shakespear was not happy with the position. The British Government's interest in his mission and in the treaty with the Amir had declined noticeably since he was called to the Foreign Office from his self-elected army post at Aldershot after the declaration of war with Turkey. On 14 January he wrote his brother a most despairing letter, telling him that he doubted whether the Government would pay the slightest heed to his recommendations and adding: 'They will probably go on messing about until they make Bin Saud so utterly sick that he will chuck his present friendly attitude.'

He also told his brother:

> Bin Saud has some 6,000 of his men in tents and thousands of Badawin all round and in a couple of days we should make a move for a biggish battle with the other big chief of Central Arabia, Ibn Rashid. From all accounts he hasn't anything like the same force so the result ought to be pretty certain, but there is never any knowing what these Badawin will do.

He had written earlier to Gertrude Bell, who was by now serving in France, telling her that he was enjoying the journey except for the cold; his water-skin had frozen in the night.

He sent a draft of the treaty to Cox on 19 January, with a covering note to the effect that the Amir would make no further concessions to Britain as far as the war was concerned, 'until he obtains in that treaty some very solid guarantees of his position'. He added that he would be leaving in a few days time and would meet the Shammar army.

They went north on the 22nd and camped near Zilfi, the head town of the Sudair region, on the following day. Ibn Rashid's Shammar army was some twenty-five miles away in the direction of Buraida. That night Ibn Saud begged Shakespear to leave him and go to the safety of Zilfi. 'If I go now, I desert not only you but my own country. I cannot do that', said Shakespear. That night too, a messenger arrived to give the Amir the astounding news that Abdullah, the Sharif's son, was leading an army from the Hijaz into his territory and was camped at Shara on the road to Riyadh. Next morning Shakespear was awakened by his little Punjabi servant, Ambush. He breakfasted and took his revolver and camera. The army of Ibn Saud went off to battle, the Amir with the cavalry, Shakespear camel-mounted to join the infantry, making northward among the *nafud* or sand dunes of Al Bittar. The camels were tied up at a deserted place known to the badawin as Baqar, the Cow, the place where Zamil, the Regent of Hail, had met his death nine months before. Shakespear was with a young townsman named Husain, who had charge of the single field-gun available to Ibn Saud. It was mounted on a dune at a position called Al Jarab, and as the Shammar army came over the horizon Shakespear, standing beside Husain and his gun, began to photograph the scene. The army of Ibn Rashid was well drilled and larger than the Englishman had been led to believe. Its horsemen engaged Ibn Saud's cavalry on the flanks.

The Saudi cavalry was giving a good account of itself and the Shammar were in some disarray after about an hour of battle in the morning sunlight of 24 January. The desert war cry *Allahu akbar* resounded across the flat empty plain beyond the dunes, and already the sand was littered with the dead and dying of both sides. Ibn Saud's son Turki was in command of the infantry, and Ibn Rashid's mounted men swept down on their position. Shakespear was busy directing Husain's field-gun fire and the enemy were being blasted effectively when suddenly it jammed. Dismayed by the failure of their prized weapon, Turki's men broke and fled towards the Wadi al Rumma, which provided cover just west of their position in the Bittar sands. Seeing the flight of the infantry, the Ajman tribe who provided a large part of Ibn Saud's cavalry force deserted the battlefield. Treacherous to the last they went off to raid the baggage camp of their own troops. Shakespear was left alone on the hill of Al Jarab. The rest of the story is best told in the words of Major Bray, who was at Indian Army HQ at the time and had access to intelligence reports.

Shakespear, to stem the panic, rushed to the gun to bring it, by his expert knowledge, again into action and was left, deserted, to face the charge alone. Ibn Rashid's horsemen swept on with muffled beat of horse hoofs, ever nearer and nearer, while Shakespear with frantic but methodical haste, sought to remedy the defect, but before he could do so, he and the gun were smothered in the wrack and when the wave swept over them and beyond, Shakepear lay a huddled heap by his silent gun.

Shakespear had been hit by bullets in the leg, the arm and the head. Only at the last moment did he remove the *topi* which he always wore in the desert, refusing the Arab *kaffiya* in which so many of his countrymen loved to be seen and photographed. As he lay by his gun mortally wounded, one of Saud ibn Subhan's slaves rode up and cut him down with his sword. He was thirty-six years old. Ibn Rashid had won a vital battle and the flame of desert rebellion was extinguished. Ibn Saud went back to Riyadh, Abdullah ibn Husain withdrew from Shara, and Cox himself met the Saudi leader to finalise the treaty with Britain, which was watered down on the insistence of the Secretary of State for India, and finally signed at Katif at the end of the year.

Major Bray later met one of Ibn Saud's infantrymen in Bahrain and reproached him for deserting Shakespear at Jarab. 'We like Shakespear very much,' he answered, 'and were sorry for his death, but by Allah the fault was not ours . . . Shakespear forgot the rule of the desert [to run away and fight another day] and so he perished.'

'The service has lost an able and gallant officer,' wrote Cox to the Viceroy. When the Foreign Office received a copy of the letter, someone appended a minute: 'A terrible loss, and doubly so now!'

Musil had arrived at Damascus from Constantinople in the middle of November 1914, to find his friend Nuri ibn Shalan still a house prisoner of the Governor as he had been since his betrayal to the Turks in 1910. Nuri begged him to speak to the Wali and to obtain a permit for him to join his tribes in the inner desert. Nuri's slaves and retainers were held prisoner at the old military barracks at Dumeir outside the city, built by Midhat Pasha in the 1870s and now in great disrepair. The resourceful Musil obtained a permit for the Prince of the Ruwalla, and left his Arab friend to make his own way to the desert while he and Khalaf went to Dumeir to seek the release of his men. They left Damascus on the Homs Road at the beginning of December.

The Austrian had noticed that the tribesmen were leaving the surroundings of Damascus and the other Syrian towns outside which they customarily camped in the hope of rich pickings; now they hurried with their sheep and camels to escape the greed of the Government. Rumblings of future tribal differences, and of the problems in store for those who would try to capture the tribesmens' loyalty, became evident from Musa's conversations along the way.

'Many wished for the defeat of the Turkish Government, while others feared that in that event the English would occupy the cultivated regions with guards so strong that it would be impossible to steal anything from the settlers.' So said the men of the Bani Wahhab. But when their chief, Saud ibn Malham, came with his sons to pay Musil homage and to show him an order from the Governor, Zakki Pasha, which he held out proudly, he said he was determined to sacrifice even himself, his children and his tribe at the behest of the Government and the Sultan in Constantinople: 'To whom God grant victory.'

But Musil had brought fresh instructions from the government which overrode Zakki's and all present were admonished to gather and listen while Mansur, Musil's servant, read out the order of the Sublime Porte: they were to join with Ibn Shalan's tribes and obey the Prince, in whose allegiance the Ottoman power had confidence. When Mansur had finished, many of the men shouted: 'Allah grant victory to the Government and the Sultan!' Many more remained silent.

Saud ibn Malham was a small plump man of about sixty-five and this was his first journey to the inner desert since his youth; he preferred his stone cottage at Homs to the tribal tent. Musil asked him if he would stand by the Government or plunder the settlements from his desert fastness. He answered evasively: 'Nuri must decide.' The Austrians travelled with Ibn Malham's tribe and with the Bani Husain of Sultan al Tayya, who were both loosely allied to the Anaiza. Their standards of morality did not seem to be high, according to Musa.

Never among the Ruwalla did I hear implications of unrestrained lechery which were frequent among these people, nor the jests about intimacies of young men with slave women, or even of young slaves with high-bred daughters. From such intimacies, perhaps, come the negro characteristics of many high-bred sons.

The Austrian had brought with him an instruction to secure if he could peace between Ibn Shalan and the Fidan and the Abda tribes, which the Government itself had stirred to attack the Ruwalla after the betrayal of Nuri in August 1910 and his arrest by the Turks, when the Ruwalla had responded by attacking the Turkish garrisons. Now, it seemed, Musil was carrying out a number of peace-keeping missions for the Turks. They had asked him to secure at least a temporary armistice between the Fidan and the Ruwalla, 'for they estimated that the war would be ended within eight months'.

The tribes, said Musa,

> saw in the Government merely a bureaucracy of tormentors who were of no benefit to the Arabs in general or the Badu in particular but, on the contrary, injured their interests whenever possible ... Had the Turkish Government guaranteed them a large booty from the war, they would have risen against the British; on the other hand, if the British had promised them that they would be allowed to loot the settlements subject to the Turkish rule, they would have risen against the Turks.

They went on towards Jauf and on 24 December were in sight of the Prince's camp near Khabra al Hayyim, in the shadow of the volcano of Umm Wuala in the black desert of Al Basaita, through which Shakespear had ridden swiftly some months before pursued by Auda abu Tayya's men. 'I sat in front of the tent until late into the night, absorbed in reminiscences of my homeland and my dear ones,' wrote Musil on Christmas Eve in that bleak year. Freezing with cold, the Austrians and their Arab companions arrived at the tents of Nuri ibn Shalan in the afternoon of 26 December. And in conversations round the camp fires of the Prince and his henchmen, Musil's own purpose began to clarify. 'Thou knowest my heart, brother,' said Nuri, 'Thou knowest that I do not trust the Government, and it does not trust me. Were it not for thee I would still be sitting in Damascus as an honourable prisoner of the Government . . . They pretended to need me in the war against the Inglees.' Musil replied: 'Of what good shall I alone be to ye? Send me into the desert and I will bring ye thousands of warriors and we shall slay the Inglees ... Why should the sons of Arabia massacre one another in the interests of a foreign Government?'

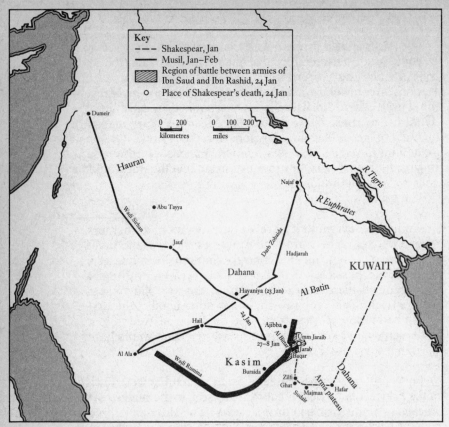

Map 9   Routes of Shakespear and Musil, 1915

And then they spoke of Ibn Rashid, and Nawwaf, the Amir's son, joined in. 'The present Governor', said Nuri, 'has not asked me for gold. He asks that I remain loyal during the war and promises after the war to help me against Ibn Rashid. Whether he speaketh the truth or a lie, I know not.' 'He lies, father,' said Nawwaf. 'How could he speak the truth when he knows that Enver Pasha considers Ibn Rashid his most loyal ally and sends him arms, ammunition and money? And what did Enver send these rifles to Ibn Rashid for? That he might more easily defeat Ibn Saud, who eighteen months before had driven the Turkish soldiers out of the province of al-Hasa . . . The same Enver Pasha has appointed Ibn Saud the governor and commandant of the whole of Nejd, had assured him of the Sultan's grace and his own favour; yet he gave to Ibn Rashid the arms with which to wage war against him. Who, then, would trust Enver Pasha?'

Neither Nuri nor his Austrian visitor spoke as Nawwaf warmed to his theme, until the young Prince paused to ask a question: 'Tell me, brother Musa, dost thou understand our Government? And this Government wants us to help it against the Inglees.' But Musa wasn't permitted to reply for the time being. Nawwaf went on with a revealing story.

'Is Enver blind that he does not see the wiles of Ibn Rashid's minister Saud and his Constantinople representative Rashid Pasha? The latter negotiated with the consul of the Frank in Damascus and promised aid to him, as well as to the Frank ambassador in Constantinople, provided they will convey their soldiers to Syria ... My men captured a messenger carrying Rashid Pasha's despatch to Hail; thus I got the information. Sometime ago there was in Hail a consul of the Engleez from Kuwait and a certain lady. Why were they there? The consul from Kuwait also came from Hail to me at al-Jauf. I was not at home at the time and he sought to gain my substitute the negro Amer for the Ingleez, and then rode from al-Jauf to Egypt. No doubt he had made a treaty against the Government with Saud ibn Subhan, and the Government and Enver have no favourite except Ibn Rashid. Shame upon such a Government: Whoever would believe that they will support us after the war is an artless child.'

As Musil was making a detailed note of his conversations with Nuri and Nawwaf, he received a visit from the rogue Shaikh of the desert, Auda abu Tayya, chief of the Howaitat, 'the most daring and most cruel man known to me in Arabia'. Auda had been put in power by the Turks in 1900 on the death of the old Howaitat chief, Arar ibn Ghazi, in the hope that he would rescue them from the depredations of other tribes in the region of Maan, which was in the tribal territory of the Howaitat. But Auda was no man's servant, and he took booty from all sides, though he did protect the Hijaz railway until the Government, afraid of his popularity, issued a warrant for his arrest, whereupon he retired to the depths of his homeland and declared war on Turkey and all its sons, keeping a careful tally of those he despatched.

The Government had asked him to come to terms with them and with the tribes that had betrayed him. He roared with laughter over Musil's camp fire and bellowed: 'Does the Government think that I don't understand?'

'Well, Auda, wouldst thou really march to the aid of the Government against Egypt?'

'The Government promises me arms and also gold at some

station of the Hijaz railway. I need both. I shall take the arms and gold, but I shall fight whoever the Howaitat fight. If they rise against the Ingleez, I shall combat the Ingleez; if they rise against the Government, I shall massacre the Government troops.'

The three Arab leaders then asked Musil if it was true that the English only fought in the middle of the sea, where no rider on camel or horse could overtake them.

In early January, Musil set off for Jabal Shammar, and Nuri had begun to doubt the wisdom of what they were doing. As he said goodbye to his Austrian friend he implored him not to go to Ibn Rashid.

'Go, Musa, to Ibn Saud. He is my brother and friend, a man honourable and loyal, but Ibn Rashid is a weakling and his minister a traitor.'

'I shall go to Ibn Saud,' said Musa, 'but it will be from the territory of Ibn Rashid.'

When Shakespear was in Jauf he had noted: 'The afternoon filled with stories of the wonderful largesse of one Musa an-Namisiya, who distributes camel loads of cartridges, sugar, clothes and tinned foods among the Ruwalla shaikhs.' Musil owed his popularity among Ibn Shalan's tribes to more than his personality.

The Austrian took a most improbable route to Ibn Rashid, bypassing the watering place of Hayaniya, where any traveller would normally call, staying all the time within the northern boundary of Jabal Shammar. On 23 January, when Ibn Saud's force was on its way from Zilfi and Ibn Rashid's Shammar were marching to meet it across the Taraffiya plain, Musil was within a stone's throw of the contending armies. When the battle was being fought at Jarab, he was at Jubail, a few miles away. Two days after the battle he was camped with Ibn Rashid in the Wadi Rumma, where Ibn Saud's infantry had hidden from the enemy horsemen after leaving Shakespear to his fate. Musil's journey was well timed and he was the only man ever to hear the details from the Rashid side. He told the story of Shakespear's death as seen from the other camp:

From the beginning of December, 1914, the minister Saud had been besieging various settlements on the border districts of Hail which had surrendered to Faisal [ibn Subhan al-Rashid] and his overlord Ibn Saud. Most of these were destroyed, the palm groves laid waste and the wells choked up. On January 23, 1915 Saud left his camp at Umm Jaraib in order to attack Ibn Saud at al-Jarab. The first attack was repulsed, and a detachment of Ibn Rashid's troops from the Lubde quarters of Hail were pursued by a party of Ibn Saud's warriors led by Faisal. But the remaining detachment under Ibn Rashid attacked again and forced the part of Ibn Saud's army which had stayed behind, to yield. A field-gun was captured, by which Shakespear was standing. Deserted by Ibn Saud's warriors, the Englishman was shot down by a slave, Ibrahim Nuwdeli, and killed with a sabre. Nevertheless, the minister Saud could not obtain a complete victory and was obliged to withdraw in the night from the vicinity of the enemy. His orderly retreat became a wild flight when express messengers brought news that his own camp at Umm Jaraib was being plundered.

It seems that after the battle the Mutair and the Ajman looted both camps. It also seems that Ibn Saud's men stayed on the battlefield until nightfall and that only Ibn Rashid's retreat prevented a further battle the next day. According to eye-witnesses who were interrogated in Kuwait, Shakespear lay on the battlefield for several days after his death, with only a blood-stained vest protecting his body from the elements.

Musil was ill at this stage of his journey. Water from a well which had given Shakespear the 'gripes' during his passage the year before was the probable cause. But the indomitable Austrian was not put off by stomach-ache and a high temperature from lengthy argument with the young Ibn Rashid and his insensate minister Saud, the killer of his own uncle Zamil. Musil had instructions from Enver himself to persuade Ibn Rashid to make peace with Ibn Saud and Ibn Shalan, and to convince all three princes if he could that obedience to the Government was their best course. But the minister Saud was in belligerent mood, and the representative of the Central Powers was eventually forced to make a journey of 450 miles to the station of Al Ala on the Hijaz railway in order to telegraph the Porte. He sent a personal message to Enver but received no reply. Not even a courteous acknowledgment. And so he returned to Kasim but Ibn Rashid had gone. He had been instructed to seek Ibn Saud, but he decided to send a note to the Amir instead, and then went on to Najaf and Baghdad, where he was cared for by the Austrian Consul, De Tahy, before proceeding to Damascus.

He arrived in Damascus on 5 June 1915. Since the previous November he had travelled more than 3,000 miles, often reduced by sickness to a state of unutterable weariness, yet he never once shirked his hard and intricate mission among people for whom he had no great liking at times. His last journey has few equals in the history of desert travel. He was a masterly agent for his country, and he and Shakespear were worthy rivals in central Arabia.

8

Councils of War

In London a Liberal Cabinet with little taste for war (except for one of its members, Churchill, who perhaps had too much) was entirely willing to place the conduct of affairs in the hands of Kitchener, who distrusted everyone around him and shared the confidences of war with no one. In Berlin, Marine and Military Cabinets, Army and Navy War Staffs, and Foreign Office submitted to the Kaiser's imposed and unconstitutional power. For twelve months of wholesale slaughter on the battlefields, whim and chance were the spouses of decision-making.

For months there was no effective war directorate in Britain: merely twenty-three brawling Cabinet ministers, every one of them distrusted by Kitchener; a Prime Minister who regularly confided in his mistress the problems and details of war; and two ministers, Churchill and Lloyd George, who constantly passed state secrets and military plans to newspaper barons. Watching the War Office in action, as frock-coated messengers scurried to the bidding of the 64-year-old Kitchener, America's Ambassador Walter Page, who had the best view of all among outsiders, observed: 'It takes your breath away.'

It was Walter Page who observed too the one profitable outcome of Britain's calamitous condition in 1914, the reorganisation of the intelligence services and the appointment of William Reginald Hall, son of the Royal Navy's first professional intelligence chief, William Henry Hall, as DNI and the most powerful figure of the Secret Service. 'Such eyes as the man has! My Lord! I do study these men here most diligently who have this vast and appalling War Job. There are the most uncommon creatures among them . . . men about whom our great-grandchildren will read in school histories; but of them all, the most extraordinary is the naval officer of whom, probably, they'll never hear.'

Hall took into alliance the Deputy Commissioner of London's police force, Commander Basil Thomson, and between them they formed the intelligence and counter-espionage organisation which was destined to wage a successful campaign throughout the world against the operations of the enemy's military and naval intelligence services, to counter the call of Enver and the Kaiser for *jihad* in the east, and to change, at a critical moment, the balance of power in the conflict.

They made an extraordinary team: Hall, the seadog born into the Royal Navy, educated at naval college, with eyes that broke the resolution of the most practised enemy agent and which closed every now and again by the shuttering action of bushy eyebrows so that he was known throughout the navy as 'Blinker'; and Thomson, son of one of the finest scholars ever to occupy the bishopric of York, scholar of Eton and New College, Oxford, Prime Minister of Tonga, Governor of Dartmoor and prison reformer before he entered the police force, and a prolific writer throughout his busy career. Thomson's room in Scotland Yard was just across the road from the old Admiralty building in Whitehall where a cluster of offices, bearing the strict injunction 'No entrance', and known as 'Room 40', became the nerve centre of the war on Britain's side; the sacrosanct lair of a brilliant team which cracked the enemy's ciphers and controlled an international network of spies.

On 5 August 1914 a War Council was formed in Whitehall, composed of senior ministers and military and naval chiefs. At its meeting on 25 November it received intelligence reports from Cairo indicating that a large Turkish army was moving through Palestine and that an attack on the Suez Canal was imminent. In the ensuing discussion Churchill put forward the theory that the best defence of Suez and Egypt lay in an attack on the Gallipoli peninsula, thus ensuring control over the Dardanelles and the ending of effective Turkish participation in the war. Kitchener thought such a course 'unwise'. It was to take twelve months of bitter wrangling, of almost incredible indecision and wanton sacrifice for the Gallipoli theory to resolve itself into one of the great disasters of the war.

Fortunately for the Allies, Germany played the same incomprehensible game with its military and naval chiefs as did Whitehall. Liman von Sanders, the general chosen to lead the Turkish First Army, was replaced by the old Prussian, von der Goltz, the Field-Marshal who had been head of the Kaiser's military mission in Constantinople for two decades before the war and Military Governor of Belgium following its invasion. Enver reluctantly agreed to Liman taking charge of the Fifth Army at Gallipoli, where he was to prove one of the great generals of the war, though the Ambassador of the Reich, von Wangenheim, devoted himself to obtaining Liman's recall by fair means or foul.

In the first days of 1915 Enver himself proceeded to the Caucasus with General Bronsart von Schellendorf at his side, to teach the Russian army a lesson. The Turco-German force was wiped out and Enver returned to his capital a somewhat wiser man, while the Russians remained to pose a threat to the Turkish rear and to the northern provinces of Persia. Liman von Sanders described Enver as a 'military buffoon' and demanded the recall of von Schellendorf.

Enver arrived back in Stamboul from the Caucasus just in time to hear of another disaster, the failure of the attack on Suez launched by the Ottoman Fourth Army under Jamal and Kress von Kressenstein in the first days of January. Staff work on the British side was not all that it might have been. The Turks were able to move an army of 20,000 men stealthily across the Sinai desert, hauling their big guns at the cost of many human and animal lives. But the man who had almost a lone responsibility for controlling a network of agents among the venal and unreliable tribesmen of the peninsula, Kitchener's nephew Alfred Parker, did remarkable work.

After the main attack had been repulsed Colonel Haldane of the 7th Gurkha Rifles led an assault on a second Turco-German force at Tor in the south. Parker and his most reliable Arab agents went ahead to flush out the Turkish agents and locate the enemy encampments. His principal agent was the Jesuit priest and Arabist, Father Jaussen, and his chief informants the girls of a convent on Mount Sinai. When the job was done the army commander paid a glowing tribute to Lieutenant-Colonel Parker, who had been Military Governor of the peninsula for three years before the war. But a more touching tribute was paid several weeks after the battle when two badawin children came out of the desert hand-in-hand and found their way to Kubri on the canal. They explained that their family deep in the desert had no food and had turned out their children, telling them to seek shelter with the Ingleez. They had walked for thirty-six miles in blazing heat without food or water, and as soon as they found a soldier they asked for Birkil Bey, the badawin name for Parker. When they were told he wasn't there they wept. But Birkil Bey was sent for and the children were looked after. Their journey through the waterless waste was considered to be beyond the capacity of the average infantryman.

In the afterglow of Suez, the Cabinet met in London and discussed the prospect of a Russian offensive in Persia which might yet destroy the ability of the Turks to defend the Gallipoli stronghold. Enthused by that transitory thought, Sir Edward Grey spoke up for the Russian ally with words which might have echoed down the twentieth century had they not been buried in Cabinet records for fifty years: 'The time has come', he said, 'to reverse the traditional hostility with regard to Russia's aims in the Middle East. It is absurd that such a huge empire has no warm water ports, except in the Black Sea.' Churchill said that territorial settlements should wait until peace was achieved. It was a piece of advice that might profitably have been followed in other areas.

The Great Debate – whether to fight to the last man in the Dardanelles or to make a strategic withdrawal before the Allied armies there and in the Balkans bled to death – was accompanied by constant talk in the Cabinet and War Council of the break up of the Ottoman Empire. It was accompanied too by an attempt to 'bribe' the Turks out of the war which brought Captain Hall and his clandestine organisation into conflict with the Government and the First Sea Lord. Fitzmaurice, the confidant of Fisher in his Mediterranean days whose recall the Germans had demanded on the grounds that he was 'poisoning the atmosphere', was in close touch with dissident elements in Turkey from his secret hideaway in the Balkans. Together with Griffin Eady, an engineering contractor with close links with Constantinople, and Fitzmaurice, Hall set out on a scheme to bring the anti-German faction at the Porte over to the Allied side, with the offer of £3 million, the sum to be increased to £4 million if the Straits were surrendered and the *Goeben* handed over undamaged. It was a plan of incredible audacity, but in the end Admiral Fisher heard about it and told Churchill. A mere £200,000 was finally offered for *Goeben*, and £100,000 for its sister, and the deal fell through.

But of all the events which interspersed the Dardanelles discussions in the fateful year 1915, nothing was of greater significance in the long term than the report presented to the Cabinet in January 1915 by Herbert Samuel, then the President of the Local Government Board, which was headed 'Palestine'. It began with the words: 'The course of events opens a prospect of change, at the end of the war, in the status of Palestine. Already there is a stirring among the twelve million Jews scattered throughout the world.' He thought it was too soon to 'attempt to realise the aspiration of a Jewish state', but that the solution which would be most welcome to the supporters of the Zionist movement throughout the world would be the annexation of the country to the British Empire. Samuel had obtained from the 'knowledgeable' Gertrude Bell a delineation of the bounds of 'Palestine Prima'.

By the time that the question came up for serious discussion again the complexion of the Cabinet had changed; a coalition came to power in the shadow of the Dardanelles disasters, following the resignation of Lord Fisher in May because of Churchill's 'constant interference in tactical and strategic matters', and the subsequent dismissal of Churchill. Six months were to pass, however, before the final decision was made to abandon the nightmare of Gallipoli.

In the meantime Enver's plan for *jihad* was being carefully evolved, and Germany's Eastern Bureau and military intelligence organisation were dovetailing into it skilfully, though with little show of esteem for their Islamic partner. The eastern world was divided for the purpose of *jihad* into four areas: the Arabian peninsula (including Syria and Mesopotamia), Persia, Afghanistan and India. Each was under the control of an officer of the Ottoman General Staff. The headquarters of the movement were in Madina, under the direction of an Indian religious teacher, Moulvi Muhammad Hassan, while the Afghan agent was the renegade Indian Barakat Allah, the representative of the CUP in Kabul who was in America early in 1914 drumming up support among Moslems there with the backing of 300,000 dollars from the German Foreign Office.

Indian intelligence was alerted to Enver's scheme in August 1914, when a youth arrived at Peshawar from the Khyber Pass and could give no satisfactory account of his purpose. He was searched and his interrogators found, sewn into the lining of his coat, pieces of linen containing messages to Indian Moslem leaders. They were told that 'the call will go forth from Mecca as soon as the Caliph of Islam is at war with Britain'. Had Ibn Saud supported it, such a call might have gone forth with devastating consequences, for the Sharif's son Abdullah had asked the Saudi leader for his guidance following Turkey's declaration.

Shakespear and Ibn Saud had sent a note to Abdullah, advising him to resist the call to *jihad*. To quote Lawrence, who in 1916 was commenting on Shakespear's account of the matter: 'Mecca however kept silent and *Jihad* fell flat . . . Abdullah's ambition, so far as we know, would have been served almost as well one way as another. This letter from Captain Shakespear, however, throws a flood of light on another side, and puts us most deeply in his debt, and in the debt of Ibn Saud.'

Determined to salvage something of his plan, Enver ordered Muhammad Hassan back to India to stir up as much trouble as he could. The Sharif invited him to Mecca before his departure, and remarkably he stayed there under the Sharif's wing, still plotting on Enver's behalf, until late in 1916, when he was eventually interviewed by British intelligence officers. They were astonished to find that the man who intended to raise the cry of holy war in India, to murder untold numbers of men, women and children, was a venerable old man with kindly eyes and a modest bearing. He was sent to Malta for internment.

In August 1915 Philippides Bey, the Chief of Secret Police in Cairo, had submitted to Wingate in Egypt a Secret Service report on the Indo-Egyptian ramifications of the Pan-Islam movement whose political firebrand was Abdal Aziz Shawish, an Egyptian living in Constantinople. The report showed that at the time of the Tripoli war Indian Red Crescent parties sent to provide medical aid were fertile sources of recruitment and conspiracy. Several well-known nationalists and anti-British personalities joined forces with Shawish, including the editor of the *Delhi Camerade*, Muhammad Ali. A number of meetings between Indian and Egyptian student nationalists and Pan-Islamites had been held in Cairo at the *Club des Ecoles Supérieures*, and in Constantinople there were Indian schools under the direction of Shawish, while in Switzerland and Germany, Egyptian Societies known as the 'Sphinx', supplied with money by von Oppenheim's Eastern Bureau, offered a warm welcome to Moslems of all nationalities and the opportunity to undermine the Allied cause. The Shaikh al Islam and the Director of Public Security were among the leading members of the Pan-Islam Party in Constantinople, and two newspapers subsidised by the Government and the CUP, *Turc Pourdi* and *Al Hedayat* circulated widely in Europe, North Africa, Syria, Afghanistan and India. Soldiers in the Egyptian and Indian armies were offered attractive terms to desert to the Turks. In Geneva *La Patrie Egyp-*

tienne carried the appeals of Shawish and the Constantinople leaders, and of Abdurrahman al Riadh their leader in Jerusalem, to Indians who might be tempted by the offer of eventual freedom from the 'imperialist yoke' in return for support for Germany and Turkey. Hall and Thomson in London spent a good deal of their time interviewing Indians passing in and out of Britain on neutral ships, one of whom presented himself at the India Office. 'A poisonous specimen,' commented Sir Arthur Hirtzel, the head of the political and secret department at the India Office, who interviewed him. Thomson successfully uncovered plots to transport arms from America to India, and to murder Kitchener, Marshal Foch and the French Prime Minister by the Berlin Moslem Committee.

But if the Indian malcontents and spies were a nuisance, the German infiltrators in Persia and Afghanistan were proving so great a menace that paranoia afflicted the War Offices in London and Delhi. Wassmuss, still bursting with anger at the conduct of the British consular men at Bushire in the first days of the war, had began to repay the enemy with vengeance and his name had become famous in Secret Service circles.

As the Afghan mission made its way through Persia to its appointed tasks, its members argued and back-stabbed interminably. Their Ambassador at Tehran, Prince Henry of Reuss, confronted by the two expeditions sanctioned by Berlin, Niedermayer's and von Hentig's, confessed in June 1915: 'On some days I am unable to cope with the situation.' Niedermayer, conscientious and difficult as ever, wrote in his diary: 'Somehow we must create for ourselves a reliable intelligence system, and make arrangements to upset the plans of the opposition. Enquiries, newsgathering, propaganda work, piling up provisions of all kinds, including weapons and ammunition.' Von Hentig, the later arrival in Tehran, was contemptuous of his fellow conspirator. 'He has been too long in Tehran, and has lost sight of his objective.' In July a telegram from Berlin to Niedermayer sent both parties on their separate ways. 'Please accelerate expedition plan,' it said.

They left Tehran on successive days in the first week of July, crossing the Dasht-i-Kavir, the Great Salt Desert, without maps to guide them to wells, vulnerable to the robber bands that were the only inhabitants of large tracts of that friendless region. The parties met up at an oasis nearly 300 miles from their starting point and from there decided to make their way across the frontier in small groups to avoid British and Russian troops patrolling the frontier. Niedermayer's group arrived at the frontier town of Kelend on 8 August and made their way to Herat to announce their arrival to the Amir, brother of the Amir of Kabul and all Afghanistan, Habibullah. They and the Germans who followed them found themselves under house arrest, and despite von Hentig's angry protestations they remained in their relatively comfortable prison for a month, forbidden to go beyond the confines of the garden.

When they were finally allowed to leave for Kabul on 6 September they were handed a note from Ambassador Wangenheim in Constantinople containing the proclamation of *jihad* in the name of the Sultan. The German caravan reached the outskirts of Kabul on 1 October 1915, where they were greeted by the Turkish colony of some ten citizens. At the citadel, the famous Bala Hissar where the British Resident and his entire staff were massacred in September 1879, a parade of troops commanded by the Turkish Hauptmann Khairi Bey, heralded their arrival. But the welcome was far from being unqualified. To their disgust the Germans found themselves billeted outside the city as guests of the Amir, who was away at his summer residence among the hills of Paghman since there was a cholera outbreak in Kabul. For nearly a fortnight the letters of Niedermayer and von Hentig to the Amir went unanswered. As they waited and listened, they found that the influence of British India was greater than they had supposed, and that while the Amir's fanatical son Nasrullah was in favour of *jihad* and an attack on India, the Amir himself was in correspondence with the Viceroy and had given a pledge of neutrality. On 13 October the Germans and Turks were taken in two motor cars to the summer residence, where they found Habibullah polite and interested in the practical advantages of siding with Germany, but positively uninterested in holy war. A subsequent meeting held out no more hope than the first. The bigoted, anti-British Nasrullah still favoured a belligerent policy, but the War Minister and the Amir himself were totally opposed to their plan.

The German agents remained for nearly six months in Afghanistan, trying their utmost to cajole the Amir into war, and arguing bitterly among themselves. On 12 March 1916 the Amir stated firmly that he had no intention of being drawn into war, but that he would permit a German or Turkish army of perhaps 20,000 men to attack Baluchistan from his territory. Britain had

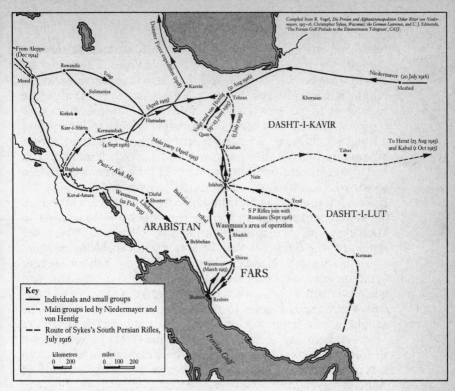

Map 10   Routes of German agents through Mesopotamia and Persia
to Afghanistan, 1914–15

given the Amir 40,000 rupees to encourage his neutrality and
with that incentive he proved as good as his word. In March the
expedition began to break up. Pathans from the North-West
Frontier region who had been sent with von Hentig returned to
their homes. In May, Niedermayer, von Hentig, Wagner, Roehr
and others of this discordant party left Kabul. The most courageous and resourceful part of the journey was yet to begin, for
von Hentig and Roehr went across the Hindu Kush to the
Pamir plateau and into Chinese Turkestan, and eventually to
China itself, running the gauntlet of Russian agents who knew
of their purpose and route. They proceeded to Peking via Kashgar, and helped the Consul there to organise Chinese raids on
Russia's trans-Siberian railway. They avoided capture and death
on many occasions, once by seeking sanctuary with a Swedish
missionary named Tornquist. They eventually travelled home
from Shanghai on 1 April 1917, on an American ship, arriving in

New York late in May after one of the epic overland journeys of the war.

Niedermayer and Wagner left their fellow countrymen in the Hindu Kush and went in disguise along the Amu Dariya, the river Oxus of old, into Russian Turkestan. They could not have returned the way they came for British and Russian forces were waiting for them. At Mazar-i-Sharif inside the Afghan border Wagner turned south-west towards Herat. Niedermayer, with henna-dyed beard and a tempting gold crown removed from a tooth, went on by horse through Russian territory, across the Kara Kum into Persia and the holy city of Meshed. He arrived in Tehran on 20 July 1916, and from there he journeyed to Hamadan, just recaptured from the Russians, where he remained with the agent Nadoly, tired and incapable of exertion. In January 1917 Nadoly informed Berlin: 'Oberstleutnant Niedermayer, whose nerve has completely broken, and can taken no further part against enemy, yesterday arrived in Baghdad where he has gone to recuperate. Have advised that he should be sent home to Germany.' He went home in February.

Other members of that ill-fated German expedition were not so fortunate. Voigt, accompanied by several Indian agents and servants, had made for Kerman across the Khash desert of Afghanistan and the Dasht-i-Lut desert of Persia. Voigt became ill with dysentery and the party was captured in August by Persians who were probably tipped off by British agents, for by then Percy Sykes's South Persia Rifles had taken Kerman. The Indians were shot and Voigt was taken prisoner. Peter Paschen was captured by Persians and handed over to the Russians in July 1916.

The hapless youth who occupied the 'Peacock' throne in Tehran was powerless to intervene as the warring parties fought their bitter clandestine battles across his territory. At Qum, virtually the German capital in Persia, Prince Henry of Reuss presided over the malevolent conflict of Turk and Teuton, failing to understand, as did most of his countrymen, the enmity between the Sunni Moslems of the Ottoman army and the Shia of Persia. In Isfahan Bakhtiari tribesmen and a pro-German Chilean revolutionary, Pugin, who had joined Oppenheim's Eastern service maintained an hilarious commune, running the ancient city like embryonic Castros.

As the Russians returned in May 1916 to the Caucasus strategy that had so nearly succeeded in 1915, and the Cossacks rode down to Tehran and then through the length of Persia to present their compliments to the British at Basra, and as Percy Sykes's Persian Rifles swept across the southern region, almost all the German agents were killed or captured. Field-Marshal von der Goltz had visited Kermanshah in November 1915, just after taking over command of the Ottoman Sixth army in Mesopotamia. The Germans had by that time trapped a British Force under General Townshend at Kut-al-Amara on the Tigris, and the Field-Marshal confidently advised that 'after Kut the Turks should advance into Persia'. In January 1916 his advice was taken and a force led by Colonel Konitz attacked the Russians, then in control of Hamadan. The Germans were defeated and Konitz committed suicide. Von der Goltz wrote after the event: 'There is nothing to be done in Persia; there is nothing but dust, cupidity and cowardice.'

But Wassmuss, operating from a fine house 7,000 feet above sea level at Shiraz, protected by the Swedish-led *gendarmerie*, did more on his own than an army could have achieved. He roamed the country at will, taking desert and mountain pass in his stride, subverting the tribal leaders to his cause, and striving by his contact with the *mujahaddin*, the 'Fighters for *jihad*', to bring all the rebels of the hot-headed south into concert.

9

The *Intrusives*

To every ruler of Arabia, to the Iman of Yemen, Husain, the Rashids, Ajaimi, Muntafiq, Mubarak and Ibn Saud, agents of both sides came, official and secret, with promises of gold and good things in exchange for an alliance.

H. C. Armstrong, *Lord of Arabia.*

'In all wars rumours romp and individuals are unjustly maligned; but the suspicions, credulity and inequity of the civilians during the first world war were in excess of any similar emotions provoked by the even greater and more immediate perils of 1940.' So wrote Harold Nicolson, and with authority, for he worked as a civilian in both conflicts, alongside the decision-makers.

Kitchener's successor in Cairo, Sir Henry McMahon, friend and fellow Grand Master in Masonry of the one-time Commander-in-Chief in India, arrived at his new station in December 1914. Until that moment, during the first five months of war, Kitchener had remained the titular Resident and Consul-General, making his decisions by proxy through the acting Resident, Milne Cheetham, conducting the affairs of Britain in the Near East as though he were still the uncrowned king of Egypt.

'We deprecated the Imperative, preferring the Subjunctive, even the wistful, Optative mood,' wrote Ronald Storrs, 'Britain had always fought for a Protectorate as against annexation; had advised, inspected, never ordered.' During the polite, hard-working regime of Eldon Gorst that may have been so. But it was hardly true of Cromer before or Kitchener after. Even before McMahon had been able to take up his new appointment the War Minister in London used the Imperative. In September the Cabinet decided to annexe Egypt, though it used the

word 'Protectorate', and the acting Resident was instructed by
Sir Edward Grey to demand the abdication of the Khedive
Abbas Hilmi, who had ruled since 1892 under the firman of the
Sultan of Constantinople which made the throne of Egypt hereditary within the family of Muhammad Ali. Kitchener had never
been able to abide the Khedive. Husain Kamil, the despised
uncle of the ruler, was put on the throne by Britain and was
given the title Sultan. He was told that the Khedival princes
would henceforth make the first call on Britain's emissary.
Husain Kamil's lips trembled with indignation according to
Storrs, who, with Cheetham, conveyed the news.

McMahon made a good impression. At his reception party a
prominent Copt observed, 'His eye is kindly.' Slight, fair,
young-looking for his fifty-two years, friendly and of quiet, cautious disposition, he represented a marked contrast to the man
who had gone before him. And unlike his predecessor he was
married, so that his subordinates and his Egyptian guests were
able to enjoy the 'generous and charming hospitality' of Lady
McMahon, presided over by the Jeeves-like butler, Jones, who
was once heard to remark to a woman guest: 'May I venture to
suggest to your ladyship a leetle less powder on the left nostril?'
But the High Commissioner inherited more than the problems
of protocol and hospitality. He was fully aware of what had been
happening before his arrival. Indeed he had dived into the deep
end on his way to Egypt. Kitchener's first message to the
Sharif's son, Abdullah, was dated 24 September 1914. It was
addressed to Milne Cheetham, the acting Resident.

> Tell Storrs to send secret and carefully chosen messenger
> from me to Sharif Abdullah to ascertain whether should
> present armed German influence at Constantinople coerce
> Calif against his will and Sublime Porte to acts of aggression
> and war against Great Britain, he and his father and Arabs
> of Hijaz will be with us or against us.

A great feast has been made by historians of the affair which
began with that message to a son of the family of the Sharif, the
Hashemites of Mecca. Indeed the liaison had an earlier provenance, for in the first days of 1914 Abdullah called on Kitchener
in Cairo, dressed in the 'pure silk robes of a prince of Mecca', to
question him 'on the British attitude to an Arab revolt'. It was a
different rebellion of which Abdullah spoke then, and Britain's

reponse was said to be unfavourable, though following an appeal
from Aziz Ali al Masri in October the Viceroy was later to tell
London that a great deal depended on the attitude of Ibn Saud.
'If under his leadership Arab revolution appears imminent and
spontaneous, we should I think assist it.' Husain's son returned
to Cairo in April to visit the Khedive, following an interview with
Enver. He had a secret meeting with Storrs at the Khedive's
Abdin Palace, and asked for an agreement between Britain and
his father similar to that between the Amir of Afghanistan and
the Government of India, in order to maintain the *status quo* in
the Arabian peninsula. The Hashemite family seems to have
been more concerned with the prospect of Ibn Saud's leadership of the Arabs than with action against the Turks.

Sharif Husain was far from being ready to commit himself to
either side by the dawn of 1915. His third son, Faisal, was deeply
immersed in the plans of von Oppenheim, Enver and Jamal, and
Abdullah, his second son, was in touch with a very special messenger, Izzat Pasha Holo. The Syrian and Mesopotamian
'Committees' meanwhile turned to him for support for a planned uprising.

McMahon's release by the Indian Government to take up the
appointment of High Commissioner in Cairo was approved by
the Viceroy on 17 December 1914. Next day the Foreign Office
confirmed his new job. In the preceding fortnight France had
caused alarm in Whitehall by proposing joint talks on the future
of Arabia. It became a matter of the utmost urgency for Britain
to establish its position with the most influential Arab princes,
and though the Sharif Husain had not been forthcoming since
Kitchener's correspondence with his son earlier in the year, the
decision had already been made to pursue him rather than per-
severe with Ibn Saud as the Indian Government would have
preferred. On his way to Cairo in December McMahon visited
Paris, where the instrument of the Foreign Office plan, Izzat
Pasha, was in exile. Izzat, who as the Sultan's second secretary
had been responsible for raising the religious funds throughout
Islam which financed the Hijaz rail scheme, had tried to buy his
way into the confidence of the Young Turks after the 1908 *coup*.
But he discovered that they were intent on bleeding him dry. He
found asylum in Nice and Paris, though he returned to his home
in Damascus to try to make amends with the CUP. He kept in
touch with old friends and new, especially the Sharif.

The Ottoman Empire had no further use for him, however,

and he returned to Paris to live luxuriously on the fortune he had made in Abdal Hamid's service. Following McMahon's call he went hurriedly to London and called at the Foreign Office on 1 January 1915, where he 'explained his views as to the future of the Caliphate'. He laid much stress on the illegitimacy of the Ottoman Caliphate and on the hatred of the Arabs for the Turks, and suggested the creation of an Arab Caliphate under the Sharif to serve as a focus and to centralise disruptive Arab elements in the Ottoman Empire. He proposed to visit Cairo to arrange meetings between McMahon and the Sharif's son. Sir Edward Grey remarked, 'subject to Lord Crewe's concurrence', HMG should tell Izzat that Britain 'would give support to an Arab Caliphate of the true race, but that the matter was for Moslems'. A copy of Grey's note was sent to Kitchener, who at the end of November 1914 had made a secret visit to Dunkirk to meet 'French politicians'. The India Office told the Foreign Office that Lord Crewe was 'most unwilling that HMG should commit themselves . . . to an Arab Caliphate of the true race'. It would not be 'agreeable to other Arab rulers'. In January McMahon told the Foreign Office that he agreed that Izzat should not be encouraged to visit Cairo. Nevertheless, Izzat kept in touch with Abdullah and with McMahon. 'He might be made use of,' said Hirtzel of the India Office. He added, 'he is, or was, an ardent Pan-Islamist', and they must avoid 'the substitution for an Ottoman Pan-Islam of what would be infinitely more dangerous, an Arab Pan-Islam'.

It was not until August 1915 that McMahon himself entered into correspondence with the Sharif, after a number of communications between Storrs and Abdullah had been exchanged, and in response to a document from Mecca which contained crucial assertions of Sharifian authority in the Arab world.

The Sharif had written to Storrs, 'The dear Honourable, may God protect him', on 14 July, saying: 'Kindly do not send any correspondence until you see the result of our operations; except the reply to the note and its enclosure, which should be through the bearer only.' The enclosure was unsigned and undated. It contained the words:

> the Arab nation sees fit to limit themselves [sic], as time is short, to asking the Government of Great Britain, if it should think fit, for the approval, through her deputy or representative, of the following fundamenal propositions,

leaving out all things considered secondary in comparison with them, so that it may prepare all means necessary for attaining this noble purpose, until such time as it finds occasion for making actual negotiations.

Allowing for Storrs's lazy translation, which was usually the work of little Ruhi, the son-in-law of Storrs's messenger Ali, and hardly ever given grammatical polish, the implications of what was by now a cumulative essay in political match-making, were clear enough. There followed a number of conditions. Firstly, England was to acknowledge the independence of the Arab countries, bounded on the north by Mersina-Adana up to the 37° of latitude, on which degree fall Birijik, Urfa, Mardin, Midiat, Amadia Island, up to the border of Persia; on the east by the borders of Persia up to the Gulf of Basra; on the south by the Indian Ocean, with the exception of the position of Aden to remain as it is; on the west by the Red Sea, the Mediterranean Sea up to Mersina. England was to approve the proclamation of an Arab Caliphate of Islam. There were in all six conditions relating to the matter which, in his covering note, the Sharif said 'is now decided'.

In its final paragraph the document which was attached to Husain's letter to Storrs read:

Consequently, the whole of the Arab nation have (praise be to God) agreed and united for the attainment, at all costs and finally, of this noble object, they beg the Government of Great Britain to answer them positively or negatively in a period of thirty days after receiving this intimation; and if this period should lapse before they receive an answer, they reserve to themselves complete freedom of action. Moreover, we [Sharif's family] will consider ourselves free in word and deed from the bonds of our previous declaration which we made through Ali Effendi.

The messenger now was a Shaikh of the Harb tribe, Muhammad ibn Arif Araifan, codenamed 'O', and the Turks were anxious to intercept him, for they knew that he was going in and out of Mecca on secretive missions.

McMahon's reply of 30 August, which 'O' carried to Mecca, was brief. It simply confirmed Kitchener's message, 'delivered to you by the hand of Ali Effendi', in which was stated 'clearly our desire for the independence of Arabia and its inhabitants, together with our approval of the Arab Caliphate when it should be proclaimed'. He went on:

> With regard to the question of limits, frontiers and bound-aries, it would appear to be premature to consume our time in discussing such details in the heat of war, and while, in many portions of them, the Turk is up to now in effective occupation; especially as we have learnt, with surprise and regret, that some of the Arabs in those very parts, far from fassisting us, are neglecting this their supreme opportunity.

Four days earlier, the High Commissioner had written to Sir Edward Grey: 'The moment has not yet arrived when we can usefully discuss even a preliminary agreement, and it might at this stage injure the Sharif's chance of the Caliphate to advertise his dealings with us.' McMahon was new to the game, but he had been Foreign Secretary in the Indian Government when detailed discussions were going on about the Arab lands. He should have known that politically and geographically there is no such place as 'Arabia'. He should have known too that for a Christian country to meddle in the matter of the Caliphate of Islam was both presumptuous and futile.

Boundaries had been drawn already in the mind of the Sharif, however, and the concept of an Arab nation under a Caliph of the Hashemite house had taken root in his thoughts, if indeed it was not planted there before. It was a notion which few Arabs had entertained since the destruction of the last Arab Caliphate when Hulaga's Tartar horde sacked Baghdad in the thirteenth century. Yet it was a notion which a self-appointed caucus of Britons in Cairo took up with alacrity, though they had not so much as consulted the one Arab prince with tribal support enough to make rebellion practicable, Ibn Saud.

War and the destruction of the Pan-Arab secret societies made a tribal rebellion inconceivable. In the changed climate, Britons who once believed that Ottoman rule was preferable to any feasible alternative became the perpetrators of a new revolu-tionary scheme and chose Husain of Mecca as its vehicle. That France would not hear of such an arrangement, that Ibn Saud in his disillusionment would do nothing to support it, and that most Arabs would as soon embrace the devil as Husain, the vas-sal of the Turk, seems not to have occurred to them.

The position of Ibn Saud in all this was crucial, a fact which seems to have been apparent to the Central Powers at an early stage of the war, for Musil's last act before leaving Najd in March 1915 to go on to Baghdad had been to write to both the Saudi leader and to his father, the Imam. He pleaded with both, as instructed by Enver, to make peace with Ibn Rashid, and to Ibn Saud he wrote: 'Please do not support him [Faisal ibn Hamud] and his relatives. Do not raid the Shammar and thus fan the flames of civil war.' The letters were signed with the signet rings of several tribal chiefs and sent to Ibn Saud at Marbat al Faras, where he was at camp after the battle of Jarab.

The irresponsible young Amir of Hail was an insignificant force when war came. He was a nuisance even to the Turks, rendering them 'no energetic aid' in Musil's words, and in 1915 he succeeded in wiping out twenty-nine of his clansmen, so that of the descendants of the founder of the Rashid dynasty only two youths apart from himself were alive in Hail, and they trembled for their lives. The irascible Faisal was with Ibn Saud, of course, and the repugnant minister Saud ibn Subhan had taken himself off to Najaf to seek the sanctuary of the Euphrates tribes. The tribes of Ibn Rashid were deserting to Ibn Saud and Faisal ibn Hamud. But the Saudi Amir was not yet ready to depose Ibn Rashid. Rejected by Britain in favour of the Sharif, Ibn Saud was content to bide his time.

When McMahon grasped the nettle of the Sharifian Revolt in August, the plan had come to fruition. Only the inflections had to be added to the promises already made, the bargains already struck on Kitchener's initiative. Yet McMahon was to be held responsible for what happened, and he seems to have had a premonition that he would be called to task in the end, for he insisted that all the important documents relating to the affair should be kept in chronological order and bound into volumes so that the record would be clear to any politician who sought a scapegoat in years to come. It did him little good. For fifty years his testimony remained in the official file of the Foreign Office, unavailable to the world at large and, in any case, too massive in content for anyone but the most leisured scholar to absorb, certainly too voluminous for the busy politician in office to digest, while blame was heaped on him; and others basked in the sunshine of contingent battles.

Among the earliest volunteers for service in France in August 1914 was Colonel Stewart Newcombe. He was awarded the

DSO for his gallantry on the Western Front, and at the end of 1914 the General Staff ordered his return to London for a 'special' assignment. Lawrence, George Lloyd and Woolley had been kicking their heels in London since the outbreak of hostilities with Germany, waiting for word from Hogarth, who was working in Cairo for 'Blinker' Hall at the Admiralty and carrying the honorary rank of Lieutenant-Commander RNVR. At the beginning of December they were ordered to proceed to Cairo under Newcombe's command. On arrival they were to report to the Director of Military Intelligence, Lieutenant-Colonel 'Bertie' Clayton. They sailed from Marseilles on 9 December 1914 and arrived at GHQ, the Savoy Hotel in Cairo, in time to spend Christmas with Ronald Storrs, Aubrey Herbert and Philip Graves, after making themselves known to the Sirdar, Wingate, and the DMI, Clayton.

It was an amorphous group which formed around Wingate and Clayton in Cairo, rushing hither and thither through the staff offices in the Savoy Hotel (next door to their dormitory, the Grand Continental), which Herbert likened to an Oriental railway station.

> We were not many; and nearly all of us rallied round Clayton, the chief of Intelligence, civil and military, in Egypt, Clayton made the perfect leader for such a band of wild men as we were. He was calm, detached, clearsighted, of unconscious courage in assuming responsibility ... he impressed men by his sobriety, and by a certain quiet and stately moderation of hope ... The first among us was Ronald Storrs, Oriental Secretary of the Residency, the most brilliant Englishman in the Near East, and subtly efficient, despite his diversion of energy in love of music and letters, of sculpture, painting of whatever was beautiful in the world's fruit ... George Lloyd entered our number ... We would not have done so much so soon without his partnership ... a restless soul, avid rather to taste than exhaust.

Mark Sykes, 'a bundle of prejudices, intuitions, half sciences', whose 'instincts lay in parody ... a caricaturist rather than artist, even in statesmanship'; Hogarth, 'our father confessor and adviser, who brought us the parallels and lessons of history'; Cornwallis, 'a man rude to look upon, but apparently forged from one of those incredible metals with a melting point of thousands of degrees'; Newcombe, Parker, Herbert, Graves, 'all of the creed, and labouring stoutly after their fashion'. Here was the cast, 'a band of wild men', set down by Lawrence, who was 'all claws and teeth', portrayed with a vigour that was to shroud events in the Middle East then and for a long time to come in shimmering, pervasive half truths. But not all those he named should be included among the 'wild men' – Newcombe, Parker and Graves were perfectly loyal staff officers.

They adopted the code name *Intrusive*, appositely, for they set themselves illicit tasks that were unique in the annals of war. All were staff officers at GHQ Cairo, subject to the disciplines of a wartime force and to the orders of the General Officer Commanding, General Maxwell, but they devised their own plan of campaign, chose their own chiefs, established their own ambitions and objectives, and pushed and plotted until Whitehall and the army commanders were enmeshed in a web which Kitchener had begun to weave in Cairo and which they resolved to finish.

Lawrence, the catalytic junior of the Cairo brigade, had to wait a year and more before his opportunity came; before a political adventure was turned to military endeavour and he was given the chance to move with an Arab army and carve for himself a niche in history. For the moment he was the backroom doctrinaire; as an historian of the Middle East was to dub him 'a doctrinaire without a doctrine'. It is interesting to recount an enemy eye-view of the brilliant and assertive Lawrence, a view formed as the Germans repaid the compliment of Hogarth's desert intelligence service and sent back their own impressions to the Oriental Bureau of the Foreign Office in Wilhelmstrasse: 'Not a man for deeds. No soldier, no natural leader of men, though he had the capacity when the need arose to weave complicated patterns. A dreamer, a man of fantasy, a secretive scholar.' The German files recorded later: 'The English officer Newcombe chose Lawrence as his companion and in December he arrived in Cairo, where he was engaged in map work and other military intelligence activities (to record and mislead Turkish troops for instance).'

The actions of the *Intrusives* were not of a conventional order. They conceived a political aim and made their own contacts and desert journeys in order to realise it. Many of their agents and co-conspirators were in Turkish-held territory, vulnerable to any indiscretion. Never before or since has there been so tragi-comic or, on occasions, so farcical an episode in the recorded history of war. But these were no ordinary soldiers. In the main they were civilians dressed in uniform, usually ill-fitting and ragtag. The only professional soldiers involved were Parker and Newcombe, and they must be cleared of any culpability, for they acted with conspicuous gallantry under the orders of the GOC, General Maxwell, in the formative stages of the 'Arab Revolt', and were not involved in the political game.

As for the *Intrusives* in general, it was the Chief of counter-intelligence on the Wehrmacht General Staff, Colonel Nicolai, who, in a criticism of his own country's methods, put his finger obliquely on the folly of those antics in Cairo which were to result in high-level political and military dissension in war, in the making of illegitimate promises, and the creation of nation states which would plague mankind for ever after. Writing of German foreign intelligence, he said that it was 'disruptive by habit. It played the spy-game much as Britain's Arab Bureau'.

Lawrence's account of the proceedings in which he, Storrs, Hogarth, George Lloyd and Herbert were the prime movers, powerfully abetted by Kitchener and Sykes in London, was not entirely accurate; neither was his version of the Cairo pecking order. But he had the gift of putting complex matters in a nutshell:

Therefore from our hybrid intelligence office in Cairo . . . we began to work upon all chiefs, far and near, Sir Henry McMahon, High Commissioner in Egypt, was, of course, our first effort; and his shrewd insight and tried, experienced mind understood our design at once and judged it good. Others, like Wemyss, Neil Malcolm, Wingate supported us in their pleasure at seeing the war turned constructive. Their advocacy confirmed in Lord Kitchener the favourable impression he had derived from years before when Sharif Abdullah appealed to him in Egypt; and so McMahon at last achieved our foundation stone, the understanding with the Sharif of Mecca.

For almost a year, the 'wild men' twiddled their thumbs in Cairo and Alexandria, doing a little map work and helping Hogarth to construct a 'Blue Book' on the tribes of Arabia, mostly with the aid of information supplied by Colonels Parker and Jennings Bramley.

Cairo and Alexandria were not the best places to be in June 1915.

It was so hot even at night that most of the European residents slept on camp beds on roofs and in gardens. Both cities were packed with the Australian and New Zealand troops who waited their turn for the bloodbath of Gallipoli, many of them making merry for the last time in their lives. It was the month in which Mark Sykes made the first of several wartime visits to Egypt as Kitchener's personal nominee on the inter-departmental committee set up under the chairmanship of Maurice De Bunsen to consider the future of the Ottoman Empire. 'I acted, Fitzgerald spoke, he [Kitchener] inspired.' As would be expected by anyone who knew him, Sykes's part in the proceedings was dynamic. By the fourth meeting he had provided the committee with plans and maps offering two possible solutions, the first demanding the partition of the entire Empire except for Anatolia among the Allies, the second involving nominal independence with European control of political and commercial interests. Either solution accommodated a British railway running for about a thousand miles between Haifa and Rowandiz.

Thus he was well equipped with a detailed plan by the time he arrived in the Mediterranean, where he had talks with Sir Ian Hamilton, then Commander of the 29th Division at Gallipoli, and with Valentine Chirol in Crete. Chirol, whose work for *The Times* had for several years been carried out against a background of intelligence work on behalf of the Foreign Office, had been banished from the foreign editorship of that newspaper by Lord Northcliffe, and was now working his way towards Delhi to set up as a freelance correspondent in the Indian capital. In Sofia, Sykes called on Fitzmaurice, still keeping abreast of events in the Balkans and in Turkey, and living between German spies placed on either side of his own house. In Cairo, Sykes made contact with the men who were to share with him the questionable fame of authorship in the division of the Arab lands and the gift of kingship.

On 14 July he wrote to the DMO in London, summarising the drift of enemy intelligence activity and the gist of Anglo-French controversy:

Just as our enemy's agents work upon conscious and unconscious instruments to keep Bulgaria and Greece in permanent opposition, in order to prevent them from combining to assist us, and by the same means endeavour to disseminate mutual suspicions in the minds of Russian and British peoples in regard to the fate of Constantinople, so it is obvious that the same forces are at work to provoke discord between ourselves and France with regard to Syria ... the idea is abroad, that Great Britain and France each desire the whole of Syria from Al Arish to Alexandretta for themselves.

Sykes regarded the Cairene atmosphere of 'suspected rivalry' between French and British interests as being due to the activities of Franco-Levantine financiers, and to Swiss forces in touch with the 'ramifications of German Constantinople finance'. CUP agents were claiming that Great Britain intended to take Syria. He was able to cite only a single newspaper article in support of these allegations. But he need have looked no farther than the men around him to find the source of the Francophobia that became apparent to him almost from the moment he took up residence at Shepheard's Hotel. He was in Cairo at the time of the first meeting of the Dardanelles Committee in London, and of Balfour's takeover from Churchill at the Admiralty. As a Roman Catholic and a firm believer in the spread of European civilisation in those parts of the East which he had come to know, and generally to dislike in his youth, Sykes was not a natural or instinctive opponent of the French claim to the guardianship of western interests in Syria; a claim which stemmed back to the Crusades. But it did not take long for Storrs, Wingate, Hogarth and their 'super-cerebral companion', Lawrence, to convince him that 'with France out of the way' Mesopotamia, Palestine and Syria could be 'controlled by Great Britain, administered as one unit ... united by language and financially self-supporting ... under the nominal rule of the Sultan of Egypt and the spiritual dominion of the Sharif of Mecca'.

The staff of General Wingate, Sirdar of the Egyptian army, were now entirely convinced of the Sharif's utility to the Allied cause, and the Sirdar had begun to take the lead in promoting his virtues, sending long, detailed and not always accurate accounts of the Sharif's sterling qualities to London. During Sykes's visit Wingate's private secretary, Captain Symes, sent a statement to the War Office 'given by a well-educated and intelligent member of a famous (Sharifian) family', explaining that Husain had 'terrified' the Turk into recognising his authority in the Hijaz, an act which 'gave satisfaction to all the Arabs and

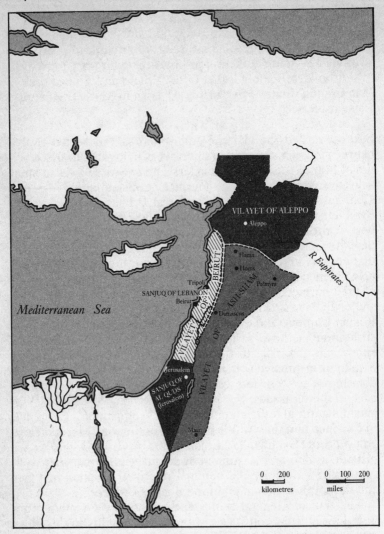

Map II   The administrative regions of Ottoman Syria

Chiefs of the Hijaz', and that the Wali himself, in order to gain favour, 'had kissed his hand publicly in front of the inhabitants'.

Just before Newcombe's party left Southampton to make their connection at Marseilles, on 5 December, a young Christian Arab, Charles Boutagy, fled from his home in Haifa aboard an

Italian ship bound for Port Said. He made his way to Cairo, where he was interviewed by Clayton following an application to join the British army. It is faithfully recorded that within a few days of his arrival in Cairo Lawrence was already creating his own network and had made contact with Boutagy, his 'first wartime agent'. In fact Boutagy was already at work when Lawrence turned up. Clayton was quite clear about the tasks assigned to his assistants in the early days of the intelligence office. 'Newcombe organised a spy service. Herbert concentrated on the secret police. Woolley specialised in propaganda. Lawrence, in many ways the least of this remarkable group of men, was in theory a cartographer.' In practice he was mostly engaged in report writing for Hogarth. 'As their leader, Clayton wanted the truth, not myths . . . each of the experts knew the general context in which they were to fit their specialities.'

As for his employment of Boutagy as an agent, Lawrence's legion of uncritical admirers, and some of his detractors, must take the blame for turning the recollections of the Christian Syrian agent when he had reached old age into assertions of fact. Some sixty years after the events in question, when Lawrence's name had been blazoned by publishers and propagandists to all corners of the world, Boutagy stated that he had been 'trained for his missions by Lawrence personally'. In fact it was Newcombe who, before the war and from early 1915, was responsible for the appointment of all Syrian agents, and it was Woolley under whom Boutagy served, through the Mediterranean station of Eastern Force at Port Said. Of course, Cairo, Port Said and Alexandria worked closely together, but Lawrence, living at the Grand Continental Hotel and working at the Savoy next door, had no part in their espionage work. On one occasion Woolley decided to send the young Boutagy back to Haifa on his 'spy' ship *Zaida*, Lord Rosebery's yacht in pre-war days, in order to meet his father, formerly the assistant British Consul at the port. In a laughable mix up Boutagy senior was arrested by the Turks and was charged with 'acting suspiciously'. He was found not guilty. From that event has grown up the idea that Charles Boutagy, who was indeed a brilliant agent (who had exceptional musical gifts which he used for constructing unbreakable cyphers), was Lawrence's agent. He was nothing of the kind. Lawrence was more concerned in 1915 with political machinations, and with the plans being hatched by Ronald Storrs and Mark Sykes.

Storrs and Sykes had a ready rapport. They had met as young men in London and both had attended the lectures of the distinguished Orientalist, Professor Browne, at Cambridge. Sykes was predisposed to take seriously the claims of the Sharif, which were urged on him by Storrs and Clayton. There were even closer links, however. Like Sykes and their chief in London, General Macdonogh, the DMI Cairo was a Catholic, as was the cryptic eminence of Turkish affairs, Fitzmaurice, so there was an early foundation of philosophical concord in what had become a close working relationship.

On one of the several evenings which they spent together, Sykes demonstrated to his host that as well as being one of the few MPs who could fill the House of Commons, an artist of outstanding ability, and a writer of immense if somewhat haphazard skill, he was also a remarkable comedian. He performed a twenty-minute parliamentary debate into Storrs's dictaphone (Storrs supplying the interruptions), with Lloyd George, F. E. Smith, John Redmond and Edward Carson (on the Irish question) among the character parts. Then they did a three-act melodrama together, making up the act as they went along with Storrs providing a musical background, Sykes doing the trotting of horses, the cracking of whips, and so on.

It was a visit to be remembered, interrupted by a journey to Aden, where the pro-Turkish tribes of the Yemen under Yahya, the 'Pope-King' of Arabia Felix, were having a great deal of success in stirring up religious feeling, so that Britain had been compelled to send reinforcements. Sykes talked to Arab prisoners of war there, and was angry to discover that they were being detained on the instructions of the Indian Government when they might be 'grist to Cairo's Arab mill'. Sykes, who to his anger was taken for an abusive Austrian spy at Port Said, had been preceded on the voyage down the Red Sea by Storrs.

Like many of the intellectuals gathered in Cairo, Storrs had a sneaking desire to prove himself in the desert, to emulate the great Victorians and follow the paths of contemporary travellers such as Shakespear, Leachman and Gertrude Bell. However he was an unmitigated disaster whenever he set foot outside the metropolitan centres of the east. At the time of his arrival with Admiral Wemyss aboard HMS *Euryalus* the Turks were threatening the border region between Aden and Asir controlled by the Sultan of Lahaj, Britain's only Arab friend in the conflict. Storrs accompanied a posse of British troops sent into Lahaj to intercept a Turkish raiding party. One of the warriors saw a suspicious movement on the balcony of the Sultan's palace, took careful aim and fired. Britain's sole ally in the south-east of Arabia lay dead, killed in the act of welcoming his guests. Storrs arrived back in Cairo late in August to take up the threads of the Sharif affair.

Sykes had proceeded to India, where he was treading energetically on the corns of the Viceroy, Lord Hardinge, a man twenty years his senior who had been Permanent Under-Secretary at the Foreign Office before his appointment to Delhi and who was, therefore, no stranger to political and diplomatic in-fighting. Hardinge kept his temper and his counsel while Sykes pored over the De Bunsen Report and outlined the schemes of Cairo, of which he knew more than his visitor might have suspected. In a letter to Valentine Chirol the Viceroy wrote: 'Sykes takes himself very seriously. He knows a great deal, but he seems unduly impressed with the importance of the Syrian Arabs.' And to Austen Chamberlain he expressed disapproval of the devolutionary proposal for Asiatic Turkey in the De Bunsen Report: 'Sykes did not seem able to grasp the fact that there are parts of Turkey [the Ottoman Empire] unfit for representative institutions.' Sykes, for his part, was disappointed with India and angered by the Viceroy's failure to grasp the merits of the schemes upon which he was now set.

From the moment Turkey entered the war, the Indian Government was faced with problems which politicians in London and political meddlers in Cairo seemed unable to comprehend. India's Moslem population was the largest in the world, dwarfing the combined populations of the Arab territories. And it was chiefly orthodox in its following, adhering to the Sunni faith, following strictly the words of the Prophet as set down in the Koran and the *Haditha* (Traditions), and accepting the Caliphate of the Ottoman Sultan, for whom they prayed regularly. They had no wish to fight the 'Soldiers of the Prophet', or to associate with the Shia Moslems of Persia and Mesopotamia whom they looked on with rather less liking than on the infidel European. The idea that some enthusiast in Egypt might lead a force into the Hijaz and precipitate a clash in which the Islamic holy of holies was damaged or desecrated was a recurrent nightmare to the Viceroy and his Government, and he warned from the beginning about the dangers inherent in the Sharif business. He described the plans of the Sharif lobby in Cairo, put to him by

Sykes, as 'absolutely fantastic' and 'perfectly fatal' in a communication to Austen Chamberlain on 6 August 1915.

Despite understandable religious reservations, the Indian troops fought with all their customary bravery and loyalty from the outset. In France and Gallipoli, Mesopotamia and at Suez, Moslem and Hindu had fought side by side and with distinction. There had been a few desertions and one serious mutiny; but white troops too had mutinied at Gallipoli. Inhuman and superhuman feats were being asked of men of many races in that first terrible year of war and it is not surprising that a few demurred. Sykes went on to Mesopotamia in September in time to see the army under General Townshend seize Kut-al-Amara. He met an old soldier of the Turkish army taken prisoner there who could not get over the fact that he was fighting alongside the Germans against the British. 'Ingliz fighting Osmanlis,' he remarked sadly, and he told Sykes: 'The Germans used to fill their ditches and kill us to defend the railway they have stolen from us.' It was good propaganda material for Sykes to take back with him. But his mind was made up. He was a convinced Sharifite now, and nothing would persuade him to approach the Arab question cautiously. As Arnold Wilson, Cox's deputy and one of the ablest administrators in the east, wrote of Sykes after meeting him in Mesopotamia, he 'had come with his mind made up, and he set himself to discover facts in favour of his preconceived notions'.

By December 1914 the Indian War Office had sent three expeditionary forces abroad, including some of its best officers and its finest regiments: the Gurkhas, Rajputs, Maharattas, Guides, Lancers and Cavalry. It had sent more than 14,000 horses with its cavalry units. And since that date repeated demands had been made on its trained resources for service in France, Gallipoli and, most importantly, Mesopotamia. Yet there was an ever-present danger of trouble at home and on the North-West Frontier, and Hardinge warned repeatedly that the drain on his resources imposed by Kitchener was leaving the sub-continent dangerously denuded of trained men of assured loyalty. He had no desire to become involved in the schemes of the British Pan-Arabists.

However, all imperial policy was now dictated by the decision of a meeting of the War Council just before it changed its name to the Dardanelles Committee, on 19 March 1915. In a discussion on the break-up of the Ottoman Empire, Grey asked for clarification of the 'Independent Moslem State' which was to include 'Arabia, Syria and Mesopotamia'. Lord Crewe, the Secretary of State for India, replied that there were two views within the India Office: the military faction preferring a strong Turkey in Asia as a bulwark against Russian and other European ambitions, the 'politicals' desiring an 'autonomous Arabia'. Kitchener agreed with the Political Department's view: transfer the Caliphate from Constantinople to Mecca under British control. If the Turkish Empire was to be sustained the Caliphate would eventually fall under the Czar's dominion, and Russia might assert itself over the Moslems of India. Haldane as always played a lone hand. It would be 'wrong to crush Germany and Turkey at the end of the war', he said. Asquith felt that it would be a 'dereliction of duty to leave others to scramble for the remains of Turkey without taking something for ourselves'. If a pun was intended there is no record that anyone laughed. At the end of the discussion a resolution was passed which read in its essential part: 'after the Straits had been forced, and Constantinople had passed into the hands of the Allies, our first desideratum would be the establishment of a Moslem entity. It would have to include Arabia, and the question would arise as to what was to go with it.' Seldom has a resolution left so many questions unanswered, or set running so many crippled hares. Throughout the discussions which took place in Whitehall and Cairo during the war years no one ever defined 'Arabia' or divulged the geographical whereabouts of the territories that were being divided and given independence and national identity.

Sykes left Mesopotamia at the end of October, travelling back by the Gulf, the Arabian Sea and the Red Sea to Cairo. On the way he wrote a twenty-two-page memorandum for the War Office in which he referred to the need for a propaganda offensive to counter the success of the CUP agents in India, where the British administration were 'afraid of the Moslems in their midst', and the inevitable meal that the Turks would make of Gallipoli. He suggested the planting of 'rumours' by native agents, 'rhymes, cryptograms, anagrams, favourable to our side', and he put foward the idea of 'a new political bureau in Cairo', to 'paralyse once and for all the enemy's activities in Persia, Afghanistan, and India, and thus deprive him of a source of diversion and menaces with which he amuses and distracts not only us but Russia'.

In October, as Sykes was on his way back to Cairo, an Arab officer of the Ottoman army, Sharif Muhammad al Faruqi, deserted to the British lines at Gallipoli. He was interviewed by Captain Smith and Lieutenant Pirie-Gordon, the naval intelligence officer on the spot, and then sent on to Cairo. He said that he represented 'a conspiracy of Arab officers' who were willing to support the Allied cause 'on certain conditions'. But if those conditions were not met, they would support the Germans, who had already made promises to them. Faruqi was promptly enrolled by Clayton as liaison officer between the High Commissioner and the Sharif of Mecca, and given the secret service codename 'G'.

He told Cairo Intelligence that he was born at Mosul in 1891, and that at the outbreak of war he was ADC to Fakhri Pasha, Commander of the Twelfth Army. When Jamal took command in Syria, he (Faruqi) was transferred to Aleppo. He had been instrumental, he claimed, in bringing together the military and civil wings of the Damascus revolutionaries, Ahad and Fattah, and he told them that the headquarters of Fattah was in London, and that there were English as well as Arab members. He supported the Sharif of Mecca, and his senior in the nationalist movement was Yasin Pasha, 'who knows more of its secrets'. Yasin was the Ottoman military commander in Aleppo, who was to remain loyal to the Ottoman authority throughout the war, though he became a leader of the nationalist movement afterwards. Jamal and Fakhri knew of their activities 'from spies'. Jamal himself had interviewed Faruqi and tried to obtain details. Ninety per cent of Arab officers in the army were members of the secret societies, he said.

By the time Sykes arrived back in Cairo on the way to London, news had arrived of more Armenian massacres and of desperate reverses at Gallipoli. And he learnt that on 21 October, as he had prepared to leave Basra, Chamberlain the new Secretary of State for India had been asked by the Dardanelles Committee to draft a telegram to the Viceroy in consultation with Sir Edward Grey and Balfour, 'explaining the situation regarding the occupation of Baghdad and its possible effect on the Arabs'. The army that had been sent to the Gulf to take over the Basra region and protect the oil installations at Abadan and Ahwaz, was to be launched on a campaign to take Baghdad and thus achieved a propaganda *coup* which would more than compensate for recent setbacks.

While in Cairo, Sykes met Faruqi, who in the meantime had been sent as yet another emissary to the Sharif. Sykes discussed with his British colleagues his plans for a political bureau and for an agreement with France, Russia and Italy, and they were enthusiastic. He also talked to Faruqi about the Sharif and telegraphed to the DMO in London, telling him that the Sharif favoured a 'Greater Arabia'. Sykes envisaged Syria as a 'French sphere of interest', while Mesopotamia would be a British sphere. France would retain control of the coastline next to its sphere. Britain would have control of the head of the Gulf next to its sphere. The dispositions of the Arab lands within the Ottoman Empire had been decided on. It only remained to conquer them.

A profusion of correspondence now passed back and forth along the Red Sea. To show its sincerity and concern the Egyptian administration began to send first grain and then money along with the messages. And McMahon trod on ever more dangerous ground. He had picked up the work of the *Intrusives*, and Sykes had returned to London to make that work a political reality; but if anything went wrong it was McMahon's head that would fall. Storrs was to observe: 'The exchange of argument and counter-argument, of reference to England (as probably reference from Mecca to Constantinople), of instructions and draftings, seemed interminable.' Clearly, even as late as September 1915, Storrs's friends in Mecca were referring their plans to Constantinople.

The Sharif's latest communication, brought by 'O' and dated 9 September 1915, was a florid affirmation of friendship and esteem. But it contained confirmation of Husain's belief that the boundaries of a Hashemite 'Arabia' had been settled. It was more than a month before 'O' returned with McMahon's reply, which was dated 24 October. It was the most crucial of all the communications between Cairo and Mecca, which the Shaikh of the Bani Harb carried in great secrecy to the Sharif. Despite the assertions of politicians and historians that McMahon was responsible for the promises made and implied at this time, the Resident's note to the Sharif was in fact drafted by Sir Edward Grey and approved by Kitchener and the India Office.

I regret that you should have received from my last letter the impression that I regarded the question of the limits and boundaries with coldness and hesitation ... I have realised, however, from your last letter that you regard this question as one of vital and urgent importance. I have, therefore, lost no time in informing the Government of Great Britain of the contents of your last letter and it is with great pleasure that I communicate to you on their behalf the following statement, which I am confident you will receive with satisfaction. The districts of Mersina and Alexandretta and portions of Syria *lying to the west of the districts of Damascus, Hama, Homs and Aleppo* [author's italics] cannot be said to be purely Arab, and should be excluded from the proposed limits and boundaries. With the above modifications, and without prejudice to our existing treaties with Arab chiefs, we accept those limits and boundaries and, in regard to those portions of the territories therein in which Great Britain is free to act without detriment to the interests of her Ally, France, I am empowered in the name of the Government of Great Britain to give the following assurances and to make the following reply to your letter:– Subject to the above modifications, Great Britain is prepared to recognise and support the independence of the Arabs within the territories included in the limits and boundaries proposed.

There followed a number of assurances about the protection of the Holy Places, an insistence on British exclusivity in advising the Sharif, and another qualification:

With regard to the vilayets of Baghdad and Basra, the Arabs will recognise that the established position and interests of Great Britain necessitate special measures of administrative control in order to secure these territories from foreign aggression, to promote the welfare of the local populations and to safeguard our mutual economic interests . . . your trusted and excellent messenger Shaikh Muhammad ibn Arif Araifan . . . *will inform you of various matters of interest but of less vital importance, which I have not mentioned in this letter* [author's italics].

A battery of questions and answers followed, diplomatic in tone, florid in form, and imprecise geographically and legally. The Sharif replied:

We renounce our insistence on the inclusion of the vilayets of Mersin and Adana in the Arab Kingdom. But the
provinces of Aleppo and Beirut and their sea coasts are
purely Arab Provinces and there is no difference between a
Moslem and a Christian Arab; they are both descendants
of one forefather.

There was no mention of Baghdad and Basra as separate enti-
ties, but 'the Provinces of Iraq are part of the pure Arab Kingdom'. To render an accord 'easy' Husain went on, 'we might
agree to leave under the British administration for a short time
those districts now occupied by the British troops, without the
rights of either party being prejudiced thereby especially those
of the Arab nation'.

In a follow-up letter from McMahon there was a guarded
reference to the position of Ibn Saud.

I am gratified to observe that you agree to the exclusion of
the vilayets of Mersina and Adana from the boundaries of
the Arab territories . . . In stating that the Arabs are ready
to recognise and respect all our treaties with Arab Chiefs,
it is of course understood that this will apply to all territories included in the Arab Kingdom, as the Government of
Great Britain cannot repudiate engagements which already
exist.

Here was a nice progression from inferred aim to accomplished
status. Kitchener had set the ball rolling in 1914 by suggesting
the possibility of an Arab caliphate. Almost exactly a year later
the idea of an 'Arab nation' had developed into an 'Arab kingdom' which would be expected to respect treaties entered into
between Britain and Arab chiefs who knew nothing of the negotiations and whose territories would be embraced within that
kingdom. Unless McMahon meant Kuwait and the other Gulf
shaikhdoms, he could only have been referring to Ibn Saud.
There were no other Arab chiefs with whom Britain had entered
into treaty relations. Cairo, and presumably the Government in
London, though Cabinet records are vague on the matter, now
accepted that the kingdom would embrace the entire Arabian
peninsula, excluding the cultivated and developed regions of the
coastal districts west of a line from Aleppo to Damascus. It is
clear that McMahon's reservation stopped short at Damascus.

The sanjuk of Jerusalem or Palestine was included along with the whole of Najd or central Arabia in that inviting package. By the same token Yemen and Asir, excepting Aden, were embraced by Husain's kingdom.

'As an earnest of our intentions and in order to aid you in your efforts in our joint cause I am sending you by your trustworthy messenger a sum of £20,000', concluded McMahon's letter of 17 December. Husain, in his reply, acknowledged two letters dated 17 December, but only one appears on the record. There are several gaps in the story resulting from missing papers, and several messages were delivered verbally. Husain wrote on 1 January 1916:

> With regard to what had been stated in your honoured communication concerning al Iraq, as to the matter of compensation for the period of occupation, we, in order to strengthen the confidence of Great Britain in our attitude and in our words and actions, really and veritably . . . leave the determination of the amount to the perception of her wisdom and justice.

As for Syria, he wrote:

> As regards the Northern Parts and their coasts, . . . all this was only done to fulfil those aspirations whose attainment is desired by the will of the Blessed and Supreme God . . . yet we find it our duty that the Eminent Minister should be sure that, at the first opportunity after this war is finished, we shall ask you (what we avert our eyes from today) for what we now leave to France in Beirut and its coasts.

The Foreign Secretary intervened on this point to make clear the inviolability of the French claim to the vilayet of Beirut and the sanjuk of the Lebanon.

On 18 February Storrs received a verbal message from Abdullah. 'My father is following up a policy which requires time, while we work out the practical details by means of a secret council of Arab notables . . . We have written certain requests, which I hope will be granted . . . I request £3,000 for myself.' Abdullah's request came with a letter from his father dated 18 February, asking for funds to be deposited at Port Sudan. 'A confidential agent will be sent.'

On 10 March McMahon sent his reply:

We are grateful to note the active measures which you propose to take ... I am pleased to be able to inform you that His Majesty's Government have approved of meeting your requests, and that which you asked to be sent with all haste is being despatched with your messenger ... We take the opportunity to explain to you a matter ... which might have given rise to misunderstanding. There are various Turkish posts and small garrisons along the coasts of Arabia who are hostile to us and who are planning injury to our naval interests in the Red Sea. We may therefore find it necessary to take hostile measures ... We give you notice of this matter in case distorted and false reports may reach you of the reasons for any action which we might be obliged to take ... The capture of Erzerum and the defeats sustained by the Turks in the Caucasus are having a great effect in our favour.

As Mark Sykes prepared to leave Egypt for London in November 1915, the Sharif's lobby in Cairo received a knowledgeable reinforcement in the shape of Gertrude Bell. At the beginning of the month Captain Hall called her to his office in London and told her that Cairo had cabled that they would like her to 'come out'. On the last day of the month she was welcomed in Cairo by Lawrence and Woolley. She was soon hard at work.

For the moment I am helping Mr. Hogarth to fill in the intelligence files with information as to the tribes and shaikhs. It's great fun and delightful to be working with him. Our chief is Colonel Clayton whom I like very much. This week Mark Sykes passed through and I have seen a good deal of him.

She lived at the gathering place of the *Intrusives*, the Grand Continental. Captain Hall, the head of Egyptian railways and brother of the DNI in London, smoothed her way wherever she went. Woolley at Port Said kept in constant touch. Her table companions were Hogarth, Lawrence, two sappers (Colonel Wright and Major Pearson) and Philip Graves, whom she had met in Constantinople when he was working there for *The Times*.

While she made herself at home in Cairo, Sykes returned to Whitehall with undiminished vigour and an 'ambitious scenario'. Bad news was rife, and the new Chief of the Imperial General Staff, Field-Marshal Robertson, referred with more than his customary emphasis to the 'side shows' which were blunting military strategy and causing much dispute at meetings of the freshly formed War Committee. The 'easterners' were pleased to have Sykes back among them. On 17 December he attended a meeting of the Committee to give evidence on the Arab question. He argued forcibly for an Egyptian offensive. Husain and his followers were pro-British but afraid of the French. Diplomacy in London and Paris combined with pro-Arab activity by officers on the spot could change all this.

Then Sykes declared that if such a policy was not adopted he feared that the Sharif of Mecca would be killed.

BALFOUR: Will be what?
SYKES: Will be killed.

Having lent a note of high drama to the proceedings, Sykes went on to paint a picture of a new Ottoman nominee at Mecca presiding over the extermination of the Christians of Syria, 'as the Armenians have been exterminated, and a real *Jihad*, threatening Britain in Mesopotamia, Persia, Afghanistan, India and the Sudan'.

The meeting agreed that Lord Crewe, who was acting temporarily for Sir Edward Grey at the Foreign Office, should contact the Ambassador in Paris, Lord Bertie, as to the advisability of Sykes making an official visit to test the reaction of the French. Bertie thought it would be a bad idea indeed and quashed it. Sykes did not give up the idea of an Anglo-French understanding, but for the moment he concentrated on his Arab plans, which had been put in train the moment he arrived back in London in December.

On 10 December, the Secretary of State for India had telegraphed the Viceroy:

To combat German and Turkish propaganda proposed to establish Bureau at Cairo under general orders of DMO, but under control of Mark Sykes, assisted by Philip Graves and Hennessy. Function to communicate information to departments and persons concerned in London, India, Mesopotamia and Mediterranean, and prepare propaganda material for Indian, British and French press.

Austen Chamberlain was in favour of an 'Islamic Bureau', citing recent examples of the success of German propaganda in India and elsewhere. On the same day Sykes outlined the functions of the Bureau: to harmonise British political activity in the Near East and keep the Foreign Office, India Office, Admiralty, War Office and Government of India informed on German and Turkish policy. He would be the head of the organisation, and its acting chief would be Lieutenant-Colonel Parker. There would be a liaison officer with the Viceroy's administration, whom Sykes suggested should be Major Hennessy, who had served in India. On 24 December Hardinge replied. 'Entirely opposed to Bureau carrying out any kind of propaganda activity in India. Although Bureau would be under control of the Director of Military Operations, doubt whether personnel named [Graves as first secretary and Hennessy as liaison officer] possess necessary military knowledge.'

Chamberlain at the India Office was resigned: 'Understand that scheme is general outline and in detailed organisation has been approved by Army Council and Sir Edward Grey; will be under supervision of CID and that intelligence will be co-ordinated with DMO.' Under-Secretary Hirtzel noted in the Political and Secret diary: 'Government of India distrust personnel and I am not surprised at their hesitation. We do not even know if Sir Mark Sykes' plan has been approved by WO and FO. I am afraid our draft reply to Viceroy will not allay doubts.'

On 6 January 1916 Asquith called an inter-departmental conference at Whitehall Place, attended by Lancelot Oliphant of the Foreign Office, Hirtzel of the India Office, Brigadier-General Macdonogh the new Director of Military Intelligence, who had been in France with Special Intelligence while the events which led to the meeting had been taking place, Freddie Maurice the DMO, Sykes, FitzGerald for Kitchener, Colonel C. N. French the head of MI1, Lieutenant-Colonel Hankey the Secretary of the Committee of Imperial Defence, and Lieutenant-Colonel W. Dally Jones, Hankey's assistant. The committee 'shall meet to consider the question of an Islamic Bureau at Cairo', instructed the Prime Minister. The most germane observation came from Macdonogh, who was fresh to the subject. He thought the committee was 'apportioning the skin of the bear before it had been shot'. An India Office minute of 14 January summarised the proceedings. 'The upshot of the inter-departmental Conference ... was to approve Sir Mark Sykes' proposals, with the material alteration that instead of being a separate body it will be merely a section of the Cairo Intelligence Department. This was insisted on by Lord Kitchener and greatly preferred by the F.O. Has advantages for our point of view too.' The Committee also rejected the title 'Islamic'. It was decided that the body should be called the 'Arab Bureau'. On 4 February Sir Edward Grey accepted the proposals with the proviso that the Foreign Office should be the primary vehicle for disseminating information. On the 15th the Viceroy approved the proposal, reluctantly, on the understanding that 'our Political Officers will not be called upon to act at dictation of Bureau and that we shall receive copies of important papers issued and received'.

Thus the Arab Bureau came into existence, with Hogarth and not Parker as its executive head under Clayton, for Kitchener's nephew had more important tasks to deal with in the Hijaz. The Indian Government, with mounting problems of its own in Mesopotamia, was about to learn that the members of the Bureau were not to be hidebound by the ground rules of the Inter-departmental Committee or subsequent agreements. New personalities were hauled aboard and Hogarth composed one of the ditties which he often reeled off on big occasions:

> 'Do you know
> The Arab Bureau?'
>
> Asked Hogarth; and answered:
> 'Clayton stability,
> Symes versatility,
> Cornwallis is practical,
> Dawnay syntactical,
> Mackintosh havers,
> And Fielding palavers,
> Macindoe easy,
> And wordie not breezy:
> Lawrence licentiate to dream and to dare,
> And Yours Very Faithfully, *bon à tout faire*.'

The day after the Viceroy's reluctant approval had come through, on 16 February, Hogarth had started a weekly news sheet called *Arabian Report*, distributed under the auspices of the Admiralty. His deputy editor was Lieutenant Cozens Hardy of the Royal Navy. By 12 March this news sheet was able to bring its elite readership up to date with the Sharif affair. A letter from the Sharif dated 18 February, it said, marked a very important step in the Arab movement against the Turks, particularly as it was written before the fall of Erzerum, capital of Armenia, to the Russians. The Sharif had stated that negotiations were completed and he was ready for action. He would proceed as follows: one son (Faisal) was in Syria and would try to persuade Arabs to oppose the Turks, or to attack the Turkish army when it approached the Suez Canal. Ali, the eldest son, was being despatched to Madina with an Arab army to occupy the Railway and help his brother in Syria . . . The Sharif needed £50,000 for expenses; also rifles, flour, barley, coffee and sugar. A request for £3,000 had been received from Abdullah, the second son and the 'power behind the throne'. In a note appended to the *Arabian Report* of 16 February, Sir Arthur Hirtzel described the Sharif's letter on the question of boundaries as 'a masterpiece of obscurity'.

The *Intrusives* had suffered a minor setback at the beginning of 1916 when, in the aftermath of the Dardanelles withdrawal, the Mediterranean command under Maxwell was merged with the Egyptian force to become the Egyptian Expeditionary Force under a new GOC, General Sir Archibald Murray, who had relinquished his job as Chief of the Imperial Staff to Robertson. He had been thought of as Kitchener's stooge at the War Office and he went to Cairo as Kitchener's man, but a reluctant 'easterner' and no supporter of side shows. He inherited a tangled web, in which the Arab Bureau, supposedly an arm of his own staff, became virtually a policy-making body, responsible not to him as the military commander but to an assortment of lesser authorities: the Royal Navy's Admiral Wemyss; the High Commissioner Sir Henry McMahon; the Sudan Government; the Sirdar of the Egyptian Army, Sir Reginald Wingate; and his own DMI, now promoted Brigadier-General, 'Bertie' Clayton. Murray soon sensed that the Bureau represented an insupportable burden for a wartime commander. He effectively sacked Clayton and appointed Major Holdich, as his intelligence chief. He took the two senior staff officers of the Bureau, Newcombe and

Parker, under his own wing, allowing the latter to act as liaison officer with Clayton's organisation and with Wingate at Port Sudan. The Bureau remained at the Savoy Hotel in Cairo while staff intelligence moved to the new GHQ at Ismailiya.

As the promises to the Sharif received tacit Cabinet approval in February, and the Arab Bureau began to take shape, Sykes and his French opposite number Picot went to Petrograd to sell their package to Foreign Minister Sazanov, and London and Cairo turned to consider a new disaster, this time in Mesopotamia.

10

The Siege

The kin of us you murdered shall be masters of your lands,
They shall batter down the bulwarks of your trust,
The city of your Sultans shall be wrested from your hands,
Your glory shall be trampled in the dust,
And the tunnels that we drove for you, the roads that we
have made,
Shall be highways for the armies of your foe.

From 'The Roadmakers: A Song of the Dead Men of Kut',
in L. Woolley (ed.), *From Kastamuni to Kedos*

When Expeditionary Force 'D' under the command of Major-General Delamain anchored off Bahrain in November 1914, the Chief Political Officer with the force is said to have told the men that their task would be to protect British oil interests at the head of the Gulf, 'otherwise the Royal Navy would be dependent on America for its oil'. Before the year was out many a general had come and gone, and the oil line from Ahwaz and the refinery at Abadan had been secured against enemy action. Fao, Basra, Shaiba and Qurna had been taken, and the men of Force 'D' settled down amidst flies and filth to enjoy their first Christmas in the land of Abraham and Nebuchadnezzar.

For men drawn from the garrisons of India, from village and town in the British Isles, from the battlegrounds of France and Belgium, Mesopotamia was a place of unknown quantity and unsuspected hazard. They called it 'Mespot', but few of them had time to describe their first impressions of it in letters home for they were pitched into the whirlwind of battle as soon as they arrived. First poignant impressions were put on paper though – the journey to journey's end in that malign, fly-infested land of dust and swamp, the sea voyage from Bombay through the Gulf

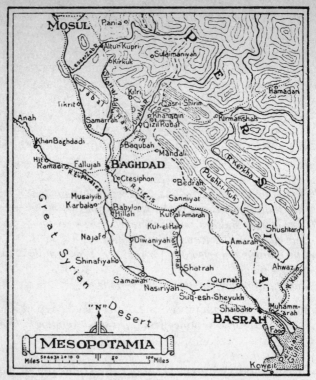

Fig. 2 Pocket map of Mesopotamia issued by Intelligence Section, GHQ Basra

waters to the silt bar at the mouth of the Shatt-al-Arab, the date plantations of Fao on the port side, the artificial island of Abadan with its smoking refineries to starboard, Shaikh Khazal's independency of Muhammerah in Persian Arabistan at a swelling of the waterway, and then the metropolis of Basra with Zubair and Shaiba towards the desert in the south-west. Eleanor F. Egan, a young woman from America intent on writing articles for the *Saturday Evening Post*, arrived early in the campaign to the consternation of the generals, carrying a letter of introduction from Britain's Ambassador in Washington Sir Cecil Spring-Rice, and as the troopship on which she made the last stage of her voyage approached she wrote in the scrap pad which she kept for occasional notes:

> 12.30 a.m. ... We are just starting over the bar. The engines have stopped; the lead is being cast; a musical

young voice rings out in the silence, calling the depths. We move slowly under our own headway. A final cast; the distant clang of an engine room signal; the engines begin to throb again, and we are under way ... very slowly, very carefully. It is a still, hot night, with not a fleck or ripple even in the path of moonlight which lies across the sea. I am thinking that for many a young man aboard this ship it really is *crossing the bar*, so many of them are likely to find the end of youth and of life in *the cradle of the world*.

Historical and military descriptions of the events which followed the advance to Qurna at the end of 1914, and beyond almost to Baghdad and back again, are legion. Some are eye-witness accounts by generals and lesser officers, and by other ranks; most are by men and women who have judged the impulses of the time, and the military vicissitudes which accompanied them, from a distance. They have in common one remarkable feature: they ignore almost entirely the official documents relating to those events and the testimony of the intelligence officers on the spot whose task it was to assess the enemy's plans and to outwit their schemes. Thus the Viceroy, Lord Hardinge, and the Commander-in-Chief India, General Sir Beauchamp Duff, have been blamed with remarkable unanimity for the grave consequences of the military campaigns of the time, though official testimony shows overwhelmingly that they opposed those campaigns with might and main. The fact was that the commanders in Mesopotamia were sucked into a vortex of military action from which there was no escape by the ambitions of the 'easterners' at home and in Cairo, by tribal skirmishes which threatened to cut off Britain's only oil supply line, and by astute German manoeuvring.

By February 1915 the activities of the German agents became alarming, not only in Persia but also along the Euphrates in Mesopotamia, where the great religious centres of Najaf and Karbala, which provided a receptive climate for the call to holy war, were ransacked by the Turks. Since November 1914 there had been attacks on the British garrisons at Bushire, oil pipelines and telegraph wires had been cut in Arabistan, and the Abadan harbour entrance blocked by a sunken 'lighter'. In September 1914 the German Foreign Office had instructed Wangenheim in Constantinople, that he 'must incite unrest in Arabia, N. Africa and Persian Gulf'. An Indian force was sent

into Ahwaz on 3 March 1915 under General Robinson to deal
with the insurgents. They fought a hand-to-hand battle with the
fanatics, whose resentment and fervour were played on so
adroitly by Wassmuss and the other enemy agents. The Rajputs,
12th Cavalry and a handful of Dorsets distinguished themselves in
the fight, but there were heavy casualties, and the wavering
tribesmen, especially the Bakhtiaris, threatened to cause a con-
flagration. Towards the end of April the Turks were advancing
on Kermanshah. General Gorringe led a division from Basra
along the Karun river to Ahwaz and then swept across the desert
to Amara in the north-west, and down again to the Karun. The
Turks who had been occupying the region were cleared and the
authority of Shaikh Khazal of Muhammerah restored. A
stretch of 142 miles of oil pipeline, badly damaged by Wassmuss's
auxiliaries at the end of February, was repaired, never to be successfully attacked again in the course of the war.

In June 1915 a notice appeared on the walls of Baghdad. 'All
Muhammadans must join *jihad*, because Turkey is between the
Devil and the Deep Sea.' Between April and September 1915,
the prospects for the British force in Mesopotamia brightened
perceptibly and General Nixon, a 'dashing' cavalry officer, 'secret, thrusting . . . with a thick moustache, a beaky nose and a
strong but ungainly physique', took over the army command
from Sir Arthur Barrett, who was sick. Already the die was cast.
Mesopotamia had become a major battleground against the
wishes of the Viceroy and the Commander-in-Chief. Politicians
at home and commanders on other fronts looked to Nixon's
army to relieve the strain and to gain the inestimable prize of
Baghdad. Why not strike now, while the iron was hot? London
blew hot and cold. Then in October 1915 it gave the go ahead
through the new Secretary of State for India, Austen Chamberlain. By November a force led by Nixon's nominee, Major-General Sir Charles Townshend, was at ancient Ctesiphon, the
gateway to Baghdad. His men were already known at home,
where the press had played up their advance, as the 'Invinci-
bles', and 4,000 of them were engaged in a hand-to-hand fight
for Chosroe's old seat of government. But the Turkish army, led
by Nureddin Pasha and with its battle plan worked out by von
der Goltz, was to prove no pushover. As the Anglo-Indian force
fought for Ctesiphon, War Office messages came through to
GHQ telling Townshend that the enemy was being reinforced
by crack units. At the end of November the British army was in

retreat. By 3 December it had been pushed back to Kut-al-Amara, the little township at a bend of the Tigris that it had taken only two months earlier. Its fate was plotted by a great military strategist of the Prussian army and it was compelled to submit to a humbling siege.

War Office, Indian and Mesopotamian intelligence underwent drastic changes as the early euphoria of the campaign gave way to the despair and recrimination of Kut-al-Amara, and one of its acquisitions was the Lady of Hail, Gertrude Bell. She went to India from Cairo in January 1916 at the behest of Valentine Chirol, youthful playmate of herself and the Viceroy when they 'did' Europe together in the last years of Queen Victoria's reign. Her primary purpose was to reconcile her friend Charles Hardinge to the plans of her colleagues in Cairo, who were deeply immersed in the schemes of the Sharif of Mecca, through the Arab Bureau. She arrived at the moment of the pull out from the Dardanelles and the confinement of Townshend's force at Kut. When she reached New Delhi in February ('there was Domnul on the platform and a Vice-regal motor car waiting outside'), the affairs of Egypt, Mecca, India and Mesopotamia had become inextricably linked.

Two months before, Hardinge had stated, not for the first time, his opposition to all that had gone on. In a letter to Wingate following a mission by Storrs to the Sharif, he told the Sirdar that the limits of the Arab state set out in a memorandum on the Sharif's claim meant 'the surrender of all the advantages for which India has been fighting in Mesopotamia during the past year and the creation of an Arab state lying astride our interests in the Persian Gulf'. India, he insisted, should not be asked to make sacrifices for Arabs who 'have been fighting against us the whole time and have no claim whatever upon us. I cannot tell you how strongly I feel upon this point.' He concluded:

these expeditions, to East Africa, Mesopotamia, Dardanelles, Salonika, and elsewhere . . . are all blunders. The war will not be won in any of these outlying spots, but in Flanders, and it is there that we should have concentrated all our strength in order to give the Germans a smashing blow at the earliest possible date . . . All these diversions mean weakness in the main theatre, and it seems to me we have been outwitted by Germany and are literally playing her game.

It was a view shared by a large part of the Cabinet, the Chiefs of Staff, the First Sea Lord, and needless to say by the French Government and General Staff. But in the end events developed an impetus of their own and the 'eastern' view dominated. The politicians led by Lloyd George turned first on Chamberlain, their colleague at the India Office, and then on Hardinge when the Mesopotamian débâcle followed on the heels of Gallipoli. Seldom has history perpetuated a more brazen untruth than that which holds even to the present day – that the Indian administration and its generals were solely to blame. Their culpability was slight compared with that of Asquith and Kitchener for their vacillation, and Balfour, Churchill, Lloyd George and Leo Amery for their clamorous campaigns for ventures against which the best military and naval brains warned them. Some motives were plain enough. In March 1915 Storrs had written to Fitzgerald, Kitchener's Secretary, of their chief's prize: viceroyalty over Egypt, the Sudan and Arabia.

By the time of Gertrude Bell's arrival in Delhi, Hardinge was being asked by Cairo to select a liaison officer to serve on the newly formed Arab Bureau, a quasi-intelligence unit attached to the General Staff, answerable to the Foreign Office, and largely paid for by the Admiralty. At first he refused. He wanted nothing to do with the Bureau or its works. But Gertrude had been well primed by her 'Beloved Boy' and by Hogarth, its leading lights, and under pressure from her the Viceroy selected A. Brownlow Fforde for a job which nobody in India would willingly undertake. More serious though was the Bureau's determination to have an officer in Basra with Force 'D'. The Viceroy would have none of the Cairo gang. What about Gertrude? He trusted her. And so she became the head of the Basra office of the Arab Bureau in February 1916 and left on 1 March to take up her new appointment. Before bidding farewell to Delhi she wrote a note to Captain Hall at the Admiralty: 'I have had a most useful fortnight here ... I have got on terms of understanding with the Indian FO, and the Intelligence Department. It is essential that India and Egypt should keep in the closest touch since they are dealing with two sides of the same problem.' She arrived in Basra on 3 March and stayed overnight with the Chief Political Officer and his wife, 'the good Coxes'. She later presented herself to the General Staff, where she was greeted by Colonel 'Bill' Beach, who offered her his bedroom by day as a workplace, and by Campbell Thompson, the man whose archaeolo-

"I've promised to visit by Dinner-time

Baghdad, and accepted the prime

Of the Head-cook's pottage, all he's rich in,

For having left in the Caliph's kitchen,

Of a nest of scorpions, no survivor."

BROWNING, The Pied Piper.

Fig. 3 Christmas card from Intelligence Section, Basra. The 'Caliph's Kitchen' theme refers to the uncovering of a German-controlled Pan-Islamic spy ring at a Basra restaurant where British officers were disguised as Pathan waiters

gical methods she had criticised on their first meeting at Carchemish in 1911 and who was now a GSO2 Intelligence at Basra.

In January, following the example of the War Office in Whitehall, India created a Directorate of Military Intelligence with Colonel Beach at its head. A small team of men had been working under his direction since the outset of the Mesopotamian campaign, patrolling the vast area from the North-West Frontier across Afghanistan and Persia to the Euphrates. Murphy had come down from Jask with the Expeditionary Force, and the Arab Bureau tried to co-opt him, but Beach refused to let him go to Cairo. Special duty officers from Simla shared the tasks of infiltrating the enemy's information sources, watching its agents, and setting up their own network. Among the most important of them was the little Pathan, Lieutenant Abdal Samad Shah, who had arrived with the staff men in November 1914, then had played a vital part in flushing out Indian and Arab enemy agents, and Major W. F. Blaker of the Royal Field Artillery, the British officer who had arrived in Basra in Pathan disguise before war was declared. He had helped to hound the German consular officials and their native supporters in the first days of the conflict, had come out of hiding and gone to fight in France. He returned to Basra in 1916. This remarkable officer was in fact a German native who had met an English girl at Brighton before the war, married her and eventually adopted her name, quickly becoming as typical an English gentleman as could be met with in the Long Room of Lord's Cricket Ground. His real name was Wilhelm Reichwald. He spoke Arabic, Farsi and Pushtu, as well as German and English, with native fluency. In the Basra region and the wild tribal territories surrounding it, these men, like their German counterparts, performed amazing feats which, in the nature of the undertakings, were most often to die with them, unrecorded and unhonoured. To the customary tasks of producing fake newspapers, identification documents, and propaganda, they added a command of disguise and dissimulation which enabled them to penetrate the political cabals, the sleezy clubs, illegal liquor distilleries, thieves' kitchens and other places frequented by Arab, Turk, Greek and Jew, and as often as not used by the Germans, as places to meet with their 'givers' and 'receivers'.

None of the newcomers to Force 'D' in 1916 was more important, however, than another German-speaking officer, Colonel

E. A. F. Redl. He was sent by Macdonogh in London to the Russian GHQ in the Caucasus at the beginning of 1916, with a Secret Service salary paid by the India Office to supplement his army pay. He arrived at Meshed in Persia in April from the Caucasus to take charge of the region Meshed–Astradbad– –Semnan–Yezd–Birjand. He added Russian to a long list of languages which he had learnt in his native Austria or had picked up since.

Of the other special agents in Mesopotamia in 1916, on the British side at any rate, most remained silent about their work throughout their lives. Campbell Thompson, 'C.T.', the Scot with the quicksilver mind and impenetrable purse, senior member of Hogarth's trio at Carchemish up to the war, came early in 1916 to join Mespot intelligence. But he never spoke of or recorded his activities.

The most dashing and famous of the 'intelligence' men to arrive in Basra, however, remained apart from Beach's team. Gerard Leachman turned up in March 1915 with instructions from the War Office in Delhi to move incognito among the tribes, working directly under the Chief Political Officer, Sir Percy Cox. He was to be a one-man band with the task of undermining the work of the brilliant German agent, Preusser, who had caused havoc along the Euphrates. Leachman and the German fought a pitched battle for the next three years, dogging each other's schemes, either one hoping to trap and kill the other. They were to end the war with a healthy mutual respect. For the moment, however, Leachman and his colleagues had but one thought, the fate of the trapped army at Kut-al-Amara.

The British force at Kut held out for five months, longer than Plevna or Ladysmith, until it was starved into submission at the end of April 1916. Townshend had intended to fight his way out at first, along his own river bank or, if he could not break through the Turkish lines, across the river; however, there were no boats, the water was mined and his men were too weak to swim. And so he rationalised his position and comforted himself with the thought that by staying where he was, he nullified the advance of the Turks and gave his compatriots time to reform; as Osman the Turk had paralysed a Russian advance and so saved the Ottoman Empire.

Hoped-for relief by the army of General Aylmer, gathered some seventy miles down river at Amara, never came. Contact with the world outside was mundane; the daily bombardment, the endless radio signals in and out of Townshend's HQ, Reuter messages relaying the world's response to their plight. Rumours and bulletins told of the mounting casualties of the relief forces, the slaughter of every animal until there was no food left for them or for the 3,000 Arabs of the town. As the position worsened the commander became increasingly tetchy with his GOC Nixon and with the generals who were straining every nerve and resource to relieve him. As Townshend strolled on the roof of his headquarters one day observing the enemy he spotted Field-Marshal von der Goltz reviewing his troops. A guard saw the aged German too and took a pot shot. Townshend reprimanded the soldier. 'I was angry,' wrote Townshend, 'for he is one of the finest military strategists in Europe.' It was not perhaps the moment to admire the enemy's prowess, but Townshend was an unpredictable officer.

By late April 1,800 men of the besieged garrison of 15,000 had died in the fighting, from bombardment wounds, or from starvation and disease. A further 1,900 had been badly wounded. And along the Tigris between Amara and Kut, 22,000 men had lost life or limb in a series of hopeless relief attempts. By 23 April Townshend was ready to admit defeat. He began to conduct the last rites of his command, and to seek surrender terms. The Turkish commander, Khalil Pasha, was willing to consider the parole of the garrison to India. He did not want the burden of feeding so many prisoners. But Enver insisted on unconditional surrender. The exhausted, half-starved collection of white and brown soldiers at Kut were still useful as a propaganda weapon. It was at this moment that two officers of the newly formed Arab Bureau arrived in Basra: Captain Aubrey Herbert and Lieutenant T. E. Lawrence.

Late in March Lord Chelmsford arrived in Cairo on his way to India to take over from Hardinge the unhappy legacy of the Mesopotamian campaign. The Prince of Wales was also in Cairo at the time, and Storrs had taken the royal visitor on several of his mandatory tours of the 'sights', especially the bazaars, where the prince met Storrs's friend, Jack Cohen, 'the final altitude of the Cairo Suq', and bought some carpets for Queen Mary. The Embassy yacht was sent down to Ismailiya to meet Chelmsford. Aboard it were the heir to the British throne; the new GOC Egypt, General Murray, and his predecessor, General Maxwell; the High Commissioner in Cairo, Sir Henry McMahon; General Birdwood, the deposed army commander

in the Dardanelles; Storrs; and the new army medical chief for
Mesopotamia, Colonel William Willcox. A week before Turkish
planes had bombed Port Said. Their pilots were not warned of
the prize that awaited them on the Ismailiya Canal that day.
Doubtless there was talk of Kut-al-Amara as of the withdrawal
from the Dardanelles both aboard the yacht and during the next
two days of conferences in Cairo.

It is known from Arab sources and from references in an
unsigned letter to Lawrence dated 26 March 1916 on the official
file, that the Cairo authorities were trying to persuade two
prominent nationalists who had served in the Ottoman army,
Aziz al Masri and Muhammad Faruqi, to join with the prominent Pan-Islamite religious leaders Dr Abdurrahman Shahbandar and Rashid Rida, to form an Arab mission in Basra. In fact,
Shahbandar was in Basra at the time with another defector from
the Turks, Nuri Said, and General Lake, who had just arrived
to take over from the disgraced Nixon as GOC, was on the point
of expelling them. At the moment of crisis Al Masri is said by

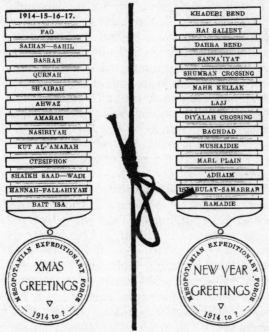

Fig. 4   The Mesopotamian campaign victories listed in Intelligence
Section's 1917 Christmas card

Arab historians to have demurred. He wanted an absolute
assurance of Arab independence and Britain could give only
'general assurances'. In fact, Kitchener vetoed the journey.
'Doesn't approve of Masri', the War Office told Cairo. The
proposed Arab delegation remained in Cairo. They were to have
been accompanied by General MacMunn, the War Office
nominee on the Basra General Staff. The General travelled
alone. There was even a suggestion that Sayid Talib should be
invited back from India to act on behalf of the Cairo brigade in
negotiations with the Turks and in talks with the Sharif of
Mecca and Arab nationalists, but that would invite too antago-
nistic a reaction from Sir Percy Cox and the generals on the
spot. And so it was left to Britons to pursue the Sharif and to try
to pluck their own from the brink at Kut-al-Amara.

On Tuesday 28 March Herbert and Storrs boarded HMS
Euryalus, Flagship of Admiral Wemyss, and proceeded through
Suez to the Red Sea. Storrs disembarked at Aden, where the
party was welcomed by Colonel Jacob, the Indian army officer
who had been in the hinterland for twelve years and was one of
the finest Arabists in the eastern service. Before the ship left on
its main mission, the Britons were introduced to a Turkish prisoner of war from the Yemen and they asked him why he had
surrendered. 'Because life is impossible in the Yemen,' he said.
'I have been six or seven years without pay, with bad food and
perpetual fighting. Human nature can't stand it.'

Wemyss and Herbert on their way to Mesopotamia were, for
the moment, in good spirits. As the *Euryalus* made its way to
Muscat and the Persian Gulf, the radio brought them news of
the world's events. *Kut-al-Amara*, of course. And on Monday 3
April, a *Zeppelin raid on London*. Saturday 8 April, as they passed Bushire, *the Russians advancing into Persia from Erzerum*.
From a German source, *the killing of a British consular agent, his
brother and four sepoys at Lingeh the day before*. By Sunday 9 April
they were at the bar of the Shatt-al-Arab, where the Admiral
and his party stepped aboard a pretty little vessel, none other
than Ambassador O'Conor's yacht; now, after service in the
Dardanelles, war-scarred and bearing the title HMS *Imogen*.
'Sir Nicholas would not have liked anyone else to command his
beloved yacht,' said Herbert. On the 10th they were at Qurna,
'beautiful and green'.

Townshend had set 1 April as the last day for survival. They
were now eight days past the accepted limit of endurance at Kut

and cholera was adding to the horror of its investment. Men were combing the bushes on the outskirts of the town for berries to keep them alive. The party disembarked at Qurna and had dinner with Gertrude Bell and Arnold Wilson, from whom they heard that a commission was on its way from London to find scapegoats and that Nixon's head was already on the block. And someone mentioned the interesting fact that Nureddin the Ottoman Commander-in-Chief, had been at Harrow with Townshend. The news would have given little comfort to the troops of either side. The Turks too, had their complaints. As soon as battle was done Arabs would swarm across the battle-fields to rob the dead and the dying, and a Turkish officer taken prisoner by the British said to Herbert: 'Let's have a truce and fight the Arabs together.'

On the evening of 11 April Wemyss and Herbert reached Ali Gharbi, at the point where the Tigris begins its leftward sweep at the head of the Iraq marshlands towards Hanna and Kut; the point to which Townshend would have retreated had his troops possessed the strength and the arms to break through the Turk-ish lines. Aylmer's relief operation had failed a month before with severe losses. The Russian breakthrough in Persia had come to a halt, the Cossacks were in retreat, and the German agents were causing chaos there. It was a black picture. Herbert, squinting through a powerful magnifying glass, for his eyes were now almost useless (though he had the temerity to go grouse shooting!), scribbled in his notebook: 'We started this campaign against one of the great military powers of the world with two brigades of Indians, who ought not to have been used at all . . . on this ground, which to them is holy. We started with the wrong types of boats [for river navigation], and also Indian Generals who looked on the expedition as a frontier campaign.' As they approached the combat lines, Herbert and Wemyss met the intrepid Leachman, who had been through the enemy lines at Kut several times in the secrecy of night, carrying messages from GHQ which could not be trusted to the wireless transmit-ters; 'A very good fellow whom everyone likes.'

At the end, planes began to drop food at Kut but it was too late. General Gorringe came and talked of the 'sorry plight of the men', and an Irish officer remarked: 'We were ready to refuse to fight against Ulster, why should Indians fight the Turks?' On 14 April Colonel Beach invited the newcomers to intelligence headquarters aboard a ship anchored beyond

Hanna. Generals Lake, Money and Williams were present along
with Major Dent of intelligence. They were interrogating a Turkish officer, an ex-schoolteacher nicknamed 'Blackbeard'. The
Turk said to them: 'I will give you all the information you re-
quire. You have failed at Gallipoli, you are held up at Salonika, and you are only visitors here. I don't mind how much I tell
you, because we are going to win.'

On 19 April a new face appeared at the hard-pressed temporary GHQ of the Tigris army. Lawrence had travelled in the rear
of the Admiral's contingent, aboard the SS *Royal George*,
occupying himself on the way with a spate of letters to Hogarth
and Cornwallis, who were running the Arab Bureau in Cairo. 'I
want to bring Gertrude Bell back with me,' he told Hogarth,
'and our Arabian office will be complete.' Before setting out he
had dashed from Cairo to Mediterranean intelligence headquarters at Piraeus, a mystery mission which doubtless involved
last-minute instructions of a verbal nature for his journey to
Mesopotamia, a journey which he was later to claim was 'for
reasons not unconnected with the fall of Erzerum'. Certainly the
fall of Erzerum to the Russians would have given a stronger
hand to the British participants in a game that was about to
begin, had they played their cards more adroitly. Gertrude Bell
and Campbell Thompson met him at Basra. 'We have had great
talks and made vast schemes,' wrote Gertrude. Herbert was
delighted to see his friend Ned. But the generals and the Chief
Political Officer were not pleased. As soon as they heard of the
plan which Lawrence had brought from Cairo and Piraeus they
dissociated themselves from it. But they were powerless to prevent its execution.

'Before this we had hopes of Mesopotamia. The beginnings
of the Arab Independence Movement had been there, under the
vigorous but unscrupulous impulse of Sayid Talib, and later of
Yasin al Hashimi and the military league . . . Unfortunately, Britain was bursting then with confidence in an easy victory: the
smashing of Turkey was called a promenade.'

Lawrence went on to explain that his mission, 'which they did
not really know', was considered to be dishonourable to a soldier, 'which I was not'. He also averred that in the end he did
nothing 'of what was in my mind and power to do'.

On their first afternoon together Herbert and Lawrence
looked out from the intelligence ship anchored at Al Wadi, at
the great blue rock of Pusht-i-Kuh visible in the distance as it

rose out of the Persian plain. Two Germans, it was said, had been offered the choice between apostasy to Islam and a journey over a sheer precipice of the rock just before the war. They chose the latter.

At Easter 1916 – a weekend to be remembered in Whitehall – the generals sat down to discuss peace terms in Mesopotamia. It was a poignant moment for both sides. On 19 April news had come from Baghdad to the Turkish command that Field-Marshal von der Goltz, the architect of their victory, had died from 'spotted fever'. Few believed that he died from natural causes. Enver still opposed the appointment of Liman von Sanders, the victor of the Dardanelles, to supreme command of the Turkish army, but Germany insisted. Enver had a minor victory, however, out of the success which his reluctant ally had planned. He appointed his uncle Khalil to succeed von der Goltz as commander of the army which had been known as Army Group 'F', became *Irakgruppe* and was to become *Yilderim*, or Lightning. And so it was with real authority that Khalil began to negotiate with Townshend, as news came from home of rebellion in Ireland.

But there were delays in the talks and Britain had not abandoned hope of breaking through. Men and animals were tormented by flies which penetrated nostrils and mouths in filthy, squelching clusters. Lawrence went down with fever. On Monday the 24th it was decided to send the river boat *Julna* up river with supplies for the starving garrison. It would run the gauntlet of enemy guns on either bank as well as mines, which would mean almost certain death for its crew. The enterprise was to be commanded by Lieutenant Firman, RN. A senior officer, Lieutenant-Commander Cowley would be number two. When volunteers were sought for the crew every man present stepped forward. In the evening, as the ship was loaded, Herbert, Beach and Leachman made a melancholy trio by the riverside amid the dead and the dying. There were no hospitals, doctors or nurses. *Julna* slid quietly upstream, a volley of gunfire subduing the sound of its engines, a majestic sunset providing the backdrop, pipers of the Black Watch sounding the eerie last rites. *Julna* did not break through. The Turks stretched a wire across the river and forced it into the shore. Firman was killed in action. Cowley was captured and never seen again, almost certainly shot in cold blood. Both were awarded VCs. The crew were taken prisoner and waited to join the men of Kut in captivity.

Aubrey Herbert's diary tells the story from there on, with a few discreet omissions.

28 April: For the last two days I have been standing by. Yesterday morning General Lake sent for me, and talked about the Turks ... Townshend has telegraphed to say that he has only food for two more days and that Khalil has referred to Enver for better terms ... We are not in a position to insist on anything. One is more sorry for Townshend and his men than words can say.

29 April: Colonel Beach came to the *Mantis* [Herbert's berth] at seven and took me off ... off to the front trenches where we met Colonel Aynslee. There Lawrence joined us. [Beach, Herbert and Lawrence went out to the trenches with a white flag.] Walked a couple of hundred yards or so ahead, where we waited, with all the battlefield smells around us.

They waited for several hours in the intense heat of morning while the Turks procrastinated. Finally they emerged from the trenches and were told that they would have to proceed blind-fold to Khalil's camp. They were guided through the Turkish lines by Leachman, the hero-figure of the army. Lawrence had hurt his knee in the trenches and couldn't ride. Beach and Herbert went on by saddle, while Lawrence made his way on foot. 'At last we came to Khalil's camp, a single round tent, a few men on motorcycles coming and going ... Colonel Beach told me to start talking.' Herbert and Khalil had met at an Embassy party in Constantinople, and the Turkish commander retained his 'lion-taming' eyes. He was asked to guarantee that there would be no reprisal against the Arabs of Kut. 'The Arabs are Turkish subjects, not British, and therefore their fate is irrelevant.' Beach asked him for an assurance that there would be no hangings or persecution, but Khalil made no promise.

Then Lawrence began to talk of the sick and wounded. Khalil said 'that he would send 500 of them down river but that he required Turkish soldiers for them in exchange ... Beach asked for the exchange of all our prisoners in Kut against the Ottomans that we had taken.' But Khalil would not take Arabs in exchange for Indian troops. 'Look these brutes have surrendered to you because they are a lot of cowards. What are you to do with men like that? You can send them back to me if you like but I have already condemned them to death. I should like to have them to hang.'

'We must see that Arabs are not sent back by mistake,' wrote Herbert.

Then Khalil made a clever suggestion. 'We would like you to send ships to transport Townshend and his men to Baghdad,' he said. 'Otherwise they would have to march, which would be hard on them.' He promised to let the British have the ships back. 'Impossible,' said Beach, though not for the official record. The army was desperately short of river transport. Khalil was angry to discover that Townshend had destroyed all guns and ammunition. One of the other Turkish officers present told the Englishmen that Townshend would have gone free, but then 'something happened, I don't know what, and now Townshend will be an honoured prisoner at Stanboul'. 'Our final understanding with Khalil was that we were to notify him when we were sending up boats so that he might clear the river. He laughed and said that he had forgotten all about the mines, which we had not.'

The negotiators said their farewells; the English party slept in the Turkish camp that night and were well looked after. Next day, Sunday 30th, Beach told Herbert to stay with the Turks and go on to Kut. He and Lawrence would come up to Kut with the boats to take the British prisoners away.

Herbert's diary does not record that three days earlier, on the 27th, Townshend had sailed upstream to negotiate with Khalil, accompanied by Lawrence and Herbert. In reply to Khalil's insistence on unconditional surrender it was suggested that the British force might be paroled in exchange for all Kut's guns and a million pounds in gold. Khalil is said to have shown interest. The two commanders agreed to meet next day, by which time the Turk could contact Enver and Townshend seek General Lake's view. On the 28th Townshend was told that Enver had rejected the offer, but that for a million pounds and the guns and stores at Kut, Townshend alone could go to India on parole.

What really happened when Herbert and Lawrence came to grips with Khalil on the 28th is told neither in official records nor in the diaries or writings of the Englishmen. They maintained an unaccustomed silence for the rest of their lives. But it is known that they offered the Turks two million pounds for the parole of the army, plus guns and ammunition. One thing was quite sure, however. The Turks and their allies had the advantage of a demoralised captive army to display to the world; they could also claim, as they did, that having failed to conquer the

Turks in war the British had resorted to corruption. It was a propaganda gift that the Turco-German alliance could hardly have dreamt of, and they made the best of it. 'We are gentlemen,' said Enver disdainfully. 'We are not to be bought with gold.' Following the Dardanelles disaster, a war correspondent told Herbert: 'After this I shall confine myself strictly to revolutions.' There was no such apt epitaph for Kut-al-Amara.

Much has been written of the long march into captivity of the 11,000 survivors of the siege; of the separation of officers and men by the Turks so that the former went up river by boat to Baghdad, while the troops, weary, hungry and sick, dragged themselves along the road to Aziziya, Ctesiphon and Baghdad, the road they had followed so hopefully six months before.

The river voyage of Townshend to Baghdad and on to 'honourable' confinement on the island of Prinkipo in the Sea of Marmara, and his conduct during the rest of the war, while those of his men who survived the journey died in thousands, is outside the scope of this essay. But theirs was not to be the last sacrifice of British blood on Mesopotamian soil. Bitter battles had yet to be fought and even after the war had ended, thousands more of their compatriots, mostly young men, were to die in the heat and dust and mud of Mesopotamia, so that it could be united under a name which once denoted a part of it, Iraq, presided over by a monarch of the Sharifian or Hashemite family of Mecca.

The straggling column of officers and men, some 2,800 Britons and 7,200 Indians, left Kut the day after the final surrender terms had been agreed, on 30 April, heading for Turkish GHQ at Shumran. The journey of eight miles was accomplished in hours. Many of the men were too ill to go on and about a thousand of them were exchanged for healthy Turkish prisoners. From there the officers and other ranks were separated, commissioned men both British and Indian going on by boat while the troops went on foot, carrying their few belongings and three dry biscuits each, their rations for three days. Those who survived the arduous journey were put to work on the Anatolian railroads and in the mines. Leonard Woolley, who met some of the officers at the prison camp at Kastamuni, told of the fate of the less fortunate. 'There was tragedy enough in Turkey, but it was rather for the men than the officers. The Turk, who cares little for his own men, cared nothing for ours, and from sickness and neglect, hunger and brutality, three-quarters of them miserably died.'

Fig. 5   Greetings from 'Intelligence', 1918–19

Perhaps the courageous story of the Kut prisoners is best told
by an inconsequential aside. When the survivors arrived in Turkey the officers and men formed football teams. A Turkish
officer who had not been introduced to the game went to watch
a match, and when it was over he remarked: 'I am a bimbashi
who (Allah be praised) has been in many wars and seen much
bloodshed. But *never* have I seen a more desperate battle than
that which you call football. The officers have indeed fought
well: are there many wounded?'

While the men marched, some 350 officers paddled up river
aboard the *Khalifa* past the arch of Ctesiphon which had been so
recently a transient monument of victory, arriving at Baghdad
after a 200-mile voyage on 13 May. There they caught their first
sight for many a month of European women – German Red
Cross nurses – and they noticed three European men gesticulat-
ing to them from one of the barred windows of the citadel in the
bazaar district. They were three adventurers of Indian intelligence – Cree, Tod and Dexter – who had arrived in Baghdad
before hostilities began, officers of MO3 Simla.

Britain had two major interests in Mesopotamia before the war: the activities of Enver's agents and the progress of the German rail system. On 3 January 1914 Major Murphy had journeyed along the Tigris to Baghdad on the same paddle-steamer as now conveyed the officer prisoners, the *Khalifa*. But his purpose had been very different. He had been sent by MO3 to call on Meissner Pasha, who had moved up from Maan on the Hijaz line to command the frantic attempt to complete the line from Haidar Pasha in Turkey to Baghdad. He was met on arrival by the head of Britain's East African military intelligence, Major Richard Meinertzhagen, a devoted bird watcher, and Captain G. R. Maitland of the 14th Lancers. After a cosy reception at Meissner's home, where there was always a welcome for the spies of all nations, and a number of meetings with agents of the Pan-Arab movement, the Britons were able to take back to Whitehall and Simla useful information on German and Ottoman plans. They discovered that the railway was in a terrible mess. Uncharacteristically, the German engineers' surveys were hopeless and there were immense gaps in the line which would take many months to complete. A stretch of some two hundred miles was missing between Tel Ubaid, where Oppenheim's men were at work, and Samarra.

At almost exactly the same time as Murphy, Meinertzhagen and Maitland met in Baghdad, Lawrence and Woolley completed their journey in the wilderness of Zin and Woolley reported to the 'extraordinarily nice' sapper whom, by an uncharacteristic indiscretion, he referred to as his 'senior officer', Stewart Newcombe. Woolley wanted Newcombe to join him and Lawrence back at Carchemish, but on referring to Cairo the senior officer was told that he must not go. A week or two later Newcombe was given fresh instructions. He was to go to Carchemish and then travel by way of Adana, across the Taurus mountains, to Constantinople. He was to take the rail route and report on the German engineers' progress. When he had completed the task the War Office decided that it needed more detailed information. The Carchemish men were therefore sent to follow Newcombe's footsteps. At Aleppo they were fortunate enough to find an Italian engineer who had been sacked by Meissner, and who was only too willing to get his own back on his German employer by giving drawings and details to the Englishmen. It was their first serious intelligence assignment, for Woolley admitted that in Sinai he and Lawrence had been stooges. It was the sapper who 'was making a military map of Sinai, and we were playing the part of the red herrings'. The rail maps and documents they obtained at Aleppo, showing two unbridgeable gaps across the Taurus and Amanus heights between Konia and Aleppo, were, said Woolley, 'the reasons why Lawrence and myself were shoved by the WO into Intelligence as soon as the war began'. It was less than the truth of the matter, but near enough.

Cree, Tod and Dexter were not so lucky as the other staff officers sent to Baghdad before the war. They were concerned with the activities of the Pan-Islamites and a particularly dangerous underground organisation known as the Persian Brotherhood, whose centre of pro-German propaganda activity was at Kadhimain. The President of the Brotherhood, Hajji Ali Akbar, lived there surrounded by followers and with elaborate printing resources provided by Germany, controlling a network of fanatical agents throughout Mesopotamia, Persia and Afghanistan. His lieutenant in Basra was Mirza Muhammad. The efforts of British intelligence officers to penetrate both Enver's Pan-Islamic movement and the widespread cells of Hajji Ali were complicated by the fact that the French Secret Service had arrived on the scene before them, and the French did not readily share confidences with their wartime allies.

The three British officers now imprisoned at Baghdad had left their departure too late. They were about to leave for Basra and a passage to India when war was declared and they were promptly arrested and taken to Turkey. Men of considerable pluck, however, they escaped from their captors and travelled via Mersina to Mesopotamia, where they joined in the defence of Kut, only to be taken prisoner again. They were then charged with 'breaking parole' and were awaiting trial in Baghdad when the captive British officers arrived there.

The officer prisoners from Townshend's army continued their journey up river to Samarra aboard the *Khalifa*, while the unfortunate troops who had made the journey on foot were herded into goods wagons and taken by rail to the same Tigris township, now a neatly laid out archaeological site which the Deutsche Orient Gesellschaft had been excavating when war was declared. As they waited among the antiquities to set out on the next stage of their journey, there was a great hullabaloo among the guards and a Daimler automobile sped past with little Enver standing to greet his troops, trying at the same time to catch a glimpse of the prisoners, armed guards either side of him. The generalissimo was on his way to Baghdad to decorate the heroes of the Mesopotamian campaign. And one of the men on whom he pinned a medal was Hajji Ali Akbar. The British officers were still at Samarra when he returned, smiling triumphantly from his open car, trying as always to look like Napoleon. The other ranks had been sent off before them towards their work camps in the north, and Enver drove along the roads where thousands of them lay down to die, having sold even their boots to buy a little goat's milk and at last run out of currency.

Nearly a year of hard fighting and relentless counter-espionage activity remained before the British force in Mesopotamia was able to break Hajji Ali's ring of agents, many of whom were working for Wassmuss in Persia. Most, it was discovered, were double agents, working for France and Germany. When Mirza Muhammad was eventually arrested in Basra, Colonel Beach had to wait until the French Consul, M. Roux, was away from his post before taking action. Within a few days the French Foreign Ministry wanted to know what Britain's intelligence service thought it was doing. Macdonogh, the DMI, told the Foreign Office that the spy had already been deported. 'Major-General Macdonogh sees no reason to interfere with the discretion exercised by the GOC Mesopotamia in this matter, and would suggest that a reply in this sense be returned to M. Cambon.'

Fig. 6   Greetings from Intelligence Section after the move from Basra to Baghdad, with a 'cuneiform' theme

That was late in 1917. By then the GOC Mesopotamia was General Sir Stanley Maude, 'Systematic Joe'. Townshend and the survivors of his army were in Turkey. The Turkish hero of the Dardanelles, Mustafa Kamal Bey now in command of the Sixth Army Corps had turned back the Russian army from Persia and Armenia and pursued the Cossacks to the Caucasus. The Arab Revolt had been declared and the world waited on the Sharif.

11

Aaron and Jamal

'As when a Prince of dispers'd Israel, chosen in the shade, Rules by no canon save his inward light. And knows no pageant save the pipes and shawms of his proud spirit.'

John Buchan, *A Prince of the Captivity.*

Lewis Einstein returned to the US Embassy in Constantinople in 1915 after an absence of six years. He had witnessed the last year of Abdal Hamid and the tentative arrival of the Young Turks. Now he resumed old acquaintanceships, revived old memories, and looked at the present through the mirror of what seemed an almost tranquil past. He spoke to the agent 'G' of the errors of the Entente: 'Their efforts had always been spasmodic . . . in the beginning they could easily have taken Baghdad . . . at Suez the Turkish army was allowed to retreat unmolested, saved only by the bright moonlight.' He went to dinner with the fanatic Izmet, Prefect of Constantinople, and the venerable Grand Vizier, Prince Said Halim, and he took with him the Princess Najieh, Enver's wife, but the Young Turks would not eat with her: a princess she might be, but still a woman. He spoke of Jamal, Minister of Marine, Governor of the Syrian provinces, and Commander-in-Chief of the Ottoman Fourth Army: 'a picturesque ruffian', as Captain Hall's personnel file called him, 'a megalomaniac, mentally aberrated with a tendency to homicide', rushing around his vilayet in a Daimler motor car, dispensing justice with cruel and arbitrary finality.

Einstein, bearing the cumbersome title 'Special Agent for Entente Affairs', became, with Ambassador Morgenthau, the periscope of the West in the Ottoman Empire. He observed the destruction of the last elements of Al Ahad, the consequence of Georges Picot's indifference, or perhaps of the sinister farsightedness of the French Secret Service, for Al Ahad looked to Britain for support in Syria. He watched the cock-a-hoop celebrations at the end of the year as Allied troops were hurried out of the Gallipoli peninsula, and noted too the toll of Turkish casualties as the wounded were crowded into the Daud barracks, to have their gashed and torn bodies treated cursorily by an overwhelmed Red Crescent. He and Morgenthau recalled the atrocities of past decades and recorded the continued persecution of the Armenians and other Christian minorities, the expulsion of the Greeks from Smyrna, and now the persecution of the Jews of Syria. 'By a final wicked touch of irony', wrote Einstein, 'the unfortunate Armenians and Greeks who had awaited the coming of the Allies were obliged to hold commemorative services to celebrate the departure of those whom they had hoped so ardently to welcome as liberators!'

Still, the Turks had shown themselves in an unfamiliar light in the Dardanelles, brave and in the main honourable. As one British staff officer was to say in retrospect, 'the army in Gallipoli may justly be considered to have been the finest that has ever taken the field in the history of the Turkish Empire'. It would have been fair to add that it had one of the finest of German generals in command, though the German War Office and Enver did everything they could to hinder his task at the height of the battle, just as Britain's politicians undermined their commanders in a conflict which all military and naval experience showed to be suicidal in its very nature.

And on Britain's side, the politicians who had been most active in their support of the Dardanelles campaign, the 'easterners', turned their vigorous attention to the Arab Revolt and to Mesopotamia. One competent observer, Philip Graves, who had shared with Lewis Einstein an on-the-spot view of the Ottoman transformation from Abdal Hamid to the CUP, wrote at that time to Lloyd George from the Intelligence Office, Cairo, reminding him that one show of relatively 'honorable' conduct on the battlefield did not presuppose an 'honorable' peace. 'What of the troops and police who have been used against the luckless Armenians,' he asked, 'or of the Turkish officials led by Talaat Bey who have done their utmost to stamp out that wretched people?' He quoted Talaat: 'I will make any idea of Armenian autonomy impossible for fifty years.'

The rape of the Christian minorities to which Britain, its allies and the enemy powers turned a blind eye, was to go on unchecked, and now Jamal in Syria was to begin a systematic persecution of the Jews. At the outbreak of war he had married an Austrian Jewess and adopted the cause of that race in Palestine. But by the autumn of 1915 he was pursuing an attractive divorcee, Madame Corbetti, in Beirut, and had relinquished his fleeting attachment to the Jews along with his wife. He had told Louis Mallet a year earlier that Egypt was the 'Alsace-Lorraine' of Turkish aspirations; that he would regain the land of the Pharaohs for Constantinople. If he had learnt a salutary lesson at the first attempt he remained unbowed and willing to try again.

In November 1915 Sarah Aaronsohn, or Sarah Abraham (she had married a Bulgarian Jew, Hayyim Abraham, in March 1914 and lived with him since in Constantinople), decided to return to her family at Zichron Yakov.

On the rail journey from Haidar Pasha station in Constantinople to Haifa she was greeted by the sight of prostrate bodies and groups of starving, terrified Armenian women and children. She found Palestine in the grip of Jamal's terror. When the Fourth Army entered Jerusalem through the Jaffa Gate in December 1914 the Jews had greeted it with banners bearing the words, 'Blessed are they that come in the name of the Lord.' Many by now knew her brother Aaron by the Arab word *Jasoos*, the Spy; a word whispered by the older people of the first Aliyah who recalled its implications in the pales of Russia and eastern Europe, spat out contemptuously by the younger generation, 'the bare-foot ones', imbued with the dogmas of revolution and workers' power.

Alex Aaronsohn had returned to Zichron Yakov from America in 1913 at the age of twenty-four only to be conscripted into the Turkish army. He had bought himself out by the time of Sarah's return and joined with Aaron and his companion, Avshalom Feinberg, to form a short-lived organisation called the Gideonites, dedicated to fighting the Ottoman power; fighting for Eretz Israel, if need be in opposition to Ha-Shomer (the Watchmen) and the workers' committees. Aaron, its leader, had lost none of his disdain for 'committee sickness', or Zionists like the notorious Dr Jacobsen, President of the 1912 Congress at Basle, who openly espoused the German cause and were as much the enemy of the new organisation as the Turks and worker revolutionaries. The Aaronsohns were reckless in their opposition to Jamal's regime, in their conviction that salvation for the Jews lay in an allied victory, and Sarah was to become the most dedicated and selfless member of Aaron's small and isolated band in its chosen work. In the backwash of Jamal's ill-fated expedition across the Sinai peninsula in January and February 1915 the Jewish spies often stood shoulder to shoulder with German officers in Fast's Hotel in Jerusalem as they exchanged military and bedroom confidences and 'Jamal' anecdotes. They had embarked on one of the most dangerous and effective espionage campaigns of the war. For the moment, however, they were unable to pass on their hard-won secrets. They had no means of communicating with Cairo, or with Parker's Sinai intelligence, which relied on Arab and Christian agents.

The youngest daughter of the family, Rivka, was sent to the American school at Beirut so that she could maintain contact with the American Consul there. Alex and Aaron were in touch with the American Consul at Jerusalem, Mr Glazebrook, a dry southerner who had been Professor of Theology at Princeton. In March, Alex stood with Glazebrook at Jaffa to watch a 'melancholy' procession as the Turks returned from Suez to the accompaniment of Jamal's claim of a 'triumphant withdrawal', and the populace led a dog, a camel and a bullock through the streets, draped in the flags of Britain, France and Russia, so that stones and filth could be flung at the unfortunate creatures.

Back in 1909, at the time of his discovery of wild wheat, Aaron had lectured to French settlers in Tunisia, noting that Jewish immigration into Palestine had begun in the same year as the French occupation of Tunisia – 1882. He spoke of the Jewish colony. 'The Jew in Palestine, just like the Frenchman here, does not put himself in the place of the native, but alongside him. It is a question of juxtaposition, and not substitution.' Soon after, Aaron went to America to visit Dr David Fairchild of the Department of Agriculture, Judge Louis Brandeis and the wealthy Shmarya Levin of the New York Zionist executive. He conjured a picture of a brilliant civilisation built by hard work on desert soil, an incandescent example to the world at large. *Vous vous croirez en une colonie française*, he had told the French settlers. Give us the support we need and we will realise Herzl's dream of Zion, he told his American hosts. 'I soon discovered that I was in the presence of an extraordinary man', said Fairchild, the son-in-law of Alexander Graham Bell.

Now the agricultural station at Athlit along the coast from his family home, built with American financial aid, was being turned into an espionage agency. By March 1915 Jamal had received orders from Constantinople to refrain from oppressive measures against the Jews, 'because the moment is politically inopportune'. The mercurial Jamal now called them 'our Ottoman brothers'. Aaron took the bull by the horns and protested to the Governor about his agricultural policies, and about his scorched-earth policy. 'What would you say if I ordered you to be hanged?' asked Jamal. 'I would say nothing, Excellency,' replied Aaron, 'but the weight of my heavy body would crack the wood so loud that the sound would be heard in America.'

Jamal no less than other influential men who came into contact with him was impressed by Aaron's knowledge and self-confidence, and he was in urgent need of the Jew's help. He gave the man who was to become the chief intelligence agent of the British army in Palestine an office at Turkish GHQ Damascus. Aaronsohn left his friend and lieutenant, Feinberg, in charge of the espionage station at Athlit. While he was in the lion's den, Feinberg and one of his recruits, the poetic Russian Jew, Liova Schneersohn, planned an escape to Cairo to contact the military authorities there.

Aaron decided that it was time to recall his younger sister, Rivka, from Beirut and send her to safety in America. And he decided that Alex should accompany her to Cairo, where he should make an attempt to contact the British. Alex could then go on to the United States with Rivka to appeal for more funds for Palestine. They were to escape on the American warship USS *Chester*, which called intermittently at Haifa to collect refugees. Helped by Mr Glazebrook and armed with false passports made out to Sephardic Jews they left for Egypt in June. Alex had been told by his elder brother: 'We can't even be sure that they will have confidence in us. Nobody is more conservative in this respect than the English.' He added: 'They may think us capable of betraying them just as we are betraying the Turks.' And he told his emissary to make it clear to the British that they acted neither for material reward nor for vengeance. 'We do it because we hope we are serving our cause.'

Alex had been warned. He was received courteously at GHQ by Captain Trumpledor, hero of the Russo-Japanese war and founder of the Zion Mule Corps, who was already working for the Egyptian Force staff, travelling back and forth to the Dardanelles, where his famous mule-borne army was playing an heroic part. Deedes at GHQ was lukewarm about Alex; Woolley thought he might be an enemy agent; Clayton was not in evidence. It was a disheartening introduction to British military intelligence for a man who was to become one of its most enterprising and longest-serving officers.

Disillusioned, Alex made his way with Rivka to America. But it became increasingly clear to Aaron that someone must gain Clayton's confidence. In early October Avshalom Feinberg left Haifa with the last of the refugees to escape from Palestine, heavily disguised in 'baroque hat, incredible eye-glasses, and a temporary seriousness of mien'. It was intended that Charles Boutagy's father should leave with him, but he was still under suspicion as the result of the incident involving British intelligence earlier in the year and it was decided that he had better stay put.

Woolley had left Cairo for the relative peace of the Port Said intelligence office (Eastern Force) and Avshalom went straight there to meet him. According to surviving accounts they discussed a scheme put forward by Boutagy for an armed uprising relying chiefly on Arab support, but Woolley though the idea unworkable. He wanted the Athlit group to concentrate on intelligence gathering and to remain small and carefully concealed. It was decided to use the monitor ship *Zaida*, which was already in communication with the Arab spy rings at Haifa and Tyre. The elegant, overbearing Woolley and the slim, resourceful Jew had struck a profitable and fearful bargain.

Feinberg and the *Zaida*'s cipher officer, Captain Weldon, worked out a signalling code at the Casino Hotel, which served as Staff HQ, Port Said. Then the Anglophile Avshalom wrote to Henrietta Szold, Secretary of the American Zionist Committee, to tell her: 'The die is cast.' And he remarked:

> Our fate is more and more linked with the Allied cause . . .
> If there is a nation whose attitude towards us is even finer
> than that of America, which is above all praise, it is that of
> the English. For if America offered its bread and its gold to
> friends who had need of it, England let this bread and this
> gold into an enemy country; sent it, almost. And with what
> delicacy, what discretion.

Woolley's spy ship took Avshalom back to Athlit on 4 November 1915, delighted with the success of his mission; and equally delighted to be in time to greet Sarah as she arrived from Constantinople. He sent a message to Raphael Aboulafia, a Russian refugee serving with Trumpledor's corps in Cairo. It said simply: 'Long live the King, and long live our country!' And with a quaint sense of English protocol: 'I shall be returning in six to eight weeks. You know my address, c/o Lt. C. L. Woolley Esq, HQ Port Said.' As for the renewed presence of Sarah, for whom he had long nursed a quiet devotion, he wrote: 'I dare not touch her, though she arouses me.' He confided in Sarah's sister-in-law his unrequited love, but added: 'Who could be good enough to be brother-in-law of a prophet?' On another occasion valour showed through a veil of sensibility: 'Adultery was good enough for King David, why not for me?' he asked.

There had been momentous events in Jamal's dominions during Feinberg's absence. The fate of the Jews of Palestine, like that of the Armenians in Turkey itself, was always uncertain. At one moment peace reigned, then suddenly the iron hand of the Ottoman master came down on them. At the beginning of 1915 the Governor of Jaffa, Beha ad Din, had recommended the deportation of both Christians and Jews from the port. In March came the instruction from Constantinople to seek the co-operation of the Jews. But as the year progressed Jamal reverted to his old ways. As he did so, however, he gave his devious mind to even more explosive matters. As Aaronsohn sat in his office as chief agricultural advisor, Jamal plotted to overthrow the Empire and sought his own aggrandisement as Sultan of a new regime.

Was there, in fact, a more dramatic and pressing reason for Feinberg's hurried journey to Egypt in October? Had Aaronsohn, seated in Jamal's HQ at Damascus, picked up the stirrings of rebellion in his mercurial chief's den? It is possible even that the artful Jamal had taken care to see that the master spy in his midst knew of his proposed insurrection. Woolley never divulged the names of his sources or the nature of the intelligence work in which he was engaged, unlike his Carchemish companion, Lawrence. Jamal's intended *coup* coincided with a projected rising of Syrian Arabs. It is possible that Feinberg went to Egypt with inside information on both contingencies.

This was the moment of Faruqi's sudden desertion at Gallipoli, of his conversations with Mediterranean and Cairo officers, and of his requests to see the Sharif's representatives in Cairo.

Soon after Faruqi's desertion from the Turkish lines at Gallipoli, the Mediterranean Group of the British Secret Service began to send through reports of high-level defections among

Arab officers in the Turkish army and even within the High Command. Russian intelligence too was alive to the same rumours, and even more anxious to exploit them. In December, military intelligence at Cairo informed the Athens Legation that it would not be justified 'in trying to ferment an Arab revolt in Syria', as such an event would give rise to savage reprisals on the part of the Turks.

On 29 December Grey circulated to the Cabinet in London the gist of a message received that day from the Russian Foreign Minister Sazanov: 'We learn from Armenian circles at Constantinople that Jamal Pasha would be prepared to lead an open rebellion against the Turkish Government and the Germans provided the Allies accepted the following terms.' Those terms were a guarantee of the integrity and independence of Turkey in Asia, to include the 'autonomous' provinces of Syria, Palestine, Mesopotamia, Arabia (presumably central Arabia and Yemen), and Armenia, with Cilicia and Kurdistan under the sovereignty of the Sultan, who would be none other than Jamal, whose family would be guaranteed the succession: at the end of the war he, Jamal, would be given financial assistance. If the Allies accepted the terms, the Syrian Governor would declare the downfall of the government in Constantinople and the dethronement of the Sultan, 'who had become prisoners of Germany', and he would enter into a campaign against them. The Allies would support a march on Constantinople with arms and supplies. Jamal agreed to the loss of the Straits and of Constantinople, and was willing to assure the safety of the Americans. The note concluded:

> Mr. Sazanov holds the view that, even in the event of Jamal's failure to overthrow the Government and dethrone the Sultan, any internal disturbance in Turkey would tend to weaken her and thus serve our common purpose, and it would therefore be desirable to enter into secret negotiations with Jamal through trusted Armenian agents.

On 30 December Count Benckendorff, the Russian Ambassador, called at the Foreign Office in London to ask Sir Edward Grey what he thought about encouraging a revolt 'on certain conditions' led by Jamal Pasha. Grey replied that he 'did not think that very much would come of it, but we wished to encourage it for all it was worth'.

In a Cabinet note Grey wrote of reservations concerning the future of the Basra and Syrian provinces, and French interests.

If, however, Jamal's movement was to have any chance of success he must get the Arabs to side with him, and he ought to have an agreement with them. If he did that, our promises to the Arabs would be satisfied by anything to which they themselves had willingly agreed. I observed to Count Benckendorff that it would be necessary to consult the French Government about Syria especially . . . I told Count Benckendorff that we had carefully abstained from any promises or discussion of the Caliphate. This we regarded as a Moslem question to be settled by Moslems.

In November 1915 there had been changes in Constantinople which reflected disaffection in the Empire. The strong men, Enver and Talaat, took the Foreign Ministry from the gentle Said Halim, who had combined the post with the Prime Ministership and gave it to the fat, genial Francophile Halil Bey, whom Fitzmaurice likened to Mirabeau Tonneau. And the German envoy, Baron von Wangenheim, whose disputes with his own Foreign Office and with Liman von Sanders grew increasingly vitriolic, was succeeded by Count Wolff-Metternich, the Ambassador in London up to the outbreak of war. But the Count was not to find an easy task awaiting him in the Ottoman capital. Wangenheim, who died shortly after his return to Berlin, had left behind a legacy of mistrust. Wolff-Metternich lasted almost a year, by which time the State Secretary Jagow was replaced by his principal Under-Secretary, the Jew Zimmermann; and the Ambassador was replaced by his understudy, von Kühlmann, the German Fitzmaurice.

At the end of December 1915, soon after Sarah Aaronsohn's arrival at Zichron Yakov from Constantinople, the *Zaida* returned to Athlit on an appointed day, but it had inexplicably changed the signalling cipher Feinberg had agreed with Weldon. After several days the adventurous Avshalom decided to don the uniform of Aaron's anti-locust brigade, and cross Sinai in an attempt to reach Woolley and find out what was happening. He was within sight of Suez when a Turkish patrol caught up with him. He was thrown in gaol at Beersheba. His guards were bribed by one of Aaron's agents working in the Ha-Shomer organisation, Yusef Lishansky, with gold supplied by the Athlit group, while Aaron protested to Jamal that the 'bloody Germans' had arrested his secretary. Jamal loathed the Germans who still laughed and sneered at his Suez campaign. Avshalom was released. But Aaron's own position had grown increasingly dangerous as Jamal jumped from one bandwagon to another, and he had begun to look for an escape route to England. Several months passed without contact with the outside world. In June 1916 Aaron sent Feinberg to Constantinople to arrange a visit to Rumania, where there were reliable British agents, ostensibly for discussions on agricultural matters. But while Avshalom was away, Woolley, whose code had been broken by the Germans, was able to send a written message ashore.

'In three weeks' time to the day, we will return.' *Zaida* did not return, however. It was never seen again.

At the beginning of July, Clayton suggested that Woolley take a holiday and so, in his own words, 'I did a few jobs and then put into the Gulf of Alexandretta'. He had made sure that his chef was provided with the ingredients of a sumptuous meal on what promised to be a luxury holiday aboard the *Zaida*. They had just finished breakfast and the Captain had gone to the bridge to relieve the First Officer when there was a mighty explosion. They had hit a mine. The crew jumped overboard and clung to pieces of wreckage as Lord Rosebery's yacht went down in twenty-eight seconds. Woolley's last recollection was of the cook lamenting bitterly that his first attempt at goose stuffed with dried peaches and pistachio nuts had gone under with the spy ship. Woolley and his companions were picked up by a waiting Turkish vessel, and they spent the next two years as prisoners of war. The Turks, it is said, gave up as hopeless the task of confining the Englishman who had dug at Carchemish and was destined to dig famously at Ur of the Chaldees; he was altogether too demanding a personality for their ordinary prisoner-of-war system, and they let him go where he liked at Kastamuni, where the officer prisoners of Kut were taken, and in Constantinople.

Woolley was an outrageous snob with a slight, somewhat accentuated lisp, to whom all men were expected to defer, even his captors. But he met his match after the war in his wife, Katherine, an artist of real ability who demanded the absolute acquiescence of all around her and permitted no contradiction of her word. One night she told her husband before she went to bed: 'Len, I am going to die this night.' Next morning he found her, true to her word, dead beside him.

The sinking of the *Zaida* was a bigger blow to Aaronsohn than to its temporary owner. He was more and more appalled by Turkish atrocities in his native land, and by Jamal's swaggering, insensitive rule. Everywhere they went, he, Sarah and Avshalom Feinberg saw the army and the *gendarmes* at work, as often as not queuing to rape a lone Armenian or Jewish girl, one or two of them holding her down to prevent too much screaming or kicking while they took it in turns to take their varied pleasures. They bestowed their favours on Arab boys with as much gusto, and revelled in the 'exquisite pain' inflicted by the bastinado, especially the caning of bare feet; and the pox, 'unnaturally acquired' was rife among young recruits. Aaronsohn loathed his masters and his opposition to them grew increasingly dangerous. But it was the burden of knowing the innermost secrets of the Central Powers to which his office in GHQ Damascus admitted him, and of significant events in Cairo and Mecca, that made a visit to London imperative.

In July 1916 he travelled to Constantinople with Liova Schneersohn, who acted as his secretary. He used the name of another Sephardic Jew, Hayyim Cohen, and carried a letter from Jamal permitting him to travel anywhere in Europe in pursuit of his scientific work. He called at the German Embassy in Constantinople for a visa to go on to Berlin, telling them that he had important information on the breeding of a new type of sesame seed, rich in oil, which would be of vital interest to a fuel-starved Reich. He left Schneersohn behind to await his instructions and arrived in Berlin in August. He was well received by the German scientific community, though what information he passed on to them about sesame breeding is not clear from his diary. Fortunately he was in Berlin at the same time as the American rabbi, Judah L. Magnes, who was there on a relief mission, and was able to give Aaron a good deal of help.

He spent a month in the German capital picking up information of the greatest value before going on to Copenhagen, where he was joined by Rabbi Magnes a few days after his arrival. It is clear that by this stage British intelligence was aware of his mission since he was able to arrange a secret meeting with the Ambassador, Sir Ralph Paget, Copenhagen being a hotbed of espionage with agents constantly watching the Embassies. Paget contacted the Berne intelligence station, which gave instructions as to Aaron's route to London. He and Magnes caught a Danish ship bound for America, which by agreement with the Admiralty was intercepted off Kirkwall in the Orkneys and Aaronsohn was 'arrested'. News of the capture of the 'Turkish spy' was leaked to the Ottoman and German authorities. At the end of October 1916 he was seated in an armchair in the headquarters of Special Intelligence, where Hall and Thomson interviewed the most famous spies of the war. But none of them had a more electrifying effect on the interviewers than the fair-complexioned Jew from Palestine.

Thomson talked to Aaronsohn over several days and found his guest, still armed with Jamal Pasha's firman and other documents which guaranteed his freedom of movement, 'a rare and remarkable individual'. The head of Special Branch, who with 'Blinker' Hall had become the antennae of the British Government at home and abroad, listened intently to Aaronsohn's secrets, to his advice on natural water supplies for the Egyptian Expeditionary Force in Sinai and Palestine, his views on the best course for a supply railroad across the desert; and to his explanation of his own part in the war, his desire to help the Allied cause not as an idealist or a false partisan, but out of duty to his homeland and the Zionist cause. On a foggy 2 November by St James's Park in London he described to Thomson the Palestinian terrain, a day's journey of exploration in Caesarea, its geology, biblical and Roman ancestry, flora and subterranean waterways. Thomson was spellbound. But it was not his impact on Thomson so much as on other more politically important figures that made Aaronsohn's visit to London at the end of 1916 an event of special significance.

At the beginning of the year, Britain's military intelligence organisation had at last assumed a coherent pattern. In the aftermath of the Dardanelles disaster and with the advent of Field-Marshal Robertson as Chief of the Imperial General Staff, the archaic structure of a military operations division trying to control war strategy and an intelligence network involving thousands of employees at home and thousands of agents strung across the world was straightened out. After a temporary reshuffle at the end of 1915 (when Brigadier-General 'Freddie' Maurice was made DMO with General Callwell in temporary charge of intelligence), Macdonogh, who had been in charge of MO5, was appointed Director of Military Intelligence. MI2 took over from the equivalent section of the old MO directorate, the Ottoman Empire, and Arabia, and added the territories of Persia, Afghanistan, Egypt, the Sudan and India to its spectrum.

MI6, the old medical division (previously absorbed by MO1, Special Intelligence) became responsible for internal supervision, and MI3 absorbed the Russian Empire, which by late 1916 was one of the most vital areas in the Secret Service deliberations of both the Allied and the Central Powers. But even the formation of a thoroughly organised Military Intelligence Directorate could not for the moment diminish the dominating role of Captain Hall's Admiralty Intelligence Division. In many of the affairs of the Middle East, including those of life-and-death concern to Aaronsohn and his colleagues in Palestine, Syria and Egypt, it was the bustling Hall, aided by the vast funds available to the senior service, who called the tune.

Soon after the declaration of war, one of Hall's men, Dr H. N. Dickson, commandeered a room in the premises to which the Royal Geographical Society had just moved in Kensington Gore from its previous accommodation in Savile Row. At that time the resources of MO4 were unable to cope with the constant cries for help from the armies in Europe. Little work if any had been done on the maps which were becoming necessary for territories in the east to which the war might spread. Dickson set to work at what was described as a 'leisurely' pace with Douglas Carruthers and Arthur Hinks, the Society's Secretary, in an effort to make up some of the leeway. As they did so, another of Shakespear's undercover missions during the 1914 journey came to light. One of the first tasks of the Kensington Gore unit was to attempt to detail a scheme worked out between Shakespear, Mark Sykes and Hogarth soon after the Captain's arrival in London; a motorised invasion of Syria from Najaf in southern Iraq along the Darb Zobaida, and thence along the road taken by Shakespear via the Hayaniya wells and Labba to Jauf and Wadi Sirhan. Such an invasion would certainly have surprised Jamal's Syrian army, and it was under active consideration in London and Cairo in December 1916. It explains Shakespear's diligent map work as he waited at Zarud for news of Saleh al Mutawah's mission to Zamil.

The Zionist cause gained impetus at this time from the appearance of a Jewish officer at the War Office. In November 1916, at the time of Aaronsohn's visit, Major Frederick Kisch was appointed GSO2, responsible for Middle East affairs including negotiations with the Sharif of Mecca. Kisch was the son of a remarkable Czech, Hermann Kisch, who emigrated to England, studied at Trinity College, Cambridge, and entered the Indian Civil Service, becoming Director General of the Indian Post Office. An early connection with the Zionist movement, not through Herzl's Congress but through the Jewish Territorial Organisation established by the journalist and author Israel Zangwill, rubbed off on the young Fred. In 1907 he graduated in second place from the RMA Woolwich and went to India, where he began a life-long devotion to Freemasonry, becoming the twenty-first initiate of the Quetta Lodge.

He later visited the lodges of Egypt and Palestine, where he found Jews, Arabs and Christians meeting freely together. At the outbreak of hostilities he left Bombay with the first India Corps to go to France. He was thirty-six years old and with his eager fellow officers he inquired: 'Are we too late?' when their troopship docked at Marseilles. Six months later Kisch was one of the few among them still alive. In October 1915 he was sent to Mesopotamia, filled with the horrifying memories of Ypres, where he fought with the Jullunder Brigade, though memories of France were soon exorcised by the new horror of war along the Tigris, in which he sustained a shoulder wound. He arrived at the War Office in September 1916 to work for Macdonogh, 'a man of remarkable attainments and kindly disposition', and settled in on the third floor with Major R. A. Steel, the GSO1 in MI2 who was also of the Indian Army, and Major W. H. Gribbon, who had served in Turkey with Lieutenant-Colonel Maunsell and had succeeded his old chief as the Turkish expert in military intelligence.

It was the time of Wassmuss's most intense activity in Persia, of the widespread anti-British feeling which that Adonis of German intelligence engendered in the wild regions of Tangistan and Arabistan, and of the prodigious thousand-mile march of Sir Percy Sykes's South Persian Rifles from India to Bushire which restored a little of Britain's battered prestige among fanatic people in Persia and across the Shatt-al-Arab in Basra province. Meetings of the section to discuss such matters were usually held in Room 328 at Whitehall Place, Sykes sketching away as he talked and listened to the professionals; Sir Denison Ross, Gertrude Bell's Arabic teacher who was head of the London School of Oriental Studies, often joining them to contribute his mite. Kisch shone among the luminaries and Sykes took a great liking to him.

War Office Intelligence Division was running out of space, and Room 328, with its wall covering of Sykes's irreverent cartoons, had to be evacuated along with several other apartments. MI2 was given new accommodation up on the roof, in vermin-infested wooden shelters. The mice became such a menace that Kisch acquired a large and ferocious tom cat to keep him company. He had no need to look far for a name. Wassmuss the scourge of the British in Persia found his namesake in the scourge of the vermin of Whitehall Place. But Wassmuss was unco-operative. He preferred pigeons to mice, and so from December 1916 onward the negotiations that accompanied Britain's war in far-off Mesopotamia, the threats of uprising in India, the Sharif affair, and other weighty matters were dealt with to the accompaniment of Wassmuss's precarious journeys along the ramparts. Many a document that was to exercise the political partisans of the future was composed, amended and sometimes blotted as officers of MI2(b) gazed through their temporary windows at his hunting exploits. When he was not stalking prey he slept peacefully in Kisch's in-tray.

Sykes had turned his fertile mind to the question of Zionism not so much out of concern for its rights or wrongs as for its usefulness to the Allied cause, and early in 1916 he had found reinforcement for his belief that its utility could be great. He went to Russia with Picot in order to clear with the Peterhof the Inter-Allied Agreement which he and the Frenchman had drawn up; a clearance demanded by the 1914 Declaration of London in which the Allied powers agreed to consult each other before determining peace terms. Sykes and Picot met with Foreign Minister Sazanov and the Ambassador, Sir George Buchanan, in March, and all went smoothly. So long as Russia received the long-coveted prize of Constantinople, Britain and France could take more or less what they liked. The Russians had occupied Trebizond and Erzerum while Sykes was in Petrograd. The Germans and Turks were in retreat in Persia and Georgia. Sykes had time to look around and he noticed the power of Zionism in Russia. He expressed in writing thoughts of using its worldwide resources in the Allied cause, and suggested that a chartered company in Palestine might satisfy Zionist aspirations. Sir Arthur Nicolson, Permanent Under-Secretary and Godfather of the Foreign Office, sent him a wire: 'Keep such thoughts to yourself.'

Sykes was the self-proclaimed amateur of the political establishment, a gentleman among players, Burton-like in temperament, choleric, mercurial, brilliant and guided in everything he did, good or ill, by the intensity of his patriotism. He had a natural affinity with men whose allegiances were devout and whose minds were yet sharp enough to match his own. He found such men at the War Office in November 1916, in Fred Kisch and the visitor from Palestine, Aaron Aaronsohn.

A few months earlier Sykes had met Rabbi Moses Gaster, friend of Herbert Samuel. The Rabbi had first opened his eyes 'to what Zionism meant'. But his pro-Zionist sentiments, like the pro-Arab sentiments which had preceded them, were largely opportunist. Zionist opinion was 'the key to the acceptance of the Allied agreements of 1916', agreements hammered out with Picot and the Russians, which had nothing whatever to do with Arab or Jewish opinion, since neither racial entity had been consulted.

But Sykes was a man of passionate if not always long-lasting conviction. One of his biographers was to write: 'the more Sykes saw of Aaronsohn, the more he liked his forthright patriotism . . . and the more Aaronsohn's confidence in Jewish colonization appealed to him. If Rabbi Gaster a few months before had provided Sykes with the grace note of Zionism in Europe, here was Aaronsohn who had actually played the trumpet in Palestine.'

12

The Sharif's Revolt

No sooner had the General Staff in Basra said a most willing farewell to Herbert and Lawrence than another representative of the Bureau arrived. This time it was the dapper George Lloyd. He was just as busy as his colleagues, and no less given to immediate and brazen assessments of those with whom he came into contact. On 27 May he wrote to Wingate, who was now taking an increasingly active part in the Bureau's affairs. It was a strange letter, castigating the Government of India, its Commander-in-Chief, and its Finance Member or Chancellor, whose parsimony was now blamed for the lack of ambulances and medical supplies in Mesopotamia.

Lloyd began with an attack on the local attitude to the Bureau: 'Cox has talked to me a great deal about this, and when I arrived I found him still not fully alive to the main objects of the thing.' Kut's surrender was but a month past and its survivors were still trudging painfully through the wilderness. The last thing in the world Cox and the generals wanted was to have to listen yet again to the enthusiasms of the Cairo brigade. But listen they must for Kitchener was still at the War Office and it was with War Office approval that the *Intrusives* descended on Basra. 'Shortly after my arrival he [Cox] received a rather testy telegram from India referring to L's [Lawrence's] visit and expressing some bewilderment as to the status of the bureau,' said Lloyd. The new Viceroy, Lord Chelmsford, and the Commander-in-Chief, General Lake, had decided that Major Blaker of intelligence should be in charge of the Bureau in Basra, under the overall supervision of Colonel Beach of course. But Cox wanted to keep an eye on it too. And so it was decided that Gertrude Bell, who was acceptable to all sides, should take it under her wing. 'Gertrude Bell seems to be the perfect person for the job', Lloyd told Wingate. That, in any case, was the job Gertrude was sent to Basra to perform.

The day after Lloyd's letter went off to Cairo, London received a wire from Lord Chelmsford. 'You are I think aware that Captain Lawrence was recently deputed here temporarily from Egypt,' he told the War Office, 'in connection with certain projects of which the Arab Bureau was one . . . In view of the modified aspect in which this institution is presented to us by Lawrence, I propose that Miss Gertrude Bell and not Major Blaker should act as corresponding officer for Mesopotamia.' It was clear that the new Viceroy was no happier than Hardinge with the activities of Cairo.

While Lloyd, Cox, General Lake and Gertrude Bell were occupying themselves with the organisational problems and status of the Bureau, Basra was brought to a standstill by three Cossack officers who rode over the hills from Erzerum to Al Gharbi on the Tigris. They received a tumultuous welcome from the British troops. The Russians had 'the time of their lives', according to Miss Bell. After that brief celebration of an all-too-rare Allied victory, the staff and politicals of Mesopotamia settled down to the reorganisation of the army and to the setting up of provisional administrations in the occupied regions; administrations which usually consisted of one young Assistant Political Officer in charge of a hostile and volatile population of tribesmen. Basra ceased to concern itself very much thereafter with the Bureau, leaving Gertrude Bell to send to Cairo regular reports and summaries of tribal history which kept Hogarth and his men informed and entertained.

Herbert and Lawrence returned to Cairo late in May 1916. As they arrived, Storrs, Hogarth and Cornwallis boarded HMS *Dufferin* at Suez to journey down to Jiddah, where they hoped to conclude the bargain with the Sharif. They were armed with £10,000 in gold, guarded by two NCOs, and a promissory note for a further £50,000. Their guidelines for negotiation were by no means precise, but the aim was clear. Grey had told McMahon in the course of the preceding talks with the Sharif that there was no time to 'discuss an exact formula', and at the foot of McMahon's reply the Foreign Secretary had written: 'What we want is Arab help *now* against the Turks.'

Neither the Arab side nor McMahon had been told at this stage that the talks which had been going on between Sykes and Picot, and between Britain, France and Russia in Petrograd since late 1915, had resulted in an agreement which was contingent on the success of the talks with the Sharif but which made a

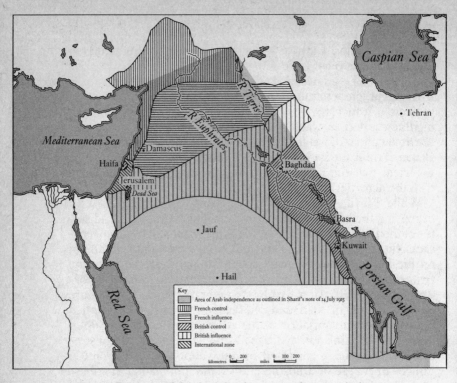

Map 12   Division of the Arab lands in accordance with the
Sykes–Picot agreement of 1916

nonsense of the claim already made by Husain and granted by
Britain. The post-war division of the Ottoman Empire would,
come what may, involve the annexation of Constantinople to
Russia and the paramount influence of France in Syria and Britain in Mesopotamia. McMahon had urged caution on his Foreign Secretary. Whatever was conceded to France must be
restricted 'to the smallest limits possible', he wrote. But Picot
had told Sykes in front of the Russian Foreign Minister that if
the 'Arab state' was allowed an outlet on the Mediterranean
coast he would not hesitate to stir up the Maronite Christians of
Syria against the Arab movement.

Had the Sharif known what was going on he would assuredly
have reverted to his old paymasters in Constantinople. As it was
he stayed aloof and waited for Britain and France to sink in a
mire of mutual suspicion. A vastly intrigued delegation of
French politicians and *agents provocateurs* awaited the arrival of

the Storrs mission. On 24 May McMahon had sent a telegram to the Foreign Secretary:

> Storrs urgently required by Abdullah, Sharif's son, to meet him on Arab coast. Sharif asking for £50,000. Abdullah for £10,000. Faisal about to arrive Mecca. News distinctly encouraging ... indicates fall of Kut has not affected Sharif and his plans. I therefore recommend strongly complying with requests of Sharif and Abdullah for money. Will send Storrs as required accompanied by member of Arab Bureau.

At this point the India Office Under-Secretary, Lionel Abrahams, stung by acid Treasury comments and Foreign Office acquiescence, drew attention to the term 'demand' which occurred repeatedly in the Sharif's communications. 'I remember a story of Washington's reply to the French ministers' *demands*. Washington told them: "*If your government asks it may have; but I will not submit to demands.*" . . . I trust that Sir Henry McMahon, in his anxiety to placate the Sharif, does not permit that potentate to impose his *demands* on us,' wrote the Under-Secretary. 'It is far from satisfactory correspondence and goes far to convince me that we want the equivalent of an Arab Bureau in London.'

Faisal, the man who was to become the legendary prince of the Arab Revolt, toyed with both sides up to the eleventh hour. He spent the first three months of 1916 at Jamal's side in Damascus, and was in close touch with Enver. While the Turks arrested every important member of the Arab Autonomy movement, the Sharif's third son was privy to the innermost secrets of the Turco-German command in Syria. On 17 March Clayton received another set of 'demands' from the Sharif. It was unsigned and undated, and requested more money and provisions. 'Rising will come either last few days of ensuing Arab month or the month after,' it read.

A month later, on 16 April, Wingate wired Clayton: 'Information obtained in conversation with "O". Sharif has communicated plans for rising to Arab chiefs. Enver has been in Madina. Left hurriedly for Damascus accompanied by Faisal. Then to Baghdad. Faisal's present whereabouts unknown to "O".' At about the same time Colonel C. E. Wilson, Wingate's special representative in the Hijaz, sent the DMI a copy of a message from the Turkish commander in the Yemen to the Sharif, telling the latter (on 24 March) that a party of Germans led by Major von Mueller had left southern India (actually Java) on 2 January, had reached Sanaa safely and was about to leave Lohaya for the Hijaz. The Sharif was asked to afford them every facility. Either the Turks knew nothing of the impending revolt or they were testing the Sharif's loyalty. Husain had forwarded the document to Wilson as 'an indication of his good faith'.

Appended to the message about von Mueller's German party was a letter from Faisal to his father, explaining that he had returned to the Meccan fold. 'In reality nothing compelled me to come back except that I have seen the general state of affairs which manifested disturbance and utter ruin.' But a few sentences on he spoke of the rumoured fall of Erzerum, Van and Bitlis to the Caucasus army, events which had not been admitted by the Ottoman High Command, and of the surrender of 45,000 Turkish troops to the Russians. Faisal had begun to sense a change in the direction of the wind in the immediate aftermath of the Turks' victory in the Dardanelles, and had decided to take his chance with Britain.

On the way to Jiddah Storrs's party was held up at the island of Qaddima near Rabegh, awaiting the arrival of HMS *Fox* with the agent-interpreter Ruhi aboard. When the ships met, Storrs was told that they would proceed to Ras Makhluk along the coast where they would be met by Araifan ('O'). While Storrs sweated and waited for Araifan (who had promised to bring with him the heads of seven Germans murdered the week before at £1 per head) the Foreign and India Offices both began to doubt the wisdom of what was being done. Hirtzel noted in the India Office Political and Secret diary apropos a communication from the Amir Faisal: 'Faisal's letter obscure, but the reverse of reassuring. It seems fairly clear that he is afraid of breaking with the Turks. He speaks of *the end of the Ottoman power* and the divisions of that Empire as *calamity*.' On 30 May the Foreign Secretary told McMahon that there was no objection to giving £10,000 to Abdullah and £50,000 to Husain, 'if there is a real uprising'.

Thus armed, Storrs steamed back towards Jiddah in convoy with HMS *Fox*, which carried the Sharif's agent. And from there on all is confusion. Storrs's account of the proceedings is less breezy than is his usual literary wont, if only because the discussions themselves and the subsequent events are more bizarre than any description could make them out to be. Araifan had received a message from Husain, addressed to Storrs, 'Honourable and respected', regretting his own inability to be present and also the absence of Abdullah, who had asked for the meeting, 'urgently', in the first place. The tables were turned before the bargain was struck. The Sharif's last sentence, after asking for guns and ammunition, read: 'My only request of you is to start operations in Syria to the best of your ability.'

The rising of the tribes had been fixed for Friday, 16 June. It transpired however that the Sharif had changed the date to the previous Saturday, the 10th. The news was given to Araifan, who went to Mecca to meet Husain, since Storrs and his Christian companions could not enter the Holy City. It was decided that Zaid, the Sharif's youngest son, should meet Storrs at Samina, six miles from Jiddah on Tuesday 6 June. On the Monday HMS *Dufferin* arrived with the British emissaries off Jiddah, and they were taken by cutter at 5.30 the next morning to the meeting place, Storrs being carried ashore by two slaves. The young prince appeared in black cloak and yellow headdress, wearing the sandals of Mecca. He was twenty years old, the Sharif's son by his second wife, a Circassian, and possessed of an easy manner and grace.

Speaking for his father, Zaid confirmed the date of the Revolt as 10 June, with uprisings in Madina to be led by Faisal and Ali, at Mecca by the Sharif himself, at Taif by Abdullah, and at Jiddah under an Amir of the Harb tribe. The conversation soon turned to money. 'Glancing hurriedly down the list of *talabs* [requests] in the first documents handed to me, I observed the mention of £50,000 with an additional £20,000, making a total of £70,000 and explained to Zaid our position in this matter, saying that the first sum would be forthcoming as soon as we had certain news that the uprising had begun and was in progress,' said Storrs. Zaid replied: 'I am then happy to be able to announce to you that it began yesterday at Madina.'

Storrs asked him what news he had of its results. Zaid corrected himself. He had meant 'was timed to begin' or 'had doubtless begun'. Storrs assured the young Prince that His Majesty's Government would be far from niggardly, once the event was 'demonstrably on foot'. Already the family which claimed descent from the Prophet's chivalrous tribe, the Quraish, had begun to quake. The Turks had 80,000 regular soldiers in

Syria, would they not take a terrible vengeance on the Sharif's
army and family unless Britain intervened? Cornwallis, who
appears to have contributed little to the proceedings, corrected
Zaid, saying there were 30,000 Ottoman troops in Syria. Zaid
refused to accept the figure.

Zaid was taken aboard HMS *Dufferin*, where he renewed a
request for arms for the Hijaz army and expressed surprise that
the ship's guns could not be removed and taken ashore for the use
of his father's troops. The Captain promised that he would return
to Jiddah on the following Tuesday (13 June) with Aziz Ali al
Masri, other Syrian officers and a Maxim gun, whereupon the
Arabs went ashore carrying Abdullah's gold and 1,000 cigarettes
for Ali and Faisal, the two smokers of the family.

Aboard ship on the evening of 6 June Storrs wrote a letter
home, in which he told his family that he had been awarded the
CMG and went on:

> What gratifies and thrills one is that, after the last twenty
> months incessant pressing of the authorities, and their tur-
> ning the smooth cheek of ill-informed criticism of Simla
> (upon whose heart I feel sure is engraved the mystic and
> blessed expression of Moslem Susceptibilities), with prick-
> ings on and heartenings up of friends in Mecca, the Arabs
> have, as Reuter will announce today, definitely thrown off
> the stupid oppression and discomforts they have endured all
> these years, and incidentally struck what should be a fatal
> blow at the religious prestige of the Turk . . . the loss of the
> two Holy Places they have so long exploited should prove in
> the end mortal to the Jews now reigning in the Bosphorus.

Storrs was about to discover that the wish is not always sire to
the event. As he disembarked at Suez following the Jiddah talks,
he was greeted by newspaper headlines in French, conveying the
sensational news: 'Les alliés honorent Kitchener.' Kitchener, the
father of the Arab Revolt, had been drowned in the icy waters of
the Atlantic on the very day that his amanuensis in Cairo had, in a
manner of speaking, sealed the agreement with the Sharif. It was
one of the truly remarkable ironies of history, almost too neat a
resolution of events to be coincidental. Britain's administrators
had urgent need to be rid of Kitchener, and he was being sent to
Russia chiefly as a device to free the War Office of his all-pervading presence.

Storrs wrote to his friend, Henry Crust: 'The loss of my dear old chief, to whom you (more than most) know how much I owe, has greatly shaken me. Three years without one disagreeable word or even look from a man with so many preoccupations . . . The effect of the news here was one of simple consternation.' Perhaps it was as well for the old warrior that he did not live to assume the blame for yet another eastern disaster.

The Sharif's 'Foreign Minister', his son Abdullah, claimed that Mecca surrendered on 13 June, without a struggle, for to engage in open warfare in the Holy City was unthinkable. On the 16th, true to his word, the Captain of HMS *Fox* sailed into Jiddah harbour and bombarded the coast, whereupon the Turks evacuated the city. But Taif held out momentarily, and Madina, the terminus of the Hijaz railroad and the most strategically important town in the Sharif's domain held out until the end of the war. So did Maan, the Turks' garrison at the junction of Syria and the Hijaz. The Royal Navy held the Red Sea coast of Arabia in an iron grip.

The British and Turkish military commanders would have been content to live with existing problems, fighting the real and inevitable battles of western and central Europe, of the Mediterranean and Mesopotamia and East Africa; but the *Intrusives* were determined to foster what Kitchener had begun, to turn political adventure into military reality.

The events which followed from that determination became known to the world as the story of 'Lawrence of Arabia'; a story of stupefying naïveté that has fascinated generations of writers, historians, scholars, poets and ordinary men and women. It is a myth to which men of academic distinction have devoted their working lives, scrambling endlessly through letters and diaries in search of the 'truth' of this and that venture, writing volume after volume of appraisal and re-appraisal, countering every attempt to put the matter into some kind of perspective with charges of calumny, deliberate distortion, bullying, muck-raking and general vilification. More biographical studies have been devoted to Lawrence than to almost any other figure in history. Publishers' offices are piled high with new attempts to exploit the legend that has grown up. Even the Germans, whose concern for documentary evidence is usually such as to reduce the most adventurous tale to an indigestible recital of factual detail, have fallen victim to the unaccountable charisma that attaches to this diminutive, talkative soldier who looked like a girl in his pristine Arab dress and of whom few Arabs had ever heard until the publishing industry and the film-makers penetrated even their awareness, so that suddenly old men of the towns and villages of Syria and the Hijaz remembered. Whenever the Germans write about one of their own desert adventurers, and there are several among them who deserve the highest praise, they include in their titles the interrogative 'Germany's Lawrence of Arabia?' It is a strangely pervasive myth, and it owes its origin and its perpetual appeal to two vital events: firstly, the appearance in Cairo of an obscure American professor named Lowell Thomas, who was invited to witness the desert war by Britain's Ambassador to the United States, Cecil Spring-Rice, at the instigation of John Buchan, then in charge of information and propaganda at the Foreign Office; and secondly, the publication by Lawrence of his own account of the 'side show' in which considerable writing talent and his acknowledged debating skill combined to produce a most colourful, memorable and grandiloquent account of the Desert Revolt.

Yet not one of the legion of writers and investigative journalists, historians and romanticists who have approached this perennial subject, ever thought of searching the papers of the two men who deployed Lawrence and the other Cairo intelligence officers in the Hijaz and the subsequent Syrian campaign: Colonels Parker and Newcombe. Both men were modest to the point of self-effacement, both supported Lawrence when his story broke deafeningly on the world in the post-war years and defended him against detractors who in their opinion were actuated more by malice than a desire to establish the truth. Newcombe befriended him to the end of his life and Lawrence was godfather to his son. Kitchener's nephew, Colonel Parker, kept his distance. Had the yarn-spinners delved deep enough, they would have discovered that he kept a day-by-day diary of events, which recorded the movements of British officers, the progress of the Sharif's campaign, details of spies and agents in Sinai and the Hijaz, and personal correspondence with Lawrence himself. That diary and other papers which tell the detailed story of the Arab Revolt lay in a locked box in the keeping of his daughter for nearly fifty years after his death in 1935, unopened and unsought. It throws a clear light on Anglo-Arab relations and the Arab Revolt of 1916.

Storrs conveyed to McMahon the young Prince Zaid's doubtful assurance: 'Risings began at Madina 5 June.' He added:

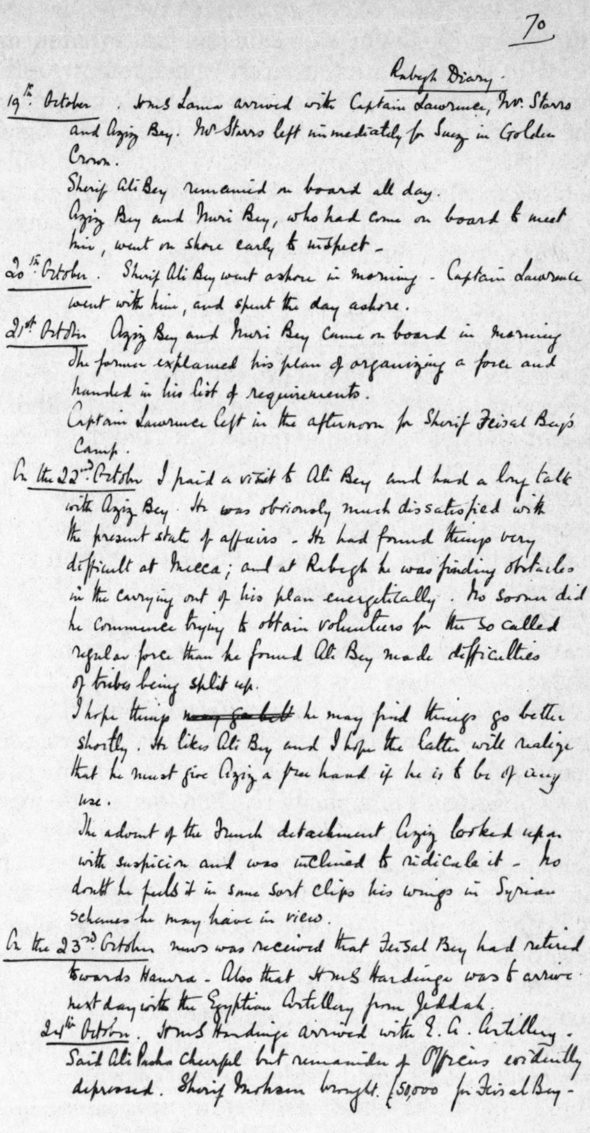

70

Rabegh Diary.

19th October . HMS Lama arrived with Captain Lawrence, Mr. Storrs and Aziz Bey. Mr. Storrs left immediately for Suez in Golden Crow.

Sherif Ali Bey remained on board all day.

Aziz Bey and Nuri Bey, who had come on board to meet him, went on shore early to inspect -

20th October . Sherif Ali Bey went ashore in morning - Captain Lawrence went with him, and spent the day ashore.

21st October Aziz Bey and Nuri Bey came on board in morning The former explained his plan of organizing a force and handed in his list of requirements.

Captain Lawrence left in the afternoon for Sherif Feisal Bey's Camp.

On the 22nd October I paid a visit to Ali Bey and had a long talk with Aziz Bey. He was obviously much dissatisfied with the present state of affairs - He had found things very difficult at Mecca; and at Rabegh he was finding obstacles in the carrying out of his plan energetically. No sooner did he commence trying to obtain volunteers for the so called regular force than he found Ali Bey made difficulties of tribes being split up.

I hope things ~~may find he be~~ he may find things go better shortly. He likes Ali Bey and I hope the latter will realize that he must give Aziz a free hand if he is to be of any use.

The advent of the French detachment Aziz looked upon with suspicion and was inclined to ridicule it - No doubt he feels it in some sort clips his wings in Syrian schemes he may have in view.

On the 23rd October news was received that Feisal Bey had retired towards Hamra - Also that HMS Hardinge was to arrive next day with the Egyptian Artillery from Jeddah.

24th October . HMS Hardinge arrived with E. A. Artillery. Said Ali Pasha cheerful but remainder of Officers evidently depressed. Sherif Mohsen brought £50,000 for Feisal Bey -

Fig. 7   A page from Colonel Parker's diary, October 1916

'Please despatch £50,000 promised. Will not be paid over until revolt confirmed.' On 9 June he told Cairo that Idrisi of Asir was ready to move with the Sharif but needed arms. Even Captain Boyle, the naval commander in the Red Sea, was caught up in the euphoria. From HMS *Fox* off Jiddah, he signalled on the 11th: 'Arabs ready to make decisive attack. We will have to pay subsidy to Sharif.' Two days later Faruqi arrived with the gold. But all was not what it seemed from Storrs's sanguine reports. Within a week of the 'rising' McMahon was telling London secretly: 'Too much has been left to the last moment and to luck.'

In July Colonel Wilson was sent down to Jiddah, which had been cleared of its 800 Turks by naval guns. He was followed in August by Parker, and the two officers had a sorry tale to report. Mecca had indeed fallen, but the Turks had withdrawn without a fight, though they had in pique damaged the *kiswa*, the shroud of the sacred *kaaba*, the holiest of Moslem shrines, before departing, a fact which the Indian administration was at pains to keep from its citizens. As Austen Chamberlain remarked in an India Office note of 22 June: 'The Government of India accept . . . with ill-concealed dislike the policy of HMG in Arabian affairs.'

'We are in for a difficult and costly business,' said Boyle, whose observation was passed by the GOC Egypt to the War Office. Even Storrs began to entertain a nagging suspicion that the Sharif was 'playing with the English'. Cairo, anxious not to become the laughing stock of friend and enemy alike when the news of Britain's complicity reached the outside world, began to promote the rumour that the Revolt was the idea of India. The Commander-in-Chief Mesopotamia and the Viceroy were dumbfounded. General Lake sent a terse report to London, referring to the 'original communication to the Sharif with regard to Mesopotamia and the Arab Kingdom . . . the decision to send certain Arab officers to Basra and an abortive project concerning Sayyid Talib'. He hoped that the 'experience gained by one or two officers from Cairo who have paid visits here . . . has resulted in considerable removal of wrong impressions'. A note in the India Office diary read: 'It is interesting to observe that Egypt led us into this adventure which is not liked by either the Secretary of State or India. Now Egypt can only say what a mess we shall be in if it fails, and protest about having the responsibility thrust upon them.'

Colonel French summed up the reaction of the War Office to

Cairo's dubious claims. He told Clayton: 'Quite between ourselves, the DMI [Macdonogh] does not like to pass Hogarth's telegrams to FO or IO'. And Clayton told French: 'The Sharif's movements ... went off rather half-cock.' The Indian Government called the Sharif's declarations the 'insensate talk of a lunatic'. Hogarth was now acting head of the Arab Bureau – Parker had declined the offer of its headship and gone down the Red Sea to do battle with the Sharif and his sons.

When Wilson was called to duty in the Hijaz in July, it was decided that he should be known as 'Mr Wilson'. Cairo concluded that, if he went as an army officer, 'India might realise the closeness of our relations with the Sharif, which at the present moment is undesirable'. In fact he was given the courtesy title of Wilson Pasha, and the temporary rank for purposes of pay of Brigadier-General, thus resolving the Arab Bureau's fears and his own disquiet. He was to be known as 'Pilgrimage Officer'. He wrestled manfully with the wily and intransigent Prince of Mecca, overworked, frustrated and often aggrieved by the old man's duplicity and constant changes of mind. He was, however, able to record one point of agreement with his host, a secret sign that would be used by the Sharif's agents and their British paymasters:

V

O

T

Parker had little more success with the Sharif's sons, discovering that they were only too ready to exaggerate the strength of the forces opposed to them, and to magnify the difficulties of offensive action. He discovered too that one of the most important coastal shaikhs, Sharif Muhammad Ali of Yanbo, was allied to the Turks and could not be bought off with British gold. By September the position had become desperate: vast sums of money were being spent, the Sharif had increased his demands to £125,000 a month, with a call for food, arms and an Allied offensive in Syria; his sons were making separate demands for money through Parker; and the Turks were in unchallenged command of the one place that interested them, Madina at the head of the Hijaz railroad.

The War Committee had met in London on 6 July. Sykes, recently returned from Russia and 'stirred with the power of Zionism' there, was called on to address the meeting on the Arab question. After obscure references to the 'physique, fire and nimbleness' of the Arab and to the fatal error of treating the Arab as 'the white man's burden', he made far-reaching recommendations, many of which were accepted. He spoke of the need to occupy Al Arish and Aqaba, to extend the Sinai military railway from Katia to Arish as quickly as possible, to tighten the hold on the Red Sea coast, to seek the aid of the Imam Yahya of the Yemen. Then to the nub of his argument. McMahon in Egypt was not up to the tasks confronting him, and Cox in Mesopotamia, though his work was exemplary, was handicapped by control from India. He should be made High Commissioner for 'Eastern Arabia', answerable to the Foreign Office, 'we should show ourselves as pro-Arabs, and [that] whenever we are on Arab soil we are going to back Arab language and Arab race, and that we shall support Arabs against external oppression by force as much as we are able, and from alien exploitation,' he concluded. The War Committee adopted most of Sykes's proposals, and it decided that the Sharif's request for £125,000 a month was excessive. However, within three weeks McMahon was told to pay the full amount, for an initial period of four months. It was to go on for the rest of the war, and to be increased substantially as time went on.

The Committee was convened again on 1 September, by which time alarming reports had come from Parker and Wilson. Sykes was called on once more to address the Downing Street gathering. Lord Crewe, Asquith's closest confidant, took the chair. The Prime Minister, Foreign Secretary and Secretary of State for India, the three ministers most concerned, were absent. Sykes was called in to address the gathering on the Arab Revolt. A pile of telegrams on the table relayed the Sharif's demands for armed help and money, and his refusal to have British or other Christian troops in the Hijaz. 'We must not let the Sharif be crushed,' said Curzon. 'We must not be negative,' said Lloyd George. Murray, the GOC, had told the War Office that it would be advisable to send a detachment of British troops to Yanbo whether the Sharif liked it or not. Sykes thought that Sudanese troops should be used but that naval guns would be the most effective weapons. It was decided to leave the major decisions regarding support for the revolt to a conference which Murray had arranged with McMahon at Ismailiya, when Wilson would report the latest news from Jiddah and be told 'to what extent the Sharif's demands . . . can be considered'.

On 10 September, Parker sent GHQ a detailed summary of

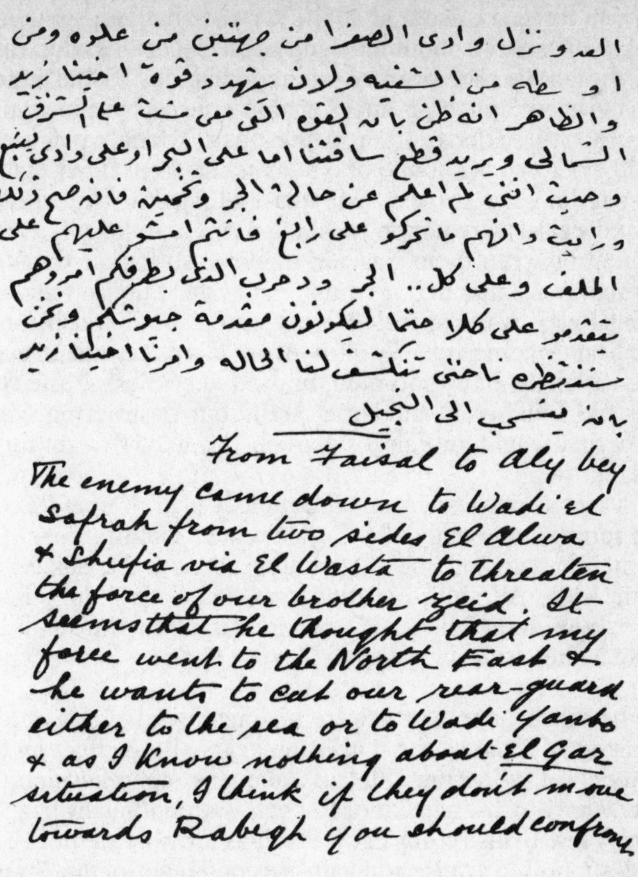

الحدو نزل وادى الصفا من جهتين من علوه ومن
او طه من الشفيه ولان سهدد قوة اخينا زيد
والظاهر انه ظن بانه لحق الذى من سنة مع الشرق
الشامى ويريد قطع ساقتنا اما على البحر وعلى وادى ينبع
وحيث انى لم اعلم من حال الغر وتحميه فانه صح زلك
وايه وانزم ما نركو على اني فانثراستر علوم على
الملف وعلى كل .. الغر ودرب الذى بطرفكم امروهم
يتقدمو على كلا هنا ليكونون مقدمة جيوشكم ونحن
سننظر ناحنى تنكشف لنا الحاله وارنا اخينا زيد
بانه يتسيب الى الجيل

From Faisal to Aly bey

The enemy came down to Wadi'el
Safrah from two sides El Alwa
& Shufia via El Wasta to threaten
the force of our brother Zeid. It
seems that he thought that my
force went to the North East &
he wants to cat our rear-guard
either to the sea or to Wadi Yanbo
& as I know nothing about El Gar
situation, I think if they don't move
towards Rabegh you should confron

Fig. 8   A letter from Sharif Faisal to his elder brother, Ali, referring
to the Rabegh campaign, with part of Colonel Parker's translation

the position in the Hijaz. It did not make reassuring reading.
The day before HMS *Dufferin* had taken Wilson and Parker to a
secret rendezvous with Faisal, close to the port of Rabegh.
Shaikh Husain of Rabegh was reluctant to support the Sharif's
cause. 'Faisal was not entirely reassured as to Husain's attitude
and expressed fears that he might still go over to the Turks.'
The situation as outlined by Faisal to the English officers was
guarded but optimistic. His force, 4,000 men armed with rifles
but with no artillery, stood in the path of the main Turkish
advance route from Madina to Rabegh, the Darb Sultani. The

Turkish force consisted of about twelve battalions, some 12,000 men, with sixteen mountain-guns and two of heavier calibre, and the intervening country was mountainous. Faisal expected the Turks to launch an attack within a period of three or four days. Ali, the elder brother of the Sharif's family was in command of a force of about 8,000 men not far from Bir al Mashi on the pilgrim road between Madina and Mecca. Unfortunately, Ali and Faisal were not on speaking terms and the only communication between them was acrimonious, so Parker was unable to discover the number or equipment of the Turks on that front.

But Faisal was hopeful. He estimated the Turkish force in and near Madina, the Twelfth Army Corps, at about twenty-nine battalions or 25,000 men, under Fakhri Pasha, 'the couragous old butcher'. Could the Arabs but destroy the Madina force, they would, in Faisal's opinion, 'advance straight through Syria to Aleppo'.

The Arab chief went on to outline a plan of operation. His own force should allow the Turks to pass southwards and then cut their lengthened line of communications and attack from the north, while Ali moved swiftly from the south. Zaid's Rabegh force would then hold the Turks or attack from the south. 'The above is the gist of Faisal's talk,' wrote Parker.

> The salient points of it were his inability to stop a determined advance by the Turks, his fears of the effect on his Arabs of a serious defeat, and his apprehension of treachery by the Shaikh of Rabegh. He continually begged for a few British troops at Rabegh as a visible sign of British support to arouse and gain the confidence of the Arabs.

But the Sharif procrastinated and Fakhri threatened. The danger of Turkish advance on Mecca now appeared very real to the leaders of the rebellion. They knew that if Fakhri led his troops into the Holy City, Husain and his sons would be the first to hang, and Husain's nominal successor Ali Haidar was already in Madina preparing a *Mahmal* (votive ark) to take with the army to Mecca. Ali Haidar was distributing money to the shaikhs and Turkish propaganda was proving effective. Taif had not yet fallen, and so the Sharif's army was confronted by Turkish armies to the north, south and east. Only along the Red Sea coast did the conspicuous presence of the Royal Navy and its newly arrived seaplanes provide evidence of Allied intention. Despite the

Sharif's continued opposition to 'Christian' intervention on the mainland, Parker recommended that a British force should be sent to Rabegh. 'A small insurance against a great risk.'

In July Robertson, the Chief of the Imperial General Staff, had suggested to Murray that Wingate might help the Sharif to sabotage the Hijaz railroad, 'as Sharif probably ignorant of art'. The GOC Egypt replied: 'Sharif averse to destroy railway as it is a Muhammadan enterprise. Am training Arabs to do demolition.' But destroying the railway involved an overland journey north of Madina through the country of the Billi tribesmen, whose chief was no supporter of the rebellion. On 16 September Parker wrote to Faisal in Arabic, as always copying an impeccable translation into his diary. He had interviewed the refractory Shaikh Suleiman Pasha abu Rifada of the Billi tribe the day before, and he told Faisal Bey: 'I regret to inform you that [his] attitude is most uncompromising.'

The Shaikh did not beat about the bush. 'Many of his Arabs were in the pay of the Turks and it was impossible to do more than to try gradually to obtain their adherence to the Sharif. Any precipitate action could, he felt, throw all the Billi in with the Turks.' When Parker tried to press him to declare his allegiance to the Allied side, the Shaikh replied: 'Better say at once that I am allied to the Turks.' He was offered money and refused it, saying that if he took money 'it would be after doing what he could, and not before'.

HMS *Hardinge* left Yanbo on 10 September and arrived off Hassaini Island opposite Umm Lejj the next morning. A party of 195 Turks was on its way south in three dhows to recapture that port. Seventy of Faisal's men were landed at Umm Lejj to await their arrival. They were not to attack the Turks but to remain hidden and communicate with HMS *Hardinge* as soon as they landed. The British ship was anchored ten miles off the town, and intended to close in when the Turks arrived and force their surrender. But Turkish intelligence was better than Britain supposed at that stage and the enemy turned back before reaching the ambush prepared for it. On the 13th the port of Wejh was shelled by HMS *Fox*, following an unanswered demand to its commander to surrender. Seaplanes attached to the fleet then went in and strafed the town with machine-gun fire. It was intended to follow up this operation by landing 500 Sharifian troops, but Faisal failed to turn up with them at the appointed time. 'It was thus impossible to force the surrender of the Turkish force,' wrote Parker.

But it was Rabegh, the vital seaport on the road between Madina and Mecca, that most concerned Parker and Wilson at this stage; along with the need to gain the support of Suleiman Pasha abu Rafida so that raids could be made on the railway through the Billi tribal territory. Parker ended his report of 10 September: 'It may appear that the garrisoning of Arabian coast towns is treated lightly in these reports. In each case, however, except in that of Aqaba, the occupation is only to tide us over a crisis in Sharifian affairs.'

Differences between the Commander-in-Chief, Murray, and the High Commissioner over the problems of the Arab Revolt had become acute by this time, and the meeting which had been promised in Murray's communication to the War Committee on 1 September was held on the next day at Murray's residence at Ismailiya. Apart from the two principals the meeting consisted of Admiral Sir Rosslyn Wemyss; Major-General Lynden Bell, Murray's Chief of Staff; Colonel Wilson from Jiddah; Colonel Holdich, the GOC's intelligence chief; Cornwallis; Storrs, and one or two other officers. It was an acrimonious gathering. Wilson was asked to make an opening statement, and he spoke of 'ifs' and 'buts', of Ali's unreliability and Abdullah's incompetence. As for Faisal, words almost failed him: 'Faisal is a man that cannot stand the racket and if they are getting at all hammered the Arabs will disappear into space.' But he went on to insist that the onus was on Britain. 'What the Arabs want is some tangible evidence that the English Government is not going to let them be crushed.'

After a discussion on military tactics, Sir Henry McMahon thanked Murray for fixing up the conference which he thought would do 'immense good'. Murray was not so sure. He recalled that he had been Chief of the Imperial General Staff before taking up his present post:

> We are absolutely clear at the War Office as to our line of policy, as are all allied nations. We have made up our minds that we will concentrate in the West every single man that we possibly can, and that we shall allow the secondary theatres of war to struggle on with the minimum of troops, and that we will on no consideration undertake fresh campaigns or fresh liabilities. We have helped with arms, but never have I or any of my staff promised that we will help this expedition with personnel.

Then it was McMahon's turn. After acknowledging the help of the GOC, he revealed the immediate cause, if not the entire historical truth, of Britain's involvement in the Sharifian affair:

but I do take exception to one thing. It was the most unfortunate day in my life when I was left in charge of this Arab movement ... It began at the urgent request of Sir Ian Hamilton at Gallipoli. I was begged by the FO to take immediate action and draw the Arabs out of the war. At that moment a large portion of the Turkish force at Gallipoli and nearly the whole of the force in Mesopotamia were Arabs, and the Germans were then spending a large amount of money in detaching the rest of the Arabs ... Could we give them some guarantee of assistance in the future in order to justify their splitting with the Turks? I was told to do that at once ... the only man we could get in touch with was the Sharif ... Now this is purely a military thing. We had nothing to do with it in Egypt; we were forced to do it at the military request, to assist Gallipoli, Mesopotamia and also as relief for Egypt. In that, I think, we have been very successful.

It was not the strict truth of the matter, but perhaps McMahon was protecting his late predecessor Kitchener and his own colleagues. In any event he did not start the venture. He had no need to lie. He had responded to irresistible pressures. He was not a policy-maker, merely an executive functionary. Nevertheless, his words persuaded Murray.

'Let me put down what you need,' said the GOC. 'I do not think I shall be able to supply the troops, and whether the WO will look upon it from the point of view of the big war or from the local point of view, I do not know.' McMahon replied: 'If I cannot get troops from the British Government, I am reduced to getting them from the French.' In a last moment of desperation, the functionary was becoming a policy-maker.

On 27 September the Chief of the Imperial General Staff instructed: 'Do not send troops to Rabegh,' in response to an urgent call from Parker. 'Only in event of collapse of Sharif,' he added. On the 29th Murray wired London: 'I am not of course in a position to say authoritatively what effect the collapse of the Sharif might have on Muhammadan opinion, but my opinion for what it is worth is that such an event might have as little effect as the evacuation of Gallipoli or the surrender of Kut.'

Faced with the hiatus of autumn 1916, Cairo decided to send Storrs back to Jiddah to try to jerk the sleepy princes of Mecca into some kind of action. He was accompanied by Lawrence, teeth and claws bared for the fight, for he was to go on to join Faisal in the desert. It was his first encounter with the Arab Revolt and from now on he was to take the desultory affair by the scruff of the neck and chronicle it into a novel of breathtaking adventure, using his own gifts and the inspiration of the great writer-traveller Doughty, whose *Arabia Deserta* he always carried with him, to make heroes of reluctant debutantes in the business of fighting a war which held out no obvious hope of plunder, and therefore had no great appeal.

The War Office decided to send its own man to see what was going on. Bray was recalled from the Western Front and told to take over as intelligence officer at Jiddah. He was called to the War Office for a briefing by Mark Sykes. In the event, Bray gave Sykes the benefit of his views on the Arabs and the Arab Revolt, whereupon Sir Mark placed a blank sheet of paper in front of him and commnded: 'Go on . . . write.'

'I can't write a word if you go on standing there,' said Bray. Sykes laughed and left the room, and Bray set down his brief report, expressing the opinion that he had expounded to the Chief of Staff in Delhi, General Sir Percy Lake, in November 1914, that the most powerful weapon available to the Allies in Arabia was Ibn Saud. But since, after the death of Shakespear, Britain had spurned the only Arab leader who could rally the tribes to its side, Bray thought it best to help the Sharif of Mecca and make the most of the Hijaz operation. He suggested that a few Indian officers and NCOs should be sent on the annual Meccan pilgrimage in October, so that they could return to India with a truthful account, thus stemming Turkish rumour which circulated there.

Sykes was wildly delighted with the idea. So were Hirtzel and the Military Secretary at the India Office, General Sir Edmond Barrow. Within days the energetic Sykes had summoned four Indian officers from France. At the beginning of August Bray and two of his Indian charges were in the Mediterranean, escorted by Japanese destroyers, on their way to Cairo, where they met Sir Henry McMahon, already familiar to Bray from pre-war days, and that 'queer mixture of brilliant men', the Bureau. On 24 August they boarded HMS *Hardinge* at Suez. On deck with Bray and the Indians, Risaldar-Major Gul Nawas and Risaldar Mir Alam (the other two had been left behind as unsuitable) were Jafar Pasha, the Turks' Commander-in-Chief in Tripoli – now translated to the Allied side – Nuri Said, the Turkish-speaking officer of the Ottoman army who had been captured in Mesopotamia, Captain Ross, the Flying Corps officer who was to play a magnificent part in future operations in the Hijaz, and Colonel Jacob from Aden; all jabbering in a cacophony of English, French, Arabic, Urdu and Hindi.

They arrived in the Hijaz to find that Storrs and Lawrence were in conference with Abdullah at Jiddah. Wilson was exhausted by a row that had developed over a statement which Abdullah proposed to issue to the world's press that, 'The nobles, ulemas and all classes of the population' had gathered to pronounce the Sharif Husain ibn Ali 'King of the Arab Lands'. From now on the Sharif's title was to be *Malik al Bilad al Araby*. The Viceroy was almost speechless though he found voice enough to tell London: 'I told you so.' Ibn Saud could hardly contain his anger. The rest of the world was amused. McMahon regretted that there was nothing he could do to prevent publicity for the Sharif's claim, and insisted that he had neither encouraged or envisaged a title other than 'King of the Hijaz'. Finally he took refuge in the suggestion that 'international usage recognised King in *esse* only and not in *posse*'. A feeble thought, but McMahon had been pushed into a hopeless corner. In the middle of the dispute at Jiddah over the Sharif's title he threw in the sponge. On 20 October he gave *carte blanche* in political matters to Wingate.

It was not a good time to introduce Bray's Indians to the scene, expected as they were to return home with a story of harmony and good feeling between Britain and its allies in the Hijaz. On the whole they seemed to share the rest of the world's indifference, though they were received with royal ceremony in the Sharif's 'beautiful palace', and gave the old man of Mecca assurances of fealty on behalf of Indian Moslems.

Lawrence and Storrs left Cairo for the Hijaz a few weeks after Bray and his companions, convinced that the misfortunes of the Revolt were due mainly to faulty leadership. 'So I went down to Arabia to see and consider its great men,' Lawrence said immodestly. He and Storrs travelled on HMS *Lama*, and even in the matter of shipboard reminiscence he was inventive. 'Storrs' intolerant brain seldom stooped to company,' he observed truthfully enough. Then, having sniffed and decided there was nobody worth talking to, Storrs (said Lawrence) turned to Aziz al Masri and began to converse in French and Arabic about Debussy. Tiring of that topic they turned to Wagner, 'in fluent

French, German and Arabic'. A fascinating debate no doubt, in Lawrence's mind, for Al Masri was not on the ship. He was already in the Hijaz fighting a losing battle with the Sharif's army. Lawrence shared a cabin with a young veterinary officer, and the nearest he came to musical entertainment was the sound of a gramophone, the gift of the ladies of Bombay. They arrived at Jiddah on 16 October, and the tale was a familiar one. Wilson was 'defiant' and 'not sure whom he represented'; admittedly a common feeling among officers attached to the Arab Bureau. And he was uninformed on matters of 'General Policy'.

It was the moment of Lawrence's first meeting with the Hashemite princes, and Abdullah did not disappoint him, mounted on a white mare, surrounded by richly armed slaves, 'through the silent respectful salutes of the town'. But Abdullah would not do. He was astute, 'but not great enough to convince us of his sincerity'.

He was certainly astute enough to reprimand Storrs with an indignant outburst when the Englishman protested that the 'promise of arms' was nothing to do with him: 'Forgive me, it was your letter and your messages that began this thing with us, and you know it from the beginning, and from before the beginning.'

There were angry and prolonged debates with Colonel Brémond, the head of the French mission which arrived soon after the announcement of the Revolt. The Colonel was shadowed by Bin Gharbrit, a spy from Morocco who was acting as political adviser on Arab matters at the Quai d'Orsay, and he wanted to know why the Pan-Islamite Rashid Rida, now living under British protection in Cairo, had been allowed to attend the pilgrimage to Mecca recently. 'We would never venture to come between a man and his religious duties,' said Storrs.

Al Masri made polite conversation and the Sharif's War Minister, Said Ali, loaned by Wingate from the Sudan army, assured the English guests that the Arabs under his command were 'a cowardly and undisciplined rabble'. The Arab commanders, like their British counterparts along the Hijaz coast, found the Sharif's army a nightmare and its sovereign chief at Mecca an indecisive dotard. Just before the second coming of Storrs, there was an urgent message from Parker to the effect that British officers trying to go ashore at Rabegh were being shot at by Ali's Arabs and demanding that the Sharif give formal permission for military landings. At 9.30 pm, Storrs's secretary Ruhi, who was at the Palace, sent back a telegraphic message via Wilson's office: 'His Highness has gone to bed and I told the Secretary not to send message until His Highness had added to it, "British officers and men allowed to land."'

The only constructive outcome of the Jiddah meetings this time was an agreement between the British contingent, Al Masri and Said Ali that Rabegh must be defended at all costs. Otherwise the main road from Madina to Mecca would be open to the Turks. Bray, who like his superior Wilson had little time for Storrs, and none for Lawrence, decided that he must return to London and talk matters over at the War Office. The Chief of the Imperial General Staff had decided that he had no Moslem troops to spare for the Hijaz and if the Sharif kept up his opposition to 'Christian troops' then he would have to sink or swim alone.

Before Bray left the Hijaz, Parker supplied a detailed report on the Rabegh situation which would provide useful ammunition for the London meetings. About 5,000 Arabs under the Sharif Ali were entrenched some four miles from shore, their left flank covered by naval guns, but the pro-Turk Shaikh Husain of Rabegh was entrenched in the hills behind the town. Parker was unable to understand why the Turks did not send a large occupying force from Madina, and thus cut the overland route to Mecca. He reported a total lack of co-operation from the Sharif Ali, and asked Wilson at Jiddah to raise the matter yet again with the Sharif Husain.

Bray stepped from his train at London's Victoria Station at 9 pm on 8 November and went straight to a telephone box to let Sykes know that he had arrived. A few minutes later he was in a taxi on his way to Sykes's Westminster home, where they talked until the early hours. 'Be at 10 Downing Street at 11 in the morning,' he was told as he took his leave.

The War Cabinet was in session when Bray was admitted. Asquith took the chair at one of the last meetings of his long and eventful premiership. Sykes, as was his way, pushed open the Cabinet Room door as though he was about to arrest the occupants of the room, leaving the young officer from the Hijaz outside, trembling at the thought of having to go in and address the august gathering. As luck would have it the Prime Minister told Sykes that the discussion of Arab matters would be put off until 3 pm, when a Select Committee would discuss the matter. But the matter could not be left on ice for four hours in Sykes's view.

He paced up and down in an ante-room, kicking chairs out of his way and banging his fist down on a pile of dispatch boxes with such force that they fell to the floor with a great clatter. The eyes of the PM's messenger bulged with surprise. 'There's not an hour to be lost, not a *moment*,' exclaimed Sykes. Bray had told him the night before, repeating Wilson's words to him before he left, that an Arab defeat at Rabegh 'would mean the end of the war in the Hijaz and the extinction of the Sharifian family'. Bray had also spoken of the difficulties of dealing with the Sharif and his family, difficulties which Storrs had tried to minimise on his return to Cairo. 'Husain repeats constantly that the Hijaz is holy territory and British troops must not fight on it; and he has no sense of urgency in dealing with the Turkish threat on his doorstep,' Bray said. It was red meat to the tiger of Whitehall, and he was not to be delayed in pursuing his meal by ministerial timetables. This time he kicked open the door and disappeared inside. A few minutes later he came out, exclaiming: 'We've got our way. All the men and ships we can spare for Rabegh.'

That evening Bray had dinner with Austen Chamberlain, who wanted to hear all about the Arab movement and its progress. On his way to the House of Commons with Sykes he ran into the Chief-of-Staff, Sir William Robertson.

'I hear you are one of those fellows who think the Arab's no damned good at all,' said the one-time private who now ruled Britain's army.

'No Sir, as guerrilla fighters I think they'll be excellent.'

'Umph,' said Robertson as he went off to his club.

'You're a fool,' said Sykes. 'You should have said the Arabs are little angels with wings.'

'Hang it all,' replied Bray. 'You don't expect me to tell the CIGS a lie!'

Before they parted Sykes gave Bray a copy of the telegram sent by the War Office to Cairo: 'Brigade of British troops, ships and all possible assistance, military and political, for Rabegh.' Bray went to the Foreign Office to pay his respects to Hardinge and show him the telegram. But Hardinge refused to see him and the telegram was handed to a secretary. Hardinge had heard enough of the Arab Revolt.

Bray had a last meeting with General Macdonogh. He shared Kisch's high opinion of the DMI. 'The greatest intelligence officer we ever had,' he said. Bray reached Cairo at the beginning of December, and like Aaronsohn, who followed him from

London to Egypt, he found an atmosphere in which embarrassment was mingled with consternation. On 6 December Sir Henry McMahon had been told to pack his bags. The office of High Commissioner was to be taken over by the administrative fusspot who had dominated the Sharif affair from the beginning as Kitchener's surrogate, General Wingate. The honest, gullible McMahon had been made the instrument of a wild and impossible scheme. At the moment when it emerged from the shadows of political ambition and intrigue into the realm of military reality, he was held to be responsible for its inconsistencies, for its perverse and impossible arrangements. His dismissal was the mark of 'our insincerity', wrote Lawrence. McMahon, 'who took the actual risk of starting it, had been broken just before prosperity began'. Lady McMahon, who possessed a lightness of touch denied to her earnest husband, observed that the Almighty had shown Himself to be 'disappointingly neutral'.

McMahon's peremptory dismissal was followed within twenty-four hours by the resignation of the Asquith coalition, and the formation of Lloyd George's administration. The chief of the 'easterners', master of political intrigue and 'skilled assassin of other men's reputations', had achieved his dearest ambition; and with that achievement everything changed, including the composition of the Secret Service. Grey, who had ruled the Foreign Office with patriarchal authority for eleven years, went with his chief. Balfour came from the Admiralty to the Foreign Office. The Earl of Derby took over the War Office. Churchill was banished from even the most minor role, at the insistence of the Conservatives, and new men emerged from the shadows of political and military authority.

But whatever new brooms were to sweep through Whitehall or the distant corridors of imperial administration, the fact remained that military decisions made with regard to Syria and the Hijaz must now be carried into effect despite the growing demands of General Haig and the High Command in France for more troops to stem the tide of German success in Western Europe. There was another factor, too, which the new Government would need to ponder: in the month before Lloyd George moved into 10 Downing Street, President Wilson had been re-elected to the White House on a ticket of continued neutrality.

Towards the end of October, with the promised Turkish advance from Madina to Mecca by way of Rabegh still threatening, Parker sent Lawrence on an extensive survey of the Wejh

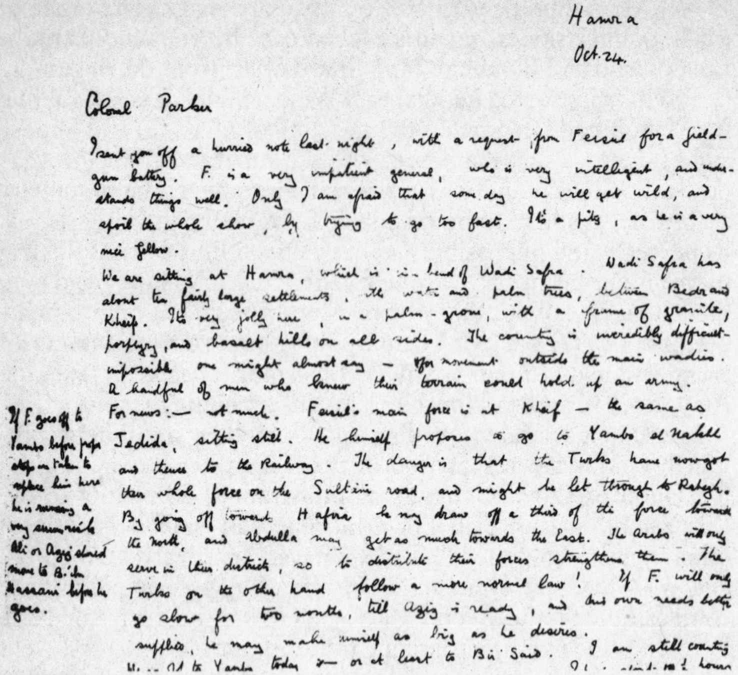

Fig. 9   Part of unpublished letter from T. E. Lawrence to Colonel
    Parker from Sharif Faisal's camp, Wadi Safra

coastal region, still garrisoned by the Turks. It was a dangerous
exercise and Lawrence, who combined a courageous spirit with
an alert if over-inventive mind, was in his element. The map
work that he had done on and off for a year or more since his
arrival in Cairo had made him a nimble cartographer and he
completed a detailed survey of the Wejh–Yanbo–Rabegh coastal
region before dashing inland to join the Arab army of Prince
Faisal north of Madina – along Wadi Safra to the village of
Hamra and the first meeting with Faisal, conveyed in a language
which seems, like that of his mentor Doughty, to caress and
whip the reader like the desert winds.

I felt at first glance that this was the man I had come to
Arabia to seek ... the leader who would bring the Arab

Revolt to full glory. Faisal looked very tall and pillar-like, very slender, in his long silk robes and his brown head-cloth bound with a brilliant scarlet and gold cord. His eyelids were dropped; and his black beard and colourless face were like a mask against the strange, still watchfulness of his body. His hands were crossed in front of him on his dagger.

Lawrence asked the Prince what his plans were, and was told that until Madina fell his army was inevitably tied down to the Hijaz, 'dancing to Fakhri's tune'. On 24 October he wrote to Parker to tell him of his meeting with Faisal.

Colonel Parker
I sent you off a hurried note last night, with a request from Faisal for a field-gun battery. F. is a very impatient general, who is very intelligent, and understands things well. Only I am afraid that some day he will get wild, and foil the whole show, by trying to go too fast. It's a pity, as he's a very nice fellow.

The strategist of the desert campaign showed incipiently in this letter from *Hamra* in Wadi Safra, his first from the Arabian desert.

For news . . . not much. Faisal's main force is at Taif . . . He himself proposes to go to Yanbo al Nakhl and thence to the Railway. The danger is that the Turks have now got their whole force on the Sultani road, and might be let through to Rabegh . . . If F will only go slow for two months, till Aziz [al Masri] is ready, and his own needs better supplied, he may make himself as big as he desires . . . strong feeling against the Turks abroad.

Faisal's motley army made its way to the coast, however, and taking Lawrence's advice retreated to Yanbo badly shaken by sporadic encounters with the Turkish force around Madina. There they waited on the consumptive elder brother, Ali, and the young Zaid, who were supposed to move up country from their base at Rabegh, still overlooked by Shaikh Husain's hostile tribesmen.
'My duty was now to take the shortest road to Egypt with the

news and the knowledge gained that evening in the palm wood, grew and blossomed in my mind into a thousand branches, laden with fruit and shady leaves', wrote Lawrence. He went down to Rabegh to report to Parker and Captain Boyle, who found his Arab headdress an unforgivable affectation. Early in November he boarded the flagship of Admiral Wemyss, HMS *Euryalus*, at Jiddah and went down to Port Sudan to report to Wingate, and then to GHQ Cairo, where Sir Archibald Murray received him politely, and Bertie Clayton listened intently.

At Port Sudan he met two remarkable officers of the Egyptian army, Joyce and Davenport, whom were to play a large part in the desert war. And he also met there Colonel Brémond, the military representative of France, whom he accused of 'having motives of his own, not military, nor taking account of Arab interests and the importance of the revolt to us'.

Wilson, Parker and Bray were not finding the Sharif and his sons anything like so amenable as Lawrence found them, and they sensed more of shady leaf and less of fruit in the relationship. 'It is unnecessary for me to dilate on the difficulty of getting the Sharif to stick to one proposal: he is constantly changing his ideas,' Wilson had told Cairo on 13 October after speaking to Abdullah for two hours on the telephone while the Sharif stood at his son's side, trying to discover whether an attack was to be made on Rabegh and, if so, whether British troops were to be used. 'I begged him to ask the Sharif to make up his mind once and for all as his decision must be final, it being impossible for him to change his requests every few days.'

On 30 October, Wilson reported: 'Situation here does not improve and Rabegh force is entirely unready either to advance or defend. Aziz al Masri has been given no control . . . He has been trying to get Sharif Ali to approve his various schemes. Latter generally approves in principal and then hinders passively . . . Have asked Parker if he would like to have talk with Abdullah and endeavour to get Sharif to give Aziz more control.'

If the problems of military co-operation with the Sharif and his army were proving almost insurmountable, political identification with the wily old man in whom even Lawrence had suspected 'crafty policy and deep ambition', had become positively dangerous. On 30 October McMahon received from Wilson in Jiddah a list of the Sharif's first ministerial council. The Prime Minister was Ali Bey, the Minister of Foreign Affairs, Abdullah and the Interior Minister, Faisal. Shaikh Abdullah

Arerag was appointed the Shaikh al Islam in defiance of the Sultan-Caliph of Constantinople. Again India had to appeal to Cairo to prevent the publication of the list, for Indian Moslems would have no truck with such a change in a position of great religious authority within Islam. These and other measures designed to demonstrate the Sharif's authority had followed a decision by Cairo, after discussions with the Foreign Office, to come clean with the Sharif and show him the treaty that Britain had signed with Ibn Saud on 26 December 1915; the treaty which Shakespear had been negotiating at the time of his death, and which Cox watered down at the insistence of Austen Chamberlain before signing it.

> Your Highness will notice that there is nothing in this treaty with Ibn Saud which is incompatible with the fulfilment of the engagements made by His Majesty's Government with your Highness. I am also instructed to inform Your Highness that His Majesty's Government is using its influence with Ibn Saud to persuade him to render Your Highness all the assistance in his power.

By 9 November Cairo was beginning to receive letters postmarked in Jiddah with the legend 'AG', Arab Government. Wilson wondered whether he should take 'official cognizance' of the Sharif's claims, and was told that he should not. Wilson remarked in answer to a complaint from India:

> In view of the exent to which Sharif owes his position, even existence, to our aid and support, we would be justified in withholding any recognition to his present action which has been taken without consulting us. To subject our relations to too severe a strain at present juncture would however appear obviously undesirable.

There was the question raised by India of Ibn Saud's reaction. 'My telegram shows how he himself does not claim right to interfere with independence of Bin Saud,' said McMahon.

McMahon's last official task was to write to the new Foreign Secretary forwarding a summary of the work of the Arab Bureau from its inception to 'the date on which I handed over its complete direction to the Sirdar'. There were testimonials to the services of the men (and the solitary woman) who had served the

Bureau: Clayton, Hogarth, Cornwallis, Lawrence, Ormsby-Gore, Wilson, Storrs, Parker, Fforde and Gertrude Bell.

Storrs was back in Jiddah trying to pacify Colonel Brémond and discipline the Sharif. A Foreign Office note observed: 'Mr Storrs writes amusingly, but he did not get very much out of the Sharif.' He did succeed in getting some good photographs of Husain, however, with his white beard and turban-like head-dress, which were sent to the press of the world. As this admission of British involvement was being broadcast, the Foreign Office was asking Special Intelligence to prevent the publication of pictures of prisoners of war taken at Jiddah and now incarcerated at Ismailiya. 'They were proof of British involvement in the Sharifian Revolt,' said the note.

13

Von Stotzingen

March 1916 was a busy month. The Sharif of Mecca had received his first substantial payment from Britain, but he was still in the service of the Ottoman Sultan. The agent Araifan had returned to Mecca from Cairo with a bag of gold and Sir Henry McMahon's note accepting most of the old man's 'demands'.

Trebizond on the Caspian had fallen to the Cossacks. Britain and France had rejected a long-cherished plan, seen from the beginning as a sensible alternative to the Dardanelles venture, to invade Syria by way of Alexandretta, and the Russian Foreign Minister had expressed his 'regret' on hearing Britain's reasons, which were not unconnected with the disaster of Kut. Lawrence and Herbert were on their way to Mesopotamia. Spies and intelligence agents were on the move everywhere.

And one day in March, Faisal, the Sharif's third son, went with Jamal to the cinema in Damascus to see a propaganda movie. It began with a view of the pyramids topped by a Union Jack. On the desert sand below Australian troops were beating Egyptian men and raping the women while a little girl went down on her knees in supplication. Suddenly, anticipating the best American 'Western' tradition, Turkish infantry appeared. The Anzacs were cut down with gun and sword. General Maxwell surrendered. The British flag was torn down, and the Egyptians appeared in their thousands to welcome their rescuers. The Ottoman Crescent flag was raised. The multitude gave thanks as the bioscope saga came to an end with the thunderous chords of the piano accompaniment.

'If this is true, Your Highness,' said Faisal, 'why go on troubling my father and myself for recruits?'

'Well, it encourages the people,' replied Jamal. 'Of course, we don't expect to conquer Egypt just yet. Our policy is to hold the British forces there at the least cost to ourselves and Germany has promised us that the last act of the war will be the conquest of Egypt and its restoration to the Ottoman Empire. On these terms I agreed to join her in arms.'

Only three months before that amiable conversation Jamal had held those now forgotten discussions with agents of the Allies, offering to lead a rebellion against his own Empire in return for money and a guarantee of power in Constantinople. And as they spoke, Faisal knew that his father had agreed with Britain the terms of his own rebellion.

Baron von Oppenheim had visited the Ottoman capital early in 1915, where he discussed with Faisal the Pan-Islamic network which Berlin had planned with Enver.

'We want to make rebellions of Moslems against Christians', said Oppenheim. Faisal thought the idea sound and asked the German where he thought they should be started. 'Everywhere,' said Oppenheim, 'India, Egypt, the Sudan, Java, Abyssinia, North Africa'; the possibilities were limitless. Faisal thought that India should be the first objective, though there was the technical difficulty of supplying arms. 'That will be put right by a German-Turk expedition into Persia,' said Oppenheim.

'What about Egypt? We can arrange to give your family office there, when it is conquered,' the German intelligence chief went on. Faisal replied that he had been in Egypt lately and had been offered the crown by Nationalists there. In fact, the British Secret Service knew that the offer had been made to the Sharif's family not in Egypt but by nationalist exiles in Greece.

In March 1916 Faisal and Jamal awaited the arrival at Damascus of another German officer, Major Freiherr Othmar von Stotzingen, a staff officer from the 27th Division of the Thirteenth Army Corps at Würtemburg. He had left Berlin on 15 March heading for Constantinople with a letter of introduction to Enver from the Countess von Schlieffen, widow of the late Chief of Germany's Imperial General Staff.

Jamal shared another secret with the Sharif's son as they conspired in the cool of a Damascus day, observed as they came and went by Aaron Aaronsohn, who kept a sharp look out from his 'Agricultural' office within Jamal's GHQ. Almost all the members of the old Ahad, now organised into the so-called 'Autonomous Syria' party, were in the Butcher's gaols awaiting the sentence of a special court. Twenty-seven leading men of the country, some members of the Ottoman parliament, at least one of them a vital link in Britain's intelligence chain, had been rounded up as the result of the perfidy of French agents and diplomats who sought to put an end to British influence in the territory. They awaited news of their fate in the knowledge that they would be tried and sentenced on the incontestable documentary evidence of Bompard, the French Ambassador at the Porte before the war, of the Consuls Ottavi and Picot, and Defrance, the French agent in Cairo.

But von Stotzingen's visit was the primary concern of Faisal at this time. His father in Mecca was keeping his options open, and the German was bent on a scheme of some audacity. Von Stotzingen arrived in Constantinople on 17 March, putting up at Tokatlian's hotel in Pera. His movements were known in detail GHQ Cairo and Room 328 in the War Office. He made a number of visits to the *Sereskerat,* Ottoman military GHQ, where he met the German intelligence officer Oberstleutnant Siefert and his opposite number in the Turkish army, Lieutenant-Colonel Seifi Bey. He also had long conversations with the communications inspectors Oberstleutnant Endres and Colonel Rushdi Bey, and with the German head of railroads Major Pfannenstal. Enver was away from Constantinople and so von Stotzingen was unable to meet the instigator of his dangerous journey.

He left by rail from Haidar Pasha station on the 26th, spent a week in Aleppo and from there went on to Damascus, where he arrived on 12 April. One at least of the purposes of his mission began to emerge there, when he was contacted by Herr Hammer, the leader of a field telegraph unit, about a faulty mast on a receiving station. But important though the establishment of a communication network may have been to the German command, a more immediately significant aspect of the mission was concerned with the Sharif's negotiations with Britain and the threat of a rebellion in the Hijaz.

Jamal, unpredictable as ever, received von Stotzingen with barely concealed antagonism, despite the fact that his mission was being carried out on the orders of Enver and the German General Staff. Jamal and his Chief of Staff, Fuad Bey – a Francophile officer who had been military attaché in Paris – appear to have done everything possible to hinder the German. Faisal was better disposed to the visitor, however, and von Stotzingen confided in him that he was on his way to the Yemen, where he intended to set up a telegraph station connecting southern Arabia with Abyssinia across the Red Sea. He was also intending to ship arms and ammunition to Abyssinia, and then go on to German East Africa, where General Smuts was commanding the British offensive against the Kaiser's factious African colony.

While in Damascus von Stotzingen met a fellow German officer, Lieutenant Fritz Grobba. British intelligence had been interested in him for some time, since his appearance in Jerusalem in June 1914 as a practising lawyer. In January 1916 he was gazetted a First Lieutenant in the Fourth Army. He spoke French and English well, and a little Arabic and Turkish. Von Stotzingen met Grobba in his room at the Victoria Hotel, and then left on 2 May, carrying an order from Fourth Army GHQ. It read:

The German Major, von Stotzingen, is ordered by the German military authorities to establish an information post in the neighbourhood of Hodaidah, for the purpose of opening up communication with German troops in East Africa. All Turkish military and civil authorities are enjoined to afford Major von Stotzingen and his staff every assistance. The wireless apparatus, brought by Major von Stotzingen, will be utilised for the purpose of forwarding orders and information from Turkish GHQ.

With the Major were two NCO wireless mechanics, Kolber and Schmidt, Hajji Muhammad (an Indian servant who had deserted from the British army during the Suez Canal attack at the beginning of the year), and a Sudanese secret-police officer whom Jamal had sent along to keep an eye on his guests. They reached Al Ala station on the Hijaz railway on 4 May, where they were met by Lieutenant Grobba and an older German, none other than Karl Neufeld, one of Oppenheim's most accomplished agents, the man Kitchener had released from imprisonment after long years in the Khalifa's notorious dungeon at Omdurman eighteen years before. They were also joined by another officer, Lieutenant Diel, an expert in telecommunications.

Neufeld had never been a man to let the grass grow under his feet. He had occupied his years in Sudanese captivity perfecting his Arabic and learning the hard way the arts of survival in the most unpropitious of circumstances. Surprisingly after his ordeal in Omdurman, he had become an apostate to Islam, and he had recently taken a young Kurdish girl as his bride. Stotzingen and his party waited for four days in the company of Neufeld and his 18-year-old bride before a promised escort of Billi tribesmen arrived to take them across the Hijaz to the coast. When the escort finally turned up it had with it a great

7 Shakespear going ashore at Bahrain on his way to meet Ibn Saud in December 1914, two months before his death. This was the last photograph taken of him

8 'Women' of the Howaitat tribe photographed by Gertrude Bell. On the right is T. E. Lawrence

9 Sir Percy Cox with Kurd and Arab shaikhs, 1918. Photograph by Gertrude Bell

deal of baggage containing equipment for a telegraphic station; a consignment that could hardly have been transported from the coast without the knowledge of the Sharif or his agents. While they waited the Germans were in constant touch with Madina.

A Turkish force of 3,500 specially picked men under Colonel Khairi Bey had travelled along the railroad to Madina ahead of von Stotzingen's party. The Allied intelligence services knew nothing about it. The Turks were the advance guard of a military mission intended to compel obedience to the Turco-German alliance by the Imams of Yemen and Asir, and to smash with a single show of force the carefully planned alliance between Britain and the Sharif. As the Sharif began to lay down his terms for rebellion to McMahon, and as Britain's generals and the Arab Bureau were occupied with the last rites of the Kut calamity, the Yemen *Mofraza* as the recruits were called, were on their way from Constantinople, where they had undergone rigorous training under the command of the artillery officer, Khairi Bey. Jamal was in regular telegraphic communication with the Sharif on the subject. On 2 April, while von Stotzingen was on his way to Aleppo across the Anatolian mountains, Jamal told the Sharif that the first trainload of *Mofrazas* was due to arrive in ten days' time. The transport of these troops, he said, was holding up rolling stock badly needed for the passage of troops for the latest Egyptian expedition. Although Husain had received substantial payments from Britain by this time, and had more or less agreed the terms of an alliance, he told Cairo nothing of the German plan. The Germans too had brought gold for the Sharif.

If the well-trained and equipped force could reach Asir and the Yemen it was almost certain to tip the allegiance of the rulers of those territories in favour of the Turks and Germans; and it would certainly make Britain jump in its negotiations with Mecca. No wonder the Sharif was insisting repeatedly at this time that British troops must not enter the Hijaz!

All possible speed was essential, Jamal told Husain, who was at that moment talking to Storrs's mission. Empty trucks must be filled with troops wanted back in Damascus from Madina. The Sharif had raised the question of the *mujahid* regiment, the 'fighters for the cause' now established at Madina and in need of arms. On 9 April Jamal told him that he would be sending 500 rifles for the regiment and £5,000. In his reply the Sharif said that his regiment had no equipment or ammunition, despite his

frequent requests. And how was he to distribute £5,000 among
1,500 *mujahaddin?* 'I will pay their expenses, for a second time,'
he told Jamal with disgust. Jamal had also told him in an earlier
letter: 'German and Austrian troops are coming to take part in
the *jihad,* under the sacred banner of the Caliphate.' The Sharif
replied: 'The arrival of Austrian and German forces will inau-
gurate a new chapter in the history of Islam.' Jamal made no
attempt to conceal his own iron fist: 'As for Faisal Bey Effendi,'
he told the old man of Mecca, 'he couldn't be spared by Army
HQ in Damascus for a single instant.'

On or about 8 May, von Stotzingen and Neufeld went with
their now united parties across country to Wejh on the coast,
where arrangements had been made for them to embark on an
Arab dhow with their equipment for the voyage down the coast
to Asir. They were surprised to find the water thick with
Admiral Wemyss's Red Sea patrol vessels and concluded that
they could not hope to proceed as planned. They decided to
make the journey by land and informed Madina that the troops
would have to do the same. They marched with their Billi camel
train along the coast road to Wadi Hamdh, which they had to
skirt for some ten miles before turning south again at Abu Zer-
aiba and striking the coast at Umm Lejj. It was late May when
they made their way through the tribal territory of the Juhaina to
the coastal town of Yanbo, where they were received by the
Turkish commandant and given quarters in the quarantine station. They remained there while Storrs's mission was at a secret
rendezvous near Jiddah, and by the time they were ready to
leave on what had now become an overland journey of almost
unimaginable difficulty, the Revolt had broken out. The rising
in Madina was soon put down by the Turks but the Sharif's forces at Taif and Mecca barred their way. They had arrived too
late for their presence to sway the balance in the negotiations
with the Sharif, and Jamal and Enver had offered too little
inducement to dissuade Husain from sealing his bargain with
Britain.

The Germans were trapped and the Arab tribesmen were
divided in their loyalties. Whichever way they went they were
likely to be in grave danger. On 9 June Grobba telegraphed the
military attaché in Constantinople: 'Mission impossible in
present political conditions.' It was decided that they should
split up into two groups and take different escape routes. Von
Stotzingen, Grobba, Neufeld and his wife took the road by

which they had come, back to Wejh. They were provided with a reliable guide and fresh Juhaina camels. About ten kilometres before Umm Lejj they were attacked by a badawin raiding party and had to flee for their lives, leaving their baggage and animals to the mercy of the attackers.

The other members of the party – Lieutenant Diel, the two NCO wireless mechanics, Jamal's policeman, the orderly Hilpert and von Stotzingen's Indian servant – were helped by three Juhaina shaikhs to commandeer a dhow to take them by the sea route to Wejh. But their movements were closely watched by Yanbo Arabs in the pay of Colonel Parker's representative on the Hijaz coast, the distinguished French Arabist, Father Jaussen.

Almost as soon as they cast off another vessel went in pursuit. The German party was overtaken not far from the shore and their craft boarded by a fanatical mob. One of the Germans was stabbed and thrown overboard to drown. The others fought off the invaders and swam for their lives. Najji Muhammad and Jamal's Sudanese policeman, the two Moslems in the group, stayed on the boat and were spared by the attackers. The remaining Germans survived remarkably and made their way along the coast to follow von Stotzingen and the others. All the belongings of the German party were taken by the Arabs, including official documents and private papers, some of which later came into the possession of British intelligence. Von Stotzingen, Grobba, Diel and the Neufelds reached Umm Lejj on 11 June. From there they went overland to Wejh and on across uninhabited desert to Al Ala, and by rail from there to Damascus.

When Grobba telegraphed Constantinople on 9 June he told the German military attaché that 'Captain Mueller and his companion' had been 'killed by Badawin near Jiddah'. Mueller's party had travelled from Java, where they had been engaged on telegraphic work connected with submarines, to the Hadramaut in the far south of Arabia. From there they had gone north-west across the Yemen by way of Sanaa and Lohaya to the west coast. They had worked their way along the coast by *sambuk* as far as Qunfidah in Asir but the inability of von Stotzingen's party to move south prevented them from joining up with their compatriots. They had gone on to Jiddah, which they had reached just before the arrival of the Storrs mission at the end of May. They had then made their way along the coast towards Yanbo with a guide provided by the shaikhs of the Bani Harb, who had given their guarantee of safe conduct. Relying on the inviolable word of the desert chiefs they had refused an armed Ottoman escort. They were nearing the village of Qaddima when they were attacked by tribesmen led by a notorious Harbi sea pirate in Britain's service, Auda ibn Zubaida. The Germans tried to save themselves by protesting that they were Moslem converts. But Auda saw the prospect of reward. The nine Germans in the party were cut down treacherously and their mutilated bodies left by the wayside. Theirs was perhaps the most remarkable of all the Arabian exploits on either side during the war. And theirs were the heads which the Sharif's agent Araifan had offered to take to Storrs at Jiddah as a token of the new alliance.

Von Stotzingen, Neufeld and Grobba arrived in Damascus early in July, their companions joining them a few days later. On 25 June, Cairo intercepted a radio message from Jamal to Fakhri Pasha, the Commander of the Madina Garrison: 'With the Yemen detachment there is £5,000 in English gold. Change this at once for paper money, and spend the gold at your discretion.' The reply to Jamal came from von Stotzingen next day: 'I beg Your Excellency to accept my most obedient thanks for your kind telegram of yesterday. With regard to the £5,000 entrusted by me to Major Khairi Bey's detachments, will Your Excellency kindly communicate with the Royal Prussian General Staff to whom the money belongs?'

On 20 July, Jamal posted the order: 'Major von Stotzingen Bey, now with the Fourth Army, unattached, and actually at Damascus, is provisionally attached with the telegraph detachment to the first Reine Abteilung: order to proceed to Beersheba will follow,'

The Fourth Army's second attempt to breach the Suez defences was under way. On 27 July, Lieutenant Diel and the NCO, Kolber, left for Beersheba. They were followed closely by von Stotzingen and Grobba. The latest Canal offensive was no more effective than the previous attempt. Nevertheless the Turco-German force commanded by Kress von Kressenstein succeeded in breaching the British defences, and at several points there was hand-to-hand fighting. In one engagement Lieutenant Grobba was captured, but succeeded in escaping, although he lost his tropical jacket and saddle-bag. Among his lost possessions was a notebook containing scribbled notes on his Hijaz journey, his contacts, accounts, and details of the plan for Khairi Bey's force to march across Arabia, from Madina to the Yemen, with the aid of the Sharif.

The discovery by Cairo of the Stotzingen party's incursion in May and June was responsible for the hurried departure of the Storrs mission, and it forced the Sharif into a premature revolt, according to an Arab Bureau admission. The agreement made with Cairo was for a rising in August. But the appearance of Khairi Bey's highly trained battalion of sharpshooters at Madina, who were intended to escort von Stotzingen and Neufeld on an unprecedented march through Arabia to the Yemen, caused panic in Mecca and Cairo. Only the massive presence of the Royal Navy in the Red Sea and the sending of artillery from the Sudan made possible the taking of Jiddah at an early stage, the thwarting of the von Stotzingen plan, and the subsequent successes at Mecca and Taif. 'The seriousness of their purpose is shown by the scale of the undertaking. There is no case on record of a Turkish force marching the length of Arabia. They were going to re-establish Turkish domination in the Peninsula, and to be an object lesson to the Arabs of the undiminished might of Turkey,' said Cairo's *Arab Bulletin* two months after the event. 'This proves that the enemy were the first to bring the Hijaz into the theatre of war, and would appear to justify our granting open active aid to the Sharif, even to the extent, if necessary, of sending troops into the Hijaz,' wrote Hogarth.

A press statement issued by the Ottoman Legation in Berne on 2 September 1916 emphasised that the Sharif of Mecca 'is a personage selected by the Imperial Government from among the numerous descendants of the Prophet and appointed by Imperial decree'. It went on:

How can one speak of a revolt of the Arabs, when one sees the flower of their youth fighting heroically in the ranks of the Ottoman army on the different fronts, while the greatest Arab leaders . . . like Imam Yahya of Yemen, Ibn Rashid of Najd, Sadun of the Muntfiq, the great Senussi of North Africa, Ali Dinar of Dafur, the Mullah of Somaliland, and many other Arab chiefs are fighting the English. . . . Thus it is an error to give the Sharif's revolt the importance of a general rising of the Arabs. Since the outbreak of the war, the ex-Sharif has . . . never ceased to importune the Government with repeated and exaggerated requests for money etc.

And then came an accusation, never proven or denied:

While the English ships were bombarding the town of Jiddah, Husain sent a telegram to the Imperial Government
informing them that he awaited their consent to the dignity of Sharif of Mecca being made hereditary, with succession to his own sons. He added that if this were granted, he
would put himself at the disposal of the [Ottoman] Government to protect the coasts from English attacks, and
would send a detachment of volunteers to support the
expedition against Egypt.

14

War and Peace

Peace talk vied with the brandished sword through the following year, and in the end fear of the consequences of a conceded peace drove both sides to a frenzy of conflict. In London meetings of the War Committee from July 1916 to the early months of 1917 were increasingly occupied with the need for an offensive into Palestine, with Jerusalem as the main objective, and with – as the Cabinet Secretary put it – 'a place called Rabegh'. Murray protested repeatedly that he must have more divisions if he was to launch a successful attack, and that he could spare no men for the Hijaz adventure. Robertson was on Murray's side and opposed to 'side shows'. But despite the lessons of the past, recounted in parliamentary reports issued in July, the 'easterners' carried all before them under Lloyd George's stewardship. Despite the need to relinquish some of his best troops for France Murray took Arish at the end of 1916. He was ordered to prepare for a major offensive in Syria. In the Hijaz military affairs assumed an ever-increasing air of unreality. In July the War Office instructed Murray in Egypt to make arrangements for the blowing up of the Hijaz rail link between Syria and Madina. Wingate offered the services of Major Garland. The Sharif declined the offer on the grounds that the Turks' only line of communication was 'a Moslem enterprise'. The Sharif, eager to promote a British invasion of Syria which would make his own military task easier and safer, in the same month started a rumour of Arab uprisings in Jamal's vilayet. When the Arab Bureau sent word to London, the War Office replied, 'we should seek confirmation of Syrian uprising and try to procure it'. But it was a false alarm. In September Berne control sent through to London warning that a Turkish force of 9,000 men under Fuad Pasha, Jamal's Chief of Staff, was marching against the Sharif. 'Their lines of communication are extremely bad and expedition need not be feared seriously,' observed the War Office.

In July too, the Idrisi, pretender to the land of Asir between the Hijaz and Yemen which was also claimed by the Sharif and the Imam Yahya, captured the important coastal town of Qunfidah; and the Imam made gestures of joining the Allied camp and began to ask for money and support.

There had been a scare at Rabegh on 7 November 1916, when Turkish planes appeared over the camp of young Zaid's Arabs, but a flight led by Major Ross drove them off. Lawrence had left Jiddah at the end of October and joined up with Faisal at Wadi Yanbo, which had been taken without resistance by the Sharif's men on 27 July but was now being threatened by Fakhri's raiding parties. Captain Boyle decided to send part of the fleet gathered off Rabegh, including seaplanes, tender and the monitor ship, M31, to Yanbo harbour to ensure its defence if the Turks came in force. Abdullah was outside Madina by the beginning of December with a force of 6,000 tribesmen, but his skirmishes did not worry Fakhri, who now posed the questions. Would he remain bottled up in Madina, or would he strike out for Mecca, either by way of Rabegh or directly through the rough tribal territory between? Parker had told Cairo intelligence on 23 October: 'Should the Turks make a determined advance on Rabegh, there is nothing to oppose them, especially as Sharif Faisal's tribesmen are said to be considerably disheartened. (Of this we shall shortly have first-hand information from Captain Lawrence.)' At the end of the month Parker left behind a truculent Ali and joined Lawrence at Yanbo. By the end of the year Fakhri had made it plain that he was more than a match for the Sharifian tribesmen. It was decided that the only way to prevent him calling the tune was to take the initiative. An attack on Wejh, occupied by about 800 Turks, was decided on.

Lawrence, encamped with Faisal's army recently defeated at Bir Abbas, summarised the matter: 'We decided that to regain the initiative we must ignore the main body of the enemy, and concentrate far off on his railway flank. The first step towards this was to move our base to Wejh: which we proceeded to do in the grand manner.' In fact, Captain Boyle, the senior officer present, decided on a naval assault backed by a small marine landing party and by Faisal's irregulars, on 24 January 1917. The resulting engagement was not a military landmark.

A show of strength was doubly needed, for the most important of the tribal shaikhs, Ibn Shalan, remained on the other side of the railway, committed to the Turks, though not with a full

heart, and the chief of the Howaitat, Auda abu Tayya, whose
writ extended from Wadi Sirhan to the Gulf of Aqaba, was still
willing to fight anyone who offered the chance of booty and a
few more scars to boast of. The Sharif's army was in disarray,
and Storrs and Hogarth were about to leave for more talks at
Jiddah. Wilson and Parker had both told Cairo that an attack on
Wejh and sorties beyond Madina along the railway provided the
best chance of persuading the most important chiefs to commit
themselves to the Sharif.

On 24 January HMS *Fox*, HMS *Hardinge* and HMS *Espiégle*
closed on Wejh, the coastal town whose chief industry was piracy. Faisal's force, with Lawrence as its adviser, was to attack
from the south-east as soon as the ships began their bombardment of the Turks, fire being directed by seaplanes under the
command of Ross. A contingent of 400 Arabs and 200 Bluejackets under Major Vickery, with Bray as their accompanying
staff officer, was landed two miles to the north, to prevent the
escape of the Turks. When Boyle gave the order to fire there
was no sign of Faisal's army. The bombardment was called off
for an hour in the hope that they would appear. But no Arab
army was in sight. Boyle decided that since the enemy had been
warned and might try to escape before Vickery and Bray had
been able to deploy their men he would have to reduce the Turkish positions. He had no choice but to forget about Faisal and
Lawrence and order the Bluejackets and the Arabs to attack
immediately following the naval bombardment. It was early
morning and misty. Only the minaret of the mosque looming
black in the half-light acted as a direction finder for the naval
gunners. The aircraft could not operate. HMS *Hardinge*, north
of the town with Vickery's men aboard, was ordered to lower
boats. Arab tribesmen leapt to them from the ship in heaps and
nearly capsized them. They reached the shore safely, however,
and found suitable shelter, where most of them fell to sleep
and contemplation. The marines and some 200 trained Arabs
were sent into battle, Vickery deciding that the others were best
left where they were. The houses of the town glistened white
as they advanced. A few Turks had occupied forward positions.
Thoughts of loot were sufficient incentive to Vickery's Arabs.
Some dropped in their tracks, but most made it to the homes of
their fellow Arabs. They killed every soul in sight, took what
they wanted and smashed everything else. When Bray arrived on
the scene the houses were littered with kapok; the Arabs had

torn every mattress apart in a frantic search for hidden treasure. Homes and courtyards flowed with Turkish and Arab blood. Here and there a few of Vickery's Arabs lay dead, their loot beside them.

A group of more disciplined Arabs engaged an entrenched Turkish force and fought a brave contest through the rest of the day, reducing the Turks by attrition. The Arabs then jog-trotted into the centre of the town exchanging fire as they went, thoughts of treasure ahead giving urgency to their step. HMS *Fox* had reduced most buildings by nightfall, and the Turks occupied only a few houses and the mosque. Bray asked them to surrender and save their lives, but they decided to fight to the end. Next morning a prisoner was sent to the mosque with Bray to ask their leader to change his mind, but he refused. One Turk asked them for a gun so that he could persuade the 'madmen' around him to give in. Eventually Bray and the prisoner retired, their white flag fluttering in a cool breeze. HMS *Fox*'s 4.7-inch gun had blown a gaping hole in the wall of the mosque, and fifteen survivors, tired and bedraggled, came out with their hands up. After more than twenty-four hours of heroic resistance the Turkish HQ in the only school building of Wejh surrendered in the early morning of 25 January 1917. The Arabs continued their looting to the end; they shot at a naval party in their excitement and were repaid for the deed. The battle was over on the 26th. Two days later Faisal and Lawrence arrived on the scene, 'a fine sight' said Bray, 'the red banner of the Sharif's army held aloft'. Afterwards Faisal and Lawrence explained to Captain Boyle that they were delayed by lack of water. Lawrence's own map, drawn at Parker's request from information supplied by Ali and Faisal and printed in Cairo for the use of the force, had shown water on the route at Abu Zeraibat and Habban. 'It was', said Bray, 'a serious lack of initiative on the part of Faisal and his British adviser not to send a contingency force ahead.'

The Turks had put up a brave fight, but they had tasted the power of naval guns and now they withdrew hastily from the coastal area. From then on Fakhri concerned himself only with holding the Prophet's city and the key town of Maan on the railway. Lawrence and Faisal planned their own private adventure. Faisal camped with his swollen army of 12,000 at Wejh. Ali was at Rabegh with a further 8,000, Abdullah at Wadi Ais with 7,000. Wilson had told Lawrence to insist that Faisal launch an attack on Madina. An emissary was sent by Wilson to give the same message to Abdullah. In reply the Sharif's son placed a tin can on the head of the messenger and took pot shots at it. The princes of Mecca did not relish a face-to-face fight with Fakhri's army. The new generals of the Sharif's force, the experienced Jafar Pasha, captured when fighting for the Senussi shaikhs in North Africa, Nuri Said and Al Masri stood by helplessly. Intelligence sources estimated the strength of the Turks at Madina as 7,400 men. They remained there until the armistice, unmolested by the 30,000 men of the Sharif's army. In July 1916 even Clayton's equable temperament began to crumble under the stress of the Sharif's inactivity. Reporting to Colonel French of Special Intelligence in London he remarked that the Sharif was 'somewhat difficile in his demands' as 'like all natives he never knows what he wants'.

By January 1917 Fakhri's peace at Madina had been disturbed by the arrival of a German Secret Service mission under Baron von Oppenheim, there to seek 'the disruption of the Anglo-Sharif alliance'.

Lawrence went to Cairo again after the fall of Wejh, dressed in the Arab garb that Faisal had devised for him, and even Colonel Brémond was impressed. He called 'to felicitate me on the capture of Wejh', saying that it confirmed his belief in Lawrence's military talent and encouraged him to expect the Englishman's help in 'an extension of our success'. Brémond wanted to occupy Aqaba with an Anglo-French force, assisted by the Royal Navy.

Lawrence had left with Bray his plan for the future campaign. It read: '1) Irregulars would not attack places and so remained incapable of forcing a decision. 2) Irregulars were as unable to defend a line or point as to attack it. 3) We must not take Madina. The Turks were harmless there, in self imposed imprisonment.'

Now he told Brémond, if his account of the conversation is to be believed, that his scheme was technically impossible. 'In my opinion Akaba, whose importance was all and more than he said would be best taken by Arab irregulars descending from the interior without naval help.' There was more bombast. 'For my part I did not tell Brémond (but he knew) that I meant to defeat his efforts and to take the Arabs soon into Damascus. It amused me, this childishly-conceived rivalry of vital aims, but he ended his talk ominously by saying that, anyhow, he was going down to put the scheme to Feisal in Wejh.'

The Sharif's sons were beginning to enjoy the rivalry between

Britain and France. In October 1916 they were told by Wilson that they would be supplied with Rolls Royces to help them in their desert campaigns. Ali responded by asking if he could have a motorcycle as well. In December 1916 Cairo received a surprise request from the French Government for £40,000 in gold which Colonel Brémond's mission wished to present to the Arabs. The Sharif himself was making merry with his newfound wealth. At the start of 1917 he sent packages of gold to Ibn Saud's shaikhs in Kasim, hoping thereby to divert their allegiance.

On 24 October 1916 Parker had written a pessimistic note to Wingate, bemoaning the decision of the War Office to refuse troops for Rabegh and to withdraw aircraft previously sanctioned, in view of the Sharif's constant changes of mind over the use of 'Christian' forces and Ali's intransigence. 'Things seems to be bad down here just at present, as you will gather from the letters I have written.' He went on: 'My opinion remains what it has always been, namely that we should land a British force at Rabegh capable of holding it ... Of course, action against the railway would have the same effect, but it has to be done *before it is too late*. I suppose it is out of the question to ask HMG to change the decision.' As for his own future he told Wingate:

> I don't know what you wish me to do myself. I offered to stay here as Wilson asked me to, and I am quite willing to stay if I can do any good – If Newcombe comes here I daresay you will like him to run things such as they are, and if you don't want me please say so. Before Lawrence arrived I had been pushing the idea of going up country and had hoped to go up. Don't think I begrudge it him especially as he will do it as well or better than anyone else ... Since he has been gone ... Ali is not inclined to agree to other trips (however) necessary. Even Al Masri is not allowed to go north to look around ... The Egyptian artillery look very sad.

On 26 October he sent a message to Cornwallis at the Savoy Hotel, Cairo. This time 'intelligence' was the subject. 'R' in Cairo wanted to establish givers and receivers within Madina. Ali had forbidden British-employed spies. He and his brothers would appoint all necessary agents. But they would not share the information with Britain. 'Ali Bey would hear of it if I employed agents without telling him, and would be suspicious of it at once,' said Parker. 'Abdullah is still loitering in Mecca. I send periodical wires asking when he is moving north.' Apart from a long report in November, it was Parker's swan song for the moment. There was nothing left for him to do in the Hijaz. Newcombe arrived in January to begin an assault on the railway that was to lead him into some of the most spectacular escapades of the war, and Parker was wanted by Murray in Cairo. 'My opinion is that unless Aziz al Masri can be got moving, or unless foreign troops hold Rabegh or unless the railway is successfully and seriously attacked there is every chance of debacle', Parker told the acting chief of the Bureau. But there was no débâcle, for precisely the reason Parker had foretold: 'What may possibly hold the Turks back from advancing on Rabegh is inability to grasp that we can be so foolish as to let them take it if they like.'

A letter from Lawrence awaited Newcombe.

Dear SFN,
So I missed you by a day! I'm very sick, but it was either that or miss Wadi Hamdth again, and that I will certainly see you at Wejh. I prepared Faisal (who is an absolute ripper) carefully for you, and had him well wound up to meet you on the morrow – and after all I took Vickery out with me instead. It won't do, you know, that sort of thing . . . I'm awfully glad you have come out . . .You'll find me as good as they say and better . . . With which modest – but not senseless saying, sleep.

There was more self-adulation; more bitching about fellow (and usually senior) officers. Vickery, one of the most valiant of all Britons in the east, had misinterpreted events in the Hijaz. Captain Boyle of the Royal Navy, the senior officer present, was 'itching' for a show. 'Try to get him a little game at Wejh. I'd like him to land north of the town, and work along the sandhills into the camp [Faisal's],' remarked the incorrigible little man.

A few weeks later, after assessing the plans of the Meccan princes, Newcombe went on his first mission along the Hijaz railway and ran straight into a Turkish patrol. He carried in his camel saddlebag some planted correspondence which he intended to drop on the route, hoping the Turks would find it and thus be misled. In the event he dropped it accidentally in the path of his pursuers. Included with the manufactured documents was Lawrence's letter. It is tempting to wonder what Fakhri in Madina made of it.

Parker's final task before returning to GHQ from the Hijaz in December had been to account for the use of Secret Service funds. He had taken a supply of gold with him for use in paying agents, but the Sharif's insistence on keeping sole charge of intelligence sources meant that his treasure chest was untouched. He transferred his funds to Major Joyce on 4 December, leaving Joyce and Bray to carry on the good work among the tribesmen, with hands tied behind their backs, while Newcombe organised a bombing campaign along the railway.

Lawrence finally left Wejh and his friend Faisal in May 1917 with companions of the Juhaina tribe and a guide from the Ataiba. They set out through Billi country on the slow four-month journey northward during which he hoped to join forces with Auda abu Tayya and take Aqaba from the rear. Faisal remained behind and brooded at Wejh until Aqaba was taken on 6 July 1917, after perhaps the most widely publicised campaign in the history of desert warfare. 'Wave a sharif in front of you like a banner and hide your own mind and person,' wrote Lawrence in the *Arab Bulletin* when he returned to Cairo.

The miracle of the Revolt was not the achievement of Lawrence and Auda in taking Aqaba, which as Bray observed could have been captured easily, as was Wejh, by sea and land attack; it was the achievement of the Turks in keeping the railway intact until almost the end of the war in spite of almost daily attacks by Newcombe and his men during 1917–18. The Turkish defence of Maan and Madina, with the railroad constantly under attack from Damascus to Madina, was 'an example of generalship unsurpassed in desert war,' said Bray. 'There is no other example in all military history of such an exposed line of communication being maintained for so long, against such odds.' Lawrence, in his account of the war, was of course obsessed by the railway. But it had nothing to do with him. His official designation after his return to the Hijaz from Cairo in October 1916, was Political Adviser to the Sharif Faisal. But Faisal was absent from the only campaign of note in which he took part.

Early in March 1917, Murray decided to 'bring the Turks to fight'. The moment seemed auspicious. Wejh had been taken and the entire Red Sea littoral was commanded by the navy, except for the single fortress of Aqaba. More importantly, Gen-

eral Sir Stanley Maude, fourth on the long list of commanders
of Expeditionary Force 'D', had taken Baghdad on 11 March,
thus avenging earlier defeats and giving the British public its
first real scent of victory in over two years of almost uninterrup-
ted reverse. And other events in the Allied camp had begun to
give a sense of urgency to the tasks of every front-line commander. As Maude's men marched through the gates of Baghdad
and another proclamation of independence was made, this time
to the Arabs of Mesopotamia, the Provisional Government of
Kerensky had taken control of Petrograd and the Czar had abdicated.

Murray's first advance along the coast from Arish to Gaza,
designed to take the ancient port by '*coup de main*' as the General explained afterwards, was repulsed by the Fourth Army
under Kress von Kressenstein on 27 March. But London was
determined to keep up the offensive. On 30 March the Chief of
the Imperial General Staff went to the War Cabinet and
obtained its approval 'to instruct General Sir Archibald Murray
to develop his success to the fullest possible extent and to adopt
a more offensive role in general'. He was told to make his object
'the defeat of the Turks south of Jerusalem and the occupation
of Jerusalem'. Murray replied that he was 'most anxious to
advance on Jerusalem', but sent the War Office a long account
of the difficulties of such a venture.

On 2 April, Sir William Robertson re-affirmed the order.
'Capture Jerusalem.' Murray was asked to outline the route he
proposed to take. On 17 April the British Expeditionary Force
began its second attack on Gaza. Three days later it was abandoned as a failure. After the battle Murray was asked his
requirements, and he replied again 'five fully equipped divisions'. His existing force consisted of three depleted divisions.
He needed two more divisions, he said, and more field artillery.
On 25 April Murray's instructions were modified. He was told to
take every opportunity to defeat the Turkish forces, and to follow up any gains with the object of driving the Turks from
Palestine, 'as and when this becomes practicable'. But Murray
had signed his death warrant by agreeing to the premature Jerusalem offensive. He was told in May that he was to be replaced,
and on 28 June General Sir Edmund Allenby, 'the Bull', arrived
from France to take command of the Egyptian force, leaving
behind him the memory of the indecisive offensive at Arras, and
of his last-minute squabble with the Commander-in-Chief, Sir

Douglas Haig, over the conduct of that battle. He was second choice for Egypt. Lloyd George had asked Field-Marshal Jan Smuts to take the job after his long battle with the Germans in East Africa, but Smuts turned it down, convinced that he would not have the backing of the War Office, who disliked the idea of diverting troops from the west for a 'side show'.

On the day of his 'resignation', 28 June 1917, Murray issued a despatch to the War Office, in which he detailed the orders and instructions that had been given him since he took command. It was a damning indictment of indecision in the War Cabinet, and in August the General asked for permission to make it public. Lord Derby, the new Secretary of State for War, permitted the publication of parts of the despatch, but not those dealing with Government policy or military planning.

Allenby had begun to make drastic changes in the Cairo staff even before he arrived. In particular, he chose his own military intelligence director, Smuts's remarkable intelligence chief in East Africa and Sidney Webb's nephew, Colonel Richard Meinertzhagen, who was in awe of nobody, not even the 'Bull'. With his appointment the intelligence division was divided into two sections, military and political, with Wyndham Deedes in charge of the latter. Both men were old hands at the game and knew every facet of intelligence activity, from office routine to the subtle requirements of appointing reliable agents and keeping an eye on their own, as well as the enemy's men. Deedes had served in Turkey before the war, where, with Fitzmaurice, he fought his own side as vigorously as the opposition, and since then he had been MI2's man in London and Cairo. In Cairo he had worked alongside Aaronsohn and after a hesitant start had come to appreciate the Jew's extraordinary qualities. But from June 1917 Aaronsohn was Meinertzhagen's right hand. 'My best agent ... was a Jew, Aaron Aaronsohn, a man who feared nothing and had an immense intellect.' Clayton was made Political Officer under the new regime. The Arab Bureau became a political vestige.

The new DMI was soon to meet Aaronsohn's team from Palestine.

Now, for the first time in my life, I found myself in close working association with Jews and soon recognized their intelligence and valour. I employed some 15, all refugees from Palestine, all of splendid physique and to my astonishment fair-headed and blue-eyed. They worked as a team, the leader being Aaronsohn. This most remarkable .man was the most daring and unassuming agent, the equal of the Dutchman Praetorius whom I had previously employed in Tanganyika. I am not at liberty to divulge many of his exploits as it would publicize methods better kept secret.

The months before Meinertzhagen's arrival and the introduction of a new regime in Cairo had not been easy for Aaronsohn. He was billeted with the General Staff at the Grand Continental and worked next door at the Savoy, though he spent much of his time at GHQ as it moved from Ismailiya to Al Arish in the wake of the advancing army. But he was an outsider; not because he was a Jew, but because his intellect and vast store of knowledge made the British staff officers uncomfortable in the pursuit of their game of breaking into 'the accepted halls of English foreign policy'. Few of the *Intrusives* were prepared to test their Sharifite philosophy in argument with the brilliant Jew in their midst.

Aaronsohn was not greatly impressed by some of the British officers stationed at Alexandria, though he worked satisfactorily with most of them. He wrote to his friend, Raphael Aboulafia about an incident involving three officers:

You are fed up with Captains Edmunds, Smith and Jones. So am I. Until the moment I started conversations with them I never allowed any man to behave to me with such indifference or lack of respect as I allow them, because their ideas and their behaviour are so different from ours ... such people and their kind of government, I've never met before. And this is our catastrophe. Avshalom should have warned us. He was with them in their decadence ... I know that the lives of hundreds of people are hanging on the slim hope of help that we can bring, and I must continue my work.

In January 1917, having been back from London for more than a month armed with the fiat of the DMI to carry out clearly defined intelligence tasks, Aaronsohn was faced with an insolent demand from junior staff officers to submit a memorandum stating his qualifications for the work. Captain Norman Bentwich, a Jewish lawyer and staff officer with the Al Arish force, was asked to return to Cairo to interview 'the Jew from Palestine, recommended by the WO'. Bentwich assured Clayton that the man whose organisation had been supplying vital information to London and Cairo for the past two years could be relied upon. Wyndham Deedes then ordered that immediate steps be taken to re-open contact with Athlit.

Aaronsohn was in Alexandria at the time of the French request for gold for the Arabs in January, working with Captain Edmunds, who was gradually coming round to his point of view on the Sharif affair. 'The Arab Revolt is being kept alive with a stream of gold,' Aaronsohn told him, 'but we will give maximum value without affecting your cash reserves.' But Aaronsohn was more interested in news that Edmunds brought him on 25 January. One of his Jewish colleagues, Lishansky, had been picked up by an Australian patrol near Al Arish and brought wounded to Port Said.

Unable to contact Aaronsohn in Cairo and aware that the British Army was preparing to advance from Al Arish at a time of conflicting stories of intensified warfare and impending peace negotiations conducted through the American President, Avshalom Feinberg and Joseph Lishansky had decided to make their way through the Turkish lines on 29 December 1916 to make contact with British HQ.

It was a long dangerous journey by the coast road and not until 20 January were they safely past the last Turkish patrols. They were dressed as Arabs and both spoke Arabic perfectly. It was misty as they reached Shaikh Zuwaid near Arish with their badawin guide. They lost their way and decided to bivouac with their camels until the next morning. Suddenly they were attacked by a party of some forty men who were pursuing the badawin guide, with whom there was a blood feud. Avshalom refused to hand the Arab over, a fight ensued and the young Jew was shot dead. Lishansky was slightly wounded in the neck but managed to crawl to the British lines, where he was found by a patrol. Avshalom, Aaron's closest friend and adviser was killed by a badawin robber, unnecessarily, for Cairo had already decided to re-establish contact with Athlit.

Aaron wrote soon after he received the news to his friend Henrietta Szold in America: 'Avshalom is dead. Upon a young woman close to me has devolved the difficult and dangerous role of first lieutenant. I dare not write her name. Rivka will whisper it to you. Take care not to divulge it.'

Wyndham Deedes called Aaronsohn to his office to express his concern and sympathy. It was a friendly meeting and it began to dispel the fog of apathy which seemed to pervade military intelligence in Cairo. Suddenly there was a spurt of activity, and the spy ship *Managam,* called to duty in place of Woolley's sunken vessel, began to visit Athlit.

On 21 February Liova Schneersohn wrote in his diary. 'A month already since I returned from Constantinople, it seems like a year.' He was waiting with Sarah, as they had waited daily, for the ship which must come eventually from Egypt. That evening the *Managam* appeared. It sent a 'liberty' boat ashore after dark with Lishansky, Leibel Bornstein of Trumpledor's Mule Corps, Boutagy and Captain Smith jammed into it. Bornstein was the first to leap ashore, exhausted and shaking with cold. He told Sarah that of her trusted band several were to return to Egypt on the *Managam.* Aaron was not permitted to go ashore, but he sent her a message by the injured Lishansky, who was to stay with her at Zichron Yakov. As the men returned to the ship the New Zealander Captain Smith asked Aaronsohn casually, 'By the way, what's your password?' Aaron turned to Liova and said, 'What shall it be?' Liova opened the Hebrew Bible he always carried with him, and his eye caught the words of 1 Samuel 15: 29 *'Nezah Yisrael Lo Yeshakker.'* 'The strength of Israel shall not lie.' And so they called themselves after the Hebrew initial letters: NILI.

Lishansky's first task was to break to Sarah the news of Avshalom's death, for she had not been told. The girl who had till now sought only to serve her brother in his work became an embittered woman, driven by remorse and revenge. She wrote to Aaron telling him that she would continue 'what my dear one began – that is all I wish'. She added: 'And vengeance, great vengeance on the wild ones of the desert and on the cruel Turk. May God give us life to continue.'

The ship had delivered funds sent to Aaronsohn from America for his own use and for distribution to the Yishuv, and now Sarah and Lishansky set out on a frantic tour of Syria, memorising as many names and addresses as they could of known sympathisers, wary of the informer and especially of their own people, who would have no truck with spies or those who would bring the wrath of Jamal and his *gendarmes* down on all their heads, though they gladly took the money. Gold went a long way in the Ottoman provinces of Syria. They travelled in the horse-drawn carriage which Aaron had kept at the Agricultural Station, driven by his friend and servant of pre-war days Abu Farid, noting as they went an arms dump in the grounds of the Carmelite sisters, starving Arab troops serving with the Fourth Army, and locations of garrisons. They were sent to Tiberias to obtain a permit to travel to Jerusalem. There they had to lie low because it was Lishansky's home territory, from which he had been expelled by the Ha-Shomer. They sent Abu Farid to obtain their permit from the *kaimakam*'s office, armed with five pounds in gold sovereigns. The order was whimsically endorsed: 'Their horses must not be interfered with in any way.'

They found few takers among their Jewish contacts for the dangerous tasks which they offered, but they had one piece of good fortune. Across the Jordan, at the rail junction of Affulah, they met the German Jewish doctor, Neumann, who was a pre-war friend of Aaron's. They took the risk of telling him of Aaron's wartime business and asked for his help. 'I'll pay with my head if I do this,' said Neumann. But he agreed to work with them and became the most valuable NILI agent in the whole of Syria during Allenby's campaign. Practically all troop movements came through the rail junction at which he was chief medical officer, and he eventually took charge of the extension of Britain's Sinai railway to the Affulah line, so that troops could be moved straight through to Damascus.

Eight days after setting out from Zichron Yakov they were in Jerusalem, resting at the Hotel Fast, where German staff officers, including the chivalrous commander Kress von Kressenstein, liked to spend their leisure moments. After a drink with some of the officers Yusef Lishansky accurately assessed the number of their fellow countrymen in Palestine at 50,000. Sarah and Lishansky arrived home at Zichron on 11 March. 'The house is always sad and lonely, and all kinds of terrible thoughts come into my mind for, after all, our work is very black, and we are always in danger,' wrote Sarah.

The *Managam* was due to start calling at regular intervals from now on. Sheets were kept in a tub ready for Sarah to hang on the washing line as soon as the ship appeared; a white sheet indicated safety, a red sofa cover danger. On the nights that the *Managam* was known to be arriving a NILI man in the village where Aaron's palm-lined private road joined the main highway held card parties and provided drinks for any troops or policemen who were about. But there were dangerous moments. A U-boat commander decided to spend an hour ashore at Athlit.

He was entertained by the coast patrol and left in the direction of Haifa; he returned in time to see the *Managam* as it was leaving for home, though fortunately too late to attack it.

Differences emerged among the Jews of Palestine, Egypt and the outside world in the spring of 1916 which centred on the distribution of funds to the needy in the war areas. At the beginning of the war a Security Committee had been established in Jerusalem to provide help for the Jews of Palestine. It was autocratic and arbitrary in its methods. The distribution of substantial funds at the beginning of 1917 by Sarah Aaronsohn and her NILI agents did not meet with its approval. Ha-Shomer, at its mountain headquarters in the Nazareth region, decided to ask the Workers' Movement in Jaffa to help break the Aaronsohn organisation 'on behalf of the Security Committee and the Yishuv'. The official newspaper of the Political Committee of the Workers' Movement stated: 'Our realistic policy in the existing circumstances is complete civilian loyalty, and every activity which removes the Yishuv from this framework must be thought of as a danger to the existence of the Yishuv.' The newspaper spoke in the main for the older settlers, who wanted to live as peacefully as they could in the midst of Jamal's soldiers and *gendarmes*, and many of whom were pro-Turkish out of their intense antipathy to Russia.

But Jamal was no respecter of the peacemaker. In March 1917, after the British offensive had been repulsed at Gaza, Jamal announced that the entire civil population of Jaffa was to be evacuated. Only farmers could remain. Those without means would be sent to the Syrian hinterland to be looked after by the Ottoman Government. Arabs were to suffer the same treatment, but non-Jewish Germans and Austrians would be allowed to remain. The German Consul at Jaffa, Freiherr von Schabinger, protested. So did the Austrian Consul. And Dr Brode, Germany's Consul-General in Jerusalem, made representations to Zimmermann in Berlin. But the Ambassador at Constantinople, Richard Kühlmann, was unhelpful. Brode was called to Jamal's office and warned not to interfere in Ottoman internal affairs, and the 'Butcher' demanded an apology from Schabinger for 'insulting the Turks'. The date fixed for the expulsion was 31 March, but Jamal changed it with characteristic suddenness to 9 April, the feast of Passover.

The world had hardly become aware of the calamity that had struck the Yishuv when 9,000 Jews were sent away on the appointed day, while thousands of Arabs were herded together and pitchforked into the wilderness with the few belongings they could carry with them. Ten days later, on 19 April, Jamal announced that Jerusalem was to be evacuated. Aaronsohn, when he heard of the decision in Cairo, sent an immediate appeal to world leaders for help in restraining the fanatical Jamal and for money to help the hundreds of thousands who were about to be displaced. He also called Sarah to Cairo to give her explicit instructions for her work in Palestine. But the loudest complaint came from the commander of the Eighth Army Corps, Kress von Kressenstein, the idol of the German officers. 'Jamal's plan bordered on insanity,' he said. And he told the German Embassy:

> The evacuation of a town in Turkey is tantamount to its complete annihilation . . . that of Jerusalem is aimed at the total ruin of its populace and of all Jewish and Christian institutions. History will burden Turkey's allies with the responsibility for this act . . . I consider it our inescapable duty to resist it energetically and reject Jamal's assurances as worthless . . . If necessary a warning should be given that all Christian officers and troops stationed in Palestine will be withdrawn.

By now Talaat had succeeded Said Halim as Grand Vizier and Kühlmann promised to raise the matter with him. But it was Zimmermann, now Foreign Minister, who intervened to stop Jamal's plan. On 26 April Zimmermann contacted the Ottoman High Command, and a few days later Enver ordered Jamal to cancel the plan. Another factor of some importance came into play as Jamal's plan to break up Palestine's Jewish population unfolded. America entered the war.

The *Managam* left Port Said on 14 April, five days after the forced evacuation of Jaffa, and picked up Sarah the next day. She was accompanied by Lishansky, who had pressed Sarah to let him join her despite the danger of their both being away at a critical time. When they reached the Grand Continental in Cairo Aaron smashed his fist down on a table with such force that he broke the glass of his wrist-watch. 'How dare you desert your post!' he roared. Yusef Lishansky stood red faced and silent while Sarah defended him, but Aaron insisted that he was endangering other people's lives as well as his own. He did not say so, but he still blamed Lishansky for encouraging Avshalom Feinberg to make that fateful journey into Sinai. Yusef was an able and daring young man with many friends among the badawin of Palestine, but Aaron thought him lacking in discretion.

The return of the *Managam* to Athlit was delayed for several days by bad weather which gave Aaron time in the evenings to brief Sarah and Lishansky on the work of the NILI group in Palestine. It was a busy and difficult time for him. Even before Meinertzhagen's arrival the staff officers in the Savoy Hotel had realised that Aaron's knowledge of the Sinai and Palestinian terrain was vitally important, as was his intelligence service through NILI and his inventive mind for devising plans to outwit the schemes of the Turco-German staff. He spent every day with Lynden Bell, the Chief of Staff, and his subordinates at the Savoy. 'Mustn't relax for a moment,' he told Sarah. 'The great ones, who have the fate of the whole business in their hands, have begun to listen to us. Now that they've got used to listening, and even to asking for advice, it is my duty to be available at all times.' He was amused to discover on arrival in Cairo that staff officers were still using the Kitchener–Condor survey of 1878 for their topographical work.

In addition to the heavy burden of military intelligence work, Aaronsohn was now dealing single-handed with the problem of broadcasting to the world at large news of what was happening to the Jews of Palestine, and with the distribution of welfare funds. He used the official cipher to keep MI2, the FO and the Zionist Bureau in Copenhagen abreast of Jamal's activities. The Copenhagen Bureau was particularly successful in persuading the non-Jewish communities of Europe and America to take the matter seriously and to provide relief funds. Equally, his informative telegrams to the DMI in London and the Foreign Office enabled political and military intelligence to keep the pot boiling in the United States. The *Manchester Guardian* commented in a leading article: 'Jamal Pasha is too cunning to order cold-blooded massacres. His method is to drive populations to starvation and to death by thirst and epidemics.' It was the message, in almost as many words, that Aaronsohn had given a few days earlier to the official news sources. Jamal, aware by now of his one-time assistant's work, pointed to Aaron Aaronsohn as the prime example of Jewish perfidy. His work was already imposing strains on the old-established institutions of international Jewry, however, as well as Jamal.

The Egyptian Committee of Palestinian refugees believed that they should have a say in the distribution of funds, and they asked Raphael Aboulafia to suggest a joint enterprise to Aaronsohn of a committee of five. 'I am not a public worker and I have no interest in committees,' replied Aaron. He said that he was acting as a private individual. 'If there is danger I take it on myself, and the responsibility I take on myself.' The results, he added, were the 'property of the people'. He did not need the help of a committee in getting money from America. 'Tomorrow there is the chance of sending our dear ones a little bread. Let's do it. We don't need committees for that.'

Sarah, the wilful child of arguments and causes that were a little deep for her at times, was the peacemaker of her days in Cairo. Everyone liked her and wanted her to stay, but she was determined to return to the family at Zichron Yakov and the station at Athlit. Aaron believed she was in grave danger from the rivalry of Ha-Shomer and the fear of the Yishuv. Captain Edmunds pleaded with her: 'Madam, The High Command has authorized me to thank you very much for all that you have done for us. They urge you not to return to Palestine. Egypt is open to you. You can stay here as long as you wish. What you have done up to now is valuable. And it is enough.'

Sarah spoke little English. She replied in French, thanking the Captain for his kindness but telling him that she must go back. 'My blood will be on my own hands, and not on others'.' She told her brother: 'If you won't find the means for me to return, I'll find my own way back.' She eventually returned with Lishansky to Athlit on 15 June after a diversion to the *Managam*'s base in Cyprus, where Yusef was given instruction in the use of explosives for blowing up sections of the Damascus railway and the Jisr Mejumi bridge over the Jordan when the moment came. Liova Schneersohn went with them. Aaron had no time now for Schneersohn's soul-searching questions and melancholy visions of the Russian motherland. Sarah and her brother had not mentioned Avshalom to each other when they were together. On Sarah's return she received a package by the next delivery of the *Managam* containing a letter from Aaron which spoke of 'the great power of silence'.

The country in which Aaronsohn was now based was the stamping ground of the conspirator and of the élite. The young intelligence officer, John de Vere Loder, gave a colourful account of the scene in his letters home.

> Life is really quite like a page out of a novel . . . The air vibrates with hushed whispers, the stairs leading to the office resound with the stealthy tread of stage villains, corpulent Egyptians with tarbooshes, down-at-heel Greeks, Syrian refugees, and terrified enemy aliens. Rifles, revolvers and ammunition pass in and out disguised as rations; in the office we keep invisible ink, secret drawers and insoluble ciphers. Letters arrive by special messengers enclosed in two or three envelopes covered with mystical seals, while the least member of the organisation is known by a number and the greatest by a single letter.

Of one colleague, William Wedgwood Benn, MP, he wrote: 'He is here with the seaplanes. He is rather a nice man, very brave and keen as mustard, but dreadfully rash and impetuous. He is always nosing around, picking up information about Egypt with which to stagger the House some day . . . He sucks in practically everything he is told.'

In February one of Aaronsohn's closest confidants in Cairo, Captain Ormsby-Gore, went to Port Said *en route* for England and dined with Loder. Ormsby-Gore had become another of Aaronsohn's converts to the Zionist cause and he was returning to London in the company of Lord Edward Cecil, who was to join with Balfour shortly in promoting the idea of the Jewish national homeland.

More visitors were on their way to the Cairo melting pot by the spring of 1917. In March Leachman was called from his lair on the Euphrates, where he maintained a lone vigil over the lawless tribes which dominated a 900-mile stretch of desert and swamp. Now Lieutenant-Colonel Leachman, he was designated by Sir Percy Cox to act as his representative in Cairo and the Hijaz in view of an impending visit to the Sharif by an Anglo-French mission headed by Mark Sykes and Georges Picot to 'advise on Allied relations with Arabs and Jews'. It was an astute choice. The man who was known to the troops in Mesopotamia as 'OC Desert', who had lived with the Arab tribes on and off for seven years, who had camped with Ibn Rashid and visited Ibn Saud in Riyadh, was unlikely to be upstaged by the Arab Bureau fraternity.

He booked in at Shepheard's Hotel in Cairo on 24 April and slept in the first comfortable bed he had know during three years of war. 'Can understand little of the Arab spoken here,' he wrote. Next day he was on his way down the Red Sea to meet the 'great ones' of the Arab Revolt. He was ill at this time from his long privations in Mesopotamia, and more sick than he knew, for he had a badly infected appendix. 'When I come back I shall have to go into hospital,' he wrote, 'I am most miserably seedy and can hardly walk upstairs.' However, he improved a little on the sea journey and was taken to Rabegh and on to Wejh, where Faisal still slept peacefully and Lawrence waited on him before his journey with Auda's Howaitat to Aqaba.

On 3 May Leachman met the Arab prince and his English adviser. Bray, who was to become Leachman's biographer, was there too and he noted the contrast as they sat in Faisal's tent:

> 'Lawrence attired in flowing white robes, but behaving with studied servility to Faisal, Leachman tall, muscular, in faded khaki, unashamedly the Englishman, and a masterful one at that. He could wear Arab clothes and play the Arab when the occasion demanded, but at other times he was Colonel Leachman of the Royal Sussex, proud to be a Christian, serving his country in the desert places where it had pleased God to call him.

Bray was inclined to exaggerate his hero's 'masterful' qualities and to overlook his faults. But it is not difficult to imagine Leachman's contempt for his princely host and the little Englishman who hovered at his elbow. Leachman was no supporter of the Arab cause. Neither was he impressed by Lawrence's Arab dress or by his pretentions. He despised the Hijaz. 'Most vile form of Arab, worse than the worst Mesopotamian specimen.' Lawrence returned the compliment. When he recalled the gathering in later years he asserted that his fellow countryman was thrown out because of his ill-treatment of his servant. In fact Leachman went quite voluntarily.

Before leaving Cairo for Wejh, Leachman had been introduced to the Egyptian Sultan, and had dined with Wingate, whom he found 'charming' but disappointing in one respect – he had gone teetotal and there was no wine at dinner, even for guests. And he had met Sykes and Picot at the Residency where he was inveigled into a long and wearisome discussion on Arab

affairs. Leachman sat throughout in silence and pained dis-
belief. 'This is an absolutely new world of soldiering. I have not
met a single officer I know. They all have about ten medals
apiece of every sort, except war medals ... if you can go to war
from Shepheard's Hotel there is no particular hardship.'

Some months before Leachman was enjoying the comfort of
that famous hotel, MI1 had investigated the activities of its chief
porter, Maurer, following the discovery of incriminating papers
on some deported Greeks. He was arrested. Further inquiries
revealed that the manager of another hotel, the National, had
been a driver with the German army before taking up his new job
and had been passing secrets to the enemy. Five others were
arrested at the same time in the two hotels. Berne station was
interested to note that soon after their detention the ex-Khedive,
who had lived in Switzerland since he was exiled by Britain and
consorted freely with the Turks there, sent a special envoy to
Mecca to speak to the Sharif. That was at the time of Storrs's first
mission to the Sharif. Now Storrs was on his way to Baghdad,
having had 'satisfactory meetings' with Sykes and Picot in Cairo.
Sykes, he noted, was delighted with Cairo's latest plan 'to open up
Central Arabia'. He called on the Sharif at Jiddah on his way.

Following Allenby's appearance on the scene Meinertzhagen
moved up with GHQ to Al Arish. Aaronsohn was called from
Cairo to join him. If the new Commander-in-Chief's orders
took priority, Aaronsohn nevertheless had other matters to deal
with, the most urgent of which was the distribution of funds to
the displaced Jews of Jaffa. Weizmann wanted the money to be
distributed through the Anglo-Palestine Bank at Jaffa, which
was controlled by a Dutchman, but Aaron had grave reservations. And he was worried about delays in the money reaching
its destination. The Foreign Office was also concerned about
the allocation of the vast sums of money which poured into the
coffers of the Relief Committee in Britain from all over the
world. 'I cannot work out what Mr Weizmann is doing', read an
under-secretarial minute on one occasion, 'his letter is very
absurd or very subtle (I expect the latter).' Sympathy for the
Jews of Palestine was by no means universal in the Foreign
Office. 'They are now suffering in a modified form the same
persecutions which the Armenians have suffered for so long
with the active participation of the Jewish elements in the Committee of Union and Progress,' noted Under-Secretary Kidston.
'Personally I should be very sceptical as to any funds ever reach-

ing the real sufferers in Palestine,' read another marginal note. 'Mr Weizmann has a great deal of money at his disposal. I do not know why he hasn't sent any. I think we might inform him that the Cairo Committee is becoming impatient.'

Aware of the chaos being caused by the deliberations of his Committee and its counterpart in Cairo, the Jewish leader decided to ask Aaronsohn to act as secretary of the Cairo committee. On 23 August he cleared with Under-Secretary Graham a telegram to Aaronsohn, care of the DMI:

> *Aaronsohn, Alexandria.* Aware of the appreciation of high authorities of your capabilities and personal work we appeal to you most emphatically to accept secretaryship of proposed new committee on lines of collective deliberations, decisions and responsibilities for necessary work. We will gladly correspond with your committee and promote your work so far as you will communicate same to us.

The appeal was signed by Weizmann and another Jew of distinction, the emigré Russian journalist, Nahum Sokolov.

Foreign Office concern went beyond the feelings of Under-Secretaries, whether for or against the Jews and other suffering minorities of Syria. 'So far as I am concerned,' wrote Sir Arthur Nicolson, 'our present attitude towards the Palestine Question is based on a compromise between ... encouraging Jewish national aspirations and ... avoiding ... suspicion in the French Colonial Party.'

In July 1917, as he wandered on the edge of the Sinai showing Anzac engineers the best water sources along Allenby's proposed route into Palestine, Aaronsohn received a message from Lishansky, telling him that the Yishuv had ceased its opposition and that NILI under Sarah's local leadership was receiving wide support. Many Jewish officers in the Ottoman army were providing it with information and Sarah and Lishovsky had established a regular pigeon post between Athlit and GHQ at Al Arish. But as Allenby's campaign gathered momentum and Aaron prepared to make his second journey to London, the NILI organisation and his family at Zichron Yakov were in grave danger. The very success of their activities made eventual discovery almost certain.

On 20 August Wingate sent a long and highly confidential report to the Foreign Secretary, Balfour. It began: 'I had intended

to report to you by despatch some of the difficulties which Mr
Aaronsohn has been experiencing both locally and *vis-à-vis* the
Zionist organisation in London, when matters were brought to a
head by a heated interview between that gentleman and Colonel
Deedes.'

It was clear from Wingate's report that there were severe differences between the political representatives of the majority of
Jews in Palestine and Aaronsohn. The latter had asked Deedes
and Wingate to issue a circular on his behalf to important Jews
throughout the world informing them of the true state of
affairs in Palestine and among the Yishuv in particular, facts
which he believed were being concealed not only by the Turks
but by the Jews themselves, whose leaders, though they had
promised not to attack or betray the NILI spies, none the less
saw no advantage in provoking the Turks. The Yishuv leaders
had nominated two men who would be sent to Cyprus to confer
with Aaronsohn. Meanwhile Aaronsohn had written a detailed
summary for intelligence. In it he went over the period of his
own close ties with Jamal, of his personal knowledge of Jamal's
intention to evacuate Jaffa, of secret meetings he had held in
Constantinople with the representative of the Zionist Congress
there, Mr Lichtheim, and with the German Ambassador and the
American Chargé d'Affaires, Hoffman Philips. There was a
fiery conclusion to his long and bitter denunciation of the Jewish
notables of Palestine. 'The denials [of Turkish brutality] coming from Palestinian Jewish notabilities are worthless: (a) having
been obtained by force, (b) being self-accusing, (c) or due to
base flattery.'

Wingate's position was clear. On 14 August he had telegraphed the Foreign Office ahead of Aaronsohn's report, asking
that he should receive 'without delay the support for which he
had asked'. An additional reason for not wishing to alienate
Aaronsohn, 'and one which may perhaps appeal to you', he told
Balfour, 'is that the military authorities attach importance to
retaining the use of the organisation he has created in Palestine'.
But there were other more pressing matters in the air in August
1917. The Arab autonomy movement now led by Dr Shahbandar
in his Egyptian exile had become increasingly suspicious of the
Sykes–Picot deal, though they know nothing of its provisions as
yet, and increasingly militant in their opposition to Anglo-
French schemes. Berne office had warned the DMI in London
that the Turks were proposing to Germany that the Arabs of

Syria and Mesopotamia should be offered autonomy, and the Cabinet in London was on the point of awarding Palestine to the Jews.

In September 1917 the Foreign Office received a cable from Wingate: 'Aaronsohn wishes to proceed to England without delay to interview Weizmann etc. This is I think only means of settling their differences. Military authorities consider his journey most desirable and are anxious that he should have no difficulties.' He arrived in London at the end of the month to renew his contact with Thomson, Hall and Macdonogh, and to take up the threads of acquaintanceship with Sykes and the Foreign Office information chief, John Buchan.

Six months before Aaronsohn's arrival, Captain Hall had achieved the supreme intelligence *coup* of the war by cracking the enemy cipher which conveyed the famous Zimmermann telegram to America, via Stockholm and Buenos Aires, using the submarine threat to America to force the President's acquiescence in an alliance between Germany and Mexico. Hall believed that the code-book used by his cipher experts in cracking the telegram, which brought America into the war on 6 April 1917, had belonged to Wassmuss. In fact it had belonged to Consul Listemann, and was among the belongings taken from the German by the subaltern Hastings when he invaded the room of his German quarry in 1914.

After Hall's men had quietly let the President know the plans of the enemy, Woodrow Wilson's *alter ego*, Colonel House, wrote to the DNI in London: 'I cannot think at the moment of any man who has done more useful service in this war than you, and I salute you.' In another note House expressed his appreciation of Britain's 'discreet silence', but added: 'The consummation of Home Rule for Ireland would have greatly accelerated the decision which the US have taken at last.'

The chief concern of all British intelligence and propaganda services from the late spring of 1917 was the power-house of world Jewry. In July 1917, as Allenby began the preparations for his campaign, von Falkenhayn, the late Chief of the German Staff, took over the command of the remnants of the 'Yilderim' group and the Syrian Sixth Army – now united into the *Asienkorps* – and to plan a counter-attack in Mesopotamia. Aaronsohn wrote in his diary for 26 July: 'Today I can say that the task I undertook has succeeded.' When he arrived in Europe little more than a year later he was to receive some painful reminders that his task was by no means finished.

Argument was fuelled by the knowledge of the very secret discussions going on in London between Balfour and Weizmann, with Lord Rothschild playing an important part on the sidelines. In June, before leaving for London, Aaronsohn appealed to America's ex-Ambassador in Constantinople, Morgenthau, for support for his cause in Palestine. President Wilson, knowing that both Britain and Germany were considering pledges to the Jews concerning the future of Palestine, while simultaneously pursuing peace initiatives, decided to send Morgenthau to Egypt to see Aaronsohn and the Zionist Committee there, and to Switzerland to contact agents of the Central Alliance. As soon as Whitehall heard of the visit, it asked Weizmann to intercept Morgenthau, who was accompanied by the American jurist and Zionist leader, Felix Frankfurter, and talk him out of the mission. Weizmann was able to cut short Morgenthau's visit, but not before a French envoy, Colonel Weil, had met the Americans at Gibraltar. Weizmann saw the 'Philanthropist', Baron Edmond de Rothschild, in Paris, and arrived in London on 22 July. Four days before his return Lord Rothschild, who was the head of the English branch of the family and the father figure of British Jewry, wrote to Balfour bringing to a climax the hopes and aspirations which had been voiced two years before in Herbert Samuel's report to the Cabinet: 'Dear Mr Balfour, At last I am able to bring you the formula you asked me for.' There was a fly in the ointment, however. The proposed declaration was opposed by only one member of the British Government: its single Jewish member.

In March 1917 Edwin Montagu, Parliamentary Under-Secretary at the India Office, had asked the Prime Minister to meet him:

> Dear PM,
> As the desert sand for rain
> As the Londoner for sun
> As the poor for potatoes
> As the landlord for rent
> As Drosera Rotundafolia for a fly
> As Herbert Samuel for Palestine
> As a woman in Waterloo Road for a soldier
> *I long for a talk with you.*

Montagu, the East End London Jew made good, wanted the Treasury. Lloyd George gave him the India Office. A bitter opponent of the Zionist cause and of the idea of a Jewish nation, he became the Prime Minister's close adviser at a time when France was war-weary and in a mood to seek peace, and when the most pressing need of the British Government was to rouse the worldwide Jewish community, especially the powerful American lobby, to all-out support of the war effort on the Allied side.

It was a time, too, when the entire 'eastern' strategy was under attack in the press; though perversely it was Hardinge, the man who as Viceroy had opposed most vehemently the entire 'eastern' adventure, who shouldered the blame, following the publication and debate of the parliamentary report on the Mesopotamian campaign in July. He was called on by press and Parliament to resign from the Foreign Office, where he was now a Principal Under-Secretary handling Middle East affairs. Hardinge asked the Government if he could be prosecuted so that he could defend himself publicly. Remarkably, the Parliamentary Commission which investigated the Kut disaster referred to none of the letters which Hardinge had written to the India Office during his viceroyalty condemning the waste of life and materials in strategically spurious ventures. And it covered up the evidence of governmental pressure on Hardinge and his military commanders to advance on Baghdad. Chamberlain, who properly accepted political responsibility, resigned in July when the Report was made public. The man who was principally to blame, Lloyd George, could hardly be expected to vacate the Premiership, and of the other great 'easterners', Winston Churchill was out of office and Kitchener dead. Lloyd George was unrepentant, indeed he continued to the end of the war his condemnation of those who saw the Western Front as the place of ultimate decision. All the same he refused Hardinge a public hearing and refused to accept his resignation. Justice had a partial victory. And he gave Chamberlain's job to the aspiring Montagu, though the King had said that he would like the Jewish MP to be the next Viceroy in succession to Chelmsford. Balfour told Lloyd George that he would be 'interested to see how the experiment succeeded'.

Montagu did not enter the debate on Palestine until August, by which time Weizmann had returned from Paris with the news that Morgenthau and Frankfurter had called off their hazardous mission to the Turks in Switzerland, and Wingate had told London:

10 No. 1 Squadron, 86th Communication Wing, RAF Mail Service at Hendon. Centre is Lt-Col. Neil Primrose, with Major Chadwick on his left. Captain Jefferson, Aaronsohn's pilot, may be seated third from left

11 Sassanian arch and palace at Ctesiphon; the last stage of the British army's disastrous march on Baghdad in 1915. Photograph by Gertrude Bell, 1909

12 Colonel A. C. Parker and Sudanese guard. Parker was Military
Governor of Sinai and first Executive Chief of the Arab Bureau

13 Britain's foremost 'Sharifites', T. E. Lawrence and Gertrude
Bell, resting at an archaeological site during the Cairo
Conference, 1921

My position with regard to Aaronsohn and his companions is still somewhat obscure though I was grateful for your private telegram of July 18th saying that general assurances of support to Zionist organisation had been given by Mr Balfour and Mr Lloyd George . . . I gather you wish me to keep Aaronsohn satisfied without telling him anything very definite.

Montagu chose this moment to make an impassioned plea to his colleagues not to go ahead with the promised declaration. He entitled his Cabinet Paper, *Anti-Semitism in the British Government.* The nub of his argument was that such a declaration would rally anti-Semitic sentiment throughout the world, and he observed: 'Zionism has always seemed to me a mischievous political creed, untenable by any patriotic citizen of the United Kingdom.' He made a further appeal, 'we have received at the India Office a series of valuable papers on Turkey in Asia from the pen of Miss Gertrude Lowthian Bell, the remarkable woman who, after years of knowledge gained by unique travel in these regions, is acting as Assistant Political Officer in Baghdad'. Gertrude, known personally to most of the men round the Cabinet table, referred to a 'non-Arab people' who looked on Palestine as 'its prescriptive inheritance'. She spoke of immigration 'artificially fostered by doles and subventions from millionaire co-religionists in Europe', and she doubted whether local Jews had any desire 'for a Jewish state' as such. And she entertained the Cabinet with Cromer's story about the Jew who told him: 'If a Jewish kingdom were to be established at Jerusalem I should lose no time in applying for the job of Ambassador in London.'

In a desperate bid to head off support for the proposed declaration, Montague quoted statesmen, rabbis, scientists and philosophers, all of the faith but having in common a distrust of Zionism and an overriding patriotism for the countries of their birth. 'I am a resolute adversary of Zionism,' wrote the French scholar and Deputy, Joseph Reinach, 'Jerusalem belongs to all the religions. We know its history for three thousand years. The Jewish Kingdom endured for scarcely five centuries.' Luigi Luzzatti, ex-Prime Minister of Italy, wrote: 'Judaism is not a Nationality, but a Religion.' And L. L. Cohen, Chairman of the Jewish Board of Guardians, had the last and most vehement word in a fiery debate:

> The establishment of a 'national home for the Jewish race' in Palestine presupposes that the Jews are a nation, which I deny, and that they are homeless, which implies that in countries where they enjoy religious liberty and the full rights of citizenship, they are separate entities, unidentified with the interests of the nations of which the form parts, an implication which I repudiate.

As the debate progressed, Montagu wrote to Lord Robert Cecil at the Foreign Office, 'no further,' enough of 'Les buts de la Guerre,' he cried.

It was all to no avail. The mind of Liberal England and of liberal Christianity was made up, and the exigencies of war, with the support of America's President for a declaration of intent, put the outcome of the debate beyond doubt. Back in February the editor of the *Manchester Guardian*, C. P. Scott, had begged Lloyd George not to let the Quai d'Orsay or the Foreign Office undermine a discussion about to take place between Weizmann, Lord Rothschild and Mark Sykes. The Foreign Secretary had long seen the return of Palestine to the Jews as an act of historical justice, and a salving of the Christian conscience of which, in his book *Foundations of Belief,* he had shown himself to be a custodian who was eminently able to argue his case. In 1905, when he headed the Conservative Government, he had argued during the passage of the Immigration Bill that the treatment of Jews in Europe was 'a disgrace to Christendom'.

Sykes's role was all-pervading. Part-author of the Sharifian promises which gave Palestine to the Arabs, and of the still secret Sykes–Picot agreement which made that land (whose extent and boundaries nobody had defined) an international charge, with Britain controlling its chief port of Haifa, he was the catalyst of the Balfour Declaration which gave it to the Zionists. As in most matters he approached Zion with the zeal of the convert.

The Cabinet discussion which took place on 3 September was interrupted by a note from the DMI on a very obtuse French scheme designed to create a Jewish state in Ibn Saud's territory of Al Hasa. The French Government had assured the Foreign Office that it was in sympathy with Zionist aspirations. Now it came up with the idea of raising a Jewish militia to take over the territory Ibn Saud had won back from the Turks in 1913. Montagu reminded the meeting that Britain had a treaty with Ibn

Saud which 'roughly promises to support [him] and his followers'. Whitehall stamped on the French plan.

Aaronsohn appeared in London in time to take part in the last stages of the debate, as the Government decided to seek the views of President Wilson. Soon after arriving in London he went with Weizmann and Sokolov to Paris to meet Baron de Rothschild. It was a time of great strain, for he had been unable to contact his sister, Sarah, before leaving Cairo, and almost as soon as he had departed Jamal's *gendarmes* fell on Athlit and the NILI organisation. Aaron wrote to his brother, Alex, who had returned from America to take his place in Cairo, telling him of his political problems and reservations, while he waited for definite news of his family and friends in Palestine.

I am leaving here tomorrow morning. I came here on Friday 21st [September] and saw the Philanthropist on Saturday afternoon . . . He listened very interestedly all the time I spoke to him and asked me questions which I answered, but he would not let me touch on certain subjects . . . He feels as we all do that if Great Britain would only rule over our land, we could attain great things; but as nothing certain is known, he cannot allow himself to speak. We must understand that he had pledged himself to silence . . . Mark Sykes came here the day before yesterday. He told me everything and showed me what a lot of enemies we have, most from among our own people, and that is dangerous to our organisation. He told me that my letter to Weizmann was like a thorn in the latter's eye. Mark Sykes begs me to make peace with them and wants me to promise not to quarrel. He says that I should listen to Weizmann and Sokolov. I told him that I was going to London not to quarrel, only to tell them their mistakes and show them the way.

There was more advice, more foreboding. 'Picot will leave Paris in two or three weeks and will come to live in Cairo, he will work with General Clayton. That is the man I told you to try to get in with.' Sykes had telegraphed to Aaronsohn to wait for him in Paris before leaving for London. Meanwhile Aaron had seen William Yale, 'who knows me from Jerusalem, where he was in the Oil Company'. Yale was now an adviser on Middle East affairs to the American Government. 'I spoke to him at great length. He takes a great interest in Eastern Questions. Get as pally as you can with him and watch him, for you will be able to get information from him which you need, especially about happenings in Egypt.' He also met another American from his earlier days in Palestine, Mr Glazebrook. 'I shall have the opportunity of seeing him again in London and through him I can reach the Ambassador.'

Finally I hope that on Monday, when I get to London, I shall hear the latest decision and I will write to you all about it. Put these things before the members of our committee ... and before our friends, Colonel Deedes, General Clayton, Lt. Fielding, Mr. Edmunds and so on.

A.A.

It was a letter written under the strain of grave events. As soon as he arrived in London in September he received the news that Jamal's intelligence men had discovered evidence of NILI's work at Athlit. One of the pigeons being used to make contact with Allenby's front-line HQ had been found at Caesarea along the coast feeding with the pet birds of the Turkish mudir. A message had been found in the cylinder attached to its leg, and though they could not decipher it the Turks realised that something was going on close at hand. HMY *Managam* was due on 10 September to bring word from Aaron. It did not arrive, and to make matters worse Sarah and her companions were hiding one of Kress von Kressenstein's adjutants who had deserted from the Turkish army, intending to put him aboard the spy ship. *Managam* eventually came into sight on the 16th, but did not anchor. There was no cloud cover and the captain had warning of Turkish activity. He turned back after signalling Athlit. The ship came for the last time on the 23rd, and Sarah sent a message to tell Cairo that the Turks were scouring the coast, that she and her companions were in imminent danger and must cease work for the time being. She had written to Aaron to protest at his silence: 'We are very cross ... but perhaps there is a reason and you are not to blame. Anyway, be successful. Who will give us our country for the New Year, so that we can be free people in our own land?' As the Turkish secret police searched the coastal villages from Haifa down to the almost deserted Jaffa and came ever closer to the home and workplace of the Aaronsohn family, talk among the local people was of 'dirty work'. Sarah and her companions were told: 'You endanger the entire Yishuv.' She wrote: 'They are perfectly justified in demanding, *Who is asking you to do this?* And if, God forbid, with all our care, we should fail, then not just a few of our leaders or twenty members of NILI will be hanged. All the Yishuv will be called to trial.'

On 1 October Jamal's men arrived at Zichron Yakov late at night. Sarah had told everyone to disperse when she was warned of the visit. She was alone with her father. Her younger brother Zvi, cousin Reuben Schwartz, Lishansky and others hid close to the house. Close enough to hear the shrieks of the young woman as the Turks beat her. They went on beating her for four days. Her father Ephraim was attacked too, but Sarah was their chief target for she had the information they wanted. Her torture was too much for the others of her group. One by one they gave themselves up in the hope that they would help Sarah by doing so. On 5 October the interrogators decided to take them all to Nazareth to be questioned by Hassan Bey, chief medical officer to the Fourth Army and a man renowned for his methods of dealing with spies. Sarah asked if she could go to her room to collect some clothes before leaving. She kept a pistol in a drawer and took it to the bathroom, where she shot herself through the mouth. The bullet lodged in her spine and she died after several hours. Alex heard a few days later, and cabled Aaron through the DMI to tell him of their sister's fate.

Aaron wrote to his American friend, Henrietta Szold: 'The hope that our heroic Sarah succeeded in shortening her tortures is gone, but she died as bravely as she lived.' They had pulled out her teeth and hair and seared her fair skin, he said, they had lashed the soles off her feet, her legs and her body. They had doubtless tried to assault her sexually. But they did not break her. Ephraim Aaronsohn contracted typhus in prison at Nazareth and was spared. Reuben Schwartz was hanged, whether by the Turks or his own hand was never established. Zvi was imprisoned in Damascus, and was an incurable invalid for the rest of his life as the result of torture. Other members of NILI were hanged. Aaron's precious botanical collection and his library were destroyed.

Lishansky took shelter among former friends of the Ha-Shomer. The Turks declared that unless he was handed over by the Yishuv the village of Zichron Yakov would be destroyed. Ha-Shomer decided that he must be assassinated, though he had been given their protection, and a murder squad was sent in pursuit of him. But they only succeeded in wounding him. He made for Allenby's advance units near Richon le Zion, but he was too weak to avoid badawin raiders. They handed him over to the Turks. Lishansky and the man who probably gave him and the others away, Naaman Belkind, were executed on the same day, 16 December 1917. There were said to have been secret representations by German officials in Palestine on behalf of many of those arrested, and some were released. Others were imprisoned and conscripted.

Thinking Jews were not unaware that the warring powers were vying with each other for their favour. In May 1917 the Ambassador in Rome, Sir Rennell Rodd, told Balfour that the Italian Foreign Minister had been asked to grant an interview to a 'Sionist', M. Sokolov.

> This he was not disposed to grant as he did not wish to treat the matter in any way officially. But from what he heard of M. Sokolov's ideas he was inclined to view them with sympathy, and he had no objection at all to the proposal to found Jewish colonies in Palestine.

A few days earlier Commander Wedgwood, MP, had asked Balfour in the House, whether 'any pledges had been given to France or Italy which might impede the establishment of an independent and integral Jewish Palestine under American or British protection'. Lord Robert Cecil, speaking on behalf of the Foreign Secretary, replied that he could not answer questions about pledges to Allies about the terms of peace. The Foreign Office diary noted that it was not an easy question to answer: 'we are at present pledged to an international administration in Palestine'.

While all sides probed to see which way the big powers would jump, there were some interesting skirmishes on the outskirts of the battle. Marmaduke Pickthall, suspected of being an enemy agent ever since his return from Constantinople at the beginning of the war, lectured a crowded meeting at the Caxton Hall in London on 9 June, on 'Muslim interests in Palestine'. Representatives of several Islamic countries were present. So were representatives of Special Intelligence. Macdonogh's men were keeping a close watch on Moslem activities at this time and they anxiously pursued the writers of several letters in Arabic to

Al Qibla, the Sharif of Mecca's magazine, run on British money. They eventually ran the culprits to earth: two very harmless old ladies who had embraced Islam, the Misses May and Ethel Etherington.

More importantly, in June the Foreign Office circulated to Cabinet ministers an article from the conservative Berlin newspaper *Reichsbote,* written by Professor Gustav Dobeler. It was, they said, a very well-informed article. It advocated a strengthening of the Turkish state through the influence of Jewry, 'precisely on the ardently coveted bridge between Egypt and India'. But the Germans should not 'disguise our purely political action in the cloak or pious hypocrisy as England, and the first champion of this idea, President Wilson, think they must do'. And it concluded:

> Just as a prairie fire is extinguished by a counter-fire, so can we foil England's latest imperialistic scheme by anticipating her own intention. The establishment of a Jewish state under Turkish supremacy would be for us a measure of defence just as the U-boat war is the only possible reply to the English blockade. Fire against fire.

The day the *gendarmes* appeared at Zichron Yakov a message arrived in London from Berne intelligence.

> A meeting is said to have taken place lately at Berlin at which Herr von Kühlmann, Jamal Pasha and a leading Zionist were present in order to discuss the Palestine Question. Certain promises were made to the Jews in order to obtain their cooperation in the new war loan. Count Bernstorff [the ex-Ambassador in America] has also, it is stated, entered into relations with Jews at Constantinople while the German Minister at Berne has held a long interview with a prominent Jew on the same subject ... It would seem that the German Government are making an attempt to counteract the effect of British effort to liberate Palestine.
>
> Berne, 2 October 1917

On 4 October Balfour sent a revised draft of the proposed formula to Colonel House, in response to a request from the President. 'In view of the reports that the German Government are making great efforts to capture the Zionist movement, the question of a message of sympathy with the movement from HMG has again been considered by the Cabinet.' On 16 October an affirmative reply came from the President. On the 22nd replies from leading Jews were circulated to the Cabinet. On 24 and 25 October there were further discussions in Downing Street, and Curzon sent an essay on 'Zionists and Anti-Zionists' in the Jewish community to the War Cabinet. Sykes observed in reply that Palestine was 'a dirty place', and that: 'If the Jews don't go there someone will. Nature abhorrs a vacuum.' Earlier the Cabinet had been treated to the views of 'the late Earl of Cromer' in the form of an article he wrote in the *Spectator* just before his death. In it he quoted Asher Ginsberg (who signed himself Achad-ha-'Am or 'One of the People'): 'Did I envy these fellow-Jews of mine their emancipation? I answer in all truth and sincerity, No! A thousand times No! The privileges are not worth the price!'

More significantly, Whitehall received news in mid-October that a Turco-German military convention had been signed in Constantinople; a blue-print for co-operation during and after the war drawn up by the principal Jew in the Ottoman Government, Javid.

On 2 November the Foreign Secretary sent the final version of his historic letter to Lord Rothschild, with its central commitment. 'HM Government view with favour the establishment in Palestine of a National Home for the Jewish Race, and will use their best endeavours to facilitate the achievement of this object.' Rothschild acknowledged the letter with his own gratitude and that of the 'large mass of Jewish people', on 4 November.

At the very moment of the promise – the promise that after 2,000 years the Jews would be allowed to return as a nation to the land from which they were dispersed – Lenin's revolutionaries stormed the citadels of Russia, many a Jew in the political vanguard, promises of freedom and emancipation and the righting of past wrongs falling from their lips. And one of the Bolsheviks' first acts of foreign policy was to reveal the Sykes–Picot agreement to the Turks and to the world; and to disavow the associated Anglo-French agreement with Russia of March 1915 which gave Constantinople to the Czar.

World Jewry was appeased by the declaration which came within a month of the destruction of NILI. Now the problem was to enlist the Jews in active support for the war effort. American troops were already fighting in Europe and a division was on its way to the Middle East. The day after the declaration to Lord Rothschild was made public the Foreign Secretary circulated to the Cabinet Sir Ronald Graham's plans for a Jewish task force.

'I held a meeting last night which was attended by Sir Mark Sykes, Dr Weizmann, Mr Sokolov and Mr Aaron Aaronsohn, to discuss the best methods of obtaining full political advantage from the new situation.' The Bolsheviks had stormed the Winter Palace and the country in which Jewry had found a new revolutionary role was thought to be the most deserving of immediate attention. 'The Zionists are now anxious to throw their full weight into the scale ... Russia is obviously the country where most could be done.' The plan was to send Sokolov, Tschlenov (President of the Russian Zionists in Britain) and Jabotinsky (founder of the Jewish Regiment in the British army and a brilliant organiser and orator) to Russia. 'I have no great faith in the capacity ... of the first two gentlemen, although they carry weight in Russian from their position, Mr Jabotinsky on the other hand is just the type of man required.' Weizmann labelled his compatriot, 'Our own D'Annunzio'.

Colonel John Buchan, appointed head of propaganda at the Foreign Office after returning wounded from France, was working closely with Jabotinsky and Aaronsohn to formulate campaigns in Russia and America. And Poliakov, the London correspondent of *Russki Slovo*, was brought in to help them.

Mr Aaron Aaronsohn will proceed to America, where his expert knowledge of conditions in Palestine will render him valuable. Mr Samuel Aaronsohn [Aaron's brother who had joined him in London] goes to Egypt. Mr Weizmann will travel to Paris to concert with Baron Edmond de Rothschild. He will then return here to supervise the central organisation. There is no question of the intense gratitude of the Zionists for the declaration.

At the end of November Wingate told London that funds were at last coming through to the Special Committee in Cairo. It was proposed to form an international committee in London composed of Weizmann; the prominent Armenian in London, James Malcolm; the Syrian Christian, Nejib Hani; and a Moslem Arab. Sykes sought approval for Arab participation from

Mecca and Cairo. 'I think that Armenian help is rated rather high,' a Foreign Office official noted. On 30 November there was a mass rally in London at which Arabs and Jews stood side by side to welcome the new *entente*.

15

Requiem for Victory

'*One of the most remarkable features in the character of our English guests was their extreme desire to do us good against our inclinations.*'

Hajji Baba, quoted in Lord Ronaldshay, *Life of Curzon*

Within three weeks of Sarah Aaronsohn's death and the destruction of the NILI network in Palestine, and a week before the publication of the Balfour Declaration, Allenby began his Jerusalem campaign with the bombardment of Gaza and the advance on Beersheba. It was among the most thoroughly planned and successful engagements of the war on the Allied side, not because of any spectacular strategic feats but because of its brilliant organisation and consequent reduction of casualties to an almost irreducible minimum. And its success was due in no small measure to the reliable intelligence provided by the NILI network in Palestine, and to the ruses which Meinertzhagen and Aaronsohn had worked out before the latter left for London, especially the so-called 'haversack' trick, which was to become famous in the annals of war.

This depended for its effectiveness on sending a senior staff officer into no man's land in front of Beersheba; an officer courageous enough to allow himself to be chased and almost certainly shot at and to drop his blood-stained haversack during the pursuit. Papers in the lost haversack were exact replicas of the real battle plan, differing only in small but vital details from Allenby's actual intentions. The Turks were almost entirely deceived. Years later Field-Marshal Lord Wavell, Allenby's biographer, wrote: 'It is now known that these papers were one of the principal influences that determined the action of the Turks before and during the battle.' Meinertzhagen, who 'knew no half measures', who was, said Lawrence, 'a strategist, a geographer, and a silent laughing masterful man', chose to make the drop himself. He was lucky to escape with his life.

Another ruse was to cause the capture of one of the most intrepid and experienced staff officers in the British army, Colonel Newcombe. He had been at the heart of the Arab Revolt since the pre-war days when he surveyed the Syrian desert under the guise of the Palestine Exploration Fund and directed the undercover activities of British and native agents. It is one of the many ironies of the Arabian adventure that because of his loyalty to Lawrence, which remained steadfast to the end of his days, Newcombe's own story as the officer responsible for the attack on the Hijaz rail line was never told, except in the elliptical manner of his hero in *The Seven Pillars of Wisdom,* and with almost total inaccuracy by Lowell Thomas in his *With Lawrence in Arabia.*

As the advance on Jerusalem entered its third and final phase at the end of October it became necessary to convince the Turks that the British force intended a wide encircling movement from the east of Hebron before advancing on the city. This was achieved by a daring diversion carried out by seventy men of 5 Company of the Imperial Camel Corps under Newcombe's command. They set out the night before the attack on Beersheba. Sixteen of the men had never ridden camels. They were taken straight from a gunnery course at Al Arish, given six days' rations and told to meet the Colonel at a pre-arranged point on the narrow-gauge railway which the army was building along the old Roman coast road as it advanced into Palestine.

Their first sight of Newcombe was not reassuring. In the words of one of the men, he arrived towards evening, 'tall, gaunt, with a scrubby ginger beard, uniform crumpled and shoddy; his appearance was far from inspiring'. The Colonel and his band of untried desert warriors joined up with 5 Company of the Camel Corps at Asluj just below Beersheba on 30 October 1917. Next morning the untutored camel riders built piles of stones from which they could swing a leg over their animals, cavalry fashion, and set off with their experienced comrades, Newcombe at the head of his motley band. He handed baksheesh to some of the badawin encountered on the road behind enemy lines, to ensure that their presence was not revealed to the Turks.

When they arrived at the Beersheba–Hebron road a party went off to cut the telegraph lines while the Lewis gunners covered them. Next day they went off to the hills which flanked the road, calmly arresting several Turkish officers who were walking

innocently along the highway in what they believed to be their
zone. Ahead of them lay Al Dhariya, which the Australian Light
Horse were due to attack at any moment. They were on the
Turks' line of retreat. 'This would appear audacity or folly, but
it was the supreme confidence of the Colonel.' A column of
Turkish infantry marched towards them and they opened fire.
'They had no chance, no time to think.' But some of the Turks,
though wounded, got away.

The British force spent the night lying on a hillside in freezing cold, hoping that next day the army would advance along the
road. But next morning an enemy aircraft spotted them, doubtless sent out on the word of the wounded infantry. A few
minutes later firing began all around. Two Vickers gun crews
were put out of action immediately. The Lewis gunners held
their position from early morning until afternoon. Anyone who
so much as sat up was shot immediately by the Turkish gunners.
They were an easy target. The Turks simply had to plaster the
hill, and they did so with venom. By late afternoon relief was still
unsighted, ammunition running out and twenty of the seventy
men were dead. Newcombe decided that he must surrender. As
Lawrence was to write: 'He was brave for six hours too long.'
The prisoners were led into Jerusalem crying for water as they
passed through the gate. So thirsty were they that they forgot
their hunger. They were marched on to Es-Salt, then to
Amman, and on to Damascus and prison camps in Turkey.
With their pernicious policy of treating officers according to the
conventions of war while other ranks were regarded as little
more than slaves, the Turks sent some of the men to work in salt
mines. Most died in captivity.

'Skinface' Newcombe was a celebrity to his captors and was
entertained royally by Jamal in Damascus before being sent to
Constantinople, where he proved an unsuspected problem.
After only a month he escaped with Captain Mousley, a Kut
prisoner, but the mast of their boat broke as they sailed the Bosphorus and they were forced to return to their gaol. He escaped
twice more, the last time with the aid of a French girl whom he
eventually took to England and married.

Before leaving Damascus he wrote to Jamal to thank him for
the treatment he and his men had received once they arrived in
the Syrian city, and asked Jamal's Chief of Staff, Izmet Bey, to
'enquire occasionally into the welfare of any British prisoners of
war here'.

Newcombe had convinced the Turks that a wide encircling movement was to be made by the cavalry force, while in fact the army marched straight through from Beersheba to Hebron. A German General of the Medical Corps who was in Hebron at the time commented: 'The place was like an ant's nest . . . Turkish gendarmes dashed through the excited populace. The main body of the English was said to be only a few kilometres off.' Allenby wired London on 31 October, 'Beersheba Ober-General Steuber attack successful'. On 16 November the British Army entered Jaffa and thus took control of the entire Plain of Philistia. On 11 December Allenby marched at its head into Jerusalem.

'Two gentlemen – very popular – sort of penny reading illustrated with living and moving pictures.' With those words the British Embassy in Washington introduced to Colonel Fisher of MI1 two Americans who were to determine for ever after the world's historical view of the war in the desert: to turn the 'Illicit Adventure' into a saga of one man's solitary endeavour in the desert.

It all began with a telegram from Cecil Spring-Rice, Britain's Ambassador in Washington, to Colonel Buchan at the Foreign Office. 'Party of Americans on way to Europe on SS *New York*. Sails November 24th. Among members of propaganda delegation, Professor Lowell Thomas.' The Arab Revolt had found its trumpeter.

At the time when Buchan was arranging for the visit of Aaronsohn and the Zionist delegation to the United States he received a letter from Lowell Thomas, who had reached Rome with his companion, Colonel Webb Hayes, son of the former President, on his way to Cairo. 'Bulletin received today states your army has captured Jerusalem . . . I want to go there at once, accompanied only by my photographer.' He was, he said 'here in Europe . . . to gather data . . . for a series of patriotic features'.

He was too late to join in the triumphant entry of Allenby and his men, marching into the Holy City of Jew, Moslem and Christian. But no matter, Lawrence whom he was soon to meet would fill in the detail: the graphic picture of the passage through the Jaffa Gate, Lawrence in his Arab attire marching as Clayton's officer of the day, of Picot's *faux pas* as he told the bull-necked Allenby: 'And tomorrow, dear General, I will take steps to set up civil government in the town', and Allenby replied: 'In the military zone the only authority is that of the Commander-in-Chief.'

Thomas met Lawrence for the first time in December, at about the same time as Meinertzhagen first came face to face with him, dressed in spotless white with a gold *agal* round his headress. 'I thought he was somebody's pleasure-boy,' said the DMI. 'Boy or girl?' asked Meinertzhagen. Lawrence is alleged to have smiled and blushed, saying 'Boy'. If Meinertzhagen was sceptical the American professor was enchanted. And he was not alone in his admiration. Wingate thought highly of him and recommended him for the VC after Aqaba. Even his arch-enemy, Colonel Brémond, recommended him for the Croix de Guerre.

By the beginning of 1918 the manhood of Britain, France and Russia had been bled almost to exhaustion; as had the men of Germany, Austria-Hungary and the Ottoman Empire. Another year would surely be beyond the capacity of any of the contestants. Only America could now sway the balance. Ludendorff, Falkenhayn's successor as Chief of the German Staff, had declared that the choice was 'victory or defeat', the only option 'a fight to the last breath'. France had been reborn under the 'Tiger', Clemenceau, and the pacifists and pro-Germans had been put behind bars. But Russia had disappeared from the Entente in the smoke of revolution. The six million Jews of Russia and the three million of America became the principal targets of British propaganda.

Buchan's Zionist propaganda unit in London under Albert Hyamson, and its counterpart in America under J. L. Kandel of Columbia University, were soon running in high gear, and even the German *Judische Rundschau* had pronounced the Balfour Declaration an event 'of world historic importance'. 'No more happy tidings could reach us', cabled the Zionists of Lenin's Russia. On the fall of Jerusalem the Chief Rabbi had conveyed to King George V the congratulations of the Jewish communities of the Empire, and he cabled Allenby: 'British Jews thrilled by glorious news from Palestine.' Such messages were grist to Buchan's mill in London and New York.

German and Turkish intelligence had not been idle during the summer, and they had found an ally in the ex-Khedive of Egypt, Abbas Hilmi, whose successor, the Sultan Husain Kamil, was critically ill in Cairo after an operation at the beginning of the year for haemorrhoids. Abbas Hilmi began to see opportunities for a return to the throne, and for a say in the affairs of Islam, in the rivalry of Britain and Germany in the Middle East. In June 1917 he was in touch with Muhammad Farid, the Egyptian nationalist who lived in Berlin.

The Germans established their own Arab Bureau in Damascus. It did not have to seek far afield for fodder. Oppenheim's new brainchild circulated the story that Britain was about to declare the Sultan it had put on the throne in 1915 'mad' and that it had decided to abandon him.

The *Albion perfide* corner of the journal it produced, *Der Neue Orient*, made hay with the Sharif affair. And while it did so Abbas Hilmi left his lair in Switzerland (to which he had retired in 1916 with a pension of £2,000 a month from Britain, and his French mistress) for Constantinople. The idea was being canvassed of an autonomous province of Syria with Abbas as the Ottoman Viceroy, as a counter to the Sharif's 'King of the Arabs'. A cryptic Foreign Office note in August 1917 said simply, 'Dangerous!' Rumbold, Britain's man in Berne wrote of Abbas: 'I do not suppose a more tortuous or untrustworthy person ever existed.' Rumbold's replacement, Lord Acton, was to add: 'But he was expected to acknowledge a man who . . . once kissed the hem of his garment.' The ex-Khedive was used by the Germans to send a messenger to the Sharif in Mecca to offer him gold and a status guaranteed by the Emperor. But German intelligence had little confidence in Abbas or his agents. He had already swindled the German Government of millions of marks in the scandalous Bolo affair, in which it was proposed to purchase the French newspapers *Le Temps* and *Figaro* and to turn them into German propaganda weapons. By Christmas 1917 Abbas was serving his new masters as a go-between with the Sharif, and his partner in crime, Bolo, had been hanged by the Clemenceau regime.

Soon after Abbas began to talk to the Sharif through his emissaries, Aziz Ali al Masri, the commander of the Hijaz army, threw in his hand. The founder member of Al Ahad, the man who had taken the lead in bringing together the princes of Arabia under the banner of Ibn Saud while he himself was a serving officer of the Ottoman army, returned to Cairo. 'He remains a friend of Britain but is unwilling, as a soldier, to take further part in the war,' wrote Wingate.

Jamal was later to say of him:

> I heard subsequently that although Aziz Bey had given me his sword of honour at the time, he placed himself at the service of the Sharif Husain during the World War when the latter, a monster of ingratitude, rose in arms against the

Caliphate and deliberately drove the world of Islam into the deplorable condition in which it finds itself today. Today it is I who cannot forgive him.

Another event helped to fuel the fires of suspicion and falsehood which occupied the world in late 1917. On 28 November the Military Press Bureau in Mesopotamia announced that General Sir Stanley Maude, the captor of Baghdad, was dead. He had been taken to the same hospital as that in which von der Goltz died soon after the surrender of Kut-al-Amara. Cholera was said to be the cause. Germany's Arab Bureau was quick to circulate the story to the neutral and enemy press that the British general had been murdered. He had become politically inconvenient to the civil administration. Rumours circulated soon after the death of the Egyptian Sultan, and the new incumbent, Ahmad Fuad, who had heard of Maude's disputes on the subject of post-war government with Cox and the civilian administrators, asked Wingate anxiously what the mystery was about.

'I was unable to enlighten him,' Wingate told Sir Ronald Graham at the Foreign Office. Graham replied: 'He died of cholera.' The Foreign Office clerk wrote on the papers dealing with Wingate's request for information: 'Room 16. *Not to be copied.* Sir R. Graham does not want to have this back.'

The matter was lost sight of in the excitement of the fall of Jerusalem, Allenby's Christmas present to the Allies. Jamal was recalled to Constantinople. Kress von Kressenstein was relieved of his command. The *Asienkorps* ceased to exist with the virtual destruction of the Sixth Army, *Irakgruppe,* and in February 1918 Liman von Sanders, victor of Gallipoli, took over from von Falkenhayn as the new commander of Army Group F, which reverted to the boastful name of the combined army, *Yilderim.* The opposing armies prepared for the final battles of 1918.

The new year came in with vigour, President Wilson's Fourteen Points for Peace giving renewed emphasis to the promises and half-promises of national independence made by Britain to the people in whose territories it had fought the war. And while America laid down the laws of peace, riots and strikes came to a hungry and demoralised Berlin. In Persia Major-General Percy Sykes's Persian Rifles mopped up the residue of German-led resistance among the tribes, though Wassmuss remained at large.

The Supreme Allied War Council, where 'easterners' were

now in the ascendant in both the British and French camps, decided on an all-out campaign against the Turks and asked Field-Marshal Smuts to lead a delegation to Allenby to 'examine his plans'. Turkey responded to the challenge by permitting Liman, the man who had called Enver 'a military buffoon' to take over the Syrian army, and by sending its two famous warships, *Goeben* and *Breslau*, into the Aegean to attack British vessels. This time the Royal Navy was ready. *Breslau* was sunk and *Goeben* limped back to port, crippled.

Trotsky, the Foreign Minister of the Bolsheviks, announced in February that Russia would 'neither fight nor negotiate' with the imperialist powers. A month later the Treaty of Brest-Litovsk was signed between the Soviets and the Central Powers.

There was stalemate on the Palestinian front, where Allenby had announced that he would do no more, whatever the Smuts mission might advocate, than secure control of the Jordan valley and cut the Hijaz railway at Amman, before the spring.

The intelligence services urgently needed rehauling again in the light of the Russian Revolution. Steel and Kisch took over the new MIO(a) devoted to Russia and 'peripheral' territories; still on the roof of the War Office, 'Zeppelin Terrace', where the other Wassmuss continued to stalk his prey and sleep in Kisch's in-tray between times. The question of whether or not to arm the White Russians, to intervene in the Revolution, was closely connected at this time with the negotiations with Turkey, for the Bolsheviks were paying attention to both Enver and the phoenix who was rising perceptibly from the ashes of the Ottoman Empire, Mustafa Kamal. Bruce Lockhart, returning to Russia as MIO's man in Moscow, thought that nothing could be gained by supporting the side which had lost the civil war. But his view did not prevail.

Undercover negotiations with the Turks assumed renewed urgency as Lloyd George, the Prime Minister reared on the village green, brought his own brand of urbanity to questions of war and peace. Since assuming office in December 1916 he had created his own Secret Service, placing little trust either in the Foreign Office establishment or in the accepted methods of naval and military intelligence. His lieutenants were old acquaintances from his days as Munitions Minister, and even before, in the years from 1908 to 1915 when, as Chancellor of the Exchequer, he had dealt with international financiers and businessmen on a scale which more orthodox politicians might have thought unbecoming. And the chief of his private intelligence service was Sir Vincent Caillard, sixty-two years old in 1918, Eton and the Royal Engineers, related on his mother's side to Disraeli, and an officer of military intelligence at Cairo during the Egyptian Campaign of 1882. He was a director of Vickers and its subsidiary, the Metropolitan Carriage, Wagon and Finance Company. His relationships with the world's armament manufacturers was intimate and perhaps his closest associate was the multi-millionaire of Avenue Hoche in Paris, Basileias Zahroff, whose shadowy figure had hovered over the vast arms deals by which Germany pursued the 'Drang nach Osten' between 1898 and 1914, infiltrating guns and ammunition to states and tribes in the east by way of Constantinople, and who played a large part in arming the great powers themselves. Zahroff was distinguished by a permanent skin disorder which errupted into a most unsightly rash in extremes of heat and cold; otherwise virtually nothing of his life or person is known.

A fellow director of Caillard's on the third floor of Vickers House in Westminster was Count Léon Ostrorog, a Frenchman who was also close to Zahroff, who had been legal adviser to the Porte before the war, and was the great European authority on Moslem law. All knew the Young Turks' leaders from their days of obscurity; all had known Abdal Hamid in his prime and in his rejection. All had been engaged in a series of peace moves which had begun with the meeting at Dedeagatch in 1915 between Fitzmaurice and Eady (the contractor who had worked in Constantinople for Vickers) and Enver's men, and which had continued with no more profit in November 1915, November 1916 and August 1917.

At different times the American Ambassador in Berlin, the Pope, Prince Sixtus and Crown Prince Charles of Austria were involved. In the highly secret meetings and correspondence which followed the advent of Lloyd George to 10 Downing Street, the Prime Minister was referred to as the 'Chairman', Caillard as the 'Treasurer' and Zahroff simply as 'Z' or 'Zedzed'. An acquaintance of both men from pre-war Germany and Constantinople was Colonel Frobenius, also known as Abdal Karim.

While Lloyd George's men held secret talks with the Turks, Faisal was negotiating covertly with Jamal while appearing to act on the orders of Allenby as conveyed to him by Lawrence. The Turco-British discussions went on as the War Cabinet in London instructed the General Staff to consider an advance through Syria 'to the vicinity of Aleppo', and the Chief of the Imperial General Staff told Allenby that a step-by-step advance was essential. 'Poof!' exclaimed Lawrence in retrospect.

Zahroff had met Enver and Abdal Karim in Switzerland in July 1917, when he offered the Generalissimo 1.5 million dollars to part company with Germany and sign a separate peace. Enver had declined the offer, though 'Z' thought that the Turkish leader might have been persuaded by £2 million. In December Bonar Law handed to Caillard a document headed, 'Summary of Chairman's Personal Views'. It read:

> To give as his personal opinion that Allies do not desire destruction of independent Ottoman State nor surrender of Constantinople but freedom of Straits to be secured. Arabia to be independent. Mesopotamia and Palestine to be protectorates on analogy of Egypt before the War. Autonomy for Armenia and Syria. Capitulations to remain abolished and generous treatment of Turkey as regards finance.

On 15 December news came from Stockholm via the Russian Embassy in London that Germany was about to launch a new offensive against the Russians and meanwhile proposed to continue along the path of 'treacherous negotiations'. The time had arrived for a new approach to Enver. Britain still hoped at this stage that Lenin and Trotsky might be induced to resume the war against Germany with Allied help.

On 9 January 1918 Lloyd George gave Caillard a copy of his terms for further talks with Enver. It consisted of just two paragraphs: the first demanding the opening of the Dardanelles and the hand-over of *Goeben* and *Breslau,* in return for five million dollars; the second, the withdrawal of all troops in Palestine to a line north of the railway from Haifa to Deraa, for which two million dollars was offered. The 'Chairman's' instructions were handed to Caillard by J. T. Davies, the Prime Minister's Private Secretary at 3.30pm on 9 January for transmission to Zahroff in Monte Carlo. Seven days later the Turks scuppered the first part of the deal by sending the warships on to the high seas. New instructions were sent to 'Z' on that day. The first paragraph was amended to read: 'We would be prepared to pay a sum of ten million dollars to secure a permanent safe passage through the Dardanelles and Sea of Marmara. This would entail the evacuation of the forts and defences ... and their occupation by British forces.' Zahroff had left Monte Carlo for Switzerland – where he was due to meet Enver and Abdal Karim – before the new terms reached him. Fortunately, however, he was delayed at the frontier by Swiss doctors who observed his dreadful skin condition, now bleeding and suppurating most unattractively, and put him into quarantine. He eventually arrived in Geneva on 27 January. The temperature was seven degrees below zero. There followed a farcical interview, in which Enver refused to leave his room. Abdal Karim therefore acted as a mobile telephone, consulting with Zahroff in his room and then trotting to Enver's room for the answer, and back again. Enver's first message was that 'Z' should tread warily as King Constantine of Greece (Zahroff's probable country of origin) had sent out agents to 'drink his blood'. The Turkish leader appeared demented. At first he thought the Palestinian terms could be met. Then he began a debate as to whether German or British rule would be preferable in that territory. Then he said that the Kaiser had told him, 'the future of Mesopotamia and Palestine would be decided on the French front'. Six months before he had been prepared to make a separate peace. Now, with Russia and Rumania crumbling, Talaat had told him, *'mais de cela je fais mon affaire!'* 'He certainly means to do away with Talaat in some way,' said Zahroff in his report to Caillard.

There was a heated argument over money, and Enver finally insisted on handing back the 1.5 million dollars that had already been paid to him, but said that he would like to hold on to $500,000 for 'a certain eventuality'. But he added: 'If I come to grief the only thing I will need is a pistol.'

On the second day Zahroff awoke thinking that the negotiations were to continue. But Enver had melted into the Swiss snows. Zahroff returned to Paris. 'I have given my heart and soul to this scheme and its failure has quite broken me up,' he wrote to his 'brother', Caillard. *'Toujours à toi. Zedzed'.* Abdal Karim had told him twice over before he left Geneva with reference to Enver: *'Il est traitre, ne le croyez pas, ne vous y fiez pas, il vous vendra. Dans ce grand monde, pour lui, il n'y a que lui.'*

When Zahroff returned to his house in Avenue Hoche he found an elegant young lady waiting for him. She held a typewritten sheet in her hand and read it to him twice over. Then she lit a match and burnt it. Its message, in French, was that at the first sign of the collapse of the Menshevik Government Germany had begun to construct baby submarines for the use of the Russians at Vladivostok. The note did not say who the 'Russians' were, but the Czar's family was murdered a few days later.

'Give the lady 2,000 francs to defray her expenses,' said the message which the lady burnt. 'I suppose your Chairman will put our Japanese ally on the scent,' wrote 'Z' to 'C' enigmatically.

There had been more general peace talks in January 1917, following an appeal by Pope Benedictus and an approach to the American President through Spain from the new Austrian Emperor, Charles, whose intermediary was his cousin and Musil's old companion, Prince Sixtus. But they too came to nothing. Negotiations were not resumed until the issues had been decided on the battlefields.

Leo Amery at Versailles became the town-crier of the 'easterners', demanding a new advance along the Tigris or Euphrates from Baghdad; a new push by Allenby; intense political activity designed to force Turkey out of the conflict; the sending of 'several hundred' officers into Armenia and south-east Russia (India Office objections should not be allowed to stand in the way); punctuated by a patronising attack on Major-General Guy Dawnay, the man who had planned Allenby's Jerusalem campaign under the Chief of Staff Chetwode, and who had been sent to the Supreme War Council by Allenby. He was, according to Amery, being sent 'with the express object of damning Palestine' and defending the 'westerners'' last trench. Dawnay was accused of 'posing' as an expert on Palestine. The accusation said more of the accuser than the accused. Amery wanted George Lloyd, Lawrence's friend, as adviser in Paris. While Amery fulminated, Weygand employed a team of officers at Supreme Headquarters to plan French strategy in the Middle East. The division of the Ottoman spoils in Asia was now a competitive exercise.

India too was an important factor in the settlements to come. Montagu, who like his famous predecessor Morley believed in keeping as much power as possible in the India Office and as little as possible in the Viceroy's Council, left London for Delhi at the end of October 1917 after losing the Palestine debate, to clip the wings of viceregal authority and sound out local opinion regarding Chelmsford's successor.

He travelled on the cruiser HMS *Bristol* and complained bitterly that Lady Allenby was aboard though he had been refused permission to take his wife on the trip. 'Lady Allenby was not a cheerful travelling companion,' he told Lloyd George. She was on her way to join her husband following the death of their only son in France.

Allenby's preparations for the final campaign in Syria were ready by March 1918, at which time a Zionist Commission headed by Weizmann was on its way to Jerusalem. Aaronsohn was among its members, having returned from America in February. He was close to his homeland but still cut off from family and friends, some of whom were in Turkish gaols, others buried in improvised graves at Zichron Yakov. The Commission was appalled by the state of the city, and by its lack of medical facilities. Allenby, determined to maintain military control of the captured towns at his rear, had refused to permit publication of the Balfour Declaration in Jerusalem. However, he did agree with the Jewish leaders that help was urgently needed, and it was decided that Aaron should cross the Atlantic yet again to press for increased political involvement as well as for more material aid from the United States. He went via Rome, Paris and London, meeting Alice Seligsberg, the head of the American Zionist Medical Mission, on the way. It was not until 7 September that he left France with Professor Levi, French representative on the Zionist Committee to America, aboard SS *Lorraine.* In the meantime he had held important talks with the Supreme Allied Command at Versailles and with the French Government.

By the time Allenby was ready to move forward, Faisal's army had been assigned certain definite roles which Lawrence, as Political Officer to the 'irregulars', was supposed to superintend. But Lawrence was depressed. He arrived at GHQ, Umm al Kaleb (Mother of Dogs) near Arish, full of contrition. 'Hogarth was there on the platform. To him I confessed that I had made a mess of things: and had come to beg Allenby to find me some smaller part elsewhere.'

At about this time an astonishing letter was delivered to Faisal. It was the time of the Zionist Commission's arrival on the scene and Aaronsohn had met Sykes, in whose name the letter was written, on the way to Cairo. Perhaps he had a hand in its composition. Dated 3 March, it read:

I write to you on this matter with great frankness . . . I know that the Arabs despise, condemn and hate the Jews, but passion is the ruin of princes and people . . . remember these people do not seek to conquer you, do not seek to drive out the Arabs from Palestine, all they ask is to be able to do what they have not done elsewhere, to return to the land of their forefathers, to cultivate it, to work with their hands to become peasants once more. This is a noble thought in the soul of the Jews, they do not seek wealth or power . . . Here are these people after 2,000 years wandering, looking for something which wealth and power cannot bring, that is the soil of the earth which bore them.

There was something of Aaronsohn's philosophy in those lines. The vision of the desert land turned to agricultural abundance by the hard work of Jew and Arab working in partnership, with Jewish money and Jewish leadership. The rest was authentic Sykes, with perhaps a dash of Lawrence in its wording. 'O Faisal, I stood by your side when we came into Jiddah, and I heard you cry when you saw Jiddah your home rising out of the water. It is the same feeling that moves the Jews to seek for Palestine.' And then: 'O Faisal . . . look on the Jewish movement as the great key to Arab success . . . Stand up for Arab rights . . . make good arrangements, but always as between friend and friend, equal and equal, and above all recognise the Jews' desire to live their national life in Palestine: recognise them as a powerful ally.' The name of the composer of the letter was carefully cut from the English version on the Arab Bureau file, though the Foreign Office index attributes it to Sykes. Letters exchanged between Faisal and his father at this time showed that the Sharif was not opposed to him meeting the Turks, especially as they were offering to withdraw to precisely the line north of the Haifa–Deraa railway which Britain had insisted on at Geneva through Zahroff, and to allow the Sharif's forces to occupy the evacuated territory. Mutual trust, in Lawrence's phrase, was thinly spread, and influenced by the astute propaganda of Oppenheim's Arab Bureau the Arabs were becoming alarmed. The presence of the Zionist Commission, the revelation of the Sykes–Picot agreement, the Balfour Declaration and rumours of secret British negotiations with the Turks combined to arouse the concern of the Sharif and the Arab nationalists. A group of seven Arab leaders under Rafiq al Azim in Cairo came together to compose a 'Memorial' to the British Government. It repudiated 'certain committees' in Paris and elsewhere, and regretted that in a statement of war aims Turkish provinces had been assured sovereignty and independence, but not the Arab provinces. They looked forward to a federal system of government not unlike that of the United States, under the Sharif of Mecca, according to the principle of 'administrative decentralisation'. And the 'Memorialists' as they came to be called asked two questions: 'Can we assure our people that (1) the aim of HMG is to assist them to obtain complete independence in all Arab countries; and (2) to form a federation like the United States.'

Wingate sent the appeal to London, and was told in reply that Britain would recognise 'the sovereign independence of Arabs in those territories which were free and independent before the war or had since been liberated by the Arabs themselves'. The implication was clear, and it was not lost on Faisal or his father, who now saw the importance of arriving in Damascus before Allenby. The declaration issued by Maude on the capture of Baghdad on 19 March 1917, composed by a Whitehall committee, was laughably equivocal: 'It is the hope of the British Government that the aspirations of your philosophers and writers shall be realised, and that once again the people of Baghdad shall flourish, enjoying their wealth and substance under institutions which are in consonance with their sacred laws and racial ideals.' Subsequent affirmations of British policy had been just as vague in the Arab view.

By May 1918, as Allenby's army was advancing steadily against Liman von Sanders's force, and while the German general was having problems with the Turco-German High Command which made political interference at British GHQ seem child's play, Faisal was supposed to be concentrating his attention on the Turkish garrison at Maan. In fact he was badgering his father for permission to return to Jiddah. On 9 May Cairo sent a message to Faisal from the Sharif: 'This proposal to come to Jiddah you must carefully consider. You and your brother [Zaid] must die at Maan or capture it and then carry out the instructions I gave you.' A week or two later Alan Dawnay, brother of Guy, who was by now in Paris, wrote to Joyce, the senior officer with the Sharif: 'The Commander-in-Chief entirely endorses the attitude of candour which we decided to adopt towards Faisal.'

By this time Faisal had appointed his own 'Commander-in-Chief', Abdullah ibn Hamza, who appeared in Cairo in April demanding arms and insisting on almost daily conferences at GHQ. And a recruiting mission for Faisal's private army had been set up in Palestine by Ibn Hamza's agent Tufiq al Halabi.

> I also saw Weizmann at Jerusalem [Dawnay told Joyce], very anxious to see Faisal and talk over Zionism, if possible before the latter's visit to Jiddah. We are arranging, therefore, to send him down with Billy Gore . . . in which case he would meet Faisal at Aqaba . . . From what I gather of the Zionist aims . . . I think there should be no difficulty in establishing a friendly and sympathetic relation between them.

Faisal had been told, in effect, to suspend operations apart from supporting Allenby as and when required. But the Sharif was pushing his son. The race for Damascus was on, and the reward for success in the field in the last stage of the war was obvious: a place at the peace table and a stake in Syria. Maan was the key bastion. But, remarkably, Maan like Madina held out to the end.

Lawrence painted a somewhat different picture of events. 'Faisal smiled wisely at Dawnay's homily, and replied that he would try this autumn for Damascus though the heavens fall, and if the British were not able to carry their share of the attack, he would save his own people by making separate peace with Turkey.' Britain had other plans for the Arab prince, however. 'High Commissioner considers that meeting of Weizmann and Faisal must take place,' telegraphed Cairo on 28 May.

There were divisions in the Arab camp and the 'Memorialists' of Cairo had made it clear to Wingate that they did not wish to be ruled by Husain and his 'unsophisticated' badawin. Faisal still wanted to go to Jiddah, but he was told that no ship was available to take him. At the meeting held a few days later at Aqaba, Faisal gave the impression that he was not opposed to a Jewish national presence in Palestine, though he was later to insist that the whole area of Palestine came within the geographical limits of the Arab Kingdom assigned by McMahon to his father. Wingate chose that moment to tell the Foreign Office that 'for all practical purposes' the Sykes–Picot agreement was 'dead'. And just before the Aqaba meeting Weizmann told Balfour, 'We shall be his [Faisal's] neighbours; we do not represent any danger to him.'

On 22 June 1918 Liman von Sanders submitted his resignation to the Kaiser. Enver had accused him of expediting Turkish drafts to the front while delaying the movement of Germans. It was the last straw in a long and weary battle with the Turks and with his own General Staff. But the Kaiser prevailed on his patriotism and he stayed to the bitter end.

Allenby left Deraa to Faisal's force aided by the 4th Cavalry. In August and September the armies of the British Empire advanced across the battlefields of Afule, Megiddo, Jenin, Nablus, Jisr al Mejamie, following in the footsteps of the Israelites when they descended on Sisera's host, and of Kléber in his contest with the Syrian horde, from which Napoleon himself had had to rescue him, to Mount Tabor and Naboth's vineyard. On 30 September the army was at the gates of Damascus. On 1 October a brigade of the Australian Light Horse entered in the early morning. The Turks had packed up and gone. Arab irregulars were already in the city. Lawrence, his objective achieved, swaggered through the ranks of his fellow officers, assuming an air of authority which puzzled General Chauvel, the commander of the Desert Mounted Corps. 'Chauvel unwillingly followed my lead, his hesitations ruled by my certainty,' said Lawrence of the coarse-grained Australian cavalry commander!

Allenby arrived on 3 October and immediately called for Faisal. He told the Arab prince that France was to be the protecting power in Syria, but that he (Faisal) acting on behalf of his father could set up a military administration in occupied territory between Aqaba and Damascus, east of the Jordan. The Lebanon would be under direct French control, and a French officer would be attached to Faisal's HQ. Faisal protested but Allenby insisted that his orders must be obeyed, 'until the peace settlement finally decided on the disposal of the Arab lands'.

Mustafa Kamal, who took over command of the Seventh Army at the last moment, led the final resistance to Allenby's advance, supported by the other Jamal Pasha (Jamal the Lesser), the last commander of the Fourth Army. The final engagement at Haritan just north of Aleppo took place on 26 October. The armistice was signed aboard a British warship anchored off the island of Mudros on 31 October. Allenby had wanted Newcombe to sign for Britain, but the War Office decided that Townshend, the senior officer in captivity, should do so. The crescent flag was dipped at last and one of the most enduring empires in all history was at an end. Turkey was to rise again under Mustafa, the Grey Wolf of Gallipoli, and the powers might still find a place for it, stripped of its Asiatic Empire. 'Germany', said Liman von Sanders, 'must bear the reproach of having failed to realise with calm, clear and expert judgement what Turkey was in a position to do with her available forces . . . It would seem as if memories of the domes of the Thousand and One Nights, or the mirages of the Arabian desert, had disturbed the critical and evenly balanced judgement of those at home.' His words applied as vividly to one side as to the other.

The Empire built by the Osmanli Turks on the ruins of Byzantium was finally brought to its knees after four years of war. It took twice as long for the peace-makers to come to compromise settlements which left the Middle East in far greater turmoil than existed in the days of the Sultans' rule. The war had taken its toll of victor as well as vanquished. The Royal Navy still ruled the waves, but not with its old dominance. America came to the Peace Conference with a widely proclaimed commitment to the self-determination of the liberated territories which did not always accord with the political realities of the vast areas of the world which were to be re-allocated; in some cases to be carved anew from deserts in which tribes had roamed from time immemorial, oblivious of nationality and contemptuous of all government.

Within a month of the world's statesmen gathering at Versailles the first blow was delivered to the Pax Britannica in the east. The efforts of Niedermayer and his companions in Afghanistan, so futile in war, suddenly bore fruit in February 1919. The war party which they had fostered murdered the Amir Habibullah while on a hunting expedition. His successor Amanullah prepared to invade India, but he was quickly brought to heel. The Royal Air Force, formed in the last months of war out of the old Flying Corps, had taken over from the navy the peace-keeping role of old and it was found that a few bombs went a long way in deterring the aggressor. The lesson was to be applied to other territories in due course, as the peace formulas of Paris were found wanting.

The Russian revolutionaries began to woo both Enver and Mustafa Kamal as the war approached its end. Enver escaped early in 1920 to the Soviets after making overtures to Britain's representatives at Paris, and attended an interim conference of the Communist Party at which Narimanov presided and Zinoviev harangued the audience. The Turk had gone to proclaim his support for the Moslem peoples of central Asia, at whose bosom his Turanian forebears had suckled. Zinoviev was making an impassioned speech when Enver entered the hall. The strutting ringleader of the Turco-German alliance waved to the delegates as he took his seat in a reserved box, while Narimanov read out the names of comrades who had given loyal service to the Bolsheviks, many of them unknown to British intelligence; Riskulov from Afghanistan, Mustafa Subhi from Turkey, Wan from China, Agarie from India; apprising western intelligence services, whose own men were among the delegates, of the links in a chain which stretched across thirty-seven lands. But they were minor links. The Bolsheviks were giving nothing of importance away. There was no mention of Enver Pasha. He left before the meeting finished with Zinoviev's steely eye fixed on him, to imprisonment at the hands of his latest accomplices. He escaped however and went briefly to a war-ravaged Berlin before returning to the Soviets at Talaat's suggestion, to Khiva and Bokhara, 'the spiritual home of Islam', as Vambery called it. It was at Bokhara that he met his end. Some say that he was shot through the heart by Lenin's men, others that his head was lopped off as he drank at a fountain. Be it as it may, Enver ended his days at the hands of a red brigade on or about 4 August 1922, while on his way to meet a certain Ibrahim near the village of Abdarra in Bokhara.

Enver's volatile comrade Talaat, the 'Danton of the Turkish Revolution', met his violent end a year earlier. In February 1921 Sir Basil Thomson, in his last days as a 'Special Intelligence' chief, asked Aubrey Herbert to meet his old friend in Germany, where he had taken refuge at the armistice. The now almost blind Englishman and the unrepentant leader of the Young Turks met in the miserable little township of Hamm near Dusseldorf. The once massive and confident Grand Vizier was reduced to a greying, emaciated shadow. They talked of old times and of the new world, and of course of the Armenian massacres. There was a sudden flash of the blue eyes which once subdued even the wrath of von Wangenheim. 'What would you have done', he asked Herbert, 'if you had had Sinn Fein enclaves all over England fighting you during the war?' He saw disaster in Britain's support for Greek ambitions in post-war Turkey. He asked kindly after Louis Mallet who had been blamed by *The Times* for Turkey's alliance with Germany and accused of 'imbecile credulity,' and spoke ill of Fitzmaurice his implacable enemy. After the meeting he went to Berlin, where he was gunned down by an Armenian.

While Balfour attended the Peace Conference, Curzon took his place at the Foreign Office and asked Percy Cox to go to Tehran to take on the unenviable task of restoring order and financial stability to the Shah's regime after the depredations of the agents and their tribal supporters during the war, and the conflicts of red and white armies afterwards. Charles Marling, the wartime Ambassador, was too ill and exhausted to cope, but in any case Cox was the man Curzon wanted for the job because he was the only diplomat in the east with the authority to deal with politicians and a royal family to whom corruption was second nature and fanaticism a way of life. Wassmuss, the 'Crazy Devil', had come out of hiding and returned to Germany. But he went back eventually to work among his 'friends' as a farmer. They promptly accused him of appropriating their land and he was hauled through the courts, finally to return to his native country to die a disillusioned man.

It was the Arab lands, however, which posed problems of the greatest complexity at Paris. The enduring portrait which events at Versailles and Sèvres have left to posterity is one of the slim, silk-clad Faisal resplendent as a Hollywood shaikh, attended by his Arab retainers, while Lawrence, his political adviser, and also in silken garb, busied himself in a frantic effort to render unto his wartime companion the spoils which Britain had promised in the heat of war.

Argument raged then, as it has raged ever after, about the meaning and exact nature of Britain's promises. It is a futile debate. The territorial limits of McMahon's pledge are quite clear. What is in doubt is not the geography of the matter, not whether we are dealing with vilayets or sanjuks or pashaliks, as the liveliest contenders in the debate constantly insist, but the legality and sanity of the promises made to the Sharif and his sons. It is as if Wellington with the authority of Government before Waterloo had promised the entire continent of Europe to the Papal Legate, save and except for the lands west of a line through Bremen, Münster, Koblenz and Metz. Historians in that case would not waste time discussing the precise geographical interpretation of the words.

When he gave himself up in the Dardanelles in 1915, Faruqi said that it was the intention of Al Ahad and its civil counterpart Al Fattah that the Sharif should be Caliph and Sultan of the new

Arab Empire. But Lawrence, who interviewed the Sharif on the subject in 1917, gained the impression that he was 'averse to the idea of receiving the office in his own person'.

Whatever the intentions of the Arab nationalists or of Husain himself, the British Government had no intention of recognising the Sharifite claims; and even if they had, there was an insuperable obstacle to their realisation in the shape of Ibn Saud. A Foreign Office memorandum said: 'Our commitments to King Husain are not embodied in any agreement or treaty signed, or even acknowledged by both parties . . . the position is complicated by the king's habit of ignoring or refusing to take note of conditions laid down by us, and then carrying on as if the particular question had been settled between us according to his own desires.' As the war drew to its close it began to dawn on the British that they might have made an error of judgment and backed the wrong man in Arabia. Thirty years later, the last head of the Arab Bureau, Kinahan Cornwallis, echoed Shakespear's words, written in 1911: 'Bin Saud stood head and shoulders above all others in power, wisdom and statesmanship.' By then Ibn Saud was the master of his rightful kingdom and America had inherited the good will which might have been Britain's if a succession of Viceroys and their officers had been listened to.

In November 1916 Ibn Saud had been invited to a durbar at Kuwait to receive a knighthood, and from there went with Shaikh Khazal of Muhammerah to Basra. He made a profound impression on his hosts in both places. 'Like an Assyrian picture,' wrote Gertrude Bell, who was at the head of the receiving line in Basra. Dr Stanley Mylrea of the American Mission, who had seen the Amir three years earlier for the first time, was to write:

> Among all the richly dressed Arabs in the room, he was easily the most conspicuous figure. His magnificent bearing still commanded the attention. The three years had only improved the attractiveness of his personality, and when presently the Chief Political Officer presented him with the KCIE and the beautiful ornament glittered on his handsome brown cloak, he would have made an unusual subject for an artist.

The Arab leader had protested then his continued loyalty to Britain even though he knew of the negotiations with the Sharif and was incensed by Husain's pretensions. 'There was never a trace of conceit in his kingly bearing and I was reminded of Mark Twain's description of King Arthur,' wrote the American onlooker. 'Armour is proud burden, and a man standeth straight in it.'

Cox told the Amir of Najd rather weakly: 'Your statesmanship will I know cause you to agree with me that it is not worth your while at this juncture raising this question between yourself and the Sharif. You can rest assured that the title which he uses or does not use has no meaning with reference to yourself.' Dr Harrison of the American Mission in Bahrain described Ibn Saud as 'a courteous host and a natural gentleman', and recorded the Amir's 'warm personal regard for the late Captain Shakespear'.

In May 1917 Ronald Storrs visited Baghdad and decided to realise the ambition of a lifetime by journeying across the desert to meet the Saudi leader of whom he had heard so much, good and bad. Clayton's men in Cairo had decided that Ibn Saud should be encouraged to attack the recalcitrant Ibn Rashid, and Storrs, armed with the promise of gold, was sent to persuade the Amir. But by then Ibn Saud was biding his time. After receiving lessons in Najdi Arabic from Gertrude Bell and listening to stories of Leachman and his new-found American companion in crime, Corporal Jack Summers – they had recently stolen a Turkish aircraft from under the noses of its owners – Storrs set off at the beginning of June 1917, 'a little nervous', with Tennyson on his lips and Henry James in his hand, borne down the Tigris, 'By Baghdad's shrines of fretted gold'. He was conveyed to Kuwait in Shakespear's beloved *Lewis Pelly*, 'no ignoble little kettle'. In Basra he found A. T. Wilson, 'sublimely and inhumanly efficient'. In Kuwait he was met by the Political Agent, Hamilton, and Shaikh Khazal, who had recently married Mubarak's Circassian widow. His escort was to be led by Shakespear's faithful camelman, Abdal Aziz. The little *jemader* was taken aback by the sight of Storrs with his new, well-pressed desert clothes and his gramophone and record collection. He chewed a straw constantly, and replied '*Salamtak*' to all the Englishman's questions: 'Don't know.'

They left Kuwait on 9 June, Storrs humming a Bach fugue as he rode towards Jahra, intermittently cursing his camel in Latin. Next day they were at the Subahiya wells. 'It had been my ambition to help in linking up Central Arabia against the Turks,' he said, 'to begin a Najdi glossary, describe the Sultani road.' Next day they met a 'raiding party' which turned out to consist of friends of Abdal Aziz, the *jemader*. But it was enough for Storrs. They returned to Kuwait on 11 June after two days in the desert, 'a touch of sunstroke' being the ostensible cause. Storrs found Shaikh Salim of Kuwait 'stingy and bigoted', lacking in 'Wein, Weib und Gesang'.

The real brief for Storrs's meeting with Ibn Saud, had it come off, had been worked out at Sykes's home, Sledmere, in Yorkshire, at the beginning of the year, when Storrs was on leave. It was to discuss Ibn Saud's obligations under his agreement with Britain; his relations with Ibn Rashid; the position of Saud ibn Subhan; trade between Kuwait, Hail and Syria; and Ibn Saud's relations with the Sharif. And more.

'The initiative in regard to proposal to attack Hail has come from Egypt and from HMG,' wrote Cox in a 'very secret' message to the DMI Cairo. At the same time Ibn Saud was asked to seek a treaty with Ibn Rashid which would detach the latter from the Turkish camp. Within a year Cox would tell a gathering of senior military and political figures in Cairo: 'If Bin Saud found a way to take Hail we should put no obstacle in the way. But the balance of power would be better preserved if Ibn Rashid continued to rule Hail.' The same meeting agreed that there was 'little likelihood' of Ibn Saud accepting Husain of Mecca as his 'temporal overlord'.

In 1917 the Turks were trying to obtain the young Ibn Rashid's assistance in defending the railway against Newcombe and his raiders, and Ibn Rashid himself had come under the influence of the Pan-Islamite Ottoman agent, Rashid ibn Lailah, who had taken up residence at Hail. And while Ibn Rashid's hungry tribesmen looked enviously towards Baghdad, where Britain now held sway, Ibn Saud's father-in-law, Suleiman ibn Daghil, who had been under house arrest in Hail, escaped and made for Cox's headquarters, where he gave Gertrude Bell a blow-by-blow account of the political situation at Hail. Cox explained in another telegram to the DMI: 'Our object is to eliminate Ibn Rashid either by winning him over or by crushing him. It matters little which alternative is pursued.' Ibn Daghil reported that the Shammar and townsfolk wanted to go over to the British side, but that the Amir of Hail was under the agent Ibn Lailah's thumb.

Whatever Britain's intentions with regard to Hail, or to the Sharif for that matter, Ibn Saud was not to be led by the nose.

As it was, Storrs, the champion of the Sharif's cause, never reached his destination and the matters which exercised Cairo and London would have to wait until a hardier emissary could be found. All the same Ibn Saud had suggested terms for a peace settlement to his adversary at Hail. As Storrs made his desultory way back to Kuwait, the Saudi chief received a characteristic reply from the young Saud ibn Rashid. 'Your terms are not agreeable. Salaam.' Cox decided that Ibn Saud had better not be pushed, 'we may depend on his loyally doing his best on the allowance we make him to . . . harass and seduce Bin Rashid's adherents . . . but I do not think we can expect much more'.

While Storrs was on his way back to Cairo, in Jiddah Colonel Wilson was talking once more to the Sharif about Ibn Saud and the Idrisi of Asir. The Sharif told him that neither the Idrisi nor Ibn Saud was to be trusted, but that the latter was 'friendly'. Ibn Rashid was 'a young fool'. The ruling family of Kuwait was 'negroid'. Shaikh Khazal of Muhammerah was 'Persian'. Therefore none of them 'could be part of the Arab Federation'.

At the end of 1917 another mission made up of H. St John Philby, one of Cox's younger 'Politicals', Colonel Cunliffe-Owen representing the new Commander-in-Chief Mesopotamia, General Marshall, and Colonel Hamilton from Kuwait was sent to Ibn Saud. In a report to Cox dated 2 December Philby referred to Ibn Saud's 'consuming jealousy of the Sharif whose assumption in correspondence of the title *King of the Arab Countries* galls him to distraction'. Philby went on to Jiddah in the new year to meet the Sharif, guided across the desert by the Amir's men.

Hogarth was sent down from Cairo to Jiddah to attend the meeting with the Sharif in the place of Storrs, who, following the Sharif's rejection of his plan to travel to Riyadh (this time by way of the Hijaz), had been made a temporary Lieutenant-Colonel and given the Military Governorship of Jerusalem by Allenby. 'Bit by bit all sorts of strings have got into my hands,' wrote Hogarth to a friend, 'and I don't know into what other hands to pass them now.'

In passing on Philby's observations following his meeting with Ibn Saud, meanwhile, Cox reported:

On Bin Saud's part there is a strong feeling of jealousy and determination not to be lorded over by the Sharif. On the Sharif's side there is a corresponding hankering for supremacy over Bin Saud and a desire to get the latter to recognise his position. I quite understand the point of view of Sir Mark Sykes that it would be convenient to get Bin Saud to make some specific recognition of the Sharif's paramount position: on the other hand, I sympathise with Bin Saud in his reluctance to do anything of the sort.

Philby arrived at Taif from Riyadh on 28 December 1918, and went on to Jiddah with the name of a small disputed township on the Najd–Hijaz border, Khurmah, ringing in his ears. Ibn Saud had received a petition from its townsmen asking for his protection. The Sharif refused to discuss the matter, claiming that Khurmah was his. Philby's instructions from Cox were to suggest that Husain send an emissary to Riyadh to discuss the matter. But the old man of Mecca was unmoved, remarking that people were saying he had 'sold his country to the English'. People would 'come to accept his estimate of Ibn Saud's unworthiness'. Philby replied: 'I was sent to Najd by the British Government to see with my own eyes, and it is my misfortune that I have arrived at conclusions widely differing from those of Your Majesty.' Hogarth, according to Philby, averted his gaze. Britain continued to back both horses, with a preference for the Sharif. Payments to Ibn Saud were still spoken of as 'blackmail' in London.

The dispute over Khurmah continued for two years, until it sparked off the final struggle for the Arabian peninsula. A new power had entered the reckoning and Ibn Saud was to use it to attain his objectives in the lands over which his Wahhabi forebears had ruled, only to find in the end he had embraced a boa constrictor.

The Ikhwan, the quiet orderly brotherhood which Musil had said began in 1908 when they formed an agricultural settlement at Al Artawiya, and which Shakespear had noted in 1914, had become, as such movements will, a zealous and fanatical desert force, driven by a puritanical and bigoted version of the faith. It was led by Faisal al Dawish, 'fat Faisal' Shakespear called him in the days when they went hunting together, though by now he had slimmed down.

By October 1918, as the war entered its final few days, the India Office in London noted that renewed fighting had broken out at Khurmah and that 'King Husain, not Ibn Saud, seemed

to be responsible'. Arnold Wilson had by this time taken over
from 'Cokus', and one of his first acts was to send to the India
Office a telegram which Philby had handed to him on his return
from his mission to Ibn Saud and the Sharif. It read:

> We have received happy news of defeat of troops of rebel
> Husain by the Ikhwan resident in Wadi Khurmah and that
> Your Excellency has arrived at Buraida to open way to
> Mecca . . . and to perform the duties of pilgrimage. I con-
> gratulate you from the bottom of my heart . . . I beg to
> inform Your Honour that if you are prepared to receive
> our assistance in the matter of arms and ammunition,
> guns, machine guns and necessary funds we are ready to
> oblige.

That letter to Ibn Saud was signed Fakhri Pasha, Commander
Hijaz Force. The War and Foreign Offices suspected another
plot by the Indian Government to undermine the Sharifian
commitment. 'Who gave it to Philby?' demanded MI2. 'Ibn
Saud, of course,' replied Wilson.

Shuckburgh, the India Office Under-Secretary, noted:
'Recent orders conveyed by the Secretary of State's telegram of
13 September, laid it down that Bin Saud was to be kept as quiet
as possible . . . In other words, our attitude towards the Hail
expedition has changed from somewhat lukewarm support to
actual discouragement.'

Within days of the armistice, Philby warned London that Ibn
Saud's patience with Husain would not last much longer. In
December 1918 when the Sharif's son, Faisal, was in London on
his way to the Peace Conference, he called at the India Office,
where he declared, 'Khurmah belongs to the Hijaz'. Philby declared equally forcefully 'it belongs to Ibn Saud'. The Amir of
Najd had written a conciliatory note a few weeks earlier to
Husain at Britain's insistence. Husain returned it 'unread' with
a contemptuous letter.

At the same time Faisal insisted that he should govern Syria
from Damascus. The French said that he should not. The
statesmen at Versailles decided to send an international commission to the country under the leadership of the Americans,
Dr H. C. King and Charles Crane, with Sir Henry McMahon
and Dr Hogarth as Britain's representatives. But France undermined the mission simply by refusing to appoint a representative

to it. As the British and American delegates set out, Faisal wrote to Allenby: 'I returned from Europe after the Peace Conference had decided to send an International Commission to the Arab country, especially Syria.' The people, he said, had decided to 'ask for their national rights', for 'the aim they cherish'.

Allenby sent a copy of the letter to Sir Henry Wilson, who had succeeded Robertson as Chief of the Imperial General Staff in July 1918. The liberator of Syria was sympathetic to Faisal. The letter showed 'how much was looked for from the proposed Commission', Allenby told the Chief of Staff.

> I don't believe that you or the French know what danger-
> ous stuff you are playing with ... The situation in the
> Hijaz aggravates the problem. This Wahhabism is of the
> nature of the fanatical Puritanism of the Cromwellians. It
> is extremely contagious; and is attractive to the wild, illiter-
> ate Arab ... I have sent Clayton to Beirut to meet the
> American Commission ... It is important that they should
> not let anyone know that they have not full recognition.

By this time the devious Faisal was negotiating with his arch-enemies, the French, seeking their intervention against Ibn Saud, and at the same time offering assistance to Ibn Saud in fighting his own father, the Sharif, and writing to Ibn Saud to protest his undying friendship, with a liberal sprinkling of quotations from the Koran.

Before leaving for Beirut and Damascus, the Americans had been advised by William Yale in Paris that the Syrians 'desired to ask for America first, Great Britain second, definitely refusing the blandishments of France'. Gertrude Bell crossèd their path in Syria and labelled their work a 'criminal deception'. Mark Sykes had, of course, been at the centre of the negotiations at Paris; but he made a tragic exit from the scene in February 1919. Tired and emaciated by overwork and anxiety he suddenly con-tracted double pneumonia and died in Paris.

He had become a wholehearted supporter of the Zionist cause. Lawrence seems to have mistaken the nature of his trans-formation:

> He had returned from a period of political duty in Syria,
> after his awful realisation of the true shape of his dreams,
> to say gallantly, 'I was wrong: here is the truth'. His former

friends would not see his new earnestness, and thought him fickle and in error; and very soon he died. It was a tragedy of tragedies, for the Arab sake.

It was with Aaronsohn that Sykes found the closest identity of view in his last days; it was in Zionism that he saw the opportunity to resolve the dilemma of the Promised Land. As for Greater Syria, he had already promised it unequivocally to France. By a remarkable irony Aaronsohn too was to die in the first days of the Peace Conference, and progressive Jewry to loose its most powerful and articulate spokesman.

A few days after Marks Sykes's sudden death had cast a shadow over the Paris Conference, a host of his former friends and enemies from the eastern theatre descended on the peacemakers. First, in early March, came Gertrude Bell, once Sykes's *bête noire* and latterly one of his closest confidantes. She was followed a few days later by the Commander-in-Chief, Allenby, who, since the signing of the armistice with Turkey in October 1918, had been in ultimate charge of all the liberated territories of the Ottoman Empire except Mesopotamia: the lands of Palestine, coastal and desert Syria, the Lebanon, Transjordan, and Cilicia known as OETA (Occupied Enemy Territory Administration). At the end of the war, on 7 November 1918, he had made a pledge to the Arab people; though a French General had ridden splendidly into Constantinople on a white charger, Faisal's irregulars had occupied Damascus, and Mustafa Kamal had taken over the Adana group of Liman's defeated Yilderim army – all symbols of other interests involved in the settlements to come.

> The aim which France and Great Britain have in view in waging in the East the war let loose on the world by German ambition, is to ensure the complete and final emancipation of all those peoples so long oppressed by the Turks, and to establish national governments and administrations which shall derive their authority from the initiative and the free will of the peoples themselves.

The birds had come home to roost. Faisal had waved Allenby's statement in Curzon's face in London. Now its composer came to mingle with Arab and Jew, with the intelligence officers turned political activists of the Arab Bureau, the Civil

Commissioner and his entourage from Mesopotamia, with Persians, Egyptians, Armenians, and all those who had a stake in the Middle East settlements; to confront the victorious powers with claim and counter-claim.

Hogarth, still the father confessor of the Cairo brigade, had written in 1917:

> The Arabian [race] claims rank too among the fighting races of the world, it claims to be of the greater civilizing races; and, finally, perhaps to be the greatest of all the races that have conceived and propagated a faith. Once it was said in mockery of a Jew, 'He saved others: Himself he cannot save;' and neither of that Jew nor of Jews in general is the jibe true. Of their semitic kinsmen, it might have been said so often, not in mockery, that we stand forewarned.

Allenby, who was about to take over from Wingate in Egypt, insisted that the Syrian Declaration meant what it said. Arnold Wilson, sensing a destructive political auction in Syria and Mesopotamia, believed it to be 'mischievous'.

'I am lunching tomorrow with Balfour who, I fancy, doesn't really care ... I hope to catch Lloyd George by the coat tails.' Gertrude Bell hobnobbed with the mighty she had known from girlhood, and peddled the Sharifian cause with Lawrence, her 'Wenigkeit', at her side. She believed that if Faisal's Committee in Damascus could hold out for six months, France would be 'kicked out' of Syria. General Gouraud, Picot's successor, whom Meinertzhagen thought 'the source of all French evil', was not to be moved. Despite determined attacks by Faisal's forces at Tripoli and Baalbek, he established a firm French presence. General Weygand, France's Political Officer in Syria was unmoved too by threat or plea. Faisal appealed to Curzon, who repeated the assurances of the McMahon–Sharif correspondence, but added: 'We have entered into obligations with the French and the Arabs. These obligations do not conflict but are complementary.' It was precisely the French objection that they did conflict, and that anyway the area under discussion, according to the Sykes–Picot agreement, was nothing to do with Britain or America.

As the argument over Syria became increasingly bitter a new element came to the fore, the resurgent nationalism of Kamal's

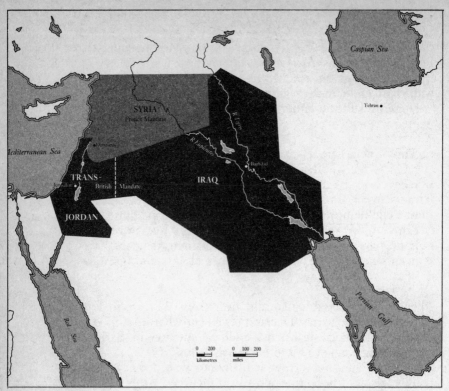

Map 13   Division of the Arab lands by the Mandates issued at San
Remo in April 1920

Turkey. Even Ibn Saud was worried, and in April 1920 Arnold
Wilson sent the Amir a reassuring note, telling him that the
Sultan, Vahid ad Din, who had succeeded Mehemet V at the
armistice, now felt strong enough to oppose the nationalists and
proposed through the Shaikh al Islam to condemn the Kamalists. By the end of April Wilson was able to tell Ibn Saud that the
Peace Conference had given the mandate for Syria to France
and for Mesopotamia and Palestine to Britain. To complete the
current Middle East picture, he mentioned that the Shah of
Persia had been entertained in Baghdad *en route* from the Peace
Conference and was on his way back to Tehran. 'Suitable
arrangements are being made for his reception,' Ibn Saud was
told. Shortly after, Cox returned to Baghdad from his mission in
Tehran. The slothful Sultan Ahmad Shah was deposed by
Colonel Reza Khan, who ushered in the Pahlavi regime. Cox's
carefully conceived Anglo-Persian Agreement of 1919, approved

even by the Bolsheviks, was promptly repudiated. 'Curzon', it was said, 'expected the impossible.'

In April 1920 Saud ibn Rashid became the latest victim of his homicidal family. His death was reported to Bahrain on the 23rd. The new Amir, Abdullah ibn Mitab, wrote to Ibn Saud immediately on his accession, asking for the ratification of an earlier treaty between the chiefs of Riyadh and Hail. Britain was concerned that Faisal ibn Rashid, the fugitive of Shakespear's day who was still with Ibn Saud, might claim the throne of Hail. But Ibn Saud had no need of compromise with anyone now. Al Ikhwan swept through the desert irresistibly, and the Saudi Amir's biggest task was to hold it back from the conquests it lusted for. Ibn Jiluwi, his governor in Al Hasa, had already found it necessary to put several Ikhwan leaders in gaol and to flog others publicly. But Ibn Saud was now on the tiger's back and he could not easily get off. The Amir dealt with Britain through Bahrain, where H. R. P. Dickson, another of Cox's young men, had been made liaison officer with the Saudi chief. His deputy was Khan Sahib Sayid Siddiq Hasan, an Indian Moslem, whom the War Office now proposed should accompany the pilgrim caravan to Mecca, a plausible cover for a spying mission into Saudi territory, where he was to contact 'secret sources'. He was told by Dickson: 'Be as circumspect as you can in all things and consult Shaikh Farhan on all matters. He is to be trusted. Bin Saud likes him and trusts him. Gather such information as you can about the Ikhwan – whether movement is growing; whether Bin Saud's influence is increasing or decreasing.' And finally:

Bolsheviks: You may say that there are signs that they want peace. They have sent a mission to England. They recently occupied Resht in Persia, but have shown no signs of advancing from there. *Turkey:* The Nationalists are anti-Sultan and anti-Allies. Have complete control of Anatolia. The Allies, however, are preventing them from approaching Constantinople. Greeks have started a successful move against their left flank.

Ibn Saud was looking for a resident doctor in Riyadh at the time of Siddiq Hasan's pilgrimage. Wilson recorded that he must be a Sunni Moslem, and he 'must be capable of furnishing required intelligence reports'.

Allenby was in constant touch with the Foreign Office on the question of the Sharif and his claim to Khurmah. He protested in a telegram from Cairo, where he was now High Commissioner, that the Foreign Office had not taken due note of Ibn Saud's own statement that he failed to see any advantage in negotiations with the King (Husain), as Najd would 'rather perish' than yield a yard of Khurmah or the near-by township of Turbah. Neither had the Foreign Office mentioned to him a remark made by Dickson in an official report which had come to his notice that 'lack of friends and excessive preaching had turned Bin Saud into a monomaniac and religious maniac'. He had earlier told the Chief of the Imperial General Staff, Wilson: 'I presume that it would not enhance our prestige if we left the salvation of Mecca and Madina to the French.' And in April 1920 he told the Foreign Office that the other Wilson, in Baghdad,

> does not seem to view with any great misgivings the rapid spread of the Ikhwan movement and the possibility of Bin Saud overrunning the Hijaz. I trust that this is not the opinion of HMG. We are under a very definite obligation to King Husain whom we have set up in the face of some opposition on the part of Indian and other Moslems, and it is our duty, and to our advantage, to support him.

Allenby, who emerged from the war with a deserved reputation for his generalship and for his personal integrity, persisted to the bitter end in his belief that the Sharif was right and Ibn Saud wrong, and that in any case Britain had a debt of honour to the old man of Mecca. In 1919 he wrote to the Foreign Office complaining of an attack by Ibn Saud's tribesmen on Turbah. The complaint was sent to the India Office, and Shuckburgh commented: 'The Cairo people have throughout taken a one-sided view of this question. It is rather absurd to characterise his [Ibn Saud's] claim as "impudent".' The word was Allenby's.

Now Allenby's plan was to bring the two contenders together at a conference in London, where all outstanding matters could be settled, including the Sharif's latest claim to Asir. But before arrangements could be made to invite the two leaders to Britain, Ibn Saud took the initiative. Even the *Intrusives*, authors of the Sharifian conspiracy and opponents of Ibn Saud's claim to be 'chief of all the tribes' of central Arabia, were forced into grudging admiration of the man who stood in the way of their schemes. In August 1919 someone, probably Cornwallis, wrote in the *Arab Bulletin* of Ibn Saud's messages to Bushire and Baghdad as 'examples of lucid communication' when compared with 'the incoherent effusions from Husain'.

On 26 April 1920 the Amir had told Dickson that he had come to terms with the new Ibn Rashid. Little more than a month later Ibn Rashid declared war on the man with whom he had just concluded this treaty. On 27 June an Ikhwan force led by the Amir's son Saud attacked the Shammar at Adwah, twenty miles east of Hail, and inflicted a heavy defeat on them. But Ibn Saud still marked time. It was not until the end of 1921 that the Ikhwan finally occupied Hail, 'Badawin with bees in their bonnets', as Philby called the fiery soldiers of the Sauds.

In October 1918 General Marshall, the Commander-in-Chief Mesopotamia, had been on leave in England when the War Office told him that the defection of Bulgaria and Allenby's victories made it likely that Turkey would sue for peace. Zahroff was back in Switzerland negotiating with Abdal Karim, Enver's envoy. Marshall had rushed back to Baghdad to make sure that as much territory as possible was occupied before the armistice. Many men were to die in the subsequent effort to police the territories won in war and to turn them into reluctant constitutional monarchies. In June 1920 there was a sudden spate of killings which began at Tel Afar following visits by Pan-Islamic agents, leading to a general uprising. On 13 August of that year Baghdad cabled the India Office: 'It is reported that Lt-Colonel Leachman was ambushed and killed on 12 August near Falluja.' Leachman had gone through most of the war with a 'grumbling' appendix, often suffering acute pain as he kept his lonely vigil among the tribes, living rough for four years. He returned home in 1919 to have his appendix removed and returned to Iraq in high spirits. But he had made enemies as well as friends among the Arabs. In August 1920 he was called to Falluja, where he was shot in the back by Khamis, the son of Shaikh Dhari ibn Mahmud, chief of the Zoba.

The assailants disappeared but seven years later, in 1927, Shaikh Dhari was taken into custody. The day after his trial for the murder of Leachman, conducted under the old Turkish law since it had not been superseded, the old man was found dead in his cell, the victim of a heart attack it was said. Terrible vengeance had been visited on the tribes of the Euphrates meanwhile.

Revolutionaries are seldom fussy about the source of their

money or arms. In Mesopotamia during 1919 and 1920 financial support came from all quarters. The day before the outbreak of violence at Tel Afar, on 2 June 1920, Wilson had interviewed a self-appointed committee of fifteen Baghdadis, and promised them a statement of policy from the British Government. On the 12th Wilson appealed to London for more troops to stem the tide of revolt. The War Office told the India Office to tell him 'not to interfere in military matters'. Next day an army convoy was attacked and wiped out near Mosul. On 17 June the Mesopotamian League, in unison with Faisal's Syrian Committee issued a proclamation to the 'Free Mesopotamians'. 'Undoubtedly you have heard about the Irish, Czechoslovaks, Armenians, Caucasians, Lithuanians etc.' They claimed the throne of 'Iraq' for Faisal's brother, Abdullah. On the 22nd Mirza Muhammad Riza, son of the chief *mujahid* of Karbala, was arrested along with ten extremists at Hillah. Security officers found a letter to the *mujahid* from the Standard Oil Company of America, showing that American funds were being distributed to the Shia extremists through the American Consul in Baghdad. Britain's funds to Husain and Faisal were being diverted to help even their bitter religious enemies at Najaf and Karbala. On 23 June a Government statement in the House of Commons suggested that all was under control, but by July the country was in open revolt. Young recruits of the Manchester Regiment, sent down to Hillah without adequate instruction, training or leadership, were decimated. And while the battle raged the American Ambassador in London called at the Foreign Office to demand 'equal opportunities' for Americans in the Mosul Oil Concessions which were being placed. 'It's a desperate state of affairs, the whole country seems to be fighting,' wrote Leachman in his last letter home.

Lonely Political Officers, trying to keep order in impossible circumstances, were picked off one by one. Troops and civilians were ambushed and murdered. But the death of Leachman, the British army's most popular soldier in the desert lands, was the last straw. Wilson submitted his resignation, finally and unequivocally, on 30 July, but not before the Commander-in-Chief, General Sir Aylmer Haldane, had been forced by events to take the action Wilson had called for all along. As order was gradually restored, the French appeared with their mandate at Damascus and Faisal and his Committees were thrown out unceremoniously. Cox returned to take Wilson's place, 'waving an olive branch'; a ready convert to Gertrude Bell's notion that Faisal should be offered the throne of a new, democratic Iraq. First he consulted the Naqib of Baghdad, the most respected and venerable of Sunni notables. The Naqib had already told Gertrude Bell that he would 'rather a thousand times have the Turks back in Iraq, than see the Sharif or his sons installed'. But Cox was persuasive.

Turkey in defeat contributed to the events of those pulsating days. While Enver and Talaat tried desperately to find a power base among central Asian Moslems and German ex-army officers, Mustafa Kamal, whose courage and political ego seemed to place him somewhere between Alexander the Great and Rasputin, gained an ever-increasing following as the Greeks marched through the Smyrna vilayet, the French occupied Cilicia, and Armenians again paid the price of foreign dominion over Ottoman pride.

As Turks waited for the decision of the Council of Four as to their future, Kamal landed on the Black Sea coast with orders from Constantinople to disband the irregular forces operating there. Across the water Enver's old friends of the Pan-Islam movement were plotting with Georgian intriguers and the German-trained officers of the Georgian Legion. On 28 May 1919 the first clash between Turks and Greeks occurred at Odemis. Kamal decided to recruit the irregulars rather than disband them. In June he issued a 'Declaration of Independence', and after a conference with General Kasim, commander of the Erzerum army, he called a meeting at Sivas. At the National Congress there in September he affirmed his loyalty to the Sultan. In December he established headquarters at Ankara, wooed by Lenin, by Faisal in Syria and by Turks who saw in him the salvation of their national pride. In January 1920 he visited Damascus and Aleppo for talks with Faisal's representatives and the Ankara assembly adopted the 'National Pact'. Kamal's forces attacked towns in northern Mesopotamia. In February the French began to withdraw from Cilicia as the mandate over Syria became a *fait accompli*. The Allies decided to establish a military occupation at Constantinople and the leading political figure of the British-supported Sultan's Government, Rauf Bey, leader of the Turkish contingent of the Turco-German expedition to Afghanistan, was exiled to Malta.

As Parliament was dissolved in Constantinople, Kamal's first Grand National Assembly met in Ankara. A month later, on 11

May 1920, Kamal was condemned to death *in absentia*. By July, as the Greeks advanced through Anatolia, Kamal's Assembly had become the only true representative body of the Turkish people. As Iraq, Syria and Egypt erupted, and the remnant of the Sultan's Government signed the Treaty of Sèvres, Kamal was drawing up a treaty with the Communist Government in Moscow. By January 1921 the Greek assault, encouraged from the outset by Lloyd George, had been reversed, and on the 20th the new Assembly adopted a Constitution based on popular suffrage. Ankara had become the effective capital of the new Turkey, and the 'Grey Wolf' of Gallipoli, Ataturk, its master. Britain maintained the pretence of the Sultan-Caliph for the sake of India. But the dual office was officially disbanded in 1922. The Fez, the Arabic alphabet, and the Sultanate itself were progressively abolished. 'Civilization means European Civilization' became the slogan of the republican regime.

In 1921 a Government re-shuffle in London resulted in Churchill becoming Colonial Secretary. At the time he was both War Minister and First Lord of the Admiralty, a combination of posts which suited him very well, but he seemed to see in the Middle East crisis an irresistible opportunity to exert himself. In a note to Bonar Law, the Lord Privy Seal and deputy Prime Minister, in the previous November he had described the Mesopotamian business as 'very nasty'. Early in January 1921 there was a whisper of the new appointment. He wrote to Lloyd George, 'I must have the power to cope with the situation in the Middle East,' and he gave the Prime Minister ten points to mull over. On 10 January he wrote: 'Dear PM, All Arab affairs must come under a Middle East Department . . . Faisal, Abdullah, Ibn Saud, King Samuel, etc.' And on the 20th: 'Trying to make up my mind whether to go to Mesopotamia.' He had elected to relinquish the seals of the War Office and the Admiralty. His subordinates were about to find the going rough.

Cox returned to Baghdad from a tumultuous Persia. He had shown himself to be more than a little tarred with the brush of oriental cunning. Before leaving at Curzon's behest in November 1918 he had declared: 'Our purpose is to keep Persia off the Peace Conference agenda . . . to negotiate freely and independently of mandates.' When he had signed and sealed the Anglo-Persian Treaty there were loud protests that he had bribed high officials of the Persian Government.

By the time Churchill arrived on the scene Cox had announced the Provisional National Government of Iraq, headed by the Naqib. Churchill appointed three principal advisers to his Middle East department: Shuckburgh, who had come over from the India Office, Lawrence and Meinertzhagen. The last two had adjoining offices and kept a close watch on each other. Lawrence, ably abetted by Gertrude Bell in Baghdad, became the proponent of the Sharif's cause. Meinertzhagen in Jerusalem had already opposed the pro-Arab policies of his former chief and had written to the Foreign Office on the subject. When he heard, Allenby called Meinertzhagen to him in Cairo and dismissed him on the spot as his Political Officer. 'I suppose you realise you would have to give your housemaid longer notice,' said Meinertzhagen. Allenby laughed and they parted on good terms.

When Churchill arrived in Cairo it was as though he had reconvened the Arab Bureau, though that self-elected body had been disbanded by Curzon in February 1920 and absorbed into the Cairo Residency, along with the *Bulletin*, which was no longer an organ of military intelligence. Cox was waiting for him, with his right-hand lady, Gertrude Bell. Lawrence, Clayton, George Lloyd, Hogarth, Hubert Young, buzzed between Residency and hotels as they had in the heady, conspiratorial days of 1915 and 1916 when the Sharifian affair was in its infancy. Now they sought to bring it to fruition. Gertrude, industrious to the last, had briefed Sir Percy well. His dispatch case was bulging with the report prepared for him by her. It was remarkably similar in its content to the ideas Churchill had been fed by Lawrence. Faisal, now rejected by the French and many of his own supporters in Syria, would be offered the throne of Mesopotamia, now to be known by the ancient name of Iraq. A buffer zone between Iraq, Syria and Palestine, to be known as Transjordan, would be carved from the desert and Husain's second son, Abdullah, offered its throne. By May 1921 Faisal was able to leave a troubled Damascus behind and prepare for a triumphal entry into Baghdad. Cox had returned there in the previous October, accompanied by Sayid Talib, the man he had exiled to India. But just before Faisal's advent Talib was arrested. He was deported in July, a month before the coronation.

Ibn Saud had sent his own son, Faisal, to Europe in 1919, so that he could put in an appearance at the Peace Conference. He was accompanied by Ahmad al Thaniyan, the kinsman of Ibn Saud who had been trained in diplomacy at Constantinople.

Bray was one of the intelligence officers deputed to look after the young prince and his companion and he was appalled at the way the Foreign Office and the Arab lobby in Paris dealt with them. He had been so angered by the Sharif's conduct at the end of 1917 that he asked for a transfer to France. Now he was in the thick of the Sharifian dispute again. He wanted to take the young Prince Faisal ibn Abdal Aziz up in a Handley Page in Paris, but Faisal's bodyguard threatened to slay himself there and then if his charge took to the air. 'Thus he lived to return to Riyadh and become king in his father's stead,' wrote Bray. In Whitehall the treatment of the Arabs was 'patronising', and Hubert Young, who joined Churchill's Middle East Department after some wartime contact with Lawrence in Syria, behaved so arrogantly that Ibn Thaniyan said afterwards: 'If Captain Young ever comes to Najd I will cut his throat.'

A meeting was arranged between the two Faisals by Jafar al Askari, who was to become War Minister of Iraq's first royalist Government. Jafar and Faisal ibn Husain sat opposite Faisal ibn Abdal Aziz and Ibn Thaniyan. The Sharif's son asked immediately: 'Who are these Ikhwan? I am told that they are not allowed to shave their beards.' It was, in Arab terms, an insulting question. Ibn Thaniyan, who had opposed the meeting in the first place, rose abruptly and took his lord and master from the room. He was stuttering with rage as they got into their car with Bray.

Faisal was soon to discover who the Ikhwan were. After taking Hail at the end of 1921 they went on to Ibn Shalan's territory and occupied Jauf. In 1924 they occupied the Hijaz and the old man of Mecca was exiled to Cyprus. Even his own sons disavowed him at the end. In December of that year Ibn Saud entered Mecca, and for the first time in his life wore the robe of the pilgrim. Ibn Dawish's fanatical force was forbidden by Ibn Saud to pillage or desecrate the shrines of the Holy Cities, for which they never forgave him; to them idolatry was the worst of sins. In the following year Ibn Saud was recognised by Britain and the world as the undisputed King of central Arabia. But not until 1930 did he eventually throw off the suffocating power of the Ikhwan, by which time the Brotherhood had served its purpose.

The prince Britain had spurned in war had won back the lands of his ancestors. He was given to colourful sayings, and perhaps the maxim he used most had a significance of which he could not then have been aware. 'If we sow well in the days of prosperity, we shall reap a ripe harvest in times of adversity,' he used to tell his tribes. And he had his own courteous words of parting which would serve for his erstwhile warriors of the Ikhwan and for Britain. 'May God unite us in Paradise.'

In August 1919 Cox had written to A. T. Wilson affirming the old divisions between Whitehall and the Indian Government over Ibn Saud. 'I congratulate you on keeping your end up so well over the Ibn Saud business. Remembering the point of view we have always had in regard to the treatment of the Sharif, I can't help chuckling at Ibn Saud getting a bit of his own back.' In 1922 Cox carried out one of the last of his official duties before retiring to England, of which he had seen little since boyhood. He went to Ujair on the Hasa coast to fix the boundaries of Iraq, Syria, Transjordan and Kuwait, and, of course, Saudi Arabia. The old Harrovian, silver-haired and immaculately dressed, treated Ibn Saud and the other Arab notables as if they were schoolboys. He simply told them where the lines would be drawn, and, suspecting the presence of oil, fixed neutral zones between Kuwait, Iraq and Saudi Arabia which would act as buffers in case of hostility or disagreement. Storrs was made Britain's first civil Governor of Jerusalem, and Herbert Samuel was appointed High Commissioner for Palestine to preside over the 'Regime of Sweet Reason' as all hell broke loose throughout the Middle East, with riots from Palestine to Kurdistan and insurrection in Mesopotamia. There was no hurry on Britain's part to implement the third of its promises, that of a Jewish homeland in Palestine.

The Jewish delegation in Paris, led by Judge Felix Frankfurter, argued and bargained. Lloyd George, Clemenceau and other leaders listened intently to Aaronsohn's personal vision of the Israel to be. Britain could not make up its mind from one moment to the next whether it had promised Palestine to the Sharif or the Jews. Meinertzhagen made no secret of his belief that the Government was 'tearing up the Balfour Declaration by degrees'. McMahon asserted all along that he had intended to 'exclude Palestine from the independent Arabia'. On one occasion Curzon challeged Meinertzhagen on his allegiance, after the intelligence officer had proclaimed the rights of the Zionists. He replied: 'My inclination towards Jews in general is governed by an anti-semitic instinct which is invariably modified by personal contact. My views on Zionism are those of an ardent Zionist.'

Sir Henry Wilson, the Chief of the Imperial General Staff

and brilliant military intelligence chief, whom Asquith never
forgave for his part in the Curragh mutiny of 1914, had an
often-repeated piece of advice regarding the disputed areas: 'Get
out of those places that don't belong to you and hold on to those
that do.' He included Ireland and Egypt in the latter category,
but not Palestine and Iraq.

At the end of the war Balfour told Wingate:

> In November 1917 the British Government declared itself
> in favour of the establishment in Palestine of a national
> home for the Jewish people, and further pledged itself to
> use its best endeavours to secure the attainment of this
> object. This declaration secured for Great Britain the sup-
> port of the Zionist Jews throughout the world, and not least
> in Palestine.

The hopes contained in that affirmation of policy must have
been in Aaronsohn's mind when he telegraphed from Washington to Wyndham Deedes at GHQ Palestine on 10 October 1918.

> 'Hearty congratulations at brilliant success. Trust you will
> take father and other surviving martyrs under your personal
> protection. Am most worried by Alec's silence, where is
> he? Please have him appoint someone to fully enquire and
> despatch here complete report on actual condition of agri-
> cultural station, surviving staff and amount of damage
> done. Please also give me your views about hurrying home
> or staying here.

He hurried home, asking Dr Eder, the head of the Zionist
Commission in Palestine, to draw from the Jewish Colonial
Trust any money needed for the house and fields at Zichron
Yakov. He sent Rivka home to Zichron, and sped to Paris, calling at Rome on the way, where he met friends of the American
Medical Mission who were based there. He found the statesmen much engrossed in the Palestine question; whenever asked
to define the region in question Lloyd George would reply, 'As
in the Bible, from Dan to Beersheba'. Unfortunately, no one
knew where Dan was.

In Paris Aaronsohn stayed at the Hotel Crillon with Judge
Frankfurter and Chaim Weizmann. He was largely responsible
for steering the talks between Faisal and representatives of Bri-

tain and France on the boundaries of the proposed Jewish state, which at that time embraced Transjordan. And it was he who obtained from Faisal the famous letter addressed to Frankfurter:

> I want to take this opportunity of my final contact with the American Zionists to tell you what I have often been able to say to Dr. Weizmann in the past. We feel that the Arabs and Jews are cousins in race, have suffered similar oppression at the hands of powers stronger than ourselves . . . We Arabs, especially the educated among us, look with the deepest sympathy on the Zionist movement . . . We will wish the Jews a hearty welcome . . . People less informed and less responsible than our leaders and yours ignoring the need for co-operation of the Arabs and Zionists, have been trying to exploit the local difficulties that must necessarily arise in Palestine in the early stages of our movements . . . Faisal.

On the day of the publication of that carefully framed statement, delegates of the Yishuv were taken by Weizmann to meet their 'semitic brother', Faisal. In the glow of the words that had been put into Faisal's mouth compliments flowed, and the Arab Prince's secretary was heard to remark: 'It doesn't hurt to say nice things.' A Jew in the gathering said: 'He speaks as though Palestine is his to dispose of.'

Aaronsohn was invited to appear before the Council of Four at Versailles to address the great men on Palestine and to make a plea for Zion. Discussing his proposed speech with William C. Bullitt, President Wilson's Special Counsellor in Paris, he wondered if the President, Clemenceau, Lloyd George and Orlando would understand his request that a particular field should be incorporated in the Jewish state. 'You see,' he said, 'it contains a unique specimen of a wild plant which should be preserved. It would be tended by the Jews, but the Arabs might neglect it.'

He was the outsider even among his closest companions in the political movement of Jewry. A scientific missionary is a 'dangerous kind of man'. 'He hated the lamenting in the candle-smeared darkness of the old synagogue, the men weeping and the women wailing . . . Lamenting was a disease of the Jew; it sickened him.'

There were deep divisions among the Jewish representatives

at the Peace Conference, just as there were suspicions, plots and counter-plots between Arab and Jew; and between the statesmen representing the victorious powers. Conversational asides were treated as statements of policy. Weizmann was quoted as saying, 'Zionism is constructive Bolshevism', and that a Palestinian state would not be 'Jewish to the detriment of its Arab-speaking inhabitants'. Faisal was the friend of the Jews at one moment, an implacable enemy the next. Frankfurter, leader of the Zionists, began to doubt President Wilson's dedication, and asked him for an unequivocal statement. Wilson gave it. 'Interesting', said a Foreign Office note, 'President Wilson brought to heel by the Zionists who refuse to be put off by sonorous platitudes.' Aaronsohn seemed to be ploughing a lone furrow.

Aaronsohn, like Herzl, believed in a Zion based on excellence, open to all the inhabitants of Palestine, and those who emigrated to it, led by Jewish genius; an outpost of civilisation, a shining example of progressive statehood which the world would look at with awe and envy. In the particular circumstances of post-Ottoman Palestine he had declared himself to the British in Cairo to be 'anti-democratic'. A dangerous man indeed!

On 10 May 1919, he left the conference chambers and the milling hotel crowds to visit London for a few days, it is said to collect maps, materials, and outfits for himself and Frankfurter to wear in Paris. He spent five days there. His movements have never been traced in detail, but he almost certainly visited the Central Zionist Office in Piccadilly to discuss the forthcoming conference at which he would have been a prominent speaker. On Thursday 15 May, just after lunchtime, he went to the Royal Air Force base at Kenley near London, where a special air service operated for the transport of mail to and from the Peace Conference, and for the use of important delegates. The pilot of the plane, a de Havilland DH4, was Captain Elgie Jefferson.

The weather was bad throughout Europe, and conditions in the English Channel were stormy, but the aircraft was given clearance to proceed on a route which was used regularly by Lloyd George, Bonar Law, Winston Churchill and members of the American peace mission. At 3.30 pm, as it was about to cross the French coast, the plane came down in Boulogne harbour. The local newspaper *Le Telegramme* reported the event on the next day.

Thursday, at 3.30 in the afternoon, a mail plane from London to Paris with two passengers on board overturned in the sea

... The sailing boat no. 328 found the wreckage and took aboard some bales which were found floating. The bales were deposited in the Marine Registry. One of the passengers was already drowned, and the crew glimpsed a second man and were approaching him some distance away when, unhappily, he suddenly went under.

It was not until five days after the crash, that news was given to the British public. *The Times* on 20 May carried a despatch from its Paris correspondent dated 18 May, headed, 'Eminent Zionist Killed: Dr Aaronsohn in aeroplane accident'. It said: 'News was received on Friday that a postal aeroplane had capsized in Boulogne harbour on its way from London to Paris, and that the pilot and passenger had lost their lives. It was not then known that the pilot's passenger was Dr Aaronsohn, the well-known Zionist leader and agricultural expert.' There followed a description of his wartime work in Cairo and his contribution to the Palestine campaign. The *Jewish Chronicle* contained a similar report on the same day, and expressed its sympathy and sense of loss to the Zionist movement in a leading article. Not until 27 May did the Zionist Office in London issue a statement. 'The Zionist Movement has lost the services of a most able adherent and interesting personality, by the tragic accident which happened on Friday 16 May,' it said. It then went on to quote *The Times* for most of its biographical detail.

There, officially, the matter rests. According to Meinertzhagen, one of Aaronsohn's admirers and closest associates in Egypt and Paris, subsequent rumours of foul play were unfounded, and the man who had worked for Military Intelligence in London and had been its chief in Allenby's campaign, was a good judge of such matters. Rivka Aaronsohn was alive in 1980, and still living at Zichron Yakov, where a museum commemorates her brother, and to which each year Jews and others pay homage at the grave of his heroic sister Sarah. She and those who most revere the name of Aaronsohn have stated that they are satisfied that the death of Aaron was due to an accident. But the mystery remains, and is deepened by investigation.

The pilot, Jefferson, is recorded in the official registry in London as having died at sea on Thursday 15 May. He had made out a will just a month before he died in the presence of Captain Gooch and Lieutenant Adams of the RAF. The Commanding Officer at RAF Kenley in those days was Lieutenant-

Colonel Neil Primrose, and he conducted an official inquiry into the matter. His report contained details of an interview with Captain Ramet, who discovered the foundering craft in his fishing boat, *Notre Dame de Boulogne*. His evidence was confined to weather and sea conditions.

The report is contained in the files of the Aaronsohn Museum in Israel, but is not on the Royal Air Force or the Post Office files in Britain. There is an Air Ministry report, however, which gives details of the service established in December 1917. Covering the period to August 1919, it says: 'On the London to Paris route three pilots and one passenger have been killed and two pilots and two passengers injured in a total of 744 flights.' An appended report gives details of the routine by which weather conditions were checked in England and France, and flights permitted. 'Provided the report is favourable the mails and any passengers are at once sent out to the aerodrome by car, the machines usually setting off at about 9 am.' There was obviously a change of routine on 15 May.

But there was a much more remarkable fact bound up with the events of that day which was never reported except in the local French press. Not one plane but two came down in Boulogne harbour at almost exactly the same time on the afternoon of that Thursday.

The report in *Le Telegramme* of 16 May went on from describing the scene found by fishing boat 328 to say:

At the same hour, in the same vicinity, another plane which left London with the first, capsized in deep water. Happily, the harbour master of the Port of Boulogne caught sight of the wreck at the moment that it began to founder and despatched a rescue team. The fuselage was only slightly damaged and the pilot was unharmed. As for the mail, it was transported in a car of l'Aviation Maritimes to Paris.

The same newspaper carried a further report the next day.

We reported yesterday a double flying accident which occurred on Thursday . . . in deep water at the Port. The bags holding documents found in the deep water have been sent off to the Marquise [Royal Air Force base near Boulogne]. The bags fished out of the water by the sailing vessel near the other wreckage were disposed of to the

Maritime Registry. The documents, whose details were of considerable interest, were destined for the Paris Peace Conference.

On the same day *France du Nord* observed: 'By a singular coincidence, not one aeroplane but two fell into the sea at almost the same time. The two passengers of the first plane were drowned. It was a unique accident, the like of which will probably never be seen again. The exact details will never be known.' That newspaper had obviously experienced some difficulty in getting at the facts, but it had found an eye-witness. He saw a plane which 'floated on the water and then drifted, driven by the wind'. Then: 'A car of the English flying camp at Marquise took the documents to Paris that evening.'

No other report was ever made, or at any rate made available to the public, on the death of the pilot or his passenger. Not a single newspaper anywhere outside the French port where the accident happened reported the true circumstances. Sixty years after, three men could be traced who were stationed at Kenley at the time of the accident, one of whom was an officer at the Paris end. One of them wrote a book about his adventures in the Royal Air Force during those pioneering days, but he said nothing about that remarkable double accident, and he could not recall it. Another remembered the removal of the squadron from Hendon to Kenley just before Easter 1919, and the first crash when General Sykes of the Air Council was being taken to Paris. The pilot was killed and General Sykes lost an eye. The same witness recalled a flight in which Captain Gooch, the man who witnessed Jefferson's will, was killed. And he remembered the occasion when Captain Vincent was detailed to take Lloyd George's lady secretary for a flip over Paris. When the plane landed she was carried from it unconscious after a rousing display of aerobatics. But none of the witnesses could recall Captain Jefferson or his passenger, or the pilot of the other mystery plane in Boulogne harbour on 15 May, whose name is unrecorded on any official file. Surviving airmen of the time have suggested that the two planes may have taken off from another airport. If so, why did Colonel Primrose's report refer to Kenley? And would the pilots not have recalled the death of a colleague wherever he set off from? It is perhaps significant that a few months after the fatal accident the RAF inspector of accidents resigned.

Fifty-seven years after an event which deprived the Zionists and Palestine of the man who many believed might have persuaded the world's statesmen to a speedy resolution of the question of the Jewish homeland, scientists from many nations held an international gathering at Zichron Yakov to pay homage to the 'pioneer father of Israel's natural science'. And compatriots remembered words uttered in the low ebb of war: 'If we fall, who will remember us? We live in the midst of an ungrateful people.'

Soon after his death, William C. Bullitt wrote:

He was, I believe, the greatest man I have known. He seemed a sort of giant of an elder day . . . like Prometheus. It is not easy to express his greatness in lifeless words; for he was the quintessence of life; of life when it runs torrential, prodigal and joyous. Many men, no doubt, are as great as he was intellectually, though I have never known his peer; but if they are great intellectually, they are not great also emotionally, as he was: great in courage, in sympathy, in desire, in tenderness, in swift human understanding, great at once in dealings with statesmen and children . . . I remember him in Washington – how the diplomatists sat open mouthed, astonished by his knowledge and insight, and were warmed by his picture of the Zion to be. I remember him in Paris . . . how from the first he foresaw the end of that tragic drama, how unerringly he picked his way through a thousand diplomatic pitfalls, how wise he was in counsel and how strong in friendship . . . The Jewish race had many brilliant leaders but when Aaron died I believe that it lost the man who, before all others, could kindle the hearts and minds of men of other nations to active sympathy. And not Zion alone will suffer for his loss.

In July 1926 Gertrude Bell, the power behind the Iraqi throne, died in her sleep from an overdose of barbiturates. Many who were in Baghdad at the time believed that she committed suicide, but the medical report and the findings of an inquiry appointed by the High Commissioner were never put on public record.

As Jew and Arab rioted and fought in Palestine, as the British taxpayer's money was used by the Arab princes to finance rebel-

lion in Iraq and British aircraft bombed Ibn Saud's tribes in a
last desperate bid to protect the Hashimite inheritance, Gertrude Bell and Lawrence had become the loudest and most articulate supporters of the cause of Arab nationalism. They had an
enormous and disproportionate influence on their country's foreign policy. 'In revenge I vowed to make the Arab Revolt the
engine of its own success, as well as handmaid to our Egyptian
campaign; and vowed to lead it so madly in the final victory that
expediency should counsel to the Powers a fair settlement of the
Arabs' moral claims.' Lawrence, like Gertrude, had forgotten
those youthful impressions of a desolate land in which 'nationality' was an empty, meaningless phrase. Yet 'The Lady' might
more readily have remembered her own words of so recent a
year as 1917:

> men who have kept the tradition of personal indepen-
> dence, which was limited only by their own customs, entirely
> ignorant of the world which lay outside their swamps and
> pastures, and as entirely indifferent to its interests as to the
> opportunities it offers, will not in a day fall into step with
> European ambitions, nor welcome European methods.
> Nor can they be hastened.

By 1920 young Britons were dying by the thousand, and their
fellow countrymen were paying burdensome taxes, to uphold
nations that had been carved from sands, swamps and pastures
over which tribes had roamed so recently; as from time immemorial. Few aspects of modern history have been the subject of
so much comment, and of so much special pleading. But few
have put the matter into more succinct words than John Connell
in an inside view of the Foreign Office, written in 1958:

> The hot winds which fanned the hearts of more than one
> generation of able and intelligent men, blasted their judge-
> ment and scorched the edges of their integrity. An ardent
> and chivalrous adventure ended in grief and squalor.
> Granted the origins of the Arab–British relationship in a
> courteous and illusory myth, it would have [been] difficult
> for the outcome to be other than what it was. But it would
> have been better for our country, and probably for the
> world, if C. M. Doughty, T. E. Lawrence and Gertrude
> Bell had not been such able and persuasive writers.

McMahon had been gullible. Asquith and Grey had been too lazy, or too occupied with other matters, to read the documents which McMahon sent them. Lloyd George and Kitchener, and for a brief period Churchill, had seen the Sharifian adventure as a useful ploy in their 'eastern' strategy. What will always remain beyond understanding is the manner in which junior staff officers who, by the standard rules of military discipline should never have left their desks in the Savoy Hotel at Cairo, except on approved intelligence missions, were able for so long to flout the wishes and the known opposition of senior officers, not least of their General Officer Commanding-in-Chief.

To the last they were allowed to jolly along their protegé, Faisal, in the face of determined French resistance, and to support the old man of Mecca in the quarrel he so foolishly picked with Ibn Saud. As Gertrude Bell so aptly observed when the peacemakers reached the conference table 'the oysters had been eaten and put down on the bill'. It was, as she said, 'useless to speculate by whom and in what proportion the bill will be met'.

Zion was to be delayed by thirty years and another Great War. Another generation of men, of politicians and spies, soldiers and philosophers, was to occupy the stage, to bring the gas chamber to the service of genocide, to bring a holocaust to suffering mankind, before at least one of the preposterous confusion of promises and treaties of 1914–18 was implemented; and then at gun point – before the children of Israel flooded into the Promised Land, and the Arabs who were to have shared in its glory and prosperity retreated into angry exile, dedicated to an eternity of retribution. The only possible victor in the Arabian peninsula, Ibn Saud, claimed his own, and America inherited the good work of the Indian Government and a share of the oil revenues of the man who in his lifetime knew great poverty and unexampled wealth. The Hashemite kingdom of Iraq, so lovingly fostered by Gertrude Bell, dissolved in predictable violence and the last survivors of the old school of Pan-Arabists were dragged through the streets by the new saviours, who little suspected that the same fate awaited them. Rampant nationalism within Islam began to turn away from the infidel West and to embrace the atheist commissars of the East. Egypt took possession of Suez; and Britain, France and Israel conspired to take it back. The shaikhs of the Gulf who survived under the protective umbrella of the Royal Navy became the richest and most powerful of men. The mullahs and ayatollahs of Persia, or Iran as they came to call it, reasserted the ancient resentments of their faith, and the faithful rejected the Pahlavi 'King of Kings'. Soviet Russia achieved the prize that had eluded the Czars for four centuries, Afghanistan, and access to the North-West Frontier and came close to Sir Edward Grey's half-promise of a warm-water port of her own. And an American President repeated almost word for word the warning of Lord Lansdowne of 1903: 'An attempt by any outside force to gain control of the Persian Gulf region will be regarded as an assault on the vital interests of the United States. It will be repelled by the use of any means necessary, including military force.' Only the name of the protecting power had changed.

Appendix A

The Arabs

Rulers and Principals of the House of Al Saud, Riyadh

Note: from the beginning of Wahhabi authority in Najd (about 1740) to 1819 Dariya, near the present capital of Riyadh, was the headquarters of the ruling family. Dariya was razed by the Turco-Egyptian army of Muhammad Ali and his son, Ibrahim, in 1819. It was partly restored in the following year but it was not until 1824, when the Turks and their allies were driven from Riyadh, that central Arabia found a new and permanent capital.

Saud ibn Muhammad al Misran, date of birth unknown, died 1724. Founder of House of Saud. Left four sons: Thaniyan, Muhammad, Fahan and Masri.

Muhammad ibn Saud ibn Muhammad al Misran, date of birth unknown. Converted to version of Islamic faith preached by Muhammad ibn Suleiman Abdal Wahhab in about 1740. Recognised as spiritual and temporal head of Wahhabis, 1747. Died 1765. (The originator of Wahhabist doctrine, Abdal Wahhab, was born in 1703 and died in 1791, by which time almost the entire Arabian Peninsula had come under the spell of his teachings.) Muhammad ibn Saud left two sons: Abdal Aziz and Abdullah.

Abdal Aziz ibn Muhammad al Saud, 1765–1803. Wahhabi power spread throughout Arabia during his reign, under the leadership of his martial son Saud. Abdal Aziz was murdered in the mosque of Dariya in 1803 by a Shiite, following a raid by his army on the Shia holy city of Karbala two years before (20 April 1801). Left two sons: Omar and Saud.

Saud ibn Abdal Aziz al Saud, 1803–14. Wahhabi influence reached its zenith under his powerful leadership. The Hijaz (Mecca and Madina) was conquered, Turkish Iraq invaded, and the Gulf states made tributary. Left sons, chiefly: Abdullah, Faisal, Nasr, Turki and Khalid. The army of Muhammad Ali, under the leadership of the Egyptian Viceroy's son, Tusan, and reinforced by the warrior clan from the region of Aqaba, the Howaitat, invaded central Arabia in the autumn of 1811. Ibn Saud evacuated Madina in November 1812 and Mecca in January 1813.

Abdullah ibn Saud, 1814–18. Resisted Turco-Egyptian advance bravely, but in September 1818 the enemy force occupied and destroyed Dariya. Abdullah was taken to Constantinople and beheaded in December 1818. Left three sons: Saad, Saud and Muhammad.

Masri ibn Saud: nominee of Turks, 1819–23.

Turki ibn Abdullah, (son of Abdullah ibn Muhammad ibn Saud ibn Muhammad al Misran, not of Abdullah ibn Saud, above) 1824–34. Killed near mosque at Riyadh, May 1834.

Faisal ibn Turki al Saud, 1834–8 and 1843–65, 'Faisal Kabeer' (the Great). War of liberation against Turkish occupying force was led by Faisal, under his father Turki, from 1821. In 1824 he drove Turks from Riyadh and established it as the capital. But Turks sowed dissension among princes of Al Saud and won support of collateral branch of family under Masri ibn Abdurrahman ibn Hassan, great-great-grandson of the original Saud, and of Khalid, Faisal's uncle, the son of Saud ibn Abdal Aziz. Faisal was proclaimed Amir on the death of his father in 1834 but deposed by Turks in December 1838 and exiled to Egypt. In the summer of 1840 Turco-Egyptian forces left inner Arabia, demoralised by constant attack and weakened by heat and disease. New pretender of Saudi family, Abdullah ibn Thaniyan, occupied Riyadh in 1841. Other pretender, Khalid, fled to Jiddah 1842. Faisal returned in May 1843, accompanied by Abdullah ibn Rashid and Shammar army under Obaid ibn Rashid. Abdullah ibn Thaniyan surrendered and died soon after. Faisal died 1865. Left four sons: Abdullah, Muhammad, Saud and Abdurrahman.

Interim amirates of Khalid and Abdullah, and Faisal's successors, Khalid, deposed in 1842, is regarded as a usurper prince, but is generally held to have been the eighth Amir in succession. Abdullah ibn Thaniyan ibn Ibrahim reigned for one year, 1842–3, before resigning in favour of Faisal. From 1865 to 1874 power was divided between Faisal's sons Abdullah, Saud and Muhammad. Abdullah lived at Riyadh and was widely regarded as the Prince of Najd; but Saud ruled in south-west and Muhammad in the north. The latter was the most capable. Civil strife between the supporters of Abdullah and Saud brought the Saudi dynasty close to ruin and led to the ascendancy of the Rashids at Hail, who were originally Faisal's Viceroys. Saud died in 1874 at Riyadh, whence he was taken by his slaves after being injured in battle with the Ataiba tribe. In 1887 Ibn Rashid took Riyadh by storm, exiled the sons of Saud, took Abdullah as prisoner to Hail and installed Faisal's youngest son, Abdurrahman, as Prince. The other son of Faisal, Muhammad, was made commander of the Riyadh garrison, but under the supervision of a warrior of Hail, Salim ibn Subhan. Abdurrahman was peace-loving, but his eldest son Abdal Aziz, about eighteen in 1887, was determined to drive Ibn Rashid from the capital. Battle raged until 1891, when Ibn Rashid re-asserted his authority at Riyadh. Abdurrahman and his sons fled to Qatar, where they were protected by the Al Thani rulers of that territory, and in 1894 they became the wards of Muhammad ibn Sabah, the ruler of Kuwait. Muhammad ibn Faisal remained at Riyadh until 1902 as Ibn Rashid's Viceroy.

Abdal Aziz ibn Abdurrahman ibn Faisal al Saud, 1902–53. Returned to Riyadh in January 1902 with his uncle, Jiluwi, and a small following, surprised and killed the Rashid governor, Ajlan, and restored the authority of the Sauds. Abdurrahman, his father, returned later but had renounced the throne in favour of his son; he was known as the Imam. Abdal Aziz left many sons, some of whom survive, including the present King and Crown Prince. He was the founder of the Kingdom of Saudi Arabia; the greatest Arab of modern times.

Rulers and Principals of the House of Al Rashid, Hail

Ali ibn Rashid, c. 1800–20. Chief of Abda section of Shammar tribe.

Abdullah ibn Ali al Rashid, 1834–7; restored 1838–47. First Amir of Jabal Shammar. Was forced by Turks to leave Hail with brother, Obaid, in 1837, but offered assistance to Turco-Egyptian occupying force and returned to capital with 250 regulars of Turkish army. Nevertheless, he regarded himself as Viceroy for Faisal ibn Turki of Riyadh. Left three sons: Talal, Mitab and Muhammad.

Obaid ibn Ali, b. 1790 d. 1869. Correctly Obaidallah. His side of family produced great warriors of Rashid army, and political leaders. He retained allegiance to Wahhabi faith, disdained by brother, Abdullah, and loyalty to Al Saud. Died at Riyadh under Abdullah ibn Faisal's stewardship. Was never Amir of Hail.

Talal ibn Abdullah al Rashid, 1847–68. Rejected allegiance to Sauds and made himself and family absolute rulers of Jabal Shammar. But he was a peaceful man who developed the agriculture of the region, and built fine mud-brick dwellings and fortresses, surrounded by palm gardens. Uncle Obaid tracked down robber bands of district. In 1855, with Obaid and brother Mitab, took Jauf basin from Ibn Shalan. Died from accidental gun wound in March 1868, the only member of his family to die from a cause other than murder or war. Left six sons, all of whom were murdered by family assassins.

Mitab ibn Abdullah al Rashid, 1868–9. A generous and valiant leader, but opposed by a faction of the family who supported Bandar, the eldest son of Talal. After Mitab had ruled for ten months he was ambushed in his castle at Hail and shot by Bandar. Left one son, aged two years, Abdal Aziz. On news of Mitab's death many members of family, including the powerful Obaid and Muhammad, the son of Abdullah (Mitab's brother), fled to Riyadh.

Bandar ibn Talal al Rashid, 1869. Only a few months after Bandar's accession, Muhammad ibn Abdullah entered Hail with a force of the Dhafir under their belligerent leader, Ibn Suwait, slew the Amir and cut down his bodyguard as they fled through the streets. Some supporters fled to the mountains of the Shammar but were pursued and murdered.

Muhammad ibn Abdullah al Rashid, 1869–97. 'Muhammad Kabeer.' Entered Hail on 25 December 1869. Brilliant politician, reluctant soldier. One of the greatest and cruellest of all Arab rulers. By 1874 he had reduced Riyadh to state of dependency and his writ ran as far afield as Asir, Aleppo, Damascus and Basra. When the inhabitants of the old Saudi towns of Kasim rebelled he destroyed their settlements. He received his arms from Kuwait, which made a fortune from gun-running in those days, and from Ujair in Al Hasa. But after the Saudi

exiles settled in Kuwait, and Abdurrahman became friendly with the son of
the Naqib of Basra, Sayid Talib, who was the Turks' governor of Al Hasa and
the chief source of supply, he became critically short of guns and ammunition
and decided to attack Kuwait. Britain, though it had no treaty rights at that
time, regarded the maintenance of the *status quo* in Kuwait as vital. Foreign
gold was distributed discreetly, and Muhammad died on 3 December 1897. It is
generally said that he died of natural causes, but his nephew Majid, the son of
Hamud ibn Obaid, said that he was poisoned.

Abdal Aziz ibn Mitab al Rashid, 1897–1906. During his reign he never set foot in the
capital, Hail, so much did he mistrust his homicidal family. He lived perma-
nently on the battlefield, trying to bolster the kingdom of his uncle, Muhammad, who died without issue. On succeeding to the title he ordered the release
of all members of the Saud family imprisoned at Hail, including some of the
'Araif', dissident Saudis who claimed the throne of Riyadh, of which Abdurrahman was now the nominal occupant. But they turned against Abdal Aziz and
schemed against him with the Sharif of Mecca. With the resumption of Ibn
Saud's authority at Riyadh, the Turks began to support Ibn Rashid with money
and arms, and in 1901 a force sent by Mubarak, the new Shaikh of Kuwait, and
Abdurrahman ibn Faisal to attack him was annihilated at Sarif (17 March 1901).
   Late in 1901 there was a general rising in the southern part of Ibn Rashid's
realm. His hold over the towns and tribes began to diminish as Ibn Saud's
power grew. In May 1904 the Turks sent an army under the command of the
Governor of Basra to his aid, which occupied Kasim for seventeen months,
until forced by sickness and the intense heat of summer to withdraw early in
1906. In April of that year Abdal Aziz ibn Rashid was attacked by his namesake
of Riyadh and defeated on the battlefield of Taraffiya. The Amir was killed in
the fighting on 12 April 1906.

Mitab ibn Abdal Aziz al Rashid, 1906–7. Recognised only by his father's followers.
After a nine-month reign he was murdered by Sultan, the son of Hamud ibn
Obaid. Mitab's brothers Mishal and Muhammad were killed too, leaving only
the infant Saud of the children of Abdal Aziz alive. He was taken secretly to
Madina, under the Sharif's protection, by his dead father's slave.

Sultan ibn Hamud al Rashid, 1907. Ruled for less than a year. In January 1908 his
brothers Saud and Faisal murdered him in his bed.

Faisal ibn Hamud ibn Obaid, sometimes known as Faisal ibn Rashid, he was never
Amir. He was the accomplice of his brother, Sultan, in the brutal murder of the
children of Abdal Aziz, and subsequently murdered Sultan. Made governor of
Jauf in January 1908, when he was visited by the English intelligence officers,
Butler and Aylmer. In September of that year, his brother Saud was killed and
he was pursued by the supporters of the late Amir, Abdal Aziz. Faisal made for
Riyadh and was granted asylum by Ibn Saud, who recognised his claim to the
governorship of Hail. But his ambition was never to be realised.

Saud ibn Hamud al Rashid, 1908. Ruled for a few months after the murder of his
brother Sultan. He himself was killed by Shammar tribesmen, supporters of

Abdal Aziz ibn Mitab, whose only surviving son, Saud, was still under the Sharif of Mecca's protection at Madina.

Saud ibn Abdal Aziz al Rashid, 1908–20. The 10-year-old Prince Saud was brought home by his supporters in September 1908 to rule through the regency of his uncles Hamud and Zamil, members of the Subhan family linked by marriage to the family of Obaid.

Regency of Hamud ibn Subhan, 1908–9. Died from poison in spring 1909. Had little influence on affairs of central Arabia.

Regency of Zamil ibn Subhan, 1909–14. Zamil had absolute power in his five years of office. At the time he became Regent the politics of Arabia were in a turbulent state. Many of the Shammar clans were deserting to Ibn Shalan, who had occupied his oasis home of Jauf on 8 January 1909, nearly sixty years after the Rashids had taken it from his father; others were going over to Ibn Saud. The Young Turks' revolution of 1908 had brought about dramatic changes in the Ottoman capital and the Empire, and Arabs began to see the prospect of self-government through the example set by their Turkish masters. In Damascus, Baghdad and Basra, where Zamil maintained agents who were in touch with Turkish leaders and aspiring nationalists, revolutionary committees were set up with the aim of throwing off the Ottoman yoke. Zamil, who inherited the Obaid concept of loyalty to Ibn Saud, recognised the overlordship of the Amir of Riyadh at the end of 1909. Arab leaders, including the Pan-Arabs of the Ahad and Fattah Committees, also recognised in Ibn Saud their natural leader. Only the Sharif Husain of Mecca, restored to his position by the Young Turks in 1908, stood aside. And Zamil, protecting the youthful Prince Saud at Hail, became the focal point of international intrigue, in which France, Russia, Germany, Britain, Austria and Turkey were involved. In 1910 he proved his anti-Turk credentials by attacking the Ottoman garrisons at Taima and Medain Saleh, installing his own governors and beheading the local supporters of the regime. In 1913, when Ibn Saud took Al Hasa back from the Turks, the Porte tried to regain the allegiance of the Rashids. The Austrians, through their agent, Professor Alois Musil, had armed Ibn Shalan, Zamil's implacable enemy, while keeping in close touch with the Rashids. Early in 1914 the Turks sent a large shipment of arms to Zamil by way of Taima. But they knew that the guns would be turned on them and plotted through the Regent's kinsman, Saud ibn Saleh al Subhan, to have Zamil murdered. Britain became aware of the plan through its Damascus Consul, Mr Devey, and Captain Shakespear was sent via Ibn Saud to investigate, and perhaps to attempt to counter the plot (other military tasks were assigned to Shakespear and he may have been acting on Ibn Saud's behalf in attempting to reach Zamil, not just the British Government's.) The Englishman arrived on the scene a few days before Zamil was shot in the desert to the east of his own path (10 April 1914). Gertrude Bell had been sent to Hail at the same time in the hope of seeing Zamil, but the ruling family had left by the time of her arrival on its contrived mission. Captain Leachman was the only European other than Ottoman officials to come to close quarters with Zamil, when he camped with the Rashids for five weeks in the Shamiya desert in 1910.

The rule of Saud ibn Abdal Aziz, 1914–20. Saud was eighteen when his uncle, Zamil, was killed. He took over the reins of government with the sinister *Saud ibn Saleh al-Subhan*, who married his half-sister Nura, as his Chief Minister. British intelligence files described the young prince as, 'Violent, irresponsible, boorish . . . a jungle youth'. Leachman reported that the young Amir was an excellent horseman and appeared to have no interest other than equestrian sport. Nevertheless, he was supported by the Ottoman Government and given a regular allowance as well as large gifts of arms. When the Ottoman Empire joined with Germany in November 1914 Britain decided to woo Ibn Saud and encourage him to put an end to the Rashid dynasty, and Captain Shakespear was sent on special duty to Riyadh. He joined Ibn Saud in the desert and planned with him and Faisal ibn Hamud to engage the Shammar in battle and to set Faisal on the throne of Hail as Ibn Saud's Viceroy and Britain's ally. In the ensuing battle with the Shammar some of Ibn Saud's tribesmen deserted and Shakespear was killed as he fought alone against the Rashid cavalry. He was cut down by the slave of Saud ibn Saleh, the same man who had shot Zamil. Musil the Austrian was near by with the two Sauds of Hail.

In March 1920 Prince Saud's own supporters decided to be rid of him and to back young Abdullah ibn Talal's claim to the throne of Hail. Saud was ambushed and killed, but his slaves immediately killed the young pretender. In the ensuing chaos, the man who had been Saud's Regent in name, though hardly in practice, since 1916, Ibn Ajil, came to an understanding with another youthful Abdullah, the son of the murdered Mitab, that he would take over. Thus an Abdullah came to the throne as the conspirators had promised. Nobody now was keen on the Princedom of Hail. The new Prince immediately threw the surviving brother of Abdullah ibn Talal, Muhammad, into prison.

Abdullah ibn Mitab al Rashid, 1920–21. In the summer of 1921 Ibn Saud, supported by Ibn Shalan and the Anaiza tribes, and by Auda abu Tayya's Howaitat, attacked Hail. Abdullah ibn Mitab sued for peace, but Ibn Saud's price was too high. Abdullah was now enjoying support from Faisal, the King of Iraq, and he decided to fight on. But in September a force of Ikhwan led by Faisal al Dawish joined the assault, and surrounded the camp of Abdullah ibn Rashid. As the final battle for Hail raged the Shammar elected their last Amir, Muhammad the son of Talal. At the end of October 1921 Ibn Saud appeared on the scene and personally conducted the siege of Ibn Rashid's capital. The Shammar fought bravely and survived under siege until early December. Abdullah ibn Rashid had died in battle. His successor was imprisoned at Riyadh with other survivors of the House of Rashid. King Husain of Mecca and his son Faisal of Iraq both encouraged the chief of the Ajman tribe, Najif ibn Kilab, to help Muhammad ibn Rashid escape. The Prince reached the palm groves of Riyadh but was discovered. He lost his left hand in the fight and was taken back to prison, where he died soon after. All his followers were killed. It was the last act of the Rashids.

Fatimah of Hail. From the last year of the reign of Muhammad ibn Abdullah in the nineteenth century to the end of the Rashid dynasty, the real power behind the throne was Fatimah, the devious and scheming woman who married Muhammad's Chief Minister, Subhan. She was the maternal grandmother of the Amir

Saud ibn Abdal Aziz. Gertrude Bell, who was a 'house' prisoner of the
Rashids in March 1914 when the murder of Zamil was being plotted, left a
graphic description of her. She believed that Fatimah was behind the Regent's
murder, as of most things at Hail. Gertrude Bell and Musil described her as the
de facto ruler.

The Sharifite House of Hashim, Mecca

The Amirs or Sharifs of Mecca were of the Qoraish, the Prophet's tribe, and descended from Hasan, son of the Caliph Ali and his wife Fatimah, the Prophet's
daughter.

The last ruling family derived its authority from the Sharif Muhammad, 'Ibn
Aun', of the Abdillah clan, who in 1827 displaced the ruling houe of Dhawi Zaid,
represented then by the Amir Ghalib. The Sharifs of the Holy Cities of the Hijaz
owned a great deal of property in Egypt, bequeathed to them by Muhammad Ali.
In the summer months the court of Mecca moved to the high ground of Taif. The
Sharifate was in the gift of the Sultans of Constantinople after Salim's victory over
the Mameluk rulers of Egypt in 1517.

Muhammad ibn Abdal Muin ibn Aun, Sharif 1827–51 and 1856–8.

Abdal Mutlib ibn Ghalib, Sharif 1851–6 and 1880–82. Mutlib was of the rival house
of Dhawi Zaid, and was appointed by the Porte on both occasions because of
dissension within the Abdillah clan.

Abdullah ibn Muhammad ibn Aun, Sharif 1858–77.

Husain ibn Muhammad ibn Aun, Sharif 1877–80. Murdered, and succeeded by
Abdal Mutlib.

Aun al Rafiq ibn Muhammad ibn Aun, Sharif 1882–1905.

Ali ibn Abdullah, Sharif 1905–7. Dismissed by Porte and exiled to Egypt under protection of Khedive.

The Sharif's duties were performed by the Ottoman Governor of Hijaz 1907–8.

Husain ibn Ali ibn Muhammad, Sharif 1908–October 1924. About sixty when he
returned to Mecca in 1908 when Kiamil the Ottoman Grand Vizier nominated
him in succession to his uncle, Abdillah, who died on his way to Mecca to fill
the vacant office. Medium height, with a white beard, dignified manner. Conspiratorial, he was in close touch with politicians of all shades in Constantinople, where he lived for twenty-five years, with the Pan-Arab and Pan-Islamic
movements, and through his son Abdullah with the British Residency in Cairo.
Consumed by jealousy for Ibn Saud, whose territory of Kasim he tried to annexe
in 1910, and whose tribal authority he tried to undermine before and during the
First World War. Made himself commander of the Mecca garrison 1916, which
he took without bloodshed on 13 June, though the Turk militia in the fort and
barracks refused to surrender until several weeks later. In March 1924 Kamal
Ataturk abolished the Ottoman Caliphate and Husain, who was visiting his

son Abdullah in Amman at the time, declared himself Caliph of Islam. On 3 October 1924, with almost the whole of the Hijaz in the hands of Ibn Saud's warriors, Husain abdicated and handed over the governorship of the province and the stewardship of the Holy Cities to his son Ali, who held out at Jiddah, the port of Mecca, for over a year while Ibn Saud imposed a blockade and finally invaded the town.

Ali ibn Husain, Sharif, October 1924–December 1925. Consumptive elder son of the Sharif Husain. Born 1880, short, slim, slightly bent in his stance, looked older than his thirty-seven years in 1917 when last British intelligence report filed. A simple, gentlemanly manner was interrupted by violent fits of temper and passion caused by his illness. Represented his father at Madina until the 1916 Revolt, when he took command of the Arab force which was supposed to blockade the Turkish garrison under Fakhri Pasha. Colonel Parker, the British staff officer responsible for the Madina and northern Hijaz operation, found him weak and vacillating.

Abdullah ibn Husain, King of Transjordan 1921–51. The Sharif's second son, Abdullah, was Foreign Minister in his father's regime, which was formed after the Revolt of 1916. Born 1882, short and stocky, strong with a merry countenance, full lips, brown beard and Semitic nose. Open and charming in manner, jested with tribesmen and not so inclined as his brothers to stand on his dignity. Deputy in the Ottoman Parliament for Mecca, not on good terms with the CUP. Frequently quarrelled with Enver. Said by intelligence reports to be a 'good dialectician'. Took command of the Arab force at Taif after rebellion declared. The small Turkish garrison held out for four months but he took the town at the end of the year. Went to Amman in 1920 to organise resistance to the French in Syria. In March of that year Syrian Congress of Arab nationalists declared him King of Iraq, and his brother Faisal King of Syria. But France repudiated Faisal and the Committee, and insisted on the wartime accords with Britain, which gave her dominion over greater Syria, being put into effect. In April 1921, following Churchill's Cairo Conference, Abdullah was offered the throne of the newly created state of Transjordan, a buffer-zone between Palestine, French Syria and British Iraq. He was declared Prince of Transjordan on 15 May 1923. He was assassinated by Arab opponents on 20 July 1951 in Jerusalem and his son Talal succeeded him.

Faisal ibn Husain, King of Iraq, 1921–33. Born 1886. Educated in Constantinople, as were his elder brothers, tall and of regal appearance. 'Far more imposing personally than any of his brothers; knows it and trades on it,' says an intelligence report (probably compiled by Lawrence, who knew him intimately). 'He is hot tempered, proud and impatient,' says the same report. Lacking in prudence, clever and not over-scrupulous. Deputy for Jiddah in Ottoman Parliament. Heavily involved in pre-war intrigues of the Young Turks' Committee and the Arab Nationalist Committees. In 1915, after visiting Constantinople, he spent much time with Jamal and the German intelligence chief, Baron von Oppenheim, at Damascus. Tried to meet Ibn Shalan, chief of the Anaiza tribes, who sent his son Nawwaf to meet him. But Jamal forbade their meeting. Returned to Syria in late 1915 on a secret mission for father at a time when Husain was playing off Britain and the Turks, and seeking the highest bidder. He returned to Madina in February 1916 accompanied by Enver and Jamal, and then went back to Syria with the Turk Commander and Governor, remaining in Damascus until the month before the Arab Revolt was declared. In June 1916 he commanded the Arab force on the Hijaz railroad, with singular lack of success.

He became Lawrence's protegé at the victory march into Damascus and at the Paris Peace Conference. At the instigation of Gertrude Bell, he was offered the throne of Iraq and crowned King on 23 August 1921. Died in 1933 and was succeeded by his son, Ghazi, who was killed in a car accident in 1939, and by his grandson, Faisal II, who occupied the throne until the army *coup* and bloodbath of 14 July 1958, when he and leading figures of the Arab independence movement and the Arab Revolt lost their lives.

Zaid ibn Husain, youngest son of Sharif Husain. Born about 1897 of a Turkish mother. Humorous, and less intense than his brothers. Became Ambassador to Britain after Second World War, but played little part in Arab politics.

Nasr ibn Ali, younger brother of the Sharif Husain. Aged fifty-four in 1917, member of Ottoman Upper House, remained in Constantinople during First World War, but was said to support his brother's rebellion.

Ali Haidar Pasha (Haidar Ali). A member of the rival Sharifian family, the House of the Amir Abdal Mutlib, recognised by the Porte as Naqib al Ashraf (representative of all the Sharifite clans), member of CUP and Ottoman Parliament. Married (second time) to Irish woman, by whom he had three children. Pan-Islamist, but well disposed to Britain, where his eldest son was educated. Maintained close contacts with Indian Moslems and Pan-Islamic agents. After outbreak of Arab Revolt he was nominated Sharif by Porte and sent to Madina, where he arrived on 26 July 1916 and issued a proclamation.

Saad ad Din Pasha, younger brother of Ali Haidar. Keen member of CUP. Married to daughter of Sultan Mehmet. Went to Hail with Eshref Bey, Ottoman officer in charge of arms consignment to Ibn Rashid, in 1914.

Ali ibn Abdullah, Amir of Juhainah, resident at Yanbo. Related to Sharif Husain by marriage. Acknowledged Ottoman authority. Replaced by Muhammad Ali al Baduwi in 1914 and fled to Suakin, but returned in June 1916. Expelled von Stotzingen and Neufeld from Yanbo and led the Sharifian force to which the Turkish garrison at Yanbo surrendered in July 1916.

The Dynasty of Muhammad Ali in Egypt (1805–1953)

Muhammad (Mehmet) Ali Pasha, Viceroy of Ottoman Sultan, 1805–48. Born 1769 at Kavala in Macedonia. Albanian by parentage. Led *Arnaut* contingent in Ottoman expedition of 1803 following the French withdrawal. Eliminated Mameluks and expropriated the wealth of the Beys. Tried to industrialise country. Invaded central Arabia in 1811 on behalf of the Sultan. 1831 rebelled against Ottoman master and took control of much of Syria. 1840 European powers intervened on behalf of Sultan. 1841 Muhammad Ali's family were granted hereditary governorship of Egypt under nominal suzerainty of Porte. To the royal firman of 13 February 1841 was attached a map showing the agreed boundaries of Egypt, which came under dispute with Britain in 1892 and 1906. It has been claimed that the Egyptian copy was destroyed in a fire and Turkish governments have never produced the Ottoman copy. Up to 1883 Britain claimed that the section of Sinai above a line drawn from Suez to Ar Rafa (near Gaza) was included in Egypt, the rest of the peninsula being Ottoman. After that date Britain drew the boundary from Rafa to Aqaba. The matter remains in doubt to the present day. Muhammad Ali retired in favour of his son, Ibrahim, in 1848. He was declared insane in 1848, and died in 1849. His successors were designated Wali (Governor) until 1867, when the term Khedive (an imprecise designation, roughly 'First Citizen') came into use.

Ibrahim Pasha, 1848. Died in year of accession.

Abbas Pasha, 1848–54. Murdered.

Said Pasha, 1854–63.

Ismail Pasha, Wali 1863–7, Khedive 1867–79.

Khedive Tewfiq, 1879–92.

Khedive Abbas Hilmi, 1892–1914. Deposed by Britain in 1914. Died in exile 1943.

Britain declared a Protectorate over Egypt, 19 September 1914, when Abbas Hilmi was deposed and given pension for life subject to him never again setting foot in Egypt. Husain Kamil was made Sultan and henceforth addressed officially as 'Majesty'.

Sultan Husain Kamil, 1914–17.

Sultan Fuad, 1917–22, King of Egypt 1922–36.

Egypt became an independent Kingdom in 1922 under 'the watchful eye of Britain', as Wavell recorded in his biography of Allenby, the High Commissioner at the transference.

King Farouk, 1936–52. Abdicated.

King Ahmad Fuad (nominal) 1952–3. Monarchy abolished.

Other Arab Personalities

Imam Yahya of Yemen; full title, Yahya ibn Muhammad Hamid ad Din al Mutawakkil, Sharif of the Kasimi House of Sheharah.

Inherited title Imam in 1904 from his father, Muhammad al Mansur, who appears to have been a usurper since there is no established connection between his family and the Imams of Sana who ruled from about 1600 AD to 1891, when Yahya's grandfather, Yahya Hamid ad Din, led a rebellion against the Ottoman power. Yahya Hamid lived an ascetic life in the northern mountains, the original centre of a Yemeni dynasty established in the tenth century by a descendant of Hasan, grandson of the Prophet.

The Imam Yahya led a second rebellion against the Turks in 1904 and captured Sana, but was driven out by the Ottoman force after a few months. He besieged Sana in 1910, but was defeated by a Turkish force led by Izzet Pasha. In 1912 he came to agreement with the Turks following a declaration of *jihad* against the Italians, who had intervened in the territory. He agreed to live at Sheharah north of Umran in return for an annual stipend. But the Turks garrisoned all the main towns, including Sana and Sheharah. He became friendly with Izzet's successor, Mahmud Nazim Pasha, in 1913 and supported the Turks from then on. In November 1915 he wrote to Enver praying for the success of the Ottoman armies. The dominant religion of the region, of which Yahya was the high-priest, was known as Zeidism, a schismatic dogma somewhere between the Shi'ite and Sunni versions of the Islamic faith. He was a bitter enemy of the Imam Idrisi of Asir to the north of Yemen. Many of his tribesmen went over to Idrisi in 1916–17.

Idrisi of Asir, full title Sayid Muhammad ibn Ali al Idrisi. Family originated from North Africa. Appeared in Arabia 1799 when Sayid Ahmad, great-grandfather of Imam Idrisi, went to Mecca. Title to territory always in dispute. Idrisi was aged about thirty-eight in 1914.

Chiefs of Aden and Hadhramaut, Sultans of Lahej. Title of chiefs of Abdali tribe since 1728. Sultan Ali ibn Ahmad succeeded in 1914. He was accidentally shot by a British soldier as he welcomed Sir Ronald Storrs to his palace in 1915. Abdal Karim ibn Fadl succeeded his cousin on 13 July 1915. Aged thirty-five in 1916. Turks occupied Lahej in 1915 and Sultan lived in Aden under British protection.

Sultans of Muscat and Oman, principal ruling family, the Albu Said, derived from Ahmad ibn Said of the Azd tribe, who in 1741 expelled the Persian allies of his tribal predecessors from the territory. Treaty relations with Britain began in 1798 and from 1891 the Sultans were under binding ties with Indian Government, from whom they received a large annual subsidy and a guarantee of protection. The reigning Sultan from 1913 was *Taimur ibn Faisal*, eldest son of Faisal ibn Turki (no connection with the Saudi Amir of the same name), who ruled from 1888 to 1913. Taimur was born in 1886. He was under constant threats from Omani shaikhs of the interior and was opposed by his uncle, Muhammad ibn Turki, who claimed the Sultanate. Arms traffic and the incitement of foreign agents were at the root of the disputes and rivalries in the territory. In May 1913 there was a serious rebellion led by Shaikh Abdullah as Salimi, and Indian troops were landed to support the new Sultan. In April 1915 Indian forces bombarded the forts of the insurgents. In autumn 1915 reinforcements had to be sent to Bait-al-Felej and an attempt by 3,000 tribesmen to take Muscat was foiled.

TRUCIAL CHIEFS

Hamdan ibn Zaid al Khalifa of Abu Dhabi, succeeded his brother, Tahnun, in 1912. A firm ruler, and pro-British but dabbled in arms traffic of Pirate Coast, allegedly to secure himself against the threat of invasion by Ibn Saud.

Said ibn Makhtum of Dubai, succeeded in 1912 his cousin, Buti ibn Suhail, with whom he was in constant conflict. Focus of arms traffic and one of the wealthiest chiefs of the coast. Warned in August 1913 after Dubai gunmen fired on HMS *Sphinx,* flagship of the Gulf flotilla.

Khalid ibn Ahmad of Sharjah, chief of the Jawasim tribe. Succeeded his cousin, Saqar ibn Khalid, in 1914. He was British Residential Agent for the Trucial area, situated at Sharjah.

Rashid ibn Ahmad of Umm al Qaiwain. A troublesome client of Britain, his chief industry was piracy. He was given the gunboat treatment in March 1914.

The Al Thani of Qatar, independent since the retreat of the Wahhabis in about 1870, when Doha, the capital, was occupied by a Turkish garrison. When Ibn Saud retook Al Hasa in 1913, the Turks were cut off at Qatar. Britain gave Ibn Saud 'verbal but not written' permission to take Qatar if he wished, following the occupation of Al Hasa. The Ottoman claim to the territory, put forward in 1871, was never recognised by the Government of India. Britain had a long-standing but not binding treaty with Qatar until 1882, when it was allowed to lapse. It was an informal Protectorate of India. The ruler from July 1913 was *Abdullah ibn Jasim al Thani.* He was pro-British and friendly with Ibn Saud, who declined Britain's questionable offer of the territory. He negotiated the final surrender of the stranded Turkish garrison in 1915. He was at odds with his brother, Khalifa. Qatar was another important and intractable centre of arms smuggling. The Al Thani rule the country to the present day.

The Khalifa of Bahrain, the Khalifa shaikhs of the Ataiba tribe who occupied Bahrain and Kuwait have been a powerful force in the Persian Gulf for more than 200 years. The shaikhs of Bahrain have been in treaty relations with Britain since 1820. In 1880 the ruler signed a treaty with Britain similar to those with Oman and the Trucial States, in extension of the perpetual Maritime Treaties of 1853 imposed by the East India Company, which outlawed piracy and forbade maritime engagements. *Shaikh Isa ibn Ali al Khalifa* succeeded in 1867. Jealous of independence and apt to intrigue with Ottoman and German agents, but intelligent, wise in counsel and energetic, he was an old man at the outbreak of the First World War. His brother, *Shaikh Khalid ibn Ali al Khalifa,* was the virtually independent ruler of the northern townships of Bahrain island, and some satellite islands. *Khalifa ibn Hamad ibn Muhammad al-Khalifa* was a prominent malcontent of the ruling house with close connections with Constantinople.

The Sabah of Kuwait, branch of the Khalifa family, said to have come originally from a settlement at Umm Kasr near Zubair on the banks of the Shatt-al-Arab. They built a fort or Kut on the coast of a place then known as Qrain when expelled from their homeland at the end of eighteenth century by Turks. Thus, Kut–Kuwait. In 1871 when Midhat Pasha the Governor of Baghdad took Al Hasa, Shaikh Muhammad ibn Sabah declared himself an Ottoman subject (the Ottoman occupying force was led by Mubarak, half-brother of Muhammad, and Sayid Talib, son of the Naqib of Basra). But in 1899, when the projected Baghdad rail scheme was under debate and Kuwait was sought as an outlet, Britain signed a secret agreement with the Shaikh forbidding alliance with other powers, and this was succeeded by another secret treaty in 1907, which leased to Britain the Shuwaikh foreshore of Kuwait harbour, the only possible debouchure for the railway in the Gulf (the so-called Bandar–Shuwaikh Lease). The first British Political Agent, Colonel Knox, arrived in Kuwait in 1904. From the departure of Knox's successor, Captain Shakespear, in 1914, neither the Shaikh of Kuwait nor Ibn Saud felt that they could rely on Britain's word and both flirted with Ottoman agents. But on declaration of war both supported the Allied cause. *Mubarak ibn Sabah*, by far the greatest of Kuwait's rulers and one of the most powerful of all Arab leaders, succeeded in 1896 after murdering his half-brother Muhammad. Compared by the editor of *The Times of India*, Lovat Fraser, with Richelieu, Mubarak was in the truest sense a Renaissance man of Arab politics, with a henna'd white beard and painted eyebrows to hide his age. He died in 1915 at the age of seventy-six. He was succeeded by his eldest son Jabir in November 1915, and by his estranged second son, Salim, on the death of Jabir in 1917.

Tribal Chiefs, Their Groups and Territories

Anaiza, probably the largest and richest of the noble (sharif) tribes, whose territory was of great strategic importance, covering the eastern fringes of Syria inland to Jauf and the western deserts of Mesopotamia. Principal area was the Hamad of Syria, which they took from the Shammar about 1770.

Main sub-divisions: *Wuld Ali*, about 8,000 tents, *dira* (grazing grounds) from Homs to Taima; principal shaikhs, *Rashid ibn Smeyr* (Hauran), *Muhammad ibn Saleh* (west of Wadi Sirhan), *Saud ibn Malham* (Homs). *Amarat*, tents uncounted, grounds run from Ana to lower Euphrates and into Najd, many sub-clans; chief man, *Fahad ibn Abdal Mehsin Dughaim ibn Hadhal*, supporter of the Pan-Arab movement, about sixty in 1914, anti-Turk, friend of Leachman and Gertrude Bell, estates at Karbala and Baghdad. *Bishr-Anaiza*, federation of Sbaa and Fidan; *dira* runs from Hama, Aleppo to Deir az Zor; leading shaikhs *Ibn Murshid*, *Ibn Hadaib*, *Ibn Mahaid* and *Ibn Gayshish*. *Hashim ibn Mahaid*, strongest of their leaders, was a true warrior of the desert, clever, and a Pan-Arab, but he was under the influence of Madame Koch of Aleppo, who was an agent of Baron von Oppenheim. *Ruwalla*, the main division of Anaiza, camped around Damascus with huge herds of camels and horses, about 6,000 tents; Amir and paramount Shaikh of Anaiza, *Nuri ibn Shalan*, owner of the rich oasis of Jauf, virtual controller of the Hijaz railway, immortalised by Lawrence and admired by Musil; but despite Lawrence's colourful account of collaboration, he remained loyal to Turks through the First World War, except in the last days of 1918 when he saw which way the wind was blowing; member of every Arab committee and league and early supporter of Young Turks; urbane, liked the high life despite his years (over sixty at outbreak of war), devious. *Nawwaf ibn Nuri Shalan*, first and favourite son of Amir, who captured Jauf for his father in January 1909; keen supporter of Arab nationalist movement, married Mishas, the daughter of his uncle, Fahad ibn Shalan, whom Nuri assassinated; later divorced her and she married Fendi ibn Saud al Malham, a distant kinsman of Ibn Saud. The first son of Nawwaf and Mishas was *Sultan ibn Shalan*, a small boy when Shakespear visited Jauf in 1914, who became the powerful leader of the Anaiza in the inter-war years.

Shammar, a huge tribe stretching from the upper reaches of the Tigris to the border of the Hijaz, tents uncounted but probably exceeding those of the combined Anaiza tribes in number. Chiefs, the Ibn Rashids of Hail, see *Rulers and Principals of the House of Rashid*. But important shaikhs outside the Rashid family led sub-divisions of the tribe, which possessed vast herds of camels and the finest stables in Arabia, and who were the fiercest of desert warriors. Most significant, the Shammar-Jerba, divided into warring camps of Wuld Farhan (children of Farhan) and Wuld Abdal Karim. Former were led by *Shaikh al Asi*, son of Farhan, the latter by *Abdal Mehsin* and *Muhammad*, the sons of Abdal Karim. Muhammad was hanged by the Turks with the connivance of his brother Farhan, and of Ibn Sadun, the chief of the Muntafiq tribe. Afterwards rival family clans were at war with each other and with Muntafiq, but all three shaikhs were keen supporters of Pan-Arab movement.

Muntafiq, a confederation of Shi'ite Euphrates tribes created out of the Ajwad, Bani Temim, Bani Saad, Bani Hukaym, Shibil, Fatlah, Bani Hassan, and other tribes and semi-nomadic communities. Battle for supremacy raged for generations between families of *Nasir Pasha* and his son, *Falih*, and *Mansur Pasha* and his son, *Sadun*, for dominance. Sadun Pasha had achieved pre-eminence by the early years of the twentieth century through his prowess in battle. Opposed to the imperial Government of Abdal Hamid, he was heir to a family tradition of conflict with Ottoman rulers and their Governors. In 1904 the Turks sent a large force to subdue the Muntafiq, but under the leadership of Sadun the tribesmen massacred the opposition at Shatra. In 1908 he gained a pardon by supporting the Young Turks' revolution. But in 1910 there was more tribal strife and the new regime at Constantinople decided to use Sayid Talib, son of the Naqib of Basra, to decoy him. Sadun was induced to board a gunboat with Talib and was arrested by the Wali and sent to Aleppo, where he died in 1911 of an alleged heart attack. The Muntafiq immediately took up arms under their new leader *Ajaimi ibn Sadun*, son of the Pasha. Ajaimi never forgave Talib for his duplicity. Talib was an early supporter of the Young Turks but quickly became their enemy and a supporter of the Arab nationalist movement. Ajaimi, determined to oppose the mercurial Talib and to avenge his father's death, took the opposite course, supporting the CUP and the Porte from 1911 onwards. When the CUP suffered a temporary eclipse in 1912, Ajaimi was outlawed by the Constantinople liberals, and briefly the sons of Falih, his father's great rival, led the tribe. But by the beginning of 1913 Ajaimi was recalled as paramount Shaikh, resumed his war with the great enemy Ibn Suwait of the Dhafir, joined forces with the Amir of Hail and caused panic around Basra.

Dhafir, tribal territory between Zubair and Samawa on the Euphrates, inland to Najd, and the Shamiya desert, for which it contested vigorously with the Muntafiq. A small tribe, but disciplined and fierce in battle. Chief shaikh was *Hamad ibn Suwait*. Tribe had been known to unite with Muntafiq, however, in fighting forces of Shaikh Mubarak of Kuwait and occasionally of Ibn Saud. Ibn Suwait was about forty in 1916, intelligent and civilised. Ibn Saud recommended him to Britain as reliable opponent of Ibn Rashid, through Shakespear, in 1915.

Mutair, sometimes Umtair. Powerful tribe with large camel herds, with camping grounds between Kuwait and northern Najd. Owed loose allegiance to Shaikh of Kuwait and Ibn Saud, liable to flirt with Ibn Rashid at times of latter's domination of central Arabia. Progenitors of Ikhwan movement, the desert 'Brotherhood' which began among devoutly religious tribesmen who were induced by their paramount Shaikh, *Faisal ibn Dawish*, to settle at Al Artawiya, east of Buraida, and become cultivators. From small beginnings in about 1908, this fanatical movement of warriors armed with a puritanical doctrine spread like wildfire in central Arabia, supported at first by Ibn Saud, who saw in its brethren a mighty military force. The Ikhwan was instrumental in Ibn Saud's eventual victory over the forces of the Sharif of Mecca in the Hijaz, over Ibn Rashid in Jabal Shammar, and in his other conquests. But in the end it became too strong for Ibn Saud to control, its leaders began to demand holy war against British-controlled Iraq and Transjordan, and Faisal ibn Dawish's warriors were bombed by the RAF and disowned by Ibn Saud at the end of 1929. Faisal, the tragi-hero of Arabia and one of its greatest warriors, died in Ibn Saud's prison on 3 October 1931, an old and broken man.

Ajman, another powerful tribe, occupying the ground between Kuwait and Al Hasa. Principal Shaikh, *Dhaidan ibn Hithlain*. One of the most fickle and, on its day, formidable tribes in Arabia. Owed allegiance at different times to Shaikh of Kuwait, Ibn Rashid and Ibn Saud. Ibn Saud married daughter of Ibn Hithlain in order to cement alliance, but whilst tribe contributed to some famous desert victories, it was also responsible for defeats and tragedies. In 1915 its desertion at Jarab, at the height of battle, was directly responsible for the death of Captain Shakespear. In 1910 the tribe had given succour in Al Hasa to the fleeing dissidents of the Saud family, the *Araif*. In the summer of 1915 Ibn Saud attacked them at Kinzan, west of Hofuf, and was defeated; and his favourite brother Saad was killed. Afterwards Ibn Saud hounded them and they sought refuge in Kuwait, which Shaikh Salim al Sabah granted, thus causing a long and angry breach between the Amir of Najd and the country he had regarded as his second home.

Bani Harb, two main branches, the Bani Salim following Ibn Rashid and the Bani Ali owing allegiance to the Sharif of Mecca. Clannish, hard fighters, with *dira* from Hijaz to Hail and south to Riyadh. They could have been a decisive force in Arab Revolt of 1916 but were disunited and too anxious to fight each other. Chiefs, *Ghati ibn Neheith* and *Mehsin ibn Ithm.*. A third section, camping on the coast around Rabegh, the Zoheid, was presided over by a robber baron, *Husain ibn Mubarak*, who was paid by both Britain and Turkey as a secret agent.

Ataiba, sometimes Utaiba. Two main branches, Ruqa and Barqa. Principal shaikhs, *Turki ibn Maslat* and *Muhammad ibn Hamdi*. They veered between Ibn Saud and the Sharif of Mecca, but were not keen on Wahhabi customs. *Dira* east of Wadi Rumma to Taif. Wealth in sheep, camels and horses, outstanding fighters, enemies of Harb.

Howaitat, tribe distinguished by colourful, indigo-dyed *thobs* or outer garments, women of exceptional beauty who are permitted to discard their *burqas* or face masks, and fearless warriors. Principal Shaikh, *Auda Abu Tayya*, was made famous by Lawrence. Musil and Shakespear both met him on his home territory at Abu Tayya, on the road from Jauf to Wadi Sirhan, and both described him as a scoundrel; a kind of Robin Hood of Arabia. There were many branches of the tribe from Hauran desert to Aqaba and Sinai, few of which had anything in common. Other leaders were *Shaikh Muhammad ibn Khailan abu Tayya*, cousin of Auda, officially Shaikh ad Dowla, responsible for collecting taxes for Turkish Government; *Ahmad ibn Muhammad*, chief of tribe on Midian coast of Sinai, pro-Turk and subsidised by Porte.

Pan-Arabs, Pan-Islamites, Nationalists and Others

Aziz Ali al Masri, Major in Ottoman Army, Iraqi by birth, trained in Constantinople, and hero of Balkan Wars, 1911–13. He was a founder member of Al Ahad (date of foundation uncertain, usually given as 1912 but Al Masri involved in Damascus committee which gave rise to 'Covenant' in 1910); the instigator of a plan to form alliance of Arab chiefs with Ibn Saud at head, leading to armed rebellion in 1915. At the same time he maintained membership of the Ottoman Committee of Union and Progress, and was a staff officer in the army. Became Enver's rival for Turkish leadership in 1914, was arrested and condemned to death for treason. Kitchener intervened to save him through rector of Al Azhar University, Cairo. Exiled to Egypt. September 1914 visited Residency regarding earlier conversation between Kitchener and Abdullah ibn Husain. Said he spoke for 'Arab movement' aiming to form secular Arab state. Kitchener doubted his sincerity earlier in the year and rebuffed his advances. In November 1914 he asked for permission to contact colleagues in Iraq. Became Chief of Staff of Hijaz army in July 1916, but constant quarrels with Husain and sons led to his resignation and retirement to Egypt in 1917.

Ali Rida Rikabi, Aleppine, highest Arab officer in Ottoman army with rank of full General, GOC Damascus under Jamal 1917, formerly Civil Governor of the Lebanon. Secret member of Al Ahad. Central figure in story of Lawrence's mysterious journey alone to outskirts of Damascus in June 1917, when the Englishman is alleged to have left Auda abu Tayya before the capture of Aqaba with a secret message from Faisal to Ali Rida. The story, told in detail in Antonius, *The Arab Awakening*, p. 221, is only inferred in Lawrence's own account, and would have been almost impossible according to Lawrence's own timetable given in *Seven Pillars*. Faisal's Chief Minister and adviser 1919–20, but he was thought to be half-hearted in his opposition to the French in Syria and was forced to resign.

Abdal Latif al Mandil, usually described as a rich landowner of Basra, he was (according to British intelligence report) a Dosiri shaikh of Bahrain with extensive property in Basra province. He was the confidant of Shaikh Mubarak, Shaikh Khazal of Muhammerah, and Ibn Saud, and the recipient of rewards from all sides in the course of negotiations between Britain, Turks and the Arab chiefs. He 'farmed' customs duty and taxes of Al Hasa for Ibn Saud in 1916 and re-organised the taxation system in the territory at Ibn Saud's request. He became a leading figure in post-war Iraqi politics and an inaugural member of the Iraq Government.

Al Asi and Ibn Farhan, sons of Abdal Karim. Both Pan-Arabs. See under 'Shammar', p. 378.

Faruki, Muhammad Sharif al, Lieutenant (staff officer) Ottoman army. Aged twenty-four when taken prisoner at Gallipoli in 1915. Born in Mosul of a distinguished Arab family claiming descent from the second Caliph, Omar ibn al Khattab. Educated Military Academy, Constantinople. Apart from Arabic he spoke Turkish and French fluently and a little Russian. He was interrogated by British intelligence (Naum Shuqair, Christian Arab working for MO2 Cairo in September 1915). Asked to see Al Masri, for whom he had 'secret message'. Wanted treaty of alliance with Britain which would not infringe complete Arab independence. Made chief intermediary with Sharif and enrolled in Secret Service September 1915, code-named 'G'.

Hashim ibn Mahaid, anti-Turk, Pan-Arab. See under 'Bishr-Anaiza', p. 377.

Izzet Pasha, private secretary (officially second secretary) to Abdal Hamid. Joined Pan-Arab movement after Young Turks came to power in 1908. Damascene, extremely wealthy, responsible for collecting religious funds for building Hijaz pilgrim railway, but irreligious and labelled by British intelligence, 'Intriguer and unsafe'. In touch with Sharif and British Foreign Office at the end of 1914 and with Sir Henry McMahon early in 1915. Lived in Paris and Nice. Acquainted with Sir Basil Zahroff.

Nuri Pasha as Said: born Baghdad, 1888. Educated Staff College, Constantinople. Captured in early days of First World War in Basra province, injured, and defected to British side while in hospital at Basra. Became second in command to Aziz al Masri – his pre-war mentor in Al Ahad – in Sharif's army. Became first Commander-in-Chief and War Minister of Iraq, 1922, and later Prime Minister. He was exiled after military *coup* of 1936, but returned as Prime Minister and Minister of Interior, and held other offices, before dying with King and other members of the old revolutionary committees in the counter-revolution of 1958. Most distinguished of Iraqi politicians.

Nuri ibn Shalan, member of all the Arab committees and of CUP. See under 'Anaiza', p. 377.

Rashid Rida, leading Islamic thinker and religious leader from Tripoli in vilayet of Beirut. Devotee of Muhammad Abduh, Islamic teacher and Mufti of Egypt from 1899 to 1905. Co-operated at first with Young Turks through the literary club, *al-Muntada al-Adabi*, which was patronised by the CUP from 1909, and the clandestine *Al Qahtaniya*, precursors of the *Hizb al Lamarkaziya al Idariya al Uthmani* (generally known as the Decentralisation Party) in Cairo, of Al Fattah (formed in Paris in 1911 by Arab students), and Al Ahad (Damascus 1911–12). He became a leading figure in the Decentralisation Party in 1912. Inclined to Pan-Islamic rather than Pan-Arab view.

Shuqari Pasha, senior Aleppine officer of Ottoman army, strongly Pan-Arab. Rashid Rida was under his influence in pre-war days when he (Shuqari) was Ottoman commander at Adana.

Jafar Pasha al Askari, brother-in-law of Nuri Pasha as Said, commander of Ottoman force which invaded Egypt with the Sannusi army from November 1915 to March 1916. Captured at Battle of Sallum. After imprisonment he decided to support Arab Revolt, and succeeded Aziz al Masri as the Sharif's Chief of Staff. He became Faisal's Governor of Aleppo in 1919, and a source of threats to British forces at Dair az Zor and Mosul. October 1920 he was invited to join the Provisional Government of Iraq under Presidency of Naqib of Baghdad. He went to Cairo with Cox for Churchill's Conference in 1921, wearing an Ottoman military helmet which gave him world-wide prominence in press photographs, and after the Conference became Chief of Staff of Iraq army. He died in the *coup* of October 1936.

Yasin Pasha al Hashimi, General in Ottoman army, left behind injured at Allenby's occupation of Damascus. A late adherent to Arab cause and an extreme exponent of Arab independence; equally, strongly opposed to French claims in Syria. But he maintained close links with the Turks, and met Mustafa Kamal 'Ataturk' in 1919. He was arrested by the British in November 1919; released to become Faisal's chief adviser and moving spirit of the Ahad al Iraq, formed in 1920 as the Mesopotamian branch of the Covenanters. He was said to have tried to reinstitute Turks in old provinces of empire out of personal ambition (Meinertzhagen). He was successively Minister of Works, Foreign Affairs and Prime Minister in post-war Iraq governments, and founder of the Iraq People's Party.

Sayid Talib an Naqib, of the family of Naqibs of Basra claiming descent from the important Sunni saint, Sayid Ahmad ar Rifai whose tomb stands in the Jazira desert. They were rich landowners. His father, Sayid Rajjab Naqib, was appointed in 1890, and used influence with Constantinople to cause dismissal of unusually honest Ottoman Wali, Hamdi Pasha, who opposed land scandals involving his family. Naqib became friendly with Shaikhs Mubarak of Kuwait and Khazal of Muhammerah, who were lucratively engaged in gun-running. Hamdi Pasha was sent back by the Porte to deal with scandals, but Naqib's son was sent to Constantinople to tell malicious stories of the Wali and force his withdrawal for a second time. Thus Talib entered political arena as the arch bully and rogue of Basra. In 1900 Talib murdered Shaikh Khazal's enemy, Abdullah Effendi Rowandiz, a popular Kurdish leader, resulting in the transfer, illegally, of large date plantations to Khazal, who was a Persian citizen though ruler of an Arab principality. In 1902 he was appointed Wali of Ibn Saud's territory of Al Hasa, but his regime was so harsh and corrupt that the Turks were forced to recall him. In 1904 the new Turkish Wali, Mukhlis Pasha, ordered the arrest of Talib and his hired band of blackguards. In 1905 he was exiled to Constantinople, where he became the friend of Prince Izzedin, who was later assassinated. In 1909 he returned to Basra as the representative of the Young Turks whom he had supported in Constantinople, but the CUP mistrusted him and sent him back to the capital, where he became acquainted with liberal element of Arab movement, and won approval of Liberal Grand Vizier, Kiamil Pasha, for his opposition to the CUP. In 1912 Talib was advised by Kiamil to make advances to Britain. He went to Cairo and Simla with letters of introduction from Britain's Consul, Mr Crow, to Kitchener and Hardinge; but his price was too high. He conceived the idea in the same year of joining Pan-Arab scheme of Ahad for revolt to be led by Ibn Saud and consequent confederacy in which he would rule Basra. In 1911 he co-operated with the Turks in capturing Sadun Pasha. Sadun's son, Ajaimi, became his sworn enemy and led the Muntafiq in support of the CUP and against Talib. The commander of Basra army supported Ajaimi and on 19 June 1913 Talib's men murdered Commandant (Farid Bey). August 1913 Enver ordered Talib's arrest, but Sayid sent a threatening address to Constantinople and Enver appeared to give in, promising Talib support. In May 1914 the British Ambassador was told that Talib was to be made Wali of Basra. At same time Djavid Pasha, Wali of Baghdad, was given secret instructions to send an army detachment to arrest him. News of the expedition reached him and he fled to Kuwait and Ibn Saud with new proposals. Rejected, he was sent back to Basra on its British occupation by Ibn Saud and exiled to India. After the First World War he returned to Basra as possible leader of country, but resumed his old ways and was exiled finally by Sir Percy Cox in 1921. He died in Munich in 1929 and his body was taken to Zubair for burial.

Appendix B

Structure of the British Military Intelligence Organisation General Staff, Cairo

From November 1914 to November 1916 Brigadier-General Gilbert Clayton was officially designated Director of Military and Civil Intelligence, with Major Wyndham Deedes as his personal secretary responsible for political intelligence. The GSO1 (intelligence) was Colonel A. C. Parker and the GSO3 Captain Holdich. The Arab Bureau was formed in June 1916 under Clayton and Parker, but was almost immediately taken over by Lieutenant-Commander Hogarth RNVR as GSO2 in executive charge, 2nd Echelon. In November 1916 Holdich was promoted to the rank of Lieutenant-Colonel and became General Murray's intelligence chief (GSO1). Colonels Newcombe, who arrived from France in 1915, and Parker remained as GSO1s of the 1st Echelon, and the Bureau, which had reported to the DMI, the Foreign Office (through the Resident), and the DNI (Captain Hall), became essentially an arm of political intelligence. In 1917 with the appearance of General Allenby, Colonel Meinertzhagen took over as GSO1 Intelligence, Deedes as GSO1 Political, and Clayton was made Chief Political Officer for Egypt and enemy-occupied territories. Officers in charge of intelligence sections changed frequently in accordance with the custom in the Secret Service.

Notes

Official Records

Wherever possible the specific file number is quoted when official documents are cited. But the research for this book has been conducted over a period of some twelve years and in some instances I have retained notes only of series of files in the many archives I have searched. In such cases others who may wish to refer to the documents in question will have to refer to the original registers and indexes.

Books

I have not given details of other authors' sources, except where stated. Again, other researchers will have to refer to the notes and indexes of the books cited if they wish to trace original sources.

Private Papers

I have made use of several collections of private papers, particularly those of the late Mr Douglas Carruthers, Colonel S. F. Newcombe and Colonel A. C. Parker. I will endeavour to lodge these with a generally accessible British archive or library, with the permission of their owners, at a later date.

When not cited in the Notes, full bibliographical details are given in the Bibliography, pp. 488–510.

Abbreviations

AA	Auswärtiges Amt, German Foreign Office, Bonn
ADM	Admiralty (British)
AIR	Air Ministry (British)
AH	Austria–Hungary, Staatsarchiv, Vienna
CAB	Cabinet Papers (British)
CASJ	*Central Asian Society Journal* (now *Journal of Royal Society for Asian Affairs, JRSAA*)
CID	Committee of Imperial Defence
C-in-C	Commander-in-Chief
CO	Colonial Office, London
DMI	Director of Military Intelligence
DMO	Director of Military Operations
DNI	Director of Naval Intelligence
DNO	Director of Naval Operations
F	France, Correspondance politique et commerciale, NS (Nouvelle Serie, from 1896)
FO	Foreign Office, London
GI	Government of India
GJ	*Geographical Journal*
GOC	General Officer Commanding
HL	House of Lords records, London, including documents from Beaverbrook Library
IGC	Inspector-General Communications
IO	India Office, London
L/P&S/	Political and secret records, India Office, London
MEC	Middle East Centre, Oxford (St Antony's)/Cambridge

MI	Military Intelligence
MO	Military Operations
PRO	Public Record Office, London
R/	Persian Gulf records, India Office, London
RGS	Royal Geographical Society, London
S/S	Secretary of State
UPM	Unpublished manuscript
US	United States National Archives, Washington
US/S	Under Secretary of State
WO	War Office, London
Z	Zionist Central Office documents, Jerusalem

1   The Battlegrounds

page

3   Kaiser's journey: *The Times*, Oct–Dec 1898.

4   Gathering at tomb of Saladin: see Alex Aaronsohn, *With the Turks in Palestine*. Although not reported in the press at the time, the Kaiser is said to have told his audience in his speech at the serai of the Wali of Damascus: 'Not splendour, not power, not glory, not honour, no earthly blessing is it that we seek here: we pine, we pray, we strive alone after the sole, the highest blessing, the salvation of our souls.' See Charles F. Horne (ed.), *Source Records of the Great War*, National Alumni, USA, 1923, comment by Dr Moris Jastrow, University of Pennsylvania.

Kitchener in London: *The Times*, 25–8 Oct 1898.

Lieutenant Winston Spencer Churchill at Rotherhithe Town Hall: *The Times*, 25 Oct. Kitchener succeeded General Sir Francis Grenfell as Sirdar of the Egyptian Army 1892, though General Wodehouse was senior candidate, on Cromer's insistence; see Cassar, *Kitchener*.

Kaiser's interference: see Rosen, *Aus einem diplomatischen Wanderleben*, and Kühlmann, *Erinnerung*.

Curzon and Kitchener: see Magnus, *Kitchener: Portrait of an Imperialist*, and Cassar, *Kitchener*.

Curzon: see article by Dr A. S. Goudie, 'George Nathaniel Curzon – Superior Geographer', *GJ*, vol. 146, no. 2, July 1980.

5   Curzon to Gulf: see Lorimer, *Gazetteer*, App. 2, Pt 2, quotes *The Times*, *Times of India* and *Pioneer* of India, 10 Nov–5 Dec 1903.

'British lake': R/15/1/475. Lansdowne, March 1902.

Lansdowne, quote: L/P & S/18/B166 (confidential print) May 1903.

Curzon, quote: Curzon, *Persia and the Persian Question*, p. 3.

6   Ottoman Empire and Persia, political and military intervention: see Lewis, *The Emergence of Modern Turkey;* Kinross, *The Ottoman Centuries;* Sir Percy Sykes, *A History of Persia;* Kazemzadeh, *Russia and Britain in Persia*. For commercial detail see Lorimer, *Gazetteer*, pp. 1,438–9.

Military intelligence: see Aston, *The Secret Service, Army List* and WO records, General.

7   Hon. Consuls, Constantinople: FO Lists.

Massy: *GJ*, vol. 26, Aug 1905, pp. 272–307, and map.

Maunsell: see Herbert, *Ben Kendim*.

8   German Secret Service: see Nicolai, *Nachrichtdienst, Presse und Volksstim-mung in Weltkrieg*, dedicated 'To my COUNTRY as a warning, and as a lesson to all who would help her win back her freedom, and who are, for that reason, threatened by her foes'. For somewhat far-fetched stories of German spies in the Ottoman Empire and elsewhere, see the account of Dr Armgaard Karl Graves, *Secrets of the German War Office*, McBride, Nast, New York, 1914. Graves, a physician and probably a South African, was recruited during the Boer War by German intelligence's Major Freiherr von Reitzenstein, and was recruited by MO3 in 1912 after being arrested in Glasgow. He worked as a double agent in America during the First World War.

Baron Max von Oppenheim: AA, Abteilung 1A, Orientalia generalia 9, Nr 1, Bd 1–12, 1886–1909; Nr 11g, Der Weltkreig (operations against Germany's enemies in Egypt, Syria and Arabia) Bd 1–19, 1914–18; Nr 11g, Der Weltkrieg (Secret) BD 1–5, 1914–15. See also Morsey, *T. E. Lawrence und der arabische Aufstand, 1916–18*. For von Oppenheim's own account, see his *Von Mittelmeer zum Persischen Golf, durch den Hauran, die Syrische Wuste und Mesopotamien*, and *Der Tell Halaf*, Leipzig, 1931. Von Oppenheim's family was designated one-third Jewish by the Third Reich, *Encyclopaedia Judaica*.

'The Spy': Storrs, *Orientations*.

Wilhelmstrasse, Institute of Archaeology: *Almanach de Gotha*, 1913, shows the Institute Director as Professor Dr L. Borchardt, responsible to the Foreign Office US/S Zimmermann through the Bureau Director Herr Mechler.

Wönckhaus, Lingeh, Feb 1896: Lorimer, *Gazetteer*. Robert Wönckhaus & Company, branch of Traun Sturken of Hamburg. According to Sykes, *History of Persia*, Wönckhaus opened premises in Baghdad, Abadan and Bushire in 1899, and lived exceedingly well on the proceeds of sea shells.

French, Russian and Austro-Hungarian Secret Services: see Nicolai, *Nachrichdienst*. The Deuxième Bureau, the intelligence wing of the French General Staff, was 'absolutely autocratic' and the 'most efficient in the world', according to Nicolai. 'Only in the days of Frederick the Great and Bismarck did Prussia and Germany compare with France.'

Okhrana: according to Nicolai, it had agents in all European capitals working through military attachés, but mostly concerned with fugitives from the Czarist regime. It was almost impossible for Germany to place agents in Russia, so it was forced to rely on Jews, who were usually open to black-mail. 'Russia infected herself but they [Britain and France] kept their own people free from the poison of espionage and spread the contagion among neutral and hostile races, especially Germany and Austria–Hungary.' Turkey was a 'hopeless place' for Germany. The General Staff 'left it to the

Turks'. See also Ronald Hingley, *The Russian Secret Police*, Hutchinson, 1970.

8   Austria–Hungary: the Secret Service chief at the turn of the nineteenth century was Baron Max von Giesl. The head of counter-intelligence was Colonel Alfred Redl, who was alleged to have passed on Triple Alliance secrets to Russia, who generally passed them to France and Britain. Thus movements and contacts of Nolde, Musil, von Oppenheim, and other agents and staff officers were known to Okhrana, as was the Alliance battle plan at the outbreak of war. Von Giesl was succeeded by General August Urbanski von Ostromiecz, founding father of the 'Black Bureau' before the First World War. Nicolai, *Nachrichdienst*.

Persian Constitution, 5 Aug 1906: Kazemzadeh, *Russia and Britain in Persia*, and in Percy Sykes, *History of Persia*.

9   Young Turks: Lewis, *The Emergence of Modern Turkey*; 'Flowery Revolution', Herbert, *Ben Kendim*, 'glowing like a rose'. Other quoted refs from ibid. Old Constitution of Midhat, 1876, suspended 14 Feb 1878, Kinross, *The Ottoman Centuries*. 'Enver announces victory from balcony of Olympos Hotel, Salonica', July 1908, ibid.

Own cricketfield: the Embassy at Constantinople always had a keen but not very good cricket eleven. In 1885 the Royal Navy sent a team ashore which beat them soundly. Abdal Hamid wanted to bestow one of Turkey's highest decorations on the victors, but he was told the gesture 'was not in the spirit of the game'. He awarded them cigarettes and Turkish delight instead. See A. C. Wratislaw, *A Consul in the East*, Blackwood, 1924.

Zionism and Freemasonry: FO 800/193A (Lowther Papers), and FO 371/1249, dated respectively 29 May 1910 (Ambassador to Sir Charles Hardinge, private letter), and May 1911 (Ambassador to Foreign Secretary). In both documents Lowther argues in language that clearly owes much to his chief dragoman, Fitzmaurice, that the CUP has been taken over by a combination of Zionist and Masonic interests. The 1910 document was inspired by a telegram from Sir Eldon Gorst, the Resident in Cairo, to London, expressing alarm at the rumoured appointment of Muhammad Farid, a senior Committee politician, as delegate to the Egyptian Grand Lodge from the Constantinople Freemasons. He traced the descent of these influences from one Emannuele Carasso, 'a Jewish Mason of Salonika, deputy for that town in the Ottoman Chamber', who some years before had founded in his home town a Lodge known as *Macedonia Risorta*, 'in connection with Italian Freemasonry'. He added: 'Talaat Bey, the Minister of the Interior, who is of Gipsy descent . . . and Djavid Bey, the Minister of Finance, who is a Crypto-Jew, are the official manifestations of the occult power of the Committee. They are the only members of the Cabinet who really count, and are also at the apex of Freemasonry in Turkey.' Elie Kedourie (*Middle East Studies*, vol. 7, no. 1, Jan 1971) analysed the former document in some detail and dismissed the Lowther/Fitzmaurice accusations as 'fustian fantasies'. Kedourie writes: 'Anti-Ottoman prejudice more or less pronounced is a standing feature of British policy from the 1880s onwards.' And 'such fictions helped to persuade the British Government to fall for and to take up Zionism'. As Kedourie says, 'Clio is an ironic muse', but the irony lies in the fact that when the British Government came to embrace the Zionist cause in Palestine the only member of the Cabinet to oppose its policy was the single Jewish minister, Edwin Montagu. Professor Lewis, *The Emergence of Modern Turkey*, discounts the idea of a dominant Zionist influence in Constantinople.

9   Fitzmaurice: see Storrs, *Orientations*.

CUP leaders: Herbert, *Ben Kendim.* See also Sir Edwin Pears, Turcophile correspondent of the *Daily News*, whose *Turkey and its People*, London, 1911, and *Forty Years in Constantinople*, 1916, are mines of information.

10   Christian persecution: Adana massacres, 1908, see Winstone, *Gertrude Bell*, pp. 119–20, actions of Major Doughty-Wylie. See also Arminius Vambery, *Freiheitliche Bestrebung im Moslimischen Asien*, Berlin, 1893, n.a. in English, and *The Coming Struggle for India*, Cassell, 1885. Records of his correspondence with Lord Salisbury and permanent officials in Whitehall from 1899 to 1911 are retained by the Foreign Office. For an account of Vambery as scholar, spy, traveller and soldier of fortune, see L. Alder and R. Dalby, *The Dervish of Windsor Castle*, Bachman & Turner, 1979. By 1900 Herzl and Vambery had Secret Service code names, *Dori* and *Schlesinger*, in British Foreign Office files. See W. N. Medlicott, 'The Near Eastern Crisis, 1875–8, Reconsidered', *Middle East Studies*, vol. VII, no. 1, Jan 1971, in his review of M. D. Stojanovic, *The Great Powers and the Balkans*, 1875–1878, CUP, 1939, quotes Gladstone, 'the one great anti-human specimen of humanity', which needs qualification in the light of modern research.

Anglo-Russian Convention : CAB 37/97–8. Anglo-Russian policy on Persia: CAB 37/99–100.

Influence of Freemasonry: from Sir Percy Sykes, *History of Persia*, it seems that Prince Malkom Khan, sometime Persian Ambassador in London, founded the country's first Masonic lodge in the 1860s, *Faramush Khana* or the house of Forgetfulness. The Prince was dismissed as Ambassador following the visit of the Shah to London in 1889 (the Shah was conducted by Vambery on his journey to the capital). From then on Malkom Khan edited the influential journal *Kanun* in London. He was joined in 1896 by a fellow Freemason, who was the father of the Persian constitutional movement, Sayid Jamal ad Din. Sayid Jamil was handed over to the Turks following the assassination of the Shah Nasr in 1896, for complicity in the crime, but he escaped to join Malkom Khan in London. The Shah's English physician, Dr Hugh Adcock, seems to have been influential in these matters. For relations between Herzl, Vambery and the Ottoman and British Governments see also Amos Elon, *Herzl*, New York, 1975, Herzl's diaries, *Tagebucher*, 3 vols, Vienna, 1922–3 and Stewart, *Theodor Herzl.*

Freemasons in India, Mesopotamia and Turkey: *Thacker's Indian Directory* and the *Bengal Freemason's Almanac* show the District Grand Master for all the east from 1873 to be Stephen Scouloudi, resident in Turkey. In 1894 the Duke of Connaught became Grand Master for Bombay. The Turkish connection is not mentioned after 1898. In 1903 Kitchener became Grand Master of the Punjab lodges.

11 Masonic connections of Shaikh Khazal: see Najdat Fathi Safwat, 'Freemasonry in the Arab World', *Arab Papers*, no. 4, Arab Research Centre, services as 'Grand Master of Iraq'. He enjoyed great influence over tribes of southern Iraq and among Shi'ite Mujahaddin. It is worthy of note that when the British Resident in the Persian Gulf, Sir Lewis Pelly, went to Riyadh in 1865 to meet the Amir, Faisal the Great, he reported, 'and from something which occurred, I could not but presume that he was a Freemason'. Pelly was himself a Mason and it is unlikely that he would have mistaken a sign. Yet it must be regarded as improbable that the strict and orthodox Wahhabi leader had been introduced to the mysteries while a prisoner in Constantinople between 1838 and 1843. See Pelly, *Report on a Journey to Riyadh in Central Arabia*, and *GJ*, vol. 145, no. 1, March 1979, review, p. 138.

Ibn Saud, titular leader: Bray, *Shifting Sands*, and L/P & S/7/248, Shakespear to Resident, 8 April 1911.

Hajji Ali Kuli Khan and Khazal: Sir Percy Sykes, *History of Persia*, May 1909. At this time Britain made a 'final' loan to the new Shah of £100,000 from Indian funds. Morley, 'no further advances', L/P & S/10/334. In December of the same year, faced with a further request for money, Sir Richmond Richie, US/S at the India Office, wrote in a marginal note: 'It will be very easy and not unreasonable for Indian politicians to ask why they should pay for the security in Persia of a constitutional system strictly denied to themselves.' L/P & S/10/334.

12 Nolde: *Reise nach Innerarabien, Kurdistan und Armenien.*

'constable': Doughty, *Arabia Deserta*. For history of Rashids of Hail see Lorimer, *Gazetteer*, and Musil, *Northern Najd*, 'The House of Ibn Rashid'.

Occupation of Al Hasa: overland force led by young Mubarak of Kuwait, aided by Khazal and Sayid Talib al Naqib of Basra. Sea invasion led by Mubarak's father, Abdullah ibn Sabah. Musil, *Northern Najd*.

Nolde: returned home via Mesopotamia, Kurdistan and Armenia, according to own account. Death at Long's Hotel, Monday 11 March *The Times*, 12 March 1895.

Death of Muhammad ibn Rashid: Musil, *Northern Najd*.

Flight of Al Saud family to Kuwait: ibid., p. 244, and Lorimer, *Gazetteer*.

Mubarak's role in last years of nineteenth century: ambivalent according to Lorimer, *Gazetteer*. Having helped to bring down Saud's kingdom and conspired with Ibn Rashid, he now gave succour to the refugee princes. The Royal Navy commander in the Gulf, Commander Baker, reported after Mubarak's accession that Kuwait was 'greatly under Turkish influence'. Britain's own position was just as equivocal. British told Shaikh he should acknowledge Turkish suzerainty, according to Lorimer, ibid.

Murder of British official, Jask: Mr Graves 1896, ibid.

Activities of Russia, Germany and Turkey: ibid.

12   French archaeological concession, May 1897: ibid.

German rail concession: CAB 37/44. Began work same year, Lorimer, *Gazetteer*.

Russian consul Isfahan, 1897: ibid.

'Mubarak turned in vain': ibid.

Officer of 'special ability': Krougloff. Ibid.

13   Threatened invasion of Kuwait: ibid.

Sir Frank Lascelles and Kaiser: Gertrude Bell, at her uncle's side during the celebrations which marked Queen Victoria's Diamond Jubilee, wrote, 'heard references to Crete . . . Bulgaria . . . Serbia . . . mobilisation'. The Empress kept looking at the Kaiser anxiously – 'she is terribly perturbed about it all . . . he is persuaded that we are all on the brink of war'. See Winstone, *Gertrude Bell*, p. 50. CAB 37/47, Lascelles's conversation with Kaiser.

Treaty with Kuwait, 6 Feb 1899: signed by acting Resident, Colonel Mead, for Britain, based on Oman treaty of 20 March 1891. Lorimer, *Gazetteer*.

Russian rail scheme: Russia joined the railroad race in 1898 by submitting a counter application to the Porte for a line from Syrian Tripoli to Kuwait in the name of Count Kapnist, On 19 Jan 1900 a German commission led by von Steinrich, Consul-General at Jerusalem, visited Kuwait but found Shaikh Mubarak 'uncooperative'. Von Steinrich told the British Consul at Basra, A. C. Wratislaw, that it was for the Porte to decide, not Mubarak. Lorimer, *Gazetteer*, and Rosen, *Aus einem diplomatischen Wanderleben*, who quotes Lansdowne's biographer, Lord Newton, as saying that Britain acceded to the German claim in order to undermine the Russian plan to build a line from Erivan to Baghdad and on to the Gulf. Newton, according to Rosen, said that a joint meeting between Foreign, War and India Office officials decided that 'the worst eontingency was a Russian line'.

Shaikh Mubarak's subsidy, Anglo-Kuwait treaty: Lorimer, *Gazetteer*.

Gilyak: ibid.

Curzon/O'Conor: ibid.

O'Conor appointed Ambassador to Porte 1 July 1898: FO List and CAB 37/47.

Curzon refused: L/P & S/18 (B164).

14   'No entanglement with Wahabees': quote from telegrams from Sir Nicholas O'Conor to India Office, 6–26 February 1904, which became the war cry of Edward Parkes, US/S FO and other permanent officials in the conflict with the India Office. L/P & S/18/B200.

Abdal Aziz ibn Rashid: Musil, *Northern Najd*. His first act was to release Saudi prisoners at Riyadh, some of whom, members of the Saud family known as the *Araif*, had ambitions of their own and turned on their liberator, and were largely the cause of strife between Abdal Aziz ibn Rashid and Abdal Aziz ibn Saud.

14   Gertrude Bell: *Arab Bulletin*, vol. 1, no. 5, Oct 1916.

Shamiyah: eastern desert, west of lower Euphrates.

Sadun Pasha and Muntafiq: Bell, *Arab Bulletin*, no. 43, 28 Feb 1917.

Battle of Sarif: 17 March 1901. Lorimer, *Gazetteer*. See also Troeller, *The Birth of Saudi Arabia*. Consul Wratislaw at Basra reported arrival of troops in 'Spring', under General Muhammad Pasha Daghestani, VI Army Corps, intending to march on Kuwait. Mehsin Pasha, Wali of Basra, dissuaded.

15   Sayid Talib, Mubarak and Sadun Pasha: see Lorimer, *Gazetteer*, and L/P & S/10/586, Sir Henry Dobbs.

August, 1901, Turks mass at Basra: HMS *Perseus* prevented incursion. Germans and Turks protested to FO. Lorimer, *Gazetteer*. Panic in Kuwait, Sept, R/15/1/471. 9 Sept, Anglo-Turkish agreement to maintain *status quo* in Kuwait and Gulf, Lorimer, *Gazetteer*. 28 Sept, Rashid force leaves Kuwait. According to Musil, *Northern Najd*, p. 281, Ibn Rashid's concentration at Kuwait weakened his position around Riyadh and facilitated uprisings, and the 'unostentatious' return of Ibn Saud to the capital.

Seizure of Riyadh: innumerable literary accounts, but little official reference. Passing reference in L/P & S/18/B164, report of Jan 1908 – Wahabees, and L/P & S/20/239, Kuwait affairs.

Wahhabi House of Saud: the term Wahhabi (spelt variously, but correctly with two aspirates) is not liked by the Saudis themselves. They use the name *Muwahiddun* ('Unitarian') for the puritanical version of the faith which was taught in Najd by Muhammad ibn Abdal Wahhab from about 1740. See Appendix A, p. 365.

Events of 1902: January, Turks take Safwan etc., Lorimer, *Gazetteer*. RN force landed, ibid.

'Amir of Najd': L/P & S/18/B164.

Viceroy: ibid.

March, Ibn Rashid asked: Lorimer, *Gazetteer*.

Kuwait, attempted *coup*: ibid., 3 Sept.

HMS *Lapwing*: ibid., 5 Sept.

FO/IO debate and O'Conor's injunction: L/P & S/18/B164, Jan 1908 – Wahabees, and L/P & S/18/B200 (FO memo from Mr Edward Parkes). And IO Home Correspondence, vol. 250, Morley to Cox, May 1907.

16   FO Memo on Persian Gulf: in L/P & S/81/B166, 12 Feb 1908.

2   **Footprints in the Desert**

17   Gertrude Bell in Jerusalem: *Letters of Gertrude Bell*, ed. Lady Bell.
Rosen: ibid.

Hogarth: ibid., 17 March 1899, Athens.

17   Hijaz railway: see W. L. Ochsenwald, *Arabian Studies*, III, 1976, and Cassar, *Kitchener*. Work began Jan 1900, funds being subscribed by world Islamic communities.

RGS and MO4: although there was never an official connection, an obvious identity of interest existed from the earliest days of the War Office Topographical Department. The Society's first professional draghtsman, W. J. Turner, was appointed in 1878 (see G. S. Holland, *GJ*, vol. 146, no. 2, July 1980) but the map room made useful acquisitions from its inception in 1830. Gertrude Bell and other Arabian travellers in the first decade of twentieth century received instruction from the map curator, E. A. Reeves. Doubtless Hogarth suggested professional training in survey techniques, as with Lawrence and other pupils. See Winstone, *Gertrude Bell*, p. 106.

18   Al Bessam: ibid., pp. 127–9.

19   Training Ottoman army and Syrian garrisons: see Murphy, *Soldiers of the Prophet*.

Musil: see list of his works in Bibliography. Also *Oesterreichisches Biographisches Lexicon*, and *Encycl. Judaica*. Reference is made in the latter work to Musil's deficiency in archaeological scholarship. He had made minor journeys as a student in Transjordania (1896) and Petraea and Palmyra (1897–8) before setting out on the first of his voyages of discovery and espionage in 1908.

20   Mark Sykes: he had visited the Middle East as a youth, travelling with his father, the eccentric Sir Tatton Sykes, to Jerusalem, the Hauran desert and Damascus in 1890; and to Jerusalem and the Druse mountains in 1897. See Adelson, *Mark Sykes*.

Britain, Turkey and Ibn Saud: L/P & S/18/B164 and B200, FO to IO, a summary of the edicts governing relations with Ibn Saud.

21   Lansdowne to S/S India: R/15/5/59. For ensuing correspondence between Colonel Knox, Political Agent Kuwait, the Resident Bushire and Foreign Department Simla, see above file and R/15/5/24.

Aaronsohn: *Reliquiae Aaronsohnianae*, Genève, Imprimerie Jent SA, 1931, 'Documents biographiques'.

23   Herzl: see Stewart, *Theodor Herzl* and Mandel, *The Arabs and Zionism before World War I*. Herzl died 3 July 1904.

Herzl and Joseph Chamberlain: see Meinertzhagen, *Middle East Diary*, discussion, 15 Oct 1902. There is little official documentation of these matters, but it is almost certain that when he referred to 'Mesopotamia' Chamberlain meant the Saudi coastal district of Al Hasa, which according to Turkish maps was part of the administrative district of Basra in Mesopotamia at the time.

Abdal Hamid to de Newlinski: Mandel, *The Arabs and Zionism*.

Aaronsohn's journey: *Reliquiae*, 'Voyage de 1904, autour de la Mer Morte et en Transjordanie'.

24   Carruthers: see his *Arabian Adventure*; correspondence and notes in pos-

session of author. Journeys in central Asia and biographical notes, see Professor Owen Lattimore, 'Douglas Carruthers Memorial Lecture', *GJ*, vol. 144, no. 2, July 1978.

25 Gertrude Bell and Carruthers, see Carruthers, *Arabian Adventure*, p. 86n.

Gertrude Bell in Syria: see Bell, *Letters*.

Gertrude Bell and Sykes: see Adelson, *Mark Sykes*, and Bell, *Letters*, 3 Feb 1905, from Ramleh.

Bani Sakhr: Gertrude Bell, *Letters*, 11 Feb from Tneib.

26 Letters from Umm al Rumanin: 3 March–16 May 1905.

Percy Loraine: unpublished letter from Gertrude Bell, in author's possession.

Aubrey Herbert: see *Ben Kendim*, and Storrs, *Orientations*.

'activity at edges': most of the journeys by British Embassy staff at this time, supplemented by the Consuls at Damascus, Jerusalem and elsewhere, were connected with the WO *Report on Syria*, which was published a year later as an intelligence and General Staff guide.

Aaronsohn: *Reliquiae*, 'Voyage de 1905, avec M. le Dr M. Blanckenhorn le long de la ligne du Chemin de Fer du Hedjaz'.

27 Herbert in Yemen: see *Ben Kendim*, and Storrs, *Orientations*.

Dogs of Stamboul: Herbert, *Ben Kendim*, and Rosen, *Aus einem diplomatischen Wanderleben*.

28 Yemen, 1905–6: Italy had opened a Consulate at Hodeida in Jan 1904 (FO 195/2174). At the beginning of March 1905 Italy threatened war if the Porte did not stop Yemeni piracy against Italian ships (FO 195/2198). On 24 March Colonel Maunsell reported to London the mobilisation of the Joan of Arc brigade in Constantinople to fight in Yemen.

Menakah and Sanaa: Herbert, *Ben Kendim*.

Caprotti: agent of Florio Rubattino, Italian shipping line which began service from Genoa to Aden, calling at Hodeida, Nov 1907 (FO 195/2286). Used to take enlisted Yemenis to Eritrea. There were disturbances at Hodeida in Sept 1907 during the visit of the Englishmen, and the Italians, determined to underline their German-backed authority in the area, sent a gunboat to the port. FO 195/2254.

Journey to Muscat, Mesopotamia and Syria: Herbert, *Ben Kendim*.

Aaronsohn: *Reliquiae*, 'Un Voyage au Djôlàn en 1906'.

29 Dr Torrance: astronomer and all-round scientist. Host to Aaronsohn family, Gertrude Bell, T. E. Lawrence and other travellers. See Stewart, *T. E. Lawrence*, and Knightley and Simpson, *Secret Lives*.

30 Discovery of wild wheat: *Reliquiae*, 'Documents biographiques', p. 28, 'La decouverte du *Tritticum dicoccoides*'. See *Bulletin de la Société botanique de Genève*, vol. 22, 1930, and index to comment in scientific press in *Reliquiae*, H. R. Oppenheimer, 'Florula Transiordanica'.

30   Leachman: born 27 July 1880. See Bray, *Paladin.*

Letter to King: 16 April 1900. Leachman, *Diary*, MEC, Oxford.

Journey in Tibet, 1905: Bray, *Paladin.*

31   Leachman diary: 'Even at this time he was guarded in reference to important matters', Bray, *Paladin.* Leachman had spent several months at the
intelligence office, Staff HQ Simla, before leaving for home.

Voyage of German ship, *Candia:* see Lorimer, *Gazetteer*, and Murphy, *Soldiers of the Prophet.*

Beauchamp Duff to DMO: R/15/5/55. Reply: 'Major-General Ewart
personally in favour of proposal to explore but necessary to seek Treasury
approval', 18 March 1907. IO to DMO: 'Secretary of State not in favour of
proposal to undertake exploration of Najd interior at present time', 9 April
1907.

Ittihad ve Teraki: Herbert, *Ben Kendim.* For a balanced view see also
Kedourie, *England and the Middle East*, Lewis, *The Emergence of Modern Turkey*, and Kinross, *The Ottoman Centuries.*

32   Limpus naval mission: see McLaughlin, *Escape of the Goeben.*

War games: ADM 116. These had been going on since Sept 1906, when
Admiral E. W. Slade, Captain of the War College, prepared a paper which
was followed by a secret report on the Dardanelles (Dec 1906). The WO
view was that the fleet could not give sufficient protection to a landing force
and that the operation should not be attempted in the event of war. The
Admiralty believed that the WO underestimated the 'extent and value of
naval assistance'. In 1908 a series of war plans was set out, including: England and France v. Germany, England v. Triple Alliance, and England v.
Germany and the United States.

Zionist office in Palestine: opened at Jaffa under management of Dr A.
Ruppin, see Philip Graves, *Land of Three Faiths*, p. 161.

Arab societies: See Tibawi, *Anglo-Arab Relations.* Advent of Zionism coincided with Arab demands in Syria. Young Turks began to attack Arab language. An open society known as *Lamarkaziyya* was formed, along with the
secret organisations Ahad (military) and Fattah (civil). Ahad and Fattah subsequently merged. See also Longrigg, *Iraq, 1900–1950*, pp. 1–40. After the
Young Turk revolution Mesopotamian deputies formed a clique under the
banner of a literary club, *Muntada al Adabi.* CUP produced 'own ruling
elite, with aims of centralization, discipline ... Not encouraging for
Greeks, Armenians, Arabs and Jews who constituted the majority of inhabitants of the Empire.'

Anglo-French naval discussions: McLaughlin, *Escape of the Goeben.*

Butler and Aylmer: see paper by Captain S. S. Butler to RGS in *GJ*, vol. 33,
no. 5, May 1909. Following the lecture, Dr Hogarth remarked 'he certainly
has wiped one white spot off the map', and Colonel Maunsell observed that
the journey had 'completed the line from Maan ... across to Baghdad'.
Another staff officer, Colonel C. E. Yate, referred to the possibility of a rail

connection over the path of Butler and Aylmer, running from Suez to Basra. *Note*: Butler and Leachman served together in India and visited Kashmir together before Butler went on special duty to Africa.

33 Murder of Mitab ibn Abdal Aziz al Rashid and his brothers: the story as told to Butler and Aylmer is repeated in substantially the same terms in Musil, *Palmyrena*, p. 19, and *Northern Najd*, History of the House of Ibn Rashid.

34 Arrived Damascus 25 Feb 1908: Butler, *GJ*.

Aaronsohn's journey: *Reliquiae*, 'Expédition à la Mer Morte et en Trans-jordanie faite au printemps de l'année 1908'.

Mutiny of Ottoman army and Anglo-Russian meeting at Reval, 9–10 June 1908: see Lewis *The Emergence of Modern Turkey*.

'Orient and Occident': Blanckenhorn, *Syrien und die deutsche Arbeit*. A distinguished geologist, Dr Blanckenhorn wrote several books on the mineral deposits of Egypt and Syria after 1891.

Howaitat tribe: these are two distinct divisions of the tribe; one occupying an extensive desert region of eastern Syria (Transjordania) and often straying as far north as the Euphrates, under the belligerent leadership of Shaikh Auda abu Tayya; the other roaming in Tor or southern Sinai, the Howaitat al Tihama, their camp being on the Red Sea coast, south of Imran. Uniquely among the Arab tribes their women are not obliged to wear the face mask, the *burqa*, though they usually did so. See Murray, *Sons of Ishmael*. But the Howaitat women were far from free of marital burdens. Musil often heard the cry *Ya zoja fik rukabti:* 'Oh husband, give my neck a rest', Musil, *Arabia Deserta*. Marriage in the tribe was indissoluble. If a man was caught *in flagrante* with another's wife, both guilty partners had to die. Ibid.

35 Avshalom Feinberg: *Encycl. Judaica*.

Aaronsohn and other visitors to Dr Torrance at Tiberias: see *Reliquiae*, 'Documents biographiques', Stewart, *T. E. Lawrence*, and Knightley and Simpson, *Secret Lives*.

Aaronsohn in America: *Encycl. Judaica*, and article by Alexandra Lee Levin in *Hadassah*, March 1977. See also *Reliquiae*, correspondence with Dr David Fairchild and letter from William C. Bullitt, 9 April 1920.

36 Musil 1908–9: see *Palmyrena*. Before setting out he had consultations in Beirut with the Austrian Consul, Herr M. Gregovich, and at Damascus with the Vice-Consul, Herr Franz Zitterer.

3 The Seeds of Revolt

37 Musil, 1909: see *Palmyrena*, pp. 19–21, and *Arabia Deserta*, American Geog. Soc. edn, Oriental Explorations and Studies, no. 2, 1927, p. 154ff.

39 Austrian arms for Arabs, and Indian Government's anxiety: see notes from

Shakespear's diary in Winstone, *Shakespear,* and Musil, *Arabia Deserta,* p. 47ff.

40 Homicidal dynasty of Al Rashid: during the discussion which followed Captain Butler's paper to the RGS on 22 Feb 1909, David Hogarth remarked: 'But, after all, what has any Eastern Sultan done? One hundred years ago the same was done in Constantinople. I should not score it very heavily against the Rashid family, considering how far they are away from civilization, that they still maintain that well-established Eastern custom.' *GJ,* May 1909. None the less, the blood lust of the Rashids was unique even in the east.

Songs of the badawin: the following are my own translations from Musil's mixture of German and Arabic – *author.*

HE: My beauty, I give thee the moon.
(Taking a coin from his shirt)
With this I buy thee
The crescent moon.

SHE: O Wolf (imitating the *samun,* the hot southerly wind)
Thou who drives away the south wind
Speak to me –
Speak my love.
I cannot imitate
The north wind.
Forgive me –
Forgive me, my love.
(She tries to imitate the *shimal,* the biting sand-laden north wind.)

The north wind
Whose eyes are insolent
Like Ali's and Abu Zaid's
And the fine folk's at the castle.
Embrace me –
Embrace me, my love.
Speak to me, O Wolf!

41 In 1907 the Royal Academy of Sciences in Vienna had published Dr Musil's massively documented *Arabia Petraea* in three volumes, dedicated to 'Their Royal Highnesses the Emperor and Empress, and the Princes and Gentlemen of Austria, Hungary and Bohemia'. This work embraced his journeys of 1896–1902. His later journeys were intended to provide a complete trigonometric survey of northern Arabia, but the task proved impossible in the time and with the resources available. See preface to *Arabia Deserta.*

Hogarth: obituary notice in *GJ,* vol. 71, no. 4, April 1928, 'A Memoir' by C. R. L. Fletcher. 'Hogarth was never *simpatico* to governments, officials or politicians, and, for one who professed the creed of "Liberalism", his contempt for democracy, as expressed in his letters, is distinctly strong, and is by no means confined to the absurdity of introducing it among backward peoples.'

41   'men in the lump': ibid.

Palmer expedition: see Sir Walter Besant, *The Life and Achievements of Edward Henry Palmer*, John Murray, 1883; and C. 3494, HMSO 1883. Correspondence respecting the murder of Professor E. H. Palmer, Captain William Gill, RE, and Lieutenant Harold Charrington, RN. Gill was an exceptionally able and courageous intelligence officer in central Asia before joining the intelligence staff in London. After his death the RGS struck a 'Gill Memorial medal', and among its recipients were Colonel Maunsell (1905) and Leachman (1912).

Professor Denison Ross: see Winstone, *Gertrude Bell*, and Adelson, *Mark Sykes*.

Gertrude Bell: Winstone, *Gertrude Bell*.

42   Hogarth family connections: see Janet Hogarth, (Mrs J. E. Courtney) *Recollected in Tranquillity*, London, 1926, and *An Oxford Portrait Gallery*, London, 1931.

Hogarth and Chirol: Chirol Papers, Department of Oriental Studies, Durham University; and Hogarth Papers, MEC, Oxford (biographical notes).

Chirol and Hardinge: Winstone, *Gertrude Bell*, and Chirol and Hogarth Papers. See also Hardinge Papers, University Library, Cambridge.

43   Lawrence in Levant: arrived Beirut 6 July 1909. See Stewart, *T. E. Lawrence*, and Knightley and Simpson, *Secret Lives*.

Pirie-Gordon: Knightley and Simpson, *Secret Lives*.

Lawrence and Woolley: Aldington, *Lawrence of Arabia*, Stewart, *T. E. Lawrence*, and Knightley and Simpson, *Secret Lives*.

Sinai: from the British occupation of Egypt, 1882, a line was drawn from Suez to Rafa near Gaza on the Mediterranean coast. The region above that line was considered part of British-administered Egypt, the region below, bordering Ottoman Palestine, as far as Aqaba was considered part of the Ottoman administrative district of Al Kuds (Jerusalem). CAB 37/9 (Egypt). In 1906 agreement was reached with Turkey whereby the whole of the Sinai peninsula would be administered by Britain, but Turkey did not renounce sovereignty. In the same year Cromer ordered boundary posts to be erected from Rafa to Aqaba to mark off British zone. See letter from W. E. Jennings Bramley to Mrs Neame, 1953, MEC, Oxford. 'I was in command of southern Sinai,' says Jennings Bramley. CAB 37/83, Turco-Egyptian frontier.

Greek rebellions: 1897 and 1906.

Report on Arabia: published by WO in 1904, based largely on maps of Victorian travellers. *Report on Syria*, 1906, prelude to detailed handbooks on all parts of Ottoman Empire, including study of 'Defence of Constantinople' by Maunsell, published in 1911. The Ottoman General Staff with its German advisers began preparation of detailed maps and topographical studies at same time. Under new DMO, Major-General Spencer Ewart, *Report on Syria* was updated in 1911 by Lieutenant Pirie-Gordon and Captain Smith.

43 Purposes of Hogarth's expedition: see Clayton, *Diary of a Mission to Ibn Saud.*

44 Baghdad railway: CAB 37/87.

Sir Gerard Lowther: Stewart, *T. E. Lawrence,* 'Several applications to Porte'. Ambassador, Sir Nicholas O'Conor, died in his office in June 1908 and was succeeded by Sir Gerard A. Lowther in July.

Jerablus lease: purchased by Layard. FO library.

Lawrence thesis: Knightley and Simpson, *Secret Lives.* Lane-Poole was working at Oxford at the time. He had been Professor of Arabic at Trinity College, Dublin.

Lawrence at Safed: ibid., and Stewart, *T. E. Lawrence.* Accounts differ slightly in detail.

'German tramp': Stewart, *T. E. Lawrence.*

'Palestine was a decent country . . .': ibid.

45 Gertrude Bell: *Letters,* 12 March 1905.

Pirie-Gordon: Stewart, *T. E. Lawrence.*

Letter held back: to Leonard Green, ibid.

Lawrence's patriotism and politics: see Knightley and Simpson, *Secret Lives,* pp. 22–7, knights of the 'Round Table' an influential group which included the Prime Minister, the editor of *The Times,* Lord Milner, and Lionel Curtis, 'who later became a close friend of Lawrence's' and was regarded as 'racist and a Francophobe'.

46 Leachman: Bray, *Paladin.* See also Bray's *Shifting Sands* for ref. to journey to Riyadh.

FO ban on travel: L/P & S/18/B200.

Morley to Viceroy: Cox, Resident at Bushire, had told Simla, 'authoritative reply necessary to protect my own reputation'. IO Home Corresp., vol. 250, 9 Nov 1906–May 1907, and L/P & S/18/B164, Jan 1908.

Zamil ibn Subhan: Musil, *Northern Najd,* p. 247ff.

47 Ibn Rashid and Ibn Saud: ibid.

For detailed account of the dispute at this time between India and FO, see Busch, *Britain, India and the Arabs.*

Percy Cox to Knox: IO Home Corresp., vol. 250, and Winstone, *Shakespear,* p. 67.

McDouall to Knox: IO R/15/5/59.

Contact with German agents: IO R/15/5/64, 21 Aug 1907.

Knox and Cox, July 1907–Sept 1908: ibid.

48 Captain Shakespear: Winstone, *Shakespear,* and Lacey, *The Kingdom,* ch. 10.

48   Jask telegraph station: IO R/15/5/55.

Ovseenko: Lorimer, *Gazetteer*.

Rich: see his *Narrative of a Residence in Koordistan and on the Site of Ancient Nineveh etc.*, 1836, and Lloyd, *Foundations in the Dust*.

Shakespear in desert: Winstone, *Shakespear*.

49   Palgrave, W.G., quote: see his *Central and Eastern Arabia*, 1865.

Shakespear and yacht: see Sir Arnold Wilson, *Loyalties: Mesopotamia*. After observing Shakespear's seamanship from deck of a British-India liner on one occasion, Wilson remarked: 'Such men are the salt of the earth.'

Lewis Pelly: it seems that Shakespear used the running and repair costs for the Agency yacht to obtain funds for paying informants and friendly desert shaikhs. As early as July 1909 Morley in London was complaining about expenditure under the headings 'Contingencies' and 'Persia'. 'Special items cannot be included under Persia,' the Indian Government was told. L/P & S/10/69.

Leachman: see Bray, *Paladin*.

Leachman: ibid.

50   MO3: Leachman visited Haldane during leave in England, autumn 1910. See ibid., and H. St John Philby, 'The Legend of Lijman', UPM in MEC, Oxford. On the way to Basra Leachman was entertained by A. T. Wilson, Cox's deputy and by E. A. Soane, British agent in Persia and Kurdistan. Philby, UPM.

Letter home: 23 April 1910, Bray, *Paladin*.

Leachman's journey: see his account, 'Description of a Journey', *GJ*, vol. 37, no. 3, March 1911, pp. 265–74.

Carruthers: see his *Arabian Adventure*.

Leachman's biographer: quotation, Bray, *Paladin*.

52   Letter to Shakespear: Winstone, *Shakespear*.

54   Shakespear's exploratory notes and field work: travel notebooks recording every hour of every day for each of his journeys in Arabia are in the RGS archives in London. For details of intelligence work, see correspondence on secret maps, and fortifications etc, with Cdr Lichfield RN and Captain C. M. Gibbon, Simla, in IO R/15/5/55.

Attempt to poison Ibn Saud: R/15/5/25. See Winstone, *Shakespear*.

Claimants to throne: the offspring of Ibn Saud's uncle Saud (the elder brother of his father, Abdurrahman) and the children of Abdal Aziz ibn Saud (the only child of Uncle Saud with issue) were known to the family as *Al Araif*, 'the lost ones', a term used for camels of uncertain ownership. See Lacey, *The Kingdom*, p. 97. Saud ibn Abdal Aziz, the grandchild of Uncle Saud, married Ibn Saud's favourite sister, Nura, in an attempt to reconcile the two sides of the family, and her husband became known as Saud

Kabeer (the 'Great' or 'Senior'). According to Lacey, the purpose of the fleeing cousins in 1910 was to 'stir the Ajman' to revolt'.

54 Capture of Riyadh: this story has been told often, and with inevitable gradations of colour. It would be superfluous to repeat it here. The interested reader should see any of works in the Bibliography dealing with the Saudi kingdom.

55 Shakespear and Ibn Saud: L/P & S/7/238–48 and R/15/5/25.

Mubarak: following an interview between the Shaikh, Cox and Shakespear on 10 Aug 1909, in which he was asked how he thought he could come closer to Britain without rousing the suspicion of Constantinople, he was considered to be more reliable than hitherto. 'I will do anything,' said Mubarak. 'I will fly the Union Jack if you like.' R/15/5/59.

56 Mubarak compared with Richelieu: Lovat Fraser, editor, *Times of India*, quoted in Sir Arnold Wilson, *Loyalties: Mesopotamia*.

Presentation of sword: Nov 1903. Lorimer, *Gazetteer*.

Shakespear's report: L/P & S/7/248, to Resident 8 April 1911, and FO 371/1249 Najd Affairs, 29 May 1911.

Age of Ibn Saud: there are differences of opinion. Musil gives 1880 as his date of birth. Admiralty intelligence files (CB 1307) indicated 'about 40' in 1917. Lacey, *The Kingdom*, went into the matter in some detail, and favours 1876. Allowing for differences in the Islamic and Christian calendars some divergence could be expected, but not four years. Lacey quotes Abdal Aziz as saying, 'I swallowed four years of my age'. Shakespear's implied date, 1880, is the officially accepted one.

57 Battle of Rakhaimiya, 13 March 1910: Leachman, *GJ*, March 1911, and Philby, UPM. Also see Bray, *Paladin*.

Shakespear's warning: delivered with tongue in cheek, on instructions from 'Foreign' Simla. Shakespear recorded that Kuwait's prostitutes were expected to give coffee pots and bedding for the newly equipped army. Warning to Mubarak repeated an earlier injunction of Resident Kemball (1901) 'not to enter into any operations calculated to involve him in difficulties in Najd or with the Turks'. L/P & S/7/238–48. See Winstone, *Shakespear*. (*Note:* location of 1910 battle is given incorrectly as 'near Sarif' in my biography of Shakespear and in many other references, including those of Arab writers. Author).

58 Ajaimi ibn Sadun and Young Turks: L/P & S/10/586.

Sayid Talib: L/P & S/10/385, Shakespear to IO.

'inviolate pride': Bray, *Paladin*.

Carruthers: *Arabian Adventure*.

Musil: see his *The Northern Hijaz*, American Geog. Soc. edn, no. 1, 1926. Also *Oesterreichisches Biographisches Lexicon*.

Gibbon: both Gibbon and Maunsell were active fellows of the RGS, and they jointly proposed Shakespear for fellowship in 1914, but Shakespear's death prevented confirmation of his election.

58 Fraser Hunter: see 'Reminiscences of the Map of Arabia and the Persian Gulf', *GJ*, vol. 54, no. 5, Nov 1919.

Shakespear and Lorimer: Winstone, *Shakespear*.

59 Shakespear's contacts: the Kuwait Agency diaries for the entire period of his tenure have disappeared from the IO. Thus there is a serious gap in the record of one of the most important periods of Persian Gulf history which can only be made up in part by reference to the Residency records (R/15). Equally mysterious is the fact that the records of the Quarter-Master-General's intelligence department, Fort William, and of the DMO's and DMI's intelligence departments at Simla, Calcutta and Delhi were not recovered from India, according to IO officials, at the granting of independence. Presumably they were destroyed.

Shakespear's personal diaries: there is a note in the records of the Royal Geographical Society, probably in the hand of Douglas Carruthers, which suggests that Shakespear handed his diary(ies) to Lieutenant-Colonel C. C. R. Murphy in 1914 then GSO1 intelligence at Jask, before setting out on his last journey. No personal diaries have survived except his typed account of his trans-Arabian journey of 1914.

Lorimer and Crow: see L/P & S/10/225–52, Persian Gulf 1909–11, and L/P & S/10/437, Persian Gulf Residency.

Arms traffic: L/P & S/11/B196. See also Lorimer, *Gazetteer*.

Gibbon to Shakespear, 16 Sept 1909: R/15/5/55.

Gov. of India to Resident, 30 Sept 1909: R/15/5/55.

Gibbon to Shakespear, 4 Nov: 'Thanks for yours of 4 Oct. Much indebted.'

60 Craufurd: appointed GSO2 Jask, 27 March 1910. Mr Spurrier to author.

Meeting of Secret Service chiefs, Simla: see Bray, *Shifting Sands*.

61 'political Svengali': the dramatic spread of anarchist doctrine and attempts on the lives of prominent officials in India, Europe and even the United States in the first decade of the century worried most security chiefs at this time. The Proudhonist programme for the destruction of the state, actively promoted by Bakunin and Kropotkin and their followers, was doubtless in Cleveland's mind. So perhaps was the delegation of the Indian National Congress to the new Viceroy, Lord Hardinge, in Jan 1911.

Britain and Germany: 'Climate of uncertainty', see Aston, *Secret Service*, Bray, *Paladin*, and C. E. Callwell, *Field-Marshal Sir Henry Wilson, Life and Diaries*, London, 1927. Aston was Chief of Staff in South Africa at this time and General Haig had taken over the Staff in India. They 'swapped information' on India, South Africa and South West Africa, where German propaganda and infiltration were most intense. Wilson, who believed that war with Germany was inescapable, took over from Spencer Ewart as DMO in Aug 1910 and immediately began discussions with his friend, General Foch, in France. Mobilisation plans were complete by 1911. In that year MO1(d) took over India, Afghanistan, Persia and other parts of the east, and MO2(b) became responsible for Austria–Hungary, the Ottoman Empire and Arabia. Asquith distrusted the new DMO and Lloyd George despised him. The feeling was mutual. Few doubted that he was the most able staff officer in the British army.

61   Trouble in India: see Chirol, *Indian Unrest*.

'Wave of crime': Cassar, *Kitchener*.

Minto–Morley reforms: India Bill before parliament Feb 1909 enfranchised 'certain classes'. Morley: 'India not yet ready for Parliamentary initiatives'. *The Times*, Feb–March 1909. Regulations were issued by the Governor-General in Council in Nov; first elections were in 1909. *The Times*, Nov–Dec 1909.

Home Rule: in 1909 the British Cabinet considered a paper on self-government for Egypt (CAB 37/102), the India Bill was enacted, and Home Rule for Ireland began its legislative progress. (CAB 37/102–8), Home Rule Bill, 11 Dec 1911.

62   Attempt on Lord Hardinge's life, 23 Jan 1912: *The Times*, 24–5 Jan. Hardinge was appointed Viceroy in June 1910 but did not arrive in India until Nov, following Morley's resignation and the appearance of the Marquess of Crewe at the India Office. IO (Gen).

'beginning of the end of Empire': Herbert, *Ben Kendim*.

Bray and travel in Turkish Arabia and Asiatic Turkey: L/P & S/10/259. C-in-C to Jask (Intelligence): 'Officers of Indian Army can no longer visit Turkish Arabia to study the language.'

Damascus, Aug 1910: see Murphy, *Soldiers of the Prophet*, Bray, *Shifting Sands*, and Bell, *Letters*. See also Gertrude Bell's *Desert and the Sown*, ch. 7.

Druse war: Murphy, *Soldiers of the Prophet*, and Bray, *Shifting Sands*. *Note*: Bray was not on Indian Army 'special list' at this time. War Office *Army Lists* ceased to publish special duty assignments in 1909.

Druses: a constant thorn in the side of the Ottoman authority. In 1839 they put up a spirited resistance to Ibrahim Pasha of Egypt, who claimed the Viceroyalty of Syria, asserting their complete independence under their own 'theocratic leadership'. In 1852 they resisted the attempt of a Christian General of the Ottoman army, Kubrisli Pasha, to control them. In 1879 Midhat Pasha imposed a *kaimakam* or Governor from the Druse family of Atrash, but they refuses to pay taxes or to serve in the Ottoman Army. In 1896 they soundly defeated a Turkish army under Abdullah Pasha at Ezra, but soon after were subdued by the army of Tahir Pasha when they agreed to pay taxes but only to serve in the army as frontier guards. See journals of John Dickson, Consul Jerusalem (1892–1906), MEC, Oxford. Dickson describes them as 'Worldly, knowledgeable people who eschew bigamy'. Gertrude Bell, *Letters*, described them in 1905 as being especially interested in foreign affairs, saddened by the death of Salisbury, knowing Chamberlain by name and being much impressed by her fiscal theories. 'They all became Free Traders on the spot.' *Letters*, p. 164.

63 Mantle of Kitchener, Condor: Kitchener first went to Palestine in Nov 1874, to join his friend from the Royal Engineers, Lieutenant Claude Condor, who had already been working on the survey for two years. They covered 1,600 square miles in Philistia, Judaea and Lower Galilee; areas covered by both Newcombe and Aaronsohn and his companions in the early 1900s. See Cassar, *Kitchener*. In the Holy Land Kitchener displayed qualities of 'hard work, thoroughness, parsimony, organisation and diplomacy – which would bring him world-wide fame'.

Newcombe: see Murphy, *Soldiers of the Prophet*, pp. 12–13, also Lawrence, *Seven Pillars*. Some detail was given to the author by Colonel Newcombe's daughter, the Baroness Elles.

Palestine Exploration Fund: founded in 1865 at the wish of Queen Victoria to discover biblical sites and 'to repel . . . onslaught of contemporary scientists upon the foundations of organised religion'. But the War Office was keenly interested and ready to lend its engineers. Cassar, *Kitchener*.

64 Yahya Atrash: Murphy, *Soldiers of the Prophet*, p. 15. Yahya and other Druse leaders were confined on the island of Rhodes.

Gertrude Bell: *Letters*, p. 80ff., 3–11 May 1900.

65 Turkish communiqué and casualties: Murphy, *Soldiers of the Prophet*.

Description of Turkish army: R/15/5/50, and *Pioneer of India*, 20 Jan 1911.

Leveson and Knott: Murphy, *Soldiers of the Prophet*, p. 12. Major Leveson 18th Hussars, Captain Knott AVC.

66 Kerak affair: ibid.

67 Riots in Baghdad and Basra: a Turkish battalion was sent from Esdki-Sham, Syria, to reinforce the Basra garrison during the Druse conflict (ibid.). The trouble in Baghdad was put down by the police. Rebellion broke out in Kurdistan a few months late, FO 371/1249. Italian invasion of Tripoli and Cyrenaica in aftermath of Franco-German dispute in Morocco, Agadir crisis, May–Oct 1911, CAB 37/107.

Outbreaks in Yemen and Asir: FO 371/1249, report by Colonel L. O. F. Stack, DMI Cairo. The C-in-C India at this time sent out a warning to all governors of districts under the 'supervision of the Government of India', a definition which embraced the Gulf region in security terms, warning of the need for the 'utmost precaution in entertaining and talking to foreigners'. R/15/5/55.

Balkan ferment, 1909–11: CAB 37/99–108. See also Herbert, *Ben Kendim*.

Battle between Ibn Saud and Sharif of Mecca: L/P & S/7/245, Shakespear to Cox, 6 Nov 1910, and L/P & S/7/248, report from Shakespear, 8 April 1911. Reports in *Al Ahram*, Cairo, and *The Times of India*, 6 Oct–2 Nov 1910. Abdullah ibn Husain, with a force of 20,000 badawin was joined by Ibn Rashid at Shara for a combined attack. Ibn Saud was forced to pay some £4,500 for the release of his brother, with the promise of annual payments. And Ibn Saud was reported to have submitted to the Sharif, but he denied this to Shakespear.

67 Trucial States: *The Times of India*, 31 Dec 1910, 'Wahhabi to the core', and FO 371/1249, report by Admiral Sir Edmond Slade.

Gertrude Bell: *Letters*, p. 220ff. WO records show two reports on Syria from Miss Bell, dated 16 Jan 1911 from Beirut and 18 Jan from Damascus. Neither appears to be on the public file.

Von Hochwaechter: see Bray, *Shifting Sands*. Bray returned to Damascus in 1913 and met 'Major H——' on latter's return from the Balkan War where he served on the staff of Mukhtar Pasha. A Greek member of the International Club was blackballed by the Germans for wearing a 'fez'. Also see Murphy, *Soldiers of the Prophet*, and Aston, *The Secret Service*.

Bray and poison attempt: see *Shifting Sands*.

68 Leachman: returned to Baghdad on the old post road by *thalul*, racing camel. He recorded the fastest time ever by camel rider. Bray, *Paladin* and Philby, UPM.

Meetings with Al Ahad: Bray, *Shifting Sands*. Branches in towns and villages throughout Syria and Mesopotamia. 'Understanding reached with some of the most powerful Arab chiefs and tribes' and with 'Christian leaders' to free Arabian peninsula. Basra to be 'flash-point' of rebellion, 'for success a revolution must have a leader ... Ibn Saud was almost unanimously elected as the natural champion of the Arab peoples'.

Secret societies: for development of independence and nationalist movements from mid-nineteenth century see Antonius, *The Arab Awakening*. Tibawi, *Anglo-Arab Relations*, asserts that the impetus at this time came from the advent of Zionism as a political movement and the attack on the Arab language by the Young Turks after 1908. Leading figures in Al Ahad, the military wing of the underground movement, were Major Aziz Ali al Masri, a staff officer in the Ottoman army, and a 20-year-old student at the military academy in Constantinople, Muhammad Sharif al Faruqi, whose family claimed descent from the second Khalifa, Omar ibn al Khattab. See Tibawi, *Anglo-Arab Relations*. At about this time, also, *Lamarkaziyya*, the Decentralisation Party, came into prominence; it was a reformist organisation based in Cairo whose leading light was Rashid Rida, an Islamic thinker who hailed from Beirut. See ibid., and Mandel, *Arabs and Zionism before World War I*. From the elections to the new Ottoman Assembly, Dec 1908, Iraqi politicians 'formed a clique with Syrian deputies', which gave rise to the 'literary club' Al Muntada al Adabi, which became the precursor of the civil wing of the movement. See Longrigg, *Iraq, 1900–1950*, p. 41ff.

'looked to Britain': Clayton, *An Arabian Diary*, 'Britain best of several poor choices'.

Shakespear and Ibn Saud at Thaj: FO 371/1249 and L/P & S/7/248, Shakespear to Cox, 8 April 1911.

69 Shakespear's journey: Winstone, *Shakespear*.

Lawrence on Shakespear, quote: *Seven Pillars*, Penguin edn, p. 266.

Kuwait borders: L/P & S/18/B166, FO memo, 12 Feb 1908. Turkish maps of the period were never very exact, but they usually labelled the Al Hasa coastal region as 'Najd'. Central Arabia from the Empty Quarter to the border of Kasim and Jabal Shammar (Ibn Rashid's territory) was simply regarded as a district of the vilayet of Basra (or at times of Baghdad) under a Mutasarif or local governor.

70　Asir and Yemen: Idrisi, an upstart 'deliverer', began attack on Asir and Turkish strongholds in Yemen in 1909. Asiri capital of Abha was cut off. End of 1910: Imam Yahya of Yemen attacked Sanaa, but revolt collapsed and Yahya concluded an agreement with Turks. June 1911: Turkish force was heavily defeated by Idrisi army, but in July joint Turkish–Sharifian force relieved Abha. FO 371/1249, and Musil, *Northern Najd*, pp. 282–3, 'Muhammad ibn Ali al-Idrisi, the founder of the independent state of al-Asir, sought Ibn Saud's friendship and help as early as 1910. The latter sent him some Ikhwan, who occupied some important settlements in northern al-Asir.' See note to p. 71, 'Ikhwan'.

Ibn Saud and Sharifian attack: see Musil, *Northern Najd*, p. 284, and L/P & S/7/248, Shakespear's report, based on conversation with Ibn Saud in 1911. See also *Arabian Report*, 1 March 1916 (in L/P & S/10/586): Sharif sent son 'to fish in troubled waters'.

'Amir of Arabia'. see *The Times*'s reports Oct–Nov 1910, quoting *Al Ahram* of Cairo, and FO 371/1249.

71　Dr C. S. G. Mylrea: *The Near East*, 11 May 1917.

Gertrude Bell: *Arabian Report*, ed. Lieut. Cozens-Hardy, 1 March 1916.

Shakespear on Ibn Saud: travel diary dept during journey of 1914, in possession of author.

Doughty: *Arabia Deserta*.

Musil on Ikhwan: 'Abdal Aziz ibn Saud in 1908 founded the settlement of al-Artawiya . . . Calling themselves Ikhwan (Brethren) they bound themselves to the observance of religious duties and to indefatigable struggle against all enemies of the *muwahhedin*, the true believers.' *Northern Najd*, p. 283.

Shakespear on Ibn Saud: FO 371/1249.

Shakespear on House of Al Saud: conquests of Ibrahim Pasha, 1811–18; conquests of Turki ibn Saud, 1824–34; rivalry of Saud and Abdullah, 1865–87; Ibn Rashid's occupation, 1897–1901. See Lorimer, *Gazetteer*.

72　Shakespear and Ibn Saud at Thaj: L/P & S/7/248 and FO 371/1249.

Ibn Saud's fears: invasion of Al Hasa in 1871, ordered by Midhat Pasha the Wali of Baghdad, when he had won support of Muntafiq tribe of Lower Euphrates, led by Nasser ibn Sadun. Musil, *Northern Najd*.

Sayid Talib: Lorimer, *Gazetteer*, pp. 972–94. The Turks offered Mubarak of Kuwait control of Al Hasa in 1904 if he would effect a settlement between Ibn Saud and Ibn Rashid. Sayid Talib ruled for a second term, 1903–5, in which time he plundered the home of one of the Gulf's richest merchants, Haji Mansur Pasha, and imprisoned his son. Even Abdal Hamid found Talib's excesses too much for his own political good.

Bandar–Shuwaikh Lease, 1907: Lorimer, *Gazetteer*.

73   Anglo-Turkish discussions: IO EUR D (Hirtzel Papers). See also Troeller, *The Birth of Saudi Arabia.*

Sir Arthur Nicolson, US/S: FO diary 7 June 1911 in FO 371/1249.

Union of Arab leaders: Clayton, *Diary*, p. 19, 'Sir Percy Cox urged the Foreign Office to follow up Ibn Saud's overtures, but Whitehall knew little of Arabia and cared less.'

Attitudes of FO/IO: FO 371/1249.

4   The Lion and the Eagle

75   'Deutschland über Allah': McLaughlin, *Escape of the Goeben.*

Anglo-Turkish Convention: IO EUR D (Hirtzel Papers): Porte shown all existing treaties with Arab chiefs, except Bandar–Shuwaikh Lease taken out by Britain on Shaikh's land in 1907. See Troeller, *The Birth of Saudi Arabia*, Britain replied to Turkish overtures, 29 July 1911.

Albania: see Herbert, *Ben Kendim.*

Kitchener in Cairo: Cassar, *Kitchener*, and Storrs, *Orientations.*

Storrs: impressions from his own story, *Orientations*; from Bell, *Letters*; Lawrence, *Seven Pillars*; Herbert, *Ben Kendim;* and from interviews with officers of administrations in Palestine, Egypt and Iraq who recalled him some sixty years later. I am particularly indebted to Colonel Gerald de Gaury, sometime Political Agent in Kuwait, and to Mr Colin Imray, late of the Colonial Police. He took up his first appointment in the east in October 1904 as assistant to the Financial Adviser in Cairo, Sir Vincent Corbett. Storrs was educated at Charterhouse and Cambridge, where his contemporaries included J. M. Keynes, Charles Tennyson, Stephen Gaselee, and Lytton Strachey. He left with a 'reasonably good' First.

On Cromer's retirement in April 1907, Sir Eldon Gorst, father-in-law of Mark Sykes, was appointed Resident. Storrs and Leland Buxton, Aubrey Herbert's friend and travelling companion, were given jobs in Audit Department. Storrs shared digs in Cairo with Philip Graves, then working for *Egyptian Gazette*, subsequently correspondent of *The Times* in Constantinople.

76   'A manly man': Cassar, *Kitchener.*

German privileges: Storrs, *Orientations.*

Ottoman Capitulations: evolved over centuries, the consequence of the Porte's traditional improvidence; all great powers enjoyed special privileges, including the right to veto external tariff charges. Thus, one country after another prevented increases in customs revenues and so achieved a balance of influence at the expense of the Ottoman prosperity. See Trumpener, *Germany and the Ottoman Empire*, Kinross, *The Ottoman Centuries*, and Caillard, *Imperial Fiscal Reform.*

Von Oppenheim and Enver: von Oppenheim did not spend a great deal of time in Berlin in the pre-war years. In 1896 he was officially diplomatic agent in Egypt; 1899 was spent in Asia Minor with occasional visits to Constantinople; in 1902 and 1904 he visited the United States; in 1905 he was official German delegate to the Oriental and Archaeological Congress in Algiers; in 1908 he was in Copenhagen; in 1909–10 in Cairo; and from 1911 to 1913 resident at his archaeological site, Tel Halaf in northern Mesopotamia. He was chief of the Intelligence Division of the German Orient Institute, but worked separately from the General Staff eastern intelligence organisation. *AA*, 1A, 9, Nr 1, 1–12. *Berichte des Freiherrn von Oppenheim*. See also German *Who's Who – Wer ist's*.

76   Entertaining Pan-Islamites: Storrs, *Orientations*.

77   German General Staff organisation: see Hermann, *Deutsche Militärgeschichte*, and Hermann Cron, *Geschichte des deutschen Heeres im Weltkrieg 1914–18*, Berlin, 1937.

Bureau of Naval Intelligence: Tappken and von Riechter, 70 Koenigergratzerstrasse, Berlin, see Graves, *Secrets of the German War Office*. 'Embodiment of Prussian efficiency.'

Frobenius, Abdal Karim: *AA*, Der Weltkrieg 11g, Bd 1–19. See *Arab Bulletin*, no. 5, May 1916. Article by Colonel Frobenius in *Die Post*, 'Advance on Baghdad'.

Fisher in Mediterranean: see his *Fear God*, 'I set to work . . . and through the patriotism of several magnificent Englishmen . . . I got a central forwarding station fixed up privately in Switzerland,' His chief aide was the Irishman Fitzmaurice! See also Thomson, *The Allied Secret Service in Greece*.

Wilson: WO records. For Fisher and Wilson see Terraine, *Impacts of War*.

Deuxième Bureau, Okhrana and Colonel Redl: Nicolai, *Nachrichdienst*.

Frock coats and quill pens: see Lockhart, *Memoirs of a British Agent*.

Agadir crisis, July 1911: CAB 37/107. For German viewpoint see Rosen, *Aus einem diplomatischen Wanderleben*. For evolution of Moroccan crisis, see Terraine, *Impacts of War*.

78   Italians in Tripoli: CAB 37/107, and *The Times*, 28 Oct 1911, *et seq.*

Balkans 1911: Grant and Temperley, *Europe in the Nineteenth and Twentieth Centuries*, p. 375ff.

Italy and Turks in Yemen: FO 195/2254.

Imam Yahya: ibid.

Grey to Tewfiq Pasha: R/15/5/59.

Baghdad railroad: CAB 37/108.

Grey: Liberal colleague, E. D. Morel, quoted in Robbins, *Sir Edward Grey*. Newton, quoted in Herbert, *Ben Kendim*.

Hogarth's team: see Stewart, *T. E. Lawrence*, and Knightley and Simpson, *Secret Lives*.

78   Lawrence's journey 1911: Knightley and Simpson, ibid., letter to mother from Jerablus, 24 June.

Guest of Dr W. B. T. Torrance: Stewart, *T. E. Lawrence.*

History of Carchemish site: Lloyd, *Foundations in the Dust.*

79   Baghdad railroad: CAB 37/108, and L/P & S/10/415 negots with Germany.

DNI: Captain Maurice Fitzmaurice was in charge of Naval Intelligence at this time, having taken over from Rear-Admiral Edmond Slade at the end of 1909. 'I got rid of Slade as a fool when he was DNI', Fisher, *Fear God*, vol. 3, p. 338. Slade was C-in-C East Indies by 1911, when he was knighted. The Admiralty's remained, as for centuries past, the senior of the intelligence services; despite the agreement of 1905 between WO and Admiralty that naval responsibilities ended at high-water mark, the DNI maintained a vast network of informants throughout the world. WO/Admiralty records, and Aston, *The Secret Service.*

80   Campbell Thomson: Mallowan, *Memoirs*, pp. 69–85.

Woolley: ibid. See also R. Campbell Thompson, *A Pilgrim's Scrip*, John Lane, 1915. 'CT' was already an experienced traveller in the desert regions with useful contacts. In 1902 he made a journey in Sinai and biblical Edom, in 1903 he was at Tarablus in northern Syria (Tripoli), and in 1904 had joined Dr Leonard King at Mosul; King had already been at work at the Nineveh site near Mosul for a year.

Von Oppenheim: *Der Tell Halaf.* See Stewart, *T. E. Lawrence*, p. 84, 'Carchemish genuine cover for a second activity', and Sir Hubert Young, *The Independent Arab*, description of visit to site and conversations with Lawrence, 1913.

Hogarth on Lawrence: Sir William Rothenstein, *Twenty-four Portraits*, Allen & Unwin, 1920.

81   Round Table fellowship: Knightley and Simpson, *Secret Lives*, pp. 23–7. 'He absorbed, via Hogarth, some of the precepts of the Round Table, and these came to be among his main motivations in Arabia.'

Campbell Thompson: only in charge for brief time, returned to Britain to marry in July. For pay of Hogarth's assistants, see Stewart, *T. E. Lawrence.*

Lawrence to brother: 20 March 1911, *The Home Letters of T.E.L.*

Gertrude Bell, 18 May: *Letters.*

Gertrude Bell and Germans: *Letters*, and travel notebooks (1905–14) containing remarks by members of Deutsche Orient Gesellschaft, RGS archives.

J. G. Lorimer: Bell, *Letters*, March–April 1911, pp. 239–48.

Goyer: notebook, 1911, RGS, and L/P & S/10/259, South Persian trade, German docs.

Willcocks: Bell, *Letters*, p.242.

82   Gertrude Bell's literary works: see Burgoyne, *Gertrude Bell: from her Personal Papers*, and Winstone, *Gertrude Bell.*

82 Bell's visit to Carchemish: *Letters*, p. 252. 'Kaimakam came over and ... told me that Mr Hogarth had left but that Mr Thompson was still at Carchemish ... and a young man called Lawrence.'

Movements of Thompson, Woolley and Lawrence: Stewart, *T. E. Lawrence*, p. 84ff.

83 Lawrence's photography and Thompson's interest in railway: ibid. See also Alfred Ehrentreich, in *Neuphilologische Monatschrift*, March 1936. James Elroy Flecker: *Some Letters from Abroad*, Heinemann, 1930. Flecker, a student of Oriental languages, worked at the Constantinople Embassy in 1910 and moved to Beirut in 1911, becoming an agent of MO2(b). But he was in failing health. His contacts were to prove useful to Lawrence and Woolley a few years hence, after his own death in 1915.

Carchemish and espionage: far too much has been made of Lawrence's mysterious contacts, movements and concepts. They are of more interest to the psychiatrist than the student of espionage. His knowledge of Musil, 'head guide to the General Staff in Damascus', Meissner 'building railways' and German staff officers, cited by Knightley and Simpson, *Secret Lives*, for example, as evidence of the use he made of his time in Syria, is no more than a mixture of guesswork and hearsay. Staff officers and their agents are never permitted to gather information beyond their clearly defined areas of activity or to possess overall strategic pictures, though Lawrence and his companions were to break the rules of military intelligence gathering a few years later in Cairo. Information on Alexandretta harbour and future plans had doubtless been picked up from Pirie-Gordon, who was conducting a survey at that time for the DNI and DMI: WO 33/738 Report on Ayas Bay, and Report on Syria, WO, 1911, Pirie-Gordon and Captain Smith.

Shakespear 1911: Winstone, *Shakespear*, ch. 13.

Mubarak to Shakespear: L/P & S/10/827, 28 Jan 1912.

Leachman at Basra: Bray, *Paladin*. Arrived 11 Nov.

84 'A miserable failure': letter to father, 5 Dec 1914.

'Shaikh rather offensive': ibid.

Sayid Talib: new efforts were being made by the Turks to woo Mubarak of Kuwait and Talib's father, the Naqib Sayid Rajab, had been chosen to lead a Turkish delegation to Kuwait to present the Shaikh with the Order of Medjidie in February: L/P & S/10/827; Shakespear refused to attend the ceremony, 2 Feb 1912. On 25 Nov 1911, Sadun Pasha, treacherously handed to the Turks by Talib in July, died in gaol in Aleppo. Turks said he suffered a heart attack, but British officials were sure he was poisoned: L/P & S/10/617, report by Henry Dobbs, 28 July 1916. Sadun's son, Ajaimi, took over leadership of Muntafiq tribes, and never forgave Talib. Both were supporters of CUP from 1908. By 1911 Talib had become secretly involved with Pan-Islamic schemes and with the Covenanters of Damascus, Al Ahad and Al Fattah. It was Talib's flirtation with Arab nationalism which drove Ajaimi into the arms of the Turks, his family's ancient enemy. He became the most reliable Arab ally of the Ottoman power.

84 Shakespear/Leachman: L/P & S/10/259. Letter to Cox, 27 Oct 1911.

85 Danish expedition: L/P & S/10/259, 21 Nov 1909.

Johnstone to Grey: ibid., 22 Dec 1909.

Captain Hunter: see Hunter, 'Reminiscences of the Map of Arabia'; and L/P & S/10/259, 31 March 1910, Lowther, Constantinople, recommended rejection.

Mubarak to Shakespear, 9 April 1911: R/15/5/64. At the exact moment of these approaches, Mubarak had heard of the Turco-German–British negotiations concerning the Baghdad railroad which arose out of the Anglo-Turkish talks in London, and in the course of which it was agreed that the line would terminate at Kadhima on the north shore of the Shaikh's territory. But the Germans told him that Britain had conceded Turkish suzerainty over Kuwait. R/15/5/59, Shakespear to Resident, 19 April 1911: 'French anxious to build line Kadhima to Kuwait' (presumably to undermine the German plan). 22 April, Mubarak on Khadima: 'Either lease it from me, or let me lease it', ibid. See CAB 37/109, Baghdad Rail, 4 Jan 1912. 23 April 1911, Resident to Mubarak: 'Khadima is already covered by our assurances.'

Thomas Brown: an Englishman who had assumed German nationality. R/15/5/8, Secret Newsletters, Foreign Simla/ Persian Gulf.

86 Simla to Resident, Bushire: R/15/5/64.

Shakespear to Political and Secret department: ibid.

Customs Master: ibid., 21 June 1911. 'German ship on way. Ali Bash [Wönckhaus agent] very friendly with Abdal Mehsin, Mubarak's customs master.'

Raunkiaer at Basra: L/P & S/10/259 and L/P & S/10/827.

Abdullah 'Germani': R/15/5/64, D'Mello (agency clerk) to Residency.

Mubarak quote: R/15/5/64.

FO to IO, Raunkiaer: L/P & S/10/259, 14 Dec 1909.

87 Raunkiaer's journey: see his own account, *Through Wahhabiland on Camelback.*

Lieutenant Davidsen: see ibid.

Raunkiaer at Basra and Kuwait: ibid. See also Winstone, *Shakespear.*

88 Voyage in *Lewis Pelly*: see Winstone, *Shakespear.*

Plot against Shaikh: L/P & S/10/827. Al Ghanim's eyes were gouged with red-hot needles while in gaol. Late in Feb Yusef ibn Salim al Badr, brother of the Shaikh's secretary, arrived from Basra to plead for the nephews who, he insisted, were not implicated. Shakespear insisted on the release of Al Ghanim, otherwise he would make 'no further calls on the Shaikh'. See Winstone, *Shakespear.*

89 Raunkiaer in Najd: L/P & S/10/827 and *Through Wahhabiland.*

91   Admiral de Richlieu: Grey to IO, L/P & S/10/259.

Shakespear's journey: Lord Lamington, L/P & S/10/827. Just before his departure for Al Qaa on 24 March, Shakespear noted that Mubarak had taken himself off to his holiday island of Failaka, that Faisal al Dawish was camped at Hafar wells and that Ibn Saud had sent him a message announcing 'a successful raid on the Ataiba', ibid. And Cox asked Foreign, Simla: 'Should we tell Shaikh what we have done?' R/15/5/59, apropos of a conversation in Nov 1911 on the Anglo-Turkish talks.

92   Musil across Palmyrene desert and in Mesopotamia: see *Arabia Deserta*, ch. XII. More detailed accounts of the places visited are in Musil's *Palmyrena* and *The Middle Euphrates*.

93   Events in Persia: Sir Percy Sykes, *History of Persia*, and Kazemzadeh, *Russia and Britain in Persia*.

1912, Meshed: 29–30 March, Sir Percy Sykes, *History of Persia*.

1909: news of CUP success in Turkey stimulus to revolution, ibid. Feb: Royalist forces besieged capital. Bakhtiaris declared for revolution. April–June: Russians ordered troops to assemble Baku. July: Bakhtiaris captured Tehran, Muhammad Ali deposed. Sultan Ahmad Shah, aged twelve, succeeded, 16 July. British troops to Shiraz. Ex-Shah to Odessa. CAB 37/100 Persia, and activities of 'Union of the Russian People'.

94   Wassmuss: Christopher Sykes, *Wassmuss*.

Sir Richmond Ritchie: L/P & S/10/334, IO to FO, 11 Dec 1909.

Shuster: see Kazemzadeh, *Russia and Britain in Persia.* 25 Dec 1910, Persian Chargé d'Affaires in Washington asked US Government to put him in touch with 'impartial financial people'. State Dep. file 3891. 51/37. Among the complicating factors in Anglo-Russian relations in Persia following the Convention of 1907 were the famous 'Willy–Nicki' talks at Potsdam in Nov 1910 which appeared to suggest the Czar's agreement to the Berlin–Baghdad rail scheme, possibly joining up with a Russian line through Persia, in return for the Kaiser's abdication of all but commercial rights in Persia. See Kazemzadeh, *Russia and Britain in Persia.* The Kaiser told the Czar: 'Help me to complete the rail link to the Gulf, and you can have what you like in northern Persia.' See Charles F. Holne (ed.), *Source Records of the Great War*, National Alumni, USA, 1923, comment by Dr Morris Jasrow, University of Pennsylvania. Another factor was the commercial loyalties of the tribal leaders. Up to this time most kept their money in Russian or British banks, according to their loyalties. By 1910 many were putting their money, and their attachments, in German hands, Kazemzadeh, *Russia and Britain in Persia.* The manager of the British bank at Shiraz in 1907 was Mr Ely Bannister Soane, now a British agent in Mesopotamia and Kurdistan. See Soane, *To Mesopotamia and Kurdistan in Disguise.* Russia's attitude in Persia 'losely related' to events in world after Bosnian and Agadir crises, 'especially German designs', Kazemzadeh, *Russia and Britain in Persia.*

95   Muhammad Ali: Sir Percy Sykes, *History of Persia*.

Arshad ad Dowla: ibid., Kazemzadeh, *Russia and Britain in Persia*, defeated near Veramin. End of Russian attempt to restore Muhammad Ali, Sept 1911.

95 'Agent of American imperialism': Z. Z. Abdullaev, Moscow 1963, quoted in Kazemzadeh, *Russia and Britain in Persia*.

Shuster 1911: his own account is colourfully presented in William Morgan Shuster, *The Strangling of Persia*, Fisher Unwin, 1912.

Treasury *gendarmerie* and Major Stokes: FO 371/1192. Shuster asked Mornard, Belgian head of Customs, to deposit receipts in Treasurer's (Shuster's) accounts. Mornard refused. The Persian *Majlis* and the manager of the Imperial Bank supported Shuster. Russian, German, Italian and French envoys supported Mornay, and Shuster was forced to back down. Then followed the row over the *gendarmerie*. FO 371/963, O'Beirne, Chargé d'affaires to Grey (FO), 20 Aug 1910: Britain and Russia agree to prevent Persia employing subjects of major powers.

Stokes: FO 371/1192, Barclay (British Minister) to Grey: 'Stokes fanatically anti-Russian, also anti-British'. 10 July 1911, Neratov (Russian Deputy F/M) suggested Russian and British officers for *gendarmerie*. Sir Edward Grey suggested Swedish commander. Shuster insisted on Stokes. Director of Anglo-Persian Oil Company, Charles Greenaway, hoped Britain would 'forbid' appointment of Stokes. 17 Aug, Grey promised Benckendorff (Russian Ambassador, London) that Stokes would not be allowed to resign Commission in Indian Army, and would not therefore be eligible. Benckendorff: 'Grey's performance undignified'. 26 Aug, Czar, in margin of telegram from Polewski, Russian Ambassador, 'No yielding'. The Russo-German agreement of Aug 1911 acknowledged Russia's 'special interests' in Persia. German interest to be confined to commerce. Kazemzadeh, *Russia and Britain in Persia*. Persian Government proposed Swedish head of *gendarmerie* in Oct. Neratov to St Petersburg: 'harmful to Russia'. Nicholas II noted in margin: 'Since it is harmful to Russia, it is impermissible. We are the masters in northern Persia.' Breaking point came in Nov 1911, when Russian troops were attacked at Tabriz and Resht, Sir Percy Sykes, *History of Persia*; Shuster appointed an Englishman, Lecoffre, financial inspector at Tabriz, Kazemzadeh, *Russia and Britain in Persia*. Cossacks hanged the culprits at Tabriz, and Russia demanded the resignations of Shuster and Lecoffre. 'By 1912 Persia had virtually ceased to exist as a state,' ibid.

5 Murder at Hail

97 Leachman's journey, Oct–Dec 1912: Bray, *Paladin*, and Philby, UPM.

Shakespear's opposition: L/P & S/10/259, Shakespear to Wilson, 26 Oct 1912, 'Objection both personal and otherwise'.

Damascus: L/P & S/10/259, 18 Nov 1912, Consul Devey to Cox. 'left here

3rd for Gahra wells, then SSE to Najd and Basra'; 21 Dec, Cox to Shakespear re Leachman's journey.

98   Journey in central Arabia: *GJ*, vol. XLIII, May 1914. Letter from Leachman to RGS, 1 Jan 1913, *GJ*, vol. XLI, p. 147;'Last November Council made grant towards expenses.'

100   Leachman left Bushire for India end-Jan 1913: Bray, *Paladin*.

Shakespear to Khafs: see Winstone, *Shakespear*, journey described from travel notes, 1913, Kuwait to Khafs, RGS archives.

Movements of Shakespear, Shaikh Mubarak, Dec 1912–Jan 1913: L/P & S/10/437.

Ibn Saud, 'natural champion': Bray, *Shifting Sands*.

Arab nationalist plans, 1913: see Longrigg, *Iraq, 1900–1950*, p. 41ff. Basra took the lead in the Arab nationalist movement.

Secret Kuwait Conference, Jan 1914: to have been attended by representatives of Sharif of Mecca, Ibn Saud, Ibn Rashid, Ajaimi Sadun, Mubarak and Sayid Talib. But in March 1913 Talib announced reconciliation with Ottoman Government. Ibid.

101   Riots in Basra: Turkish General, Farid Bey, was murdered and Talib believed responsible, but there was no proof. Ibid.

Warship: HMS *Alert*, ibid.

Hakki Pasha: *The Times* (10 Feb 1913).

Shakespear to Kubbar: L/P & S/10/437. In fact, Murphy was taking over at this time. Craufurd left officially on 13 April, 1913. Mr Spurrier to author.

102   Taking of Katif: L/P & S/10/384, 15 May. Occupation of Al Hasa and movements of *John O'Scott*, ibid. *The Times*, 23 May 1913: 'Al Hasa has surrendered to Arab chief Ben Sa'ood.'

FO reprimand: in FO 371/1820, 24 June 1913. Shakespear's journey, said Sir Edward Grey, 'does not seem to have been a necessary condition of any mission with which he has been charged'. L/P & S/10/437.

'nothing but personal matters': Shakespear's report to Resident, 15 May 1913, in L/P & S/10/384. Resident to Foreign, India, 20 May, ibid. Government to Resident, 22 May ibid. But there was a warning of events to come. 'The Amir and his brothers and the Najdi notables . . . seemed to consider that Turkey's misfortunes and present weakness furnished the best opportunity for Najd to rid itself of all shadow of Ottoman suzerainty.'

Oil delegation from India: led by H. H. Hayden, a geologist, Feb–March 1913. L/P & S/20/C176. In Jan a proposal by Admiral Sir John Fisher was presented to the Cabinet in London. It stressed the need to protect and develop oil supplies in preparation for emergency. CAB 37/114.

Bray at Damascus: *Shifting Sands*, p. 50ff.

103   Young Turks: *The Times*, 18 Jan 1913, *coup d'état* expected. Muhammad

Shevket appointed Grand Vizier. See Lewis, *The Emergence of Modern Turkey*; party led by Enver invaded Cabinet, Nazim, War Minister, shot dead.

103   Armenians: *The Times*, 8 Jan. 'Anti-Armenian outrages': orphanage burnt at Hadjin.

104   Jamal: see Djemal Pasha, *Memories of a Turkish Statesman*.

Azmi Bey: *The Times*, 30 Jan.

Morgenthau: see 'The Turkish Conspiracy' and other articles in *Land and Water*, 9 May–24 Oct 1918.

Aziz Ali al Masri: Djemal Pasha, *Memories*. See also Barclay, *The Turco-Italian War and its Problems*.

105   Renewed opposition in Turkey: *The Times*, 18 Aug reported extensive fire in Constantinople. St Sophia and several oil depots were ablaze; on 28 Aug 'many arrests', 26 March, anti-Armenian demonstrations at Adana. Kinross, *The Ottoman Centuries*: Adrianople surrendered in March to Bulgarians; bad weather had prevented a force led by Enver Bey from landing on Bulgarian flank. Counter-revolution threatened and Shevket was urged to resign. British and French banks refused further aid to Turkey. Herbert, *Ben Kendim:* funds were collected for Turks in Egypt and India.

Murder of Shevket: 15 June 1913. Shot on way to War Office. Djemal Pasha, *Memories*. Said Halim appointed Grand Vizier, Enver War Minister. Shevket had occupied both posts. Although (D)jamal gives 15 June as date, *The Times* reported the murder on the 12th.

Letter from Gertrude Bell: *The Times*, 27 Jan 1913.

Lowther: see Kedourie, 'Young Turks, Freemasons and Jews', *Middle East Studies*, vol. 7, no. 1, Jan 1971, and FO 800/193A (Lowther Papers, PRO).

Sir Louis Mallet's appointment: *The Times*, 4 Nov 1913.

Aubrey Herbert: *Ben Kendim*.

Bray: *Shifting Sands*.

106   Gertrude Bell in Damascus: *Letters*, p. 253ff.

Porte's approval: India Office records (Register Z/L/P & S/7/40) entry for 8 Jan 1914, 'Miss Bell, Turks no objections', file no. 1202/12, not found in Political and Secret records.

Lawrence and Wooolley: Stewart, *T. E. Lawrence*, and Knightley and Simpson, *Secret Lives*.

Lawrence and Mr Bell: see Lawrence, *The Home Letters of T.E.L*, 30 Sept 1913 from Aleppo.

German bridge builders: see Woolley, *As I Seem to Remember*. Details of first meeting between Lawrence, Woolley and Newcombe 1913. 'Kitchener told Newcombe to go to Carchemish.' Woolley to Newcombe: 'Our camp is a stone's throw from bridge over the Euphrates which is being built by German Baghdad Railway Company.'

Newcombe on special duty: Army Lists, 1911–13, and quarterly reports of

Palestine Exploration Fund. See also C. W. L. Woolley and T. E. Lawrence, *The Wilderness of Zin*, Palestine Exploration Fund, 1915. Newcombe 'mapped a larger area than any of his assistants'.

106   Lorimer succeeds Cox: R/15/5/59, 8 Dec, Cox to IO.

107   Carruthers in London: see Carruthers, *Arabian Adventure*, p. 86. 1913: 'she tried to persuade me to join with her on her proposed Arabian venture. I demurred, but offered her my man'. Later Carruthers placed her 1,500 miles of survey on the map.

Lawrence and Miss Bell: *The Home Letters of T.E.L.*, to A. W. Lawrence, signed 'Ned'.

Gertrude Bell's notes on Syrian stage of journey: BM 45158C Add. Her travel notebook for 1911 with three pages catalogued '1905' was deposited in the British Museum manuscript room by Lady Richmond, Gertrude's half-sister, at an unspecified date. These documents were obviously kept separately from the other travel notebooks and diaries, which were presented by her family at a later date to the University of Newcastle upon Tyne. Gertrude herself had left field notebooks and some 200 photographic negatives with the Royal Geographical Society. But the three pages in question could not have been for the year 1905. She went nowhere near the places named at that time. They must have referred to the 1913 journey.

Miss Baird: unpublished letter to Lady Bell, 14 Nov 1913, University of Newcastle upon Tyne.

Journey to Bair: Bell, *Letters*, p. 253ff. Photographs: RGS collection.

Lawrence and Woolley: *The Wilderness of Zin*. See also Woolley, *As I Seem to Remember*, p. 88ff., 'Why I got into Intelligence. What made the WO do it?' Winter 1913–14, Route 'in *Numbers 33*'.

108   Kenyon: intro. to *The Wilderness of Zin*.

Sinai: Knightley and Simpson, *Secret Lives*. In his letter to Storrs, Newcombe gives a sketchy account of the Sinai frontier from the battle of Nasib in 1883 to the outbreak of war. 'Cromer insisted on surveying the Rafa–Aqaba frontier and erecting boundary posts visible one from the next. Any passage across that line by Turkish troops meant war.' Newcombe does not give a date. See note to p. 399, Jennings Bramley to Mrs Neame, 1953, agreement with Turkey, 1906. 'War nearly did break out in 1906 after the secret agreement had been reached, when the Turks occupied Aqaba.' Knightley and Simpson say: 'Newcombe, of course, did not have all the facts'. In fact, he was the one man who did know very nearly all, but he never divulged his information or sources. Author.

109   'leg pull': letter from Newcombe to Sir Ronald Storrs, 1953, quoted ibid.,

Parker: Army Lists, and private papers in possession of author.

Jennings Bramley and Jarvis: I am grateful to Sir Duncan Cumming and to Colonel Parker's daughter for personal information on these officers, and on Parker himself.

Woolley and Lawrence: *Wilderness of Zin*.

109 'Gertie': Lawrence in *The Home Letters of T.E.L.*

Gertrude Bell held up at Ziza: *Letters*, pp. 265–6. T.E.L. and Woolley arrived 5 Jan (in Gaza on 6th).

'Beloved boy: usual form of address in letters.

New path: see Hogarth, description of journey in *GJ*, vol. LXX, no. 1, July 1927.

110 Guarmani: Jerusalem to Hail and Khaibar, 1864. See Freeth and Winstone, *Explorers of Arabia*.

Carruthers: Dec 1909–March 1910. 28 Dec 1909, 'by train for Maan . . . seeking Meissner Pasha at Tabuk'. To northern Hijaz with letter of safe conduct from Meissner. See *Arabian Adventure*. Notes on maps and correspondence with military intelligence, Cairo, in possession of author.

Musil, 1910: see *Northern Hijaz*, 1927.

Woolley and T.E.L. to Beersheba: Lawrence was accompanied by his Carchemish friend, Dahoum. Gertrude Bell makes no reference to her countrymen or to Dahoum in her letters, nor they to her. She stayed overnight with Dr Mackinnon and his family in Damascus on the way down, however, and Lawrence called on the hospitable doctor. See Bell, *Letters*, p. 264, and Stewart, *T. E. Lawrence*.

Stirling: see Herbert, *Ben Kendim*, p. 147.

'suspicion of map makers': *Wilderness of Zin*.

Newcombe: ibid.

Itinerary of Lawrence and Woolley: ibid.

Gertrude Bell: *Letters*, 272–5, and unpublished letters, Newcastle University.

111 Photographs Lawrence: the photograph which Gertrude Bell took of the Howaitat woman, with Lawrence clearly shown in the group in Arab dress, is the only clue to their meeting at this time, apart from their undoubted meeting at Ziza rail junction on 5 Jan, since both parties were at that place on the same day. But this is not surprising in view of the clandestine nature of their journeys, which were clearly being directed by Newcombe and Hogarth, and by MO2 in London, which now embraced the Ottoman Empire and Arabia. My attention was drawn to the presence of Lawrence in the photograph by Nigel Dennis in his review in the *Sunday Telegraph* of my *Gertrude Bell*, 10 Sept 1978, and I am grateful to him.

Muhammad abu Tayya: Bell, *Letters*, p. 273.

Gertrude Bell at Hail: see Winstone, *Gertrude Bell*, p. 126ff.

112 'at the lowest ebb': she was in the throes of a highly charged love affair with Major 'Dick' Doughty-Wylie, who was to die and be awarded a posthumous VC at Gallipoli, when she left England for central Arabia. Some years later she told the American anthropologist Dr Henry Field of her tribulations on the journey to Hail, and he wrote: 'She was tired. She was very ill . . . she lay in her sleeping bag . . . Her head swam. A nosebleed pre-

ceded deep sleep. The Beduins were anxious about their Bint Bell,' *Arabian Desert Tales.*

112 *John O'Scott* and Indian troops for Al Hasa: L/P & S/10/384, Shakespear to Political Resident, 15 May 1913; Resident to Government of India, 20 May. Shakespear: 'News received with greatest surprise in Kuwait.' Troops of Ibn Saud assembled at Hofuf, 4 May; 300 men took the town on foot. And a clue to the subject of discussion between Shakespear and Ibn Saud at Khafs in April: 'I confess that I was surprised by the suddenness of Bin Saud's attack . . . I thought he would wait to see what effect movements for self-government in other Arab provinces would have.'

Expulsion of Turks from Bahrain and Qatar: ibid. Crow, Basra, to Marling, Chargé d'Affaires Constantinople, 14 June.

Ibn Saud 'Governor': ibid. Cox to India, 30 May.

Holderness: FO 371/1820, 3 July 1913, in reply to Mallet (7 June), 'Regarding recent events in Najd'. General attitude of HMG, 'to consolidate the power of central Government in Asiatic Turkey'. In same document: 'Sir Edward Grey is, moreover, far from convinced that the ultimate triumph of Ibn Saud over the Turkish authorities is assured.' See also L/P & S/10/B200, 'Non-interference in Najd', 3 July 1913.

FO observations: ibid.

113 Cox and Shakespear to Mubarak and Ibn Saud: L/P & S/10/437. Between 5 and 7 July a very secret meeting with Shaikh Mubarak was held on board HMS *Sphinx.* Shaikh Khazal was present, and on the British side Major Haworth from the Indian General Staff joined Cox and Shakespear. R/15/5/59, and L/P & S/10/437. In the following month, immediately after the signing of the Convention (which was never ratified because of the declaration of war in 1914 and the intervening influence of Germany in Constantinople), the Foreign Office suggested to India that the Shaikh of Kuwait should be asked to grant an oil concession to Britain. L/P & S/20/C176. See note to p. 415, visit of Hayden's mission, Feb 1913. Foreign, Simla, told London, 'Anglo-Persian Oil Company willing'.

'still stalling': FO 371/1820, Oct 1913.

Anglo-Turkish treaty: CAB 371/115 (negotiations with Hakki Pasha). Held up by differences over Baghdad Railway and Customs matters. See Clayton, *Diary,* 29 July 1913, and FO 371/1820.

Shakespear's activities: L/P & S/10/384 and FO 371/1820, 11 Aug 1913.

Ibn Saud, 'mutasarif in Najd': L/P & S/10/384, S/S to Foreign, India. New Ambassador to Constantinople, Sir Louis Mallet, reported, 'Turks about to recognise *fait accompli'.*

Shakespear and Trevor, meeting with Ibn Saud: Shakespear went to Muhammerah for talks with Shaikh Khazal, then on to Bahrain aboard *Lewis Pelly* to pick up Trevor, and thence to Uqair for meeting at end of December. L/P & S/10/437.

114 Turkish arms for Ibn Rashid: see Musil, *Northern Najd,* p. 248ff. And

Shakespear's private diary of journey across Arabia (in author's possession) refers to supply of arms by Turks to Ibn Rashid and Musa al Namisa, Musil the Austrian, to Ibn Shalan's Anaiza. L/P & S/10/384, Shakespear reports from Nakhl, Sinai, 'Consignment of Turkish arms to Bin Rashid. Motor car in charge of three Europeans. Designed to strengthen Rashid against Ibn Saud.'

114 Gertrude Bell's route: evidence of the distortion of news in the desert was provided by an Arab whom Shakespear met at Jauf, who had been in the United States and Brazil as a cab-driver. He told Shakespear of a European Christian who had visited Hail twenty days before. He had orders from Constantinople and came by train to Tabuk. Finding Ibn Rashid away he went on to Karbala. 'Business with Ibn Rashid,' he whispered confidentially, 'not an explorer or antiquary.' He referred to Gertrude Bell.

Zamil ibn Subhan: in Sept 1913 Shakespear reported to the Government that Zamil was on good terms with Ibn Saud and the Turks were sufficiently concerned to have invited Shaikhs Khazal and Mubarak to Basra to effect a compromise between Ibn Saud and the Porte. L/P & S/10/437.

Attacks on Turks: Musil, *Northern Najd*, p. 248.

Shakespear and Faisal ibn Hamud: ibid.

Shakespear hands over: R/15/5/27.

115 'told Cox': 27 Nov 1913, copy of letter in Shakespear's private papers. Loch, from GHQ to join Lorimer. R/15/5/55.

Places and people visited *en route:* from personal travel notes typed by Shakespear in London, but unpublished at the insistence of the FO. Interim report on journey to Grey at Kuwait from Zilfi, 27 Feb. R/15/5/55.

Lorimer: Winstone, *Shakespear*, p. 144. 20 Jan 1914. *Note:* Foreign Secretary conveyed approval of Turks and Mallet, Constantinople, 7 Jan 1914, after repeated requests from Viceroy. L/P & S/10/259.

Loch: R/15/5/55.

Journey: see Winstone, *Shakespear*, p. 145ff., and Douglas Carruthers, 'Captain Shakespear's Last Journey', *GJ*, May–June 1921.

Death of Lorimer: no event in the tumultuous year which led up to the outbreak of the First World War was more tragic in significance, or more inexplicable, than the death of John Gordon Lorimer. He was the outstanding man in a galaxy of brilliant administrators, historians, linguists and writers in the Indian Civil and Political Services. He combined all the talents. His *Gazetteer of the Persian Gulf,* commissioned by Curzon following his tour of the Gulf in 1903, a study of the tribes of the North-West Frontier, and a grammar and dictionary of the Waziri variant of the Pushtu language, remain as the only testaments to his remarkable skill and energy. Not a single file relating to events at Bushire at the time of his death survives, though several documents are spread among the political and secret records. Of these, the most significant (in L/P & S/10/437), dated 11 Jan 1914, is to the Foreign Secretary, Simla, and refers to the pressure of work which he found at Bushire. He wrote, ominously: 'If Loch were to go [through overload of work] I do not know what would happen.' On 16 Jan (IO register Z/L/P & S/7/37) he wrote to India regarding 'proposed extra remuneration for Resident Surgeon N. E. H. Scott'. On 8 Feb 1914 he went to his private apartment at the Residency during working hours, and some time later an assistant found him lying dead on the floor, a gun by his side. Captain R. L. Birdwood, who edited the *Gazetteer* for press and who was his First Assistant, held an inquiry, at which the evidence of the Residency Surgeon, Major S. Hunt, was heard. A verdict of 'death from wounds caused by the accidental discharge of an automatic pistol' was recorded. No cause of death was given on the certificate issued by Major Hunt (no. PSR 5681A Consular Deaths, London). On 5 March, more than three weeks after the event, Reuter issued a statement which appeared in *The Times*, 6 March: 'It appears that Mr. Lorimer was extracting the cartridges from his revolver in order to send it as a pattern to Bombay, and inadvertently left one in the barrel'. J. G. Lorimer's brother, Major David Lorimer, was British Consul at Kerman at the time of the Resident's death. His wife, Emily Lorimer, (Tutor at Somerville College, Oxford, 1907–10 and daughter of Judge Overend of Dublin) wrote to her parents on 11 Feb 1914: My own darling Father and Mother, You will not expect much of a letter this week. We are still stunned by the awful news from Bushire ... of all people Gordon, so prudent and cautious, so used from his boyhood to handling firearms, should have been the last to have an accident. When you think of him, just in the flush of health and strength and success, with a brilliant career behind him and the whole world still before him ... it seems such waste, waste, waste'. (Letters of Emily Lorimer in India Office records). 'Deceased's wife was living with him at time of his death', IO Annuity records L/AG/34/14A/10. Probate granted to John Parker Watson and Annie Mercer Watson, Edinburgh. No date. (L/AG/21/8/38).

The Turks had a strange snobbery about titles and were particularly impressed by military rank while disdainful of civilians. It was decided in 1911, when he was Resident at Baghdad, to give J. G. Lorimer the honorary rank of Lieutenant-Colonel (IO Register Z/L/P & S/7/37, 14 March 1911), and though he never used it, some of his junior colleagues, including Shakespear, addressed him as 'Colonel'.

116   Shakespear at Riyadh: Clayton, *Diary*, 12 March, 'Bin Saud pressed for agreement with Britain.'

Notes of Shakespear's journey from Zarud, 6 April: taken from route log (RGS archives) and from his private diary (typed, in my possession, author).

Letter to Ibn Rashid from Shaikh Mubarak in Arabic: Shakespear's private papers.

119   Correspondence: Henry Talbot Shakespear, Colonel C. C. R. Murphy and Carruthers. 8 Feb 1917, Major H. T. Shakespear (Meerut) to Murphy GSO1 Simla: 'As regards his Arabian journey being in an official capacity, I think all such references should be avoided. He had very great difficulty in

obtaining sanction from HMG to embark on the journey at all, and it was supposed to be a purely geographical enterprise.' 10 Feb 1917, Murphy to Carruthers from Simla: 'I hope it is what you want.' Further correspondence recorded in Carruthers papers with IO, MIO(3), MI1, 8–29 Oct, 22 Nov 1918.

121 'near Abu Ghar': Shakespear seems to have been misinformed about the place of Zamil's death. Grey, the Political Agent, records that he was murdered near Al Baqar. Al Mutawah, see Winstone, *Leachman*, Quartet, 1982. Ali Mutawah, Ibn's Saud's amir at Ayun.

122 French attempt to arrange treaty with Ibn Rashid: on 15 Feb 1914 while Shakespear was on his way to central Arabia, France withdrew its minority interest in the Baghdad railroad scheme in return for recognition of preferential rights in Syria and Arabia. See Charles F. Horne (ed), *Source Records of the Great War*, National Alumni, USA, 1923, comment by Dr Morris Jastrow.

Rashid Pasha at Damascus: Musil, *Northern Najd*, p. 248. Pact with Saud ibn Subhan, ibid. While Musil's version of events is difficult to believe, and while it must be admitted that rumous spread like a locust invasion in the desert, the fact remains that the Austrian's source of information, Nuri ibn Shalan, was the most impeccable in northern Arabia.

123 End of Arab Revolt: L/P & S/10/437. At end of Feb Shaikh Mubarak met the Wali of Basra to discuss rebellion. Mubarak thought it unlikely that Britain would support Ibn Saud. Kuwait agency diary, undated note by Colonel Grey, Political Agent. Colonel Knox took over as Acting Resident at this time. In correspondence on subject with Grey he was terse. Addressed PA as 'Dear Sir'. Nobody much liked the taciturn Grey. R/15/5/55. Turkish War Office trying to arrange meeting with Ibn Saud through Mubarak. L/P & S/10/437.

Abdullah in Cairo: L/P & S/10/523. Cheetham to Grey (F/S) 13 Dec 1914, relays report from Storrs: 'In month of February Abdullah, the second son of the Sharif, called on Earl Kitchener, to enquire whether Britain would intervene if the Turks deprived his father of the hereditary office of Sharif of the Holy Places. No definite reply was given.'

Shakespear in Cairo: See Winstone, *Shakespear*, p. 183.

to Ibn Saud: ibid., p. 185. 'On the road we heard of the murder of Zamil ibn Subhan, and I grieve for he was a good man . . . God knows what will now happen to the affairs of Ibn Rashid. Doubtless you are aware that the Turkish Government has sent many thousands of rifles and magazine arms to Hail . . . and will shortly make war on your tribes.'

Gertrude Bell at Palmyra: unpublished letter, see Winstone, *Gertrude Bell*, p. 140.

6   War: Most Urgent

124 Outbreak of First World War and attitude of Sir Edward Grey: see Ter-

raine, *Impacts of War*. A good précis of events is given in Grant and Temperley, *Europe in the Nineteenth and Twentieth Centuries*, p. 384ff.

124   Alliance battle plans: in the absence of Russian and Austrian documentation, it is generally assumed that the Russian knowledge of German-Austrian plans came from Alfred Redl's Kundschaftsstelle in Vienna. But Nicolai, *The German Secret Service*, says: 'German officials in Geneva were persuaded by the ex-Russian Consular Secretary Von Eck to sell vital secrets.' See also Kautsky, *Die deutsche Dokumente zum Kriegsausbruch*, vol. III.

Declaration of war: Kitchener Secretary of State for War, CAB 42/1. 3 Aug, entire Cabinet agreed to declaration with exception of Morley and Burns.

Kitchener: see Cassar, *Kitchener*, 3 Aug prepared to leave for Dover. Balfour: 'Ask for K's retention in London.'

125   Prince Louis: see Terraine, *Impacts of War*, and McLaughlin, *Escape of the Goeben*.

War plan, 1906, and obligations to France: Terraine, *Impacts of War*.

Two German cruisers: McLaughlin, *Escape of the Goeben*.

Italy and Triple Alliance: Grant and Temperley, *Europe in the Nineteenth and Twentieth Centuries*, p. 407.

Fisher and King: McLaughlin, *Escape of the Goeben*.

126   Fisher and Churchill, 1911: ibid. My italics: author.

Secret treaty, 2 Aug: see Trumpener, *Germany and the Ottoman Empire, 1914–18*. Trumpener quotes Gottlieb Schmitt and Soviet sources for suggestion that while German-Turkish negotiations were in progress, and the Anglo-Turkish Convention still awaited ratification, Porte proposed an alliance with Russia (via Talaat) as a means of achieving closer relations with France. Jamal Pasha, Navy Minister in August 1914, was said to be in charge of negotiations.

Nauen to Admiral Souchon: see James, *The Eyes of the Navy*, p. 60. Message no. 51, 4 Aug.

Alliance with Turkey: *note:* according to War Office records, *Nauen* did not begin to operate as military transmitter until 22 Aug, author. Admiralty did not decypher message until several months later, James, *The Eyes of the Navy*.

127   Cambon and Grey: McLaughlin, *Escape of the Goeben*. It should be added that on 2 Aug Grey told Cambon: 'If the German fleet came through the Straits of Dover to attack French ports, the Royal Navy would go into action.'

Fisher to First Lord: ibid.

'told Lord Esher': ibid.

Souchon: see Morgenthau, *Secrets of the Bosphorus*.

128   'the tortures of Tantalus': Churchill, *The World Crisis*.

'the real drama': McLaughlin, *Escape of the Goeben*.

128 Ambassador Mallet: Trumpener, *Germany and the Ottoman Empire*, Morgenthau, *Secrets of the Bosphorus*, and Kühlmann, *Erinnerung*, p. 453: 'Der englische Botschafter Sir Louis Mallet war anscheinend kein diplomatisches Genie.'

129 'action against Russia': McLaughlin, *Escape of the Goeben*.

Baron Wangenheim: Morgenthau, *Secrets of the Bosphorus;* Kühlmann, *Erinnerung*, 'Sondermission in Konstantinopel', p. 440ff., says that when he arrived in Constantinople, at the time of the *Goeben* affair, Wangenheim was 'distinctly nervous'.

Fitzmaurice: McLaughlin, *Escape of the Goeben*.

Sultan Osman I and *Rashadieh:* ibid., and Trumpener, *Germany and the Ottoman Empire*, pp. 24–7.

130 Limpus: McLaughlin, *Escape of the Goeben*.

Said Halim: ibid.

'full-scale row': CAB 37/22, Admiralty Orders and telegrams re escape of *Goeben* and *Breslau*, 26 Nov 1914.

Souchon's log: McLaughlin, *Escape of the Goeben*.

Venizelos: see Thomson, *The Allied Secret Service in Greece*, 6 Aug 1914. Venizelos awakened at 2 am by German Ambassador, 'coal should be given to two merchant ships'. Venizelos knew coal destined for *Goeben* and *Breslau*, 'our duty as neutrals'. The merchant ships, loaded with paper for South Africa, rendezvoused with warships at Naxos.

Nauen, 10 Aug: James, *Eyes of the Navy*, p. 61. Transmitted 2.15 pm.

131 Souchon: McLaughlin, *Escape of the Goeben*.

Enver and von Kressenstein: ibid.

Turks mobilise: see Murphy, *Soldiers of the Prophet*. After the war Murphy, as staff officer in Constantinople, was able to question senior enemy officers and examine documents.

Limpus: FO 371/1241. And see McLaughlin, *Escape of the Goeben*.

Limpus takes leave: FO 371/1241, Mallet to Grey, 14 Sept.

132 Kaiser, 'John Bull . . .': McLaughlin, *Escape of the Goeben*.

Captain H. W. Richmond: later Admiral Sir H. W. Richmond, commanding Dreadnought class HMS *Conqueror*, and 2nd Battle Squadron, Grand Fleet; and C-in-C, East Indies. In 1913 appointed Assistant DNO under Rear-Admiral Arthur C. Leveson. He took outspoken exception to Churchill's invasion of the naval operations room during the *Goeben* fiasco, and to the subsequent conduct of naval and military operations. He was generally thought to have the best tactical brain in the navy. In 1915 he was banished to Italy as Naval Attaché. See Arthur J. Marder, *Portrait of an Admiral: The Life and Papers of Sir Herbert Richmond*, London, 1952.

Chief of Naval Staff: Admiral of the Fleet Sir Frederick Charles Doveton Sturdee, naval historian. Fisher could not work with him and he was replaced by his ex-assistant and DNI, Admiral Oliver, at the end of the year.

132 Prince Louis of Battenburg: Admiral of the Fleet, first Marquess of Milford Haven, Louis Alexander Mountbatten, First Sea Lord, 1912–Nov 1914. Unfairly the butt of public and press anger at the *Goeben* affair and the disasters which followed, with suggestions even of pro-German sympathies deriving from his ancestry. Lord Louis commented on his resignation: 'When I joined the Royal Navy there was no German Empire.' McLaughlin, *Escape of the Goeben.*

Court of Enquiry: see Sir Julian S. Corbett, *Naval Operations*, Official History, vol.I, p. 54ff., and summary in McLaughlin, *Escape of the Goeben.*

German merchantman at Chanak: see Murphy, *Soldiers of the Prophet*, and McLaughlin, *Escape of the Goeben.*

Mines: European side of Straits mined on 24 Aug. Trumpener, *Germany and the Ottoman Empire.*

133 Turkey purchased ships: McLaughlin, *Escape of the Goeben*, 11 Aug.

Wangenheim, Turco-German mission: AA/A16840/14 Weltkreig 11/Bd1.

'chattering, egotistical Jew': *Arab Bulletin*, no. 23, 26 Sept 1916. Adds: 'prewar favourite of Kaiser and Kaiserin'.

Von Oppenheim to Wangenheim: AA/A16840/14 Weltkrieg 11, Bd1. See Vogel, *Die Persien und Afghanistanexpedition*. A complete account from German, British, Persian and Russian sources of the German mission to Afghanistan.

134 Enver to Russian Attaché: 5 Aug, ibid, quotes military files IBZI.II, 6 Nrs 6/8/69/100/244 (Die internationalen Beziehungen im Zeitalter des Imperialismus). See also Trumpener, *Germany and the Ottoman Empire*, Enver, possible alignment with Entente.

Russian Ambassador, Benckendorff, to Sazanov, 9 Aug: Vogel, *Die Persian und Afghanistanexpedition.*

Territorial integrity: 18 Aug, Sazanov to Benckendorff, ibid.

Row over *Goeben:* McLaughlin, *Escape of the Goeben.*

Events in Constantinople: Trumpener, *Germany and the Ottoman Empire.* Murphy, at Jask, received details of intercepted messages from MO3 agent sent to Basra. 'Turkey's entry into war imminent,' 1 Sept. (Note in Carruthers's private papers.) But on 2 Sept Mallet reported optimistically to FO. L/P & S/10/462, Mallet to Grey.

Kaiser agreed to loan: see Trumpener, *Germany and the Ottoman Empire.*

First contingent left for Constantinople 10 Sept: Voigt diary, quoted Vogel, *Die Persien und Afghanistanexpedition.*

Said Halim to Mallet: FO 371/2141.

135 Rumania: Trumpener, *Germany and the Ottoman Empire.*

Enver: opinions of Kaiser and Churchill, McLaughlin, *Escape of the Goeben.*

135   Expeditionary Force 'D': L/P & S/10/462, Viceroy to IO, 13 Oct. Murphy, *Soldiers of the Prophet*, p. 47.

Cromer: report to Cabinet, 16 Oct 1914, CAB 37/121.

Vice-Generalissimo: Trumpener, *Germany and the Ottoman Empire*. Enver was appointed War Minister Jan 1914.

Arrest of Herr Harling: Murphy, *Soldiers of the Prophet*.

Military attaché's report: FO 371/2141, dated 28 Oct.

German submarines to Constantinople: FO 371/2141. Russian Secret Service reports, telegraphed from Petrograd to London, 3 Nov.

Ottoman fleet to Black Sea: Trumpener, *Germany and the Ottoman Empire*. Souchon: 'Mission of war'. Orders to 'seek provocation at sea before attacking Russian coast'.

136   Fisher: *The Times*, 28 Oct. See Marder in *Fear God and Dread Nought*, vol. III, p. 39ff., and same author in *Portrait of an Admiral*, p. 124ff. Also Fisher, *Memories*, passim. Exclamation: 'On re-appointment Fisher prayed at Westminster Abbey, and afterwards was heard to exclaim'. He was seventy-four when he resumed his old job, and on his first day back at the Admiralty worked twenty-two hours at a stretch.

Advance British force, Muhammerah: Murphy, *Soldiers of the Prophet*.

Russian Ambassador at Porte, Benckendorff, recalled: Vogel, *Die Persien und Afghanistanexpedition*.

Porte to Sazanov: IBZ I, II, 6. Trumpener, *Germany and the Ottoman Empire*.

Ambassadors leave capital: Vogel, *Die Persien und Afghanistanexpedition*.

Viceroy's proclamation: FO 141/710, Indian Government declaration to Arab Nation, 31 Oct. Issued 2 Nov. Friedman, *Germany, Turkey and Zionism, 1897–1918*.

Egypt: declaration of martial law, 2 Nov. Tibawi, *Anglo-Arab Relations*.

Czar declares war: Trumpener, *Germany and the Ottoman Empire*. Javid, unhappy about the German alliance, and other Jewish members of the Ottoman administration resigned.

Bombardment of forts: see James, *The Eyes of the Navy*, p. 60, and McLaughlin, *Escape of the Goeben*, p. 156.

Von der Goltz: recalled from Belgium, 23 Nov, Vogel, *Die Persien und Afghanistanexpedition*, command of First Army, 24th, Trumpener, *Germany and the Ottoman Empire;* 28th, to Constantinople, Vogel, *Die Persien und Afghanistanexpedition*.

137   Niedermayer's party: ibid., quoting Voigt diary, 23 Nov, 'animosity between Wassmuss and others'.

'showplace': ibid.

Allegiances of tribes at beginning of war: ibid. See also Sir Percy Sykes, *A*

History of Persia; Christopher Sykes, *Wassmuss,* and Kazemzadeh, *Russia and Britain in Persia.*

137 Germans to Baghdad and Persia: Vogel, *Die Persien und Afghanistanexpedition.*

138 Second German mission: sanctioned 1 Jan, ibid.

Von Hentig: Secretary in the diplomatic corps, ibid.

Barakat Allah: Professor at San Francisco, friend of Habibullah's brother, a Pan-Islamite. Ibid.

Mahendra Pratap and Indian agents: L/P & S/10/899.

C. J. Edmonds: 'The Persian Gulf – Prelude to the Zimmermann Telegram', *CASJ,* vol. XLVII, no. 1, Jan 1960.

141 'Persian neutrality': Christopher Sykes, *Wassmuss.*

142 Anglo-Persian Oil Company: CAB 37/119. Proposed agreement with APOC, Winston Churchill, 11 May.

Attacks on oil installations: see Sachar, *The Emergence of the Middle East,* p. 54, and Sykes, *Wassmuss.*

7 The Flickering Flame

143 Mubarak to Ibn Saud, with note from British Government: L/P & S/10/387.

Correspondence relating to Shakespear's instructions and journey to Ibn Saud's camp, with messages between Bushire, Kuwait, Bahrain and Shakespear, in L/P & S/10/384–91. See Winstone, *Shakespear,* p. 185ff., and Lacey, *The Kingdom,* pp. 113–17.

144 Diary and secret papers: note in RGS archive: 'Diary handed to C. C. R. Murphy 1914'. Probably made by Carruthers.

Viceroy: eventually arrived at Basra 4 Feb 1915. Murphy, *Soldiers of the Prophet.*

Death of Birdwood: ibid., and Sir Arnold Wilson, *Loyalties: Mesopotamia.*

Sayid Talib to Kuwait: L/P & S/10/387.

145 Shakespear on Sayid Talib: L/P & S/10/384.

146 Crow to Constantinople, 20 April: R/15/5/27.

Knox/Trevor: ibid.

Ibn Saud to Mubarak, 16 April: ibid.

Aboard SS *Ferrara:* the delegation actually arrived on Mubarak's yacht, *Mishrif.*

147 Restoration of Ottoman authority in Al Hasa: Britain's motives at this time are hard to understand. On 25 April Foreign Dept, India, had told the Resident that HMG would no longer 'press mediation' with Ibn Saud, that there was no longer objection to direct negotiations between Turks and

himself, and set out 'desiderata' based on a note to Hakki Pasha dated 9 March. That note included the injunction, 'Bin Saud not to interfere in territories or politics of Gulf rulers, including Qatar'. On 29 April, when Turks were demanding the right to re-post garrisons at Uqair and Katif, Ibn Saud was told that in return for his acquiescence in the Turks' plan, he would be given 'verbal permission' to occupy Qatar. But Ibn Saud had never claimed Qatar. He only wanted a guarantee that the Turks would not be allowed to keep a garrison there and thus threaten him from the north. See R/15/5/27, correspondence March/April 1914.

Viceroy to IO, 13 Sept 1913, contained in note from Eyre Crowe, U/S FO to IO, 1 April 1914. R/15/5/27. Viceroy added: 'We have nothing to fear from Turkey, now that we have reached an agreement with her in the Persian Gulf'.

An alternative scheme devised by Sayid Talib and the Turks, according to Gertrude Bell in a subsequent intelligence document, was to encourage Ibn Saud to attack Kuwait. *Arab Bulletin*, no. 43, 1917. Perhaps the knowledge of that possibility drove Britain's negotiators to extremes of political caprice.

147   Annual pension from Turks: £250 a month. To fly Ottoman flag, R/15/5/27.

148   Treaty between Ibn Saud and Turks: dated 4 Rajab, 1332 (15 May 1914), found among Turkish records at Basra. L/P & S/10/385. According to Lacey, *The Kingdom*, p. 572, the Saudi authorities claim this document to be a forgery. It is difficult to see why. It reflects no discredit on Ibn Saud, but a great deal on Britain, and as Shakespear insisted (letter to brother 14 Jan, Winstone, *Shakespear*, p. 203) on Grey and Knox. See Shakespear to Resident, 20 Nov 1914 in L/P & S/10/387.

Ibn Saud to Talib: L/P & S/10/385.

Viceroy to London, 10 May 1914: L/P & S/10/384.

Mallet to F/S, 12 May 1914: R/15/5/27.

Shakespear to Resident, 20 Nov 1914: L/P & S/10/387.

Shakespear to Ibn Saud: ibid.

149   Basra to London, via India, Viceroy 9 Oct: L/P & S/10/462 (War). 'Sayyid Talib came to see me last night. He says Turkey seems resolved on war ... He would like to enter into negotiations with regard to attitude in case of hostilities. He desired me to ask Your Excellency to remind Lord Kitchener of a conversation with him in Cairo 3 years ago and to say that the time has come.' Reply: FO to Mallet, 10 Oct (incomplete cypher; tel. no. 655), 'Talib's message will be conveyed to Lord Kitchener, but he should bear in mind that war is not inevitable'.

Correspondence, Oct 1914: L/P & S/10/259, 387, and 462.

Ibn Saud raids Mutair and Ajman: *Arab Bulletin*, no. 43, 28 Feb 1917, Gertrude Bell.

Crewe to Ibn Saud, via India, 4 Oct 1914: 'Your friend Captain Shakespear is on his way to you', Winstone, *Shakespear*, p. 193. Cox to Foreign, 16 Nov,

'Captain Shakespear apparently contemplates staying with Bin Saud according to original instructions'. L/P & S/10/387.

149 Shaikh of Kuwait to Ibn Saud: L/P & S/10/259.

Colonel Grey to Bushire: Winstone, *Shakespear*, p. 197.

Shakespear to Grey, 11 Dec 1914: ibid., p. 198.

'last will and testament': signed 5 Dec. Registry, London.

150 Journey: reports to Resident, L/P & S/10/387. And Winstone, *Shakespear*.

'welcomed his guest warmly': Shakespear's first report, dated 2 Jan, was wired to London, and the Cabinet was pleased to learn that Ibn Saud 'still adhered to Britain'. CAB 37/123.

Sayid Talib: L/P & S/10/532. Negotiations by Sir Percy Cox, 7 Jan, and memo from F. E. Crow, 5 Jan. To Bombay as 'State guest'. Allowance 1,200 rupees per month, L/P & S/10/387. Report from Shakespear based on conversation with Talib's father, Sayid Rajab the Naqib, L/P & S/10/586, Dec 1915.

151 Visit of emissary of Abdullah ibn Husain, 17 Jan 1915: *Arab Bulletin*, no. 25, 7 Oct 1916. And Winstone, *Shakespear*, p. 22.

Letter to brother, Lieutenant-Colonel H. T. Shakespear, 14 Jan: ibid., p. 203.

To Gertrude Bell, 5 Jan: ibid. Address: 'A little North of Majmaa'.

Shakespear to Cox, 19 Jan: L/P & S/10/387.

152 Battle of Jarab: see Winstone, *Shakespear*, p. 205ff. Statements of Shakespear's servants, present at Jarab, R/15/5/88.

Major Bray: see *Shifting Sands*, p. 64.

153 Treaty with Britain, Dec 1915: L/P & S/390. Reservations of Sir Edward Grey and Lord Crewe: L/P & S/10/387, FO to IO, 29 Jan 1915.

Shakespear: IO/FO obituary, L/P & S/10/586.

Musil, Nov 1914: see *Arabia Deserta*, pp. 377–474.

157 Shakespear at Jauf, 28 April–1 May 1914: travel notes, RGS.

158 Musil at scene of Shakespear's death, 14 Jan–6 Feb 1915: see *Northern Najd*, pp. 46–57.

159 Battle of Jarab and description of Shakespear's death: see *Northern Najd*, notes on the History of the House of Ibn Rashid, pp. 248–50.

Field-gun: the gun, which has achieved some notoriety as the immediate cause of Shakespear's death, was probably one of the six Erhardt 4.7-inch light pieces which the Turks took to Kasim from Samawah on the Euphrates in late May 1904, at the start of their 'benign occupation' till 1906. The field-guns were each carried on a litter between two mules, and were left behind when the Turks retreated in the face of Ibn Saud's success against Ibn Rashid. R/15/5/24 and FO 406/20–21. And see Longrigg, *Iraq*.

'lay on the battlefield': evidence of Khalid and others, R/15/5/88, 19 June 1915.

160   Musil to Mesopotamia and Damascus: see his *The Middle Euphrates*, pp. 128–33.

8 Councils of War

161   For a rounded view of the British Cabinet in the first year of war, I have used Cassar, *Kitchener*, Churchill, *The World Crisis*, Terraine, *Impacts of War*, and Burton J. Hendrick (ed.), *The Life and Letters of W. H. Page*, 3 vols, Heinemann, 1922.

Kitchener: Churchill, *The World Crisis:* 'When he gave a decision it was invariably accepted as final. He was never, to my belief, overruled by the War Council or the Cabinet in any matter, great or small'. But Churchill had a vested interest in perpetuating the idea of Kitchener's absolute dominance of decision-making procedures.

Page: *Letters.*

Commander Thomson: often cited as Head of the Metropolitan Police Special Branch. According to official police records, he was Assistant Commissioner from 23 June 1913 to 30 Nov 1921, and Director of the Criminal Investigation Department. He took charge of Special Branch in 1918 and was succeeded by the Hon. Trevor Bigham as Director of the CID.

162   War Council, meeting 25 Nov 1914: CAB 42/1. Original members of Council: Prime Minister, H. H. Asquith; Chancellor of Exchequer, Lloyd George; Foreign Secretary, Sir Edward Grey; First Lord of Admiralty, Winston Churchill; First Sea Lord, Admiral Lord Fisher; Secretary of State for War, Field-Marshal Lord Kitchener; Chief of the Imperial General Staff, Lieutenant-General Sir J. Wolfe Murray; and A. J. Balfour, co-opted from Opposition (Conservative Party). Lord Haldane, the Lord Chancellor, and Admiral Sir A. K. Wilson, Chief of Naval Staff, were co-opted in 1915.

Von der Goltz: see Trumpener, *Germany and the Ottoman Empire*; 24 Nov, given command of First Army.

Liman von Sanders: ibid., 31 Oct, Wangenheim asked Bethmann Hollweg to recall Liman – 'nervous, introspective', persecuting Embassy staff.

163   Enver and von Schellendorf: Liman's views, ibid., quotes AA, 139, Turkei.

Caucasus: the adventure of Enver and von Schellendorf was, ironically, a response to early Russian disasters in the Caucasus which gave rise to the Grand Duke's call to the Allies to stage a counter-attack to relieve his army, 2 Jan 1915. See the official history, Brigadier-General J. E. Edmonds, *Military Operations, France and Belgium*, vol. 1.

The desire to relieve pressure on the Russian front is generally held responsible for the determination to go on with the Dardanelles venture. But Churchill was already pushing for it in Cabinet. See Sachar, *The Emergence of the Middle East*, and Cassar, *Kitchener*.

163 Suez campaign: CAB 42/1 and CAB 37/124 Military ops against Turkey, 2 Feb, WO 33/796 (report of Colonel Haldane). CAB 37/125. Events 25 Jan–8 Feb.

Parker: private diary, 3–6 Jan. Arab attacks on Tor villages. Principal Arab agent, Issairi Effendi, on duty in Syria. Saad Bey Rifaat made chief agent in southern Sinai. Clayton (DMI Cairo) to Parker: 'Convent will help in getting intelligence through Arab contacts'.

Convent: agents on Parker's books: 'Monks and Nuns of Convent of St. Catherine, and Monastery of Mount of Moses.'

Parker diary: payments to Father Jaussen, Feb–May 1915, listed.

Children and Birkil Bey: Murray, *Sons of Ishmael.*

164 Russian offensive: Cabinet discussion, CAB 42/2 3 March. Also CAB 37/125, meeting of full Cabinet, same day. See Cassar, *Kitchener.*

Fitzmaurice: joined Admiralty intelligence Jan 1915, and took up residence in Sofia. The Germans soon discovered where he was living and placed an agent in the next-door house. Hall believed that had Fitzmaurice been in Constantinople at the time of the *Goeben* business he would have warned the Government in time. There was little he did not know of intrigue in the capital. Fisher found him in London and recruited him. But after fifteen years his memory was confused. 'Find Maurice Fitzgerald,' he told Hall. He was probably mixing him up with the ex-DNI, Maurice Fitzmaurice. Eady and Fitzmaurice met Turkish emissaries at Dedeagatch on the Bulgarian coast in late Feb 1915. The go-between was the adopted son of the Chief Rabbi of Constantinople. See James, *Eyes of the Navy,* pp. 60–64, McLaughlin, *Escape of the Goeben,* pp. 44, 84, and Fisher, *Fear God,* vol. 3, p. 158.

Samuel: 'The Future of Palestine', CAB 37/123, dated 21 Jan 1915.

165 Fisher's resignation, 12 May 1915: see Fisher, *Fear God,* correspondence with Churchill, Asquith and King George V, March to June, pp. 167–265, and Marder's summary.

Churchill dismissed: Admiral Sir Stanley Colville to King, 'he was, we all consider, a danger to the Empire', See McLaughlin, *Escape of the Goeben,* p. 94. Asquith asked all ministers to submit resignations on 17 May. The Coalition Government was formed on 25 May. Balfour took over the Admiralty and Austen Chamberlain the India Office. Grey remained at the Foreign Office.

When Prince Louis resigned as First Sea Lord in 1914 he told Churchill that 'he sincerely trusted that he would not go off with the navy alone to attack the Dardanelles and thus alert the Turks, because Kitchener refused to support him with the army'. Earl Mountbatten of Burma to author, 13 March 1979.

Germany's Eastern Bureau, and Turco-German General Staff organisation: see Bray, *Shifting Sands,* for account of activities in Syria, India and Madina. Also Vogel, *Die Persien und Afghanistanexpedition.* Official files, AA, IA Weltkrieg 11f, Unternehmungen und Aufwiegelungen gegen unsere Feinde in Indien, WO 106/710–31 (papers of DMO and DMI).

166   Lawrence on Shakespear: *Arab Bulletin*, no. 25, 7 Oct 1916.

Philippides: FO 371/2921.

167   Hall and Thomson: see James, *Eyes of the Navy*, and Sir Basil Thomson, articles in *The Times*, 14 Nov 1921, and the *Sunday Express*, 1 Dec 1935.

Afghanistan: Vogel, *Die Persien und Afghanistanexpedition*.

Niedermayer, July 1915: AA, Wk. 11e, Bd 18.

168   Nasrullah: H. H. Dodwell (ed.), Cambridge History of the British Empire, vol. 5, CUP, 1932.

170   Russians in Persia: Christopher Sykes, *Wassmuss*, took Kasr Shirin 7 May.

171   Cossacks in Basra: Gertrude Bell, *Letters*, 27 May.

Persian Rifles: Sir Percy Sykes, *History of Persia*, and *The South Persian Rifles*.

Von der Goltz: Christopher Sykes, *Wassmuss*.

Wassmuss: ibid.

9   The Intrusives

172   Harold Nicolson: quote from his *George V, His Life and Reign*, London, 1952, cited by Terraine in *Impacts of War*.

McMahon: L/P & S/11/85, 18 Dec 1914.

Storrs: *Orientations*, p. 191ff.

173   Protectorate: FO 371/2930. S/S to Acting Resident Cheetham, 19 Sept 1914. Declaration announced 18 Dec, on appointment of McMahon as High Commissioner, L/P & S/11/85 and CAB 41/35. See also PRO 30/57–44, Cromer to Kitchener, 'Dismemberment of Ottoman Empire'.

Firman of Sultan: first issued in 1867. See Stewart, *The Middle East*.

McMahon: see Storrs, *Orientations*.

Jones: ibid. Previously O'Conor's butler, Constantinople.

Kitchener to Cheetham: L/P & S/18/B222, and FO 882, 24 Sept 1914. Mallet, in Constantinople, had been consulted by the FO before Kitchener's message was approved, and he commented, 'support of Arab Movement' might be an 'effective weapon'. FO 371/2139, 4 Sept 1914.

Abdullah to Cairo, Feb 1914: L/P & S/10/523 and FO 371/2140. See also Clayton, *An Arabian Diary*. No precise date.

174   Viceroy: FO 371/2140, 8 Dec, following approaches by Al Masri to Cheetham and Clayton between July and Oct 1914. L/P & S/10/523, 9 Aug, story from 'the famous Aziz al Masri'; FO to Cheetham, 11 Aug, 'impress strongly on Al Masri need to keep quiet and leave Arabs alone'; Cheetham to FO, 24 Aug, 'reliable agent to Al Masri' with 'warning'. Consul G. P. Devey to Mallet, 29 July, Arab Revolutionary Committee 'Voice of Ages', 'This shall

be the last year of slavery'; report by Clayton following interview with Far-uqi, nationalist deserter, 30 Oct; Cheetham to Grey, 13 Nov, 'Al Masri's idea, revolution in Mesopotamia'; Grey to Cheetham, 14 Nov, 'Arab move-ment should be encouraged'; Cheetham to FO 16 Nov, interview with Al Masri: 'Must find Nuri as-Said, Muhammerah'. (Nuri Said was at Basra; this was the period of Sayid Talib's mission to Ibn Saud and the alleged payment to Talib of a large sum of money by the Basra merchant Abdal Latif Pasha Mandil on behalf of Ibn Saud.) IO, Viceroy informed of Al Masri's plan, 19 Nov; P. Graves, MI Cairo, on 'Mesopotamian scheme', 6 Dec; Hirtzel, IO, 'I was always suspicious of this scheme', 8 Dec. And see FO 371/2141, 9 Nov, McMahon to Grey, 'Venerated friend of Bin Saud in Cairo'. See also Tibawi, *Anglo-Arab Relations*, 'Al Masri rebuffed'.

174 Second meeting: 18 April 1914. Storrs's report in L/P & S/10/523.

Faisal in 1915: *Arab Bulletin*, no. 42, 1916. See also Clayton, *Arabian Diary*, May 1915, returned to Mecca with 'price of cooperation of Arab secret societies'.

Syrian and Mesopotamian 'Committees': Lawrence, *Seven Pillars*, p. 49. 'In January 1915, Yasin, head of the Mesopotamian officers, Ali Riza, head of the Damascus officers, and Abdul Ghani al Areisi, for the Syrian civilians, sent down to him a concrete proposal for a military mutiny in Syria.'

French proposals: L/P & S/11/85, 3 Dec 1914; and L/P & S/10/523, 16 Dec, M. E. Jung, Paris correspondent of *L'Egypte* suggested England, France and Russia proclaim Arab independence. L/P & S/11/85, 17 Dec. Govern-ment of India approved McMahon's participation in talks on Arabia. 12 Dec, IO to FO, correspondence with Sharif 'dangerous'. L/P & S/10/523, FO apologised to IO for not keeping it informed. See Meinertzhagen, *Mid-dle East Diary*, 'Secret agreement with France', early 1915, allotting Greater Syria to France and port of Haifa and Palestine to Britain.

McMahon and Izzat: L/P & S/11/85, 4 Jan.

Izzat and Young Turks: L/P & S/20/132, Personalities.

175 Izzat at FO: L/P & S/10/523.

Kitchener to Dunkirk: see Aston, *The Secret Service*.

IO to FO (Hirtzel) 6 Jan: L/P & S/10/523.

McMahon to FO, 13 Jan: ibid.

McMahon to Sharif: 'Apparently dated' 30 Aug 1915. L/P & S/18/B222. This file contains all the correspondence between the Cairo Residency/ High Commission (from Dec 1914) and the Sharif and his son, Abdullah. Antonius, *The Arab Awakening*, gives 30 July as the date of McMahon's first letter.

'previous declaration': this consisted of a shorthand note made by Ali Bey of a discourse by the Sharif which took place 'in privacy at night on the roof of his palace'. It was full of complaints about the Ottoman Caliphate and intimated that he (the Sharif) was no longer bound to 'Enver and his cli-que'. It concluded: 'Say, Ali, are you satisfied?' 'Yes, sir.'

176 Araifan, 'O': L/P & S/10/586, Arab Revolt.

177 High Commissioner to Grey, 26 Aug 1915: L/P & S/18/B215.

Caliphate: L/P & S/10/523. Dec, Lord Crewe asked *Daily Mirror*, *Nation* and *Morning Post* to be 'careful' in editorial comments.

178 Musil to Ibn Saud: Musil, *Northern Najd*, p. 180ff.

Faisal ibn Hamud: usually called Faisal ibn Rashid, the same.

Amir of Hail: Musil, *Northern Najd*.

McMahon's responsibility: see note in his hand attached to file FO 882 in the PRO.

179 Lawrence and others to Cairo: see Knightley and Simpson, *Secret Lives*, pp. 42ff. The authors of this generally well-researched book say that Lawrence and Woolley approached Newcombe for war jobs, and then turned to Hogarth. In fact it was Colonel Hedley, head of MO4, who recommended Lawrence to Cairo. Newcombe was serving in France at the time (Oct 1914). Cairo had already asked for reinforcements for its skeletal intelligence service, and Hedley had thought of sending Marmaduke Pickthall, a rabid Turcophile who had lived in Constantinople up to war, but he was considered too dangerous, and Lawrence was chosen in his stead. See Liddell Hart Papers, 1914-15, King's College, London, Aldington, *Lawrence of Arabia*, and Woolley, *As I Seem to Remember*.

Herbert, Savoy Hotel: Lawrence, *Seven Pillars*.

180 'band of wild men': ibid.

GOC, General Maxwell: The position of General Sir J. G. Maxwell, GOC-in Chief, Force in Egypt, was anomalous from the beginning. Sir Reginald Wingate, Sirdar of the Egyptian Army, was essentially in charge of all the Staff facilities. Clayton was Director of Military and Civil Intelligence, under Wingate's control. Colonel A. C. Parker was Clayton's GSO1, responsible for the Sinai and the Red Sea coast. Colonel Jennings Bramley had returned from southern Sinai to the Savoy Hotel. Slatin Pasha was Inspector-General of Police and head of the Secret Service in the Sudan. Wingate's secretaries, Captain G. S. Symes and Captain R. J. R. Rees-Mogg, were effectively running the Staff offices for the Sirdar, while the GOC's Adjutant-General, Lieutenant-Colonel W. H. Drake, fought a losing battle in his attempt to set up adequate Staff facilities for the Expeditionary Force. As Jamal and his deputy, Kress von Kressenstein in Jerusalem, planned the first Suez attack, Maxwell's resources were almost non-existent. But the General played along with Wingate and by and large supported the Arab Bureau's schemes.

Oriental Bureau on Lawrence: see Ehrentreich, 'Lawrence of Arabia', in *Neuphilologische Monatschrift*.

'Doctrinaire': Kedourie, *England and the Middle East*.

181 Lawrence's account: *Seven Pillars*.

181 Wemyss: Admiral Sir Rosslyn, C-in-C, Red Sea. Colonel Neil Malcolm, GSO on Maxwell's staff.

Map work and tribal 'Blue Book': see Gertrude Bell, *Letters*, p. 294ff., Nov–Dec 1915. Details in notes and diaries of Colonel Parker (in author's possession).

Cairo and Alexandria, June 1915: Storrs, *Orientations*.

182 Sir Mark Sykes and Maurice De Bunsen: see Adelson, Roger, *Mark Sykes*, pp. 180ff. Adelson notes that Sykes was at the same school as George Macdonogh, the DMI, that both were Catholics and both 'believed in making something big out of the operations in the East'. Macdonogh 'paved' his way in 'the world of Military Intelligence'. But at this time Macdonogh was not the DMI, and Kitchener was Sykes's mentor.

Sykes, quote: ibid., p. 180.

De Bunsen Report: CAB 42/3, 30 July 1915.

Chirol: Rebecca West in *Sunday Times*, 20 July 1958, review of Burgoyne, *Gertrude Bell: from her Personal Papers*.

Sykes on 'enemy agents': FO 882/13, to DMO, 14 July 1915.

183 'suspected rivalry', CUP agents: Sykes quotes French military attaché, Constantinople, article in *Revue hebdomadaire*, 5 June 1915. See Adelson, *Mark Sykes*.

'with France out of the way': FO 882/13, Sykes to DMO, 16 July 1915.

Sharifian family: report from Symes. L/P & S/18/B211, and L/P & S/10/523, 3 Aug 1915. Forwarded by Wingate to S/S.

184 Charles Boutagy: see Knightley and Simpson, *Secret Lives*, pp. 42–4.

185 'faithfully recorded': ibid., p. 42.

Clayton on duties of Cairo staff: see Clayton, *An Arabian Diary*.

Lawrence as cartographer: according to Sir Ernest Dowson, then Director-General of the Survey of Egypt, Lawrence's particular assignment was map work, for which Hogarth had recommended him to MO4 in London. Dowson says that he saw Lawrence several times a week in Cairo and that he was engaged in writing 'geographical essays' and special papers. See R. L. Bidwell, *Arabian Studies*, III, MEC, Cambridge, 1976.

Employment of Boutagy: the Boutagys were friends of the Aaronsohns and of Dr Torrance at Tiberias, and it is probable that Lawrence knew father and son through the latter from his pre-war travels in Syria. See Alex Aaronsohn, *With the Turks in Palestine*, and Engle, *The NILI Spies*. An account of the Haifa escapade involving Boutagy senior is given in Knightley and Simpson, *Secret Lives*, p. 42ff., in which Lawrence is said to have been the instigator; and Lawrence is represented as Woolley's superior officer. Both were Second-Lieutenants. See also Woolley, *As I Seem to Remember*, for description of Boutagy's anonymous activities.

Storrs and Sykes: Storrs, *Orientations*.

186   Imam Yahya, 'Pope-King': Herbert, *Ben Kendim.*

Sykes in Yemen: see Adelson, *Mark Sykes.*

Aden, July, 1915: CAB 37/131, operations at Lahaj and Aden. Reinforcements for Aden. Death of Sultan of Lahaj.

187   Storrs in Yemen and death of Sultan: see Storrs, *Orientations.*

Sykes in India: see Adelson, *Mark Sykes.*

Hardinge on Sharif lobby: to A. Chamberlain, 6 Aug 1915, Hardinge Papers, University Library, Cambridge. See Adelson, *Mark Sykes*, p. 189.

Sykes at Kut: ibid., p. 192.

Sir Arnold Wilson: see his *Loyalties: Mesopotamia.*

Indian Expeditionary Forces: WO 33/716.

Hardinge, warnings: CAB 37/126, private telegram.

War Council, 19 March: CAB 42/2. Partition of Turkey in Asia.

189   Sykes, memo to WO: FO 882/13, 28 Oct 1915. See Adelson, *Mark Sykes.*

190   Sharif Muhammad al Faruqi: FO 882/13, 17 Oct 1915; met Sharif Faisal in Aleppo, April 1915, and sent to Gallipoli by Jamal, Tibawi, *Anglo-Arab Relations*; L/P & S/10/523, McMahon to FO, statement on Sharif of Mecca, to intelligence officers, 11 Oct; and L/P & S/18/B292, Faruqi, aims of Arab Party. Tibawi, *Anglo-Arab Relations.* Faruqi interrogated by Naum Shuqair, Anglophile Arab nationalist leader, on 12 Sept, and expressed a wish to see Al Masri. See FO 371/2490 and FO 141/1732.

Chamberlain: took over at IO in May 1915.

Dardanelles Committee: became War Committee on 4 Nov, CAB 42/4.

Telegram to Viceroy: CAB 42/1 and CAB 37/136.

191   Sykes and Faruqi: FO 882/13, 21 Nov, to DMO, Callwell.

Faruqi interviews with intelligence: Aubrey Herbert sent a long report to MI2 which was passed to Hirtzel at the IO. On 6 Nov Hirtzel observed that one of the 'good Sharif's sons' was on way to assist Ibn Rashid to attack Ibn Saud, and that Faruqi had offered no evidence for story of Ottoman troops and officers 'ready to revolt at the Young Arabs' signal'. And on the same day he told FO: 'the discretion of Sir Henry McMahon has been exercised without due regard to Indian interests'. L/P & S/10/524.

Storrs: *Orientations.*

Sharif's communication: WO 33/969, and L/P & S/18/B222, Grand Sharif of Mecca to his Excellency the Most Exalted, the Most Eminent, the British High Commissioner in Egypt, 9 Sept 1915.

McMahon to Sharif: WO 33/969 and L/P & S/10/B222, 24 Oct 1915.

'drafted by Grey': see McMahon corr. file 131,Oct 1915, MEC, Oxford.

192   Sharif's reply, 5 Nov: ibid. Letter unsigned. *Note:* in WO 33/969, it is stated (p. 24) that McMahon's letter was sent 'without prejudice to interests of France', and that at the time of these negotiations neither Sir Henry

McMahon nor the Sharif had knowledge of negotiations then in progress between Britain, France and Russia which led to the Sykes–Picot agreement. The Indian Office noted, L/P & S/10/523, 27 Oct: 'Assurances to Sharif incompatible with recommendations of Inter-departmental Committee' (De Bunsen proposals), and Chamberlain wrote in margin of note from Hirtzel, promises 'unfortunate'. See also Antonius, *The Arab Awakening*.

193 McMahon to Sharif, 17 Dec 1915: L/P & S/18/B222.

Arab Kingdom and Caliphate: CAB 42/6, 16–17 Dec, 'The Arab Question' and 'Evidence of Sir Mark Sykes'.

194 Husain's reply, 1 Jan 1916: L/P & S/18/B222. For notes on Sharif's demand for compensation for 'occupation of Iraq' see WO 33/969.

Foreign Secretary intervenes: WO 33/969. See Tibawi, *Anglo-Arab Relations*, Grey to Benckendorff, Russian Ambassador, 'Arabs have appealed to British Government', French and Russian interests.

Abdullah to Storrs, 18 Feb 1916: WO 33/969. Letter and verbal message in L/P & S/18/B222 undated. 'It is unworthy of the greatness of Great Britain to think that we believe false rumours,' verbal message. Letter from Sharif, 18 Feb, confirms secret sign with British agents. Messenger's code name 'Elias'.

195 McMahon to Sharif, 10 March: L/P & S/10/B222.

Gertrude Bell in Cairo: Winstone, *Gertrude Bell*, pp. 160ff.

196 Sykes, 'ambitious scenario': Adelson, *Mark Sykes*.

Robertson, 'side shows': CAB 42/7. See Cassar, *Kitchener*, on 'Easterners' and Cabinet squabbles. Kitchener offered his resignation on 30 Nov, but Asquith refused to accept it.

Sykes, War Committee evidence: CAB 42/6.

Lord Bertie to Crewe, 21 Dec 1915: FO 800/58. See Adelson, *Mark Sykes*, pp. 197–8.

S/S to Viceroy, 10 Dec: L/P & S/10/576.

197 Sykes on Cairo Bureau: FO 882/2, and L/P & S/10/576. See also L/P & S/10/523, Sykes's memo, 9 Dec 1915.

IO to FO, and attitude of Government of India: CAB 42/7 and L/P & S/10/576, Chamberlain to Grey, 30 Dec 1915.

Inter-departmental Conference, 6 Jan 1916: FO 882/2, and L/P & S/10/576.

198 Hogarth ditty: Storrs, *Orientations*.

199 *Arabian Report*: L/P & S/10/525.

Hirtzel: ibid.

Sir A. J. Murray, GOC Egypt: succeeded his namesake, General Sir J. W. Murray as CIGS in Sept 1915. Nominated as new GOC Egypt, Jan 1916.

New General Staff organisation, Cairo: Clayton replaced by Holdich in March 1916. But Clayton remained intelligence chief of Sirdar, Sir Reginald Wingate. WO records. Holdich made temporary Lt-Colonel, GSO1.

200   Sykes and Picot to Petrograd: L/P & S/10/525, Buchanan to Foreign Sec-
       retary. Impending visit, 19 Feb 1916. Left for Russia in March. See Sykes
       and Picot on 'Arab Question' 5 Jan 1915, CAB 42/11, and meetings of Sir A.
       Nicolson's committee re Sykes–Picot negotiations in FO 882/2, FO 371/2767
       (Turkey), 21 Jan, agreement provisional until Russian consent obtained.

10   The Siege

201   Expeditionary Force 'D': L/P & S/10/462, Admiralty to IO, 25 Aug 1914,
       Expeditionary Force at Karachi, 'ready at short notice'. 30 Oct 1914,
       advance force at Muhammerah. 3 Nov, force at anchor fifteen miles off
       Fao. 6 Nov, Fao fort bombarded by HMS *Odin*, second contingent at Bah-
       rain. CAB 37/122, and Mesopotamian Commission Report, 1917, Cd 8610.
       See Murphy, *Soldiers of the Prophet*, for details of the Bahrain landing.
       Troops under Lieutenant-General Sir Arthur Barrett landed at Basra on 7
       Nov.

       Chief Political Officer, Sir Percy Cox: see Braddon, *The Siege*, pp. 16–17.
       Braddon quotes B. F. Lake, but there is no official corroboration of the
       statement, though it represents a fair account of Britain's initial intention.

202   Eleanor Franklin Egan: see her *War in the Cradle of the World*, Harper, 1918.

203   Viceroy and C-in-C: see CAB 37/162. Paper by Lord Hardinge, 'Mesopota-
       mia', Dec 1916.

       German agents, Feb 1915: for events from the beginning of the year see
       CAB 37/123, 20 Jan, IO Report, *Situation in Basra*. L/P & S/10/384–91, 25
       Jan, 15,000 Turks with Arabs at Nasiriya. For attacks on oil lines see
       Christopher Sykes, *Wassmuss*, and Vogel, *Die Persien und Afghanistanexpedi-
       tion.*

       Najaf and Karbala: L/P & S/10/478, 27 Jan 1915. Turks plunder. 'Unwise to
       publish.'

       Bushire, Abadan, Arabistan: activities of German agents, L/P & S/10/462.
       Viceroy to S/S, 21 Aug 1914, 'nervous of attack on Abadan'. Proposed to
       send HMS *Odin* and *Lawrence* with 100 sepoys. Tug belonging to
       Wönckhaus was to be used to sink derelict lighter in Shatt-al-Arab.

       German FO: see Trumpener, *Germany and the Ottoman Empire*, 6–8 Sept
       1914, Zimmermann to Wangenheim.

204   Situation in April, Generals Robinson and Gorringe's actions: see Sir
       Percy Sykes, 'Persia', *Encyclopaedia Britannica*, 11th edn, vol. 32, p. 60ff., and
       Official History, *Mesopotamia.*

       Wassmuss auxiliaries: see Sachar, *The Emergence of the Middle East*, Christ-
       opher Sykes, *Wassmuss*, and Vogel, *Die Persien und Afghanistanexpedition.*

       Baghdad notice, *jihad:* WO 157/776 (Intelligence, GHQ Basra).

       General Sir John Nixon: description from Braddon, *The Siege*, p. 24. Took
       over from Barrett in April 1915.

204 'against the wishes of the Viceroy and the C-in-C': the idea that has become 'accepted history', that the advance on Baghdad was planned and carried out by India in defiance of the Cabinet and WO in London, advanced by Braddon and others, and that hospital and sanitary conditions were ignored by the army commanders on the spot, is ridiculous, and largely derives from the *Mesopotamian Commission Report* of 1917 and its minority addendum, ill-conceived documents which brought about the resignation of Austen Chamberlain as Secretary of State for India. See CAB 37/124, Dardanelles and Mesopotamia; CID Paper, 'Conduct of the War', 22 Feb 1915, Russia's deteriorating position and calls for help from Grand Duke Nicholas, mutiny of Indian troops at Singapore, reinforcements for Mesopotamia, 18 Feb; Wingate Papers, Durham University, Box 469/8, George Lloyd to Wingate, Arab Policy, 30 Jan 1915, Wingate urges 'occupation of Baghdad to impress Arabs'; CAB 42/2, Future Settlement of Turkey in Asia and Arabia; private telegram from Viceroy, 18 March, Sir Percy Sykes, 'Persia', *Encyclopaedia Britannica*, advance north begins in April to counter Turkish advance in Persia; Cox had urged advance as early as 23 Nov 1914, according to Murphy, *Soldiers of the Prophet*. See CAB 37/136, telegrams advance on Baghdad, 21 Oct 1915, and CAB 37/148, Townshend ops 11 Nov–3 Dec, CAB 37/149, Townshend's attitude. CAB 42/1, troops from France to Mesopotamia (25 Oct), Chamberlain to Viceroy, 'If Nixon satisfied force is sufficient, may march on Baghdad'.

Battle of Ctesiphon: Braddon, *The Siege*, p. 30ff.

Nureddin Pasha: WO 157/776 (Intelligence file, GHQ Mesopotamia), 28 May 1915, Nureddin arrived as new Wali of Baghdad with troop reinforcements, 22 May.

Von der Goltz: Trumpener, *Germany and the Ottoman Empire*. Relinquished command of First Army, 24 Oct. Appointed C-in-C Turkish Sixth Army.

205 Kut-al-Amara: taken by Townshend's force 28 Sept. See Cassar, *Kitchener*, Nixon wanted to advance on Baghdad, Kitchener 'violently opposed'.

War Office changes: in April 1915, MO5 (Counter-Intelligence) was named 'Security Intelligence' and made a sub-directorate of Special Intelligence, the old MO6, under Brigadier-General G. K. Cockerill. At that time MO5 had a staff of 4 officers. By Dec it had 83 officers and 23 civilians on the payroll. On 29 Dec 1915, Brigadier-General F. B. Maurice became DMO and Major-General C. E. Callwell remained in temporary charge of intelligence. On 3 Jan 1916, Major-General G. M. W. Macdonogh, who had been Chief of Intelligence with Field-Marshal French's army in France, became DMI. In a wholesale re-deployment, MI1(c) became 'Special Duties', accommodated at a secret address, as were MI5 and 'Special Intelligence'. MI2(b) embraced the Ottoman Empire, Arabia, Persia, Afghanistan, and Tripoli, and 'information emanating from Egypt, Sudan and India'. MI4 remained the topographical unit.

Gertrude Bell: *Letters*, 27 April 1916, from GHQ Basra, 'I don't hold a brief for the Govt. of India but it is only fair to remember that K. drained India white of troops and of all military requirements, including hospitals and doctors'; CAB 37/128, 14 May, last meeting of War Council; *The Times*, 14 May, 'Criminal neglect by Government'; CAB 37/131, Ops in Mesopotamia, 14 July. Moberly, *Official History of the War, Mesopotamia*, vol. 2, 'First Campaign for Baghdad', warning from India 'not to undertake operations above Baghdad'. On 30 Aug Nixon sent memo to India recommending advance. Sept, Hardinge to Chamberlain (Moberly, p. 3), 'pointed out great effect in East of capture of Baghdad', but would not recommend 'unless reinforcements from France or Egypt were made available'. And see Fisher, *Fear God*, vol. 3, p. 338: 'The Tigris advance to Baghdad was solely due to Balfour (advised by Slade) but the fact is being concealed, and all is put down to Nixon ... The General on the spot ... (Townshend) protested strongly. I've seen a letter from him to that effect. But the Government wanted to get Baghdad to cover the evacuation of the Dardanelles!' Fisher to Admiral Jellicoe, 6 April 1916.

It must be said on the other side that on 27 Sept Sir Percy Cox, Chief Political Officer with Force 'D', expressed view to India that 'Baghdad is within our grasp' and 'could be accomplished without reinforcing our troops'. Sir Arthur Hirtzel at IO: 'I entirely agree'. L/P & S/18/B220.

205   Gertrude Bell: see Winstone, *Gertrude Bell*, pp. 167–73.

206   Hardinge to Wingate: FO 882, 28 Nov 1915.

'easterners' and 'westerners': the polarities of ministers are more or less apparent from the records of the War Council, Aug 1914–May 1915, CAB 41/1–2, the Dardanelles Committee, which succeeded the Council in June 1915 and lasted until Oct 1915, CAB 42/3–4, and the War Committee, Nov 1915 to Dec 1916. After Lloyd George's occupation of 10 Downing Street on 7 Dec 1916, power was concentrated in a small War Cabinet and the issues arising from the 'side shows' were largely academic, though Leo Amery, British political representative at Supreme Allied Headquarters in Versailles, continued to lambast the 'Western Front' merchants and to promote the Arab Bureau's policies. See Lloyd George papers, House of Lords, and intro to *List of Cabinet Papers 1915 and 1916*, PRO. And see Terraine, *Douglas Haig*.

Kitchener's prize: Kitchener Papers. PRO 30/57/47.

Gertrude Bell and Viceroy: Arab affairs, see FO 371/2013, G.L.B. to Lord Robert Cecil.

Primed by 'Beloved Boy': Lawrence, *The Home Letters of T.E.L.*, 4 Jan, 'Miss Bell is doing great work for me', and 25 Jan, 'Miss Bell went to India yesterday.' In fact, she left on the 28th aboard HMS *Euripides*; Winstone, *Gertrude Bell*.

Appointment of A. Brownlow Fforde: L/P & S/10/576.

Arab Bureau: formally established 10 Jan 1916, CAB 42/7.

Gertrude Bell to Captain Hall: *Letters*, Lady Bell, Vice-Regal Lodge, 18 Feb 1916.

206 Gertrude Bell in Basra: *Letters*, 3 March–16 April 1916.

Gertrude Bell at GHQ: *Letters*, 27 April onward.

208 Indian Army Intelligence: IO records, Indian Army Lists, and information from private sources. I am particularly grateful to George B. Blaker.

Murphy and Arab Bureau: see his *Soldiers of the Prophet*. On return to India he was in charge of *Gazetteer of Arabia*, largely based on notes and map work of Shakespear, Leachman and Gertrude Bell. See Bell, *Letters*, p. 302.

Blaker: officially listed as Captain W. F. Reichwald, Assistant Military Secretary and interpreter to C-in-C until June 1914. Took English name when he went to fight in France in 1915.

209 Redl: L/P & S/11/101.

Leachman: arrived 11 March; Bray, *Paladin*.

Preusser: L/P & S/10/462, Secretary of State to Viceroy, Dr Conrad Preusser, activities in Cairo, now in Syria, 26 Oct 1914.

British force at Kut-al-Amara: see Moberly, *Mesopotamia*, Braddon, *The Siege*, and Townshend's own account, *My Campaign in Mesopotamia*.

210 Von der Goltz at Kut: Townshend, *My Campaign*.

Arrival of Herbert and Lawrence: see Herbert, *Mons, Anzac and Kut*, Lawrence, *The Letters of T. E. Lawrence*, Lawrence, *Seven Pillars*, p. 59, and Gertrude Bell, *Letters*, 9 April–26 May 1916.

Lord Chelmsford, Prince of Wales, etc., Cairo: see Storrs, *Orientations*, p. 192.

211 Arab sources: see Tibawi, *Anglo-Arab Relations*.

Unsigned letter to Lawrence, *en route* for Basra: FO 882/15.

Al Masri: L/P & S/10/525 (22 March) Faruqi and Al Masri to Mesopotamia: 'Lord Kitchener doesn't approve of Masri'. In same correspondence, S/S Chamberlain asks, 'Is Sharif going to turn up trumps after all?' Perhaps attempts were being made to bring Sharif into negotiations with Turks at Kut. Ibid., 30 March, General Lake to WO. 'Unable to concur in deputation of Faruqi and Al Masri to Mesop.' Dr Shahbandar and Nuri Said, 'Inexpedient to keep here'. Nuri Said, captured in 1915, was a patient in American Mission Hospital, Basra; see Dorothy Van Ess, *Pioneers of the Arab World*, p. 117. Abdal Rahman Shahbandar, friend of Jamal, Turkish C-in-C Syria, ibid. Left Damascus for Basra 2 Nov 1915.

General Lake: officially assumed command 19 Jan. *Army List*.

212 Arab historians: see Tibawi, *Anglo-Arab Relations*.

Kitchener vetoed: L/P & S/10/525.

MacMunn: FO 882/15, 26 March, Cairo to TEL: Nationalist leaders to Basra. MacMunn on way. 'He knows all about you.'

Talib: FO 882. And Lawrence, *Letters of T.E.L.* p. 265.

Herbert and Storrs: see Storrs, *Orientations*.

212 Colonel Jacob: ibid.

Turk POW: Herbert, *Mons, Anzac and Kut.*

213 Basra, Qurna and Kut: ibid., Gertrude Bell, *Letters*, Braddon, *The Siege.*

Leachman: Herbert, *Mons, Anzac and Kut.*

214 'Blackbeard': ibid.

Lawrence: FO 882/13, 22 March. T.E.L. left Cairo for Basra and Kut.

'bring Gertrude Bell back': Stewart, *T. E. Lawrence.*

'dashed to Piraeus': Ehrentreich, *Lawrence of Arabia*, 'Important mission to Greece in Spring of 1916'. See R. Bidwell, 'Questions to Biographers of T. E. Lawrence', *Arabian Studies*, III, MEC, Cambridge, 1976, quotes Graves, *Lawrence and the Arabs*, p. 84, 'to contact Levant group of British Secret Service'.

Erzerum: CAB 42/9. See Aldington, *Lawrence of Arabia.*

'met him at Basra': Lawrence, *The Home Letters of T.E.L.*, 18 May.

'great talks': Gertrude Bell, *Letters*, 9 April. See Stewart, *T. E. Lawrence*, p. 143.

Cox and generals: WO 33/969, telegrams between Viceroy, S/S and General Lake, April 1916. CAB 42/29. Précis of correspondence about Mesopotamian expedition, and CAB 42/31, 8–11 April, revised documentation about Townshend and Kut. See also Aldington, *Lawrence of Arabia:* Hubert Young (on Cox's staff) 'shocked'. Generals 'snubbed' Lawrence. 'He never forgave them.'

'hopes of Mesopotamia': Lawrence, *Seven Pillars*, ch. 7.

215 Herbert and Lawrence: Herbert, *Mons, Anzac and Kut.*

Easter 1916: CAB 42/12. Kut, Ireland.

Von der Goltz: died 19 April, Trumpener, *Germany and the Ottoman Empire.*

Julna: Corbett, *Naval Operations*, Official History.

216 Negotiations: Herbert, *Mons, Anzac and Kut*, and Moberly, *Mesopotamia.* See also Townshend, *My Campaign*, Braddon, *The Siege*, and Wilson, *Loyalties: Mesopotamia.*

218 March to captivity: see Woolley (ed.), *From Kastamuni to Kedos*, written by many hands; Sandes, *Tales of Turkey*, and *In Kut and Captivity*; and Keeling, *Adventures in Turkey and Russia.*

219 Football: Sandes, *Tales of Turkey.*

220 Murphy and other staff officers in Baghdad: see Murphy, *Soldiers of the Prophet.*

Meissner Pasha and Baghdad Rail: AA, Turkei 152, Bd 79, Roessler to Bethmann Hollweg, 20 Oct 1914, and Rosenberg to Zimmermann, 27 Nov 1914. Also, Andrae, *Lebenserinnerungen eines Ausgräbers*, p. 175; details of Meissner's career. Visited Deutsche Orient Gesellschaft in Assyria, 1914.

Woolley and 'senior officer': see Woolley, *As I Seem to Remember*, p. 88ff.

221 Mirza Muhammad and Haji Ali: MI5 document 241559.

Officers awaiting trial: Keeling, *Adventures in Turkey and Russia*, p. 10.

Enver in Baghdad: ibid.

222 Macdonogh to FO, MI5, 16 Dec 1917: in FO 371/3062.

223 Sir Stanley Maude: took over in Aug 1916 from Sir Percy Lake.

Mustafa Kamal: Kinross, *Ataturk: the Rebirth of a Nation*.

Counter-offensive against Russians: Lewis, *The Emergence of Modern Turkey*, pp. 239–40, and Christopher Sykes, *Wassmuss*.

11 **Aaron and Jamal**

224 Lewis Einstein: Secretary and Chargé d'Affaires, US Embassy Constantinople, 1915. Special Agent, Entente Affairs, 1915–17. See his *Inside Constantinople*.

Jamal Pasha: Admiralty intelligence file 'Personalities in Turkey', in L/P & S/20/C132A.

Destruction of Al Ahad and Syrian nationalist movement: *Arab Bulletin*, no. 1, 6 May 1916, sentences on 'Autonomous Syria' members.

225 Persecutions: Einstein, *Inside Constantinople*, and Morgenthau, *Secrets of the Bosphorus*.

'finest of German generals': Liman von Sanders and enmity of Enver and General Staff, see Trumpener, *Germany and the Ottoman Empire*, and Sachar, *The Emergence of the Middle East*. Liman left for Gallipoli with his trusted Chief of Staff, Colonel Kazim Bey, to take command of Fifth Army on 24 March 1915. Mustafa Kamal was given command of the 19th Division. Trumpener, *Germany and the Ottoman Empire*.

Philip Graves: correspondent of *The Times* to outbreak of war. Staff Officer (GSO3) 1915. HL/D/20/2/18, Graves to Ll.G. 15 Sept 1915.

Rape of Christian minorities: see eye-witness report on 'the gentlemanly Turk' from Sir Arthur Crosfield to Lloyd George, HL/G/5/7/33, 7 Feb 1927. 'For ever since . . . the Turkish controversy became a factor in British politics, it is the Liberal Party which – with the exception of one or two periods of momentary error – has held the right end of the stick, while . . . a large part of the Tory party has been, as all events have proved, absolutely in the wrong.'

226 Jamal and Austrian Jewess: Admiralty Intelligence file CB 1307 in L/P & S/20/132A.

Madam Corbetti: ibid.

'told Louis Mallet': ibid.

Sarah Aaronsohn, marriage: *Encycl. Judaica*. See also Engle, *The NILI Spies*. There is a suggestion in *With the Turks in Palestine* by Alex Aaron-

sohn, brother of Aaron and Sarah who was to become a life-long Anglophile and servant of British military intelligence, that her marriage was one
of convenience. She is said to have 'escaped' to Constantinople when Alex
and his friends were ordered to hand in their arms and he was 'smashed in
the face' with a rifle butt.

226 Journey from Haidar Pasha: Engle, *The NILI Spies*.

Fourth Army, Jerusalem: Storrs, *Orientations*, and Meinertzhagen, *Middle
East Diary*.

Activities of Aaronsohns and Avshalom Feinberg, 1914–15: see Engle, *The
NILI Spies*, and Alex Aaronsohn, *With the Turks in Palestine*. Perhaps the
most authentic account is given in the novel *Behold the Fire* by Michael
Blankfort, in which the Jews of Zichron Yakov are given fictional names but
the British, Turk and German military officials are represented factually.
Aaron Aaronsohn appears as Judah Singer and Sarah as Rachel.

Avshalom Feinberg: see article by Rabbi Rabinowitz, 'Shalom Avshalom'
in *The Jewish Herald*, 27 Dec 1967, on the occasion of the reinterment of his
remains at the military cemetery on Mount Herzl.

Dr Jacobsen: L/P & S/20/132A, 'Personalities in Turkey'.

227 Fast's Hotel: Alex Aaronsohn, *With the Turks in Palestine*.

Alex and Mr Glazebrook at Jaffa: ibid.

Aaron in Tunisia: Aaron Aaronsohn, 'La Colonisation Juive en Palestine',
in *Bulletin de la Societé Botanique de France*. Report of a lecture given at
Tunis on 24 April, 1909. See Stewart, *The Middle East*, 'To the Arabs, arguments that the Jews were "returning" to the land of Israel had a disturbing
echo: the two Catholic colonisers in North Africa, France and Italy, often
stressed that North Africa had been Latin once and was becoming Latin
again.'

Aaron in America, 1909: Alexandra Lee Levin, 'Aaron Aaronsohn, Pioneer
Scientist, Spy and Friend of Henrietta Szold', *Hadassah Magazine*, March
1977. Mrs Levin quotes Justice Felix Frankfurter, 7 June 1961: 'I do not
need all the fingers of my two hands to include him among the most
memorable persons I have encountered in life.' Henrietta Szold had met
the Aaronsohn family during a visit to Palestine. Aaronsohn returned to
America in 1913, when he was in great demand as a speaker, ibid.

Agricultural Station, Athlit: incorporated under the laws of the State of
New York, on 10 Feb 1910. Aaronsohn was Executive Director, Julius
Rosenwald of Sears, Roebuck was appointed President, Professor Morris
Loeb Vice-President, and Paul M. Warburg Treasurer. Henrietta Szold
was Secretary of the organisation in America. The station was established
in same year at Athlit between Haifa and Caesarea, near the ruins of a Crusader castle.

228 Jamal and Jews: in Jan Jamal invited a distinguished Ottoman Jew, Albert
Antebi, to his office to be interviewed by the Jew-baiting *mutasarif* of Jaffa,
Beha ad Din. Antebi gave a good account of himself and Beha was made to

look foolish. Nevertheless, Jamal made his *Mutasarif* Secretary for Jewish Affairs in Syria in the following month. See Friedman, *Germany, Turkey and Zionism,* and Sachar, *The Emergence of the Middle East.* On 2 March Jamal made a friendly speech at the Herzliyah High School in Tel Aviv (Jaffa). Friedman, *Germany, Turkey and Zionism.*

228   Aaronsohn, quote: see Engle, *The NILI Spies.*

Aaronsohn appointed Agricultural Adviser, Syria, Spring 1915: *Encycl. Judaica.* At the same time Albert Antebi was appointed Special Adviser, and Moshe Wilbushewitz made Chief Civil Engineer of the province. See Sachar, *The Emergence of the Middle East.* Friedman, *Germany, Turkey and Zionism,* says the appointment was effective in June, and Sachar says 'Summer'; but political records suggest that Aaronsohn was in Damascus by April.

Alex and Rivka to Cairo: see Alex Aaronsohn, *With the Turks in Palestine,* and Engle, *The NILI Spies.* Alex's account says that Sarah accompanied him, but she was still in Constantinople. Presumably a slip of the pen.

Refugees from Haifa: Glazebrook, Ambassador Morgenthau in Constantinople and Captain Decker of the USS *Tennessee,* played vital and generous roles in rescuing thousands of refugees from Palestine in the face of Jamal's purges. See Alex Aaronsohn, *With the Turks in Palestine,* and Friedman, *Germany, Turkey and Zionism.* For Morgenthau, see L/P & S/20/132A.

Zion Mule Corps: see Sachar, *The Emergence of the Middle East.* 10,000 Jews were in camps in Egypt. Jabotinsky, a Russian journalist, and Trumpledor organised them into the Volunteer Jewish Legion and Zion Mule Corps, March 1915.

Alex's reception in Egypt: Woolley to Leonard Woolf, quoted in letter to Anita Engle, 11 June 1957, see *The NILI Spies.*

229   Avshalom to Egypt: unpublished report to Miss Szold from Alexandria, 1915, ibid.

Zaida: papers of John de Vere Loder (Lord Wakehurst), MEC, Oxford.

Avshalom on English help: to Henrietta Szold, Secretary of the New York Zionist Executive, with 200-page report on Palestine and the work of Aaronsohn's team. Judge Louis Brandeis, head of the Executive, commented: 'This is one of the most excellent and most important documents I have ever read in my life.' See Engle, *The NILI Spies.*

'into an enemy country': FO 382/1639. Correspondence with MI1(b), transfer of money to Palestine.

230   Avshalom and Sarah: quote from Blankfort, *Behold the Fire.* Feinberg was engaged to Sarah's younger sister, Rivka, then in America. Fifty years after his death, Rabbi Rabinowitz was to describe Rivka as 'his bride', *Jewish Herald,* 27 Dec 1967, but he must have been mistaken. Rivka remained 'Miss' Aaronsohn till her death in 1981.

Beha ad Din and Jamal: see Friedman, *Germany, Turkey and Zionism,*

Sachar, *The Emergence of the Middle East*, and Mandel, *The Arabs and Zionism before World War I*.

230   Jamal's *coup:* first intimation reached London at end of Dec, but Russian agents in Constantinople had been in touch with Petrograd for some weeks. CAB 37/139, 29 Dec 1915. And L/P & S/10/525, Sazanov to Buchanan, 'Armenian agents in touch with Russian Government'. See also Tibawi, *Anglo-Arab Relations*, Grey to Benckendorff, Dec, 'Arabs have appealed to the British Government'.

Rising of Syrian Arabs: the plot was undoubtedly known to Jamal. On 2 Nov Dr Abdal Rahman Shahbandar, the English-speaking Syrian leader, escaped from Damascus and arrived at Basra in disguise in December with Tufiq ibn Rajib al Halabi, a personal friend of Jamal. 'Escaped here to avoid arrest,' said a Force 'D' telegram. L/P & S/10/525, 2 Jan 1916. On 31 Oct General Maxwell had wired from Cairo to the Indian C-in-C at Delhi, suggesting that in view of Arab plans and defections 'we should seize this excellent opportunity of issuing a proclamation giving verbatim text of our proposals to Sharif of Mecca and Arab Party.' Needless to say, India was less than enthusiastic. L/P & S/10/525. On 12 Oct Maxwell had told Kitchener it was Young Arabs' 'moment of action'. L/P & S/10/523.

Faruqi's desertion: FO 882/13, 17 Oct, and L/P & S/10/523, statements to intelligence officer, 11 Oct. Almost as soon as he arrived in Cairo at the beginning of Oct, the Sharif of Mecca appointed Faruqi his representative, see Tibawi, *Anglo-Arab Relations*.

'high-level defections': message from British Minister Athens, 15 Oct, relayed by Admiralty to London and repeated to GOC Cairo, 17 Oct. FO 882/4.

231   DMI Cairo to Athens, Dec 1915: Graves, *Lawrence and the Arabs*, quoted by Bidwell, *Arabian Studies*, III, MEC, Cambridge, 1976. *Note*: Kitchener arrived in Athens 20 Nov, see Cassar, *Kitchener*.

Cabinet: 29 Dec, CAB 37/139.

232   Changes at Constantinople, Nov 1915: see Trumpener, *Germany and the Ottoman Empire*.

Halil Bey: Admiralty Intelligence file. L/P & S/20/132A.

Wangenheim was succeeded temporarily in July by Prince Zu Hohenlohe-Langenburg, following continued disagreement with Liman von Sanders and the death of Colonel von Leipzig, the Military Attaché in Constantinople, from 'accidental shooting'. Enver's friend Bronsart suggested his successor, Colonel Otto von Lossow (later to gain notoriety in Hitler's rise to power), as Liman's Chief-of-Staff, Trumpener, *Germany and the Ottoman Empire*. Wolff-Metternich took over in Nov; and was recalled in Aug 1916 when Kühlmann, 'more friendly' to Turks, took charge. Kühlmann, *Erinnerung*.

Zaida: see Engle, *The NILI Spies*. There seems to be confusion about the identity of the monitor ship used for Syrian coastal missions at this time. Engle refers to the *Managam*, which was not used until August 1916, before which it was used in the Red Sea and Gulf of Aqaba under the direction of Colonel A. C. Parker, to make contact with agents in southern Sinai and on the Hijaz coast. Parker diaries (in author's possession).

232   Sarah Aaronsohn: arrived home 24 Dec 1915. Engle, *The NILI Spies*.

Feinberg's journey and capture: ibid., and Blankfort, *Behold the Fire*.

233   Feinberg to Constantinople: Engle, *The NILI Spies*.

Woolley and *Zaida*, July 1916: Woolley, *As I Seem to Remember*.

Woolley as POW: see his own account, ibid., and *From Kastamuni to Kedos*.

'outrageous snob', and story of wife: see Mallowan, *Memoirs*.

234   Turkish atrocities: Alex Aaronsohn, *With the Turks in Palestine*. There was widespread starvation at this time, from which Arabs, Jews and Christians suffered equally, and even the Ottoman army was on minimum rations. Some 200,000 Maronite Christians died in the Lebanon alone (see Levin, 'Aaron Aaronsohn'), Armenians were still being slaughtered throughout the Empire. Jamal had only just started on the Jews. See Sachar, *The Emergence of the Middle East*.

Aaron, journey to London: *Yoman*. See also Blankfort, *Behold the Fire*, for a colourful fictional account with a basis in fact. The organised nature of the journey and the extent of his contacts is indicated by the fact that he was able to send a message through the British Copenhagen Embassy to Cela Feinberg (sister of Avshalom) in Berlin, for transmission to Liova Schneersohn in Constantinople. See Engle, *The NILI Spies*.

235   Danish ship: boarded 1 Oct 1916, FO 382/1639.

Interviews with Hall and Thomson: Engle, *The NILI Spies*.

Military intelligence: see note, p. 439.

236   Dr Dickson and RGS unit: RGS records. See James, *Eyes of the Navy*.

Shakespear's route to Jauf: *Arab Bulletin*, no. 33, 4 Dec 1916, conceived in the summer of 1914 by Shakespear, Mark Sykes and Hogarth in London. On 24 Nov 1916, Captain Marrs surveyed the section of the road from the Euphrates to Shaqra at the request of the War Office. Details were sent to Carruthers at the RGS intelligence unit on 27 Nov. Marrs thought motorised units could negotiate the Darb Zobaida. MI Basra to Carruthers, 27 Nov 1916.

Kisch: see Bentwich, *Frederick Kisch*. Appointed GSO2 in MI2(c), Room 328, Nov 1916.

238   Sykes and Picot to Russia, Feb–March 1916: see Adelson, *Mark Sykes*, ch. II, 'Arabs, France and Zionism'.

Inter-Allied Agreement: generally known as Sykes–Picot Agreement. Concluded in Feb 1916, subject to Russian approval. L/P & S/10/525, Buchanan, 19 Feb. Impending visit of Sykes and Picot, ibid., 17 March. IO to FO, Petrograd negotiations 'very satisfactory . . . We can now let the Grand Sharif go ahead with a good conscience'. See Antonius, *The Arab Awakening*, Appendix B, S.–P. Agreement, notes defining Russian share exchanged between Sazanov and Paléologue (French Ambassador), 26 April 1916. File copies of the 'Sykes–Picot' agreement are undated and no date is given by Antonius, *The Arab Awakening,* or by other historians. Meinertzhagen, *Middle East Diary,* however, gives 16 May 1916 as date of signature following agreement on Russian, British and French shares; Brown Area, Palestine, to be internationally administered, with ports of Haifa and Acre to Britain.

238   Fall of Erzerum: CAB 42/9.

Sykes and Sir Arthur Nicolson: see Friedman, *The Question of Palestine,* quoted in Adelson, *Mark Sykes,* p. 206.

239   'key to acceptance': Adelson, *Mark Sykes.*

Aaronsohn quote: ibid.

12   The Sharif's Revolt

240   Lloyd to Wingate: FO 882, 27 May 1916, and L/P & S/10/576.

Major Blaker: L/P & S/10/576, Viceroy to S/S, 15 May: Message regarding Bureau status 'ambiguous ... Please explain precise purport of words ... Major Blaker has been appointed special liaison officer by GOC Force "D", but there are apparently other officers, e.g. Lawrence, who have been sent to Mesopotamia with special instructions of which we are unaware'.

241   Gertrude Bell: L/P & S/10/576, Viceroy to S/S, conveying tels of 22 May from GOC: 'In view of somewhat modified aspect in which this institution is presented to us by Lawrence, I propose that Miss Bell and not Major Blaker should act as corresponding officer in Mesopotamia.'

'Captain Lawrence deputed': ibid., 28 May. See also FO 882/18, Lawrence's report on mission to Basra and Kut, May 1916, and Clayton to Wingate, Durham University, Sudan Archive, 12 June.

Cossack officers from Erzerum: Gertrude Bell, *Letters,* 27 May 1916.

Storrs and others to Jiddah: L/P & S/10/597.

Grey to McMahon: 1 Nov 1915, FO 882/16.

242   'restricted "to the smallest limits" ': McMahon to Grey, 7 Nov 1915, FO 371/2486.

Picot to Sykes, Maronites: FO 371/2767. See Tibawi, *Anglo-Arab Relations,* and Adelson, *Mark Sykes.*

243   McMahon to Foreign Secretary, 24 May: L/P & S/10/597.

Lionel Abrahams: ibid., 21 May. FO to IO, 26 May, 'Word should be "requests" '.

Arrest of Arab 'Autonomy' members: Jamal's proclamation of 6 May, *Arab Bulletin,* no. 2, 12 June 1916.

Faisal: *Arab Bulletin,* vol. 2, March 1916, FO Library collection, 'Faisal's Table Talk'. See L/P & S/10/597, May 1916, Faisal to Sharif. Explains return to Mecca due to 'fall of Erzerum'. Also *Arabian Report*, 22 May 1916, Sharif's 'fear that Turks in Syria have discovered his plans'. FO 371/2013, 24 March, McMahon to Sharif by secret messenger, 'Erzerum'.

243   Wilson Pasha (Colonel C. E.) to Clayton: FO 882, 17 March 1916.

Wingate to Clayton, conversation with 'O': L/P & S/10/525, 15 April, and FO 882, 16 April.

244   Party of Germans: L/P & S/10/597.

Faisal's return: letter written in March.

Storrs's party: see *Orientations*.

Araifan: L/P & S/10/597.

Germans murdered by badawin: ibid., McMahon to FO, 1 June 1916.

Hirtzel: ibid., 19 May.

Foreign Secretary to McMahon, 30 May: ibid.

Storrs in Jiddah: description from FO 882, L/P & S/10/597, L/P & S/10/586 *(Arab Bulletin)*, and Storrs, *Orientations*.

Kitchener's death, HMS *Hampshire:* CAB 42/15, 6 June 1916.

246   Kitchener and Storrs: see L/P & S/10/586. Storrs's memory, as was often the case, failed him in his record of events of this time in *Orientations*. He says that he returned to Cairo on 7 June and that he first learnt of Kitchener's death at Suez. In fact, he was interviewing the Sharif's young son, Zaid, on 6 and 7 June *(Arabian Report*, XIXA), after which meeting Storrs wired 'Arbur' (the Bureau's telegraphic address), 'Sharif committed to open revolt'. He actually returned to Egypt on the 10th. But Storrs always told a good story and was never too fussy about facts.

247   Fall of Mecca: L/P & S/20/131 (Arabian Personalities, Sharif). 'Fort and barracks surrendered later.' The date on which the Sharif raised his standard in revolt and issued a proclamation (FO 371/2776) 5 June, is the accepted beginning of the 'Arab Revolt', but there was no fighting on that day. See CAB 42/16, reports by Sykes and Gertrude Bell.

248   Parker and Newcombe records: Newcombe was, of course, at the centre of the Lawrence controversy when Richard Aldington's *Lawrence of Arabia* was published in 1955. Churchill and other prominent figures jumped to Lawrence's defence by asserting that Newcombe, the 'other' hero-figure of the campaign, attested to his achievements. But it is interesting that few of the writers involved ever paid the slightest attention to Newcombe's personal story, mentioned in passing in *Seven Pillars*, with its remarkable incidents of captivity, escape and romance; neither did they seek out the first Director of the Arab Bureau, Colonel Parker. Lawrence's self-appointed Cicero, the American Lowell Thomas, defended his subject with the aid of Newcombe, whose name he could not even spell correctly. On 22 July 1954, when Aldington's book threatened, he wrote to Dr G. C. Ramsay: 'I am sure you remember . . . how Newcomb was the first high ranking officer to be captured by the Turks. Although ill and an old man, he is still alive, and

he says that every word of what Lawrence wrote was true, and that none of the things he told about were impossible for a man as unusual as "T.E.". Colonel Newcomb's views will carry great weight.' I am indebted to the daughters of both Colonel Newcombe and Colonel Parker for so generously showing and lending me their papers when I inquired.

248   'Storrs conveyed': L/P & S/10/597, 8 June, McMahon to FO, 'From Storrs today'.

250   'McMahon was telling London': ibid., 11 June, McMahon to FO.

Wilson to Jiddah: ibid., McMahon to FO, 10 July: 'Most important send competent officer to Jiddah. Suggest Wilson.' C. E. Wilson was Commandant of Troops (Sudan) and Governor of the Red Sea Province. On 8 July Wingate confirmed need for 'Political Officer' at Jiddah.

Parker to Jiddah: Parker diary, '14 August, left Cairo 7 am. General Dobell. Saw Jennings Bramley. GHQ, saw Alan Dawnay. Lunch J. B. Major Mackenzie, letters for Wilson, £300 gold for me.' Arrived Jiddah 17 Aug.

Damage to *Kaaba*: FO 141/710.

Damage to *Kiswa*: Parker's diary and L/P & S/10/597.

Indian Government: 'Greatly disturbed . . . Hope news will be suppressed', *Arabian Report*, 13 June 1916.

Austen Chamberlain: L/P & S/10/597.

Captain Boyle: ibid.

'the idea of India': L/P & S/576. Storrs, *Orientations*.

Lake: L/P & S/10/576, 11 June, to Government of India, FO, IO, WO and Arab Bureau.

251   Col. French, MI1, to Clayton: WO 33/969, 13 July 1916.

Clayton to French: WO 33/969, 27 July.

'talk of a lunatic': *Arab Bulletin*, no. 14, 7 Aug 1916. Revolt 'a bombshell' in India. See also CAB 37/152, 'Views of Indian Muslims'.

Mr Wilson: 'India might realise . . .' L/P & S/10/598, 21 July.

Secret sign: DMI Cairo to MI2, in L/P & S/10/598, 12 Aug 1916.

Parker: personal diary, 11 Sept 1916. 'Ruhi and Arabs returned 4 pm from Umm Lijj. Brought Sharif Ghalib, brother of Sharif Muhammad Ali, aboard.' Reports on Shaikhs for and against Sharif Faisal, interviews 12–16 Sept, 16 Sept aboard HMS *Dufferin*. Shaikh Suleiman Pasha abu Rifada back from Jamal, 'pockets filled with gold'.

'Vast sums of money': L/P & S/10/598, 6 July, FO to McMahon. 'Consider £125,000 month excessive. £50,000 should be enough.' WO 33/969, Appendix 4a, p. 46, monthly subsidy to Hijaz began in 1916 at £125,000 per week.

Parker: interview with Faisal, 9 Sept.

Turks at Madina: 'M' Berne to DMI. '9,000 Turks under Fuad Pasha against Sharif', WO 33/738. Parker, 18 Sept, Umm Lijj. 'Turks from Madina on way to recapture.'

251 War Committee: CAB 42/16, CAB 37/151, Arab Revolt/Mesopotamia.

252 Sharif's subsidy: there are considerable discrepancies in FO and WO accounts of amounts paid. WO 33/969, increased to £225,000 per month in 1917, £100,000 from Jan 1918. The WO reference to £125,000 per week from 1916 is probably a misprint.

War Committee, 1 Sept: CAB 42/19.

Difficulties of Parker and Wilson: Parker diary, 19 Aug to GHQ (Intelligence). 'Unable to carry out tasks at Wejh and Dibba.' WO 33/738, GOC to McMahon, Wilson reports: 'Sharif begs no landings on Hijaz coast.' Parker, 6 Sept, interview with Araifan and Zaid on *Dufferin*.

Murray's Conference: WO 33/820 (Secret Telegrams). And FO 882, Hijaz Rising.

Parker to GHQ, 10 Sept: Diary, and letter to Amir Faisal Bey, 16 Sept, ibid.

254 Fakhri Pasha: Lawrence, *Seven Pillars*, p. 58.

Faisal's opinion: Parker, 10 Sept to GHQ.

Ali Haidar: appointed Sharif of Holy Cities by Sultan in Aug. *Arab Bulletin*, no. 14.

255 CIGS to GOC: 10 July (tel. 5334) WO 33/820.

GOC reply: 14 July (tel. 5370) ibid.

Parker to Faisal: Parker, diary.

Shaikh Suleiman Pasha: Parker, diary, 15 Sept 1916.

Umm Lejj and Yanbo: ibid.

256 Meeting, Murray and High Commissioner: WO 33/738.

257 CIGS instructed: WO 33/905.

Murray wire: ibid.

258 Bray to Jiddah: see *Shifting Sands*.

With Mark Sykes at WO: ibid.

259 Abdullah, statement to world press: issued 30 Oct 1916. FO 882/5, FO 371/2776 and L/P & S/18/B292. The dispute between the Sharif and the British was concerned with the wording of an appeal to 'The Peoples of Iraq'. A revised version was produced and sent by McMahon to FO on 13 Oct. FO 371/2776.

Viceroy: FO 371/2776, correspondence Foreign, Simla, and Cairo, 3–8 Nov.

'McMahon regretted': FO 371/2776. McMahon to Sirdar, 31 Oct, and FO on 9 Nov.

'A feeble thought': ibid. On 9 Nov he suggested to Foreign Simla that 'Champion of the peoples of Arabia' might be better than 'titular head of the Arab peoples'. The Viceroy had questioned the Sharif's right to any title which gave him precedence over the other Arab leaders, particularly Ibn Saud (Tel. 6 Nov to Sirdar).

'*carte blanche* . . . to Wingate': ibid., McMahon to Sirdar, 20 Oct, copy to

Foreign, Simla, sent to FO 9 Nov. 'Best arrangement . . . political authority in Hijaz . . . you to have *carte blanche.*' Parker, diary, 17 Oct, message from Wilson: 'Wingate now i/c.' WO 33/905, 4 Oct, to GOC: 'Assistance to Sharif in hands of Sirdar.'

259 Bray's Indians: FO 371/2776. Captain N. N. E. Bray, 18th K.G.O. Lancers to DMI, War Office, 19 Oct 1916, 'Report on visit of Risaldar-Major Gul Nawas Khan, 18th (K.G.O.) Lancers and Risaldar Mir Alam Khan, 34th Poona Horse, to Sharif of Mecca, Sept–Oct 1916'.

Lawrence and Storrs: left Cairo 13 Oct. FO 882/5.

'consider its great men': Lawrence, *Seven Pillars.*

turned to Al Masri: ibid.

Al Masri in Hijaz: Parker, diary. For Storrs's comment on Lawrence's story, see *Orientations.*

260 Abdullah: Lawrence, *Seven Pillars.* See also Storrs, *Orientations,* and extract from Storrs's diary in FO 882/5, 19 Oct.

'indignant outburst': Storrs, diary, in FO 882/5. 'He gave a fairly accurate historical summary of the negotiations . . . citing textually a phrase in a letter from Maxwell (which I have never seen), placing at their absolute disposal, so far as I could gather, a very considerable proportion of the British army.'

Bin Gharbrit: Storrs, *Orientations.*

Rashid Rida: ibid.

Said Ali: ibid.

Parker, landing at Rabegh: FO 371/2776, 1 Oct; Wilson to Sharif: 'Colonel Parker sent with other officers to arrange defence . . . must be allowed to land.' Parker, diary, 13 Oct; 'Bray and Boyle still have trouble.'

Message from Ruhi, 9.30 pm, 1 Oct: FO 371/2776, 1 Oct.

261 Rabegh must be defended: WO 33/738. Lawrence, Jiddah, to DMI, 17 Oct: 'Meeting today. Wilson, Storrs, Abdullah, Aziz al Masri and self present.' CAB 42/21, 3 Oct, Arab Question. Parker, diary, 18 Oct, from Wilson: 'High Command holding back aircraft. Planes to return to Cairo on orders of Sirdar.' Diary, 23 Oct, re decision of HMG not to land troops in Holy Places. 'Arab army inchoate and fluctuating.' Military situation 'bad'. FO 371/2776, Parker to Arab Bureau, 30 Oct; 'Rabegh force entirely unready.' WO 33/728, 30 Oct from Parker and Lawrence: 'Faisal's Arabs fear Turkish planes.' FO 371/2776, 29 Oct, HMG authorises planes for Rabegh.

CIGS: CAB 42/22.

Parker report: FO 371/2776, 7 Oct. This document, prepared for the Arab Bureau and sent by the Residency to FO, 22 Oct, was compiled in two parts, dated 7 and 10 Oct. It showed that on the 10th Lieutenant Perry of the Royal Engineers began to blast a channel through the Rabegh reef, on instructions from Captain Boyle, the senior naval officer, Red Sea. As Parker worked on the report aboard HMS *Euryalus* on 8 Oct, Nuri Said reported the capture by the Turks of Bir Abbas and Safra. Note in Parker's diary: 'Pressure of Kress.'

261   Bray in London: see his *Shifting Sands.*

262   Kisch and Bray on Macdonogh: see Bentwich, *Frederick Kisch,* and Bray, *Shifting Sands.*

Cairo, Dec: Aaronsohn arrived 12th, Engle, *The NILI Spies.* Bray, no date.

263   McMahon: FO 371/2925, 6 Dec, Wingate to succeed McMahon.

'our insincerity': Lawrence, original introduction to *Seven Pillars*, suppressed from 1st edn. See Knightley and Simpson, *Secret Lives.* See *Seven Pillars*, p. 58, 'his shrewd insight, and tried, experienced mind understood our design at once and judged it good'.

'who took actual risk': *Seven Pillars,* p. 172.

Lady McMahon: Gertrude Bell, *Letters,* 15 Feb 1918.

Lloyd George, 'other men's reputations': see Terraine, *Impacts of War.*

New administration: CAB 37/161. Lloyd George Prime Minister and War Cabinet formed, 7 Dec. Balfour Foreign Secretary, 11th.

Churchill banished: *The World Crisis.*

President Wilson: re-elected Nov 1916.

Lawrence in Hijaz: Parker, diary, 19 Oct, to Arbur, question of Lawrence going up to see Faisal. *Arab Bulletin,* no. 31, 21 Oct, account by T.E.L.: 'Journey in Desert with Nuri [Said] and Faisal; Rabegh and Yanbo.' Parker, diary, 21 Oct, Lawrence left for Faisal.

264   'to the village of Hamra': Parker, diary. Letter from T.E.L., Hamra, 24 Oct. Requests from Faisal: 'Aziz al Masri organising regular force at Rabegh.'

265   'I felt at first glance': *Seven Pillars,* p. 92.

Letter to Colonel Parker, 24 Oct 1916: unpublished, Parker papers.

'My duty now': *Seven Pillars,* p. 99.

266   'to report to Parker and Boyle': Parker, diary, 31 Oct. 'Reports most favourably on morale of Sharif's army.'

Boyle's view of Lawrence: see Bray, *Shifting Sands;* but Clayton to Sykes, FO 881/14, 'Lawrence is of course essential and unique', and Colonel Wilson to Wingate, 'a bumptious ass', Bidwell, *Arabian Studies,* III.

Lawrence to Port Sudan and Egypt: *Seven Pillars,* pp. 114–15. See Tel. no. 9, 9 Nov, Sirdar to Government of India, report on Hijaz, following discussion with Lawrence and Admiral Wemyss.

Colonel Brémond: it is interesting to compare Wilson's view, FO 371/2776, 26 Oct, McMahon to Grey, quoting Wilson, 'relations between Colonel Brémond and myself are all that I could desire'.

Wilson on Sharif: FO 371/2776.

30 Oct: ibid.

266 'crafty policy': *Seven Pillars.*

Sharif's ministers: FO 371/2776.

267 Ibn Saud, treaty: FO 371/2776, 3 Oct, Husain shown treaty.

Sharif's claims: L/P & S/18/B292, 6 Nov. FO instructs Wingate to tell Sharif: 'Caliphate should be left open until end of war.' FO 371/2776, 7 Nov, High Commissioner Cairo to Govt of India. 'Neither Wilson nor Brémond attended ceremonies', (Husain's Coronation ceremonies first week of Nov). Parker diary, 19 Nov: 'Ali hurt at British refual to recognise father's declaration [of Arab sovereignty].'

'Wilson remarked': FO 371/2776.

Ibn Saud's reaction: ibid.

McMahon to Foreign Secretary, 19 Dec: FO 371/895. Also in FO 371/3043, FO 371/4213 and FO 882, 19 Dec.

268 Storrs's return to Jiddah: FO 371/893. Cairo 9 Dec.

Foreign Office comment: ibid. See also CAB 37/161, 15 Dec, Arab Revolt, Rabegh, Yanbo.

Prisoners: FO 396/16 MI1 to DMI Cairo, Dec 1916, Major J. L. Fisher.

13   Von Stotzingen

269 Payment to Sharif: L/P & S/10/597, Sharif to McMahon, 'received your honourable letter dated 10 March, together with the sum demanded'. Dated in Arabic 25 Jamd Awal 1334. Unsigned. See also FO 882, 16 March 1916, Clayton to Wilson, 'Araifan', preparations for revolt; and L/P & S/10/525 (9 March), Grey to Chamberlain, copy to Kitchener. Note by Hirtzel, IO. 'Now we are paying the Sharif and asking him not to take military action.' WO 33/820, 8 June 1916, 'Sharif wants £50,000 promised provisionally, and a further £20,000 for his N. force at Madina,' DMI Cairo to DMI London.

Trebizond: Moberly, *Mesopotamia*, Official History.

Alexandretta: L/P & S/10/526, 8 March, Buchanan, Petrograd, to Grey. 'Sazanov regrets.' And CAB 42/11, Sir George Buchanan/ Arab Question.

Faisal and Jamal at cinema: *Arab Bulletin*, vol. 2, 1917, pp. 78–9.

General Maxwell: in March Maxwell returned to Britain and divided control of the Mediterranean/Egypt theatre of operations was abandoned. Murray was in sole command. See Cassar, *Kitchener.*

276 Oppenheim and Faisal in Constantinople: *Arab Bulletin*, vol. 2, no. 42, 15 Feb 1917, p. 79.

Faisal and crown of Egypt: offer made 'in Piraeus', ibid.

Von Stotzingen: details in the following pages regarding the Arabian missions of Major Freiherr von Stotzingen, and Captain Mueller's 'Java' party, taken from *Arab Bulletin*, 6 June 1916–30 Aug 1919, *Arabian Report*, 6 Aug 1916, Appendix C, in L/P & S/10/586, German Foreign Office file, AA, Weltkrieg, Nr 11g (Major von Stotzingen), and Morsey, *T. E. Lawrence.* Two collections of the *Arab Bulletin* were used: IO/L/P & S/10/657–8, and the Foreign Office Library file. Different numbering systems are employed, i.e. edition numbers and dates, volume numbers and pages. Either enables the researcher to find the references cited.

270   Letter from Countess von Schlieffen: *Arab Bulletin*, vol. 1, p. 133 (Appendix). Baron von Stotzingen 'knows English and French perfectly'. Has 'spent four winters in Africa in the years before the war and travelled in the company of Arabs . . . does not intrude his personality and has not those characteristics which often make the Germans disliked in foreign parts'. She added, 'the duties which the gentleman in question is to take over in the east is in a certain sense the result of a decision of Your Excellency'.

Jamal and Faisal: *Arab Bulletin*, vol. 1, p. 134. 'Note by Cairo', p. 138, 'Jamal had reason to be nervous about the Arab attitude towards Germans, and probably some foreknowledge of the coming revolt in the Hijaz, which was not imparted to von Stotzingen.'

Sentences on 'Autonomous Syria' members: *Arab Bulletin*, no. 2, 12 June, citing *Al Akha al Othmani*, Beirut, 6 May 1916. Twenty were sentenced to death, seven to imprisonment or exile.

Faisal and von Stotzingen: *Arab Bulletin*, vol. 2, p. 78.

272   Lieutenant Fritz Grobba: son of a nurseryman, doctor of law, served as a Referendar, lower grade of judicial service, at Gartz near Stettin, in 1913. On 24 June 1914 reached Jerusalem for a year's 'Sabbatical' prior to entering Consular Service. Joined Turkish Fourth Army 3 Jan 1916. Became chief of German Middle East intelligence under the Third Reich. *Arab Bulletin* vol. 1, p. 263 and Grobba, *Männer und Mächte im Orient.*

German party. Listed German members of the mission were: Major von Stotzingen, General Staff; Lieutenant Grobba, interpreter; Lieutenant Diel, wireless; Herr Neufeld, interpreter; NCO Kolber, wireless operator; NCO Schmidt, wireless operator; Heinrich Hilpert, orderly.

274   Germans at Yanbo: the party appears to have been concealed for nearly two weeks. On 1 June the Sharif ordered all Turks from Mecca, and on the 11th Storrs and Hogarth reported the Revolt 'genuine and inevitable'. The German heads had a price. L/P & S/10/597 and WO 33/820, DMI 11 June.

275   Parker's Hijaz agents: Parker, diary, letter to DMI, 6 Jan 1915: 'Have been trying to contact Hijaz Arabs since late December [1914]. Appointment of agents, £2½ per month.'

Father J. Jaussen: correspondence Jan–Aug 1915 between Father Jaussen and Parker and Newcombe, in Parker papers marked, 'Pour l'usage personnel du Colonel Parker et du Major Newcombe.' Parker accounts for 1914 show (4.3.15) paid by Father Jaussen on his trip to Suleiman al Rabia, 6 shillings; expended on various items not specified during trip to (?) Desair £3.72

(sic). Cost of stores for Father Jaussen and Captain Anderson (10–28 March 1915) £16.78, etc. See also *Arab Bulletin*, vol. 1, p. 18, 'Hijaz Intelligence'.

275 Deaths of Captain Mueller's party: L/P & S/10/597, 1 June and *Arab Bulletin*, no. 2, 12 June, Summary. McMahon to Grey. Date of murders not known but probably about third week of May. Offer of their heads made by 'secret messenger O' (Araifan) on 27 May. On 18 April Sharif sent letter to McMahon claiming to have sabotaged Hijaz railway 'to increase discomfort' of Turks. 'It will be absolutely necessary therefore that a sufficiency of British troops should land at a convenient point [in Syria] . . . to occupy railway connecting Syria with Anatolia, so as to make it easy for our friends . . . to rise up'. On 24 May McMahon assured Sharif that a strict blockade of Hijaz coast would operate from 25th. L/P & S/10/597.

276 Fritz Grobba's diary: *Arab Bulletin*, vol. 1, 19 Sept 1916, pp. 263–74, including other Stotzingen papers.

277 Premature revolt: *Arab Bulletin*, vol. 2, 1917, p. 249.

Seriousness of purpose: vol. 1, p. 272, 'Conclusion'.

Hogarth: *Arab Bulletin*, vol. 2, p. 250.

Press statement, Berne, 2 Sept 1916: *Arab Bulletin*, vol. 1, p. 340ff.

14 War and Peace

279 War Committee meetings: CAB 37/151, July, Arab Revolt: CAB 37/153, Aug, Situation in Syria and N. Palestine; CAB 42/20, Sept, Arab Revolt; CAB 37/157, Oct, Future of Asia Minor, Italy Invited to Stake Claims; CAB 42/21, Oct, Rabegh/Arab Revolt; etc.

Need for offensive: CAB 37/151/151 and HL/F/24/2/8(b), The Narrative of War Committee and War Cabinet Decisions in Regard to General Murray's Operations, 1916–17, Sir M. P. A. Haukey, Secretary War Cabinet, to Lloyd George, 7 Feb 1920. Murray's advance to Al Arish recommended by Asquith at War Committee 6 July 1916 (W. C. 53, Min. 5). 'The Chief of the Imperial General Staff should direct the Commander-in-Chief in Egypt to make all possible preparations for the occupation of Al Arish and Aqaba.'

'place called Rabegh': Hankey, HL/F/24/2/8(b).

Parliamentary reports: CAB 42/16, 11 and 28 July 1916, Mesopotamia and Dardanelles.

'took Arish': CAB 42/24, 19 Nov, paper by Captain T. E. Lawrence; CAB 37/161, 15 Dec, Al Arish, Arab Revolt, Rabegh.

Blowing up Hijaz rail: WO 33/820, 10 July, CIGS to GOC; 'Wingate might help with destruction of railway. Sharif probably ignorant of art.'

Uprisings in Syria: WO 33/820, 1 July, DMI, London, to Clayton.

Fuad Pasha marching against Sharif: WO 33/738, Maurice, from Berne.

280 Idrisi takes Qunfidah: L/P & S/10/598, 1 July. 4 July, Brigadier-General W.

C. Watton, Aden, to Foreign Simla: 'Idrisi not actively hostile to Imam but, in common with most decent Arabs, regards him as a dishonest and disreputable ruler'. 6 July, Chamberlain to War Committee: Imam, 'a little money might help'.

280 Scare at Rabegh: WO 33/728.

Major Ross: see Lawrence, *Seven Pillars*, p. 118, 'Rabegh, shaken by the first appearance of Turkish planes on November the seventh'. Ross, 'who spoke Arabic so adeptly and was so splendid a leader that there could be no two minds as to the wise direction of his help'.

Yanbo surrenders, 27 July: L/P & S/10/598, 30 July.

Lawrence at Yanbo: Parker, diary, (19 Oct 1916), 'Question of Lawrence going to see Faisal'; 30 Oct, 'leave Rabegh for Yanbo to meet Captain Lawrence'; 31 Oct, 'have advised L to report to Sirdar at Port Sudan'; 31 Oct, 'arrive Yanbo, Lawrence with Abdal Kidr'. See Lawrence, *Seven Pillars*, ch. xx. T.E.L. does not give dates of his wanderings at this time, but movements can be followed from Parker's diary. The senior officer's version of events differs greatly from Lawrence's. Parker, 4 Oct, 'Turk advance on Bir Abbas two days ago, Faisal won't fight decisive action.' Parker to Cairo, diary, 23 Oct, 'Military situation bad.'

Faisal defeated at Bir Abbas: FO 371/2776, 10 Oct, Parker.

Lawrence to Wejh: intro to Book II, *Seven Pillars*, 'Opening the Arab Offensive'. Before the British force decamped from Rabegh, Joyce (who arrived from Egypt with 250 men, aircraft and guns on 11 Nov), Parker, Davenport and Nuri Said were refused permission by the truculent Prince Ali to inspect his troops 'unless ordered by Mecca'. He also refused Nuri Said troop 'returns'. Parker's diary, 11–14 Nov.

281 Sharif's army in disarray: WO 33/728, Parker to Clayton, 3 Nov: 'Reports of Turkish advance exaggerated'. See also FO 371/2776, 22 Oct, report from Colonel Parker dated 7 Oct; and WO 33/728, 17 Nov, report by Captain Lawrence, 'Sharif's position' giving a much more sanguine account, and ibid., Arbur to DMI, 18 Nov, 'Sharif's forces on move'. Parker to Arbur, Parker, diary, 29 Nov, 'Aziz al Masri complaints', 'Meccan intrigues and Turkish strategy', and, 6 Dec, 'Zaid retiring on Yanbo, Faisal at Nakhl al Mubarak in Wadi Yanbo, Abdullah somewhere on eastern road, Ali at Rabegh'.

Storrs and Hogarth at Jiddah: FO 882/5, 19 Oct 1916.

Action at Wejh: WO 33/905 and WO 33/758 (secret telegrams) messages Jan–Feb 1917; and *Arab Bulletin*, no. 41, 6 Feb 1917, report by Captain N. N. E. Bray, 18th Bengal Lancers. See also Bray, *Shifting Sands*, and Lawrence, *Seven Pillars*, for very divergent accounts.

282 'shot at a naval party': WO 33/905, 'brigade of 24 men from HMS *Fox* captured 55 of enemy and killed twelve'. Lt Stewart, Royal Navy, killed by Arab.

Captain Boyle and 'serious lack of initiative': Bray, *Arab Bulletin*, no. 41, and *Shifting Sands*.

282   Map: GSGS 4011, Published by Survey of Egypt, 21 Feb 1917.

'brave fight': WO 33/905. Arbur to DMI, message from Newcombe, 7 Feb 1917, 'of Turks who escaped from Wejh only 70 reached safety, rest killed'.

Sharif's forces: Bray, report, 6 Feb, *Arab Bulletin*, no. 41.

283   Clayton to French: WO 33/969, 27 July 1916.

German mission at Madina: WO 33/905, 17 Jan, Arab Bureau to DMI.

Lawrence to Cairo: *Seven Pillars*, diary of movements: 27 Jan boards HMS *Hardinge* at Wejh, 28 Jan Cairo.

Colonel Brémond: *Seven Pillars*, p. 172ff.

Lawrence's plan: Bray, *Shifting Sands*.

284   Rolls Royces for Sharif's sons: Bray, *Shifting Sands*.

French request for gold: FO 371/2925, 19 Dec 1916.

Gold to Kasim: WO 33/905, 1 Jan 1917.

Parker to Wingate, 24 Oct: Parker, diary.

WO refusal of troops and aircraft: WO 33/905, 27 Sept, CIGS to GOC.

Ali's intransigence: Parker, diary, Aug–Sept 1916.

Parker to Cornwallis, 26 Oct: Parker, diary. 'R' was the DMI's designation.

285   Parker, report: 29 Nov 1916, 'Meccan intrigues, Turk strategy', Parker, diary.

Newcombe's arrival: WO 33/728, 9 Dec 1916. 'Newcombe very urgently required Jiddah. Wilson ill.' FO 882/6, 15 Jan, Wilson to Newcombe, 'My representative in all military and political matters.'

Lawrence to Newcombe: MEC, Oxford, letter dated 17 Jan 1917.

Newcombe's saddle-bag: returned to owner by Ismet Bey in April 1936 and acknowledged by Newcombe in letter of 24 April 1936, MEC, Oxford.

286   Parker, Secret Service fund: diary. Summary of Hijaz situation, 6 Dec 1916, to Sirdar.

Lawrence, movements from March 1917: *Seven Pillars*. See also Knightley and Simpson, *Secret Lives*, p. 80ff., alleged visit to Damascus. J. M. Wilson quotes Lawrence to Clayton: 'I've decided to go off alone to Damascus, hoping to get killed on the way'. intro., T. E. Lawrence, *Minorities*, Cape, 1971.

'wave a Sharif': *Arab Bulletin*, no. 60, Aug 1917.

Bray observed: *Shifting Sands*.

Murray's plans, March 1917: HL/F/24/2/8(b).

287   Baghdad taken: see Sir Percy Cox in Gertrude Bell, *Letters*, p. 409ff. See also *Arab Bulletin*, no. 47, 1 April 1917, Gertrude Bell, 'Influence on Moslem Minds'.

Proclamation of independence, 19 March 1917: CAB 27/22. See also Adelson, *Mark Sykes*, pp. 223–5; drafted by Sykes, amended by Chamberlain, finalised by Curzon, Hardinge and Milner.

287 Advance to Gaza: see Wavell, *Allenby*.

War Cabinet, 30 March: HL/F/24/2/8(b).

Attack on Gaza: ibid.

Revised instructions to Murray: ibid.

General Allenby to Cairo: see Wavell, *Allenby*, p. 154

288 Field-Marshal Smuts: ibid.

Murray's despatch, 28 June: HL/F/24/2/8(b). The GOC re-applied for permission to publish on 20 Oct 1918. He was given authority to publish the non-strategic and non-political parts.

Departure of Murray: FO 371/2927, Wingate to Balfour.

Meinertzhagen: see Wavell, *Allenby*, and Meinertzhagen, *Middle East Diary*.

289 British attitude to Aaronsohn and colleagues: most British officers worked amiably with both British and expatriate Jews in Cairo, but there is evidence of anti-Jewish bias on Hogarth's part (see Fletcher, 'Memoir of D. G. Hogarth', *GJ*) 'I go up, now and again, to Jerusalem, but always find the atmosphere of priests and Jew-fanatics and politico-ecclesiastical intrigues rather uncongenial,' letter dated 14 April 1918. And Clayton (Durham University, Box 139/1) letter to Wingate, 3 Aug 1916: 'Widespread influence of Jews'. Most anti-Russian, 'therefore anti-British'.

Aaronsohn's team: Meinertzhagen, *Middle East Diary*, pp. 5, 211.

'the accepted halls': Lawrence, *Seven Pillars*, p. 58.

Aaronsohn to Aboulafia: Engle, *The NILI Spies*, and Aaronsohn, *Yoman*.

Bentwich: an enthusiastic Zionist. See interview, 1909, in FO 371/3083, evidence of Montagu, 9 Oct 1917.

290 Contact with Athlit: L. B. Weldon, *Hard Lying*, Jenkins, 1925.

Aaronsohn to Edmunds: see Engle, *The NILI Spies*.

Peace negotiations: HL/F/3/7/13, Feb 1917, Lloyd George to Balfour, Sir Francis Hopwood and peace negotiations. Hopwood was Director of the Intelligence Division, controlled by the FO to act as liaison between the various branches of the Secret Service. First message from MI1 (Berne) 24 Feb.

Feinberg and Lishansky: *Encycl. Judaica*, and Engle, *The NILI Spies*.

Death of Feinberg: Engle, *The NILI Spies*.

Aaron to Henrietta Szold: Lee Levin, *Hadassah*.

Wyndham Deedes: Engle, *The NILI Spies*.

291 *Managam:* sent from Suez, where it had operated as a Red Sea and Gulf of Aqaba monitor ship under Parker's orders, to Mediterranean in July 1916, as replacement for SS *Zaida*. Captain Smith had been working with Parker in Sinai before joining the Port Said operations of MI. Parker, diary.

291   Liova Schneersohn, diary: Engle, *The NILI Spies.*

NILI: ibid., and *Encycl. Judaica.* The initials are, of course, phonetic.

Sarah and Lishansky: description of the journey to Galilee and Jerusalem taken from Engle, *The NILI Spies* and Blankfort, *Behold the Fire.*

Funds from America: the gold supplied to the Aaronsohns via Cairo was intended to be the last American money to arrive in 1917. FO 382/1639, American funds for Jews in Palestine, 13 Jan and Feb (no date), cessation of relief. But America's entry into the war brought about a resumption in April.

293   Differences among Jews: Engle, *The NILI Spies.* For a history of the Labour movement in Palestine see Sachar, *A History of Israel.*

Security committee: Arthur Ruppin was allowed to distribute funds by the Turks. 'Enjoyed the confidence of Arthur von Zimmermann,' Sachar, *A History of Israel.*

Ha-Shomer and the Aaronsohn organisation: Engle, *The NILI Spies.*

Jamal's announcement: see Friedman, *Germany, Turkey and Zionism.*

German protests: ibid.

'insulting the Turks': ibid.

Date of expulsion: ibid., and Sachar, *The Emergence of the Middle East,* and *A History of Israel.*

294   Jerusalem to be evacuated: Friedman, *Germany, Turkey and Zionism.* Jamal's decision was characteristically abrupt, and both German and Allied protests were justified. But most writers on these events ignore the fact that the order was issued as the British army advanced on Gaza and the Turks' C-in-C expected a full-scale advance to Jerusalem. The second attack on Gaza was repulsed by the Turks on 20 April. HL/F/24/2/8(b).

Von Kressenstein's protest: Kress von Kressenstein, *Mit den Türken zum Suezkanal.* See also Friedman, *Germany, Turkey and Zionism.*

Talaat, Grand Vizier: succeeded Prince Said Halim Feb 1917, retaining Interior Ministry. Nesimi Bey took over Foreign Ministry from Khalil Pasha at same time, and Javid re-entered Cabinet as Finance Minister. See Trumpener, *Germany and the Ottoman Empire.*

Zimmermann to High Command: Friedman, *Germany, Turkey and Zionism.*

America entered war: 6 April 1917.

Sarah Aaronsohn and Lishansky to Cairo: Engle, *The NILI Spies.*

295   'Mustn't relax for a moment': ibid.

Using Kitchener–Condor Survey: ibid.

Using official cipher: FO 371/3055, Wingate to FO.

Work of Aaronsohn and NILI: see Elieza Livneh (ed.), *NILI* (in Hebrew), Tel Aviv, 1961, and Friedman, *Germany, Turkey and Zionism,* p. 354: 'It was the Aaronsohn group, a small but efficient spy-ring in Palestine, which was responsible for giving the news to the world.'

295 Copenhagen Bureau: Zionist Central Archive, Jerusalem, Z 3/616–80, (Das Kopenhagener Zionistische Büro), AA Turkei 195, and FO 382/1639. For comprehensive list of sources on Zionist propaganda, work of Aaronsohn and other Jewish figures, and communications between London and Berlin through Copenhagen, see Friedman, *Germany, Turkey and Zionism*, p. 354ff., and bibliographic notes, pp. 430–31.

Manchester Guardian: 9 May. Similar reports in *The Times, Daily Telegraph, Morning Post* and *Le Temps:* Friedman, *Germany, Turkey and Zionism.*

Jamal and Aaronsohn: ibid.

296 Egyptian Committee: FO 371/1639, 11 May 1917.

Aaronsohn, quoted: Engle, *The NILI Spies.*

Captain Edmunds, quoted: ibid.

Sarah to Aaron: ibid.

Return to Athlit: ibid, left Cairo 16 May. Reached Palestine 15 June, *Encycl. Judaica.*

297 John de Vere Loder, later Lord Wakehurst: letters to his mother from Casino Palace Hotel, Port Said, 3 and 11 Dec 1916, MEC, Oxford.

Ormsby-Gore and Lord Edward Cecil to Port Said: Loder to mother from Base Commandant, Port Said, 25 Feb 1917.

Leachman: see Bray, *Shifting Sands.*

Anglo-French mission: FO 371/3053, 25 April 1917. 'Aaronsohn should act for Weizmann.'

298 Meeting at Wejh: ibid. Bray, *Shifting Sands.*

Leachman on Hijaz Arabs: letter home, 10 May 1917.

Lawrence on Leachman: see *Letters of T. E. Lawrence*, p. 224, letter 126 to Alec Dixon, 29 Dec 1925.

Leachman in Cairo: FO 882, 2 May, meeting at Residency. See also Bray, *Shifting Sands* and *Paladin.*

299 Arrest of Maurer and others: FO 371/2672, 'German Espionage in Egypt', MI1, 15 June 1916, GOC to CIGS, 13 June.

Ex-Khedive's envoy to Sharif: *Arab Bulletin*, no. 4, 16 June 1916.

Storrs to Baghdad: L/P & S/10/388, 5 April 1917, 'Sykes and Storrs to Mesopotamia at once'. Sykes remained in Egypt. See Storrs, *Orientations.*

Sykes delighted: ibid.

Allenby in Egypt: took command of Egyptian Expeditionary Force 28 June 1917. See Wavell, *Allenby.* Murray departed 16 June, FO 371/2927. Meinertzhagen arrived Cairo 24 May: Meinertzhagen, *Middle East Diary.*

Funds for displaced Jews: FO 382/1639 and FO 371/3053.

Through Anglo-Palestine Bank: FO 371/3055. Wingate to Graham, 4 July 1917, 'Our relations with Aaronsohn are somewhat difficult . . . mode of transmission of money was never laid down.'

Foreign Office concern: FO 382/1639.

299   Minute on Weizmann: FO 382/1639, Minute, 15 Aug 1917. And HL/F/2/28, 23 July, Graham to Hardinge about Weizmann.

Kidston: ibid, 15 Aug.

Mr Weizmann: FO 382/1639, minute dated 22 Aug.

300   Weizmann to Aaronsohn: ibid. Forwarded to Sir Ronald Graham from 67 Addison Road, London W14, 23 Aug 1917, signed Weizmann and Sokolov.

Sir Arthur Nicolson: FO 371/3055, minute 5 July in response to Wingate's telegram of 4 July. Kidston added the minute: 'I do not know who Aaronsohn is, but I entirely agree with the intimation made to him that the funds of the Jewish Committee at Cairo should be kept in the Bank until such time as it may be possible to distribute them on the spot in occupied territory.' He knew perfectly well who Aaronsohn was, having dealt with several FO papers involving his movements.

July 1916, message from Lishansky: Engle, *The NILI Spies*, quotes letter, 20 July, to friend in England, S. Tolkowsky.

Wingate to Balfour: FO 371/3062, 20 Aug 1917, enclosing report on Palestine and the Zionists by A. Aaronsohn. Some Jews in Cairo and London believed that Aaronsohn exaggerated the scale of the Jaffa expulsions. But Parker, who went in with the advance force, reported that of a population of 65,000 only 2,000 remained. Diary, 20 Dec 1916.

301   Arab autonomy movement: Arab prisoners of war released at Sykes's instigation, had formed the first Arab Army, the Arab Legion, in Egypt, and had rallied to Dr Shahbandar, in the 'late summer'. See Bray, *Shifting Sands*.

Berne to London: Turks offer to Syrians and Mesopotamians, FO 371/3060.

302   Cabinet, London: Lloyd George Papers, House of Lords; see notes to p. 305ff.

Aaronsohn to London: FO 382/1639, Wingate to Foreign Secretary, 2 Sept 1917. 3 Sept, FO to WO and Home Office, 'Please give facilities.'

Hall, and Zimmermann telegram: see James, *Eyes of the Navy*, pp. 152–3, 7 Feb and 30 March 1917.

German codebook: see C. J. Edmonds, 'Prelude to the Zimmermann Telegram', *CASJ*, vol. XLVII, no. 1, Jan 1960.

Colonel House to Hall, 6 April 1917: James, *Eyes of the Navy*, p. 154.

'another note': House to J. A. Baker, 4 April, HL/F/3/2/16.

Von Falkenhayn: see Wavell, *Allenby*, p. 171, 'von Falkenhayn, one of the ablest and most experienced of the German commanders [sent] to take charge of . . . "Yilderim". It was to be transported down the Euphrates to strike at the British left-flank in Mesopotamia.' Wavell also says, 'Mustafa Kamal [later Ataturk, the first President of the Turkish Republic] was offered command of the Turkish portion of the force, but declined to serve under a German staff.' Wavell was not entirely correct. In fact, Kamal took command of the Seventh Army Corps under von Falkenhayn on 5 July and relinquished the job two months later, on 20 Sept. See Kinross, *Ataturk*, and Vogel, *Die Persien und Afghanistanexpedition*, (July), 'Asienkorps'. Enver undermined von Falkenhayn's plan.

303   Secret discussions: FO 371/3083, July 1917.

Morgenthau: HL/F/3/2/28, 23 July 1917, minute in Foreign Office diary by Sir R. Graham: 'Dr Weizmann returned from Paris last night.' Weizmann reported Morgenthau 'extremely vague' and 'ill-equipped for task'; Frankfurter described as an 'extremely capable gentleman'.

Peace initiatives: FO 371/3083, July 1917, Noel Buxton MP to Hardinge: 'Need to detach one of Germany's allies.' Correspondence Paget and Townley. Secret session of House of Commons, Bonar Law's declaration. HL/F/3/2/38, July 1917, Sir E. Goschen (former Ambassador Berlin) to Sir Eric Drummond: 'More conversations with Germany rumoured.' Sir Samuel Hoare, meeting in Berlin between Archduke Frederick of Austria and German officials. Goschen: 'No, would have noticed arrival of Archduke . . . British intelligence not that dumb.'

French envoy, Colonel Weil: HL/F/3/2/28. Weizmann and the British Government were particularly concerned at this time by the rise to prominence of the pro-German and largely Jewish Caillaux faction in France. One of Caillaux's henchmen, Professor Bache, told Weizmann that France was hoping to conclude 'an honorable peace' and that it would be directed not against Germany 'but against England'. He added: 'We shall not continue to fight for England's absurd ideas of conquest in Mesopotamia or Palestine.' After a recent speech by Caillaux in the French Chamber, said Weizmann in his report to the FO, people were saying, 'En voila un qui comprend.' 'Only the Americans could combat his influence'.

Rothschild to Balfour, 18 July 1917: FO 371/3083 and HL/F/3/2/34.

Montagu to Lloyd George, 28 March 1917: HL/F/39/3/11.

'wanted the Treasury': ibid., 1 May 1917. 'Need for a Liberal loyal to you. Suggest Exchequer for myself.' He added: 'I do not think Chamberlain is doing the IO well.'

304   Parliamentary Report: Report of Mesopotamian Commission, June 1917, Cd 8610. Debated in Parliament 11 July 1917. Chamberlain resigned on day of debate. *The Times*, 12 July.

Hardinge: HL/F/3/2/26, 9 July 1917, Balfour to Lloyd George. Demand for Hardinge's resignation. Balfour hoped that he would be allowed to defend Hardinge in the House.

Montagu as Viceroy, King George's views: HL/F/3/2/24, 18 July, Balfour to Lloyd George.

Wingate to London, about Aaronsohn; assurances by Balfour and Lloyd George: FO 371/3083, 28 July, to Graham, FO.

345   Montagu's plea: ibid.

Gertrude Bell: ibid.

305 M. Joseph Reinach, 12 April 1917, and Sig. Luigi Luzzatti (Prime Minister 1910) in *Jewish Exponent*, 18 May 1917, ibid., L. L. Cohen, ibid.

306 Montagu to Cecil: ibid., 14 Sept.

C. P. Scott to Lloyd George: HL/F/45/2/4, 5 Feb 1917, 'My dear George, I hope you will be able to see Weizmann about the Palestine Question.'

Balfour, 1905: Tibawi, *Anglo-Arab Relations*.

Sykes: see Storrs, *Orientations:* 'When the Zionists obtained the sympathy of this Englishman they gained an ally hardly less valuable than Balfour himself.' And see Adelson, *Mark Sykes:* 'Sykes was too caught up in his Allied-Arab-Armenian-Zionist vision to lose heart over what he saw as Bureaucratic defeatism.' Original draft of Balfour Declaration was produced by Sykes and Sokolov. Balfour rejected it as too long and detailed. A revised formula was sent formally by Rothschild to Balfour on 18 July (at this time Sykes was acting as Assistant Under-Secretary FO, appointed by Lloyd George as part of his strategy to combine the offices of Prime Minister and Foreign Secretary). See Adelson, *Mark Sykes*, p. 235.

Cabinet, 3 Sept: HL/F/3/2/34.

French plan for Jewish state in Al Hasa: FO 371/3062, 29 Sept 1917, DMI to Hardinge, 'proposal by Dr M. L. Rothstein . . . cannot be entertained'.

307 Whitehall on French plan: FO 371/2930,MI2 to FO, 29 Sept.

Aaronsohn, arrival in London, 18 Sept: FO 382/1639. According to FO 371/3062, Aug 1917, Aaronsohn intended to go immediately to America.

Views of President Wilson: HL/F/3/2/34, 3 Sept. Reply from Colonel House, 12 Sept.

Jamal's *gendarmerie*, Athlit, 4 Sept 1917: see Engle, *NILI Spies*.

Aaronsohn to brother Alex: dated 'Oct 1917' written in Hebrew. Text taken from copy in misc papers, MEC, Oxford, ref. DS151 A3.

308 Movements of HMS *Managam:* Engle, *The NILI Spies*. *Managam* was commanded at this time by Captain Weldon of Port Said intelligence. See his *Hard Lying*, Jenkins, 1925.

Events from 10 to 30 Sept: Engle, *The NILI Spies*. See *Encycl. Judaica*, 'NILI', 'internal conflicts' and 'grave suspicions over circumstances of Feinberg's death'. Belkind, member of NILI arrested, gave information to the Turks.

309 Sarah to Aaronsohn: Engle, *The NILI Spies*.

Jamal's men at Zichron: letter from Alex to Aaron quoted by Lee Levin in *Haddasah*, March 1977.

Death of Sarah: ibid. See also *Encycl. Judaica*, 'Sarah Aaronsohn' and 'NILI'; and Aston, *Secret Service*, p. 184: 'Her fate was terrible, but no torture could elicit from her anything to incriminate her brother.'

Aaronsohn to Henrietta Szold: Lee Levin, *Haddasah*.

End of NILI: *Encycl. Judaica*, 'NILI'.

310 Rodd to Balfour: FO 371/3062, 10 May, Rome.

Commander Wedgwood: Parliamentary Question, *House of Commons Order Paper*, 9 May.

Cecil's reply: *Parliamentary Debates*, 9 May 1917.

Marmaduke Pickthall: proceedings of Central Islamic Society, in FO 371/3062.

311 Letters to *Al Qibla:* Brigadier-General Cockerill, Director of Special Intelligence, to U/SS, FO, 1 Dec 1917, in FO 371/3062.

Article from *Reichsbote*: 'A Jewish Republic in Palestine', FO 371/3062.

Berne to London: MI2 to FO, 2 Oct, in FO 371/3062.

312 German support for Jewish claims in Palestine: the strong Zionist lobby in Berlin had counted Foreign Minister Zimmermann among its supporters until Aug 1917, when he was replaced by von Kühlmann the Ambassador in Constantinople, in the shadow of the famous telegram controversy. Kühlmann was replaced at the Porte in Sept by Count Bernstorff the ex-Ambassador in Washington. But the German Government and High Command remained anxious to placate the Zionists. See Gustav von Dobeler, 'A Jewish Republic in Palestine', *Reichsbote*, May 1917, trans. in FO 371/3062. They were hotly opposed by their Turkish allies, however. The CUP was no more anxious than Abdal Hamid had been to divide the Empire. From the moment of their intervention in the war, a neo-Turanian ideology became the strongest influence in CUP councils; back to their central Asian origins. See FO 395/16, Memorandum on neo-Turanian movement by Arab Bureau, May 1916. And see Kühlmann, *Erinnerung;* recalled to take up Ambassadorship at the Hague and made Foreign Secretary. For detailed account of CUP 1908–18, see Lewis, *The Emergence of Modern Turkey*, p. 209ff.

Cabinet, 4 Oct: HL/F/3/2/34, and FO 371/3083. Draft submitted to War Cabinet by Lord Milner.

President's reply: FO 371/3083.

Replies of leading Jews: ibid.

Cabinet, 24–5 Oct: HL/F/3/2/34. and FO 371/3083. Also, 25th, Graham to Hardinge, HL/F/3/2/20.

Curzon: FO 371/3083.

Sykes: ibid.

Cromer: *Spectator*, 12 Aug 1916.

Turco-German military convention: 18 Oct 1917, signed by General Herman von Stein and Enver. See Trumpener, *Germany and the Ottoman Empire*.

Foreign Secretary to Rothschild: FO 371/3083, 1 Nov, War Cabinet minute 227, message of sympathy for Zionist aspirations. FO 395/86, 2 Nov, Balfour Declaration. Also in HL/F/3/2/34(a).

312   Rothschild to Balfour, 4 Nov: FO 371/3083.

Bolsheviks: overthrow of Provisional Regime, 7 Nov. Lenin's Foreign Ministry almost immediately informed Turks of provisions of Sykes–Picot agreement. Jamal, 'seeking reconciliation with Husain', sent him details. But in releasing information to world in speech at Beirut on 6 Dec 1917, Jamal 'taunted Husain'. See Kedourie, *England and the Middle East*, ch. 7.

Anglo-French agreement, March 1915: precursor of Sykes–Picot agreement. CAB 42/2.

313   Sir R. Graham's plan, 10 Nov: FO 371/3083.

'Russia . . . where most could be done': no doubt informed Jews saw hope in Trotsky's influence at Lenin's side. But hopes were soon dashed. Many senior officials in London believed that both Lenin and Trotsky were secret agents of Germany (see Lockhart, *Memoirs of a British Agent*, p. 197). The Czarist Secret Service chief, Vladikavkaz, claimed irrefutable evidence that Trotsky was in the pay of Germany (Keeling, *Adventures in Turkey and Russia*).

'I have no great faith': FO 371/3083, Graham to Foreign Secretary.

'Our own d'Annunzio': Weizmann, quoted by Hirst, *The Gun and the Olive Branch*.

Colonel Buchan, working with Jabotinsky and Aaronsohn: FO 371/3083.

International Committee: ibid., 14 Nov 1917.

314   Mass rally: FO 371/3062, 30 Nov, rally 'next Sunday.'

15   Requiem for Victory

315   Allenby's campaign: see Wavell, *Allenby*, ch. VIII, 'The Taking of Jerusalem, June–October 1917'.

Meinertzhagen and Aaronsohn: see Meinertzhagen, *Middle East Diary*, and Wavell, *Allenby*, pp. 167, 261–2.

'haversack' trick: executed 28 Oct 1917. One of the most secret devices of the war, both Meinertzhagen and Wavell suggest that it had a decisive effect on the campaign but neither gave details, insisting that the trick was best kept secret. Aston, *Secret Service*, pp. 191–6, gives a colourful account in which Meinerzhagen is represented as 'Mannering' and a letter from the Colonel's wife announcing the birth of their child played a significant part.

Lawrence on Meinertzhagen: *Seven Pillars*, p. 393.

316   Newcombe, attacks on Hijaz railway: see Wavell, *Allenby*, p. 178. 'Colonel S. F. Newcombe . . . had been with Lawrence in the Hijaz in the early part of 1917. He came back to Egypt in July on account of sickness, and himself suggested and organised the raid on the Hebron road.' FO 882/4, 14 June, report by Newcombe, proposals for operations against railway. A few days later he was injured in raid and invalided to Cairo.

316   Newcombe's loyalty to Lawrence: Newcombe correspondence, MEC, Oxford; and private papers, correspondence, with Lowell Thomas, J. A. Kelly and others 1920–54 (in author's possession).

Newcombe's diversion: only detailed account is by Lance Corporal C. H. Geraghty of the 2/21st Btn, London Regiment (Surrey Rifles) in *Barrak*, Irregular Newsletter of the Old Boys of the Imperial Camel Corps, Aug 1971.

'set out the night before': 30 Oct, ibid.

Description of Camel Corps' engagement: ibid., and Wavell, *Allenby*, p. 178.

317   Lawrence: quoted in Geraghty, *Barak*.

Newcombe, POW: letter from Newcombe to Ismet Bey, 18 Nov 1917, MEC, Oxford. And private papers, unpublished essay (in author's possession), no date.

'with aid of French girl': Elsie Chaki. Geraghty describes her as 'a beautiful Syrian girl', but she was of French nationality, daughter of a pre-war official in the Ottoman capital (Baroness Elles to author, Nov 1981). Newcombe, in his description of his captivity refers to her simply as the cousin of his interpreter Marco, 'a wealthy fellow, educated in France'.

Wrote to Jamal/Ismet Bey: letter to Ismet, 18 Nov.

318   'like an ant's nest': Ober-General Steuber, quoted in Geraghty, *Barak*.

Beersheba, Allenby to London: Wavell, *Allenby*, p. 180.

Jaffa: ibid., 'Pursuit in Philistia', p. 182ff.

Jerusalem: actual surrender 9 Dec, Turks vacated on 8th, Feast of Hanukah. See Sachar, *Emergence of the Middle East*, and Wavell, *Allenby*.

'Two gentlemen': FO 395/86, Butler (Washington) to Lieutenant-Colonel J. L. Fisher, MI1 (Special Intelligence), 13 Dec 1917.

Spring-Rice to Buchan: ibid., 20 Nov 1917.

Lowell Thomas to Buchan: FO 395/86, 10 Dec 1917.

Entry into Jerusalem, 9 Dec: Lawrence, *Seven Pillars*, ch. LXXXII. Wavell, *Allenby*, 'a simple but impressive ceremony'.

Picot: *Seven Pillars*, p. 464.

Thomas and Lawrence: see Stewart, *T. E. Lawrence*, Knightley and Simpson, *Secret Lives*, and Thomas's own account, *With Lawrence of Arabia*.

Meinertzhagen and Lawrence: see Meinertzhagen, *Middle East Diary*, 'not much impressed'.

319   Lawrence, recommendations for VC and Croix de Guerre: see Stewart, *T. E. Lawrence*.

Ludendorff: see his *My War Memories*, vol. 1, quoted in Grant and Temperley, *Europe in the Nineteenth and Twentieth Centuries*, p. 414.

France and Clemenceau: ibid., p. 418.

Buchan and American Zionist propaganda: FO 395/86, Buchan to Butler, correspondence Dec 1917. Jewish Branch of FO Information Department under auspices of Hyamson, 29 Dec 1917.

319 *Judische Rundschau:* FO 395/86, extract cabled to America 14 Dec 1917, FO minute. 'First occasion on which a great power has officially declared itself in relation to Zionism.'

Russian Zionists: ibid., Buchan to Butler, 22 Dec.

Chief Rabbi: ibid.

Illness of Sultan Husain Kamil: FO 371/2926, Wingate to FO, 1 Feb 1917, *et seq.*

Abbas Hilmi, pro-German activities: FO 371/2930 (31 Aug/1 Sept 1917), circulated to King and War Cabinet, Abbas Hilmi to Constantinople, in touch with Austrians and Germans; Berne intelligence to Sir Horace Rumbold, Ambassador, 6 Oct 1917, information from Czech in touch with ex-Khedive's solicitors, Rosenberg and Bettelheim; treaty with German Government, 'till peace concluded, Turkey will pay Abbas Hilmi annual rent of £200,000 Turkish'.

June 1917: FO 371/2927, 2 June, Berne to Lord Robert Cecil, FO Muhammad Farid has left Berlin for Stockholm. 'Not disposed to give ex-Khedive any advice'. Socialist connections. Enemy agents (MI1 report) FO 371/2926, 2 March, Cecil to Graham, FO, 'time for Colonial Office to take over Egypt'. Graham, 'first step to annexation and would be seen as such'.

320 German Bureau, Damascus: AA Nr 11g, Der Weltkrieg, Bd 1–19 (Unternehmungen und Aufwiegelungen gegen unsere Feinde). Von Oppenheim and his agents were well established in Syria and the Hijaz from 1909 but did not establish the equivalent of Britain's Arab Bureau, with its propaganda arm, until June 1917, when it began to disseminate the journal *Der Neue Orient,* described by British FO as 'excellent' (FO 371/3062). Also AA, Nr 11g, adh. Bd 1 and 2, Syrien und Arabien, 1916–18.

Sultan 'mad': FO 371/2925.

Abbas Hilmi (1914–17): FO 371/2930, Berne to FO (report July 1917). Abbas Hilmi wanted to visit London in June 1914, but Kitchener refused permission. His mistress, Mlle Lusanges, joined him in Switzerland when Louis Mallet, Ambassador in Constantinople, refused him permission to return to Cairo in Aug 1914 after a visit to Paris. Given £2,000 per month by Britain, 'never to set foot in Egypt again'.

Autonomy for Syria and Mesopotamia, Abbas Hilmi Viceroy: FO 371/3060, Aug 1917.

Rumbold. FO 371/2930, July 1917.

Acton: ibid.

'used by the Germans': FO 371/2930, British Legation, Berne, 'Memorandum Concerning Present Activities of ex-Khedive', 11 Dec 1917. 'At Constantinople conducting intensive campaign ... among the Arab chiefs.' Given two million francs towards expenses. 5 Oct, Rome Embassy to FO; Turkey, rumour of reconciliation with King of Hijaz under German auspices with support of ex-Khedive. Ibid., 17 Nov, Bertie, Paris, to FO: 'French authorities in possession of paper signed by Count Richthofen on behalf of Turkish, German and Austrian governments, guaranteeing ex-Khedive . . . £100,000 Turkish and promising to recognise his claim to throne of Egypt.' Abbas Hilmi claimed Britain asked him to act as intermediary with Arab chiefs. Turks accepted a similar offer to undertake a mission on their behalf.

320   Bolo affair: FO 371/2930, British Legation Berne to FO, 15 Oct 1917, 'shows conclusively that on visit to Switzerland (1915) he [ex-Khedive] was acting as German agent'.

Aziz Ali al Masri: Wingate to Hardinge, FO, 25 Sept 1917.

Jamal: see Djemal Pasha, *Memories*.

321   Death of General Maude: FO 371/3062, 29 Nov 1917, Wingate to FO.

Death of Sultan, 9 Oct 1917: FO 37/2928, Wingate to FO. 'Died at Abdin Palace, 12.10 pm today.' 'Devotion to duty hastened premature demise. Prince Ahmad Fuad succeeded.'

Sultan Ahmad Fuad, mystery: FO 371/3062, 29 Nov.

Circumstances of Maude's death and disputes with civil administrators: see Bell, *Letters*, 22 Nov, from Samarra: 'The I.G.C. [MacMunn] came to my house and said . . . C-in-C dangerously ill of cholera . . . not expected to live. It was almost incredible to us all. There had been little cholera in the town . . . nothing very serious . . . yet how fortunate when the man dies before the name.' See Winstone, *Gertrude Bell*, p. 230 (unpublished letter), 'Maude! Maude! Anyone more totally removed from the remotest idea of self-government in Asia it would be impossible to conceive.'

Graham: FO 371/3062. Message attached to note of 29 Nov.

Jamal recalled, Dec 1917: Trumpener, *Germany and the Ottoman Empire*.

Kress von Kressenstein: assumed command Eighth Army, Oct 1917, relinquished command Dec. Ibid.

Liman von Sanders: given command of Army Group F following dismissal of von Falkenhayn at request of Enver and his Chief of Staff, von Seeckt. German Ambassador Constantinople, Count Bernstorff: 'Only Liman can pull off victory.'

Persian tribes: Sir Percy Sykes, *A History of Persia*.

Supreme Allied War Council,Paris, 22 Jan 1918: see HL/F/2/1/4, L. S. Amery to Lloyd George, 5 June 1917, 'Eastern approach', and HL/F/6/1/3, 29 Dec, Amery to Lloyd George: 'To eliminate Turkey with all possible speed is the most urgent need . . . The French, I may say, are showing the keenest interest in the Turkish question and General Weygand has three officers on his staff here at work upon it.'

322   Smuts to Allenby: WO 106/729, 28 Jan, War Cabinet, Smuts to proceed to Egypt. See Wavell, *Allenby*, pp. 204–5, 'policy of the *Easterners*. The Prime

Minister had his way'. And see HL/F/2/1/4, Amery, 5 June: 'Smuts is one of the rare men who have got precisely the type of mind required.'

322   *Goeben* and *Breslau*, 16 Jan 1918: See Trumpener, *Germany and the Ottoman Empire*, and McLaughlin, *Escape of the Goeben*.

Trotsky, quoted: *The Times*, 11 Feb 1918.

Treaty of Brest-Litovsk: 3 March 1918.

Allenby: see Wavell, *Allenby*, p. 203.

Overhaul of intelligence services: see Bentwich, *Frederick Kisch*.

Lockhart: see his *Memoirs of a British Agent*, ch. 5, return to Moscow.

Lloyd George and attitude to Foreign Office, etc.: the best inside account of Cabinet rivalries and machinations of period after 1916 is given in Admiral Fisher's letters, *Fear God and Dread Nought*, to C. P. Scott, Admiral Jellicoe and others, vol. 3, p. 398ff. I have used Fisher's comments and impressions extensively (author).

323   Caillard: *Who's Who* and *Army Lists*. Seems to have taken up Secret Service appointment in March 1917 (FO 371/3051 Lord Murray to Sir E. Drummond). Died March 1930.

Zahroff: see Lewinsohn, *Der Mann im Dunkel*, and *The Man Behind the Scenes;* Davenport, *Zahroff – High Priest of War*, and McCormic, *Pedlar of Death*. See also Fisher, *Fear God and Dread Nought*, vol. 3, p. 619, letter to Sir Ernest Hodder-Williams, 'Sir Basil Zahroff, the richest man in the world (not excepting Rockefeller)'.

Count Ostrorog: HL/F/6/1/19, 2 Oct 1918, Caillard to Lloyd George. FO 371/3062, 6 Oct, CUP agents in Britain; suggestion that Ostrorog agent of CUP in London, but cleared by Special Intelligence.

Peace moves: March 1915 (CAB 37/126 Petrograd discussion); Nov 1915 (CAB 42/5, Peace rumours in Holland); Nov 1916 (CAB 42/24 German peace feelers through Belgium. Prince Sixtus). And CAB 37/159 (Terms of possible peace deal); Aug 1917 (FO 371/3083, appeal of Pope Benedictus XV).

Frobenius: AA, Abteilung 1A, Orientalia generalia 9 Nr 1, and Der Weltkrieg Nr 11g, B 1–19, 1914–18. Author of *Des deutschen Reiches Schicksalsstunde* ('The Reich's Hour of Destiny'), see *Times Literary Supplement*, 13 Aug 1914. See also *Arab Bulletin*, vol. 2, 1917, p. 79, he was at Jiddah in Nov calling himself 'Abdal Karim Pasha'.

Faisal and Jamal, secret talks: see Lawrence, *Letters*, no. 397, p. 670, to William Yale, 22 Oct 1929, 'Faisal and Jamal carrying on peace negotiations all 1918, while England secretly negotiated with Talaat. Poof!'

War Cabinet to General Staff: WO 106/729, 14 Jan 1918, CIGS to Allenby. WO 106/729, 12 Jan. And HL/C137/391, 5 Oct, War Cabinet Jaffa–Jerusalem line. Allenby's instructions.

324   Meeting with Enver, July 1917: HL/F/6/1/1, Caillard to Lloyd George, 1 Aug 1917. 'Z' reports, 'if the money had been his, he would have risked the £2

million, as he thinks it would have been well worth while'. Memo from Zahroff enclosed.

324 'separate peace': HL/F/6/1/3, first communication from Caillard to PM, Vickers House, 23 Nov 1917. 'Z' reported on 18 Nov: 'A-K will arrive next week.' Caillard, 'an opportune time'. Turks might ask for Anglo-French guarantee of Public Debt, 'about £150 million'.

'Chairman's personal views': HL/F/6//1/16(b), 6 Dec 1917.

Instructions for 'Z': HL/F/6/1/7, 9 Jan 1918.

'Turks scuppered': *Goeben* and *Breslau* attacked RN bases in Aegean, 16 Jan. *Breslau* sunk, *Goeben* crippled. See Trumpener, *Germany and the Ottoman Empire*.

'New instructions': HL/F/6/1/11 (undated note from J. T. Davies to Mr Vincent, from 10 Downing Street). Caillard sent Davies a copy of his note to Zahroff on 26 Jan, explaining that their 'friend' had started for Switzerland before latest instructions could reach him.

325 'Z' 's journey and meeting with Enver: HL/F/6/1/13. Notes written to Caillard from train, 29 Jan. Reached Geneva on 27th, two days later than expected. 'E' arrived next morning.

Description of meeting: ibid.

'young lady waiting': HL/F/6/1/14. Note signed Zahroff. Postscript: 'She either came direct from "E", or if she came from "AK" it must be on "E"'s instructions.' Note connected with alleged instructions from German High Command to Trotsky; probably forgery. See Lockhart, *Memoirs of a British Agent*, p. 231.

326 Death of Czar and family: about mid-Feb according to tradition.

General peace moves: FO 371/3083, Appeal of Pope, 1 Aug 1917. James, *Eyes of the Navy*. Emperor Karl of Austria to King of Spain. Message intercepted by Room 40, 20 Feb 1918. Spanish Ambassador called on President Wilson, 24 Feb.

Amery: HL/F/2/1/4. Letters to 'My dear PM', 26 and 29 Dec 1917, Sir William Robertson's report on future operations in Palestine 'farcical', and, 21 Jan 1918, Dawnay. A meeting of the Supreme War Council was held in Paris on 22 Jan (HL/F/2/1) and the meeting endorsed a plan for decisive offensive against Turkey. See Wavell, *Allenby*, p. 202.

Weygand: HL/F/2/1/4.

Montagu to India: HL/F/40 (Box file), correspondence between Montagu and Lloyd George, Oct 1917–Dec 1920. 23 Oct 1917, from HMS *Bristol:* 'I want to do everything in my power to preserve . . . brotherhood of the people who are going to create a revolution in the Government of India, but this is going to be very difficult.'

327 Allenby: see Wavell, *Allenby*, ch. IX, 'The Final Campaign'.

Zionist Commission: see Philip Graves, *Land of Three Faiths*, arrived Jaffa 4 April. Palestine Office of Zionists under Dr Thon.

327   Aaronsohn: left America end Jan 1918, *Encycl. Judaica*. See also Levin, *Haddasah*, 30 Jan. Wires Henrietta Szold before leaving.

Allenby, refused publication: Wavell, *Allenby*, p. 199, n. Declaration made when third battle of Gaza in full swing. 'Few realised its significance or danger at that time.'

Aaronsohn to America, April 1918: *Encycl. Judaica*.

Aaronsohn in Europe: *Encycl. Judaica*; and Engle, *The NILI Spies*.

Aaronsohn to America, 7 Sept: FO 371/3388.

Lawrence at GHQ: *Seven Pillars*, p. 514, 21 Feb 1918.

Letter to Faisal: FO 882, doc. HM/18/1, 3 March 1918.

Letters between Faisal and father, 9 May 1918: Faisal to Husain ibn Ali, and reply. Forwarded by Wilson to Arab Bureau. MEC, Oxford. See also Tibawi, *Anglo-Arab Relations*. p. 272ff, and Lawrence, *Seven Pillars*, pp. 572–3.

328   'Memorial': FO 371/3380, 7 May 1918, Wingate to FO. See Tibawi, *Anglo-Arab Relations*, p. 274; and Antonius, *The Arab Awakening*, statement to Arab officers, 16 June.

329   Baghdad declaration: CAB 27/22, and appendices to War Cabinet notes, March 1917, CAB 23/2. And Adelson, *Mark Sykes*, pp. 223–4.

Message to Faisal, 9 May: MEC, Oxford.

Liman von Sanders: see his *Funf Jahre Turkei* (relevant passages translated by MI3 for Cabinet in CAB 44/13). From Liman's war diary, 13 April 1918: 'At the close of my statement I requested Enver to lay before the Sultan my request to be recalled from command of the Yilderim Army Group.'

Cairo to Faisal: paraphrase of telegrams Bassett, Jiddah to *Arbur*, Cairo, 8 May 1918, for transmission to Faisal, 9 May, at Aqaba, message from King; MEC papers, Oxford.

Dawnay to Joyce, Cairo, 27 May: 'Faisal should understand, therefore, that, for the time being, he cannot look for British co-operation East of the Jordan' (because of renewed German offensive on Western Front and shortage of troops). MEC papers, Oxford.

Abdullah ibn Hamza and agent: Dawnay to Joyce, 27 May. See Wavell, *Allenby*, pp. 212–13, and n.; Shaikhs of Bani Sakhr at GHQ; 'irresponsibility of Arab warfare'.

330   Lawrence's version: *Seven Pillars*.

'High Commissioner considers': Wilson, Jiddah to Commandant, Aqaba. Tel. WO 93/285, 27 May. 'King very much against' Faisal visiting Jiddah, and Tel. 750/116, 28 May, *Arbur* to Wilson.

Arab divisions: FO 371/3380; and Antonius, *The Arab Awakening*, p. 270.

Conference, Aqaba: *Hedgehog* (Staff HQ Cairo) to Commandant, Aqaba, 29 May. '*Spey* sailing 1 June, carries Weizmann and Ormsby-Gore. It is most desirable that they return *Imogen* on 5 June, make necessary arrangements with Faisal.' Conference took place 4 June. See Knightley and Simpson, *Secret Lives*, p. 117.

330 Faisal and Jewish national presence: see Tibawi, *Anglo-Arab Relations;* Lenczowski, *The Middle East in World Affairs;* Antonius, *The Arab Awakening;* Kedourie, *England and the Middle East.*

Wingate to FO: CAB 27/27, 16 June. See Knightley and Simpson, *Secret Lives*, p. 72.

Weizmann to Balfour: document, 30 May, Scottish Record Office. See Knightley and Simpson, *Secret Lives*, p. 117.

331 Liman von Sanders: see *Funf Jahre Turkei;* and Trumpener, *Germany and the Ottoman Empire*, Sept 1918, for relations between Liman, Enver and von Seeckt.

Allenby's campaign, Aug–Sept: Wavell, *Allenby*, p. 215ff.

Damascus, Sept: ibid., p. 238ff.

Lawrence in Damascus: *Seven Pillars*, ch. CXIX.

Allenby's orders: Wavell, *Allenby*, pp. 242–3. 'Lawrence worked feverishly to aid the Arabs.' And: 'After Faisal had left, Lawrence said that he could not consent to work with a French officer and asked for leave, which was granted.'

Aleppo campaign, 5–31 Oct 1918: ibid. See also Stewart, *T. E. Lawrence.*

Newcombe: unpublished MSS, escape from captivity. It appears that the Turks asked both Newcombe and Townshend to go to Mudros, but Newcombe stood down for the senior officer.

Turks led by Rauf Bey, aboard HMS *Agamemnon*: see Lewis, *The Emergence of Modern Turkey.*

332 Liman von Sanders: *Funf Jahre Turkei.*

Peace Conference: opened officially 18 Jan. Temperley, *History of the Peace Conference.*

War party in Afghanistan, murder of Habibullah: *The Times*, 22–4 Feb 1919. Attack on India, *Morning Post*, 20 March 1919.

Enver and Mustafa Kamal: see WO 33/969. Up to June 1920 Enver still playing off Britain against Russia. At meeting on 7 June in St Moritz Pan-Islamites and Arab nationalists drew up a treaty between Enver and Bolsheviks. Faisal's agent, Amir Shaikh Arslan, in touch with Litvinov in Copenhagen. Anti-British demonstrations followed in Syria, Mesopotamia and India. Insurrection in Mesopotamia sparked off by explosion at Tel Afar near Mosul, 3 June 1920.

333 Enver in Russia: WO 33/969. See also Kurt Okay, *Der Grosse Freund Deutschlands*, Berlin, 1935.

Overtures to Britain: WO 33/969. 'Enver's approach synchronized exactly' with Islamic Congress at St Moritz on 7 Jan, attended by Talaat, Jamal,

Javid, the Shaikh al Islam, the Druse chief Amir Shaikh Arslan and Muhammad Mukhtar.

333 'interim conference': this was probably the 'Oriental Mission' held in Moscow, Jan 1920. WO 33/969. At that meeting, attended also by Lenin, it was decided 'not to begin an armed movement [against the Imperialist Powers] until the Bolsheviks were prepared to occupy the Caucasus, after which there was to be a union of the forces of . . . Azerbaijan and Turkey.'

Enver in Germany: WO 33/969, British mission at Paris and Whitehall 'seriously perturbed' by 'insight into preparations for anti-Constitutional disturbances in Britain', rail strike, Irish troubles, etc. Enver announced intention, should he receive 'cold shoulder' from Britain, of proceeding to Moscow to pursue anti-British campaign with Bolsheviks. See same document for relations between Faisal, Enver, and Bolsheviks, and disturbances in Mesopotamia. See also HL/F/6/1/23, Caillard to Lloyd George, 12 Oct 1918, list of leading rebels and revolutionaries in Great Britain. 're. Revolutionary Movement'. Included G. D. H. Cole, Sylvia Pankhurst and James Maxton as well as leading TU officials and Sinn Feinners.

Death of Enver: Okay, *Der Grosse Freund Deutschlands.* Alternative account in Fitzroy Maclean, *A Person from England*, Cape, 1958.

'Danton': J. Oestrup quoted in Lewis, *The Emergence of Modern Turkey.*

Thomson, last days: in 1919 a division of Special Branch was formed under Thomson with the specific task of combating Communist infiltration. He reported directly to the Home Secretary and not to the Police Commissioner, but worked closely with Caillard, and with his old colleagues of military and naval intelligence. In 1921 he was accused by the Home Secretary, Mr Shortt, of 'insubordination' and of 'withholding vital information' from the Government. Thomson denied the charge but refused to serve under the Police Commissioner, Sir William Horwood. In Dec 1925 he was compromised by a prostitute in Hyde Park and arrested, *Daily Express*, 12 Dec 1925. The man who was chiefly responsible for the internal security of Britain in wartime ended his career in disgrace. Metropolitan Police and WO records. See Thomson, *The Allied Secret Service in Greece*, and *The Story of Scotland Yard.*

Herbert and Talaat: see Herbert, *Ben Kendim.*

Mallet: blamed by *The Times*, 4 Aug 1917, for permitting Turco-German alliance. Mallet's defence, FO 371/3060, 30 Aug 1917.

334 Cox to Tehran, 1919: see Kazemzadeh, *Russia and Britain in Persia*, pp. 678–9. Quotes Buchanan to Czar, 14 March 1915, 'After war Russia and Britain will be two most powerful empires in world.' Settlement of Persian question vital to world peace.

Wassmuss: Christopher Sykes, *Wassmuss.*

Interpretation of promises to Sharif: see Cd 1700, *British Policy in Palestine*, correspondence between Zionists, Arabs and Colonial Office, 1922. Arabs claimed HMG gave undertaking of independent National Government in Palestine. Colonial Office insisted that McMahon's letter of 24 Oct

1915 excluded Palestine ('portions of Syria W. of district of Damascus'). The Arabs were wrong about McMahon's wording, 'Vilayet refers to Syria'. This should be vilayet of As-Sham. In fact, the document referred to 'districts' west of a 'line' terminating at Damascus. Palestine cannot possibly be said to be west of district of Damascus. It was not the Arabs who were wrong. It was the wording itself. Author.

335 Intentions of Arab nationalists: see Tibawi, *Anglo-Arab Relations,* Wingate to Sir Edward Grey (avoiding McMahon): Arab leaders Al Morghani and Ali Rida define Arabia as 'Peninsula and Palestine, Syria and Iraq'. FO authorised Wingate to refer to 'Peninsula and Holy Places' and to say it will 'remain in hands of an independent Moslem state'. Dated 15 March 1915. See FO 371/6237, Nov 1916. Report by Hogarth, *Territorial Agreement with Sharif,* including map, cited in Knightley and Simpson, *Secret Lives,* p. 106.

Foreign Office memo: L/P & S/18/B292.

Sir Kinahan Cornwallis: see *The Arab War,* London 1940, intro. to Gertrude Bell's dispatches for the *Arab Bulletin.*

Abdal Aziz to Kuwait and Basra: L/P & S/10/387, 29 Nov 1916, and *Arab Bulletin,* nos 33, 38, 1916 reports by Gertrude Bell. See also FO 395/133 and L/P & S/18/B248 'A Ruler of the Desert'.

Dr Mylrea: *The Near East,* 11 May 1917.

336 Cox told Amir: IO/R/15/5/27, 11 Feb 1917. Ibn Saud had asked in ciphered message: 'Does Sharif sign himself King of Arabs?' And see *Arab Bulletin,* vol. 2, no 5, 24 June 1918, Colonel Wilson to Wingate: Sharif 'Claims promise made to him in letter from Cairo recognised him as King of Arabia, not Hijaz. Limited recognition rankles with him.'

Dr P. W. Harrison: *Arab Bulletin,* no. 70, 21 Nov 1917.

Storrs in Baghdad: see *Orientations,* Bell, *Letters,* 3–11 May, and Winstone, *Gertrude Bell,* p. 197.

Storrs's journey: L/P & S/10/388. See *Orientations.*

337 Storrs at Sledmere: Adelson, *Mark Sykes,* p. 240.

Sykes's brief to Storrs: L/P & S/10/388, May 1917, with *aide memoire* for Storrs.

Cox to DMI: L/P & S/10/388, June 1917 file, message repeated to FO. See also *Arab Bulletin,* no. 53, 1917. Message from Cox, 6 June, 'Rumour that Turks and Ibn Saud in collusion to attack Hail and Hijaz railway.'

Cox in Cairo: *Arab Bulletin,* vol. 2, no. 3, 1 April 1918. 'The Future of Arabia.' Meeting at Residency, Cairo, 23 March, 1918. Cox was on his way to England. Wingate in chair.

Rashid ibn Lailah: L/P & S/10/388, 7 June 1917. 'Of the moneys entrusted to him for Hail he has appropriated about three-quarters, investing it in property in Constantinople.' Also L/P & S/10/387, Gertrude Bell to DMI, 3 Aug 1917.

Suleiman ibn Daghil: ibid. Native of Buraida. His daughter married Ibn

Saud and had one son. He owned and edited Baghdad newspaper, *Al Riyadh*, before the First World War. He escaped from Hail to Fahad Bey's Anaiza and then to Baghdad. Report on Hail included in report from Cox to Foreign, Simla, 23 Dec 1917, L/P & S/10/388.

337   Cox on Saudi Amir: L/P & S/10/387, May–June 1917.

338   Correspondence between Ibn Saud and Ibn Rashid: ibid.

Wilson and Sharif: *Arab Bulletin*, no. 60, Aug 1917.

Philby mission: L/P & S/10/388, Dec 1917. This mission was intended to meet Storrs at Riyadh. IO intended that Major Bray should lead the delegation, but Cox preferred Philby. Earlier, IO had suggested Leachman.

Philby to Cox: ibid. Message received 16 Dec.

Philby to Sharif: ibid. He left Riyadh for Taif 8 Dec 1917. It was intended that the meeting should take place at Taif and that Ibn Saud should send a representative 'on friendly mission to Sharif'. Storrs would then accompany the delegates back to Riyadh for talks between the two sides. IO note, 22 Nov, 'King Husain has revoked approval, cannot guarantee safe passage.' Under-Secretary Shuckburgh: 'Tiresome.' Hirtzel: 'Sharif and Bin Saud like oil and vinegar.' Wingate, 27 Nov: Husain insists 'Storrs' journey not feasible'.

Hogarth to Jiddah: ibid. Following Husain's decision not to allow Storrs to travel to Riyadh by way of the Hijaz, Hogarth was deputed to join the talks at Jiddah. Storrs was made Military Governor of Jerusalem 28 Dec. Philby arrived Jiddah from Taif 31 Dec. Hogarth arrived 5 Jan 1918.

Hogarth, quoted: *GJ*, April 1928. Letter 22 Dec from Helwan.

Cox on Ibn Saud and Sharif: L/P & S/10/388, 23 Dec.

339   Khurmah dispute: L/P & S/10/389. Policy towards Ibn Saud. Also L/P & S/10/388 and 390; and FO 371/4144, 7 Jan 1919, note from IO, 'The Najd–Hijaz Dispute'.

Philby's instructions: L/P & S/10/388, Philby/Storrs Mission, Dec 1917.

Philby to Sharif: L/P & S/10/390, 12 Nov 1918, Philby's report on mission. See Monroe, *Philby of Arabia*.

Payments to Ibn Saud: L/P & S/10/387, 8 Dec 1917, Philby to Cox: 'Bin Saud in serious financial straits. Might be induced to attack Hail if kept happy financially. Suggest dole of £50,000 for minor objectives.' Shuckburgh (IO): 'I would hesitate to pay further blackmail to Bin Saud or anyone else until we are sure that we cannot get on without their assistance.'

Ibn Saud and Ikhwan: L/P & S/10/389, 3 Sept 1918, 'Secret Ikhwan'. A great deal on this subject is to be found in Philby and other writers on central Arabia. A recent account is given in Lacey, *The Kingdom*, ch. entitled 'Al Artawiya'. But although Lacey quotes the present writer as saying that Shakespear was the first to refer to the 'Brotherhood' in Feb 1914, he is mistaken. In the course of the conversation recorded in Winstone, *Shakespear*, p. 151, Shakespear told Arab companions that he had met Ikhwan in 1911. And

Musil, *Northern Najd, Notes on Family of Ibn Saud,* refers to the establishment of Al Artawiya as an Ikhwan settlement in 1908. (Author)

339 Shakespear on Faisal al Dawish: see Winstone, *Shakespear.*

Renewed fighting at Khurmah: L/P & S/10/389. And see L/P & S/18/B308 (Najd–Hijaz Dispute), memo by Shuckburgh, 7 Jan 1919, with Appendix 1, memo by Philby, 13 Aug 1918, 'Ibn Saud's Claim to Kurmah'. For other side of dispute, FO 882, 15 Dec 1918, Wingate to Wilson, Jiddah: Policy in dispute between Ibn Saud and Husain.

Wilson took over from Cox: took over officially on 15 Sept 1918, when Cox succeeded Marling at Tehran (FO List).

340 Telegram from Fakhri Pasha: L/P & S/10/387, 16 Oct 1918, Philby to Wilson. FO to IO and Wilson's reply to Shuckburgh re telegram, IO minute, 1 Nov.

'Shuckburgh noted': L/P & S/10/387. IO diary, 16 Oct 1918.

'Philby warned London': L/P & S/10/387. Philby from Basra to Baghdad, transmitted to London/Cairo, 29 Nov 1918.

Faisal at India Office: L/P & S/18/B308. Visit 27 Dec 1918.

Philby: ibid.

Amir to Husain: ibid.

King–Crane Commission: see Wavell, *Allenby,* p. 260, 'to retain Iraq and Palestine, Britain's Prime Minister had agreed that Syria should be placed under French mandate. The American report was not even made public.'

341 Faisal to Allenby, 28 May 1919: HL/F/47/8/22.

Allenby to Sir Henry Wilson, 6 June 1919: ibid.

Faisal, devious schemes: IO/R/15/1/557, vol. iii, 8 April 1920. News of mission from Faisal in Damascus to Ibn Saud. Faisal said to have offered Ibn Saud 'full support against father Husain'. Faisal to Ibn Saud, 29 Feb 1920, from High Command, North Arabian Army HQ, 'to strengthen the friendship and regard (existing between us) for the continuance of which I hope and pray'.

'advised by William Yale': see Kedourie, *England and the Middle East.* Commission left for Syria in July 1919. Gertrude Bell, L/P & S/18/B337, 'Syria in October 1919'. Wilson, *Loyalties,* vol. II, Commission did not visit Mesopotamia but included section on 'supposed wishes of the people'.

Death of Mark Sykes, 16 Feb 1919: see Adelson, *Mark Sykes.*

Lawrence on Sykes: *Seven Pillars,* p. 57.

342 Gertrude Bell in Paris: arrived 2 March, IO Register Z/L/P & S/7/47.

Allenby in Paris: gave evidence 20 March. Wavell, *Allenby.*

Occupied Enemy Territories: see ibid., p. 257.

Mustafa Kamal: see Kinross, *Ataturk.* Took command 31 Oct 1918.

342   French General: Franchet d'Esperey. The white horse was a gift from local Greeks. See Lewis, *The Emergence of Modern Turkey*.

Faisal's supporters in Damascus: Kedourie, *England and the Middle East*; Stewart, *The Middle East*.

Allenby's pledge and Anglo-French Declaration, 7 Nov 1918: CAB 27/24, 'Britain and France in agreement in desire to see independent governments', quoted in Knightley and Simpson, *Secret Lives*, p. 101. Also WO 33/969 and HL/F/205/3/23, 'published in November issue of the *Palestine News*, official journal of Egyptian Expeditionary Force, and appearing in translation in the Arabic and French press of Beirut, Syria, in November 1918.' See also Wavell, *Allenby*, p. 260, and Antonius, *The Arab Awakening*, App. B.

343   Hogarth, quoted: *Arab Bulletin*, no. 48, 21 April 1917.

Allenby, High Commissioner: appointed day following his appearance at Paris, 21 March 1919, and Wingate, who had been ordered to London in February to discuss the question of the nationalist Egyptian leader Zaghul was dismissed peremptorily. See Wavell, *Allenby*, p. 268.

Arnold Wilson: see Kedourie, *England and the Middle East*, 20 Nov 1918, Wilson to S/S, 'Dissents from Sharifite Settlements' and Anglo-French Declaration, 'mischievous'.

Gertrude Bell at Conference: Winstone, *Gertrude Bell*.

Curzon, quoted: HL/F/205/3/23, 9 Oct 1919, summary of British position regarding pledges to Arabs; Earl Curzon to His Highness Sharif Faisal. 'Your Highness would appear to be under a misapprehension . . . the said documents in no sense represent an agreement between the French and British Governments.'

344   Wilson to Ibn Saud: IO/R/15/5/557, 28 April 1919, Civil Commissioner Baghdad to Political Bahrain.

Mandates, Syria and Mesopotamia, and Shah's visit to Baghdad: ibid.

Shah deposed: Pahlavi regime, Feb 1921: see Waterfield, *Sir Percy Loraine*; also Philip Graves, *The Life of Sir Percy Cox*; and Kazemzadeh, *Russia and Britain in Persia*. At the time of its signature, 9 Aug 1919, the agreement was described as 'a triumph for Curzon's policy of barring the way to India'.

345   Death of Saud ibn Rashid: IO/R/15/1/557. News brought to Bahrain by Abdal Aziz al Qusaifi. Dickson to Wilson, 23 April 1920.

Ibn Jiluwi: see Harrison, *The Arab at Home*, and H. R. P. Dickson, *Kuwait and Her Neighbours*.

Dickson, mission into Saudi territory: R/15/1/557, 13 July 1920, instructions to Khan Sahib Sayid Siddiq Hasan from Major H. R. P. Dickson.

Doctor for Ibn Saud: ibid., Wilson to Dickson, April 1920.

Allenby on Ibn Saud: IO/R/15/1/557, 19 April 1920, repeated to Baghdad.

346   Told CIGS: HL/F/47/8/22, 6 June 1919, Secret. 'My dear Henry . . . no doubt you have seen Bols, who will have told you all.'

346 Allenby to Foreign Office, 1920: IO/R/15/1/557, 23 April 1920.

Allenby to FO, 1919: L/P & S/10/390, 28 May.

Husain and Ibn Saud to London: ibid., Allenby to FO, 19 April 1920.

Ibn Saud's messages: *Arab Bulletin*, no. 114, 30 Aug 1919.

347 Amir told Dickson: ibid., Dickson to Baghdad, 7 May. Terms of treaty: Hail's foreign relations to be conducted through Ibn Saud; all matters concerning Shammar tribe in Ibn Saud's hands.

Attack at Adwah: ibid. Report from Kuwait, 27 June.

Ibn Saud occupies Hail: CO 730/19, 2 Nov 1921. See also Clayton, *An Arabian Diary*, Introduction.

The Ikhwan: *Arab Bulletin*, no. 108, 11 Jan 1919.

General Marshall: Bray, *Shifting Sands*.

Zahroff back in Switzerland: HL/F/6/1/18, 21 Sept 1918, Lloyd George to Caillard.

June 1920, spate of killings: WO 33/969, 3 June 1920. 'Explosion' at Tel Afar. Evidence of visits by agents connected with Moscow 'Oriental Mission'. *The Times*, 12 June, British officer killed at Tel Afar. *The Times*, 30 June, Kurds attack Assyrians. In March 1919 MI(o) had recorded a decision of the Kurdish National Committee to 'cast off British yoke', and to declare independence 'under Turk Sovereignty'; and in June 1920 that Iraq and Irish risings 'almost simultaneous'.

Death of Leachman, 12 Aug 1920: L/P & S/11/175.

Arrest of Shaikh Dhari: Bray, *Paladin*.

348 Wilson, interview with Baghdadis: Bell, *Letters*, p. 426.

Wilson, more troops: L/P & S/11/75, 12 June.

Army convoy attacked: *The Times*, 15 June.

Proclamation to 'Free Mesopotamians': L/P & S/11/75, 17 June.

Arrest of Mirza Muhammad Riza and others: ibid., 22 June. See p. 221.

Standard Oil Company Funds: ibid., 22 June.

Funds from Faisal to Shia: see Kedourie, *England and the Middle East*, quotes Al Firaun, July 1920. Faisal sent £26,000 in gold to Euphrates leaders, but not one penny reached Ayatollah al Shirazi or any Shia leader of revolt. See Wilson, letters, BM Manuscript Dept MSS (52455–9) correspondence with Cox about Gertrude Bell, July 1920, Sayid Talib in conversation with Yusef Effendi, latter dissatisfied with Sharifians. Promised £100,000 to Sunni adherents, sent only £16,000. And see L/P & S/11/75, 23 July 1920, interview with General Haddad on allied policy, IO note: Sharifians under Abdullah 'laughing stock in field'.

Government statement: Kedourie, *England and the Middle East*, 23 June, and *The Times*, 24 June.

348   Open revolt: see press reports, July–Aug 1920: Manchester Regiment at Hillah, *The Times*, 4 Aug.

American Ambassador to FO: *The Times*, 30 July.

Leachman's last letter: Bray, *Paladin*, 5 June.

Wilson's resignation: L/P & S/11/175, 30 July, to Cox in London.

General Haldane: for part of Gertrude Bell in delaying military action, see Winstone, *Gertrude Bell*,, p. 224, and Gertrude's comment (in L/P & S/11/175): 'The thing isn't made any easier by the tosh T. E. Lawrence is writing in the newspapers.'

French at Damascus: see Longrigg, *Iraq*, July 1920, collapse of Faisal's Goverment in Syria. And Tibawi, *Anglo-Arab Relations*, 20 May, Faisal ordered to leave Damascus; 1 Aug, Faisal ordered to move on from Deraa to Haifa. Herbert Samuel received with official honours. 'The least Britain could do.' *Observer*, 8 Aug, quoted by Kedourie, *England and the Middle East*, 'French merely followed tyrannical ways of the British'; following lead of T. E. Lawrence.

Cox, return to Baghdad: *The Times*, 4 Oct, 'resumes duties'. He did not arrive in Baghdad, however, until the 11th; see Gertrude Bell, *Letters*, p. 407.

349   Naqib: see Kedourie, *England and the Middle East*, p. 208, quotes Wilson.

Cox persuasive: Bell, *Letters*, 23 Oct, 'Naqib undertakes to form Provisional Government'; statement by Cox.

Turkey, events from end of war: see Lewis, *The Emergence of Modern Turkey*, and Kinross, *Ataturk*. Izzat, the last wartime Grand Vizier, succeeded by Ahmad Tewfiq Pasha, 7 Nov 1918; Kamal returned to Constantinople, 13 Nov, the same day as the Allies entered; court-martial proceedings begun against Enver and Jamal, 26 Nov; Sultan Vahideddin dissolved Chamber of Deputies, 21 Dec; Enver and Jamal cashiered, 1 Jan 1919; Sultan appointed brother-in-law, Damad Farid Pasha, Grand Vizier, 4 March 1919; Kamal appointed Inspector-General Ninth Army, Anatolia, 30 April.

Kamal at Samsun, Black Sea: *Morning Post*, 19 May 1919

'plotting with Georgians': *Morning Post*, 15 May. From 'Special Correspondent'.

Turks and Greeks clash: Lewis, *The Emergence of Modern Turkey*, p. 240.

Declaration of Independence, 21 June: Kinross: *Ataturk;* see also Lewis, *The Emergence of Modern Turkey*, Kamal had secret meetings and conferred with General Kasim.

'affirmed his loyalty to the Sultan': Kinross, *Ataturk*, Conference 4–13 Sept. According to Kinross, Kamal had resigned from the army in July and been 'dismissed by Sultan's Government'. At National Congress held in Erzerum (23 July–6 Aug) he was elected President. The 'National Pact' promulgated. Kasim was instructed to arrest him by the Sultan but refused.

HQ at Ankara, 27 Dec 1919: Kinross, *Ataturk*. Sultan's Government had resigned on 5 Oct, ibid.; negotiations between Government and Kamalists at Amasya, Lewis, *The Emergence of Modern Turkey*.

349 To Damascus and Aleppo: *The Times*, 20 Jan.

National Pact: adopted by Ankara Assembly, 28 Jan. Kinross, *Ataturk*.

Attacked Mesopotamian towns, Jan 1920: Lewis, *The Emergence of Modern Turkey*.

Evacuation of French from Cilicia: garrison left Marash 9 Feb, Kinross, *Ataturk*. Persecution of Armenians, general French withdrawal.

Mandates confirmed at San Remo, April 1920: CO 730/57.

Allied military occupation, 16 March 1920: Kinross, *Ataturk*.

Deportation of Rauf and others: ibid.

Parliament dissolved: Lewis, *The Emergence of Modern Turkey*. Last meeting of Imperial Parliament, 18 March.

First Grand National Assembly: ibid. Kamal called to emergency meeting at Ankara, 19 March; Assembly met 23 April.

350 Kamal condemned, 11 May: Kinross, *Ataturk*.

Greek advance: Lewis, *The Emergence of Modern Turkey*. Turks driven to Sakarya river, July 1920.

Treaty of Sèvres, signed by Porte 10 Aug 1920: Kinross, *Ataturk*.

Draft treaty, Moscow and National Government, 24 Aug: ibid. Pact ratified 1925, denounced by Soviets 1944 after trial of Pan-Turanian fascists. Lewis, *The Emergence of Modern Turkey*.

Greek assault. Lloyd George's role: HL/F/12/3/9, Venizelos to Ll.G., 'Immediate invasion of Turkey'. See also Thomson, *The Secret Service in Greece*, and Philip Graves, *Land of Three Faiths*, p. 77, following 'unhappy' speech by Lloyd George, Turkish nationalists attacked Greeks. Within three weeks not a Greek soldier was left in Asia, Aug 1922. Greek advance was checked at battle of Inonu, 6–10 Jan 1921. Kinross, *Ataturk*.

Ankara: became official capital, 9 Oct 1923. Republic proclaimed 29 Oct. Ibid.

Ataturk: adopted 29 Nov 1934, with law requiring surnames, ibid.

Sultan-Caliph: abolished 3 March 1924, ibid. Sultan Mehmet V Vahideddin fled on British warship. Abdal Majid made Sultan, 13 Nov 1922, Lewis, *The Emergence of Modern Turkey*.

Fez and religious societies banned 30 Aug 1925: Kinross, *Ataturk*.

Social changes: new Civil Law Code, Feb 1926. Treaty of Ankara between Britain, Turkey and Iraq signed 5 June 1926. General amnesty for all prisoners and fugitives, except murderers of Colonel Leachman. CO 730/106.

Civilisation: Lewis, *The Emergence of Modern Turkey*, quotes Abdullah Jevdet, 1911.

Churchill, Colonial Secretary: see his *World Crisis: The Aftermath*.

350   Churchill to Bonar Law: HL/F/9/2/45, 10 Nov 1920.

Churchill to Lloyd George: ibid., 4 and 12 Jan 1921.

To Lloyd George, 20 Jan: HL/F/9/2/55.

Cox, Nov 1918: L/P & S/20/C193, 18 Nov, to Viceroy.

'loud protests': see Waterfield, *Sir Percy Loraine.*

351   Provisional Government, Baghdad: CO 730/1, 15 Dec 1920. See also HL/F/12/3 (Lloyd George Papers). Syrian and Mesopotamian Committees meet Damascus, 9 March 1920, to elect Abdullah King of Mesopotamia, and Faisal King of Syria.

Churchill's advisers: see Meinertzhagen, *Middle East Diary.* Late in 1918 Meinertzhagen left Cairo to become deputy to the DMO, General 'Freddie' Maurice. He later worked with MI2 before going to Jerusalem as Allenby's Political Officer. He was offered the jobs of Secret Service chief in Ireland or Churchill's assistant.

Meinertzhagen's dismissal: see Wavell, *Allenby.*

Arab Bureau: officially ceased to function 19 Feb 1920. IO/R/15/5/15.

Cairo Conference: opened 12 March, ended 25 March. See Longrigg, *Iraq.*

Decisions of Cairo Conference: see CO 730/1, 4 April, Interim Report; HL/F/25/1/16, 16 March 1921, Lloyd George to Churchill, 'We have repeatedly hinted to France . . . Faisal acceptable for Iraq if supported by population'; and HL/F/9/3/11, 18 March, Churchill, Cairo, to PM, 'Faisal formula'.

Expulsion of Sayid Talib: CO 730/1, 16 April 1921, dinner with Percival Landon, correspondent of *Daily Telegraph;* arrest and exile.

Coronation of Faisal: Bell, *Letters,* p. 497ff; also CO 730/17, Gertrude Bell, 13 Aug, Articles, *The Amir Faisal of Mesopotamia.* Faisal enthroned Baghdad, 23 Aug 1921.

Visit of Prince Faisal to London: Bray, *Shifting Sands,* and Gerald de Gaury, *Faisal: King of Saudi Arabia,* London, 1966.

352   Ikhwan: capture of Hail, Dec 1921, Clayton, *An Arabian Diary;* Ibn Saud's clemency at Hail, CO 730/19, 1 Feb 1922; friendly letter from Ibn Saud returned by Sharif with demand for restoration of Ibn Rashid, CO 730/37, July 1922; conquests in north Arabia and Hijaz, CO 730/72, 1924–5.

Ibn Saud at Mecca: Holy City given up without a fight, but Jiddah was defended under Sharif's eldest son, Ali, and under siege for six months. See Philby, *Forty Years in the Wilderness,* pp. 113ff., and Lacey, *The Kingdom,* p. 190ff.

Ikhwan: CO 730/105, 14 June 1926, Air Staff Intelligence, Nasiriyah, report by W. Dent, 'Intrigues against Ibn Saud by Faisal al Dawish'. See Dickson, *Kuwait and Her Neighbours.*

Ibn Saud's sayings: Bray, *Shifting Sands,* and Philby, *Arabian Jubilee.*

353   Cox to A. T. Wilson: letter, 23 Aug 1919, MS 736C.

353   Cox, one of his last duties: left Baghdad 19 Jan 1923, for Lausanne, where he represented Britain in formulation of Peace Treaty with Turkey. He returned to Baghdad briefly in March 1923 with a draft protocol to treaty with Iraq, which proposed a reduction of the British mandate from twenty to four years. Sir Henry Dobbs appointed High Commissioner, Baghdad, 22 Aug 1923. Peace with Turkey, recognising the existence of the state of Iraq within frontiers which included the vilayet of Mosul, signed at Lausanne 20 Sept 1923. CO 730/41–2.

Uqair Conference: CO 730/26, Nov–Dec 1922; Clayton Papers, Durham University, Box 471/11, Protocols of Uqair, to be read with Treaty of Muhammerah; Clayton, *An Arabian Diary*, pp. 34–7.

Treated notables as schoolboys: Dickson, *Kuwait and Her Neighbours.*

Suspected oil: L/P & S/18/C176, 17 Sept 1913, visit of Mr H. H. Hayden to Kuwait; and L/P & S/11/73, 23 March 1914, Admiralty to IO, Oil Commission to Gulf, Mr E. H. Pascoe to join.

Herbert Samuel, High Commissioner: see Sachar, *The Emergence of the Middle East*, Britain's mandate for Palestine announced at San Remo, 25 April 1920. Four days later military regime at end. Samuel selected by Curzon. Wyndham Deedes Chief Secretary of administration, Norman Bentwich, barrister and Zionist Attorney-General, Storrs (previously Military Governor) Governor of Jerusalem.

Regime of Sweet Reason': ibid.

'all hell broke loose': Nabi Musa riots, activities of Haj Amin Al Husaini, 'Mopsi' (Israeli Communists), inter-Jewish and Arab-Jewish clashes; see ibid., and Philip Graves, *Land of Three Faiths*. See also *The Times*, 1–15 April, frontier agents were inciting tribes to attack British in Mesopotamia; disturbances in India; raids on Upper Euphrates. Lewis, *The Emergence of Modern Turkey*, May 1920, riots in Anatolia. Nationalists fighting Greeks, French, Armenians and fellow Turks. Philip Graves, *Land of Three Faiths*, Feb, Moslems attacked Jews and Christians, Matullah; 5–6 May, Arabs attacked Jews on Plain of Sharon. Tibawi, *Anglo-Arab Relations*, Christians in Marjayun area were massacred by Turks; Moslems attacked Maronites. Druses and Maronites joined forces; 19 May, riots in Damascus. And Nabi Musa riots, April 1920. See also Meinertzhagen, *Middle East Diary*, April 1920. Waters-Taylor, senior officer of Military Administration, was admonished by the GOC for a pro-Arab speech at Gaza. This Waters-Taylor was a frequent visitor to Haj Amin. Meinertzhagen recommended that London replace the Military Administration with a High Commissioner. He was dismissed by Allenby a week later. He took the witness stand in defence of the Jews arrested during the riots.

McMahon: letter to CO, 12 March 1922, cited by Philip Graves, *Land of Three Faiths*, p. 52, 'Why not West of Jordan? Arabs might find more suitable frontier.'

Meinertzhagen, Balfour Declaration: Sachar, *The Emergence of the Middle East*, despatch to Curzon, 14 April 1920.

353 Meinertzhagen on Zionism: *Middle East Diary*, 26 Sept 1919.

Sir Henry Wilson: Wavell, *Allenby*, p. 279. (I assume that he would not include Iraq and Palestine in latter category from tone of his Intelligence summary WO 33/969 during his term as CIGS; author.)

354 Balfour to Wingate: FO 882, doc. 147225, Nov 1918, 'HMG and Balfour Declaration'.

Aaronsohn to Deedes: FO 371/3395.

Aaronsohn to Europe: *Encycl. Judaica*, to Rome Oct 1918.

Lloyd George, Dan to Beersheba: Meinertzhagen, *Middle East Diary*.

355 Letter, Faisal to Frankfurter: Meinertzhagen, *Middle East Diary*. See also Caplan, *Palestine Jewry and the Arab Question*, and Knightley and Simpson, *Secret Lives*, for relations and discussions between Arab and Jewish delegates and their protagonists. According to Meinertzhagen, the letter was compiled by Faisal, Lawrence, Weizmann, Frankfurter and Meinertzhagen, as from Delegation Hedjazienne, on 1 March.

Faisal's secretary, Auni Abdal Hadi: Caplan, *Palestine Jewry*.

Aaronsohn and Bullitt: *Reliquiae Aaronsohnianae*, 9 April 1920, letter from William C. Bullitt to Alex Aaronsohn.

'the outsider': quotes from Blankfort, *Behold the Fire*.

356 Weizmann, quoted: to Meinertzhagen, 30 Jan 1919; see *Middle East Diary*.

Not to the detriment of Arabs: FO 159/375: see Knightley and Simpson, *Secret Lives*, p. 118.

Faisal: ibid. See also Kedourie, *England and the Middle East*, and Antonius, *The Arab Awakening*, App. B.

Frankfurter and President Wilson: FO 371/4171, letter from Felix Frankfurter to President from Organisation Sioniste, 10 Place Edouard VII, Paris, dated 8 May 1919. Comment in FO diary, 3 June 1919.

Aaronsohn, like Herzl: FO 371/3062, report on Cairo Zionists from Wingate to Foreign Secretary, 20 Aug 1917, containing statement by Aaronsohn written in Hebrew. 'His aims . . . the regeneration of the Jews in Palestine and his political views . . . anti-democratic and anti-opportunist.' Kidston's note, 11 Sept, 'The internal feuds in Jewry are too complicated for the mere Gentile to follow.'

Aaronsohn to London, 10 May: Levin, *Haddasah*, March 1977.

Events of 15 May: pieced together by author from evidence of RAF personnel and reports in French press. See notes to p. 359.

Special air service: report by L.A.R. 'The R.A.F. Paris–London Service', issued by Air Ministry Press Bureau, 12 March 1919. 'The R.A.F. detachment carrying out this work – officially known as No. 2 Communication flight – is situated a few miles outside Paris [Buc airport; *author*]. The machines used are Handley Pages and DH4s.' Details are given of weather conditions under which flights may be made, and times (average 2½ hours, record 1 hour 50 minutes). 'Most interesting machine on this service is a specially converted DH4 to carry two passengers and the pilot.' Among notable people carried were, 'Mr Bonar Law, Mr Winston Churchill, Sir John Beal, Sir W. Robinson, Colonel Lawrence, Major Astor, and Senators Norton and White'. The service was first notified by General Groves, Director of Flying Operations, to Postmaster General, 11 Dec 1918, Hendon to Buc. 'It is proposed in a few days time to begin . . .' Documents in Post Office Records, PO 19387, 1919.

356   Pilot, Jefferson: report by Lieutenant-Colonel Neil Primrose, Commanding Officer Communication Squadron, Kenley, in possession of Aaronsohn House, Zichron Yakov.

357   Zionist Office statement: FO 371/4171, 27 May 1919, 'The Late Aaron Aaronsohn', from Central Office, 175 Piccadilly, London.

Meinertzhagen: *Middle East Diary*.

Rivka Aaronsohn: died 1981.

Jefferson: Registry, London (No. 93) 1920. Last Will and Testament, 10 March 1919. Probate granted to widow, 23 Jan 1920.

358   Colonel Primrose's report: details cited was given to the author by Aaronsohn House, Zichron Yakov, 8 May 1980.

Air Ministry Report: AIR 1/162, report on Aerial Mail Services Jan–Aug 1919.

359   Sixty years after: in the course of my inquiries into Aaronsohn's death I contacted Aaronsohn House, Israel, the Central Zionist Organisation in Israel, the Mayor of Boulogne, the Port Supervisor at Boulogne, the Chamber of Commerce, Boulogne, the Ministry of Defence (including Air Historical Branch), the Israel Broadcasting Authority (9 May 1979, at a time when a television programme was being made on Aaronsohn), the Records Department, Postal Headquarters London, and the following personnel of the RAF who served in the London–Paris service, with whom I was put in touch by the kind assistance of the editor of *Airmail* magazine: Sir Victor Goddard, who was involved in an attempt to establish an airship service between Croydon, Paris and Brussels which preceded the aeroplane service, Mr William C. Tice, who worked as a clerk to Lieutenant-Colonel A. B. Burdett on the Inter Allied Aeronautical Commission of Control, Mr C. Cook, who was a Corporal in the Royal Flying Corps and who served with No. 1 Communication Squadron at Hendon and Kenley as a mechanic, Wing Commander (Retd) E. J. G. Hill, who was posted to the 86th Communication Wing at Hendon in Feb 1919 as a Corporal Wireless Mechanic and who moved with the CO, Colonel Primrose, to Kenley 'just before Easter' 1919, and Wing Commander (Retd) R. H. McIntosh, who was known to his colleagues as 'All-Weather Mac' and who wrote a book with that title. None had a clear recollection of the pilot, Captain Jefferson, and none remembered the accident.

I wrote to Aaronsohn House during the lifetime of Rivka Aaronsohn on several occasions, and asked if I could make an appointment to see Miss

Aaronsohn. I was told that she could not entertain visitors (letter 6 June 1980) and I did not press the request in view of her age and ill health. However, I asked on four separate occasions: Are you satisfied, and is Miss Aaronsohn satisfied by the accepted accounts of Aaron Aaronsohn's death; and did you know that not one plane but two crashed simultaneously on that day? I received no answer to the questions, although in every other matter I received the most thorough and courteous help from the Aaronsohn and NILI archives. I asked the same questions of all the Israeli organisations cited (including Naomi Kaplansky, the producer of the Radiodiffusion-Télévision Israélienne programme on the history of Zionism which included my subject). In no case did I receive a direct answer, though all the inquiries were replied to politely. I applied by letter and in person to the port and municipal authorities of Boulogne for harbour records which must unquestionably have been kept of this and other accidents. I was given no answer. On one occasion I was told that 'such records are not kept'.

Most remarkable of all is the fact that there is no official record of the crash, even at Lloyd's, where air accidents were recorded in those days; and none of the personnel at Kenley had any recollection of the accident or the people involved, nor did they ever hear of a pilot being rescued from the water on that occasion. Yet one of them retained his RAF logbook in which the most detailed records were kept. He was Wing Commander Hill, and after a lengthy correspondence during 1979 we spoke on the telephone. I made a shorthand note of the conversation. Commander Hill: 'I still cannot remember this affair. I referred to my log book today and there is no mention of an accident at this time. It was at this time that the squadron moved from Hendon to Kenley. But No. 3 Squadron remained at Hounslow.' Author: 'But there weren't so many pilots in those days. You were all very close. If these planes took off from, say, Hounslow, or one from Paris and one from London, and both came down and one of your pilots was drowned, would you have heard about it?' Commander Hill: 'Without question. In any case it would have been headline news.'

Wing Commander McIntosh served at Kenley during May 1919. Like the others he knew Gooch and Knott, and recalled the 'flip' with Lloyd George's secretary and other matters; but none clearly remembered Elgie Jefferson. Mr Cook loaned me a photograph of the Kenley team. None of the witnesses could identify Jefferson. McIntosh recalled Colonel Primrose, whom he served under in the Middle East. *Author.*

359　Resignation of inspector of Accidents: G. B. M. Cockburn resigned 30 Sept 1920, AIR 1/37/15/1/249/1.

360　Aaronsohn, quoted: Kadish Luz, Speaker of the Knesset, 'Shalom Avshalom' by Rabbi Rabinowitz in *Jewish Herald*, 27 Dec 1967.

William C. Bullitt: letter to Alex Aaronsohn, 9 April 1920, *Reliquiae Aaronsohnianae.*

Gertrude Bell: see Winstone, *Gertrude Bell* (rev. and paperback edns) which give the opinions of Sir Max Mallowan and Dr Henry Field, two visitors in last days, which support the widely held belief that she committed suicide. There is no direct medical evidence, however.

361 Lawrence, quoted: *Seven Pillars*, p. 283.

Gertrude Bell, quoted: Cornwallis (ed.), *The Arab War*, Gertrude Bell's contributions to the *Arab Bulletin*.

John Connell, quoted: see his *The Office*.

362 Gertrude Bell, quoted: 'Syria in October 1919', in L/P & S/18/B337.

363 American President, quoted: from President Carter's State of the Union Address, Jan 1980.

Bibliography

General

Aaronsohn, Aaron, *Yoman, 1916–18* (diary in Hebrew), Tel Aviv, 1970.

—— 'Agricultural Explorations in Palestine', *Bulletin*, 180, US Dept of Agriculture, 1910.

Aaronsohn, Alex, *With the Turks in Palestine*, Bümplitz-Bern, 1916; Constable, 1917.

Aaronsohnianae, Reliquiae, with journeys 1904–8 and *Florula Transiordanica*, ed. H. R. Oppenheimer, Geneva, 1931.

Abdullah ibn Husain, King of Transjordan, *Memoirs*, ed. P. Graves, Cape, 1950.

Adamec, Ludwig W., *Afghanistan, 1900–23*, Berkeley, L. A., 1967.

Adelson, R., *Mark Sykes: Portrait of an Amateur*, Cape, 1975.

Ahmad, Jamal Muhammad, *The Intellectual Origins of Arab Nationalism*, OUP, 1960.

Albertini, Luigi, *The Origins of the War of 1914*, 3 vols, London, 1952–7.

Alder, L., and Dalby, R., *The Dervish of Windsor Castle*, Bachman & Turner, 1979.

Aldington, Richard, *Lawrence of Arabia*, Collins, 1955.

Alexander, C., *Baghdad in Bygone Days*, London, 1928.

Amana, Muhammad, *Arabia Unified*, Hutchinson/Benham, 1980.

Ancel, Jacques, *Manuel historique de la question d'Orient*, Paris, 1931.

Anchieri, Ettore, *Constantinopoli e gli Stetti nella politica russa ed Europa*, Milan, 1948.

Anderson, M. S., *The Eastern Question, 1774–1923*, Macmillan, 1976.

Andrae, Walter, *Der Anu-Adad-Tempel in Assur*, Leipzig, 1909.

—— *Die Festungswerke von Assur*, Leipzig, 1913.

—— *Lebenserinnerungen eines Ausgräbers*, Berlin, 1961.

Antonius, George, *The Arab Awakening*, Hamish Hamilton, 1938.

Archbold, W. A. J., *Afghanistan, Russia and Persia*, The Cambridge History of the British Empire, vol. 4, ed. H. H. Dodwell, CUP, 1929

Armstrong, H. C., *Lord of Arabia*, Arthur Barker, 1934.

Arthur, Sir George, *Life of Lord Kitchener*, 3 vols, London, 1920.

Asquith, Lord Oxford and, *Memories and Reflections*, Cassell, 1928.

Aston, Sir George, *The Secret Service*, Faber & Faber, 1930.

Atiya, E., *The Arabs*, Penguin, 1955.

—— *Palestine Essays*, Copenhagen, 1972.

Babinger, Franz, *Sonderdruck aus Islam*, Berlin, 1923.

Baker, Randall, *King Husain and the Kingdom of Hijaz*, Oleander Press, 1979.

Balfour, Lord, *Speeches on Zionism*, Arrowsmith, 1928.

Barber, C. H., *Besieged in Kut and After*, Edinburgh, 1917.

Barber, Noel, *Lords of the Golden Horn*, Pan, 1976.

Barbour, N., *Nisi Dominus: A Survey of the Palestine Controversy*, Harrap, 1946.

Barclay, Sir Thomas, *The Turco-Italian War and its Problems*, Constable, 1912.

Baring, E. (1st Earl of Cromer), *Modern Egypt*, 2 vols, London, 1908.

—— *Ancient and Modern Imperialism*, London, 1910.

—— *Political and Literary Essays*, London, 1914.

Barker, A. J., *The Neglected War*, Cassell, 1967.

Bar-Zohar, Michael, *Spies in the Promised Land*, trans. from French by Monroe Stearns, Davis-Poynter, 1972.

Bayer, Yusuf H., *Turk inkilabi tarihi* (History of the Turkish Reform), 9 vols, Istanbul/Ankara, 1940–57.

Bean, C. E. W., *The Story of Anzac*, Sydney, Australia, 1921.

Becker, C. H., 'Deutschland und der Islam', in *Der Deutsche Krieg*, ed. Ernst Jäckh, vol. 3, Berlin, 1914.

Bein, Alex, *Theodor Herzl*, London, 1957.

Belhaven and Stenton, Lord, *The Uneven Road*, John Murray, 1955.

Bell, Gertrude, *The Desert and the Sown*, Heinemann, 1907.

—— *Amurath to Amurath*, Heinemann, 1911.

—— *Letters*, ed. Lady Bell, 2 vols, Benn, 1927.

Ben-Gurion, David, *My Talks with Arab Leaders*, Jerusalem, 1972.

—— *A Personal History*, New English Library, 1972.

Ben-Hanan, Elie, *Our Man in Damascus*, Hale, 1971.

Benoist-Mechin, Jacques, *Arabian Destiny*, Elek Books, 1957.

—— *Le Roi Saud, ou l'Orient à l'heure des relèves*, Paris, 1960.

Bentwich, Norman, *Wanderer between Two Worlds*, Kegan Paul, 1941.

—— and Kisch, M., *Brigadier Frederick Kisch: Soldier and Zionist*, Vallentine, Mitchell, 1966.

Bérard, V., *La Révolution turque*, Paris, 1909.

Berchem, M. van, and Fatio, E., *Voyage en Syrie*, Cairo, 1913.

Berger, Elmer, *The Jewish Dilemma*, New York, 1956.

Berkes, Niyazi, *The Development of Secularism in Turkey*, McGill, 1964.

Bernstorff, Count Johann M., *Erinnerung und Briefe*, Zurich, 1936.

Besson, Yves, *Ibn Saud: Roi Bedouin*, Lausanne, 1980.

Bidwell, Robin L., *Travellers in Arabia*, Hamlyn, 1976.

—— 'Queries for Biographers of T. E. Lawrence', *Arabian Studies*, III, MEC, Cambridge, 1976.

Birdwood, Lord, *Nuri as-Said, a Study in Arab Leadership*, Cassell, 1959.

Blaisdell, D. C., *European Financial Control in the Ottoman Empire*, New York, 1929.

Blanckenhorn, M., *Syrien und die deutsche Arbeit*, Weimar, 1916.

Blankfort, Michael, *Behold the Fire*, Heinemann, 1965.

Blunt, W.S., *The Future of Islam*, London, 1882.

—— *A Secret History of the Occupation of Egypt*, London, 1907.

—— *My Diaries, 1888–1914*, London, 1919.

Boustead, Colonel Sir Hugh, *The Wind of Morning*, Chatto & Windus, 1971.

Bowman, Humphrey, *Middle East Window*, Longmans, 1942.

Boyle, Clara, *A Servant of Empire*, Methuen, 1938.

Braddon, Russell, *Boyle of Cairo*, Wilson, 1965.

—— *The Siege*, Cape, 1969.

Bray, N. N. E., *Shifting Sands*, Unicorn, 1934.
—— *Paladin of Arabia*, John Heritage, 1936.
Brémond, E., *Le Hedjaz dans la guerre mondiale*, Paris, 1931.
Broadley, A. M., *How We Defended Arabia*, London, 1884.
Brockelmann, Carl, *Geschichte der islamischen Völker und Staaten*, Berlin, 1939.
Buchan, John, *A Prince of the Captivity*, Hodder & Stoughton, 1933.
Bullard, Sir Reader, *Britain and the Middle East*, London, 1950.
—— *The Camels Must Go*, Faber, 1951.
Burgoyne, Elizabeth, *Gertrude Bell: from Her Personal Papers*, 2 vols, Benn, 1958–61.
Burne, A. H., *Mesopotamia, the Last Phase*, Aldershot, 1936.
Burns, Lt-General E. L. M., *Between Arab and Israeli*, London, 1962.
Busch, Briton Cooper, *Britain, India and the Arabs*, University of California Press, 1971.
Bush, Eric W., *Gallipoli*, Allen & Unwin, 1975.

Cadogan, Lord, *The Cadogan Diaries*, ed. David Dilks, Cassell 1971.
Caillard, Sir Vincent Henry Pensalver, *Imperial Fiscal Reform*, London, 1903.
—— (posthumous) *A New Conception of Love*, a story written from the 'Great Beyond', attrib. Zoë Caillard, Rider, London, 1934.
Caillard, Zoë, *Sir Vincent Caillard Speaks*, Rider, 1932.
—— *An Extraordinary Flight*, Stockwell, London (undated), British Library, 1940.
Callwell, Sir C. E., *The Life of Sir Stanley Maude*, Constable, 1920.
Calverley, Eleanor T., *My Arabian Days and Nights*, New York, 1958.
Candler, E., *The Long Road to Baghdad*, 2 vols, Cassell, 1919.

Cantwell Smith, W., *Islam in Modern History*, Princeton University Press, 1977.
Caplan, Neil, *Palestine Jewry and the Arab Question*, Frank Cass, 1978.
Carré, J.-M., *Voyageurs et Ecrivains Français en Egypte*, Cairo, 1932.
Carruthers, Douglas, *Arabian Adventure to the Great Nafud*, Witherby, London, 1935.
Cassar, George H., *Kitchener: Architect of Victory*, Wm Kimber, 1977.
Chapot, V., *La Frontière de L'Euphrate*, Paris, 1907.
Cheesman, R. E., *In Unknown Arabia*, Macmillan, 1926.
Chesney, F. R., *The Expedition for the Survey of the Rivers Tigris and Euphrates*, 2 vols, London, 1850.
Childers, Erskine B., *The Road to Suez*, London, 1962.
Chirol, Sir Valentine I., *Indian Unrest*, London, 1910.
—— and Lord Eversley, *The Turkish Empire*, London, 1923.
Churchill, Sir Winston, *The World Crisis*, 4 vols, Thornton Butterworth, 1923–6.
Clayton, Sir Gilbert, *An Arabian Diary*, intro by K. Collins, University of California Press, 1969.
Coke, R., *Baghdad, City of Peace*, London, 1927.
Conder, C. R., *Heth and Moab: Explorations in Syria, 1881–82*, London, 1892.
Connell, John, *The Office*, Allan Wingate, 1958.
Copeland, Miles, *The Game of Nations: The Amorality of Power Politics*, Weidenfeld & Nicolson, 1969.
—— *The Real Spy World*, Weidenfeld & Nicolson, 1974.
Cornwallis, Sir Kinahan, *Asir Before World War I* (1916 Handbook), intro. by R. L. Bidwell, Falcon/Oleander, 1978.
Courtney, J. E., *An Oxford Portrait Gallery*, London, 1931.

—— and Courtney, W. L., *Pillars of Empire*, London 1918.

Crankshaw, Edward, *Bismark*, Macmillan, 1981.

Curtis, Michael (ed.), *People and Politics in the Middle East*, New Jersey, 1971.

Curzon, George, Marquis of Kedleston, *Indian Speeches of, 1898–1901*, compiled by C. S. Sinha, 2 vols, Calcutta, 1900–1902.

—— *Lord Curzon in India: A Selection from his Speeches as Viceroy, 1898–1905*, Macmillan, 1906.

—— *Russia in Central Asia in 1889, and the Anglo-Russian Question*, Longmans, Green, 1889.

—— *Persia and the Persian Question*, 2 vols, Longmans, Green, 1892.

—— *Tales of Travel*, Hodder & Stoughton, 1923.

Curzon, Grace Elvina, Marchioness of Kedleston, *Reminiscences*, London, 1955.

Dane, E., *British Campaigns in the Near East*, 2 vols, London, 1918.

Davenport, G., *Zahroff – High Priest of War*, Boston, 1934.

Deacon, R., *History of the British Secret Service*, Muller, 1962.

—— *The Israeli Secret Service*, Hamish Hamilton, 1977.

De Gaury, Gerald, *Rulers of Mecca*, Harrap, 1951.

—— *Three Kings of Baghdad*, Hutchinson, 1961.

De Novo, John A., *American Interests and Policies in the Middle East, 1900–1939*, University of Minnesota Press, 1963.

Dickson, H. R. P., *The Arab of the Desert*, Allen & Unwin, 1949.

—— *Kuwait and Her Neighbours*, Allen & Unwin, 1956.

Dickson, Violet, *Forty Years in Kuwait*, Allen & Unwin, 1971.

Dickson, Brig.-Gen. W. E. R., *East*

Persia: A Backwater of the Great War, London, 1924.

Dilks, David, *Curzon in India*, 2 vols, Hart-Davis, 1969–70.

Djemal, Ahmad (Jamal Pasha), *Memories of a Turkish Statesman, 1913–19*, New York and London, 1922.

Dodwell, H. H., *Central Asia*, The Cambridge History of the British Empire, vol. v, ed. H. H. Dodwell, CUP, 1932.

Dorys, G., *Abdul-Hamid intime*, Paris, 1909.

Doughty, Charles, *Travels in Arabia Deserta*, Cape, 1936.

Dranov, B. A., *Chernomorskiye prolivy*, Moscow, 1948.

Dunsterville, Major-General Lionel C., *The Adventures of Dunsterforce*, London, 1920.

Dussaud, R., *Missions dans les régions désertiques de la Syrie moyenne*, Paris, 1903.

—— *Les Arabes en Syrie avant l'Islam*, Paris, 1907.

Dyer, R. E. H., *The Raiders of the Sarhad*, London, 1921.

Earle, Edward Mead, *Turkey, the Great Powers, and the Baghdad Railway, A Study in Imperialism*, New York, 1923

Edelman, Maurice, *Ben Gurion*, London, 1964.

Edib, Halidé, *The Turkish Ordeal*, London, 1928.

Edmonds, C. J., *Kurds, Turks and Arabs*, OUP, 1961.

Einstein, Lewis, *Inside Constantinople*, Murray, 1917.

Elton, Lord, *Among Others*, Collins, 1938.

Endres, Franz Carl, *Der Weltkrieg der Turkei*, Berlin, 1920.

Engle, Anita, *The NILI Spies*, Hogarth, 1958.

Erdmann, Hugo, *Im Heiligen Krieg nach Persien*, Berlin, 1918.

Erzberger, M., *Erlebnisse im Weltkrieg*, Berlin, 1920.

Euting, J., *Tagbuch einer Reise in Inner-Arabien*, 2 vols, Leyden, 1914.

Evans, R., *Brief Outline of the Mesopotamian Campaign*, London, 1926.

Ewing, W., *Arab and Druse at Home*, London, 1907.

Fatemi, Nasrollah, *Diplomatic History of Persia, 1917–23*, New York, 1952.

Field, Henry, *Arabian Desert Tales*, Sygernetic Press, New Mexico, 1977.

Fischer, Adolf, *Orient*, Berlin, 1924.

Fischer, Fritz, *Krieg der Illusionen: Die deutsche Politik von 1911 bis 1914*, Dusseldorf, 1969.

Fisher, Admiral Lord, *Fear God and Dread Nought*, 3 vols, Cape, 1952–9.

Fletcher, Arnold, *Afghanistan, Highway of Conquest*, Cornell University Press, Ithaca, NY, 1965.

Fraser, D., *The Short Cut to India*, Edinburgh, 1909.

Fraser, Lovat, *India under Lord Curzon and After*, London, 1921.

Freeman, Edward A., *The Ottoman Power in Europe*, London, 1877.

Freeth, Zahra, *Kuwait was My Home*, Allen & Unwin, 1956.

—— *A New Look at Kuwait*, Allen & Unwin, 1972.

Friedman, Isaiah, *Germany, Turkey and Zionism, 1897–1918*, OUP, 1977.

Frobenius, Hermann, *Des Deutschen Reiches Schicksalsstunde*, 14th edn., Berlin, 1915.

—— *The German Empire's Hour of Destiny*, Preface by Sir Valentine Chirol, trans. W. H. B., John Lang, 1914.

Furlonge, Geoffrey, *Palestine is My Country: The Story of Musa Alami*, London, 1969.

Gehrke, Ulrich, *Persien in der deutschen Orientpolitik während des Ersten Weltkrieges*, Stuttgart, 1960.

Ghanima, J. R., *The Trade of Iraq in Ancient and Modern Times*, Baghdad, 1922.

Giannini, A., *Documenti per la Storia della Pace orientale*, Rome, 1933.

Gibb, Sir H. A. R., *Modern Trends in Islam*, Chicago, 1947.

—— and Bowen, H., *Islamic Society and the West*, OUP, 1950.

—— *Studies in the Civilization of Islam*, ed. M. Stanford J. Shaw and William R. Polk, Routledge & Kegan Paul, 1962.

Gilbert, Martin, *The Arab-Jewish Conflict: Its History in Maps*, Weidenfeld & Nicolson, 1979.

Gillard, David, *The Struggle for Asia*, Methuen, 1977.

Gleich, Major-General Franz von, *Von Balken nach Baghdad*, Berlin, 1921.

Glubb, Sir John Bagot, *The Story of the Arab Legion*, London, 1948.

—— *A Soldier with the Arabs*, Hodder & Stoughton, 1957.

—— *Britain and the Arabs*, Hodder & Stoughton, 1959.

—— *War in the Desert*, Hodder & Stoughton, 1960.

—— *Arabian Adventure*, Cassell, 1978.

Goltz, Feldmarschall Colmar Freiherr von der, *Denkwürdigkeiten*, ed. Baron F. von der Goltz and W. Foester, Berlin, 1929.

Gooch, G. D., and Temperley, H. W. V. (eds), *British Documents on the Origin of the War*, London, 1926–38.

Gottlieb, W. W., *Studies in Secret Diplomacy during the First World War*, London, 1957.

Grant, A. J., and Temperley, H. W. V., *Europe in the Nineteenth and Twentieth Centuries*, Longman, 1963.

Graves, Dr Armgaard Karl, *Secrets of the German War Office*, McBride, Nast, NY, 1914.

Graves, Philip, *Land of Three Faiths*, Cape, 1923.

—— *The Life of Sir Percy Cox*, Hutchinson, 1941.

Graves, Robert, *Lawrence and the Arabs*, Cape, 1935.

—— with Liddell Hart, B. H., *T. E. Lawrence to his Biographer*, Faber, 1938.

Graves, R. W., *Storm Centres of the Middle East, 1879–1929*, London, 1933.

Greaves, Rose L. *Persia and the Defence of India 1884–1892: A Study in the Foreign Policy of the 3rd Marqess of Salisbury*, London, 1959.

Grey, Viscount Edward of Fallodon, *Twenty-Five Years*, London, 1928.

Grobba, Fritz, *Männer und Mächte im Orient*, Frankfurt, 1967.

Grothe, H., *Meine Vorderasienexpedition, 1906–7*, Leipzig, 1912.

Guhr, H., *Als türkischer Divisions-Kommandeur in Kleinasien und Palastina*, Berlin, 1937.

Habib, S., *Ibn Saud; Warriors of Islam: The Ikhwan of Najd and their Creation of the Saudi Kingdom, 1910–30*, Brill, Leiden, 1978.

Haig, Field-Marshal Earl, *The Private Papers of Douglas Haig*, ed. Robert Blake, Eyre & Spottiswoode, 1952.

Haldane, Lt-General Sir Aylmer, *The Insurrection in Mesopotamia, 1920*, London, 1922.

—— *A Soldier's Saga*, Blackwood, 1948.

Hallgarten, George W. F., *Imperialismus vor 1914*, 2 vols, Munich, 1963.

Hankey, M. P. A., 1st Baron, *The Supreme Command, 1914–18*, 2 vols, London, 1961.

Harrison, Dr Paul W., *The Arab at Home*, Hutchinson, 1924.

H. R. [Harun al Rashid], *Marschall Liman von Sanders Pascha und Sein Werk*, Berlin, 1932.

Hedin, Sven, *Persien und Mesopotamien*, Leipzig, 1923.

Heikel, M., *The Road to Ramadan*, Collins, 1975.

—— *The Sphinx and the Commissar: The Rise and Fall of Soviet Influence in the Modern World*, Collins, 1978.

Hendrick, J. Burton, *The Life and Letters of Walter Page*, 3 vols, Heinemann, 1922–5.

Hennig, Richard, *Die deutschen Bahnbanten in der Turkei*, Leipzig, 1915.

Hentig, Werner Otto von, *Meine diplomatenfahrt ins verschlossene Land*, Berlin, 1918.

—— *Mein Leben eine Dienstreise*, Göttingen, 1962.

Herbert, Aubrey, *Mons, Anzac and Kut*, Hutchinson, 1919.

—— *Ben Kendim*, ed. Desmond McCarthy, Hutchinson, 1924.

Hermann, Carl, *Deutsche Militärgeschichte*, Frankfurt, 1966.

Herzfeld, Hans, *Die Liman-Krise und die Politik der Grossmachte in der Jahreswende 1913–14*, Berlin, 1933.

Herzl, Theodor, *The Diaries*, ed. Marvin Lowenthal, Gollancz, 1958.

Hesse, Fritz, 'Persien' in *Weltpolitische Bücherei*, ed. Grabowsky, vol. 26, Berlin, 1932.

Hewins, Ralph, *A Golden Dream: The Miracle of Kuwait*, W. H. Allen, 1963.

Hill, G., *With the Beduins*, London, 1891.

Hilprecht, H. V., *Explorations in Bible Lands during the Nineteenth Century*, Edinburgh, 1903.

Hirst, David, *The Gun and the Olive Branch*, Faber, 1977.

Hitti, Philip K., *History of the Arabs*, Macmillan, 1937.

—— *History of Syria*, Macmillan, 1951.

Hogarth, David, *A Wandering Scholar in the Levant*, London, 1896.

—— *The Nearer East*, London, 1905.

—— *The Penetration of Arabia*, Clarendon, 1922.

Holden, David, *Farewell to Arabia*, Faber, 1966.

Hornby, E., *Sinai and Petra: Journals, 1899 and 1901*, London, 1901.

Hourani, A., *Minorities in the Arab World*, Royal Institute of International Affairs, 1947.

—— *Arabic Thought in the Liberal Age, 1798–1939*, OUP, 1962.

Howard, H. N., *The King–Crane Commission*, Beirut, 1963.

—— *The Partition of Turkey: A Diplomatic History*, University of Oklahoma Press, 1931.

Howarth, David, *The Desert King*, Collins, 1964.

Huber, C., *Journal d'un Voyage en Arabie*, Paris, 1891.

Hunt, John, *Life is Meeting*, Hodder & Stoughton, 1981.

Hurewitcz, J. C. (ed.), *Diplomacy in the Near and Middle East: a Documentary Record*, Princeton, NJ, 1956.

Hurgronje, C. Snouck, *The Holy War 'Made in Germany'*, New York, 1915.

Husaini, Ishak Musa, *The Moslem Brethren*, Beirut, 1956.

Hutchinson, E. H., *Violent Truce*, New York, 1956.

Hutton, W. H., *Constantinople: The Old Capital of the Empire*, London, 1900.

Huxley, Leonard (ed.), *Our Indians at Marseilles*, trans. from French, Smith, 1915.

Inchbold, A. C., *Under the Syrian Sun*, London, 1906.

Ingrams, Doreen, *A Time in Arabia*, John Murray, 1970.

Ingrams, Harold, *The Yemen: Imams, Rulers and Revolutions*, John Murray, 1963.

Ireland, P. W., *Iraq: A Study in Political Development*, Cape, 1937.

Issawi, Charles, *Egypt in Revolution*, OUP, 1963.

Jabotinsky, V, *The Story of the Jewish Legion*, New York, 1945.

Jäckh, Ernst, 'Die deutsch-türkische Waffenbrüderschaft', *Der Deutsche Krieg*, ed. L. Jäckh, vol. 24, Berlin, 1915.

Jalabert, Louis, 'Du roman en pleine histoire. L'aventure de quelques Allemands en Afghanistan et en

Perse pendant la Guerre', *Etudes*, Paris, 1937.

James, Admiral Sir William, *The Eyes of the Navy*, Methuen, 1955.

Jarvis, C. S., *Yesterday and Today in Sinai*, Blackwoods, 1938.

Jäschke, Gotthard, 'Mitteilungen: Zum Eintritt der Türkei in den Ersten Weltkrieg', *Die Welt des Islams*, Berlin, 1955.

Jaussen, A., and Savignac, R., *Mission archéologique en Arabie*, Paris, 1909.

Jeffries, J. M. N., *Palestine: the Reality*, Longmans, 1939.

Jones, E. H., *The Road to En-Dor*, John Lane, 1919.

Joseph, Bernard, *British Rule in Palestine*, Public Affairs Press, Washington DC, 1948.

Jung, Eugène, *La Révolte arabe, I. De 1906 à la révolte de 1916*, Paris, 1924.

—— *L'Islam et l'Asie devant l'Imperialisme*, Paris, 1927.

Kamal, Mustafa, *Egyptiens et Anglais*, Paris, 1906.

Kampffmeyer, G., *Urkunden und Berichte zur Gegenwärtsgeschichte des Arabischen Orients*, Berlin, 1924.

Katz, Samuel, *Battleground: Fact and Fantasy in Palestine*, W. H. Allen, 1973.

Kautsky, Karl, *Die deutschen Dokumente zum Kriegsausbruch*, 4 vols, Berlin, 1919.

Kazemzadeh, Firuz, *Russia and Britain in Persia: A Study in Imperialism, 1864–1914*, Yale 1968.

Kearsey, A., *Notes on the Mesopotamian Campaign*, London, 1927.

Kedourie, Elie, *England and the Middle East*, Bowes & Bowes, 1956.

—— *The Chatham House Version and Other Middle Eastern Studies*, Weidenfeld & Nicolson, 1970.

—— *In the Anglo-Arab Labyrinth*, CUP, 1976.

Keeling, E. H., *Adventures in Turkey and Russia*, Murray, 1924.

Kelly, J. B., *Eastern Arabian Frontiers*, Faber, 1964.

——*Britain and the Persian Gulf, 1795–1880*, OUP, 1968.

——*Arabia, the Gulf and the West*, Weidenfeld & Nicolson, 1980.

Kerner, Robert J., 'The Mission of Liman von Sanders', *Slavonic Review*, VI, 1927–8.

Khadduri, Majid, *Independent Iraq, 1932–1958*, OUP, 1960.

—— (contributor), *Arab Contemporaries: The Role of Personalities in Politics*, Johns Hopkins UP, 1973.

Khairallah, K. T., *Les Régions arabes libérées*, Paris, 1919.

Kheirallah, George I., *Arabia Reborn*, University of New Mexico Press, 1952.

Kiernan, R. H., *The Unveiling of Arabia*, Harrap, 1937.

Kiesling, Oberstleutnant Hans von, *Mit Feldmarschall von der Goltz Pasha in Mesopotamia und Persia*, Leipzig, 1922.

Kimche, Jon, *Seven Fallen Pillars*, Secker & Warburg, 1950.

—— *The Unromantics: The Great Powers and the Balfour Declaration*, Weidenfeld & Nicolson, 1968.

Kingsmill, A. G., *The Silver Badge*, Stockwell, 1966.

Kinross, Lord, *Ataturk: The Rebirth of a Nation*, Weidenfeld & Nicolson, 1964.

—— *The Ottoman Centuries*, Cape, 1977.

Kitchener, Lt H. H., and Conder, Lt C. R., *Survey of Western Palestine*, Palestine Exploration Fund, 1881.

Knightley, Philip, and Simpson, Colin, *The Secret Lives of Lawrence of Arabia*, Panther, 1971.

Kohn, Hans, *A History of Nationalism in the Middle East*, New York, 1929.

Koldewey, R., *The Excavations at Babylon*, London, 1914.

Kraus, Theodor, and Donitz, Karl, *Die Kreuzerfahrten der Goeben und Breslau*, Berlin, 1933.

Kressenstein, General Friederich Freiherr Kress von, *Mit den Türken zum Suezkanal*, Berlin, 1938.

Kühlmann, Richard, *Erinnerung*, Heidelberg, 1948.

Kunke, Max, *Die Kapitulationen der Türkei*, Munich, 1918.

Lacey, Robert, *The Kingdom*, Hutchinson, 1981.

Laffin, John, *The Arab Mind*, Cassell, 1978.

Landes, David, *Bankers and Pashas*, London, 1958.

Lanzoni, A., *Il Nuovo regime turco e l'avvenire della Mesopotamia*, Rome, 1912.

Laqueur, Walter Z., *Communism and Nationalism in the Middle East*, London, 1956.

—— *The Israel–Arab Reader: History of the Middle East Conflict*, London, 1969.

Larcher, Maurice, *La Guerre turque dans la guerre mondiale*, Paris, 1926.

Lawley, Sir Arthur, *A Message from Mesopotamia*, London, 1917.

Lawrence, T E., *Seven Pillars of Wisdom*, Cape, 1935; Penguin, 1962.

—— *T. E. Lawrence by his Friends*, ed. A. W. Lawrence, Cape, 1937.

—— *The Letters of T. E. Lawrence*, ed. D. Garnett, Cape, 1938.

——*Secret Despatches from Arabia*, ed. A. W. Lawrence, Golden Cockerel Press, 1939.

—— *Oriental Assembly*, ed. A. W. Lawrence, London, 1939.

—— *The Home Letters of T.E.L. to his Brothers*, Blackwell, 1954.

—— *Letters to T. E. Lawrence*, ed. A. W. Lawrence, Cape, 1962.

Lebkicher, Roy, Rentz, George, and Steineke, Max, *The Arabia of Ibn Saud*, New York, 1952.

Lee, D. Fitzgerald, *'D' Force (Mesopo-*

tamia) in the Great War, London, 1927.

Lehmann, Walther, Die Kapitulationen, Weimar, 1917.

Lenczowski, George, The Middle East in World Affairs, Ithaca, NY, 1956.

Leslie, Sir Shane, Mark Sykes, His Life and Letters, London, 1929.

Lewin, Evans, The German Road to the East, London, 1916.

Lewinsohn, R., The Man Behind the Scenes (Zahroff), trans. from German, Der Mann im Dunkel, London, 1929.

Lewis, Bernard, Notes and Documents from the Turkish Archives, Israel Oriental Society, 1952.

—— The Emergence of Modern Turkey, OUP, 1961.

—— The Arabs in History, Hutchinson, 1977.

Libbey, W., and Hoskins, F. E., The Jordan Valley and Petra, New York, 1905.

Liddell Hart, B. H., T. E. Lawrence, Cape, 1935.

—— A History of the First World War, Faber, 1934.

Litten, Wilhelm, Persische Flitterwochen, Berlin, 1925

Lloyd, Seton, Ruined Cities of Iraq, OUP, 1942.

—— Twin Rivers, OUP, 1943.

—— Foundations in the Dust, intro. by Sir Leonard Woolley, OUP, 1947.

Lloyd George, David, The Truth about the Peace Treaties, Gollancz, 1936.

—— War Memoirs 1914–18, 6 vols, London, 1933–7.

Lockhart, R. H. Bruce, Memoirs of a British Agent, Putnam, 1932.

Loder, J. de V., The Truth about Mesopotamia, Palestine and Syria, London, 1923.

Long, P. W., Other Ranks at Kut, Williams & Norgate, 1938.

Longrigg, S. H., Four Centuries of Modern Iraq, Clarendon, 1925.

—— Iraq, 1900–1950, Royal Institute of International Affairs, OUP, 1935.

—— Oil in the Middle East, RIIA, OUP, 1968.

Lonnroth, E., Lawrence of Arabia, London, 1956.

Lord, John, 'Duty, Honour, Empire': The Life and Times of Colonel Richard Meinertzhagen, Hutchinson, 1971.

Lorimer, J. G., Gazetteer of the Persian Gulf, Government Press, Bombay, 1913.

Ludendorff, General von, My War Memories, Hutchinson, 1920.

Luers, Hans, Gegenspieler des Obersten Lawrence, Berlin, 1936.

Lufti, as-Sayid Afaf, Egypt and Cromer: A Study in Anglo-Egyptian Relations, Murray, 1968.

Lyautey, P., Le Drame oriental, Paris, 1924.

Lyell, T., Ins and Outs of Mesopotamia, London, 1923.

McCormic, Donald, Pedlar of Death, Macdonald, 1965.

McIntosh, Wing-Cdr R. H., and Spry-Leverton, G., 'All-Weather Mac', Macdonald, 1963.

Mack, John E., A Prince of Our Disorder: Life of T. E. Lawrence, Weidenfeld & Nicolson, 1976.

MacKenzie, David, The Serbs and Russian Pan-Slavism, 1875–8, London 1967.

McLaughlin, Redmond, The Escape of the Goeben: Prelude to Gallipoli, Seeley, 1974.

MacMunn, Sir George, Afghanistan from Darius to Amanullah, London, 1929.

Magnus, Sir Philip, Kitchener – Portrait of an Imperialist, Murray, 1958.

Maine, E., Iraq from Mandate to Independence, London, 1935.

Malik, Y., The British Betrayal of the Assyrians, Chicago, 1936.

Mallowan, Sir Max Mallowan's Memoirs, Collins, 1977.

Mandel, Neville J., *The Arabs and Zionism before World War I*, University of California Press, 1976.

Mangold, Peter, *Superpower Intervention in the Middle East*, Croom Helm, 1978.

Mansfield, P., *The Ottoman Empire and its Successors*, Macmillan, 1973.

Manuel, F. E., *Realities of American–Palestine Relations*, Washington, 1949.

Marder, Arthur J., *From the Dreadnought to Scapa Flow*, London, 1961.

Marlowe, John, *The Seat of Pilate*, Cresset, 1959.

—— *Late Victorian: The Life of Sir Arnold Wilson*, Cresset, 1967.

Marriot, J. A. R., *The Eastern Question*, Oxford, 1940.

Marshall, General Sir William, *Memories of Four Fronts*, Benn, 1929.

Martchenko, M., *Un Voyage en Perse pendant la révolution russe. Les agissements allemands*, Strasbourg, 1920.

Masad, Paulus, *Libnan wa Suriya qabl al intidab wa baadun* (Arabic), 'The Lebanon and Syria before and after the Mandates', Cairo, 1929.

Mason, A., and Barny, F. J., *History of the Arabian Mission*, New York, 1926.

Massey, W. T., *Allenby's Final Triumph*, London, 1920.

Massignon, L., *Mission en Mésopotamie*, 2 vols, Cairo, 1910–12.

Meinertzhagen, Richard, *Middle East Diary*, Cresset, 1959.

—— *Army Diary*, Oliver & Boyd, 1960.

—— *Diary of a Black Sheep*, Oliver & Boyd, 1964.

Mikusch, Dagobert von, *Wassmuss der deutsche Lawrence*, Berlin, 1938.

Miller, William, *The Ottoman Empire and its Successors, 1801–1927*, Frank Cass, 1966.

Molesworth, G. N., *Afghanistan 1919*, London, 1962.

Monroe, Elizabeth, *Britain's Moment in the Middle East, 1914–1956*, Chatto & Windus, 1963.

—— *Philby of Arabia*, Faber, 1974.

Moorhouse, Geoffrey, *The Diplomats: The Foreign Office Today*, Cape, 1977.

Morgenthau, Henry, *Secrets of the Bosphorus*, Hutchinson, 1918.

—— *Ambassador Morgenthau's Story*, New York, 1918.

Morris, James, *The Hashemite Kings*, Faber, 1959.

—— *Pax Britannica, the Climax of an Empire*, Faber, 1968.

Morsey, Konrad, *T. E. Lawrence und der arabische Aufstand, 1916–18*, Osnabrück, 1976.

Mousa, Suleiman, *T. E. Lawrence: An Arab View*, OUP, 1966.

Mühlmann, Carl, *Deutschland und die Türkei, 1913–14*, Berlin, 1929.

—— *Das deutsch-Türkische Waffenbündniss im Weltkrieg*, Leipzig, 1940.

Muir, Sir William, *The Caliphate, its Rise, Decline and Fall*, ed. T. W. Weir, Grant, 1924.

Müller, Karl H., *Die Wirtschalftliche Bedeutung der Bagdadbohn. Laud und Leute der asiatischen Türkei*, Hamburg, 1917.

Murphy, C. C. R., *Soldiers of the Prophet*, Hogg, 1921.

Murray, G. W., *Sons of Ishmael*, Routledge, 1935.

Musil, Alois, *Arabia Petraea*, 3 vols, Vienna, 1907–8.

—— *Kusejr Amr*, 2 vols, Vienna, 1907.

—— *Northern Hijaz*, American Geographical Society, 1926.

—— *Arabia Deserta*, AGS, 1927.

—— *Northern Najd*, AGS, 1928.

—— *Palmyrena*, AGS, 1928.

Nadoly, Rudolf, *Mein Beitrug*, Wiesbaden, 1955.

Nicholson, R. A., *A Literary History of the Arabs*, CUP, 1907.

Nicolai, Colonel W., *Nachrichtdienst, Presse und Volksstimmung in Weltkrieg*, Berlin, 1920.

Nicolson, Harold, *Peacemaking 1919*, London, 1933.
—— *Curzon: The Last Phase, 1919–25*, London, 1934.
Nogales, Rafael de, *Vier Jahre unter dem Halbmond*, Berlin, 1925.
Nolde, Baron E., *Reise nach Innerarabien, Kurdistan und Armenien*, Brunswick, 1895.
Nuri Said Pasha, *Arab Independence and Unity*, Government Press, Baghdad, 1943.
Nutting, Anthony, *The Arabs*, Hollis, 1964.
—— *No End of a Lesson*, Hollis, 1964.

O'Connor, Frederick, *On the Frontier and Beyond: A Record of Thirty Years' Service*, London, 1931.
Oncken, Hermann, *Das deutsche Reich und die Vorgeschichte des Weltkriegs*, 2 vols, Leipzig, 1933.
—— *Die Sicherheit Indiens. Ein Jahrhundert englischer Weltpolitik*, Berlin, 1937.
Oppenheim, Max Freiherr von, *Von Mittelmeer zum Persischen Golf, durch den Hauran, die Syrische Wuste und Mesopotamien*, Berlin, 1900.

Palgrave, W. G. *Central and Eastern Arabia*, Macmillan, 1865.
Papen, Franz von, *Der Wahrheit eine Gasse*, Munich, 1952.
—— *Memoirs*, trans. Brian Connell, Deutsch, 1952.
Parfit, Canon J. T., *Twenty Years in Baghdad and Syria*, London, 1916.
—— *Mesopotamia: The Key to the Future*, London, 1917.
Patterson, Lt-Colonel J. H., *With the Judaeans in Palestine*, London, 1922.
Pears, Sir Edwin, *Turkey and its People*, London, 1911.
—— *Forty Years in Constantinople*, London, 1916.
Pechmann, Dr Gunther Freiherr von, and others, *Virtuti pro patria*, for Der

königlich bayerische Militär-Max-Joseph-Orden, Munich, 1966.
Peez, Alexander von, *Englands Rolle im Nahen Orient*, Vienna, 1917.
Pelly, Sir Lewis, *Report on a Journey to Riyadh*, Intro. by R. L. Bidwell, Cambridge, 1978.
Percy, H. A. G., Earl, *Notes from a Diary in Asiatic Turkey*, London, 1898.
Perlmann, M., *Arab-Jewish Diplomacy, 1918–22*, New York, 1944.
Philby, H. St J., *Report on the Najd Mission 1917–18*, Government Press, Baghdad, 1918.
—— *The Heart of Arabia*, Constable, 1922.
—— *Arabia of the Wahhabis*, Constable, 1928.
—— *Arabia*, Benn, 1930.
—— *Arabian Days*, Robert Hale, 1948.
—— *Arabian Jubilee*, Robert Hale, 1952.
—— *Forty Years in the Wilderness*, Robert Hale, 1957.
—— *Arabian Oil Ventures*, Middle East Institute, Washington, 1964
—— *Saudi Arabia*, Arno Press, New York, 1972.
Pingaud, A., *Histoire diplomatique de la France pendant la Grande Guerre*, Paris, 1938.
Polk, William R., *The United States and the Arab World*, Harvard University Press, 1965.
Pomiankowski, Joseph, *Der Zusammenbruch des Ottomanischen Reiches*, Zurich, 1928.
Preston, R. M. P., *The Desert Mounted Corps*, Constable, 1921.

Raban, Jonathan, *Arabia Through the Looking Glass*, Collins, 1979.
Rashid, Ibrahim (ed.), *Documents on the History of Saudi Arabia*, 3 vols, Salisbury, NC, 1976.
—— *Saudi Arabia Enters the Modern World: Secret US Documents on the*

Emergence of the Kingdom of Saudi Arabia as a World Power, 1936–1949, 2 vols, Salisbury, NC, 1980.

Raswan, Carl S., *The Black Tents of Arabia*, Hutchinson, 1935.

Raunkiaer, Barclay, *Through Wahhabiland on Camelback*, intro. by Gerald de Gaury, Routledge, 1969.

Rawlinson, A., *Adventures in the Near East, 1918–22*, London, 1923.

Rawlinson, Sir Henry C., *England and Russia in the East*, London, 1875.

Raynfield, F. A., 'The Dardanelles Campaign' (unpublished), Imperial War Museum, London, n.d.

Rendel, Sir G. W., *The Sword and the Olive: Recollections of Foreign Diplomacy, 1913–1954*, John Murray, 1957.

Rentz, George, 'Saudi Arabia', *Modernization of the Arab World*, ed. J. J. Thompson and R. C. Reischauer, Princeton, NJ, 1966.

Repington, Lt-Colonel C. à C., *The First World War*, 2 vols, London, 1920.

Reuther, O., *Das Wohnhaus in Bagdad und anderen Stadten des Irak*, Berlin, 1910.

Reventlow, Ernst Graf zu, *Indien: Seine Bedeutung für Grossbritannien, Deutschland und die Zunkuft der Welt*, Berlin, 1917.

Reynardson, H. B., *Mesopotamia, 1914–15*, London, 1919.

Richmond, Lady, *The Earlier Letters of Gertrude Bell*, ed. Elsa Richmond, Benn, 1937.

Riddell, Lord, *Intimate Diaries of the Peace Conference and After*, London, 1933.

Ridley, M. R., *Gertrude Bell*, Blackie, 1941.

Rihani, Ameen, *Ibn Sa'oud of Arabia*, Constable, 1928.

Ritter, A., *Nordkap-Bagdad, das politische Programm des Krieges*, Frankfurt, 1916.

Robbins, Keith, *Sir Edward Grey*, Cassell, 1971.

Robinson, R. D., *The First Turkish Republic*, Harvard, 1963.

Rodinson, Maxime, *Islam and Capitalism*, Penguin, 1977.

Rohde, Hans, *Der Kampf um Asien*, 2 vols, Stuttgart, 1924.

Rohrbach, Paul, 'Weltpolitisches Wanderbuch, 1897–1915' (unpublished), n.d.

Romein, Jan, *Das Jahrhundert Asiens. Geschichte des modernen asiatischen Nationalismus*, Berne, 1958.

Ronaldshay, Earl of, *The Life of Lord Curzon*, 3 vols, Benn, 1923.

Rooseveldt, Kermit, *War in the Garden of Eden*, London, 1920.

—— *Jew Counter Coup: The Struggle for the Control of Iran*, McGraw-Hill, 1979.

Rose, Kenneth, *Superior Person: a Portrait of Curzon and his Circle*, Weidenfeld & Nicolson, 1969.

Rosen, Dr Friedrich, *Aus einem diplomatischen Wanderleben*, Berlin, 1931.

Rousan, Mahmoud, *Palestine and the Internationalization of Jerusalem*, Ministry of Culture, Baghdad, 1965.

Ruppin, A., *Palestine Emigration and Immigration*, Royal Institute of International Affairs, 1926.

Rutter, Eldon, *Holy Cities of Arabia*, 2 vols, London, 1928.

Ryan, Andrew, *The Last of the Dragomans*, London, 1951.

Rybitschka, Emil, *Im gottgegebenen Afghanistan*, Leipzig, 1927.

Sachar, Howard Morley, *The Emergence of the Middle East, 1914–24*, Penguin, 1969.

Sachar, Morley, *A History of Israel from the Rise of Zionism to Our Time*, Blackwell, 1976.

Sackville-West, Vita, *Passenger to Tehran*, Penguin, 1943.

Sadleir, G. F., *Diary of a Journey Across Arabia* (1819), Government of Bombay Press, 1866.

Saleh, Zaki, *Mesopotamia 1600–1914, a Study in British Foreign Affairs*, Baghdad, 1957.

Sampson, Anthony, *The Arms Bazaar*, Hodder & Stoughton, 1978.

Samuel, Viscount, *Memoirs*, Cresset, 1945.

Sandes, E. W. G., *In Kut and Captivity with the 6th Indian Division*, London, 1924.

—— *Tales of Turkey*, London, 1924.

Sanger, Richard H., *The Arabian Peninsula*, New York, 1970.

Sarre, F., and Herzfeld, E., *Archaeologische Reise im Euphrat-und-Tigris Gebiet*, 4 vols, Berlin, 1911–20.

Schieder, Wolfgang (ed.), *Erster Weltkrieg. Ursachen, Entstehung und Kriegsziele*, Cologne, 1969.

Schmidt, Dana Adams, *Yemen: The Unknown War*, Bodley Head, 1968.

Schmitt, B. E., *The Coming of the War*, New York, 1930.

Schrenck-Notzing, Caspar, *Hundert Jahre Indien: Die Politische Entwicklung, 1875–1960*, Stuttgart, 1961.

Schweinitz, H. H. Graf von, *In Kleinasien 1905*, Berlin, 1906.

Seeckt, Oberst-General Hans von, *Aus meinem Leben, 1866–1917*, Leipzig, 1938.

Seton-Watson, R. W., *Disraeli, Gladstone and the Eastern Question*, London, 1935.

Sherson, E., *Townshend of Chitral and Kut*, London, 1928.

Singhal, Damstar, and Singhal, Prasad, *India and Afghanistan, 1876–1907*, University of Queensland Press, 1963.

Skrine, Sir Clarmont, *World War in Iran*, London, 1962.

Smith, Gary V., *Zionism: The Dream and the Reality, A Jewish Critique*, David & Charles, 1974.

Soane, E. B., *To Mesopotamia and Kurdistan in Disguise*, London, 1912.

Sokolov, N., *History of Zionism*, intro. by A. J. Balfour, Longmans, 1919.

Soussé, A., *Araber und Juden in der Geschichte*, Lausanne, 1977.

Sperling, Otto, *Mein Traum Indien*, Berlin, 1934.

Spring-Rice, Sir Cecil, *Letters and Friendships of*, ed. Stetten Gwynn, 2 vols, London, 1929.

Stark, Freya, *Turkey: A Sketch of Turkish History*, Thames & Hudson, 1971.

—— *Beyond Euphrates (1928–33)*, John Murray, 1951.

Stein, Leonard, *The Balfour Declaration*, Valentine, Mitchell, 1961.

Stewart, Desmond, *The Middle East: Temple of Janus*, Hamish Hamilton, 1972.

—— *Theodor Herzl, Artist and Politician*, Hamish Hamilton, 1974.

—— *T. E. Lawrence*, Hamish Hamilton, 1977.

—— and Haylock, John, *New Babylon, A Portrait of Iraq*, Collins, 1956.

Stitt, G. M. S., *A Prince of Arabia, Ali Haidar Sharif*, Allen & Unwin, 1948.

Stojanovic, M. D., *The Great Powers and the Balkans, 1875–8*, CUP, 1939.

Storrs, Sir Ronald, *Orientations*, Nicholson & Watson, 1937.

Streck, M., *Die alte Landschaft Babylonien nach den Arabischen Geographen*, 2 vols, Leyden, 1900–1901.

Sumner, B. H., *Russia and the Balkans*, London, 1937.

—— 'Der russische Imperialismus in Ostasien und im Mittleren Osten, 1880–1914', in *Imperialismus*, ed. Hans-Ulrich Wehler, Cologne, 1970.

Sykes, Christopher, *Wassmuss: the German Lawrence*, Longmans, 1936.

—— *Two Studies in Virtue*, Collins 1953.

—— *Crossroads to Israel: Palestine from Balfour to Berlin*, Collins, 1965.

Sykes, Sir Mark, *Through Five Turkish Provinces*, London, 1900.

—— *The Caliph's Last Heritage*, London, 1915.

Sykes, Sir Percy, *A History of Persia*, 2 vols, Macmillan, 1930.

—— *History of Afghanistan*, London, 1940.

Taylor, A. J. P., *Europe: Grandeur and Decline*, Pelican/Hamish Hamilton, 1967.

—— 'The Trouble-Makers: Dissent over Foreign Policy, 1792–1939', *The Ford Lectures*, Hamish Hamilton, 1957.

Temperley, H. W. V., *England and the Near East*, Longmans, 1936.

—— *History of the Peace Conference*, British Institute of International Affairs, 1920–24.

Terraine, John, *Douglas Haig: the Educated Soldier*, Hutchinson, 1963.

—— *Impacts of War, 1914–18*, Hutchinson, 1970.

Thesiger, Wilfred, *Arabian Sands*, Longmans, 1960.

—— *The Marsh Arabs*, Penguin, 1978.

—— *Desert, Marsh and Mountain: The World of a Nomad*, Collins, 1979.

Thomas, Bertram, *Alarms and Excursions in Arabia*, London, 1930.

—— *Arabia Felix: Across the Empty Quarter of Arabia*, Cape, 1938.

Thomas, Lowell, *With Lawrence of Arabia*, Hutchinson, 1925.

—— *The Boy's Life of Colonel Lawrence*, New York, 1927.

Thompson, R. Campbell, *A Century of Exploration at Nineveh*, London, 1929.

Thomson, Sir Basil, *Allied Secret Service in Greece*, London, 1931.

Tibawi, A. L., *Anglo-Arab Relations and the Question of Palestine, 1914–21*, Luzac, 1977.

Tibble, Anne, *Gertrude Bell*, A. & C. Black, 1958.

Tichy, Herbert, *Afghanistan: Das Tor nach Indien*, Leipzig, 1940.

Tirpitz, Admiral A. von, *My Memoirs*, 2 vols, Hurst & Blackett, 1920.

Townshend, General C. V., *My Campaign in Mesopotamia*, Thornton Butterworth, 1920.

Toynbee, Arnold J., *The Islamic World since the Peace Settlement*, Survey of International Affairs, 1925, Royal Institute of International Affairs/OUP, 1927.

—— *A Study of History*, vol. VIII, CUP, 1954.

—— *Acquaintances*, OUP, 1962.

Trevelyan, Humphrey, Baron, *Worlds Apart*, Macmillan, 1971.

—— *The India We Left*, Macmillan, 1972.

—— *Diplomatic Channels*, Macmillan, 1973.

Trinkler, Emil, *Quer durch Afghanistan nach Indien*, Berlin, 1925.

Troeller, Gary, *The Birth of Sa'udi Arabia: Britain and the Rise of the House of Sa'ud*, Frank Cass, 1976.

Trumpener, Ulrich, *Germany and the Ottoman Empire, 1914–18*, Princeton, NJ, 1968.

Tuson, Penelope, *The Records of the British Residency and Agencies in the Persian Gulf*, Foreign and Commonweath Office, 1979.

Twitchell, K. S., *Saudi Arabia: With an Account of the Development of its Natural Resources*, New York, 1958.

Upton, Joseph M., *The History of Modern Iran: An Interpretation*, Cambridge, Mass., 1961.

Vambery, A., *Freiheitliche Bestrebung in Moslischen Asien*, Berlin, 1893.

—— *The Coming Struggle for India*, Cassell, 1885.

Van Ess, Dorothy, 'Gertrude Bell', *Pioneers of the Arab World*, no. 3, Historical Series of Dutch Reformed Church of America, Michigan, 1974.

Van Ess, John, *Meet the Arab*, Museum Press, 1947.

Villars, J. B., *T. E. Lawrence: or the Search for the Absolute*, trans. from French by P. Dawney, Sidgwick & Jackson, 1958.

Vital, David, *The Origins of Zionism*, OUP, 1975.

Vogel, Renate, *Die Persien und Afghanistanexpedition Oska Ritter von Niedermayers, 1915–16*, Osnabruck, 1976.

Wahba, Hafiz, *Arabian Days*, Arthur Barker, 1964.

Waterfield, Gordon, *Sir Percy Loraine, Professional Diplomat*, John Murray, 1973.

Wavell, A. J. B., *A Modern Pilgrim in Mecca*, London, 1912.

Wavell, Field-Marshal Viscount, *Allenby: Soldier and Statesman*, Harrap, 1946.

Webster, C. K.,*The Foreign Policy of Palmerston*, Bell, 1951.

Weizmann, Chaim, *Trial and Error*, Hamish Hamilton, 1949.

White, Freda, *Mandates*, London, 1926.

Wigram, W. A., *The Assyrian Settlement*, London, 1922.

—— and Wigram, E. T. A., *The Cradle of Mankind*, London, 1914.

Wilber, Donald N., *Afghanistan, its People and its Society*, New Haven, Conn. 1962.

—— *Contemporary Iran*, New York, 1963.

—— *Iran Past and Present*, Princeton, NJ, 1967.

Wilson, Sir A. T., *The Persian Gulf*, Allen & Unwin, 1928.

—— *A Bibliography of Persia*, Clarendon Press, 1930.

—— *Loyalties: Mesopotamia 1914–17*, OUP, 1930.

—— *Mesopotamia, 1917–20: A Clash of Loyalties*, OUP, 1931.

—— *Persia*, Benn, 1932.

—— *The Suez Canal*, OUP, 1933.

—— *South-West Persia: A Political Officer's Diary*, OUP, 1941.

Wilson, Sir Henry, *His Life and Diaries*, 2 vols, London, 1927.

Winder, R. Bayly, *Saudi Arabia in the Nineteenth Century*, New York, 1965.

Wingate, Sir Ronald, *Not in the Limelight*, Hutchinson, 1959.

Winstone, H. V. F., *Captain Shakespear*, Cape, 1976: Quartet, 1978.

—— *Gertrude Bell*, Cape, 1979, Quartet, 1980.

—— and Freeth, Zahra, *Kuwait: Prospect and Reality*, Allen & Unwin, 1972.

—— *Explorers of Arabia*, Allen & Unwin, 1978.

Wittlin, Alma, *Abdul Hamid, the Shadow of God*, trans. from German by N. Denny, London, 1940.

Wood, E. F. T., Viscount Halifax, *Lawrence of Arabia*, London, 1936.

Woodward, E. L., *Short Journey*, London, 1942.

Woolley, Sir Leonard (C. L.) (ed.), *From Kastamuni to Kedos*, Blackwell, 1921.

—— *As I Seem to Remember*, Allen & Unwin, 1961.

Wright, Denis, *The English Among the Persians*, Heinemann, 1977.

Wright, Q., *Mandates under the League of Nations*, Chicago, 1930.

Yapp, M. E., *Strategies of British India, Britain, Iran and Afghanistan, 1798–1850*, Clarendon Press, 1980.

Young, Sir George, *Corps de Droit Ottoman*, 7 vols, Oxford, 1905–6.

Young, Sir Hubert, *The Independent Arab*, John Murray, 1933.

Young, Kenneth, *Arthur James Balfour*, Bell, 1963.

Younghusband, Lt-General Sir G. J., *Forty Years a Soldier*, London, 1923.

Zaki, Salih, *Origins of British Influence in Mesopotamia*, New York, 1941.

Zeine, Z. N., *The Struggle for Arab Independence*, Beirut, 1960.

Zetland, Marquess of, *Lord Cromer*, London, 1932.

Ziemke, Kurt, *Als deutscher Gesandter in Afghanistan*, Stuttgart, 1939.

Zugmayer, Professor Erich, *Eine Reise durch Vorderasien im Jahre 1904*, Berlin, 1905.

Zwemer, Rev. S. M., *Arabia: the Cradle of Islam*, Edinburgh and New York, 1900.

Official and Institutional Publications and Documents

BRITISH MUSEUM AND LIBRARY

Papers of Sir Arnold Wilson, MS 736 C.

Notebook of Gertrude Bell, 1913 (attrib. 1905), MS/45158A–C.

Letters of Sir Basil Thomson, 1908, MS/Add 46066 f. 15.

CARNEGIE ENDOWMENT

Report of International Committee of Inquiry into the Balkan Wars, Washington, 1914.

COMMAND PAPERS, ISSUED BY ORDER OF PARLIAMENT, HMSO

1897: C 8304, *Turkey*.

1914: Cd 7628, *Rupture with Turkey*.

1915: Cd 8253, *General Townshend's Appreciation before Kut*.

1917: Cd 8610, *Report of the Mesopotamian Commission*.

      Cd 8490/371, *Reports on the Dardanelles*, 2 parts.

1919: Cmd 5964, *Statements Made on Behalf of His Majesty's Government During the Year 1918 in Regard to the Future Status of Certain Parts of the Ottoman Empire.*

1920: Cmd 960, *Treaty of Sèvres*, 10 Aug 1920.

      Cmd 1061, *Review of the Civil Administration of Meso-potamia, 1914–1920*, by Gertrude L. Bell.

1921: Cmd 1176, *Draft Mandate for Mesopotamia* (Iraq).

      Cmd 1195, *Franco-British Convention*, 23 Dec 1920.

      Cmd 1226, *Correspondence with Government of USA Regarding Economic Rights in Iraq.*

      Cmd 1351, *Petroleum in Iraq.*

      Cmd 1500, *Final Draft of Mandates*, for Iraq, Syria and Palestine.

1922: Cmd 1757, *Anglo-Iraq Treaty*, 10 Oct 1922.

      Cmd 2217, *Use of Royal Air Force in Iraq.*

1923: Cmd 1814, *Lausanne Conference.*

      Cmd 1929, *Treaty of Lausanne*, 24 July 1923.

1924: Cmd 2120, *Anglo-Iraq Protocol*, 30 April 1924; and *Agreements.*

1925: Cmd 2562, *Turco-Iraqi Frontier.*

      Cmd 2563, *Incidents on Turkish Frontier.*

      Cmd 2565, *Agreement with Najd.*

1926: Cmd 2587, *New Anglo-Iraq Treaty*, 13 Jan 1926.

      Cmd 2679, *Anglo-Iraq-Turkish Treaty*, 7 June 1926.

1927: Cmd 2998, *Draft Revised Treaty with Iraq*, 14 Dec 1927.

1929: Cmd 3440, *Statement of British Policy in Iraq.*

1930: Cmd 3627/3675, *Anglo-Iraq Treaty and Exchange of Notes.*

1937: Cmd 5479, Royal Commission on Palestine, Minutes of Public Sessions.

1939: Cmd 5957, *Correspondence between Sir Henry McMahon*

and the Sharif of Mecca.

Cmd 6974, *Report of a Committee Set Up to Consider Certain Correspondence between Sir Henry McMahon and the Sharif of Mecca in 1915 and 1916.*

COMMITTEE OF IMPERIAL DEFENCE, HISTORICAL DIVISION

Official History of the War, published 1920–33, HMSO.

Military Operations Gallipoli, C. F. Aspinall-Oglander.

The Campaign in Mesopotamia, 4 vols, F. T. Moberly.

Military Operations in Egypt and Palestine from the Outbreak of War to June 1917, G. MacMunn and Cyril Falls.

Military Operations in Egypt and Palestine from June 1917 to End of War, Cyril Falls.

Naval Operations, vol.3, *The Dardanelles Campaign, The Mesopotamian Campaign*, Sir Julian Corbett; *Mesopotamia*, vols 4–5, Sir Henry Newbolt.

Official History of Australia in the War of 1914–18, published Angus & Robertson, Sydney, 1921–35.

C. E. W. Bean, *The Australian Contingent, British Expeditionary Force.*
—— *The Story of Anzac.*
H. S. Gullett, *Sinai and Palestine.*

Geographical Journal, (GJ) Journal of the Royal Geographical Society

'Journey of Captains Butler and Aylmer from Nejef through Jauf to Damascus, vol. XXXIII, no. 5, May 1909.

'A Journey in North-West Arabia', Lecture 24 Jan 1910, Douglas Carruthers, vol. XXXV, no. 3, March 1919.

'Captain Leachman's Journey in Spring 1910', and award of Gill Memorial Medal, vol. XXXVII, no. 3, March 1911.

'A Journey through Central Arabia', Captain G. Leachman, vol. XLIII, no. 5, May 1914.

'Mapping Arabia', F. Fraser Hunter, vol. LIV, no. 6 Dec 1919.

'Captain Shakespear's Last Journey', Douglas Carruthers, vol. LIX, nos 5 and 6, May/June 1922.

'Gertrude Bell's Journey to Hail', Dr D. G. Hogarth, vol. LXX, no. 1, July 1927.

'Memoir of D. G. Hogarth', C. R. L. Fletcher, vol. LXXI, no. 4, April 1928.

'Douglas Carruthers and Geographical Contrasts in Central Asia', Owen Lattimore, vol. 144, part 2, July 1978.

'George Nathaniel Curzon – Superior Geographer', A. S. Goudie, vol. 146, part 2, July 1980.

'The Centenary of the RGS Drawing Office', G. S. Holland, vol. 146, part 2, July 1980.

Journal of Central Asiatic Society (CASJ), now *Journal of the Royal Society for Asian Affairs*

'Central Mesopotamia', Perceval Landon, vol. III (i), 1916.

'Baghdad', Colonel Sir Thomas Holdich, vol. IV (ii), 1917.

'Mesopotamia and Syria after the War', Demetrius Boulger, vol. IV,(iii), 1917.

'Mesopotamia, 1914–21', Lt-Colonel Sir Arnold Wilson, vol. VIII (iii), 1921.

'The Qanum al Aradhi', Colonel Evelyn B. Howell, vol. IX (i), 1922.

'The Assyrian Adventure of 1920', Lt-Colonel F. Cunliffe-Owen, vol. IX (ii), 1922.

'The British Museum Archaeological Mission in Mesopotamia in 1919', Dr H. R. Hall, vol. IX (iii), 1922.

'The Early Days of Arab Government in Iraq', A Correspondent in Baghdad, vol. IX (iv), 1922.

'Storm Waves in the Mohammadan World', Sir Valentine Chirol, vol. IX (iv), 1922.

'Three Difficult Months in Iraq', A Correspondent in Baghdad, vol. X (i), 1923.

'Arabia and the Hijaz', Lt-Colonel C. E. Vickery, vol. X (i), 1923.

'Current Affairs in Iraq', A Correspondent in Baghdad, vol. X (ii) 1923.

'Palestine', Sir Wyndham Deedes, vol. X (iv), 1923.

'Trans-Jordan', H. St J. B. Philby, vol. XI (iv), 1924.

'The French in Syria, 1919–24', Major D. McCallum, vol. XII (i), 1925.

'Recent History of the Hijaz', H. St J. B. Philby, vol. XII (iv), 1925.

'The Triumph of the Wahhabis', H. St J. B. Philby, vol. XIII (iv), 1926.

'Five Years' Progress in Iraq', Jafar Pasha al Askari, vol. XIV (i), 1927.

'Problems in Northern Iraq', Dr W. A. Wigram, vol. XV (iii), 1928.

'Syria', H. Charles Woods, vol. XIV (ii), 1927.

'Arabia: An Unbiased Survey', Ameen Rihani, vol. XVI (i), 1929.

'The Iraq-Najd Frontier', Anon, vol. XVII (i), 1930.

'Ideas and Ideals of Modern Islam', D. S. Margoliouth, vol. XVII (i), 1930.

'A Note on the Iraq Treaty of Alliance, 1930', Lt-Colonel F. Cunliffe Owen, vol. XVII (iv), 1930.

'Damascus to Hail', Eldon Rutter, vol. XVIII (i), 1931.

'Iraq: The New State', Sir Nigel Davidson, vol. XIX (ii), 1932.

'The Next Twenty Years in Asia: A Survey and a Forecast', Lt-Colonel Sir Arnold Wilson, vol. XIX (iii), 1932.

'The Assyrians in Iraq', Brig.-General Sir Percy Sykes, vol. XXII (ii), 1934.

'A Kurdish Lampoonist: Shaikh Riza Talabani', vol. XXII (i), 1935.

'The Arab Position in Palestine', Fakhri Bey Nashashabi, vol. XXIII (i), 1936.

'The Jewish Position in Palestine', Dr Chaim Weizmann, vol. XXIII (iii), 1936.

'The Desert Beduin and His Future', Major C. S. Jarvis, vol. XXIII (iv),1936.

'Treaty Making in the Middle East', Archer Cust, vol. XXIII (iv), 1936.

'The Persian Gulf: Prelude to the Zimmermann Telegram', C. J. Edmonds, vol. XLVII (i), 1960.

'Links with the Past', Sir Evelyn B. Howell, vol. L (iii), 1963.

'Arab-Persian Rivalry in the Persian Gulf', John Marlowe, vol. LI (i), 1964.

'The Kurdish War in Iraq: A Plan for Peace', C. J. Edmonds, vol. LIV (i), 1967.

'Postscript to Asian Empire', Lord Trevelyan, vol. LV (iii), 1968.

'Gertrude Bell in the Near and Middle East, C. J. Edmonds, lecture, delivered 25 June 1969, vol. LVI (iii) 1969.

London Gazette

Reports by Commanders-in-Chief, Expeditionary Force 'D'

General Sir J. Nixon, April–Sept 1915 (5 April 1916).
Oct–Dec 1915 (10 May 1916).
General Sir Percy Lake, Jan–April 1916 (10 Oct 1916).
General Sir Stanley Maude, Aug

1916–March 1917 (10 July 1917)April–Sept 1917 (10 Jan 1918).
General Sir W. R. Marshall, Oct 1917–March 1918 (28 Aug 1918).
April–Sept 1918 (20 Feb 1919).
Oct–Dec 1918 (11 April 1919).

Official Archives

INDIA OFFICE LIBRARY AND RECORDS, LONDON

Political and Secret Records

L/P & S/3, Home Correspondence, 1807–1911.

L/P & S/7, Correspondence with India, 1875–1911.

L/P & S/10, Subject files, 1902–31, Persian Gulf Residency, Kuwait and Bahrain Agencies, Kuwait, Arabian affairs, War, Persia, Afghanistan, enemy agents.

L/P & S/11, Subject files, 1902–31. Pan-Arabs, German agents, oil, Persia, the Idrisi, Baghdad Rail, Pan-Islamic Indian agents in Britain and America, death of Leachman.

L/P & S/14, Subject files, 1902–31. India and Afghanistan.

L/P & S/18, Memoranda. Tribes, Central Asia, Russian and German incursions, Aden and Yemen, Ibn Saud, Russia and Afghanistan, Hijaz rail, Relations with Turkey, Mesopotamia, Najd, Sharif of Mecca, Turkey and Palestine, Arab Movement, War in Mesopotamia, Palestine, Work of Civil Commission in Mesopotamia, Reports by Residents and Political Agents, Syria, Russian secret agents, Personalities in Arabia and Turkey, Handbooks.

L/P & S/20, Political and Secret Library. Subjects as above.

R/15/5 Records of the Persian Gulf Residency, Bushire (1), and Political Agencies at Bahrain (2), Kuwait (5), Muscat (6).

PUBLIC RECORD OFFICE, LONDON

Cabinet records

CAB 37/1–122, Cabinet Papers, 1880 to 1914.

CAB 37/123–162, Cabinet Papers, 1914 to 1916.

CAB 42/1–2, War Council, Aug 1914–May 1915.

CAB 42/3–4, Dardanelles Committee, June–Oct 1915.

CAB 42/5–26, War Committee, Nov 1915–Dec 1916.

CAB 1, Miscellaneous records, 1914–19.

CAB 27, *Ad Hoc* committees.

CAB 24, G Series, Memoranda.

Foreign Office Records

FO 371, Turkey, Turkish Arabia, Egypt.

FO 372, Egypt, Personnel, Enemy agents, Prisoners of War, Correspondence with GOC (War Office).

FO 382, Contraband, enemy agents, Aaronsohn's movements in Europe and arrival in Britain.

FO 395, Enemy propaganda, Correspondence with Special Intelligence and DMI, Aaronsohn, Weizmann, Morgenthau, Lowell Thomas, Anglo-American affairs, Balfour Declaration.

FO 406, Confidential Prints, Eastern Affairs.

FO 424, Confidential Prints, Ottoman Empire.

FO 686, Jiddah records.

FO 882, Arab Bureau records.

ROYAL AIR FORCE RECORDS

AIR 1/408/15/239/1, Aircraft Park, Mesopotamia, 1915–18.

AIR 1/408/15/240/1, Middle East Brigade, RFC, Oct 1916–Oct 1917.

AIR 1/426/15/260/1, Notes from War Diaries Mesopotamian Expeditionary Force 'D'.

AIR 1/162/15/124/4, Report on Aerial Mail Services Jan–Aug 1919.

AIR 1/37/15/1/249/1, Resignation of Mr G. B. M. Cockburn, Inspector of Accidents, 30 Sept 1920.

AIR 1/426/15/260/3, Mesopotamia. Take-over of security by RAF, March 1920–April 1921.

AIR 1/426/15/260/5, Bombing of Kuwait at Request of High Commissioner.

AIR 1/427/15/260/11–12, Baghdad Internal Security, May 1919–Sept 1922.

AIR 1/675/21/13/1726, Agent dropping 1915.

COLONIAL OFFICE RECORDS

CO 781, Register.

CO 730/1–44, Intelligence Summaries, 1921–3.

CO 730/45–106, Intelligence Summaries, 1924–6.

WAR OFFICE RECORDS (Ministry of Defence)

WO 157/687–747, Intelligence Summaries 1914–20.

WO 33/731–981, Secret Telegrams, Mediterranean and Egypt to WO, 1914–20.

WO 106/710–31, Correspondence of DMO and DMI.

PRO 30/57, Kitchener Papers.

WAR OFFICE LIBRARY, Ministry of Defence, London

Army Lists.
Indian Army Lists.

FOREIGN OFFICE LIBRARY, LONDON

Arab Bulletin, 1915–19
Diplomatic and Consular Lists, British and Foreign, 1880–1930.

AUSTRIAN RECORDS

Oesterreichischer Staatsarchiv, Vienna. Austro-Hungarian Foreign Ministry (AHFM). Files mostly incomplete and poorly recorded. Of limited value.

FRENCH RECORDS

Ministère des Affaires étrangères, Quai d'Orsai, Paris (F).

Correspondance politique et commerciale.

F/NS (Nouvelle Serie) 1–6, Politique interieure, 1895–1914.

F/NS 7–15, Présence anglaise, 1896–1913.

F/NS 16, Armée–Marine, 1896–1913.

F/NS 17–25, Politique étrangère, 1895–1914.

Turquie: Correspondance politique et commerciale

F/NS 104–24, dossiers général, 1895–1914.

F/NS 129–35, Palestine, 1896–1914.

F/NS 136–8, Sionisme, 1897–1914.

F/NS 139–45, Arabie–Yemen, général, 1896–Dec 1914.

F/NS 146–8, Pèlerinage de la Mecque, 1896–1917.

F/NS 149–52, Mesopotamie, Gofe persique, 1896–1914.

Defense nationale

F/NS 153–9, Armeé, 1897–1914.

F/NS 161–3, Marine, 1897–1914.

F/NS 164–308, Politique étrangère de la Turquie.

Guerre 1914–18, Turquie
F 845–65, dossiers général, 1914–18.
F 867–886, Syrie–Palestine, 1914–18.
F 1197–1201, Sionisme.
F 1681–1701, Arabie, 1915–18.
F 1702–10, Hedjaz, 1917–18.
F 1563–74, Egypte, 1914–18.

GERMAN RECORDS

Archiv des Auswärtiges Amt, Bonn, (AA)
Abteilung IA
Orientalia generalia 9, Nr 1. Berichte des Freiherrn von Oppenheim über orientalische Verhältnisse. Bd 1–12, 1886–1909.
Persien Nr 3. Akten betreffend die Militär-Angelegenheiten Persiens, Bd 5–6.
Persien Nr 23. Akten betreffend den Anschluss Persiens an die Zentralmachte und an die Tükei, Bd 1–5.
Persien Nr 24. Geldangelegenheiten unserer Aktion in Persien, Bd 1–2.
—— Die deutsche Irakgruppe, Bd 11–16.
Afghanistan Nr 1. Akten betreffend allgemeine Angelegenheiten Afghanistans, Bd 17–18.
Der Weltkrieg Nr 4. Neutralitätserklärungen.
—— Nr 11e. Unternehmungen und Aufwiegelungen gegen unsere Feinde in Afghanistan und Persien, Bd 1–34.
—— Nr 11e adh. Handschreiben an den Emir von Afghanistan und an indische Fürsten.
—— Nr 11f. Unternehmungen und Aufwiegelungen gegen unsere Feinde in Indien, Bd 8–9.
—— Nr 11g. Unternehmungen und Aufwiegelungen gegen unsere Feinde in Egypten, Syrien und Arabien, 1914–18, Bd 1–19.
—— Nr 11g adh. Syrien, Arabien, 1916–18, Bd 1–2.
—— Nr 11g (geheim dass.) 1914–15, Bd 1–5.

CENTRAL ZIONIST ARCHIVE, JERUSALEM (Z)

Z1, Documents of Central Office, Vienna, 1897–1905.
Z2, Documents of Central Office, Cologne, 1905–11.
Z3, Documents of Central Office, Berlin, 1911–14.
L2, Documents of Zionist Office, Jaffa, 1908–14.
L5, Correspondence of Zionist representative, Constantinople, 1908–14.
KKL, Correspondence of Jewish National Fund.
H, Papers of Theodor Herzl.
W, Papers of David Wolffsohn.
A18, Papers of Nahum Sokolov.

Private Papers and Academic Collections
IN AUTHOR'S POSSESSION

Papers and letters of Mr Douglas Carruthers, courtesy Mrs Rosemary Carruthers.
Papers and letters of Colonel Gerard Leachman, courtesy Brigadier John G. Parham, Mrs Hetman Jack Parham and Miss Belinda Parham.
Papers and letters of Colonel Stewart Newcombe, courtesy the Baroness Elles.
Diaries, letters and documents of Colonel A. C. Parker, courtesy Mrs Anne Edgerley.
Correspondence of Admiral Sir Herbert Richmond with Sir Julian Corbett and others, courtesy Lady Plowden, Mrs Mary Wilson and Mrs Valentine Vester.

Papers of Captain W. H. I. Shakespear, courtesy Major-General J. D. Lunt.

ST ANTONY'S COLLEGE, OXFORD (Middle East Centre)

Papers of Viscount Allenby, 1918–25. Reports and letters of George Antonius. Diaries of Colonel Sir John Ardagh. Papers relating to the Balfour Declaration. Diaries and letters of Gertrude Bell. Correspondence of Norman Bentwich during period of service as Legal Secretary to Government of Palestine (1921–9). Diaries and correspondence of Mr Humphrey Bowman. Correspondence of Mr Harry Boyle relating to Egypt, 1902–21. Papers of Major C. D. Brunton, Sir Reader Bullard, Sir Milne Cheetham, Sir Valentine Chirol, Sir Gilbert Clayton, Sir Kinahan Cornwallis, Lord Cromer, Sir Wyndham Deedes, Colonel H. R. P. Dickson, Mr John Dickson, Mr C. J. Edmonds, Sir William Everett, Mr Felix Frankfurter, Mr Richard Graves, Dr D. G. Hogarth, Sir Vyvyan Holt, Mr Cecil Hourani, Mr Lionel Jardine, Mr Jennings Bramley, Ismet Karadogan, Sir Arthur Kirby, Colonel T. E. Lawrence, Colonel G. E. Leachman, Lord Lloyd, Baron Wakehurst (J. de V. Loder), Brigadier S. H. Longrigg, Sir Harry Luke, Colonel Richard Meinertzhagen, Miss Elizabeth Monroe, Dr C. S. G. Mylrea, Mr L. F. Nalder, Colonel S. F. Newcombe, Mr H. St J. Philby, Sir George Rendel, Colonel H. P. Rice, Mr Keith Roach, Sir Thomas Russell, Viscount Samuel, Mr Lionel Smith, Sir Ronald Storrs, Sir Mark Sykes, Sir Charles Tegart, Abdul Latif Tibawi, Mr W. Tudor-Pole, Mr Woodrow Wilson, Sir Ronald Wingate, Mr William Yale, Sir Hubert Young. Minutes and Agenda of Cairo Conference, 1921. De Bunsen Committee Report, 1915. Document relating to Sharif of Mecca and Arab Revolt.

UNIVERSITY OF NEWCASTLE UPON TYNE

Letters, diaries and papers of Gertrude Lowthian Bell.

UNIVERSITY OF DURHAM

Correspondence and papers of Gertrude Bell, Sir Valentine Chirol, Sir Gilbert Clayton, Col. Frank Balfour.

BODLEIAN LIBRARY, OXFORD

Correspondence and papers of Colonel Richard Meinertzhagen.

ROYAL GEOGRAPHICAL SOCIETY

Letters and notebooks of Gertrude Bell, Captain Shakespear, and Douglas Carruthers. Maps of Bell, Leachman, Carruthers, Musil, Butler and Aylmer, and General Staffs of Britain, Turkey, France and Germany.

YALE UNIVERSITY

Papers of Ernst Jäckh.

HOOVER LIBRARY, STANFORD, USA

Papers of Dr Heinrich Kanner of Vienna.

MUSEUM AND LIBRARY AARON-SOHN, ZICHRON YAKOV, ISRAEL

Archive of NILI and the Aaronsohn family.

Published Documents from Official Archives
(See also books under 'General')

Die europäischen Mächte und die Türkei während des Weltkrieges, Konstantinopel und die Meerengen. Nach den Geheimdokumenten des ehemaligen Ministeriums für Auswärtige Angelegenheiten. Redaktion von E. Adamow, 2 vols, Dresden, 1930.

Die Grosse Politik der europäischen Kabinette 1871–1914. Sammlung der diplomatischen Akten des Auswärtiger Amtes, hrsg. Johannes Lepsius, Albrecht Mendelssohn-Bartholdy, Friedrich Thimme, 40 vols, Berlin, 1922–7.

Deutsche Reichgeschichte in Dokumenten 1849–1934. Hrsg. von Johannes Hohlfeld, 4 vols, Berlin, 1934.

Die Internationalen Beziehungen im Zeitaler des Imperialismus. Dokumente aus den Archiven der Zarischen und der Provisorischen Regierung, ed. M. M. Pokrovski, 5 vols, issued by the Central Committee, USSR, 1931.

Documents diplomatiques français, 1871–1914, 42 vols, Paris, 1929–59.

I Documenti Diplomatici Italiani, Rome, 1954.

Newspapers, Magazines and Specialist Journals

Al Ahram, Cairo, 1910–30.

Arab Papers, no. 4, Najdat Fathi, Safwat, 'Freemasonry in the Arab World', Arab Research Centre, 1980.

Army Quarterly, miscellaneous issues, 1920–30.

L'Avenir, Paris, 3 Jan–12 Aug 1919.

Daily Express, Jan 1919–Dec 1930.

France du Nord, May 1919, Aaronsohn.

Figaro, April 1854–Dec 1942.

Hadassah Magazine, March 1970, Aaronsohn.

Jewish Chronicle, May 1919, Aaronsohn.

The Jewish Herald, 27 Dec 1967, Feinberg.

Land and Water, USA, 9 May–24 Oct 1918, Henry Morgenthau.

Middle East Studies, Elie Kedourie, 'Young Turks, Freemasons and Jews', vol. 7, no. 1, 1971.

Morning Post, 1880–1920.

Neuphilologische Monatschrift, Leipzig, 1936. A. Ehrentreich on 'T. E. Lawrence'.

The Palestine News, 1918–19. Journal of Expeditionary Force 'E'.

Pioneer of India, 1911–18.

Al Qibla, Jiddah, 1916–18. British-financed journal of Sharifian forces in the Hijaz.

The Round Table, miscellaneous copies, 1914–20.

Le Telegram, Boulogne, May 1919, Aaronsohn.

The Times, 1880–1930.

The World, 8 July 1874–25 March 1922.

The World Today, Lt-General MacMunn on 'Lawrence of Arabia', nos L and LI, Nov–Dec 1927.

Index

A=Appendix
n=notes

Aaronsohn, Aaron, 21ff., 28ff., 34ff.,
110, 226ff., 236, 239, 262, 270, 288ff.,
315, 327, 342, 353ff.
Aaronsohn, Alex, 226ff., 307ff.
Aaronsohn, Ephraim, 22, 309
Aaronsohn, Rivka (Rebecca), 227ff.,
290, 357
Aaronsohn, Samuel, 313
Aaronsohn, Sarah, 35, 226ff., 290ff.,
307ff., 315, 357
Aaronsohn, Zvi, 309
Aaronsohn Museum, Zichron Yakov,
358
Abadan, oil installations, 142, 190, 201–2
Abbas Hilmi, Khedive of Egypt, 76,
173ff., 299, 319, 320
Abbasia Police School, Cairo, 109
Abbasids, see Caliphate
Abda, Shammar tribe, 155
Abdal Aziz ibn Abdurrahman al Saud,
see Saud, Ibn
Abdal Aziz ibn Mitab al Rashid (Ibn
Rashid), 14, 33
Abdal Aziz ibn Muhammad al Saud
(Ibn Saud), 365A
Abdal Aziz ibn Salim, 145
Abdal Hamid II, Sultan, 6, 9, 10, 13, 23,
34, 104, 175, 224–5
Abdal Hamid Bey, Col., 63
Abdal Karim, 323ff., 347
Abdal Samad Shah, 208
Abdin Palace, Cairo, 174

Abdullah Arerag, Shaikh, 267
Abdullah ibn Ali al Rashid, 367A
Abdullah ibn Askar, 101, 105
Abdullah ibn Faisal al Saud, 366A
Abdullah ibn Hamza, 329
Abdullah ibn Husain, Sharif (Amir of
Transjordan), 67, 70, 123, 151ff., 165–
6, 173ff., 194, 199, 243ff., 280ff., 348,
351, 372A
Abdullah ibn Mitab al Rashid, 345, 347,
370A
Abdullah ibn Mubarak al Faraikh, 52
Abdullah Pasha, 63
Abdullah ibn Ustad Ahmad ('Ger-
mani'), 86
Abdurrahman ibn Faisal al Saud, 12,
91, 116, 178
Abdurrahman al Riadh, 167
Aboulafia, Raphael, 229, 289, 296
Abraham, Hayyim, 226
Abraham, Sarah, see Aaronsohn, Sarah
Abrahams, Sir Lionel, 243
Abu Farid, 292
Abu Ghar, 121, 422n
Abu Harara, 93
Abu Tayya (place), 111
Abu Zeraibat, 282
Abyssinia, 28, 270, 271
Ackloni, Emil, 85
Acton, Lord, 320
Adams, Lieut., 357
Adana, 176, 193, 220
Aden, 28, 75, 186, 212
Admiralty, passim
Adrianople, 105
Affulah, 292

Afghanistan, 10, 133, 165ff., 196, 349, 363; German agents in, 133ff. 167, 332

Africa, SS, 28

Afule, 331

Agadir crisis, 77, 125

Agarie (Indian Communist), 333

Agriculture, US Dept of, 35

Ahad, Al (The Covenant), 68, 100, 103, 123, 190, 224, 270, 334

Ahmad Riza Pasha, 10

Ahwaz, oil pipeline, 145, 190, 201, 204

Ajaimi ibn Sadun, Shaikh of Muntafiq, 15, 58, 137

Ajlan, Rashid Governor, 54

Ajlan, valley of, 3

Ajman tribe, 55, 149, 152, 159

Akleh, Faridah, 44

Ala, Al, 159, 272, 275

Alam, Risaldar Mir Khan, 258ff.

Albania, 75

Aleppo, 20, 45, 135, 137, 190ff., 220, 271, 331

Alexandretta, 183, 192, 233, 269

Alexandria, 181, 290; Intelligence office, 185

Ali Bey, Colonel, 63

Ali Dinar, 277

Ali Effendi (Cairo messenger), 175, 176

Ali Haidar Pasha, Sharif, 254, 373A

Ali ibn Husain, Sharif, 199, 246, 256, 260, 261, 282ff., 372A

Ali Muhammad (Persian Governor), 139

Allenby, Field-Marshal Lord, 287ff., 299ff., 315, 319, 322, 323, 327, 331, 338ff., 346ff., 351; capture of Jerusalem, 318

Allenby, Lady, 327

Amadia, Kurdistan, 176

Amanullah, Amir of Afghanistan, 332

Amara, 204, 209

Amarat tribe, 51

American Mission of Dutch Reformed Church, 87, 336

American Mission School, Beirut, 83, 227

Amery, Leopold, 206, 326

Amman, 317, 322

Amu Dariya, river, 170

Anaiza (Saudi Arabia), 98, 117

Anaiza tribal federation, 32, 36, 51ff.

Anatolia (Turkey in Asia), 7, 22, 62, 182

Anderson, Dr, 44

Andrae, Dr Walther, 81

Anglo-French Entente, 5, 75, 76; war plans, 124ff.

Anglo-French Mission to Hijaz, 297

Anglo-French-Russian Agreement (1915), 312

Anglo-Persian Oil Company (later AIOC and BP), 142

Anglo-Persian Treaty, 344, 350

Anglo-Russian Convention (Persia), 10

Anglo-Saudi Treaty, 150ff., 267

Anglo-Turkish Convention, 73, 75, 78, 84, 85, 100, 102, 112, 113

Ankara (Angora), 349

Anzacs, 182, 269

Aqaba, 7, 43, 110, 252, 283, 286, 330, 331

Arab Bulletin, passim

Arab Bureau, 189, 196ff., 205, 206, 240ff., 279, 288, 297, 351

Arab Revolt, pre-war plans for, 32, 72, 100, 153; Sharifian rebellion, 174ff., 181ff., 223, 240ff.

Arabia, SS, 143

Arabian Report, 199

Arabistan, 137, 203, 237

Araif (Saudi pretenders), *see* Saud, Ibn

Araifan, Shaikh Muhammad ibn Arif, 176, 191, 192, 243ff., 269, 276

Arar ibn Ghazi, 157

Ararat, Mount, 136

Ardagh, Sir John, 6

Aridh, 115

Arish, Al, 183, 252, 279, 287, 290, 294ff., 316

Armenia, 9ff., 231, 324, 326; massacres of populace, 9, 103, 190, 196, 225ff., 333, 349

Armfield, Rev. H. T., 42

Armistice (Mudros), 331

Armstrong, H. C., quoted, 172

Armstrong-Vickers, 129

Arnold Forster, H. O., 6

Arras offensive, 287

Arshad ad-Dowla, 95
Artawiyah, Al, 71, 339
Ashmolean Museum, Oxford, 42ff.
Asienkorps, see Yilderim
Asir, 70, 186, 273, 280, 346
Asquith, Earl of Oxford and, 32, 189, 197, 206, 261, 354, 362
Assassins, the, 45
Athens, 231
Athlit, Agricultural Station, 227ff., 290, 291, 295, 300, 370ff.
Auda abu Tayya, Shaikh of Howaitat, 35, 40, 111, 155, 157, 286, 298
Auda ibn Zubaida, pirate, 276
Austria–Hungary (Habsburg Empire), 5, 8, 39, 77, 124, 134
Aylmer, Capt. L., 32ff., 98
Aylmer, Lt-Gen. Sir Fenton, 209, 213
Aynslee, Col., 216
Ayun (Kasim), 98
Aziziya, 218
Azmi Bey, 104

Baalbek, 343
Babylon, 28, 92
Bachmann, Dr W., 81
Badawin (bedouin, collectively badu), passim
Baedeker, guide, 44
Baghdad, 13, 28, 31ff., 67, 87, 92, 133, 159, 170, 190, 192, 203ff., 218, 224, 287, 304, 347; Proclamation of (1917), 287, 329
Bahrain, 88, 99, 112, 135, 201
Bair, 107, 111
Baird, Winifred, 107
Bakhtiari tribes, Persia, 10, 95, 137, 171, 204
Bala Hissar (Kabul), 168
Balfour, Arthur James, 1st Earl of, 6, 183, 190, 196, 206, 303ff., 310, 311, 330, 354
Balfour Declaration, 305ff., 319, 328, 334, 353
Balkan Wars, 31, 43, 67, 75, 78, 105
Baluchistan, 168
Bandar Abbas, 48
Bani Hassan, tribe, 154

Bani Khalifa, tribe, 68
Bani Lam, tribe, 137
Bani Sakhr, tribe, 25ff., 58
Bani Wahhab, tribe, 154
Baqar, Al, 152
Barakat Allah (Indian revolutionary), 138, 165
Barclay, Sir George H., 95
Barrett, Gen. Sir Arthur, 144, 204
Barrow, Gen. Sir Edmond, 258
Basaita, Al, 155
Basle, 226
Basra, 7, 15, 31, 67, 87, 98, 101, 135, 137ff., 144, 150, 171, 190, 192, 201ff., 232, 237, 240, 336
Battenburg, Prince Louis of, 125, 132, 136
Bayern, Princess Theresa von, 134
Beach, Col. W. H., 206, 208, 213, 215, 222, 240
Beersheba, 110, 276, 315ff.
Beha ad-Din, 230
Behbehan, 138ff.
Beirut, 28, 44ff. 107, 193ff.; Jesuit College at, 19
Belhaven and Stenton, Baron, see Hamilton, Major
Bell, Alexander Graham, 227
Bell, Gertrude, 14, 17, 19, 25, 41, 64, 71, 78, 105ff., 109ff., 123, 151, 157, 186, 195, 205–6, 213ff., 240, 268, 305, 335, 342ff., 349, 360ff.
Benckendorff, Count, 136, 231–2
Benedictus XV, Pope, 323, 326, 470n
Bentwich, Capt. Norman, 289
Benzinger, Dr, 24
Berkeley University, 35
Berlin–Baghdad rail scheme, 12, 13, 78ff.
Berlin Moslem Committee, 167
Bermann, Dr, 30
Berne, intelligence station, 77, 279, 299
Bernstorff, Count von, 76, 311
Bertie, Lord, 196
Bessam, Muhammad ibn Abdullah, 18, 107
Bieberstein, Baron von, 9
Billi tribes, 255, 272

Bir Abbas, 280
Birdwood, Capt. R. L., 144
Birdwood, Gen. Sir W. R., 210
Birijik, 176
Bismarck, Prince Otto von, 8
Bitlis, 244
Blaker, Lt-Col. W. F., 208, 240
Blanckenhorn, Dr Max, 24, 34
Boer War, 20, 30
Bokhara, 333
Bolo Pasha, 320
Bolsheviks, 312ff., 345; revelation of Sykes–Picot agreement, 312
Bompard, M., 271
Bonar Law, Andrew, 325, 350, 356
Bornstein, Leibel, 291
Bosphorus, *see* Constantinople
Boulogne, 356ff.
Boutagy, Charles (and father), 184, 229, 291
Boyle, Capt., RN, 250, 266, 280
Brackenbury, Gen. Sir Henry, 6
Bramley, Lt-Col. A. W. Jennings, 109, 181
Brandeis, Judge Louis D., 35, 227
Bray, Lt-Col. N. N. E., 50, 62ff., 67–8, 102, 105, 152, 258, 281ff., 298, 352
Brémond, Col. Edouard, 260, 266, 268, 283, 319
Breslau, warship, 125ff., 322, 324
Brest-Litovsk, Treaty of, 322
Bristol, HMS, 326
Brode, Dr (Consul), 293
Brodrick, St John (Lord Midleton), 20
Brown, Thomas, 85
Bubiyan island, 15
Buchan, John (Lord Tweedsmuir), 81; quoted, 224, 248, 302, 313, 318
Buchanan, Sir George, 238
Buenos Aires, 302
Bulgaria, 78, 182, 347
Bullard, Sir Reader, 149
Bullitt, William C., 355, 360
Buraida, 88, 98, 117, 122, 149, 152
Burazjan, Khan of, 139–40
Bushire, British Residency, 48, 138ff., 203, 237

Butler, Capt. S. S., 32ff., 98
Buxton, Leland, 27ff.

Caesarea, 235
Caillard, Sir Vincent, 323ff.
Cairo, 87, 124, 149, 172ff., 234, 269, 314, 318; Pan-Islam Movement in, 166; Zionist Committee in, 300, 303, 313
Caliphate, 175, 177, 187, 189, 232, 274, 335, 350
Callwell, Brig.-Gen. C. E., 143, 235
Cambon, Paul, 222
Cambridge University, 186, 236
Candia, Hamburg–Amerika liner, 31
Caprotti, Sig., 28
Carchemish (Jerablus), 78, 82, 106, 111, 220, 233
Carden, Adm. Sir Sackville, 136
Carmel, Mount, 44
Carmelite Convent, Sinai, 292
Carol, King of Rumania, 135
Carruthers, Douglas, 24, 50, 58, 107, 110, 119, 236
Carson, Sir Edward, 186
Carter, President Jimmy, 363
Casino Hotel, Port Said, 229
Caucasus, 163, 223
Caxton Hall, London, 310
Cecil, Lord Edward, 297
Cecil, Lord Robert, 306, 310
Central Powers, 97, 125, and *passim*
Chakhdara, RIMS, 143, 144
Chamberlain, Sir Austen, 187, 188, 190, 196ff., 206, 250, 262, 267, 304
Chamberlain, Joseph, 23
Chanak, Dardanelles, 132
Charles, Emperor of Austria, 323, 326, 470n
Charterhouse School, 30
Chauvel, Gen. Sir Henry, 331
Cheetham, Sir Milne, 172–3
Chelmsford, Viscount, 210, 240, 250, 259, 304, 326
Chester, USS, 228
Chetwode, Gen. Sir Philip, 326
China, 169
Chirol, Sir Valentine, 42, 82, 182, 187, 205

Churchill, Sir Winston, 4, 125ff., 135, 142, 161–2, 164, 183ff., 206, 263, 290, 304, 307, 350ff., 356, 362

Cilicia, 231, 349

Clayton, Gen. Sir Gilbert, 179, 185, 190, 195, 228, 233, 251, 283, 288, 318, 336, 351

Clemenceau, Georges, 319, 320, 353

Cleveland, Sir Charles, 60, 62

Cohen, L. L., 305

Committee of Imperial Defence (CID), 197

Committee of Union and Progress (Young Turks), 9ff., 27, 31, 103ff.

Connell, John, 361

Conservative Party, 6

Constantine, King of Greece, 325

Constantinople, 9, 28, and *passim*

Copenhagen, 85, 91, 125, 234; Zionist Bureau at, 295

Corbetti, Mme, 226

Cornwallis, Sir Kinahan, 179, 214, 241, 245, 256, 284, 335, 347

Cossacks, 170–71, 223

Cowley, Lt-Comm., 215

Cox, Maj.-Gen. Sir Percy Z., 47, 56, 86, 94, 97, 102, 106, 112ff., 115, 139, 144, 150, 153, 201, 206, 209, 212, 240, 252, 267, 297, 320, 334, 336, 349ff.

Crane, Charles, 340

Craufurd, Brig.-Gen. Sir G. S. G., 60, 88, 101

Cree, Capt., 219, 220

Crete, 12, 32, 43

Crewe, Lord, 84, 97, 112, 143, 149, 189, 196, 252

Crillon Hotel, Paris, 354

Cromer, Evelyn Baring, 1st Earl of, 4, 20, 75, 76, 82, 135, 172, 305, 312

Crow, F. E., 87, 101, 146, 149

Ctesiphon, 204, 218, 219

Cumberbatch, Henry, 102

Cunliffe Owen, Lt-Col. F., 135, 338

Curragh mutiny, 354

Curzon of Kedleston, 1st Marquess, 4, 5, 13, 15, 20, 31, 43, 56, 252, 312, 334, 342ff., 353

Cyprus, 296

Dahana, sand belt, 91, 99, 101, 150

Damascus, 3ff., 17, 19, 25ff., 62, 92, 97ff., 107, 119, 122, 153, 164, 192–3, 243, 269, 271, 275, 292, 317, 330ff., 348

Darb Zobaida (Sultani), 51, 119, 236, 253

Dardanelles, 32, 130, 136, 164, 188, 199, 205, 206, 214, 215, 223, 244, 257, 269, 324, 325

Dardanelles Committee, 183, 188, 190

Daud Barracks, Constantinople, 225

Daud Bey Daghistani, 50

Davidsen, Lt, 87

Davies, J. T., 324

Dasht-i-Kavir, desert, 167

Dasht-i-Lut, desert, 170

Davenport, Major W. A., 266

Dawish, Faisal al, 339, 352

Dawnay, Col. Alan, 329, 330

Dawnay, Maj.-Gen. Sir Guy P., 326

Dead Sea, 23

De Bunsen, Sir Maurice, 182

De Bunsen Committee, 182, 198; Report, 187

Dedeagatch, 323

Deedes, Col. Sir Wyndham H., 228, 288, 290, 301, 308, 354

Defrance, M., 271

Delamain, Brig.-Gen. W. S., 135, 201

Delhi, 106, 182, 205; Coronation durbar at, 83

Delhi Camerade, 166

Dent, Major W., 214

Denusa, 130

Deraa rail junction, 62, 324, 331

Derby, Earl of, 263, 288

Deutsche Orient Gesellschaft (archaeological expedition), 12, 43, 81, 82, 221

Deuxième Bureau, 77, 103

Devey, George P., 102

Devonport, HM Dockyard, 130

Dexter, Capt., 219

Dhafir tribe, 14

Dhari ibn Mahmud, Shaikh of Zoba tribe, 347

Dhariya, Al, 317

Dickson, Dr H. N., 236

Dickson, Lt-Col. H. R. P., 345ff.

Diel, Lt, 272ff.
Disraeli, Benjamin, Earl of Beacons-field, 323
D'Mello, L. M. (Kuwait Agency Clerk), 150
Dobeler, Prof. Gustav, 311
Dodecanese islands, 78
Doughty, Charles, quoted, 71, 98, 258, 361
Druses, 25ff., 34, 62ff., 103
Duff, Gen. Sir Beauchamp, 31, 203, 204
Dufferin, HMS, 241, 246, 253
Dumeir, 153

Eady, Griffin, 164, 323
East Africa campaign, 205, 247
Eastern Bureau, German Foreign Office, 166, 180
Eder, Dr, 354
Edmonds, C. J., 138ff.
Edmunds, Capt., 289, 296, 308
Edward VII, King, 125
Egan, Eleanor F., quoted, 202
Egypt, 75ff., 119, 172ff., 226, 269ff., 278, 350, 354
Egyptian Exploration Society, 108
Einstein, Lewis, 224ff.
Eisenhut, Karl, 139ff.
Empty Quarter, Saudi Arabia (Rub al Khali), 49
Endres, Lt-Col., 271
Entente powers, 75, *passim*
Enver Pasha, 9, 76, 104, 105, 125, 130, 131, 133ff., 143ff., 156, 162ff., 174, 178, 210, 215, 217ff., 221, 225, 232, 243, 270, 271, 322ff., 332, 333, 349
Eretz Israel, *see* Palestine
Erfah Bey, 110
Erzerum, 195, 199, 238, 241, 244
Esbaita, 110
Esher, Lord, 127
Espiègle, HMS, 281
Etherington, the Misses, 311
Eton College, 162
Euphrates, river, *passim*
European concert, withdrawals from, 13
Euryalus, HMS, 186, 212, 266
Evans, Sir Arthur, 42

Ewart, Gen. Sir Spencer, 7, 77
Expeditionary Force 'D', Mesopota-mia, 135ff., 144
Ezra, battle of, 63

Fahad Bey ibn Hadhal, Shaikh of east-ern Anaiza tribes, 51
Fahad ibn Muammar, 70
Fairchild, Dr David, 35, 227
Faisal ibn Abdal Aziz al Saud, Crown Prince (later King), 351–2
Faisal ibn Husain, Sharif (King of Iraq), 174ff., 199, 243ff., 269ff., 280ff., 298, 323, 327, 329, 340ff., 351ff.
Faisal ibn Rashid (Faisal ibn Hamud al Obaid), 34ff., 46, 114, 116, 123, 158, 178, 345, 368A
Faisal ibn Turki al Saud, 366A
Fakhri Pasha, Gen., 190, 254, 276, 280ff., 340
Falkenhayn, Field-Marshal Erich von, 302
Falluja, 347
Falticeni (Rumania), 22
Fao, 143, 201–2
Farhan, Shaikh al Rahama, 345
Fars, 93
Faruqi, Muhammad al, Sharif, 190ff., 211, 230–31, 334
Fast's Hotel, Jerusalem, 227, 292
Fatima, Princess of Hail, 111
Fattah, Al (civil wing of Arab Coven-ant), 190
Feinberg, Avshalom, 35, 110, 226ff., 290, 291, 295
Ferrara, SS, 146
Fetki Pasha, Field-Marshal, 63
Fforde, A. Brownlow, 206, 268
Fidan tribe, 155
Fielding, Lt, 308
Figaro, 320
Firman, Lt, 215
Fisher, Adm. Lord, 77, 125ff., 136, 142, 165
Fisher, Lt-Col. J. L., 318
Fitzgerald, Col. Oswald, 182, 206
Fitzmaurice, Gerald, 9, 129, 164, 182, 186, 232, 333

Foch, Marshal Ferdinand, 77
Foreign Office, *passim*
Fox, HMS, 244, 247, 255, 281ff.
France, 8, 174, 177, 183, 191, 192, 232, 306ff.
France du Nord, 359
Franco-Prussian War, 6
Frankfurter, Judge Felix, 303, 304, 353ff.
Franz Josef, Emperor, 92
Freemasonry, 9ff., 105, 237
French, Col. C. N., 197, 250, 283
French, Field-Marshal Sir John (Earl of Ypres), 133
Frobenius, Col. Hermann, 77, 323
Fuad, Sultan of Egypt (later King), 469n
Fuad Pasha, General, 271, 279

Galicia, 125
Galilee, 28
Gallipoli, *see* Dardanelles
Garland, Major H., 279
Gaster, Rabbi Moses, 239
Gaza, 110, 287, 293, 315
Gazetteer of Persian Gulf, 58, 144
Geneva, 166, 325
George V, King, 83, 125, 133, 319
Georgia, 238
Georgian Legion, 349
Geraghty, L-C C. H., quoted 316, 467n
Germany, 4ff., 8, 12, 59, 61, 85, 124, 138, 203ff., 320, 328
Ghadaban, Shaikh of Bani Lam, 137
Ghanim, Saqar al, 88
Gharbrit, Ibn, 260
Ghat, 89, 90, 115
Gibbon, Capt. C. M., 58ff.
Gideonites, 226
Gill, Capt. William J., 41
Gilyak, Russian warship, 13
Ginsberg, Asher, 312
Gladstone, W. E., quoted, 3
Glazebrook, Mr (American Consul), 227, 308
Gleichen, Col. the Count von, 43

Goeben, German warship, 125ff., 164, 322, 324
Golan, 28
Goltz, Field-Marshal Colmar von der, 19, 32, 63, 136, 162, 171, 204
Gooch, Capt., 357ff.
Gorringe, Gen. Sir George, 204, 213
Gorst, Sir John Eldon, 20, 75, 172
Gouraud, Gen. Henri, 343
Goyer, Dr, 81
Graham, Sir Ronald, 300, 313, 321
Grand Continental Hotel, Cairo, 179, 195, 294
Graves, Philip, 179, 195, 196, 225
Greece, 43, 182, 270, 333ff., 349; persecution of nationals, 10
Greene, Sir Conyngham, 87
Grey, Sir Edward (Earl of Fallodon), 67, 78, 85, 95, 100, 112ff., 124, 130, 131, 143, 149, 164, 173, 177, 188, 190, 191, 194, 196ff., 231, 241, 244, 263, 362, 363
Grey, Lt-Col. W. G., 113, 114, 145ff.
Gribbon, Lt-Col. W. H., 237
Grierson, Maj.-Gen. Sir James Moncrieff, 6
Grignon, Agricultural College, 22
Grobba, Fritz, 272ff.
Guarmani, Carlo, 110

Habban, 282
Habibullah, Amir of Afghanistan, 138, 168, 332
Hadjin, 103
Hadramaut, 275
Hafar wells, 150
Haidar Khan, 139
Haidar Pasha (rail terminus), 220, 226, 271
Haifa, 25, 44, 226, 228, 229, 324
Haifa–Deraa railroad, 328
Haifa–Rowandiz rail scheme, 182
Haig, Field-Marshal Earl, 263, 288
Hail, 11, 14, 98, 109ff., 116, 178, 337, 340, 345, 347, 352; arms for, 114, 147
Hajji Ali Akbar, 221, 222
Hajji Ali Kuli Khan, 11
Hajji Muhammad, 272
Hakki Pasha, 101, 112

Haldane, Lt-Gen. Sir Aylmer, 348
Haldane, Col. C., 163
Haldane, Col. J. A., 31, 44
Haldane, Richard Burdon, Viscount, 189
Halim, Prince Said, 126, 129ff., 134, 136, 224, 232
Hall, Capt. William Henry, RN, 42
Hall, Vice-Adm. Sir W. Reginald, 161ff., 164, 167, 179, 195, 206, 224, 235, 302
Hama, 192
Hamad desert, 40
Hamadan, 170
Hamdani, Rashidi messenger, 118, 122
Hamilton, Gen. Sir Ian, 182
Hamilton, Major R. E. A. (Baron Belhaven and Stenton), 336, 338
Hammer, Herr, 271
Hamra, 264–5
Hamud ibn Sabah, 13
Hamud ibn Subhan, 39
Harb tribe, 276
Hardinge of Penshurst, Baron, 42, 62, 144, 147ff., 153, 174, 187, 188, 190, 196ff., 205, 206, 262, 304
Hardinge, RIMS (and HMS), 255, 258, 281
Hardy, Lt Cozens, 199
Harling, Herr, 87, 135
Harrison, Nora, 44
Harrison, Dr Paul, 336
Hasa, Al, 11, 54, 56, 68, 72, 99, 102, 112, 146, 345; proposed Jewish state, 306
Hashemite dynasty, passim
Ha-Shomer (Watchmen), 226, 232, 292ff., 309
Hassan Bey, 309
Hassan, Moulvi Muhammad, 165ff.
Hassan Riza Bey, 87
Hastings, Lt Leslie, 63, 302
Hauran desert, 25, 34, 62ff.
Haversack ruse, Palestine campaign, 315
Hayaniya wells, 119, 158, 236
Hayat Daud, 139
Hayes, Col. Webb, 318
Hazil, 100

Hebron, 316–17
Hedley, Col. W. Coote, 434n
Helles, Dardanelles, 131
Henry, Prince of Reuss, 167, 170
Hentig, Werner von, 138, 167ff.
Herat, 168, 170
Herbert, Hon. Aubrey, 7, 9, 27ff., 62, 105, 110, 179ff., 210ff., 240, 333
Hermon, Mount, 30
Herzl, Theodor, 23, 227, 237, 356
Hijaz campaign, 244ff.
Hijaz railway, 17, 24, 45, 63, 78, 107, 110, 157, 174, 251ff., 279, 316, 322
Hillah, 348
Hilpert, Herr, 275
Hindenburg, Field-Marshal Paul von, 125
Hindu Kush, 169
Hinks, Arthur, 236
Hirtzel, Sir Arthur, 197, 199, 244, 258
Hit, 32
Hochwächter, Major von, 63, 67, 103
Hodeida, 27
Hogarth, Dr D. G. (Lt-Cdr RNVR), 17, 41ff., 78ff., 107, 179ff., 198–9, 206, 214, 236, 241, 251, 281, 338ff., 351
Hogarth, Rev. George, 41
Hogarth, Janet (Mrs J. E. Courtney), 42
Holderness, Sir Thomas W., 112
Holdich, Col. G. W. V., 199, 256
Holmes, Miss, 44, 83
Homs, 92, 192
Hotel Grossman, Tiberias, 28
House, Col. Edward, 302, 311
Howaitat tribe, 34, 40, 111, 298
Hozier, Capt. Sir Henry, 6
Huber, Charles, 98
Hulaga Khan, 177
Hunter, Capt. F. Fraser, 58, 85
Husain, Saudi gunner, 152
Husain ibn Ali, Sharif of Mecca, 38, 70, 123, 166, 174ff., 183, 191ff., 205, 212, 241ff., 269ff., 280ff., 320, 329, 335, 339ff., 346ff., 352, 362, 371A
Husain Kamal, Sultan of Egypt, 173, 319, 320
Husain of Rabegh, Shaikh, 253, 261, 265

Hutaim tribe, 40
Hyamson, Albert, 319

Ibrahim ibn Subhan al Rashid, 111, 123
Ibrahim Nuwdeli, slave, 159
Ibrahim Pasha, Kurd, 81
Ibrahim Pasha of Egypt, 71, 99
Idrisi of Asir and Yemen, Sayid Muhammad al, 70, 72, 250, 280, 338, 375A
Ikhwan, 71, 339, 345ff., 352
Imogen, Embassy yacht, 212
Imperial Military Geographical Institute, Vienna, 19, 20, 93
India, 60ff., 133, 165ff., 187ff., 196, 240, 270; Viceroy's proclamation, 136
India Office, *passim*
Intrusive, Arab Bureau code name, 180 and *passim*
Irakgruppe, German army in Mesopotamia, 215
Iraq, 193, 348, 350; Provisional Govt, 351; kingdom, 351ff.
Ireland and Home Rule agitation, 62, 67
Isfahan, riots at, 170; agents in, 12, 170
Ismailiya, GHQ Egypt, 200, 256
Isvolsky, Alexander, 10
Italy, 28, 78, 125, 191; Turco-Italian War, 78, 91
Izmet Bey, 224, 317
Izzat Pasha Holo, 10, 174

Jabal Druse, 22, 25
Jabal Shammar, 52, 110, 119, 122, 158
Jabal Tubaiq, 111, 119
Jabal Tuwaiq (escarpment), 99, 115
Jabir ibn Mubarak al Sabah, 57
Jabir ibn Sabah, 13
Jabotinsky, Vladimir, 313
Jacob, Lt-Col. H. F., 212
Jacobsen, Dr, 226
Jafar Pasha al Askari, 258, 352
Jaffa, 230, 293, 299, 318
Jagow, Graf von, 232
Jahra, 84, 336
Jamal Pasha, Ahmad, 103, 131, 134, 163, 174, 190, 224ff., 243, 269ff., 279, 291, 293, 301, 307, 311, 317, 320ff.
Jamal Pasha, Gen., 331
Jarab, Al, 152, 158, 159, 178
Jarvis, Lt-Col. C. S., 109
Jask, 8, 48, 135
Jauf, 32ff., 46, 119, 155, 236, 352
Jaussen, Père A., 163, 275
Java, 244, 270, 275
Javid Pasha, 10, 312
Jefferson, Capt. Elgie, 356
Jellicoe, Adm. the Earl, 126
Jerablus, *see* Carchemish
Jericho, 24, 35
Jerusalem, 17, 25, 28, 226, 272, 279, 287ff., 292, 294ff., 315ff., 321, 338
Jewish Chronicle, 357
Jewish Mission, Safed, 44
Jewish Regiment, 313
Jewish Security Committee, 293
Jewish Territorial Organisation, 237
Jewish Workers' Movement, Political Committee, 293
Jews, persecution of, 225ff.
Jiddah, 27, 241ff., 274, 275, 278, 281, 329
Jihad (holy war), 133, 138, 165, 196, 204
Jiluwi, Abdullah ibn, 101, 102, 116, 345
Jisr al Mejamie, 331
Jodrell, Dr J., 81
John O'Scott, SS, 102, 112
Johnstone, Sir Alan, 85ff.
Jones (butler), 173
Jones, Capt. 289
Jones, Lt-Col. W. Dally, 197
Jordan, 351, 355; river, 292; valley, 23, 322
Joyce, Lt-Col. P. C., 266, 286, 329
Jubail, 158
Judische Rundschau, 319
Juhaina tribe, 274–5, 286
Julna, river boat, 215

Kabul, 168
Kadesh, 110
Kalti, *see* Carchemish
Kandel, J. L., 319
Kara Kum desert, 170
Karasso Pasha, 9
Karbala, 28, 33, 92, 203, 348

Karun river, 142, 204
Kashgar, 169
Kasim (Najd), 98, 100, 159
Kasim Bey, Gen., 138, 349
Kasr Amr, 19
Kastamuni, PoW Base, 218, 233
Katif, 102
Kelend, 168
Keller, Countess, 76
Kenley, RAF base, 365ff.
Kenyon, Sir Frederick, 108
Kerak, 24, 45, 66
Kerensky, A. F., 287
Kerman, 93, 170
Kermanshah, 171, 204
Khafs, 100ff., 106, 114
Khairi Bey, Col., 168, 273ff.
Khalifa, river boat, 219ff.
Khalil Pasha, Gen., 210, 215ff.
Khazal, Shaikh of Muhammerah, 11, 72, 100, 113, 136, 145, 202, 204, 335, 338
Khiva, 333
Khurmah, 339ff., 346ff.
Kidston, George, 299
King, Dr H. C., 340
King–Crane Commission, 340ff.
Kipling, Rudyard, 5
Kisch, Lt-Col. Frederick, 236, 239, 322
Kisch, Hermann, 236
Kitchener, Field-Marshal H. H., Earl of Khartoum, 3ff., 31, 61, 75, 104, 109, 123, 124, 133, 149, 161, 162, 172ff., 188ff., 198, 206, 240, 246–7, 263, 304, 362
Kleber, Jean Baptiste, 331
Knesevich, A., 110
Knesevich, Emil, 110
Knott, Capt. G. P., 65
Knox, Lt-Col. S. G.., 47, 139, 145ff.
Kober, Leopold, 58
Kolber, Herr, 272, 276
Konitz, Col., 171
Kontilla, 119
Kressenstein, Gen. Friedrich Freiherr Kress von, 131, 163, 276, 287, 292, 294, 308, 321
Kubri, 163
Kudairat, Ain al, 110

Kühlmann, Richard von, 232, 293, 294, 311
Kurdistan, 7, 137, 231, 353
Kusaiba, 98
Kut-al-Amara, 137, 171, 188, 205ff., 269, 317
Kuwait, 11, 13, 15, 47ff., 68ff., 83ff., 87ff., 98, 100, 102, 144, 336ff.; Bandar–Shuwaikh Lease, 78

La Patrie Egyptienne, 161
Labba, 236
Lahaj, 186
Lake, Gen. Sir Percy, 211, 214, 217, 240, 250, 258
Lansdowne, Lord, 5, 20ff., 27, 363
Lapwing, HMS, 15
Lascelles, Sir Frank, 13, 17
Lawrence, Col. T. E., 43ff., 69, 78ff., 106ff., 129, 166, 179ff., 206, 210ff., 240, 247ff., 280ff., 315ff., 323ff., 331, 335, 341ff., 351ff., 361
Layard, Sir Henry, 79
Leachman, Lt-Col. Gerard E., 30ff., 49ff., 74, 83, 97ff., 100, 103, 115, 122, 186, 209, 213ff., 297ff., 336, 347, 348
Lebanon, 44ff., 194, 331
Lenin, Vladimir, 312, 324, 333, 349
Leveson, Major C. H., 65
Levi, Professor, 327
Levin, Shmarya, 227
Lewis Pelly, agency yacht (later armed tug), 59–60, 88, 101, 115, 144, 336
Lichtheim, Mr, 301
Limpus, Adm. Sir A., 32, 130, 131
Linders, Dr Theodor, 138
Lingeh, 135ff.
Lishansky, Yusef, 232, 290ff., 300, 309
Listemann, Dr Helmuth, 94, 138ff.
Lloyd, Lord, 7, 179, 240ff., 326, 351
Lloyd George, David, Earl of Dwyfor, 77, 186, 206, 225, 252, 263, 279, 304, 306, 322ff., 327, 343ff., 350, 353, 355ff., 362
Loch, Capt. S. G., 115ff.
Lockhart, R. H. Bruce, 322
Loder, John de Vere (Lord Wakehurst), 297

Lohaya, 244, 275
London, Declaration of (1914), 238
Long's Hotel, London, 12
Lorimer, Major D. L. R., 91
Lorimer, J. G., 49, 50, 58ff., 81, 87, 106, 115, 144
Lorraine, SS, 327
Lotus, SS, 107
Louis, Prince, *see* Battenburg
Lowther, Sir Gerard, 9, 44, 73, 105
Ludendorff, Field-Marshal Erich von, 125, 319
Luzzatti, Luigi, 305
Lynden-Bell, Maj.-Gen. Sir Arthur, 256, 295

Maamar, Fahad ibn, 117, 119
Maan, 58, 110ff., 157, 220, 247, 282, 286, 329
Macdonogh, Brig.-Gen. Sir G. M. W., 197, 198, 209, 222, 235, 237, 251, 262, 302
McDouall, W., 47
Macedonia, 8, 78
Mackenzie, Sir Donald, 42
McMahon, Col. Sir Henry, 102, 115, 172ff., 191, 193, 210, 241ff., 269, 330, 331, 340, 353, 362
McMahon, Lady, 263
MacMunn, Gen. Sir George, 212
Macpherson, Capt. C. F., 100
Madagascar, 94
Madan, 51
Madina, 17, 38, 165, 199, 243, 247ff., 273ff., 280, 283, 286
Magnes, Judah L., 234
Mahbub, slave minister of Al Saud, 90
Mahendra Pratap, 138
Maitland, Capt. G. R., 220
Majid ibn Ajil, Shaikh, 51
Majid ibn Hamud, 33
Majmaa, 101, 115
Malcolm, James, 313
Malcolm, Col. Neil, 181
Mallet, Sir Louis, 105, 112, 128ff., 136, 147, 226, 333
Managam, HMY, 292ff., 308
Manchester Guardian, 295, 306

Mandates, 344ff.
Mandil, Abdal Latif ibn, 380A
Marbat al Faras, 178
Mardin, 176
Margoliouth, Prof. David, 41
Margoliouth family, 41
Marling, Sir Charles, 334
Marmara, Sea of, 218, 325
Marquise, RAF base Paris, 358
Marshal, Gen. Sir William, 338, 347
Mary, Queen, 210
Masjid-i-Sulaiman, oil region, 142
Masri, Aziz Ali al, 104, 174, 211ff., 246, 259ff., 283ff., 320
Massy, Col. P. H. H., 7
Mathi, Muhammad al, guide, 32
Maude, Lt-Gen. Sir Stanley, 223, 287, 321, 329
Maunsell, Col. Francis, 7, 8, 43, 59, 143, 237
Maurer, German agent, 299
Maurice, Maj.-Gen. Sir Frederick, 197, 235
Maxwell, Gen. Sir John, 180ff., 199, 210, 269
Mazar-i-Sharif, 170
Mecca, 19, 191, 234, 243ff., 269, 274, 277, 314, 352
Megiddo, 331
Mehemet V, Sultan, 10, 104, 129, 133
Meinertzhagen, Col. Richard, 220, 288, 295, 299, 315, 318–19, 343, 351, 353, 357
Meissner Pasha, 19, 24, 58, 220
'Memorialists' of Cairo, 328
Mensheviks, *see* Russia
Mersina (Anatolia), 176, 192ff., 221
Meshed (Iran), 93, 170, 209
Meshed Ali, *see* Najaf
Mesopotamia, 7, 133, 165, 171, 183, 188, 189, 191, 196, 200ff., 231, 242, 247, 324
Mesopotamian League (Iraq Covenant), 348
Messina, 125
Metternich, Count Wolff von, 232
Mexico, 302
Middle East Department (Colonial Office), 350ff.

Midhat Pasha, 9, 153
Midiat (Kurdistan), 176
Military Intelligence (General Staff), 6, 43, 76ff., 235; in Cairo, 384A
Military Operations (General Staff), 7, 43, 50, 76, 235
Military Reports, 7, 43
Milne, Adm. Sir Berkeley, 127ff., 136
Milner, Alfred, Viscount, 81
Minto, Lord, 42, 47, 61
Minto–Morley reforms, 61
Mirza Muhammad Riza, 221, 348
Mishal ibn Abdal Aziz al Rashid, 33, 369A
Mitab ibn Abdal Aziz al Rashid, 33, 369A
Mofraza (Turk army recruits), 273
Money, Gen. Sir A. W., 214
Mongolia, SS, 43
Montagu, Edwin, 303ff., 326
Montenegro, 78
Moresch, Herr, 81
Morgenthau, Henry, 104, 127ff., 224, 303, 304
Morley, John, Viscount, 75, 84, 326
Mosul, 137, 348; oil concessions, 348
Mousley, Capt., 317
Mubarak al Sabah, Shaikh of Kuwait, 11ff., 47, 55ff., 72, 83ff., 87ff., 98, 100, 113, 117, 143, 145ff.
Mueller, Major von, 244, 275
Muhammad ibn Abdal Aziz al Rashid, 33
Muhammad ibn Abdullah al Rashid, 11ff., 46, 55
Muhammad Ali, of Egypt, 173, 373A
Muhammad Ali, Pan-Islamite, 166
Muhammad Ali, of Yanbo, 251
Muhammad Ali Mirza Shah, 10, 11, 95
Muhammad Farid, 319
Muhammad al Murawi, guide, 107
Muhammad ibn Sabah, of Kuwait, 12
Muhammad abu Tayya, 111
Muhammerah, 11, 136, 202
Mujahiddin, 273
Muntafiq, tribal federation, 14ff., 57ff., 137, 378A

Murphy, Lt-Col. C. C. R., 62, 64, 68, 101, 119, 135, 144, 208, 220
Murray, Gen. Sir Archibald, 199, 210, 252, 255ff., 279
Murray, Gen. Sir J. Wolfe, 199
Muscat, 28, 212
Musil, Prof. Alois, 19, 35, 37ff., 58, 92ff., 103, 110, 122, 143, 153, 178
Mustafa Kamal (Ataturk), 223, 322, 331, 332, 342, 344, 349ff.
Mustafa Subhi, 333
Mutair tribe, 149, 159
Mutawah, Ali al, 118ff.
Mutawah, Saleh al, 98, 118ff., 236
Muzaffer ad-Din, Shah, 10
Mylrea, Dr C. S. G., quoted, 71, 335

Nablus, 331
Nachrichtdienst, 77 and *passim*. See also Germany
Nadoly, Rudolf, 170
Nafud, desert, 58
Najaf (Meshed Ali), 32, 92, 159, 178, 203, 236, 348
Najd (central Arabia), 11ff., 20ff., 37ff., 46, 73, 85
Naji Bey, Col., 63
Najieh, Princess, 224
Nakhl (Sinai), 109, 147
Naqib of Baghdad, Sir Sayid Abdul Rachman, 349, 351
Naqib of Basra, Sayid Rajjab, 382A
Narimanov, 332
Nasrullah, Amir, 168
National Hotel, Cairo, 299
National Hotel, Damascus, 98
National Pact, Ankara, 349
Nauen, German secret transmitter, 126, 130
Naval Intelligence, 42, 79. *See also* Hall, Admiral
Nawas, Risaldar-Major Gul Khan, 258ff.
Nawwaf ibn Nuri al Shalan, 37ff., 46, 156
Nazareth, 293
Nazim Pasha, 104, 105, 135

Neale, Capt. W. G. (later Sir Gordon), 139ff.

Nearchus, RIMS, 141

Negev desert, 110

Nejib Hani, 313

Neue Orient, 320

Neufeld, Karl, 272ff.

Neumann, Dr, 292

New York, 55, 318

Newcombe, Lt-Col. S. F., 63, 68, 106ff., 178ff., 220, 248, 284ff., 316ff., 331, 337

Newlinski, Philipp Michael de, 23

Newton, Lord, quoted, 78

Nicholas II, Czar of Russia, 136, 287, 326

Nicholas, Grand Duke, 125

Nicholson, Field-Marshal Lord, 6, 60

Nicolai, Col. W., 77, 103, 181

Nicolson, Sir Arthur, 10, 73, 238, 300

Nicolson, Sir Harold, quoted, 172

Niedermayer, Oskar Ritter von, 133ff., 137ff., 142, 167ff., 170, 332

NILI, espionage network, 291, 300, 315

Nixon, Lt-Gen. Sir John, 204, 211

Noel, Major Edward W., 139ff.

Nolde, Baron E., 11ff.

Northbrook, Earl of, 6

Northcliffe, Lord, 182

North-West Frontier, 59, 188

Nureddin Pasha, 204

Nuri Said Pasha, 211, 258, 283

Oakes, Capt. T. T., 140

Obaidallah (Obaid) ibn Ali al Rashid, 33, 367A

Occupied Enemy Territory (OET), 342ff.

O'Conor, Sir Nicholas, 13, 15, 21, 47, 212

Odemis, 349

Odessa, 136

Oil: in Persia, 142, 201; Kuwait, 102; Mosul, 348

Okhrana, 77

Oman, 59, 147, 375A

Omdurman, 4, 13, 272

Oppenheim, Baron Max von, 8, 76, 80, 133, 166, 170, 174, 220, 270, 283, 320, 328

Orlando, V., 355

Ormsby-Gore, Capt. the Hon, W. A., 268, 297, 330

Osman, General, 209

Ostrorog, Count Léon, 323

Ottavi, M., 271

Ottoman Empire, 6, 9ff., 15, 20, 32, 43ff., 61ff., 75, 101, 125, 133ff., 174, 182, 187, 189, 191, 242, 332; army of, 18, 34, 63, 65, 144, 225, 238; Capitulations and public debt, 66, 76, 128, 324

Ovseenko, M., 48

Oxford, University of, 41ff., 162

Packe, Major F. E., 62

Page, Walter, 161

Paget, Sir Ralph, 234

Pahlavi, Iranian dynasty, 344, 363

Palace Hotel, Damascus, 106

Palestine, 22, 23, 106, 162, 164, 183, 226ff., 235, 239, 279, 301, 324

Palestine Exploration Fund, 63, 106, 109, 316

Palgrave, W. G., 98, 115

Palmer, Prof. E. H., 41

Palmyra, 92, 123

Pamirs, 170

Pan-Arab movement, *see* Ahad and Arab Revolt

Pan-Islam movement, 166 and *passim*

Parker, Lt-Col. A. C., 109, 163, 180ff., 197ff., 227, 248, 281ff.

Parker, Alwyn, 112

Paschen, Peter, 170

Pashawar, 165

Peace Conference, Paris, 332ff.

Peace negotiations, 164, 323

Pearson, Major, 195

Peking, 169

Pelly, Sir Lewis, 72

Pennsylvania, University of, 43

Persepolis, gunboat, 31

Persia, 5, 6, 9ff., 48, 133, 137, 165, 167ff., 196, 203ff., 238, 334, 350, 363

Persian Gulf, 4, 10, 11, 16, 75, 189, 363

Pfannenstal, Major, 271

Philby, H. St J., 338
Philippides Bey, 87, 166
Philips, Hoffman, 301
Philistia, 318
Pickthall, Marmaduke, 310
Picot, F. Georges, 102, 122, 200, 224, 238ff., 241ff., 271, 297, 307, 318, 343
Piraeus, intelligence station, 77
Pirie-Gordon, Lt H., 8, 43, 45, 190
Plevna, siege of, 209
Poliakov, 313
Port Said, intelligence station, 185
Port Sudan, 266
Praetorius, agent in E. Africa, 289
Preusser, Dr Conrad, 81, 209
Primrose, Lt-Col. Neil, 358
Prinkipo, 218
Pugin (Chilean agent of Germany), 170
Pusht-i-Kuh, mountains, 214

Qaddima island, 244
Qaddima village, 276
Qatar, 112, 147
Qibla, Al, 311
Quai d'Orsay, Paris, 133
Qum, 170
Qunfidah, 275, 280
Quraish, Prophet's tribe, 245
Qurna, 201, 203, 212

Rabegh, 244, 253ff., 279ff., 298
Rafiq al Azim, 328
Rahmy Bey, 10
Ramet, Capt., 358
Ramsey, Sir William, 42
Rashadieh, warship, 129
Rashid dynasty of Hail, 33, 47, 98, 103, 112, 122
Rashid ibn Lailah, 337
Rashid Pasha (agent of Ibn Rashid), 114, 122, 157
Rashid al Rida, 211, 260
Raudhatain (Kuwait), 84
Rauf Bey, 137, 149
Raunkiaer, Barclay, 74, 85ff., 115
Rawlinson, Sir Henry C., 50
Redl, Col., 77

Redl, Col. E. A. F., 209
Redmond, John, 186
Reichsbote, 311
Reichwald, Capt. W. F., see Blaker
Reinach, Joseph, 305
Rémond, Georges, 104
Reuter, 210, 246
Reza Khan, Pahlavi, 344
Ribdi, Ali al, 118
Rich, Claudius J., 48, 50
Richlieu, Admiral de, 85ff.
Richmond, Admiral Sir Herbert, 132
Rigai wells, 84
Ritchie, Sir Richmond, 73
Riyadh, 11, 72, 74, 84, 99, 100, 106, 115ff., 153
Robertson, Field-Marshal Sir William, 7, 196, 199, 235, 255, 257, 262, 287
Robinson, Gen., 204
Rodd, Sir J. Rennell, 310
Roehr, Herr, 169
Ronaldshay, Lord, 315
Rosebery, Earl of, 185
Rosen, Dr Friedrich, 17, 78
Rosh Pinah, 30ff.
Ross, Sir E. Denison, 41, 237
Ross, Major, 259, 280ff.
Rothschild, Baron Edmond de, 22, 30, 303, 307, 313
Rothschild, Lord, 303ff.
Roux, M., 222
Royal Air Force, 332
Royal Danish Geographical Society, 85ff.
Royal Geographical Society, 8, 17, 59, 236
Royal George, SS, 214
Royal Navy, 13 and passim
Ruhi Effendi, 176, 244, 260
Rumania, 134, 135, 233, 325
Rumbold, Sir Horace, 320
Rushdi Bey, Col., 271
Russia, 5, 8, 11, 12, 77, 134, 189, 191, 238ff., 322, 325, 363
Russki Slovo, 313
Russo-Persian rail scheme, 13
Ruwalla tribe (Anaiza federation), 34, 40, 154

Saad ibn Abdurrahman al Saud, 70, 116
Sabaea, 70
Sadairi, Saad ibn Abdal Mehsin al, 115
Sadleir, Capt. G. F., 99
Sadun Pasha ibn Mansur, Shaikh of
   Muntafiq, 14ff., 54
Safed, 30, 34
Safwan, 15
Said Ali, Col., 260
St Petersburg, 200, 238, 241ff., 287
Sakaka, 33
Salim ibn Hamud of Hail, 33
Salonika, 214
Salt, Al, 316, 317
Samarra, 92, 220, 221
Sami Pasha, 62, 65ff.
Samuel, Sir Herbert, 164, 303
San Francisco, 138
Sanaa, 28, 244, 275
Sanders, Gen. Liman von, 126, 132, 136,
   162, 163, 215, 225, 232, 321, 322, 329ff.
Saniyah, battle of, 144
Sarif, 14
Saturday Evening Post, 202
Saud, Ibn: Abdal Aziz ibn Adurrahman
   al Saud, Amir of Najd and King of
   Saudi Arabia, 11, 15, 38, 46, 47, 54ff.,
   68ff., 85, 91, 98ff., 106, 112, 116ff., 120,
   143ff., 149ff., 156ff., 165–6, 174, 177–8,
   193, 258, 259, 267, 284, 297, 335ff.,
   351ff., 362, 366A
Saud ibn Abdal Aziz al Rashid, 38, 46,
   53ff., 93, 112, 117, 151ff., 156ff., 178, 277,
   297, 336ff., 345
Saud ibn Hamud al Rashid, 33
Saud ibn Malham, 154
Saud ibn Saleh al Subhan, 38, 93, 100,
   112, 120, 157ff., 178, 337
Savoy Hotel, Cairo, 179, 200, 295, 362
Sayid Siddiq Hasan, Khan, 345
Sazanov, Count Sergai, 134, 136, 200,
   231, 238, 242, 269
Schabinger, Freiherr von, 293
Schellendorf, Gen. Bronsart von, 163
Schlieffen, Countess, 76
Schmidt, Herr, 272
Schneersohn, Liova, 228, 234, 291,
   296

School of African and Oriental Stu-
   dies, 41
Schwartz, Reuben, 309
Scotland Yard, 162
Scott, C. P., 306
Seifi Bey, Col., 271
Seligsberg, Alice, 327
Senussi, North African dynasty, 277
Serbia, 78
Sèvres, Treaty of, 350
Shahbandar, Dr Abdurrahman, 211, 301
Shaiba, 201–2
Shaikh al Islam, 166
Shakespear, Capt. Henry, 107, 119
Shakespear, Capt. W. H. I., 48ff.,
   68ff., 83ff., 87ff., 99ff., 103, 106,
   112ff., 139, 143ff., 157, 166, 186, 236,
   258, 267, 336
Shalan, Nuri ibn, Shaikh of Ruwalla
   and Amir of Anaiza tribes, 36ff., 46,
   72, 103, 122, 153ff., 280, 352
Shamiya desert, 14
Shammar tribes, 14ff., 40, 51ff., 93, 116,
   120, 151ff., 178, 347
Shara, 152
Sharif of Mecca, *see* Husain ibn Ali
Shatt-al-Arab, 135, 139, 142, 143, 202ff.,
   237
Shawish, Abdal Aziz al, 166
Shepheard's Hotel, Cairo, 183, 298ff.
Shevket Pasha, Mahmud, 66, 104, 105
Shia, Moslem sect, 187 and *passim*
Shiraz, 93, 138
Shuckburgh, Sir John, 340, 351
Shuster (Iran), 138
Shuster, W. Morgan, 94ff.
Siefert, Lt-Col., 271
Simla, 60ff.
Sinai, 23, 34, 108ff., 119, 163, 221, 232,
   235, 300, 374A
Sinn Fein, 333
Sivas, 349
Sixtus, Prince of Bourbon, 92ff., 323,
   326, 470n
Slubba, 32, 51
Smith, F. E. (Lord Birkenhead), 186
Smith, Capt. Ian, 8, 190, 289, 291
Smith, John, 20

Smuts, Field-Marshal Jan, 288, 322
Smyrna (Izmir), 28, 349
Sofia, 82
Sokolov, Nahum, 300, 307, 310, 313
Soskin, Dr Selig, 22
Souchon, Adm. Wilhelm, 126ff., 135
Spectator, 64, 312
'Sphinx', Egyptian secret society, 166
Sphinx, HMS, 59, 113
Spring-Rice, Sir Cecil, 202, 248, 318
Stack, Sir Lee Oliver Fitzmaurice, 62
Standard Oil Company of America, 348
Steel, Major R. A., 237, 322
Steuber, Ober-Gen., 318
Stirling, Dr, 110
Stockholm, 302
Stokes, Lt-Col. C. B., 95
Storrs, Sir Ronald, 27, 75, 76, 172ff., 179, 183ff., 194, 205, 210ff., 241ff., 274ff., 281, 299, 336ff.
Sturdee, Admiral Sir S. C. D., 132
Subahiya, Kuwait, 146ff., 336
Subhi Bey, Col., 144
Sudair region, 101, 115, 157
Sudan, 196, 270
Suez, 4, 109, 162, 188, 199, 224
Suleiman Askari Bey, 137
Suleiman ibn Daghil, 337
Suleiman abu Rifada, Shaikh, 255–6
Sultan Ahmad Shah, 10, 344
Sultan ibn Hamud al Rashid, 33, 37
Sultan Osman I, warship, 129
Summers, Corp. Jack, 336
Sunni, Moslem sect, 187
Supreme War Council, Paris, 326, 327
Survey of Egypt, 295
Survey of India, 58, 85
Suwait, Hamud ibn, 14
Switzerland, Pan-Islamites in, 156, 299, 303
Sykes, Lady (Edith), 20, 25
Sykes, Sir Mark, 7, 20, 25, 179ff., 236ff., 241ff., 297ff., 302, 306, 327, 337ff.
Sykes, Maj.-Gen. Sir Percy, 93, 134, 170, 171, 237, 321
Sykes, Sir Tatton, 20

Sykes–Picot Agreement, 238 ff., 306, 312, 328, 330
Symes, Capt. G. S., 183
Syria, 7, 31, 165, 183, 191–2, 194, 199, 224, 231–2, 242, 245, 263, 269, 279, 291, 324, 331ff., 348ff.
Szold, Henrietta, 229, 290, 309

Tabor, Mount, 331
Tadmor, *see* Palmyra
Tahy, Herr de, 160
Taif, 247, 254, 274, 277, 339
Taima, 46, 111, 114
Talaat Pasha, 9, 104, 131, 225, 232, 294, 333ff., 349
Talib, Sayid al Naqib, 15, 58, 72ff., 76, 83ff., 101, 144ff., 212, 250
Tanganyika, 289
Tangistan, 138–9, 237
Taraffiya, 158
Taurus Mountains, 20, 137, 220
Tehran, 10, 93, 95, 167, 170, 171
Tel Afar, 347, 348
Tel Ahmar, 82
Tel Ubaid, 220
Telegramme, Le, 356ff.
Temps, Le, 320
Tewfiq Pasha, 78
Thaj, 68
Thaniyan, Ahmad al, 99, 351ff.
Thomas, Lowell, 248, 316, 318
Thomasberger, Herr R., 19, 36, 58, 92
Thompson, R. Campbell, 8off., 206, 209, 214
Thomson, Sir Basil, 161ff., 167, 235, 302, 333
Tiberias, 28ff., 292
Tibet, 30
Tigris, river, *passim*
Tih, Al, 110
Times, The, 42, 105, 196, 333, 357
Tod, Lt-Col. J. K., 219, 221
Tokatlian's Hotel, Constantinople, 271
Tornquist, missionary, 169
Torrance, Dr, 29, 35, 44, 78
Townshend, Maj.-Gen. Sir Charles, 171, 188, 204, 209ff., 331
Transcaspia, 5

Transjordan, *see* Jordan
Trans-Siberian Railway, 170
Trebizond, 238, 269
Treidel, Joseph, 22, 29
Trevor, Major A. P., 113, 146
Triple Alliance, 75 and *passim*
Tripoli (N. Africa), 78, 91
Tripoli (Syria), 45, 343
Trotsky, Leon, 322, 324
Troubridge, Rear-Adm. E. C. T., 128, 132
Trucial Coast, 147
Trumpledor, Joseph, 228, 291
Tschlenov, 313
Tufiq al Halabi, 330
Turbah, 346
Turco-German Alliance, 124 and *passim*
Turco-Persian border dispute, 136
Turco-Saudi Treaty, 147
Turkestan, 5, 169
Turkey, *see* Ottoman Empire
Turki ibn Abdal Aziz al Saud, 152
Turki ibn Saud, 71, 366A

Ujair, 99; conference at, 353
Ukhaidar ruins, 92
Umm Jaraib, 159
Umm Kasr, 15
Umm Kaleb, Sinai GHQ, 327
Umm Lejj, 255, 274
United States of America: Aaronsohn in, 35; entry into war, 133
Ur of the Chaldees, 233
Urfa, 45, 82, 176

Vahid ad Din, Sultan, 344
Vambery, Armin, 333
Van, Ottoman vilayet of, 244
Van Ess, Rev. John and Mrs, 87
Versailles, 326
Vickery, Col. C. E., 281ff.
Victoria, Queen, 205
Victoria Hotel, Damascus, 25, 64, 106, 272
Voigt, Gunther, 170

Wadi Ais, 282

Wadi Araba, 110
Wadi Hamdh, 274, 285
Wadi Rumma, 152, 158
Wadi Safra, 264
Wadi Sirhan, 25, 32ff., 37ff., 58, 111, 236
Wadi Yanbo, 280
Wagner, Kurt, 169, 170
Wahhab, Muhammad ibn Suleiman Abdal, 365A
Wahhabi creed, 15, 71
Wales, Edward, Prince of, 210
Wallin, Dr G. A., 98, 100
Wan (Chinese Communist), 333
Wangenheim, Baron Hans von, 128ff., 134, 137, 163, 168, 203, 232, 333
War, declaration of, 124 and *passim*
War Cabinet, 260 and *passim*
War Committee, 196, 252, 256, 279
War Council, 162, 164, 188
War Office, *passim*
Warton, Capt. C. P. F., 140
Washington (USA), 138
Wassmuss, Wilhelm, 94, 137ff., 167, 171, 204, 222, 237, 321, 334
Watzinger, Professor, 35
Wavell, Field-Marshal Lord, 315
Wechsel, Herr, 81
Wedgwood, Commander, 310
Wedgwood Benn, W. (Viscount Stansgate), 297
Weil, Col., 303
Weizmann, Dr Chaim, 299ff., 303ff., 327, 330, 354ff.
Wejh, 255ff., 280ff., 298
Weldon, Capt. L. B., 229, 232
Wemyss, Adm. Sir Rosslyn, 181, 186, 212ff., 256, 266
Weygand, Gen. Maxime, 326
Wilhelm II, Emperor, 3ff., 17, 23, 61, 129, 133-4, 136, 161, 325, 331
Willcocks, Sir William, 81
Willcox, Col. (later Sir) William, 211
Wilson, Sir Arnold T., 97, 188, 213, 336, 339, 343ff.
Wilson, Col. C. E. (Pasha), 243ff., 281ff., 338
Wilson, Field-Marshal Sir Henry, 77, 97, 143, 341, 346, 353

Wilson, President Woodrow, 263, 302, 311, 321, 355

Wingate, Gen. Sir F. Reginald, 123, 166, 179ff., 205, 240ff., 263, 266, 279, 284, 298, 300ff., 320, 321, 329, 330, 343, 354

Woolley, Sir C. Leonard, 43, 80ff., 106ff., 179, 185, 201, 218, 220, 228ff.

Wönckhaus, R., and Co., 8, 85ff., 113, 135, 139

Wright, Col., 195

Wuld Ali, tribe, 114

Yahya, Imam of Yemen, 72, 73, 78, 103, 186, 252, 277, 280, 374A

Yahya Atrash, Shaikh of Druse, 64

Yale, William, 307

Yanbo, 251, 252, 274

Yasin Pasha, Gen., 190, 214

Yemen, 27, 76, 91, 186, 212, 244, 271, 273, 277

Yilderim, Turco-German Army Group, 215, 302, 321

Yishuv, Palestine Jewry, 291 and passim

Young, Capt. Hubert, 351ff.

Young Turks, see Committee of Union and Progress

Yusef, Sadar, 93

Zahroff, Sir Basil, 323ff., 347

Zaid ibn Husain, Sharif, 245ff., 280

Zaida, HMY, 185, 229, 233ff.

Zakki Pasha, 154

Zarud, 117ff., 236

Zamil ibn Subhan, Regent, 40, 46ff., 100, 112, 114, 120, 159, 236

Zangwill, Israel, 237

Zichron Yakov, 22 and passim

Zilfi, 89, 115, 122, 150, 152

Zimmermann, Dr Arthur, 8, 233, 293, 294, 302

Zin, wilderness of, 108, 220

Zinoviev, 332–3

Zionists, 9, 23, 32, 105, 165, 226, 227, 235, 238ff., 251, 299ff., 319, 330, 353ff.

Zionist Medical Mission, Rome, 327, 354

Ziza, 107, 109, 110

Zubair, 84, 202

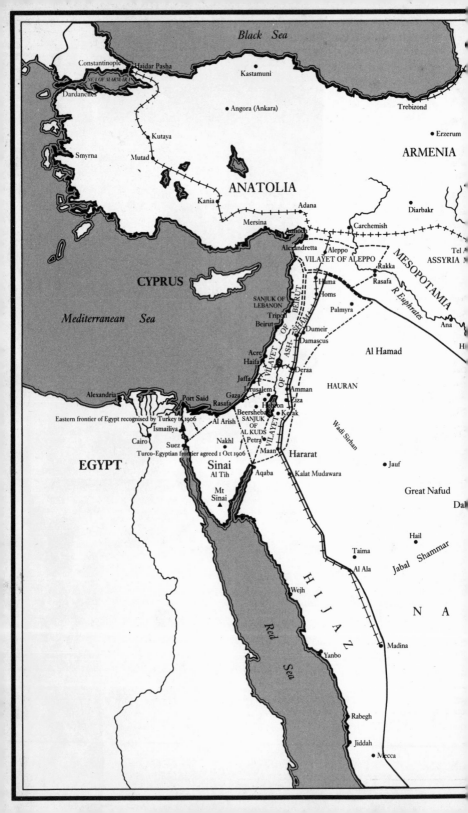